MW00390429

WINDOWS 2000

Windows 2000 Developer's Guide

Windows 2000
Developer's Guide

RAJ **RAJAGOPAL**
SUBODH **MONICA**

Osborne/**McGraw-Hill**

Berkeley New York St. Louis San Francisco
Auckland Bogotá Hamburg London Madrid
Mexico City Milan Montreal New Delhi Panama City
Paris São Paulo Singapore Sydney
Tokyo Toronto

Osborne/**McGraw-Hill**
2600 Tenth Street
Berkeley, California 94710
U.S.A.

For information on translations or book distributors outside the U.S.A., or to arrange bulk purchase discounts for sales promotions, premiums, or fund-raisers, please contact Osborne/**McGraw-Hill** at the above address.

Windows 2000 Developer's Guide

This work reflects the opinions of the author and is not intended to represent the opinions of the MITRE Corporation.

Book p/n 0-07-212463-6 and CD p/n 0-07-212464-4
1234567890 CUS CUS 01987654321
ISBN 0-07-212465-2

Publisher	**Proofreader**
Brandon A. Nordin	Stefany Otis
Vice President & Associate Publisher	**Indexer**
Scott Rogers	Jack Lewis
Acquisitions Editor	**Computer Designer**
Ann Sellers	Gary Corrigan
Project Editor	Kelly Stanton-Scott
Jennifer Malnick	Michelle Galicia
Acquisitions Coordinator	**Illustrator**
Timothy Madrid	Michael Mueller
Technical Editor	**Cover Design**
Greg Guntle	Amparo DelRio
Copy Editor	**Series Design**
Robert Campbell	Peter F. Hancik

This book was composed with Corel VENTURA™ Publisher.

To my daughter, Sheila, who is eager to see her name in print; to my son, Venkat, who I hope one day will be equally eager to see his name; to my wife, Chitra; and to my parents.—Raj

To my wife, Indu, and my son, Kapish, for their understanding and putting up with all the long hours; and to my parents.—Subodh

CONTENTS

Part II

Advanced GUI and OS Services Programming

Part III

Windows 2000 Communications Programming

Part IV

Windows 2000 Multimedia and Database Programming

Part V

Appendixes

ACKNOWLEDGMENTS

We would like to thank Arthur "Choon" Choi for his help in the area of database programming, Keng T. Loh in the area of ActiveX programming, and Donald Asonye in the area of sockets programming. We would like to thank Narayanan Vasudevan for his suggestions and constructive comments in the area of Windows Security. We would like to thank Greg Guntle for his technical reviews and useful tips and the staff at Osborne including Scott Rogers, Wendy Rinaldi, Ann Sellers, Robert Campbell, Timothy Madrid, Jennifer Malnick, and Jody McKenzie—without their support and hard work, this book would not have been possible.

INTRODUCTION

In our experience of developing applications, we have found that, in a given project, selected parts of the operating system are used more heavily than others. For example, in a communications-oriented Windows 2000 project, one may use sockets a lot, while in an Internet-oriented application, one may use WinInet and ISAPI a lot. We have always felt the need for a book that provides a quick introduction to a topic concerning the operating system and that includes some examples that we could use to become productive quickly. This book is aimed at fulfilling these needs for the advanced programmers who have used Windows 2000 for a while, but who are still looking for something to jumpstart their learning a new Windows 2000 topic.

With this in mind, this book addresses a number of programming topics in Windows 2000 including Active Directory, Security, OLE 2, ActiveX, WinSock2, ODBC, ADO, WinInet, ISAPI, OpenGL, Common Controls, Audio, Video, 3D, Animation, GDI, and more. Each topic is introduced at such a level that programmers can easily pick up the concepts of the topic and immediately follow with the examples, allowing them to be productive in a very short time. The examples are kept simple to better enable the understanding of the concept rather than being drowned in code. Thus at places the error checking is deliberately skipped to keep the code simple.

The CD includes the complete source and project files of all the programs in the book.

Happy Programming!!

PART I

Windows 2000 Programming Foundations

CHAPTER 1

Windows 2000 Overview

Windows 2000 is the place to be for programmers. Windows operating systems are outselling competing operating systems (OSs) and network operating systems (NOSs) such as UNIX and NetWare, and Microsoft has done a good job of fixing the security and performance problems of prior versions of Windows. Microsoft has two families of Windows products, one aimed at consumers and their PCs at home, and the other aimed at businesses. The former includes products such as Windows 95, Windows 98, and the expected "Windows Me." The latter includes all versions of Windows NT and Windows 2000.

While Windows 95 and the newer Windows 98 still enjoy a huge installed base, the distinction between them and equivalent business (Windows 2000) editions is narrowing. Starting with version 4.0, Windows NT has the same end-user interface as Windows 95, and this trend is continued in Windows 98 and Windows 2000. The Win32 API (Application Programming Interface) has become a common development mechanism for both the Windows operating systems families of products. Starting with Windows 2000, Windows operating systems will start getting all the benefits of 64-bit programming.

With the prices of memory, processors, and other hardware continuing their downward spiral, the minimum system requirements to run Windows 2000 are getting more and more affordable. Windows NT and Windows 2000 do not have any 16-bit code and are more stable than Windows 95; Windows 2000 is the base for Microsoft's BackOffice set of products. Although UNIX still has a sizable mission-critical application base, many UNIX application vendors have ported or developed equivalent applications to run on Windows 2000. Also, third-party products let customers port their UNIX applications to Windows 2000. Windows 2000, with the Internet Information Server (IIS) and the capability to access data from corporate databases, can be a strong player in the fast-growing corporate intranets.

Are you sold on Windows 2000 yet? This book is for and by Windows programmers. Its focus is to give you the Windows 2000 programming concepts you need along with sample code you can cut and paste into programs you will be writing. The CD is packed with all the source and executables of all programs in the book as well as utilities we use every day to be more productive.

Part I presents a quick overview of Windows 2000 from a programmer's perspective. Windows NT came in two flavors—Windows NT Workstation and Windows NT Server. Windows 2000 comes in four flavors—Windows 2000 Professional, which is the equivalent of Windows NT Workstation, and three variations of the server, Windows 2000 Server, Windows 2000 Advanced Server, and Windows 2000 Datacenter Server. For the most part, programming for Windows 2000 Professional is the same as programming for any variations of the Windows 2000 Server. Accordingly, all programming topics presented apply to all flavors of Windows 2000 unless specifically noted. A summary of the similarities and differences between Windows 2000 Professional and Windows 2000 Server variations is included later in this chapter.

The purpose of this chapter and other chapters in Part I is to provide you with a list of Windows 2000 topics that you should be familiar with before getting into advanced Windows 2000 programming. If you have been working with Windows for a while, then you may be familiar with some of the topics presented. Since the rest of the book presumes that you are familiar with these topics, you may want to peruse the list in this chapter and ensure that you are comfortable with the list of topics. If you need a more detailed coverage of any individual topic, refer to an introductory book such as *Windows 2000 Programming from the Ground Up,* by Herbert Schildt, published by Osborne/McGraw-Hill, 2000.

Microsoft provides programming languages, APIs, SDKs (software development kits), class libraries, a development environment, and so on, to facilitate programming for Windows 2000. The topics that a Windows 2000 programmer should be familiar with or aware of include

▼   Windows 2000 architecture overview
■   Programming languages and development environment
■   Application Programming Interfaces
■   Software development kits (SDKs)
■   Microsoft Foundation Class (MFC) library
■   Graphical device interface (GDI)
■   Internet and network programming
■   Component Object Model (COM), COM+, and Distributed COM
■   Object linking and embedding (OLE)
■   Multimedia
■   Data access
■   Registry
■   Active Directory
▲   Windows Distributed interNet Application Architecture (DNA)

Now we'll look at each of the topics in greater detail.

WINDOWS 2000 ARCHITECTURE OVERVIEW

Windows 2000 architecture is best explained using Figure 1-1. This shows the different components that make up the Windows 2000 architecture, the modes in which they operate, the interaction between the components, and so on.

Kernel and Microkernel

The operating system (OS) is the one program that is always running when the computer is on. It uses real memory, disk space, and other resources. It is the necessary "overhead" to keep the computer up. The aim of operating system designers is to keep this overhead as low as possible while still delivering all the services an OS should deliver. The way

Windows 2000 keeps the overhead low is by keeping the base operating system as small and as tight as possible. Only those functions that could not reasonably be performed elsewhere remain in the base operating system or *kernel*. This microkernel-based approach of Windows 2000 is similar to Mach, a microkernel-based operating system developed at Carnegie-Mellon University.

The kernel is the nucleus of the operating system. (See Figure 1-1 for the relationship of the kernel to the other parts of the operating system. The kernel is just above the layer

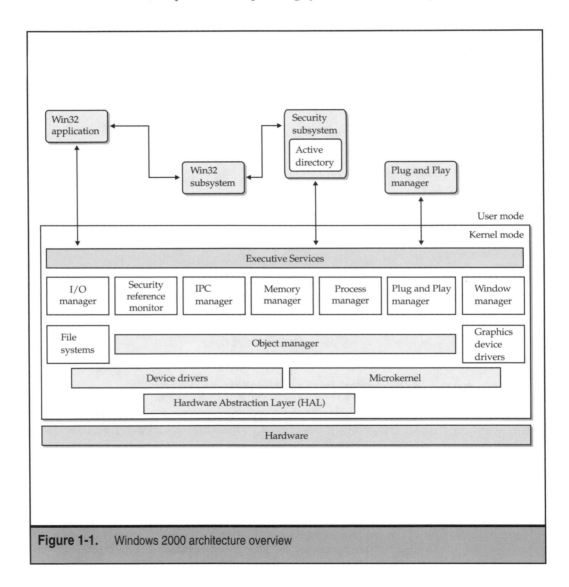

Figure 1-1.   Windows 2000 architecture overview

of code that shields the hardware, the *Hardware Abstraction Layer [HAL]*, which will be discussed later in this chapter.)

The kernel is resident in memory and cannot be preempted (except by some interrupts). Some of the functions the kernel performs are

▼   Handling hardware exceptions and interrupts

■   Scheduling, prioritizing, and dispatching *threads,* the basic unit of execution

▲   Synchronizing execution across processors in a multiprocessor environment

Operating Modes

A simple programming principle to keep in mind is that your program takes turns with others and the Windows 2000 operating system during the execution of your program. If your program runs in a multiprocessor system, then more than one program (or even threads of the same program) can be simultaneously executing in multiple processors. But the concept of programs taking turns still applies. Memory, disk space, and other resources are shared by all the executing programs. Mechanisms are necessary to keep applications separate from the operating system and other applications. Windows 95 application separation was not very good, and it caused application memory to be corrupted, resulting in the infamous General Protection Faults (GPFs).

The way Windows 2000 solves this problem is to run the operating system code in a privileged processor mode known as *kernel mode*. Operating system code running in the kernel mode has access to system data and hardware. Applications run in a non-privileged processor mode known as *user mode* and have limited access to system data and hardware. Thus, if an errant program misbehaves, the operating system gets control and can terminate it without other programs being affected. Windows 2000 uses the protection mechanisms (also called *rings*) provided by the processor (also known as the central processing unit, or CPU) to implement mode separation. When an application program is executing, the operating system is not using the CPU and really does not

Note for UNIX Programmers

Though UNIX and Windows 2000 are similar in many ways, one of the differences is the kernel. Windows 2000 uses a microkernel-based approach, where the core kernel functions are kept as small as possible and the other functions of the operating system are performed in nonprivileged portions of the operating system called protected subsystems. This approach is in contrast to UNIX, where it is not uncommon for the kernel to be a lot bigger and encompass many more operating system functions. One consequence of a bigger kernel is that it needs to be changed more often compared with the Windows 2000 kernel.

know what the application is trying to do. However, the operating system gets the CPU to check if the application attempts to execute at a ring level not appropriate for the application. If the application misbehaves, the CPU raises an exception and invokes the operating system, which is now in control, to deal with the application.

When an application needs to have access to the hardware—for example, when an application wants to print or read data from a disk—it invokes the operating system services, usually through a set of well-defined interfaces, called *Application Programming Interfaces (APIs)*.

Hardware Abstraction Layer (HAL)

Operating systems, including Windows 2000, are designed to run on more than one hardware platform, and platform-specific details are masked from the rest of the operating system by the Hardware Abstraction Layer (HAL). Windows 2000 is designed to run on Intel, Alpha, and PowerPC platforms, although IBM and others have recently announced that they are dropping support for Windows NT on the PowerPC and Microsoft recently announced dropping support for Alpha. Hardware can vary in instruction sets (reduced instruction set computing, or RISC, versus non-RISC), word sizes (64-bit versus 32-bit, and so on), and even the number of processors. Most parts of the operating system are not concerned about these hardware differences, thanks to the Hardware Abstraction Layer.

Processor Support

Up until recently, most computing at the desktop and server levels used machines that had only one CPU. *Multiprocessing,* where multiple processors exist on the same physical machine, have been used in mainframes for some time. With the advent of cheaper processors and operating systems that support multiple processors, multiprocessing is becoming more commonplace in desktops and servers.

Asymmetric multiprocessing (ASMP) is where the operating system uses one or more processors for itself and schedules and runs the application programs in the remaining processors. Operating systems that support *symmetric multiprocessing (SMP)* do not impose such restrictions on processors. The capability to run any program on any processor provides better load balancing (in ASMP, the processor that runs the operating system may be idle while applications are waiting to use the other processor[s]). Fault tolerance is also improved in SMP because the failure of a processor dedicated for the operating system in ASMP means the machine is not operational, even though other processor(s) may be operational. The price to pay for improved load balancing and fault tolerance is complexity. SMP operating systems are more complex to build and maintain. Windows 2000 and many UNIX operating systems support SMP; SMP support is usually transparent to applications.

Note for UNIX Programmers

Unlike UNIX, this portion of the operating system in Windows 2000 is not changed locally by a system administrator, and is updated only by upgrades issued by Microsoft.

Executive

In Windows 2000, the *Executive* refers to the operating system code that runs in kernel mode. Besides the kernel and the Hardware Abstraction Layer, the Executive includes modules that provide services for applications, such as memory management, I/O handling, object handling, process management, security monitoring, and a local procedure call facility. These modules are not implemented as a layered hierarchy, one on top of the other. Rather, they are implemented as peer managers, which interact with each other.

Process Manager

A *process* is the execution instance of a program. Each process has its own memory address space (four gigabytes [GB] in Windows 2000 Professional and Server[1] and many UNIX systems) where the code that makes up the process resides. Each process also owns resources required for the process, including files, threads, and so on. The Process Manager portion of the Executive manages the creation, management (including suspending and resuming processes), and deletion of processes (and threads). The Process Manager, like other key operating systems services such as the Security Reference Monitor, gathers valuable performance data that helps system administrators monitor the system performance.

Even though a process is an execution instance, the process itself does not execute. A process is made up of one or more *threads,* the basic units of execution. A process has at least one thread, and multiple threads can be created. Each thread has its own memory. Threads are a convenient and efficient way to split functions that can be done in the background, while the main thread continues with other processing. In multiprocessor systems, two or more threads of the same process can be executing in parallel, thereby having portions of the same program executing in parallel. However, the price to pay for the convenience and efficiency is the need to *synchronize* threads. If you use a thread to perform a big sort in the background, your main thread has to ensure that the sort input data has not changed, and the main thread must be notified when the sort is done. As you will see in Chapter 9, using threads is one way to take advantage of the programming facilities in Windows 2000, and you can synchronize threads using communication techniques such as semaphores.

---

[1] Advanced Server and Enterprise Server can support more than 4GB. Please see Table 1-2.

Note for UNIX Programmers

Unlike UNIX, processes in Windows 2000 are not executable by themselves. Windows 2000 does not automatically establish a parent/child relationship when one process creates another.

Memory Manager

As mentioned earlier, each process gets its own address space of 4GB. Most desktops and servers do not have that amount of real memory. Considering that there will be multiple processes at the same time, it is obvious that some mechanism must map the process address space to real memory. This mapping is done by the Virtual Memory Manager. The "virtual" in "virtual memory" indicates that most (or all) of a process memory is not real memory. Contents of the address space that are not held in real memory are held on the disk (see Figure 1-2).

During the course of execution, programs may need additional memory. A program requests additional memory either because program control gets transferred to part of the code that is not resident in memory, or because the program needs more memory for

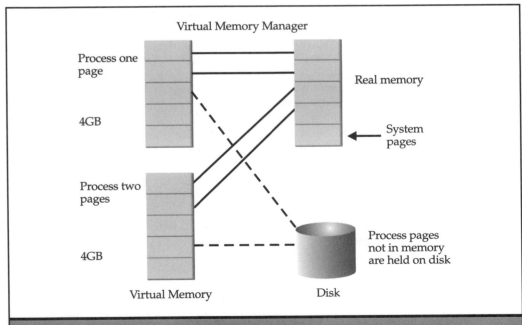

Figure 1-2. Virtual memory management

application data storage. In either case, since real memory is limited, some contents of real memory have to be swapped out. The process of swapping memory contents is called *demand paging*. A *page* is the minimum amount of memory that will be swapped in or out. The typical page size is 4 kilobytes (K). Both the process address space and the real memory are divided into pages. Each process thus has a million pages (4GB/4K). If you have 32 megabytes (MB) of real memory, then you have 8,000 real memory pages (32MB/4K).

The technique of selecting which pages will be moved out is called *first in, first out (FIFO)*. The operating system keeps track of which pages came in first and selects those for swapping out. The idea behind this technique is: the more recent a page, the greater the chances that it will be used and needs to be kept in real memory. The Virtual Memory Manager uses a *page table* (actually the page table is a multilevel table), which holds status information about all memory pages. A business application programmer normally does not have to worry about how the operating system internally manages memory using memory management routines.

Virtual memory management attempts to strike the proper balance. If too much memory is allocated to processes, fewer processes will run and real memory occupied by some processes will not be accessed fast enough and will be wasted. Allocating too little memory to processes may cause frequent swapping of pages, resulting in a situation where the operating system is taking up a lot of CPU time that could have otherwise been used by application processes (the system is said to be *thrashing* when this occurs). To compound the situation, the memory access patterns will vary between processes, and what is optimal for one will not be for another. The operating system monitors the number of pages allocated and used by each process (also called the *working set*) and automatically fine-tunes memory allocation.

Windows 2000 uses 32-bit linear memory addressing. *Linear memory* means that the whole memory is considered one big layout, and each memory address is one value in the 32-bit address space. Contrast the linear memory model with the segmented memory model of Windows 3.1, where memory is considered to be composed of 64K segments. If you are familiar with programming using segmented memory, then consider the 4GB memory as one *huge* segment where you don't have to worry about far and near pointers. The 4GB limit comes from the 32-bit address (2^{32}). Half of the process address space (2GB) is used for the application process, and the other half, for system functions (related to the application process).

Note for UNIX Programmers

UNIX uses linear memory addressing, too. In addition, Windows 2000 and UNIX use demand paging. Both systems support memory-mapped files, which is a technique of speeding up file access by keeping files in memory rather than on disk. In addition, both systems use heaps, which are unstructured memory. However, there are differences. Windows 2000 has a richer API set for virtual memory management and for managing heaps.

NEW IN WINDOWS 2000:   Windows NT introduced ways that applications can get 3GB (please see KB ID: Q171793 for more details). Windows 2000 is extending the process limit. For example, the Windows 2000 Enterprise Server with 64-bit addressing will raise the limit to 64GB.

Input/Output Manager

The part of the Windows 2000 Executive known as the Input/Output (I/O) Manager deals with all input and output, including input from and output to displays, disks, CD-ROM drives, and so on. The I/O Manager uses what is called a *uniform driver model.* In this model, every I/O request to a device is through an *I/O request packet (IRP)*, regardless of the specific type of I/O device. The device specifics are handled at a level below the I/O Manager. The I/O Manager performs the I/O task asynchronously. The process that issued the I/O request is preempted by the operating system, and it waits until it gets a signal that the I/O has been completed.

The I/O Manager of Windows 2000 uses a number of subcomponents such as the network redirector/server (Remote Access Server or RAS), the Cache Manager, file systems, network drivers, and device drivers:

▼   *Network redirector/server (RAS)*   This is covered in Chapter 3.

■   *Cache Manager*   In both Windows 2000 and UNIX, the *cache* is used to store frequently accessed data from disk (such as file data) to speed up future requests for data. Unlike some other systems with fixed cache sizes, Windows 2000 allows the cache size to vary depending on the amount of available memory.

▲   *Device drivers*   The need for device drivers is very simple. Windows 2000 can have hundreds of printers, disk drives, CD-ROM drives, and other peripherals attached to it. The low-level code to drive each of these devices is unique to the device. For example, the line-feed command for an HP printer would be different from the command for an Epson printer. It could even be different for different printer models from the same manufacturer. If a word processing application wants to print, it wouldn't make sense for the Windows 2000 base operating system to format the output, including the device-unique codes. The job of formatting output for the specific device is taken care of by device drivers (see Figure 1-3).

The Windows 2000 base operating system interacts with all device drivers in a standard way. By contrast, Windows 95 supports two ways—a device driver could be a protected-

Note for UNIX Programmers

Both Windows 2000 and UNIX consider all forms of I/O data as a string of bytes or a file, and both systems implement task preempting for I/O requests.

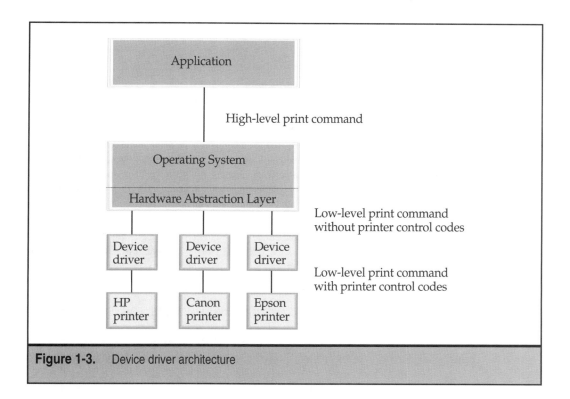

Figure 1-3. Device driver architecture

mode device driver, or it could be a real-mode device driver. As discussed earlier, Windows 2000 restricts low-level hardware access, and not supporting real-mode drivers is another example of the same design principle. Windows 2000 includes *device driver kits (DDKs),* which are equivalent to SDKs, for writing device drivers. Device drivers are normally written only by peripheral manufacturers or software companies that specialize in writing device drivers. Device drivers are low-level programs that business application programmers do not normally worry about.

NEW IN WINDOWS 2000:   To support plug and play, Windows 2000 uses a slightly different serial device driver model than Windows NT 4.0. Windows NT 4.0 serial device drivers that depend on the Windows NT 4.0 *Serial.sys* load order cannot function in Windows 2000 without some modification.

The *file system* subcomponent deals with accessing, reading, and updating files. File systems are covered in Chapter 4.

Object Manager

This part of the Executive creates, manages, and deletes objects. Almost everything in the Windows 2000 operating system is an object. For example, memory, processes, devices, and so on are all objects. Objects have properties associated with them, and the functions of the object are invoked by *methods*. From the time an object is created to the time it is deleted, it has an associated *handle* that uniquely identifies the object.

Security Reference Monitor

Security in computer systems is getting a lot more attention thanks to hacking and viruses. With the increasing popularity of the Internet, the scope of hacking and of viruses has increased dramatically. Virtually any computer with external connections and/or floppy disk drives is susceptible to hacking and viruses. To combat this, operating systems have been increasing their security functions. Many agencies of the federal government have been working on the security problem along with interested groups in the computer industry for a long time. One result of these efforts is a scale indicating the level of security functions provided by an operating system. The scale ranges from D (least secure level) to A (most secure level), with intermediate classifications. The level most operating system vendors aim for and that is required in many federal computer procurements is C2. Windows 2000 meets the requirements for the C2 security level.

Windows 2000 implements a security system wherein all resources such as files have an associated security level. All users of the operating system, including system administrators, other users, and applications, have an associated security level. The security information is specified in an *access control list*. When a user wants to access a resource, the security levels are compared to determine if the user will be allowed to access the resource. Of course, security is a lot more complicated than that. Security is pervasive throughout Windows 2000 and is a part of many APIs and MFC classes. APIs and MFC classes will be covered throughout this book. Most of the setup and maintenance of security functions are handled by the system administrator.

NEW IN WINDOWS 2000:   With Windows 2000, Microsoft is attempting to transform Windows from a workstation and server operating system to an operating system that can be used across all classes of hardware in an enterprise from a desktop to a mainframe class. To this end, Windows 2000 is significantly more secure than Windows NT. Some of the major security-related enhancements include

Support for strong authentication using public-key infrastructure technology including certificates
Support for secure channels based on Secure Sockets Layer (SSL) 3.0
CryptoAPI, which supports industry-standard protocols for data integrity and privacy across
   public networks
Support for the industry standard Kerberos version 5 authentication protocol
Integration with Windows 2000 Active Directory

Chapter 22 covers Windows 2000 security features in more detail.

Local Procedure Call Facility

Applications *(clients)* request services from the protected subsystems *(servers)*. For example, a Win32 application requests services from the Win32 subsystem. Although the phrase "client/server" may conjure up the vision of a small Windows desktop accessing a big server across a network, there is no restriction that clients and servers cannot coexist on the same physical machine. For clients and servers distributed across a network, the most common communication mechanism is the industry standard *remote procedure call (RPC)*. When the client and the server are on the same physical machine with common resources such as shared memory, there is scope for optimizing the communication mechanism. Such an optimization is called the *local procedure call.*

Protected Subsystems

The operating system functions not performed by the kernel are performed by a set of nonprivileged servers known as protected subsystems (see Figure 1-1 in the first section of this chapter). When your application makes a Win32 API call, these calls are handled by the protected subsystems. One of the advantages of the protected subsystems approach is that it permits modular development of new protected subsystems without affecting either the base operating system or the other existing protected subsystems. The same is true for enhancements to protected subsystems. For example, if Microsoft wants to drop support for OS/2 or POSIX applications, then essentially all that needs to be done is to drop the code contained in those protected subsystems.

NEW IN WINDOWS 2000: Microsoft indeed dropped the OS/2 subsystem code from the previous edition and announced that OS/2 applications will not be supported in future releases. For POSIX applications, please see the next box for UNIX Programmers.

Although Windows 2000 is designed to run POSIX and OS/2 applications, do not expect to be able to pass data or files between a Windows application and a POSIX (or OS/2) one. Nor can you expect to see the graphical user interface Windows is famous for—both POSIX and OS/2 support only character-mode applications. This is because the Win32 subsystem is the primary subsystem and supports the programming of text, graphics, networking, and all other functions available in Windows 2000. The OS/2 and POSIX subsystems, on the other hand, are "compatibility mode" subsystems with just text support, and without graphics or network support. The lines between the OS/2 or POSIX subsystems and the Win32 subsystem in Figure 1-1 indicate that for many application calls, the OS/2 and POSIX subsystems actually call the Win32 subsystem. Microsoft documentation is specific on the differences in how Windows 2000 handles Win32 and POSIX (or OS/2) applications.

Quoting from "Microsoft Windows NT from a UNIX Point of View," a white paper from Microsoft:

"The POSIX and OS/2 subsystems provide 'compatibility-mode' environments for their respective applications and, by definition, are not as feature-rich as the Win32 subsystem."

A more technical quote from the Windows NT resource kit:

"With this release of Windows NT, POSIX applications have no direct access to any of the facilities and features of the Win32 subsystem, such as memory mapped files, networking, graphics, or dynamic data exchange."

Translated, no access to graphics means that the popular Windows graphical user interface is not natively available for a POSIX application, and you are restricted to console text applications. No networking means no WinSock, Point-to-Point Protocol (PPP) support, and the like. You get the picture. In providing POSIX support the way it did, Microsoft ensured that Windows 2000 can be used in federal and state acquisitions bids that mandate POSIX compliance, while ensuring that there is enough incentive for users to switch and take advantage of the other Win32 features.

Besides the protected subsystems, Windows 2000 also supports *virtual machines*. All the DOS programs, for example, run in a virtual DOS machine (VDM). The same mechanism is also used to run 16-bit Windows applications (also called *WOW* for Windows on Win32 applications). The same 16-bit Windows application that may run and cause a GPF and shut down Windows 3.1 will not be able to do that here, since the application only affects the virtual machine, not the whole operating system. The price for this protection is that some 16-bit applications (games and other applications that access the hardware or attempt to enhance performance through nonstandard means), will not run in Windows 2000. More than one virtual machine can be active at the same time.

Note for UNIX Programmers

There are third-party tools that let you run an application written using the Win32 API on many UNIX systems. Microsoft has a licensing program called Windows Interface Source Environment (WISE). The goal of WISE is to enable programs written to the Win32 API to run on different platforms such as UNIX and Macintosh. WISE SDKs provides source code compatibility, and the application source code must be recompiled for the different systems the application needs to run on. Examples of WISE SDKs include MainWin from Mainsoft and Wind/U from Bristol Technologies.

PROGRAMMING LANGUAGES
AND DEVELOPMENT ENVIRONMENT

Microsoft supports program development by providing a number of language compilers and an integrated development environment. Languages supported include general-purpose programming languages such as Visual C++, Visual Basic, and Fortran, as well as special-purpose languages such as HTML, Visual J++, and Perl (Practical Extraction and Report Language).

Hypertext Markup Language (HTML) is the language used for developing World Wide Web pages and supports embedding multimedia content such as graphics into Web pages. HTML also supports *hyperlinks*; viewers click a hyperlink (typically displayed in a different color than the rest of the text) and go to the address (*URL*, or Universal Resource Locator) pointed to by the link.

Perl, which has its origins in UNIX, is a free-form interpreted language used to scan and extract information from text files and to print reports using the extracted information. Windows 2000 supports Perl 5.

Fortran is used primarily for many scientific and some engineering applications. Microsoft's Fortran PowerStation supports the latest Fortran standard—Fortran 90.

Java is the programming language developed by Sun Microsystems; it differs from traditional programming languages in one important way: Java compilers do not produce run-time executables for a specific environment, unlike traditional programming languages. The Java compiler outputs *Java byte codes*. These byte codes are interpreted by a Java Byte Code Interpreter, which can be embedded into many applications. The most common example of applications that embed Java interpreters is a World Wide Web browser. Visual J++ is Microsoft's implementation of Java. Visual J++ enables you to create, edit, compile, run, and debug Java programs within an integrated development environment.

Visual Basic provides the ability to build applications without a lot of programming by use of prebuilt programming components or objects. It includes many features of other programming languages such as branching, condition evaluations, and assignments. Visual Basic, however, uses English-like constructs rather than terse programming constructs.

Keep in mind that you are not tied to any programming language. For the most part, you can invoke programs written in one language from another language. All major development efforts typically use more than one language. Learning programming languages is like learning to drive cars. Once you get a basic feel for the road, you can drive most cars relatively easily. Once you have learned to program in one language and understand logic, algorithms, and the like, you can program in any other language after a short learning curve.

Microsoft provides an integrated program development environment called the *Developer Studio*. The Developer Studio supports development of Visual C++ and other languages. The functions provided by the Developer Studio include

▼ Source code management

■ Editing and compiling program source

■ Link editing and make files

■ Project management

▲ Debugging

Microsoft integrates new functions related to program development into the Microsoft Developer Studio. Most of the programming examples in this book will be written in C++ and developed and tested through use of the Developer Studio.

Other software vendors also provide development environments. Corel has taken over the development environment developed by Borland International and subsequently by Inprise. This environment includes language compilers, editors, and tools, including the C++ compiler, the Object Windows Library (OWL), and so on.

APPLICATION PROGRAMMING INTERFACES

Windows Application Programming Interfaces started with Win16, the 16-bit API used by Windows 3.1 applications. Win32 is the 32-bit version used by Windows 2000. Win32 was a subset of the Win32 API set that could be called by 16-bit applications. Wing is an API set for graphics. Although there is a huge installed base of 16-bit applications, advances in hardware and software make it likely that most future programming will use the Win32 API, which this book will focus on. You can tell whether system files and DLLs are 16-bit or 32-bit versions by looking for "32" in the filename. For example, *Kernel32.dll, Gdi32.dll, User32.dll,* and *Regedt32.exe* are all 32-bit functions.

The Win32 APIs are categorized as shown in Table 1-1.

Category	Functions
Controls	Combo box, dialog box, edit, header, hot-key, image lists, list box, list view, progress bar, property sheet, rich edit, scroll bar, status, tab, toolbar, toolkit, track bar, tree view, and up-down controls Example: CreateUpDownControl
Graphics (GDI)	Advanced graphics functions including animation Example: CAnimateCtrl

Table 1-1. Win32 API Categories and Functions

Category	Functions
Windows management	Windows, window class, window properties, and window procedures; cursors; menus; hooks; icons; Multiple Document Interfaces (MDIs); keyboard accelerators; keyboard inputs; mouse input messages; message queues; timers; and clipboards Example: InsertMenuItem
Console	Shell-related functions Example: TextOut
System services	Access files and databases, exception handling, network transports, performance monitoring, processes, threads, and security Example: GetOpenFileName
Network	Handle network connections, manage network configuration, domain administration, network management, remote access service, and Windows Socket interface Example: GetExtensionVersion
Multimedia	Audio, media control, video, joystick, and other special inputs/outputs Example: mciSendString

Table 1-1.   Win32 API Categories and Functions *(continued)*

Win32 Extensions

Microsoft has extended the Win32 APIs and included support to

▼   Develop desktop applications that integrate telephone functions by use of the Telephony Application Programming Interface (TAPI)

■   Develop asynchronous communications applications by use of the Remote Access Server (RAS)

■   Provide applications with database access by use of Data Access Objects (DAO)

▲   Develop electronic commerce applications by use of Exchange SDK

SOFTWARE DEVELOPMENT KITS

Microsoft provides a number of *software development kits (SDKs)*. SDKs are self-contained kits including specifications, programmer reference documentation, example source code, and so on. Each SDK focuses on one topic. Windows 2000 provides a number of SDKs. These include

▼ *Win32 SDK* The Win32 SDK enables you to develop code using the Win32 API (refer to the "Application Programming Interfaces" section earlier in this chapter).

■ *MAPI SDK* The MAPI SDK enables you to develop MAPI-compliant applications. The MAPI SDK is available in 16- and 32-bit versions. The 32-bit version is part of the Win32 SDK. C, C++, and Visual Basic examples are included in the MAPI SDK.

■ *OLE SDK* The OLE SDK contains the COM specification. The OLE SDK enables you to develop code using the Microsoft object linking and embedding (OLE) interface.

■ *ODBC SDK 2.1* This enables you to develop Open Database Connectivity (ODBC) drivers and ODBC-compliant applications.

■ *DAO SDK* The DAO SDK enables you to develop DAO applications.

■ *RAS SDK* The RAS SDK enables you to develop applications by use of the RAS API. You can use the RAS API to write applications to establish, communicate, and terminate connections with remote machines.

■ *Exchange SDK* The Exchange SDK enables you to develop client and server programs based on the Microsoft Exchange Server.

■ *SMS SDK* This SDK is used for developing applications for the Systems Management Server. The SMS Server and the SNA Server are add-on server products that run on top of Windows 2000. These are covered later in this chapter.

■ *Systems Network Architecture (SNA) SDK* This SDK is used for developing applications for the SNA Server.

▲ *Active Directory Service Interfaces (ADSI) SDK* This SDK enables users, such as administrators, or applications to access and manipulate LDAP, NetWare, and Windows 2000 directories. ADSI also includes Active Data Object (ADO) and OLE DB interfaces. ADSI itself is not language specific and will work with Visual Basic, Visual J++, and Visual C/C++.

MICROSOFT FOUNDATION CLASSES (MFC)

The Microsoft Foundation Class (MFC) library is an application framework for developing applications by use of the Win32 API. The framework is a collection of C++ classes. Classes simplify programming and promote code reuse. Using MFC classes will save you a lot of time. MFC is integrated within the Visual C++ development environment. For example, if you develop an application using AppWizard, you have the MFC classes available for your use. MFC is built on top of the Win32 API and attempts to shield the programmer from some of the details of API programming. Programs developed using MFC port well across the different Windows platforms, unless there are platform-specific constraints. If you have some old 16-bit code, Microsoft has an MFC migration kit that assists you in migrating that code. MFC has been keeping pace with recent Microsoft development technologies. The latest version of MFC includes full OLE support, Data Access Objects (DAO) support, common controls support, thread synchronization support, and so on.

This book will include many programming samples and exercises using the MFC.

GRAPHICAL DEVICE INTERFACE (GDI)

The *graphical device interface* deals with the graphical end-user interface (as opposed to character-based interface) that Windows and Microsoft have become famous for. Windows includes a lot of support for you to develop GDI applications including Win32 APIs, MFC classes, prebuilt controls, and so on. Some of the common GDI objects you will use include

▼ Pens
■ Brushes
■ Fonts
■ Bitmaps
▲ Metafiles

User interface programming is covered in more detail in Chapter 2.

While Windows is famous for its graphical interface, Windows 2000 does support character-based applications. Character-based applications run in the Windows 2000 *shell,* which is an enhancement to the command prompt that supports character-based applications and is a good alternative to regular graphical windows programming for quick-and-dirty applications.

INTERNET AND NETWORK PROGRAMMING

Microsoft provides a number of ways to help you develop programs involving the Internet. Some of the ways include

▼ Internet server classes

■ AppWizard for creating Internet applications

▲ World Wide Web access from the Developer Studio

The latest release of MFC has added five new Internet server classes to implement the Internet Server API (ISAPI). These classes are

▼ **CHttpServer**   Creates an Internet server extension

■ **CHttpServerContext**   **CHttpServer** uses this to handle multiple concurrent requests

■ **CHttpFilter**   Creates an Internet server filter to screen messages to and from an Internet server

■ **CHttpFilterContext**   **CHttpFilter** uses this to handle multiple concurrent requests

▲ **CHtmlStream**   **CHttpServer** uses this to send an HTML stream back to the client

You can create Internet server extensions and filters using these classes and the ISAPI extension wizard. Visual C++ includes the example MFCUCASE, which illustrates creating Internet filter DLLs using MFC classes. Visual C++ also includes the example HTTPSVR, which illustrates using MFC and WinSock classes to implement a simple World Wide Web HTTP server. The HTTP server supports form creation and execution of Common Gateway Interface (CGI) server applications by use of the standard HTML constructs. In addition, ASP provides a Web server–scripting environment.

Network Programming

Besides the Internet, Windows 2000 also includes functions to support network programming. These functions include

▼ Windows Sockets (WinSock) support

■ Remote Access Server (RAS) support

■ Messaging Application Programming Interface (MAPI) support

▲ Telephony Application Programming Interface (TAPI) support

TAPI includes the APIs to integrate telephone functions with your applications. For example, using TAPI you can programmatically place or receive a telephone call, hang up, place a call on hold, transfer calls, enable conference calls, and monitor calls. Of course, you need a line device such as a phone, fax card, modem, or an Integrated Services Digital Network (ISDN) card and a connection to the public phone network.

MAPI is more than an API. MAPI is a messaging architecture that is designed to bridge multiple applications on one side to multiple messaging systems on the other across heterogeneous hardware platforms and networks. MAPI shields users from the differences of various messaging systems—in particular, mail systems.

For example, you can use MAPI to develop applications that communicate with different messaging systems for fax, voice, and so on.

You can use MAPI in different ways:

▼   You can use Simple MAPI by using the Visual C++ (or Visual Basic) API interface.

■   You can use Common Messaging Calls (CMC), which is another form of API that supports the XAPIA standard.

▲   You can use OLE messaging.

COMPONENT OBJECT MODEL (COM) AND DISTRIBUTED COM

COM specifies how objects interact; it does not matter whether the objects are within a single application or spread across different applications. COM specifies basic interfaces that are used by all COM-based technologies such as OLE and ActiveX. One of the important elements of COM is its specification for component interoperability at the binary level. Binary components imply that the source language used to generate the binary or even the platform/vendor used to generate the binary is not relevant. The binary need only follow COM interoperability rules to use and be used by other COM-based binaries. Besides the binary nature of components, COM also specifies the communication rules between COM components. There is no restriction that the components be restricted to a machine or process. Thus, you have the communications between objects across networks, the basis for networked OLE functions. COM also specifies the rules for sharing memory between components, handling exceptions in the case of errors, and dynamic loading of components as required.

Distributed COM (DCOM) extends the COM model and constructs to let objects interact seamlessly across a network. DCOM is the new name for what used to be called networked OLE. Each DCOM object provides useful functions, and a set of functions is called an *interface* (which, in reality, is a table of pointers to the functions). Each DCOM object can have multiple interfaces. When an application that you are developing wants to use functions available in a DCOM object, you can invoke the DCOM object. The exact invoking mechanism is handled transparently by the operating system. Your application does not know where the object resides, which could be across a network or in the same process. In addition, the interfaces to the objects your application invokes can be changed and your application will remain unaffected (unless you want to take advantage of the interface changes). DCOM objects' functions are implemented as dynamic link libraries (DLLs). This means that your application need not be recompiled if the DCOM object's functions are changed. DCOM builds on remote procedure calls (RPCs).

In Windows 2000, COM+ builds on COM's integrated services and features, making it easier for developers to create and use software components in any language, using any tool. COM+ includes Transaction Services and Message Queuing Services for reliable distributed applications.

OLE

The following describes a user's view of OLE. Your job is to provide the programming to make this happen. Let's start with a very brief recap of OLE basics and OLE 1.0. OLE provides the capability for an application like Word to include a spreadsheet object and to permit editing of the spreadsheet using Excel, but without quitting Word.

The object—the spreadsheet in this case—can be *linked* from or *embedded* into the Word document. If the object is linked, it remains as an independent spreadsheet and can be independently edited by use of Excel. But if you open the Word document that has the spreadsheet linked to it, the Word document will reflect the updates made to the spreadsheet. This behavior is an advantage if this is what you wanted, and a problem if you opened the Word document and were surprised to find the updated spreadsheet. When the Word document embeds the spreadsheet, it completely contains the spreadsheet. The size of the Word document increases (approximately) by the size of the embedded spreadsheet. You can send the Word document to another Windows machine (across the world), and you can still see the document including the spreadsheet (assuming that machine has the right versions of Word and Excel). The Word document is also called a *compound document*.

OLE is based on the Component Object Model (COM). OLE lets you write platform- and language-independent objects. It specifies the interaction rules between objects. OLE lets you programmatically implement the preceding scenario in your own application.

OLE has since expanded beyond compound documents. It is used for a variety of component software–based programming functions such as reusable custom controls, data transfer, drag-and-drop embedding, OLE automation, and in-place activation. As mentioned before, OLE is based on COM; an OLE-compatible application should follow the COM rules for functions and interfaces. Many interfaces are available for OLE applications, and many OLE applications use only a small subset of the interfaces. The one interface all OLE applications should implement is the **IUnknown** interface, which is like an entry point for all other interfaces. In fact, it includes the **QueryInterface** function that provides the list of the other interfaces available. Another important programming concept associated with OLE that you should be familiar with is called *OLE automation*. OLE automation is the mechanism by which one application can access, control, and manipulate another application's objects. OLE is covered in more detail in Chapter 13.

MULTIMEDIA

Windows 2000 includes support for you to develop multimedia applications. Multimedia applications are those that incorporate video, sound, and complex graphics. You can program at a high level using the **MCIWnd** window class, you can have more control using the Media Control Interface (MCI) API, or you can even use multimedia structures such as **AVIFilePrevKeyFrame**. Other services provided by Windows 2000 for multimedia programming include a multimedia timer and I/O support such as joystick services. You can write sophisticated graphics programs in Windows 2000 using OpenGL.

OpenGL

OpenGL was originally developed by Silicon Graphics Incorporated (SGI) for its graphics workstations. Using OpenGL, you can create applications with high-quality color images and animated 3-D graphics. OpenGL is independent of the windowing systems, operating system, and hardware.

Windows 2000 OpenGL components include

▼ OpenGL commands

■ OpenGL utility library (GLU)

▲ OpenGL programming guide auxiliary library

The Windows Graphic Library APIs and the new Win32 APIs for pixel formats and double-buffering also help in OpenGL programming. Microsoft Visual C++ has some OpenGL examples.

DATA ACCESS

Windows 2000 provides a number of ways for applications to store and retrieve data. Where applications use files, Windows 2000 supports multiple file systems such as New Technology File System (NTFS), File Allocation Table (FAT) and FAT variations such as FAT32, and so on; these are covered in Chapter 4.

Windows 2000 applications can also store and retrieve data from many databases, including smaller ones such as Access or enterprise databases such as SQL Server or Oracle. One popular way to access databases is the *Open Database Connectivity (ODBC)* method using the standard language for database retrieval, the *Structured Query Language (SQL)*. Microsoft has recently introduced *Data Access Objects (DAO),* which improves upon the functionality of ODBC. ODBC is covered in Chapter 20. DAO is covered in Chapter 21.

REGISTRY

The *Registry* is the name given the configuration information databases in Windows 95, Windows 98, and Windows 2000 (although at this point they are not compatible). The Registry replaces the INI files used in prior versions of Windows and is an alternative and better method for dealing with configuration information about hardware, applications, users, and so on. Note that for compatibility reasons, the old INI files are still supported. The Registry can be updated by use of a built-in Registry Editor. The Registry can also be programmatically accessed by use of APIs.

ACTIVE DIRECTORY

A *directory* stores information about different entities such as users, application, and devices in a network. Developers can use a number of standard interfaces to write applications that utilize information stored in the Active Directory. All Active Directory functions are available through LDAP, ADSI, and MAPI for extending and integrating with other applications, directories, and devices. Active Directory programming is covered in more detail in Chapter 10.

WINDOWS DNA

With the Windows DNA, programmers can build secure, reliable, highly scalable solutions that ease the integration of heterogeneous systems and applications. Windows DNA programming is covered in more detail in Chapter 16.

WINDOWS 2000 EDITIONS

As mentioned earlier, Microsoft Windows 2000 actually comes in four flavors: Windows 2000 Professional and three variations of Windows 2000 Server. Windows 2000 Professional is designed to be the client machine, with fewer resource (memory and disk space) requirements compared with the Windows 2000 Server family. There is more commonality between the Windows 2000 products than there are differences. You can think of the Server functions as a superset of the client functions. All Windows 2000 products provide rich networking capabilities including Transmission Control Protocol/Internet Protocol (TCP/IP) support and remote access services. All of the products also have the same file systems support, include basic NetWare integration functions, and provide basic security functions. Probably most important from a programming perspective, both products support the Win32 API, including GDI support for end-user interfaces. This means that the same Win32 program that you write will work on both products.

There are differences between the client and server Windows 2000 products, however, and the important ones from a programming perspective are summarized here:

▼   If you develop server applications—for example, using the BackOffice products or the Internet Information Server—then those may not work under Windows 2000 Professional.

■   Windows 2000 Server products includes a special disk device driver called *Ftdisk.sys,* which takes advantage of fault-tolerant capabilities such as disk mirroring, duplexing, and parity striping of Redundant Array of Inexpensive Disks (RAID).

■   Windows 2000 Server includes TCP/IP-related networking enhancements such as Dynamic Host Configuration Protocol (DHCP) support (which permits dynamic IP address assignment), Windows Internet Name Service (WINS) support (which provides dynamic NetBIOS name registration and resolution), and a Dynamic Domain Name Service, which adds on the benefits of dynamic support to regular Domain Name Service functions.

■   Another networking difference concerns RAS. The RAS service in Windows 2000 Server supports multiple simultaneous RAS connections (some versions support 256 connections), while the RAS service in Windows 2000 Professional allows only a single connection.

■   Windows 2000 Server provides Internet support using the Internet Information Server (IIS). IIS is a full-fledged Internet server that supports the Hypertext Transfer Protocol (HTTP), File Transfer Protocol (FTP), Gopher, and other Internet services. Windows 2000 Professional, on the other hand, uses Peer Web Services, which is functionally equivalent to the IIS, with one important difference being that it limits the number of incoming connections to ten. This limitation restricts the number of users and Internet functions that can be supported by Windows 2000 Professional.

▲   Windows 2000 Server can integrate Macintosh clients, has extensible security functions, supports integration with and migrating from NetWare, supports "roving" users by storing user-profile information and letting the user have the same environment wherever he or she logs on, can provide a single logon for multiple domains, and so on.

Table 1-2 summarizes features of the different Windows 2000 Editions.

There are more differences between the client and server Windows 2000 products. To summarize: Windows 2000 Professional is not designed to run such server applications, and the two products are designed for different requirements. If Windows 2000 Server is used where Windows 2000 Professional would suffice, it would amount to cracking a nut with a sledgehammer. On the other hand, if you attempt to save money and try to run server applications on the Professional edition, chances are that there will not be enough horsepower for it to run the application (if it were possible to run at all).

	Windows Professional	Windows Server	Windows Advanced Server	Windows Datacenter Server
Windows NT equivalence	Windows NT Workstation	Windows NT Server	Windows NT Server	Windows NT Server
Target audiences	Business desktops, notebooks	File, print, intranet, networking	Line of business, e-commerce	Large critical applications: OLTP, data warehouses, ASPs, and ISPs
Max. CPUs supported by one system	2	4	8	32
Memory supported	4GB	4GB	8GB	64GB
Clustering	None	None	Two-node failover, 32-node network load balancing	Cascading fail-over among four nodes, 32-node network load balancing
Minimum system requirements	133 MHz Pentium-compatible CPU, 64MB RAM, 2GB disk space	133 MHz Pentium-compatible CPU, 256MB RAM, 2GB disk space	133 MHz Pentium-compatible CPU, 256MB RAM, 2GB disk space	To be announced

Table 1-2.   Windows 2000 Editions

ADD-ON SERVER FUNCTIONS FOR WINDOWS 2000 SERVER

Besides the Windows 2000 Server products, Microsoft produces a number of add-on server products that add unique functions to the Windows 2000 Servers. These unique functions include database access, systems management functions, functions for the Internet, and so on. Your programming tasks are likely to include one or more of these add-on products. The following presents a brief summary of these add-on products. Figure 1-4 shows an overview of the add-on products and the common programming tools for the add-on products.

SQL Server

The Structured Query Language (SQL) Server is a relational database management system. It is comparable to and a competitor of database systems from Oracle, Sybase, and Informix. Some of the functions provided by the SQL Server are

▼   Storing and retrieving data

■   Capability to run application logic common to many applications in one place, instead of each application duplicating the logic

■   Database administration functions such as backup and recovery

■   Communication between databases when data required for an application is in another database

▲   Interface support to permit applications to access data (such as ODBC, DAO, and so on)

Common programming tools for the SQL Server include SQL, ODBC, and DAO.

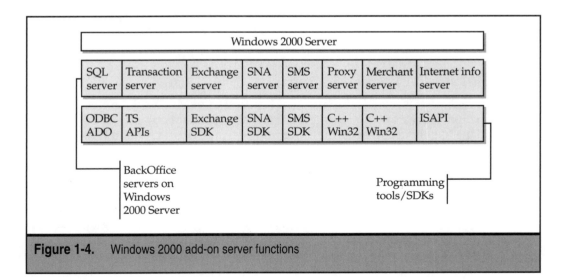

Figure 1-4.   Windows 2000 add-on server functions

Systems Management Server

The Systems Management Server (SMS) is a tool for administrators to manage servers and client workstations from a central location. Some of the functions provided by the SMS are the following:

▼ SMS stores and updates configurations of hardware and software for servers and clients on a network.

■ Remote software distribution permits clients' software to be automatically updated from the SMS. Besides the actual program files, configuration information for the client could be provided as well.

■ SMS provides an end-user interface as well as the capability to access its functions programmatically.

▲ SMS helps desk support functions, including the capability to monitor client workstations remotely.

The SMS SDK, which includes System Management APIs, is used to program the SMS.

Proxy Server

The Microsoft Proxy Server acts as a gateway on top of the Windows 2000 Servers and the Internet Information Server to provide a secure access to the Internet. All Internet users' requests are routed through the Proxy Server, which includes caching functions and will attempt to satisfy a user's request with a cached copy. The Proxy Server eliminates having a dedicated Internet gateway, since it (and IIS) can run on any Windows 2000 Server. It supports TCP/IP and Novell's Internetwork Packet Exchange/Sequenced Packet Exchange (IPX/SPX) protocols, the Secure Sockets Layer (SSL) interface, and the European Laboratory for Particle Physics (CERN) Proxy standard.

Merchant Server

The Merchant Server is a new add-on server function from Microsoft designed to facilitate transaction processing and exchanges between merchants online. Both the Proxy Server and the Merchant Server can be programmed by use of the C++ and Win32 APIs.

Microsoft Transaction Server

The Microsoft Transaction Server is a recent addition to the Microsoft BackOffice family. Microsoft Transaction Server is a transaction processing system. It includes different components including a Transaction Server run-time environment, a graphical user interface, and so on. Of interest to the programmer is an Application Programming Interface specifically meant for developing applications for the Transaction Server. Some of the important features of the Transaction Server of interest to the programmer include these:

▼ Developers can build Transaction Server applications as software components using tools that support ActiveX, including Microsoft Visual Basic, Visual C++, and Visual J++.

■ Transaction Server includes a component packaging service to facilitate integration, installation, and deployment of many components as a single application.

■ Transaction Server manages a pool of ODBC connections to a database.

■ Transaction Server automatically provides transparent transaction support to applications running on the server. The application does not need to use low-level transaction control primitives (or fundamental elements) to accomplish this.

■ Transaction Server uses DCOM for component-to-component communications across a network. Microsoft is trying to license DCOM as an open-industry standard through the Open Group.

■ Transaction Server works with many resource managers, including relational databases, file systems, and image stores, that support a transactional two-phase commit protocol. This enables businesses to leverage existing investments in UNIX and mainframe data stores.

■ Win32 "fat" clients and HTML "thin" clients can access Transaction Server applications concurrently.

▲ Administrators can easily partition an application across multiple servers by deploying an application's components into several packages, with each package running on its own server.

IIS Server

The Internet Information Server (IIS) provides Internet-related functions for its Internet clients, including

▼ File transfer using the File Transfer Protocol (FTP)

■ Searching the Internet through a Gopher

▲ Domain Name Service (DNS) to translate or look up Universal Resource Locators (URLs)

The ISAPI is used to program Internet-related functions. MFC also includes new Internet-related classes.

SNA Server

The SNA Server is used to interface with IBM's networks that use the Systems Network Architecture. The SNA Server enables applications to interface with legacy applications and to retrieve legacy data.

The SNA SDK is used to program the SNA server functions.

CONCLUSION

We have looked at a range of Windows 2000 topics that provide an overview of the different functions in Windows 2000. These topics lay the groundwork for future chapters, and you should be familiar with the programming topics mentioned. The remainder of the book builds on these topics. For example, ODBC is covered in Chapter 20; DAO, in Chapter 21; ISAPI, in Chapter 16; OLE, in Chapters 12 and 13; and TAPI is covered in Chapter 18.

CHAPTER 2

User Interface Programming

Programming the user interface is one of the most challenging and rewarding areas of Windows 2000 programming. You already know that people can understand a lot better what they can *see*. A well-designed user interface and demo help to show the application you are developing much better than reports, charts, and other documentation about the application. The good news for you is that Microsoft has standardized the user interfaces of its primary products. First, Windows NT 4.0 got the same interface as Windows 95, and this common interface is being carried forward to follow-on products such as Windows 98 and Windows 2000. Second, Microsoft is trying to further standardize the desktop as an Explorer-based one for which it doesn't matter whether the items on the desktop are from the local machine or from the network. This interface is already becoming available in the Visual Studio, the Microsoft Developers Network, and so on. Why is this standardization important to you? One obvious reason is that if you have used one Microsoft product, you can be comfortable with others. More important, Microsoft includes a lot of prebuilt code to support user interface programming, and use of the prebuilt code will lead to the same standardized interface. This means that even without seeing a single dialog box in your application, your end users are already trained in many end-user aspects of your application.

THE WINDOWS USER INTERFACE

User interface programming involving Windows 2000 differs from other programming environments, such as mainframes and even many UNIX environments, in Windows 2000's capability to customize and in its built-in support for the customization. Most mainframe and some UNIX environments display the application screens to the user, but the user can do little to customize them. Many of the functions that are taken for granted in Windows 2000 user interfaces, such as adjusting the size of the window, changing background and foreground colors, changing fonts, scrolling, moving the position of a window on the desktop, and reducing a window to an icon, are either not available or restricted in the other environments. The good news on customization for you as a programmer is that you get all of this functionality for very little effort. Windows 2000 has a lot of built-in code that provides much of the functionality for supporting the Windows 2000 user interface.

Besides the window management and customization support, Windows 2000 includes a number of built-in standard user-interface elements to ease the task of user interface programming. These include standard functions to ask the user to choose from a list of alternatives, to provide the user with a list of available choices for a field, and so on. These built-in elements are the bread and butter of Windows 2000 user interface programming.

In this chapter, we will review the basics of user interface programming for Windows 2000, including a few of the built-in controls. Windows operating systems have always included a number of built-in APIs and controls to support user interface programming. Windows 2000 expands on the built-in APIs and controls while also including support for advanced user interface features, such as common controls and world transforms. These advanced features add pizzazz to your user interface. A more detailed discussion of some of the built-in elements, together with programming examples, appears in Chapter 6 and Chapter 7.

As a programmer, you are not constrained to use any of these built-in elements. However, unless you want to try things on your own, use these built-in elements as much as possible. If you use them, you have already in effect trained your end user in some aspects of using your application. For example, if you open a Windows application that you may not know how to use, you still may have some idea where to find the application functions if you see File, Edit, Window, and Help on the menu bar. Since your application end user has most likely used other Windows applications at home or work, you make his or her life a lot easier by being consistent with other Windows applications.

WINDOWS 2000 USER INTERFACE PROGRAMMING

Windows 2000 provides different ways that you can program to support user interfaces:

▼ Windows basic and common controls
■ Programming interfaces to support graphics (GDI support)
■ ActiveX controls
■ OpenGL support
■ Control classes supplied by the MFC
▲ Windows 2000 shell and shell extensions

This chapter covers the basic controls, and using the MFC to program controls. Chapter 6 addresses GDI programming. Chapter 7 addresses advanced controls and the shell and its extensions. Chapter 14 addresses ActiveX controls, and Chapter 19 addresses OpenGL programming. Before we start looking at programming simple controls, let's look at two ways that you can program these controls.

APIs VERSUS MFC PROGRAMMING

You can program user interfaces (and most other functions) in Windows 2000 either directly using the Win32 API or by using the MFC. Win32 APIs were introduced in Chapter 1.

Programming using the MFC is the same as C++ programming using classes. In fact, the MFC is a class library, encapsulating or wrapping Windows 2000 programming elements such as dialog boxes in the MFC classes. You program using the MFC by using an existing class (or deriving from an existing class) and creating an object of the existing or derived class. Once an object has been created, you call member functions of the class to manipulate the object. It is important to note that use of the MFC is not a completely different way of programming. The MFC calls the same Win32 APIs that you can write to directly. The MFC shields some of the details associated with APIs and in some cases performs some small housekeeping functions that tend to save you time and effort compared with programming directly to the Win32 APIs. Also note that the MFC encapsulates most of the Win32 API. Note that there are some APIs that the MFC doesn't encapsulate. This is because the MFC provides classes for the anticipated needs of most programmers, but it is not meant to be a C++ run-time library. In cases where the MFC does not have the classes for some function that you want to program, you can use the MFC for the other functions and call the Win32 API directly from within the MFC.

While many programmers use the MFC for the added convenience, as an advanced Windows 2000 programmer, you should be familiar with both Win32 API and MFC programming. Let's review some basic controls, their characteristics, and programming aspects.

BASIC CONTROLS

It is impossible to use Windows 2000 for long and not come across the word "control." *Controls* are the building blocks of user interface programming. The interaction between a user and your program takes the form of messages passed back and forth between your program and controls. Controls are child windows to let the user make selections, input or edit data, and so on. Controls are typically used in dialog boxes, although they are used in other windows as well. Some common examples of controls include check boxes, combo boxes, edit boxes, list boxes, and scroll bars. The Windows operating systems have always provided a number of predefined controls, and more controls were added for Windows 2000. The advanced controls are called *common* controls; let us call the older, simpler ones *basic* controls.

Windows 2000 provides the programming tools for you to include controls in your program. You can add controls to your dialog box using the Visual C++ dialog editor. The MFC includes a class for each of the controls. **CWnd** is the base class for all control classes (and all other window classes as well).

Next, let's look at how to program controls—predefined and custom controls, disabling controls, and stand-alone controls.

PROGRAMMING CONTROLS

You can create a control in two ways. You can specify a control's associated windows class to the **CreateWindowEx** function. Alternatively, you can specify the controls to be included in the dialog box template. Typically, you would include more than one control in your dialog box or window. To distinguish one control from another, each control has a unique identifier called a *control identifier*. If you use **CreateWindowEx**, the control identifier is specified using the *hMenu* parameter. If you use a dialog box template, the control identifier is specified in the ID member of the DLGITEMTEMPLATE structure.

NEW IN WINDOWS 2000: **CreateWindowEx** supports some additional parameters for Windows 2000 to support message-only windows and layered windows.

A *message-only* window simply dispatches messages but has nothing else in common with other windows. It is not visible, has no Z order, cannot be enumerated, and does not receive broadcast messages. It enables you to send and receive messages.

Layered windows are used when a complex window is set up as layers. Since Windows 2000 automatically composes and repaints layered windows and the windows of underlying applications, performance is significantly improved and layered windows are rendered smoothly, without the flickering typical of complex window regions. You use layered windows when you have a window that has a complex shape, or when you animate the window shape, or if you want to use alpha blending effects. Windows 2000 supports alpha blending by making some of the layers partially translucent.

Once created, a control sends messages when it is accessed by the user (these are **WM_COMMAND** messages). These messages, called *notification messages,* are sent to the parent window. The notification messages include the control identifier and information about the event that caused the notification message. The control includes the control identifier in the notification message either by using the **GetDlgCtrlID** function or by retrieving the identifier from the *hMenu* member in the **CREATESTRUCT** structure while processing the **WM_CREATE** message. The application receives these messages and takes appropriate action. The application can manipulate the control using functions such as **ShowWindow** or **EnableWindow,** or it can send control messages (if the control's window class supports control messages).

NEW IN WINDOWS 2000: **ShowWindow** provides an option to minimize a window, even if the thread that owns the window is hung.

Control messages can be predefined, such as **WM_SETFONT**, or application defined. Application-defined messages are sent using a function such as **SendDlgItemMessage** to send messages. All messages from the application to the control go through to the window procedure.

Predefined Versus Custom Controls

You can use the controls that are predefined by Windows 2000, or else you can create your own custom controls. There are many advantages to using predefined controls. *Predefined* controls have a set of built-in *styles* that you can choose from. Styles specify the appearance and behavior variations for the control. Windows 2000 also provides a lot of code to support the built-in controls, which translates into less work for you. To get a custom look, you can use your own custom controls.

The most elaborate and time-consuming way to do this is to define your own window class. You then register your window class the same way you would register any other window class. (Remember, each window class must have a unique name.) You then specify the name of your window class in the **CreateWindowEx** function or in the dialog box template. You must also write the window procedure to draw the control, process any input messages from the keyboard and mouse, and send notification messages to the parent window. In addition, your window procedure may need to process control messages sent by the parent window or other windows.

There are a couple of easier ways to make custom controls. First, you can create a subclass of a predefined control class. In this case, instead of writing a window procedure to handle all the messages, you can write a subclass procedure to handle selected messages and pass all other messages to the original window procedure for the control. Finally, for some predefined controls such as list boxes and combo boxes, you can designate them as owner-drawn controls by specifying the appropriate style. Windows 2000 still does most of the work associated with the control, such as detecting user interaction and notifying the application. Drawing the control, however, is left to the parent window of the control. Thus, you can choose to vary the appearance of your control.

USING PREDEFINED CONTROLS

Having looked at different controls and some programming aspects in general, let's look at some common predefined controls and user interface programming functions provided by Windows 2000.

TIP: There are excellent examples of different user interface elements and how to navigate. You already have the examples—just refer to your Windows 2000 and Visual C++ program interfaces.

Menu

You probably will never develop a Windows 2000 user interface application without a menu. Your menu, which typically is the first one your user sees, provides a snapshot of all functions provided by your application. Windows 2000 provides a lot of support to help you in creating your menu.

The menu (or more accurately the *menu bar*) is the bar displayed just below the *caption bar* displaying the choices your program provides to the user. For example, the Microsoft Word menu is shown in Figure 2-1.

Menu Characteristics

The menu shows a list of items that the user can select by clicking them (or selecting them by means of the keyboard). When selected, each item typically brings up a *pull-down menu* (also called a *submenu*) indicating more choices. Menu bars have consistency guidelines that are a good idea for you to follow in your application. For example, File is typically the first item, and Help, the last. Within each pull-down menu, horizontal bars group similar items together. Items that have additional levels of choices are indicated by an ellipsis (...). Typically, a description for each item in the menu bar shows up either as a tooltip or as text in the status bar. It is also common for a user to select a

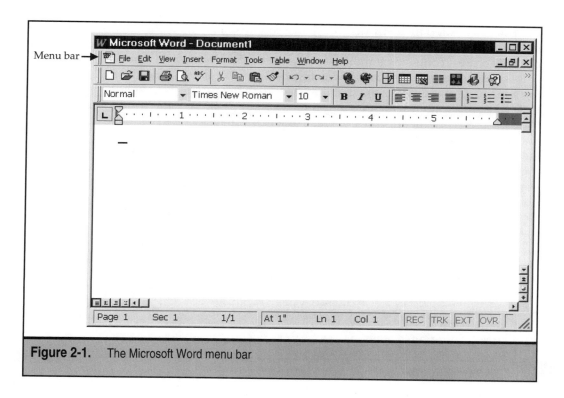

Menu bar →

Figure 2-1.   The Microsoft Word menu bar

menu item by typing a letter when the menu or submenu is active (usually the first letter, unless the letter is already being used). Each window (except for some very simple ones) typically has a menu, but having a window is not a prerequisite for a menu. You can program *floating menus* to appear anywhere on the desktop. The *pop-up menu* that appears when you click the right mouse button on an empty area of the desktop is an example of a floating pop-up menu. You can dynamically add or change menu items according to the context in your application.

Programming Menus

From a programming perspective, you can consider each menu item as a command that you have to process. Windows 2000 passes the command menu item, and your program processes the command and responds to the message. The steps involved in adding and processing a menu in your program are as follows:

1. Create the menu.
2. Display the menu at program startup.
3. Handle messages from the menu.
4. Destroy the menu (if necessary).

You can create a menu by defining it in a resource file. You can edit a resource file using resource editors built into Microsoft Visual C++, or you can edit them by hand. You can also create menus dynamically and by using the Visual C++ AppWizard. You can edit the menu resource AppWizard generates to add or delete menu items. When creating a menu, you should ensure that the ID for each menu item is unique, because this ID tells your application which item you are working with. Submenus do not have IDs. When you create a menu, you also create the items that belong to the menu. Some items may have other items nested below them, which are called *submenus* or *pop-ups*. You create pop-ups when you create the menu as well. You also specify options associated with menu items, such as if the item is to be inactive or grayed (you can programmatically turn these on later—for example, in Word some of the edit options are grayed out until you open a file).

In step 2, you cause a menu to be displayed at program startup by specifying the name of the menu in the *lpszMenuName* parameter of the window class.

In step 3, you start using the menu. The user makes a selection by clicking a menu item (or using the keyboard). This causes a **WM_COMMAND** message to be sent to the window that owns the menu. One of the parameters passed in the message is the ID of the menu item selected by the user. This lets you take appropriate action in your program and respond. Your response depends on your application. If you are using the MFC, the MFC framework converts the **WM_COMMAND** message into a function call that can be used in your program's other classes, such as document or view classes.

NEW IN WINDOWS 2000:   If a menu is defined with a MENUINFO.dwStyle value of **MNS_NOTIFYBYPOS**, **WM_MENUCOMMAND** is sent instead of **WM_COMMAND**.

Finally, if your menu is associated with a window, then the menu is destroyed and its memory released when the window is closed. If your menu is not associated with a window, then you should explicitly destroy your menu using **DestroyMenu**.

You can change a menu by adding or deleting menu items. If you add a menu item, you modify the menu resource to add the item and add message-handling functions to process the new menu item. Message-handling functions can be developed by use of the ClassWizard.

Dialog Box

A *dialog box* permits more complex interaction, including the ability for the user to input text using the keyboard.

A dialog box (or *dialog*, for short) is actually a placeholder wherein other controls such as list boxes, edit boxes, and so on can reside. As such, the dialog box is the parent for the other controls that reside in it.

Dialog Box Characteristics

There are two types of dialog boxes: *modal* and *modeless*. The user must respond to a modal dialog box before he or she can switch focus to another window in the application (and this includes the parent window of the modal dialog box). Figure 2-2 shows the Save As dialog box in Word, which is a modal dialog box. You can move a modal dialog box around on the desktop.

A modeless dialog box permits the user to switch focus to another window in the application. Figure 2-3 shows the Find dialog box in Word, which is a modeless dialog box.

Modeless dialog boxes provide more options to the user, and they are also more difficult to program, since you have to cater to more possibilities of user actions compared with the modal dialog box.

Programming Dialog Boxes

Before you can use a dialog box in your program, you must define it. The usual method to define a dialog box is by use of the dialog editor. Some of the parameters you specify to define a dialog box are the dialog name, a caption for the dialog, and the style of the dialog. The style specifies such things as whether support for Maximize and Minimize should be included, whether the dialog box should include a system menu when created, and so on. By default, a modal dialog box is visible when created, whereas a modeless dialog box is not. If you are creating a modeless dialog box and want it automatically visible, ensure that you have made it visible.

Your program creates (displays) a dialog box by calling either the **DialogBox** API (for modal dialog boxes) or **CreateDialog** (for modeless dialog boxes). You pass the name of the dialog box as a parameter, and Windows 2000 looks for a dialog box with the name

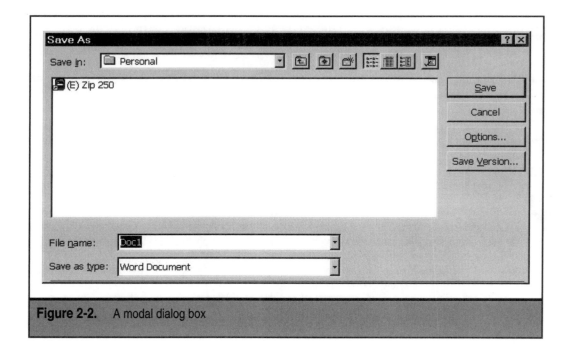

Figure 2-2.   A modal dialog box

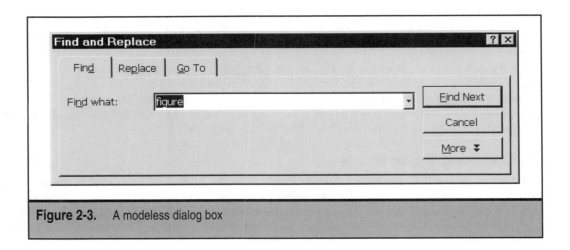

Figure 2-3.   A modeless dialog box

you specify in your program's resource file. **DialogBox** returns control to your program with an exit status. **CreateDialog** returns a handle that your program should use for future requests associated with the dialog box.

A dialog box has its own message queue, and the messages from the dialog box are not sent to your program's main window function. Dialog box messages are handled by *dialog functions* (also called *dialog procedures*). Although we refer to the messages the dialog box function receives as dialog box *messages,* keep in mind that the messages are actually triggered by the user accessing one of the controls within the dialog box. Each dialog box has its own dialog function. The dialog function is a callback function. The message sent to the dialog function includes the ID of the control that caused the message to be sent. The main difference in programming modal and modeless dialog boxes lies in message processing. In the case of a modeless dialog, your main window function may receive messages while the modeless dialog is active. So you need to check if the messages are actually meant for the modeless dialog box and not process them in your main window function. You use the **IsDialogMessage** function to check and route dialog box messages.

When you no longer need the dialog box, destroy it using **EndDialog** (for modal dialogs) or **DestroyWindow** (for modeless dialogs).

TIP: You may be creating dialog boxes outside **WinMain** (for example, in the window procedure). Since the dialog box needs access to the current instance handle, you have to ensure that a copy of the current instance handle is available to the dialog box. You could use a global variable for this purpose.

Dialog Boxes Using the MFC   If you use the MFC, you can create a dialog box either by hand or by using the dialog editor. When you create the dialog box, you also include the controls that are part of the dialog. Then you use the ClassWizard to derive a class from **CDialog**. You code your message-handling functions as required. Depending on where the dialog box is invoked, you may need to modify your existing resources and message-handling functions to include the new dialog.

Message Box

Another common control you will use in your program is the *message box,* which is actually a special and simple form of a dialog box. You are likely to use this often.

A message box is a simple window used to show a message to a user. The message box is removed after the user has acknowledged the message. Figure 2-4 shows a message box.

Message Box Characteristics

The severity of the message varies. It can convey information or a warning, or even notify the user of a serious error. Besides one or more buttons, a message box can include an icon, and you can color-code the icon to indicate its severity. For example, you can use red to indicate serious errors. When you display a message to a user, you want to ensure that the user has read the message. The way to ensure this is to get the user to acknowledge the message (using a mouse click, for example). You should include at least one button (usually this is the OK button). You can also provide more button choices for user acknowledgment, where appropriate. For example, if the user's request cannot be fulfilled due to a resource not being available (printing when the printer is out of paper, or reading a floppy disk drive that has no floppy disk), then you can ask the user if the operation is to be retried. A message box commonly provides the user with Abort, Retry, and Ignore options. (Ignore skips that particular request but proceeds with other requests.)

While it is a good programming practice to get the user to acknowledge messages you display, there are some exceptions. An acknowledgment from the user may be optional, for example, in a status message that indicates progress of the user's request (such as a print request). If you don't want your program to wait for an acknowledgment, you can program to display the message for a certain amount of time or until an event occurs (such as successful completion of printing) and programmatically remove the message. Keep in mind, though, that you cannot use a modal dialog (including a message box) if you plan to do this, since by definition the modal dialog will wait for the user's response.

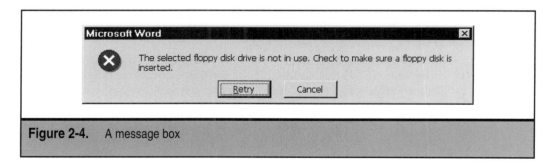

Figure 2-4.   A message box

Programming Message Boxes

You can program a message box using the **MessageBox** API. You can pass the title of the message box window as a parameter. You can also use styles to ask Windows 2000 to include some buttons automatically. The most common button is the OK button, which is specified by including the **MB_OK** style. Including the OK button lets the user click the OK button to acknowledge the message. Other buttons you can include are Abort, Retry, Cancel, and so on. The message box returns the user's choice of acknowledgment.

NEW IN WINDOWS 2000: Microsoft recommends that you use MB_CANCELTRYCONTINUE instead of MB_ABORTRETRYIGNORE—doing so causes the push buttons to display Cancel, Try Again, Continue. Another change in **MessageBox** relates to the use of MB_DEFAULT_DESKTOP_ONLY. In Windows NT 4.0 and earlier, use of this option causes **MessageBox** to fail if the current input desktop is not the default desktop. In Windows 2000, **MessageBox** does not return until the user switches to the default desktop if the current input desktop is not the default desktop.

Message Boxes Using the MFC   Using the MFC, you invoke a message box using one of the MFC classes like **AfxMessageBox**. You can pass as parameters the text that is to be displayed in the message box and the styles you want. There are two forms of **AfxMessageBox**. The one whose prototype is shown next lets you provide a pointer to a string to display in the message box.

```
int AfxMessageBox( LPCTSTR lpszText,
                   UINT nType = MB_OK,
                   UINT nIDHelp = 0 );
```

Where *lpszText* points to a **CString** object or null-terminated string containing the message to be displayed in the message box, *nType* is the style of the message box, and *nIDHelp* is the Help-context ID for the message (0 indicates the application's default Help context will be used).

The other form of **AfxMessageBox** uses an *nIDPrompt* parameter of type UINT, which is a unique ID used instead of the *lpszText* parameter to reference a string in the string table.

Scroll Bar Control

A scroll bar is a very important control, and one that you are most likely to use in programming user interfaces. This is the bar to the right and at the bottom of many windows, with arrows at the ends and a small box in the middle that can slide along the scroll bar.

Scroll Bar Characteristics

Scroll bars are used to scroll the contents of the window they border on. The vertical scroll bar moves the window contents up or down. The horizontal scroll bar moves the contents right and left. The scroll bar can be used to move the contents in one of two ways—either by clicking the arrows or by clicking, holding, and dragging the sliding small box. The latter method tends to be faster than the former. The scroll bars that are present in almost all windows are called the *standard scroll bars.* Scroll bars can also be used as stand-alone controls, providing the same functionality as standard scroll bars. When used in this manner, the controls are referred to as *scroll bar controls.* Standard scroll bars have a default range of 100, while scroll bar controls do not have a default range and have to be set programmatically.

Programming Scroll Bars

To include a standard vertical scroll bar, you can specify the **WS_VSCROLL** style in **CreateWindow**. Use **WS_HSCROLL** to include a horizontal scroll bar. When the user uses the scroll bar in one of the two ways mentioned earlier, your program gets a **WM_VSCROLL** message for a vertical scroll bar or a **WM_HSCROLL** message for a horizontal scroll bar. The parameters passed with **WM_VSCROLL** or **WM_HSCROLL** indicate whether the scrolling was for a line or a page, and the direction of the scroll (Up, Down, Right, Left). Unlike some other controls, Windows 2000 does not automatically update the scroll bar's position. You have to do that in your program. Windows 2000 provides you the **SetScrollInfo** and **GetScrollInfo** APIs to help you update the scroll bar position. **SetScrollInfo** and **GetScrollInfo** work for both standard scroll bars and scroll bar controls.

Static Control

The use of the word "control" in "static control" is actually inaccurate, because a *static control* doesn't do anything. That is, it doesn't generate or receive any messages. Once you define a static control and it shows up on the display, that's it. Sometimes you need to put up some text on dialogs, or group a bunch of controls to indicate to the user that the controls belong to a group. You would use a static control for these purposes. Static controls are summarized in Table 2-1.

As their names suggest, CTEXT, RTEXT, and LTEXT are used to display static text in a centered, right-aligned, or left-aligned manner. GROUPBOXes can be used judiciously to make your dialogs more intuitive and are another way to spruce up your user interface.

Figure 2-5 shows the Page Setup dialog in Word. Besides the text, it shows that the header and footer margins are a group, since both share the common property that they are measured from the edge of the page. When you change one margin, the grouping makes you think about the other margin as well.

Static Control	Function of the Control	Parameters
CTEXT	Display text centered in a predefined area	Text to be displayed, area where the text is to be displayed
RTEXT	Display text right-aligned in a predefined area	Text to be displayed, area where the text is to be displayed
LTEXT	Display text left-aligned in a predefined area	Text to be displayed, area where the text is to be displayed
GROUPBOX	Draw a box to group other controls	Title of box, area where the box is to be displayed

Table 2-1.   Static Controls

OTHER BASIC CONTROLS

Windows NT provides many more basic controls. Some of these controls are listed in Table 2-2. If you are not familiar with programming any of these, refer to *Windows 2000 Programming from the Ground Up,* by Herbert Schildt, Osborne/McGraw-Hill, 2000.

ADDING CONTROLS BY HAND

As stated earlier, you can either add controls to a dialog box with the dialog editor, or add them yourself with code. You can create your own control object by embedding the C++ control object in a C++ dialog or frame-window object. Like many other objects in the MFC framework, controls require two-stage construction. You should call the control's **Create** member function as part of creating the parent dialog box or frame window. For dialog boxes, this is usually done in **OnInitDialog**, and for frame windows, in **OnCreate**.

Note for UNIX Programmers

If you have programmed user interfaces using X Window/Motif in the UNIX environment, then programming for the Windows environment is similar. Window sizing and navigation functions are very similar between Windows 2000 and UNIX.

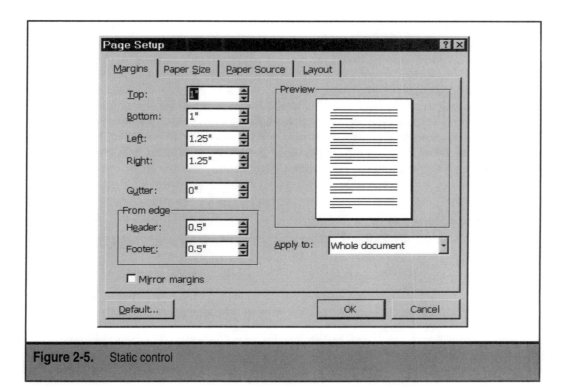

Figure 2-5.   Static control

Control	Function of the Control
List Box	Provides a list of alternatives for the user to choose from
Edit Box	Lets user input data
Check Box	Provides the ability to turn an option on or off
Radio Button	Provides a list of mutually exclusive options
Combo Box	Combines the functionality of a list box and an edit box

Table 2-2.   Other Basic Controls

DISABLING CONTROLS

One of the ways you can make your program really user friendly is by making it impossible for users to select options that don't apply to their situation. From your program's context, you know what valid input your user can provide at a given time. It would be too expensive to create a separate dialog for the controls a user needs at each point. A more effective solution is to use an existing dialog and to disable the controls that are not applicable. Disabling a control causes that control to be displayed in gray. The user cannot select a grayed control. Figure 2-6 and Figure 2-7 are two output screens from Windows 2000 diagnostics that illustrate disabling controls. The buttons for Properties and Refresh are grayed out in Figure 2-6, as they are not applicable. The same buttons are enabled in Figure 2-7.

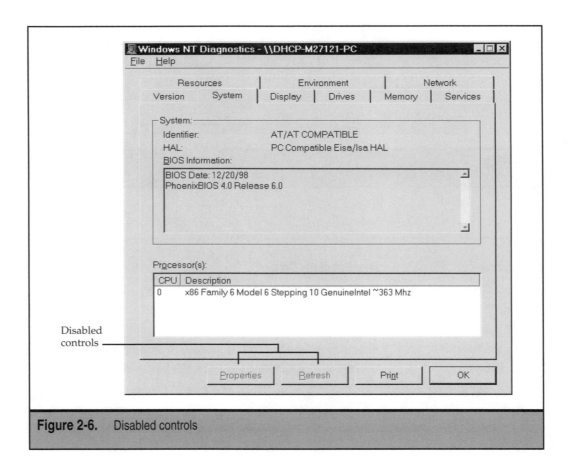

Figure 2-6. Disabled controls

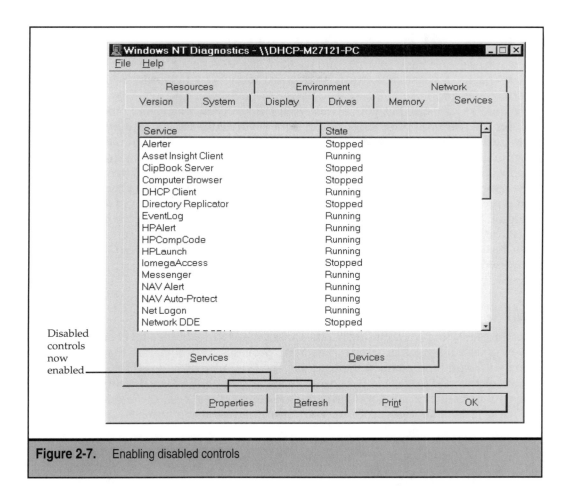

Figure 2-7. Enabling disabled controls

STAND-ALONE CONTROLS

Although controls are normally used within a dialog box, you can program controls to be stand-alone. Of course, stand-alone controls must still be within the client area of the main window. The control could be a basic control such as Button, ComboBox, ListBox, and so on. You can also customize the control by using the styles associated with the controls, just as you would if the control were within a dialog. You create a stand-alone control using **CreateWindow**. You pass the name of the control and the associated style you want as parameters. Messages from a stand-alone control are handled by the control's parent window procedure.

USER INTERFACE: BEYOND CONTROLS

We have seen some basic controls, and we have also seen how to derive custom controls. Besides basic and custom controls, there are other ways you can spruce up your user interface.

Windows 2000 also lets you include your own icons, bitmaps, and other graphics in the user interface you program. You can significantly enhance the usability of your program by suitably using these graphical elements in your program. You can use icons for programs, resources (such as printers), operations, and so on. Some programs include a small icon and a slightly larger icon to represent the same object in different situations. For example, the small icon is typically used when the window of a program (that the icon represents) is minimized. You can also use bitmaps. A *bitmap* is a pixel-level representation of a graphic image. Bitmap sizes vary. Small bitmaps (about the size of thumbnails) are used for menu choices. You can use the built-in graphics functions to draw lines, rectangles, circles, and so on. Windows 2000 provides support for GDI, and this is addressed in Chapter 6.

THE MFC CONTROL CLASSES

As is the case with programming in other areas, the MFC includes a lot of support for developing user interface programs. The MFC provides control classes that you can use when you want to implement the controls. The MFC also provides classes that provide variations that add pizzazz to your controls, such as the ability to include bitmaps instead of text for buttons, and support for dragging list items. Table 2-3 lists three such classes.

These classes let you spruce up your user interface using bitmaps, draggable lists, and so on.

ACCELERATOR KEYS

Another way to spruce up your user interface in Windows 2000 is to use *accelerator keys*.

When you program user interfaces, you invariably come across a dilemma—how to structure your user interface so that a first-time user can use it easily *and* so that it supports power users. You can optimize for one user set, but that invariably means affecting the other user set. For example, if you make your interface flow easily through a bunch of windows, the power users may have to navigate more windows than necessary. Of course, the choices are application dependent, and you may have a simple way out. For example, if your application is designed primarily for decision-support purposes and is used occasionally by managers and executives, you want a very simple user interface, one that is very tolerant of user errors. But more often than not, your user base is likely to be an assortment of users with varying degrees of familiarity with computers.

Control Class	Function
CBitmapButton	Permits you to use bitmaps instead of text for button labels. You can use up to four bitmaps for each button to show the different states of the button (normal, selected, focused, disabled).
CCheckListBox	Provides the functionality of a list box with added check boxes that the user can check. Used only for owner-drawn controls.
CDragListBox	Improves on the functionality of a regular list box by including the ability for the user to drag items in the list. By default, the dragged items are moved, but you can customize the drag to perform a copy instead of a move.

Table 2-3.   Additional MFC Control Classes

This dilemma is not unique to business application programming. Programmers who write software for games face a similar problem: how to make the game interesting for the first-time player, while still keeping it challenging for the power user? Their solution is to alter the program behavior using play skill levels. For business programming, you normally do not want to ask (or otherwise figure out) if the user is a beginner or an advanced user. But you can develop the user interface more toward the beginner and program some functions that will help the power user. One such function is *accelerator keys*.

You can let a user branch to another window in your application, bypassing the menu system by using accelerator keys. Often an experienced user knows where to branch to within the menu system, but he or she has to make a bunch of tedious menu selections to get there. For the users who are paid by the number of transactions they process, going through the menu system is more than an annoyance, it is loss of productivity and money. Pressing the accelerator keys jumps the user directly to the window and brings the window to the top of the Z order. (The Z *order* of a window indicates the window's position in a stack of overlapping windows along an imaginary z-axis.) Besides the alphabet and number keys, accelerator keys can also include *virtual keys*—keys that do not have an ASCII equivalent, such as the SHIFT key, CTRL key, and so on.

Programming Accelerator Keys

Programming for accelerator keys involves two steps:

1. Define the accelerator keys.
2. Include the accelerator keys in your program.

You can define accelerator keys using an accelerator key table in your resource file.

You can include the accelerator keys in your program by using two APIs—**LoadAccelerators** and **TranslateAccelerator**. You call **LoadAccelerators** right after creating a window, and it loads the accelerator table and returns a handle. **TranslateAccelerator** sends a **WM_COMMAND** message including the ID associated with the translated accelerator key. This is transparent to your program and will appear to your program that the **WM_COMMAND** was generated by the user making a menu selection. However, there is a difference. You should ensure that when you get a message as a result of **TranslateAccelerator**, you don't call **TranslateMessage** and **DispatchMessage** as you normally would in processing messages. For the most part, it should not make any difference to your program whether the user pressed an accelerator key or used the menu. But you can figure it out if you need to by looking at **WM_COMMAND** parameters.

Note that while the primary use for accelerator keys is with menus, the accelerator-key mechanism is general enough for you to perform any function you want that is triggered by the accelerator key. The accelerator key concept is very similar to hot keys. Both accelerator keys and hot keys enable some keyboard combination to be used as kind of a shortcut to perform a function. The HotKey control lets you define a keyboard combination that can be pressed by the user to perform some immediate function in your application. The HotKey control is covered in Chapter 7.

Besides standard and common controls, Windows 2000 provides other controls, most notably ActiveX controls. ActiveX controls, formerly known as OLE controls, can be used in dialog boxes in your applications for Windows 2000 or in HTML pages on the World Wide Web. ActiveX controls are covered in Chapter 14.

TEXT SUPPORT IN USER INTERFACES

Although the graphical interfaces with windows, icons, bitmaps, and so on are the ones most programmed for and used, Windows 2000 has special support for text. There are two ways that text can be displayed under Windows 2000. Older character-based programs can be run in the Windows 2000 shell. This is more of a compatibility mode solution for the older programs, which are usually DOS-based and assume that the whole screen is available to them. If you want to develop programs that have just a text interface under Windows 2000, there is a better method—one that lets you display text in a window. You can use the APIs Windows 2000 provides for text support.

APIs for Text

The most common API for text is **TextOut**. You can pass the character string you want displayed and the (x,y) coordinate locations to **TextOut** (coordinates are relative to the window and not absolute coordinates). The coordinates are logical coordinates, and Windows 2000 maps these logical coordinates to physical coordinates according to the mapping mode. In the default mapping mode of **MM_TEXT**, logical coordinates and physical coordinates are the same—pixels—and thus you specify the coordinates in pixels. For example, if your coordinates are *(x,y)*, Windows 2000 locates the starting point for the text display by moving *x* pixels right and *y* pixels down (since the coordinate origin is the upper-left corner).

When you display text, Windows 2000 uses the default colors for the text and the background, but you can change them using **SetTextColor** and **SetBkColor**, respectively. In cases where the physical display is not capable of displaying the color selected, Windows 2000 chooses the closest color that the device is capable of. In Windows 2000, as with many other systems, different colors are specified as different combinations of the three fundamental colors—red, green, and blue (RGB). Windows 2000 provides a macro, the RGB macro, that helps you specify the color of your choice. The macro accepts three parameters, one for each of the three colors. Each parameter is a value between 0 and 255, with 0 being the lowest intensity and 255 being the highest intensity. Thus, RGB(0,0,0) is the absence of red, green, and blue—black, and RGB(255,255,255) is a combination color that has the maximum of red, green, and blue—white. The RGB macro returns a 32-bit value, which has a special type called COLORREF. You use this type in your program to specify your color choice. You can also set the background mode (which is either Opaque or Transparent) using **SetBkMode**.

Text Metrics

One of the differences between Windows 2000 and other operating systems is the evolution in support for text and graphics. Many other operating systems supported text and were subsequently enhanced to display graphics and color. Windows 2000, on the other hand, always had graphics support as a primary objective, and text support is also present. One consequence of this difference in evolution is that in other systems you will not find functions that you would normally take for granted, such as a text cursor. If you display text in a window, you (not Windows 2000) have to worry about whether there is enough space to display additional text. There is no concept of a cursor that automatically advances according to the number of characters. In addition, knowing the number of characters you displayed is not enough, since most text you display will be proportional. The actual space occupied on the display will be different for two strings with the same number of characters (as long as the characters themselves are different). What you need to do is calculate the actual space occupied by what you displayed and adjust the starting coordinates of your next display request accordingly. You need to know the font characteristics (height, distance between lines in pixels). The API that you use to get font characteristics is **GetTextMetrics**.

NEW IN WINDOWS 2000:   Windows 2000 provides a set of features (through the Win32 API) that you can use to program special user-interface functions that make it easier for persons with disabilities to use your program. These features are beyond the scope of this book.

CONCLUSION

Designing and writing good user-interface programs is more an art than a science. As a user interface programmer, your job is similar to that of an artist. You have the tools (basic controls, custom controls, icons, bitmaps, graphics, and so on), and you have a set of blank screens. Using the tools, you paint a set of screens that constitutes your program's user interface. You can make a big difference in your users' perception of your application by what you do with your user interface. As mentioned before, you can also make a difference in user productivity.

In Chapters 1 and 2, we have looked at an overview of Windows 2000 and user interface programming aspects. Continuing to lay the groundwork for 2000 programming foundations, we will look at the communication mechanisms that Windows 2000 provides in Chapter 3.

CHAPTER 3

Windows 2000 Communications and Networking

Although PCs started out as personal, self-contained computers, it soon became apparent that communicating with other computers is highly desirable, since that is how many tasks related to the PC get accomplished—by communication and collaboration. Thus, while DOS had limited communications features and you typically bought communications software packages, Windows 2000 has integrated networking with built-in functions to communicate in a variety of ways. For example, Windows 2000 not only supports dial-up networking, but it also includes support for a number of clients (including Apple Macintosh) and protocols. The ever increasing use of e-mail and the Internet has given communications programming an important role, one that you should be familiar with as an advanced Windows 2000 programmer.

In terms of computers, the word "communications" has different meanings. There are communications between different programs (processes) *within* a computer—*interprocess* communications. There can also be functions requiring communications (such as file transfers) between two programs each running in a different computer. The link between the two computers can be a cable or telephone lines. There are software packages that provide such links, and you normally do not program for such applications (unless you are a developer of one of the communications packages).

Then there are communications where the computer is attached to a network with a *network adapter card,* and you write business applications that communicate using the adapter card and communications facilities provided by the operating system. This is the type of communications discussed in this chapter. Using this, you can have both peer-to-peer and other forms of communication for distributed computing, including client/server communications.

Even if you have programmed with Windows 2000, you will find many business applications where communications functions are limited and you have little chance to program them. If such has been your experience, then this chapter will help you understand the communications mechanisms available in Windows 2000 and set the stage for an in-depth study in Part III.

We will start with the International Standards Organization (ISO) model for communications between two applications. This is also called the *seven-layer model* or the *Open System Interconnection (OSI) model.* We will briefly review the communications mechanisms that Windows 2000 provides. We will then look at *distributed computing,* a programming paradigm in which communication plays a key role. Then we will look at some Windows 2000 communications functions associated with the Internet.

Note for UNIX Programmers

If you have programed using UNIX communication mechanisms, then it will be easy for you to write communications programs using Windows 2000. Windows 2000 provides TCP/IP support and includes the Windows version of Sockets, called WinSock. WinSock (short for "Windows Sockets") is compatible with Berkeley Software Distribution (BSD) sockets. WinSock includes BSD-style sockets as well as Windows-unique extensions.

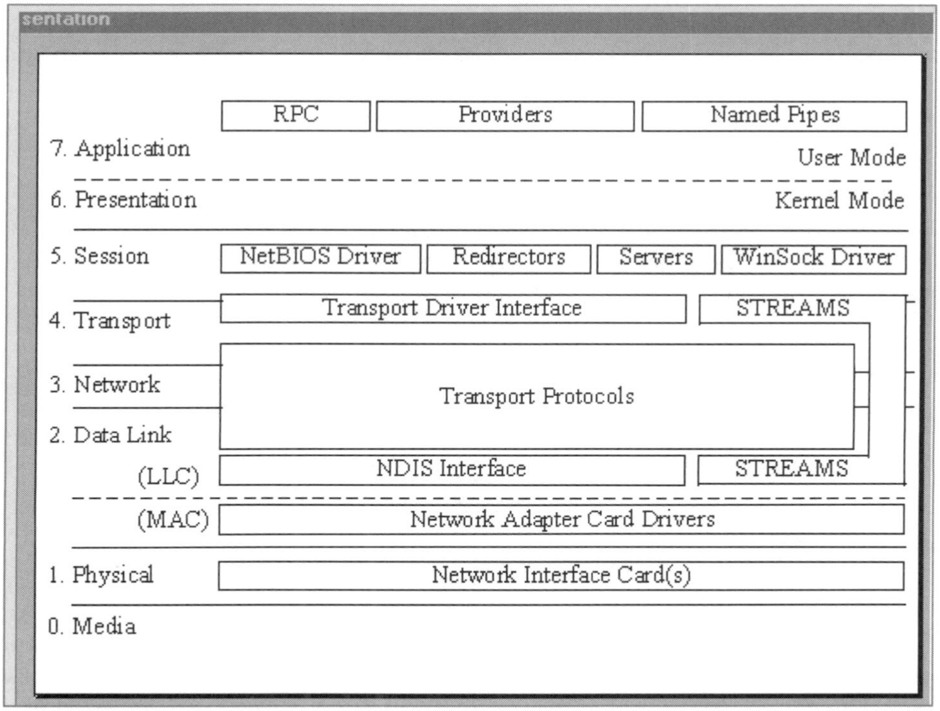

Figure 3-1.   The ISO seven-layer model and associated Windows software components

THE ISO COMMUNICATIONS MODEL

Figure 3-1 shows the ISO seven-layer communications model. Although strictly speaking there are eight layers (0–7), from a programming perspective you don't have to worry about the bottom layer—the *media layer*. This model has been used for quite a while. Note that this is a reference model, not a commercial product or design. The beauty of this model is that you can fit the role of any communications-related program into one or more of the seven layers.

Before we look at the other layers, let's review some characteristics that are true for all the layers above the media layer. The purpose of each of the other layers is to provide services to the next higher layer. The aim is to provide services that are transparent. If you call a Win32 API, you know you pass control and get control back. Your program doesn't know exactly what happens in between. The same concept applies here. Lower layers shield the higher layers from the actual implementation details. There is also division of labor between the layers. When an application in one computer communicates with another application in another computer, several functions must be taken care of. These functions include breaking down the data into manageable *packets*, ensuring that data has been properly transmitted (including retransmission, if necessary), translating between *communications protocols* if required, and so on. The different layers are meant to take on different functions. In practice, a product that primarily addresses the functions of one layer may include some functions in other layers. Transport protocols span the functions of multiple layers. Let's look briefly at the services of each layer.

The Media Layer

The bottom layer is the media layer, which is all the media used to connect computers and networks—whether these are copper or fiber-optic cable or even wireless. From a programming perspective, there is no software in this layer.

The Physical Layer

The *physical layer* is where the *network interface card (NIC)* (also called *network adapter card*) fits in. The NIC has the physical hardware connectors to connect to a network external to the computer. It shields device drivers from the properties of the media.

The Data Link Layer

The *data link layer* is divided into two sublayers—the *media access control (MAC) layer* and the *logical link control (LLC) layer*. The MAC sublayer hosts the device drivers that control the NIC, as mentioned in the physical layer section. The MAC sublayer sends and receives data in *frames* (which is just a way of grouping bits). One of the added functions of the MAC sublayer is to ensure that the communications are error free. For example, it retransmits frames if it does not receive positive acknowledgment that the frames it sent were received. The LLC hosts the Network Device Interface Specification (NDIS), a specification jointly developed by Microsoft and 3Com. As with other layers, NDIS shields the details of the NIC from the transport protocols.

The Network and Transport Layers

The *network layer* and *transport layer* functions are provided by transport protocols. The transport protocols fit in both the network layer and the transport layer. Windows 2000 supports many transport protocols—TCP/IP, NetBEUI Frame (NBF), NWLink, Microsoft Data Link Control (DLC), and AppleTalk.

The TCP/IP protocol is the de facto protocol standard that is common in the Internet. TCP/IP includes an addressing mechanism and routing based on the addresses. The ability to route avoids the need to broadcast messages. Avoiding broadcasting and sending messages to portions of the network helps reduce network traffic. The NBF protocol is derived from *NetBEUI* (NetBIOS Extended User Interface). NetBEUI is the protocol used in older Microsoft networks, such as those for Windows for Workgroups, and is an extension of NetBIOS (Network Basic Input Output System). The NWLink protocol is an NDIS-compliant version of the transport protocol used in Novell networks—IPX/SPX (Internetwork Packet Exchange/Sequenced Packet Exchange). AppleTalk is the protocol used by Apple

Macintosh networks. The unit of data that is moved in the network and transport layers is a *packet,* which is not related to or dependent upon frames. The functions provided by the network and transport layers include adjusting packet-routing based on network traffic, checking for errors in packets, and retransmitting them, if necessary.

Windows 2000 also supports STREAMS, developed by AT&T for UNIX System V, Release 3.2. Windows 2000 includes STREAMS support for the same reason it supports the POSIX subsystem—compatibility. Inclusion of STREAMS support enables existing STREAMS-based transport protocol drivers to work with Windows 2000.

The Session Layer

The Transport Driver Interface (TDI) enables software at the *session layer,* such as a network director, to choose from different lower-level transport mechanisms, such as TCP/IP or IPX/SPX. This illustrates the power of the ISO model. Lower-level mechanisms are shielded from the upper layers, and software at one level is not tied to the details of the software at another level. TDI lies between the transport layer and the session layer. Transport protocol device drivers are written to the TDI interface.

At the session layer level are the drivers such as WinSock (short for "Windows Sockets") and NetBIOS drivers.

WinSock

A *socket* is a connection's endpoint. Two sockets, one at each end, form a complete communication path. A communication path formed by sockets provides a bidirectional communications mechanism. WinSock 1.1 supports two types of sockets—*stream sockets* and *datagram sockets.* Stream sockets are used for the bidirectional transmission of a large stream of data. Streams are normally used for transmitting and receiving unduplicated data (packets are sent and received only once) and sequenced data (the order in which the data packets are sent is preserved). Stream sockets guarantee data delivery. As mentioned before, grouping the data into packets is handled by the lower-level transport layer. Datagram sockets are connectionless, unreliable communications mechanisms suitable for data communications where you don't care about guaranteed data delivery. The message buffers allocated for datagram-type sockets are small. Datagram sockets use the User Datagram Protocol.

WinSock has had two releases. The first release aimed at providing independence from TCP/IP stacks. That was a stepping stone for the next release, which not only supports TCP/IP but also supports other protocols including DECnet.

WinSock 2 not only expands on the socket types but also provides a dynamic way for applications to query the available transport protocols and their properties using the **WSAEnumProtocols** function. Socket type definitions appear in *Winsock2.h.*

Programming Windows Sockets Windows Sockets is implemented as a DLL— *Winsock.dll.* You can use the MFC for Windows Sockets programming. The MFC includes socket objects, with encapsulated handles of the type SOCKET. Socket handles are similar to window handles. You use the handle to get to an instance of the socket or window. You then use socket classes to perform the actual messaging functions. The MFC includes two classes for sockets programming—**CAsyncSocket** and **CSocket**. **CAsyncSocket** is more advanced and includes all the functionality of sockets APIs. **CSocket** is a simplified version for serialized data communications such as packing and unpacking data for stream sockets. You can derive your own classes from these two classes and override the member functions they contain, **OnConnect**, **OnSend**, **OnAccept**, and so on.

NetBIOS

NetBIOS stands for Network Basic Input Output System. As with WinSock, NetBIOS fits in the session layer. The functions that NetBIOS provides include establishing logical network names and establishing connections between the logical names. The Win32 NetBIOS function is primarily for compatibility. You would use this function for porting current NetBIOS applications that are not being rewritten. If you have programmed using IBM's NetBIOS specifications, note that there are some minor differences in the way Microsoft implemented the specification.

Redirector

When you communicate, you access resources on another computer and vice versa. *Redirector* and server are a pair that provide complementary communications functions. The redirector handles accessing the remote computer, and the server responds to remote requests. The redirector provides transparency. It redirects an I/O request to the right device across the network when the file or device to be accessed is not on the local machine. It interfaces with the server on the remote machine. The redirector is a file system driver. The application's file I/O request does not change whether the file is local or remote. The redirector also redirects print requests in the same manner. The redirector interfaces with the I/O Manager Executive component. The Windows Executive and its components were covered in Chapter 1. Redirectors also perform some network housekeeping functions.

Server

The term "server" is used to denote different things. In Windows 2000 Server, the term refers to the whole operating system (and sometimes includes the machine the operating system is running on). In SQL Server, the server refers to the software that is on top of the Windows 2000 Server and that provides database services. In the context of this paragraph, the server is the component that talks to redirectors. When a server receives a request from a redirector, it accesses the local resources and returns the result to the requesting redirector. The server is also a file system driver and handles print requests as well as file I/O requests.

Note for Unix Programmers

The ability of the redirector to provide transport file access is similar to the functionality in UNIX file systems such as the Network File System (NFS) and the Andrew File System (AFS). File systems are covered in Chapter 4.

Both the redirector and the server execute in the kernel mode for a reason. Both may handle large amounts of data, and it is easier to handle large amounts of data with other kernel-mode components such as the I/O Manager and the Cache Manager executing in kernel mode than in user mode (such as a protected subsystem). At any given time, many redirectors and servers can be active.

Redirector/server pairs are a modular way to expand the network connectivity of Windows 2000. Windows already includes such software to let Windows 2000 coexist in NetWare networks. Third-party redirector/server pairs are also available.

The Presentation Layer

The *presentation layer* handles formatting and translating data, including such functions as code and character set conversion. For example, this layer handles ASCII to EBCDIC (which stands for Extended Binary Coded Decimal Interchange Code, a character set that is commonly used in IBM mainframes) translation, compression/decompression, and encryption/decryption of data. This layer also establishes and terminates sessions. This layer allows the layer above, the application layer, to interpret the meaning of the data.

The Application Layer

The top layer, the *application layer,* is where the business application you write fits in. All your program knows (and cares about) is the interface to the layer just below—the presentation layer. All the other layers are concerned only with the successful transmission of data. The actual content of the data and its meaning are relevant only at this level.

We looked at the different layers of the ISO's OSI model. Now let's take a step-by-step look at how the different layers of the model are used when two applications communicate.

THE OSI MODEL AND A WINDOWS 2000 APPLICATION

Having looked at the ISO's OSI model, let's look at what happens when a Windows 2000 application issues a request for a remote file I/O access. The sequence of events that happen when your program requests an I/O operation is as follows:

1. Your program (at the application layer level) makes an I/O request, using a Win32 API for file I/O, and the I/O Manager gets the request.

2. The I/O Manager formats your request into an I/O request packet (IRP). The IRP is sent to the redirector (at the session level) through a *provider* (for each redirector there is a provider at the application level). The right provider is selected by a multiple provider router.

3. The redirector determines if the request can be satisfied locally or whether the request needs to be sent to a remote computer (let's go with the remote version).

4. The redirector sends the request to a network transport driver (at the transport level).

5. The network transport driver adds header information for the network and transport and invokes the NDIS driver (at the data-link layer level).

6. The NDIS driver adds data-link headers and invokes the lower level.

7. The physical layer and the media layer carry the IRP plus all the other headers to the server (on the remote machine).

8. The NDIS driver on the server removes the data-link headers and passes the rest of the data to the server network transport driver.

9. The server network transport driver removes the headers its counterpart on the requesting machine added and passes the rest of the data up the chain.

10. The server completes the I/O and sends the data back. Now it follows the same path described in the previous steps, except that the data flow is from the remote machine's server to the requesting machine's redirector. For brevity, let's skip the lower layer steps and assume that the data has come back to the redirector of the requesting machine.

11. The redirector gets the results (including the requested data, hopefully) and passes the results to the I/O Manager.

12. The I/O Manager returns the data to your program.

While the number of steps and the whole operation may seem time-consuming and complex just for a file I/O, in practice it is very fast and not that complex. The added headers and checks at different levels ensure not only an error-free transmission, but also retransmissions that are transparent to the application. Your application will never know that it got its data on the second attempt because the first attempt had a recoverable error.

COMMUNICATIONS MECHANISMS IN WINDOWS 2000

Having looked at a generic reference model and an application scenario of how that model is used with Windows 2000 components, let's look at all communications mechanisms in Windows 2000. Windows 2000 supports a number of communications mechanisms to facilitate you writing programs that require communications services. The mechanisms include

▼ *Win32 API*   such as the one we looked at for file I/O.

■ *WinSock APIs*   covered in Chapter 15.

■ *WNet*   provides a network-independent interface for managing network connections.

- *Remote procedure calls (RPCs)*   provide the capability to invoke procedures that are physically resident on another machine as though they were present in the local machine.

- *Remote Access Server (RAS) services*   lets remote users have the same functionality as if they were connected directly to a computer network, by the use of one or more RAS servers.

- *Named pipes*   connect two Windows applications and facilitate communication between the applications.

- *Mailslots*   are similar to named pipes. You can use mailslots to let your process communicate with other processes.

- *Support for protocols*   includes support for TCP/IP, NBF, NWLink, Microsoft Data Link Control (DLC), and AppleTalk.

- *Internet-related communications mechanisms*   include:

  Telnet   lets your computer become a terminal to a remote server.

  FTP   allows for file transfers between remote computers.

  Ping   checks if a remote server is responding.

- *Microsoft SNA Server*   provides communication with legacy systems that support IBM's Systems Network Architecture. SNA Server supports programming using the Common Programming Interface for Communications (CPI-C) and Advanced Program-to-Program Communications (APPC) interfaces. The SNA Server was briefly covered in Chapter 1.

- *Open Database Connectivity (ODBC)*   enables applications to communicate with databases to retrieve, store, and update data. ODBC is covered in Chapter 20.

- ▲ *Object linking and embedding (OLE)*   allows applications to communicate with each other and to make functions of one program available to another. OLE can also be used to provide complex communications functions between applications across networks. OLE is covered in Chapter 13.

Let's briefly look at some of the communications mechanisms.

WNet

WNet functions let you connect and disconnect network resources and the associated end-user interfaces. For example, the **WNetAddConnection2** function makes a persistent connection or redirects a local device to a network resource. The local device could be any local resource such as a disk or printer. WNet also includes functions to enumerate resources (**WNetEnumResource**) or even the current network user name (**WNetGetUser**). The WNet end-user interface includes **WNetConnectionDialog**, which displays a network-connection dialog box. **WNet** enumeration functions use the **NETRESOURCE** structure shown next:

```
typedef struct _NETRESOURCE {   /* network resource structure */
    DWORD   dwScope;
    DWORD   dwType;
    DWORD   dwDisplayType;
    DWORD   dwUsage;
    LPTSTR  lpLocalName;
    LPTSTR  lpRemoteName;
    LPTSTR  lpComment;
    LPTSTR  lpProvider;
} NETRESOURCE;
```

dwScope defines the enumeration scope. It could be RESOURCE_CONNECTED to get currently connected resources, RESOURCE_GLOBALNET for all network resources, or RESOURCE_REMEMBERED for remembered (persistent) connections.

dwType indicates whether the resource is disk (RESOURCETYPE_DISK), printer (RESOURCETYPE_PRINT), or any (RESOURCETYPE_ANY). Type is specified as a bitmask.

dwDisplayType specifies how the network object is displayed in the user interface. It could be RESOURCEDISPLAYTYPE_DOMAIN to display the object as a domain, RESOURCEDISPLAYTYPE_GENERIC to indicate that the display type does not matter, RESOURCEDISPLAYTYPE_SERVER to display the object as a server, or RESOURCE DISPLAYTYPE_SHARE to display the object as a share.

dwUsage is only applicable when *Scope* is RESOURCE_GLOBALNET. It could be RESOURCEUSAGE_CONNECTABLE to indicate a connectable resource whose name is pointed to by *RemoteName* or RESOURCEUSAGE_CONTAINER to indicate a container resource.

lpLocalName is the name of a local device if *Scope* is RESOURCE_CONNECTED or RESOURCE_REMEMBERED. It is NULL if the connection does not use a device. Otherwise, it is undefined.

lpRemoteName is the remote network name if the resource is a network resource, or the network name associated with the name pointed to by *LocalName* if the resource is a current or persistent connection.

lpComment is a provider-supplied comment, and *lpProvider* is the name of the provider owning this resource. *Provider* can be NULL.

Remote Access Server (RAS) Services

RAS allows two-way communications between the Windows 2000 Server and clients supported by the Windows 2000 Server. RAS lets a remote computer provide all the functions as if it were directly connected to the network. Functions provided by RAS at the client include providing an end-user interface, starting and ending RAS connections between the remote computer and the Windows 2000 Server, and providing RAS status and configuration information. At the server, RAS provides administration, security, and connection-management functions.

NEW IN WINDOWS 2000:   The programmatic interface for the Remote Access Server (RAS), available as a downloadable component for Windows NT 4.0, is integrated within Windows 2000 with one difference. The naming convention is different between the two Application Programming Interfaces (APIs). Functions under Windows NT 4.0 RAS typically begin with "RasAdmin." The equivalent functions under Routing and RAS begin with "MprAdmin." For example, the callback function **RasAdminGetIpAddressForUser** in Windows NT 4.0 has the equivalent function **MprAdminGetIpAddressForUser** in Routing and RAS.

Named Pipes

A *named pipe* is a high-level communications mechanism you can use in your process to communicate to another process. The process you are communicating to can be anywhere on the network (unlike an anonymous pipe) and need not be related to your process. Windows 2000 implements a named pipe as a file object. If you are familiar with accessing files using file system drivers, then you know how to use named pipes. In fact, you use read and write operations on named pipes as you would for files.

TIP: The file-system object and driver analogy is applicable in many other areas of Windows 2000 programming such as mailslots.

Usually a server opens a named pipe with a name clients already know, or passes the handle or the name of the pipe to clients through an interprocess communication (IPC) mechanism. Once a client knows the name, it opens the named pipe (provided it has the authorization to do it), and the server and the client communicate using read and write on the pipe. Named pipes can support both one-way and two-way communications. When clients open a named pipe by using its name, separate instances of the named pipe are created, even though the pipes may have the same name. These separate instances have unique handles and memory buffers (you can also have unbuffered pipes if you want to). The use of separate instances permits more multiple clients to simultaneously communicate using the same pipe name. Pipe access can be overlapped or synchronous. Named pipes can use any underlying transport protocols that are available for communication between a client and a server. One of the nice features of named pipes is *impersonation,* which lets a server impersonate a client. This has security implications. When a server impersonates a client, it is the client's access privileges that determine whether an access can be performed.

Programming Named Pipes

Some of the functions you may use for communicating using named pipes are **CreateNamedPipe**, **TransactNamedPipe**, and **CallNamedPipe**. The typical programming sequence would be to call the functions **CreateFile**, **TransactNamedPipe**, and **CloseHandle**. You can use **WaitNamedPipe** if **CreateFile** cannot open the pipe immediately. Alternatively, you can call one function—**CallNamedPipe**. The **CallNamedPipe** function connects to a message-type pipe, writes to and reads from the pipe, and then closes the pipe. **CallNamedPipe** waits for an instance of the pipe, if one is not available. The prototype for **CallNamedPipe** is shown next:

```
BOOL CallNamedPipe( /* Connect , Write, Read, and Close a named pipe */
              LPCTSTR  lpNamedPN,
              LPVOID   lpInBuf,
              DWORD    nInBufSize,
              LPVOID   lpOutBuf,
              DWORD    nOutBufSize,
              LPDWORD  lpBytesRead,
              DWORD    nTimeOut
);
```

lpNamedPN is the named pipe name, *lpInBuf* is a pointer to the input buffer that contains the data written to the pipe, *nInBufSize* is the input buffer size in bytes, *lpOutBuf* is the pointer to the output buffer that holds the data read from the pipe, *nOutBufSize* is the output buffer size in bytes, *lpBytesRead* is a pointer to a variable that stores the actual number of bytes read from the pipe, and *nTimeOut* is the time to wait for the named pipe to be available. You can specify the time-out duration in milliseconds, or you can specify to wait indefinitely (NMPWAIT_WAIT_FOREVER), to not wait if the pipe is not available (NMPWAIT_NOWAIT), or to wait for the default specified when the pipe was created using the **CreateNamedPipe** function (NMPWAIT_USE_DEFAULT_WAIT). The return value is nonzero if the function succeeds and zero otherwise.

Mailslots

Mailslots are similar to named pipes in that by using mailslots your process can communicate with other processes. The file system analogy of named pipes applies to mailslots as well. But there are differences between the two (otherwise you wouldn't need two different communications mechanisms). The similarities and differences between named pipes and mailslots are summarized in Table 3-1.

Note for Unix Programmers

If you have programmed using named pipes in UNIX, then Windows 2000 named pipes are very similar. Note, however, that named pipes in Windows 2000 are not compatible.

Feature	Named Pipes	Mailslots
Communication type	Two way	One way
Message delivery	Processes know if messages sent	Processes don't know for sure if messages sent
Programming	Using file system APIs	Using file system APIs
Scope	Between any two processes	Local to the creating process and to processes that inherit from the creating process
Typical use	Between two processes	Broadcast

Table 3-1.   Comparing Pipes and Mailslots

When you create a mailslot, you are a mailslot server. Other programs (mailslot clients) can store messages in the mailslot, and the messages are appended to the end and remain in the mailslot until you retrieve them. You can be a mailslot server and a client at the same time. There are basically two classes of mailslots—first class and second class. Windows 2000 implements only second-class mailslots. Second-class mailslots are a connectionless messaging mechanism. When you use second-class mailslots, keep in mind that the message delivery is not guaranteed. This absence of a guarantee makes mailslots suitable for broadcast messaging and for identifying computers and services available on a network. You can broadcast to one computer or all computers in a domain. (A *domain* is a group of workstations and servers that have a common group name.)

TIP: If you are familiar with programming using Microsoft OS/2 LAN Manager, then using mailslots should be easy, since mailslot APIs in Windows 2000 are a subset of those in Microsoft OS/2 LAN Manager.

Programming Mailslots

You can use mailslots in your program by using the mailslot APIs, which are **CreateMailslot** to create a mailslot, **GetMailslotInfo** to read a message from a mailslot, and **SetMailslotInfo** to set the mailslot's time-out value for a read. You create a mailslot and set a time-out, if applicable. Other programs write messages to the mailslot using **CreateFile** and **WriteFile** functions, and you read them using **GetMailslotInfo**. The prototype for **CreateMailslot** is shown next:

```
HANDLE CreateMailslot(LPCTSTR lpszName, DWORD cbMaxMsgSz,
```

```
        DWORD dwRdTimeout,

        LPSECURITY_ATTRIBUTES lpSecAttr);
```

lpszName is the mailslot's name. It can include multiple directory levels and must be unique.

cbMaxMsgSz is the maximum message size allowed for a message (in bytes). Set *cbMaxMsgSz* to zero if you do not want a limit.

dwRdTimeout specifies the time to wait for a mailslot message (if the mailslot is empty) in milliseconds. If *dwRdTimeout* is zero, the function returns immediately if there is no message. You can also wait until a message arrives in the mailslot (use MAILSLOT_WAIT_FOREVER).

lpSecAttr is the pointer to a SECURITY_ATTRIBUTES structure (shown next) that determines whether the returned handle can be inherited by child processes.

```
typedef struct _SECURITY_ATTRIBUTES { /* Security Attribute Structure */
        DWORD   nLength,

        LPVOID lpSecurityDescriptor,

        BOOL bInheritHandle
} SECURITY_ATTRIBUTES;
```

PROTOCOLS

Protocols are an important part of communications. Let's review some common protocols supported by Windows 2000, such as TCP/IP, NetBEUI, and IPX/SPX.

TCP/IP

TCP/IP actually comprises two major functions. *TCP,* which stands for Transmission Control Protocol, covers messaging details, while *IP,* which stands for Internet Protocol, covers addressing and routing messages. TCP/IP is probably the most commonly used protocol today due to two related developments: the adoption of TCP/IP as the protocol when Berkeley UNIX started including network functions, and the growing popularity of the Internet, which was already using TCP/IP.

TCP/IP Features

TCP/IP is a robust, time-tested protocol. Some of its robustness comes from its support for transmission reliability features. Compared with competing protocols such as NetBEUI, TCP/IP has proved itself in demanding applications. It includes support for applications to interface with sockets. The socket support enables higher-level functions such as FTP, Ping, and firewalls to be built on top of TCP/IP. Consistent with the OSI model, it shields the functions built on top of it from the details of the lower-level layers.

It is a general-purpose protocol and is used for a wide range of applications—unlike, for example, IPX/SPX, which is used heavily for network file and print services in Novell NetWare networks. TCP/IP supports message routing by including a routing *gateway address* for all messages not meant for a specific TCP/IP network segment.

TCP/IP Addressing

Each computer running TCP/IP must have three addresses—a unique address that lets other computers locate it, another address to indicate the network that it is a member of (called the *subnet mask*), and the gateway address to route messages, as mentioned before. Each of these addresses is a 32-bit number expressed in dotted decimal format (such as 112.233.34.115). This addressing scheme provides for scalability. The explosive growth of the Internet has caused the number of IP addresses to run out, and efforts are under way to increase the address size. A TCP/IP network can be segmented so that each segment carries the traffic only for addresses within the segment.

TCP/IP, while popular, does have some drawbacks. TCP/IP requires a good deal of configuration work. If you have tried to get connected to an Internet service provider (ISP) and played around with WinSock to get connected, then you have a good idea of the configuration work involved in setting up TCP/IP.

NEW IN WINDOWS 2000: Microsoft Active Directory replaces NetBIOS as the primary name resolution and directory service in Windows 2000. Active Directory uses DNS as the location service. Accordingly, on a Windows 2000 system, you can run TCP/IP without NetBIOS or Windows Internet Naming Service (WINS).

NetBEUI

NetBEUI stands for NetBIOS Extended User Interface. IBM introduced NetBEUI in 1985 to support communications across PC networks. The protocol is old (at least in terms of computer years) and has some problems associated with an old design. For example, NetBEUI allows only 254 simultaneous sessions, which was probably a large number when NetBEUI was designed. In addition, NetBEUI was not designed to provide reliable connectionless communications.

NetBEUI Features

NetBEUI is not as robust as TCP/IP. Unlike TCP/IP, which is a general-purpose protocol, NetBEUI is optimized for print and file sharing within the local network. Also, NetBEUI is not as well standardized as TCP/IP. One of the extensions supported by NBF is the removal of the 254-session limit. NetBEUI doesn't support routing, so if you segment your network, you lose communications functions across segments. This also means that NetBEUI is not very scalable. But NetBEUI is easy to configure.

IPX/SPX

IPX stands for Internetwork Packet Exchange, and *SPX* stands for Sequenced Packet Exchange. IPX/SPX is the protocol suite widely used in Novell networks. Novell recently provided TCP/IP support for NetWare (which is a testimony to the popularity of the TCP/IP protocol). IPX/SPX is similar to NetBEUI in that both are primarily used in small networks, and file and print sharing are the major applications. IPX/SPX is a connection-oriented, routable protocol. It is easy to configure.

The features of TCP/IP, NetBEUI, and IPX/SPX are compared in Table 3-2.

As mentioned before, TCP/IP has complex configuration and setup procedures. Let's look at some functions provided by Windows 2000 to mitigate this problem.

TCP/IP CONFIGURATION AND SETUP SOLUTIONS

As noted earlier, configuration and setup is a major issue with TCP/IP. One of the solutions to the system administrator having to set up TCP/IP configuration in each client machine is to set up the configurations in a server and download the configurations to clients. This is the idea behind the Dynamic Host Configuration Protocol (DHCP). The system administrator sets up (at least) one DHCP server that stores the configuration information for the entire network, including client configurations. This works fine for client workstations that are in-house. For dial-up remote clients, a RAS server can be set up to act on behalf of a remote computer as a DHCP client. The RAS server requests and gets a pool of IP addresses and configuration information from a DHCP server. RAS manages this pool by allocating and deallocating addresses when remote computers log on and log off.

Features	TCP/IP	NetBEUI	IPX/SPX
Initial design purpose	General communications	File and print sharing	File and print sharing
Setup and configuration	Complex	Simple	Simple
Robustness in handling demanding applications	Robust	Not so robust	Robust
Routing support	Routable	Not routable	Routable

Table 3-2. Comparing TCP/IP, NetBEUI, and IPX/SPX

NEW IN WINDOWS 2000:   Windows 2000 Server includes an enhanced implementation of DHCP. Enhancements include integration of DHCP with DNS, enhanced monitoring and statistical reporting for DHCP servers, multicast address allocation, rogue DHCP server detection, and more.

Programming Using DHCP

A DHCP client broadcasts a Discover request on startup. Any DHCP server that receives the Discover can respond with an Offer, which among other things contains configuration information, including a proposed IP address. The Offer is not broadcast but is sent directly to the client issuing the Discover. If the DHCP client and DHCP server are not on the same subnet, the Offer is sent through a router back to the DHCP client. The client receives the Offer and accepts with a Request. The Request is broadcast and includes the accepted IP address. If more than one DHCP server responded to the Discover, the server that issued the accepted IP address is the one that will carry on future communications with the client.

The DHCP server completes the setup with an ACK. ACK includes complete configuration information. When the client receives the ACK, it completes setting up the TCP/IP stack and is now a *bound* DHCP client that can start using the IP address. The client is said to have *leased* the configuration from the server, since a time limit is specified for the use of the IP address given to the client. The client can renew the lease or get a new lease from another server (if the server that issued the first lease is unavailable, for example). The DHCP protocol caters to network interruptions. The client and server periodically exchange information to keep configuration updated. For example, if a client with an active lease moves from one subnet to another (for example, when a portable or even a desktop machine is moved around), the ongoing lease is terminated and a new lease is set up. The ongoing lease cannot be used because the subnet address is part of the IP address, and moving to another subnet causes the IP address to change.

Note for UNIX Programmers

If you have programmed using NFS or Domain Naming Service (DNS), then the concepts of centralizing configuration information are the same. However, in NFS the configuration information is locally held and is periodically downloaded. In DNS, a server stores the configuration information, but the address-name mapping is static. Also, unlike DNS, WINS doesn't support a network hierarchy or *zones*.

WINDOWS INTERNET NAMING SERVICE (WINS)

WINS provides dynamic name registration and resolution on TCP/IP. WINS complements DHCP, but DHCP is not a prerequisite for WINS. WINS provides a dynamic name resolution method along with DHCP. The functions of WINS are similar to those of DNS, with one major difference. DNS resolves TCP/IP host names to static IP addresses. WINS is specifically designed to resolve NetBIOS names on TCP/IP to dynamic addresses assigned by DHCP. WINS is fully interoperable with other NetBIOS Name Servers (NBNS).

When a WINS client is started, it contacts a WINS server directly (unlike a broadcast used by a DHCP client). WINS primary and secondary server names are specified in the client's TCP/IP properties sheet. The information sent by the WINS client includes the computer name, an IP address, and so on. If the WINS client is also DHCP enabled, then the IP address will have been obtained dynamically from a DHCP server. If the WINS client is not DHCP enabled, the IP address is a static number obtained from a network administrator and manually entered as part of the TCP/IP configuration information. IP addresses must be unique. If DHCP assigns the addresses, then it ensures the addresses are unique. If DHCP is not used, then they are manually assigned and the person assigning the addresses (usually the network administrator) has to ensure that they are unique.

NEW IN WINDOWS 2000:   In Windows 2000, WINS has several enhancements, including server enhancements, client enhancements, and enhancements to the management tool. These enhancements make networks easier to manage and result in a more robust solution for mapping NetBIOS names to IP addresses.

WINDOWS 2000 MACINTOSH SUPPORT

Windows 2000 Server includes functions to be an AppleShare file server for Macintosh clients. File server functions are provided by the Macintosh Services component. Macintosh Services also includes the AppleTalk print server and fully functional, native AppleTalk router functions. Macintosh Services supports the AppleTalk Filing Protocol (AFP). Using Windows 2000 as an AppleShare file server enables some of the other functions built into Windows 2000, including RAID support, multiprocessor support, security functions, and so on. Using Windows 2000 as an AppleTalk print server lets Mac clients print to any printer that can be attached to Windows 2000, including network printers and non-PostScript printers. Windows 2000 includes a PostScript interpreter to convert the data stream into a (bitmap) format that can be handled by a non-PostScript printer. Since the number of printers supported is large, this provides a significant advantage for Windows 2000 compared with many other print servers. As an AppleTalk router, you can use a variety of network cards, including Ethernet, FDDI, and so on.

DISTRIBUTED COMPUTING

Distributed computing is the next logical step in the evolution of communications. First you have peer-to-peer, where the communication is between two peers, such as applications. Then you have client/server communications, the next step, where a client application talks to different server applications for application, print, and file services. Distributed applications are applications portions of which can reside on heterogeneous systems at different nodes in a network but work together to fulfill the functions of the applications. To accomplish this, the applications need an environment that will provide distributed services, a mechanism to pass messages between applications, mechanisms to accomplish distributed transaction processing, the capability to access data from different databases, and so on. Such an environment has been specified by the Open Software Foundation (OSF), a nonprofit industry consortium formed to further the use of open distributed computing, and is called the Distributed Computing Environment (DCE). While distributed computing systems are a better match to the real world and have some advantages, keep in mind that they also tend to be more complex. The DCE specifies six core services:

▼   *Remote procedure call (RPC)* services to let an application access services provided by another computer on the network

■   *Active Directory services* to locate any named object on the network by use of a single naming model

■   *Threads* services to be able to execute multiple threads

■   *Distributed time* services to maintain one time across all computers on the network by synchronizing the system clocks of different computers

■   *Security* services to authenticate users, authorize access to resources, and provide user and server account management on a distributed network

▲   *Distributed file* services to access files anywhere on a network

Windows 2000 natively includes only full RPC support. Windows 2000 adds directory services. You can use third-party software to provide the other services.

Remote Procedure Call (RPC)

RPC was invented by Sun Microsystems. Based on this initial work, the Open Software Foundation issued DCE RPC. DCE is the heterogeneous distributed computing environment envisioned by OSF, and RPC is the mechanism in DCE for interprocess communications.

RPC gives you the ability to invoke procedures that reside on another machine as if they were present in the local machine. The details of the network are transparent to your application. Your application also does not have to worry about data translation that may need to occur in heterogeneous environments—for example, between Windows' *little-endian* convention and UNIX's *big-endian* convention. RPC fits in the application layer of the ISO model. As with other layers, RPC is dependent on other lower-level mechanisms. In Windows 2000, RPC can use named pipes, NetBIOS, or Windows Sockets to communicate with remote systems. RPC interfaces are specified by use of the Interface Description Language (IDL) and compiled by use of Microsoft's IDL language compiler (MIDL). MIDL converts IDL into C syntax. When you compile your interfaces using the IDL compiler, *stub functions* (which are dummy functions that call the actual functions on the remote machine at run time) are generated on the local machine. Your program calls only these stub functions. The stubs convert the passed procedure parameters into the network data representation (NDR) format. At run time, RPC run-time libraries and the underlying network code call the real remote procedures with the NDR-formatted parameters. A *binding* is established between the RPC client and the RPC server at run time. A variation of the RPC called LPC (local procedure call) is used for communication across local systems within a computer.

DIAL-UP NETWORKING AND RAS

Dial-up networking, as the name suggests, offers networking capabilities normally available to LAN-attached desktops to remote dial-in computers. For example, your laptop could function as your desktop and perform the same functions—access mail, file, and printers. You can also access the Internet by dialing in and using the RAS server as an Internet gateway. Some limitations do apply to RAS-based network connections. Dial-up networking is the client portion of RAS. The server portion of RAS is remote access administration. RAS connections can be made using regular phone lines and a modem. RAS also supports X.25 and ISDN connections. RAS supports up to 256 concurrent sessions (in the Windows 2000 Server). These sessions can be incoming or outgoing. RAS supports IPX, TCP/IP, and NetBEUI at the network layer and Point-to-Point Protocol (PPP) and Serial-Line Internet Protocol (SLIP) at the transport layer. While RAS connections can use any combination of the network layer protocols, the transport layer protocol has to be either PPP or SLIP.

Some common RAS functions are in Table 3-3.

Note for UNIX Programmers

If you have programmed using ONC RPC or DCE RPC, then you can easily program using Windows 2000 RPC. Windows 2000 RPC is interoperable with DCE RPC, and there are porting tools that let you port ONC RPC to DCE RPC.

RAS Function	Action Performed
RASADFunc	Application-defined callback function
RasConnectionNotification	Specifies an event object that the system sets to signaled state when creating/terminating a RAS connection
RasDial	Establishes a RAS connection between a RAS client and a RAS server
RasDialFunc2	Application-defined callback function invoked by RasDial on state changes
RasDialDlg	Establishes a RAS connection using a specified phone-book entry
RasEntryDlg	Property sheets to manipulate phone-book entries
RasEnumConnections	Lists active RAS connections including handle and phone book
RasGetConnectStatus	Status of a current RAS connection
RasGetEntryDialParams	Retrieves connection information from last successful call for a phone-book entry
RasGetErrorString	Converts RAS error code to an error string
RasMonitorDlg	Property sheet that describes the status of RAS connections
RasHangUp	Terminates a RAS connection

Table 3-3.   Common RAS Functions

CONCLUSION

In this chapter we looked at the OSI reference model, which is the "granddaddy" of computer communications. We looked at the communications mechanisms provided by Windows 2000 and how these mechanisms relate to the OSI model. We took a step-by-step look at how communications work. We then looked at some of the Windows 2000 communications mechanisms in more detail. This chapter lays the groundwork for Part III, where we will look at sockets, Internet-related programming, MAPI, and RAS in greater detail.

CHAPTER 4

Windows 2000
File Systems

Continuing with Windows 2000 programming foundations, let's take a look in this chapter at the support in Windows 2000 for accessing data such as file systems and databases. Windows 2000 supports multiple file systems. Besides the file systems themselves, Windows 2000 also includes features such as *memory-mapped files* and *asynchronous input/output* that you can take advantage of in your programs to speed up file processing. We will also briefly look at Windows 2000 support for Redundant Array of Inexpensive Disks (RAID), which provides better fault tolerance and performance compared to regular disks.

FILE SYSTEMS

Separating data from executable code so that the same executable can run using different sets of data probably began when programmers first started to program. The early data storage was through files of different types. Now it is more common to use databases, particularly for business mission-critical data (although many databases internally use files to store the data). This trend has become even more popular with the advent of desktop databases. Database programming using ODBC is covered in Chapter 20. MFC support for databases and the ADO SDK is covered in Chapter 21. As a business programmer, you may still use files occasionally when the effort and cost of setting up and using a database system outweigh the benefits of using a database.

Windows 2000 support for file systems lets your applications create, read, write, update, and delete files and directories. Windows 2000 supports multiple file systems. The file systems supported by Windows 2000 include the *New Technology File System (NTFS)*, the *File Allocation Table (FAT) file system* (and some variations of FAT such as *protected-mode FAT* and *FAT32*), the *Compact Disc File System (CDFS)*, and, up to Windows NT 3.51, the *High-Performance File System (HPFS)*. Keep in mind that file systems are not mutually exclusive. You can have one partition in your hard drive formatted for FAT and the other formatted for NTFS, and Windows 2000 can access and write to both.

FILE ALLOCATION TABLE (FAT)

The FAT file system had its origins in the DOS operating system and suffers from the problems of an old design not keeping pace with advances. One of the problems is the FAT file-naming system. All files handled by FAT should follow what is called the *8-dot-3 system*, where the filename can be up to 12 characters—with the first up to 8 characters followed by an optional dot (mandatory, if there is an extension) followed by an extension of up to 3 characters. Actually, the full name of a FAT file is *drive:\directory\filename.ext* (*directory* could include subdirectories). All other fields except *filename* are optional. This design may suffice when disk capacities are very small and there are only a few files. It becomes a major problem with many software development efforts where there typically are hundreds of files. In addition, FAT is not case sensitive. One solution to this problem was a variation of FAT called *VFAT* or *protected-mode FAT*. VFAT supports long filenames of up to 255 characters and other file data, such as date last accessed, in extended FAT structures. VFAT is compatible with FAT.

Another problem with FAT is clustering. Available disk space is usually broken down into *clusters,* which are further broken down into *sectors.* A sector typically is a half kilobyte (512 bytes). The number of sectors per cluster varies (for example, the sectors per cluster is 4 for a 1.2MB floppy disk and 32 for a 512MB hard drive). Allocations are usually in cluster multiples. Thus a 1K data file that occupies 4 sectors on a 1.2MB floppy will take up 32 sectors or 16K on the 512MB hard drive. The rest of the space is usually wasted. Accordingly, if you have a lot of small files on a big hard drive, there will be a lot of wasted space using FAT. Microsoft introduced FAT32, a variation of FAT that addresses this clustering problem. FAT32 uses only 4K clusters (for disks up to 8GB) to avoid wasting disk space. FAT32 also supports disks with capacities up to 2 terabytes. FAT32 is supported by Windows 95 (OSR2), Windows 98, and now by Windows 2000, but not by Windows NT. FAT32 is compatible with FAT and any Windows operating system that supports FAT32 can also read files created with FAT.

NEW IN WINDOWS 2000:   One of the things new in Windows 2000 is support for FAT32. Windows NT 4.0 did not support FAT32. If you want to dual-boot with Windows 98 and Windows 2000, keep in mind that the large partition support that works on both Win98 and Windows 2000 is FAT32, not NTFS.

FAT's big advantage is its low overhead, and for this reason it is the only file system available to support floppies and very small hard drives. In fact, on small drives, FAT access will even be faster than NTFS or HPFS. Since FAT has been around a while, there are many volumes and floppy disks with the FAT file system. To maintain compatibility, all operating systems since DOS—including Windows 3.*x*, Windows 95, Windows 98, Windows NT, Windows 2000, and OS/2—support FAT.

NEW TECHNOLOGY FILE SYSTEM (NTFS)

NTFS is the file system designed to address many of the limitations of FAT. Probably the most significant change is the removal of the FAT requirement that filenames use the 8-dot-3 format. But that is just the beginning. NTFS also includes much better recovery (without having to use stand-alone file recovery utilities), security features (consistent with Windows 2000's C2 security classification), support for Unicode filenames, and so on. NTFS not only supports multiple extended attributes, but it also allows applications to define their own extended attributes.

NEW IN WINDOWS 2000:   Windows 2000 supports NTFS version 5 and provides additional features, particularly for security. Some of the new features in Windows 2000 include more granular control of permissions and additional flexibility in propagation and blocking features compared to Windows NT.

While Windows 2000 (using NTFS) supports long filenames, it also supports the 8-dot-3 filenames. In fact, whenever a file is created with a long filename, it internally generates a short name in the 8-dot-3 format. Table 4-1 compares the features of FAT and NTFS.

File System Feature	FAT	NTFS
File naming	8-dot-3	255-character maximum, no extension required
Security	Not secure	Enhanced security
Multiple data stream	No	Yes
File recovery	Poor—need stand-alone recovery tools	Good—don't need stand-alone utilities in most cases
Unicode support	No	Yes
Special functions for POSIX	No	Yes
MS-DOS aliases	N/A	Automatic
Floppy disk support	Yes	No
Extended attributes	No	Yes
Overhead	Low	High

Table 4-1.   Comparing FAT and NTFS Features

HIGH-PERFORMANCE FILE SYSTEM (HPFS)

Microsoft dropped support for HPFS in Windows NT 4.0. HPFS is similar to NTFS in that it allows long filenames, extended attributes, and so on. Windows NT supported HPFS (up to version 3.51) primarily for backward compatibility (for systems that dual-boot OS/2 and Windows NT).

COMPACT DISC FILE SYSTEM (CDFS)

With increasing program sizes and large multimedia content, CD-ROMs have become the most common distribution mechanism for software. CDFS has been the file system used to store files on a CD-ROM. Windows 2000 supports the ISO 9660 standard (level 2).

Note for Unix Programmers

UNIX systems have their own file systems, such as the Network File System (NFS) and the Andrew File System (AFS). Third-party tools are available to let Windows 2000 applications access these file systems and vice versa.

> ### Note for UNIX Programmers
> Thanks to an international standard (ISO 9660), CDFS is supported by many UNIX operating systems and Windows NT. You should be able to exchange CDs between two operating systems supporting CDFS.

We've looked at different file systems. Now let's take a look at programming aspects of file systems.

UNIVERSAL DISK FORMAT (UDF)

UDF is the successor to CDFS. UDF is a file system defined by the Optical Storage Technology Association (OSTA). The ISO standard that addresses UDF is ISO 13346. The current public version of UDF is version 1.50 (OSTA has very recently approved a draft of the 2.0 version).

UDF is targeted for DVD, CD-ROM, and data exchange between operating systems. The standard supports a number of advanced features, including:

▼ Long and Unicode filenames, access control lists (ACLs), and streams

■ Read/write

▲ Bootability

Windows 2000 supports read-only operations for UDF. Windows 2000 supports UDF version 1.5. Microsoft plans to support writability in future versions of Windows 2000.

FILE SYSTEM PROGRAMMING

File system programming falls into three categories:

▼ Volume- and drive-related programming

■ Directory-related programming

▲ File-related programming

Let's review each of these categories.

Volume and Drive Functions

The functions available for your applications related to volumes and drives are summarized in Table 4-2.

Function	Information Returned or Action Performed
GetVolumeInformation	Retrieves volume name, volume serial number, file system name (FAT, NTFS), file system flags (whether the file system is case sensitive, supports Unicode, and so on), maximum filename length, and so on.
SetVolumeLabel	Sets or deletes the label of a file system volume.
GetDiskFreeSpace, GetDiskFreeSpaceEx	Retrieves volume organizational data such as bytes/sector, sectors/cluster, number of free clusters, and total number of clusters.
GetDriveType	Indicates whether the drive (specified drive letter) is a removable, fixed, CD-ROM, RAM, or network drive.
GetLogicalDrives	Identifies the volumes present.
GetLogicalDriveStrings	Retrieves a null-terminated string for each volume present.

Table 4-2. Volume and Drive Functions

Let's look at the prototype of one of the volume and drive functions—
GetDiskFreeSpaceEx—which you would use anytime you want to ensure that there is enough space on the disk for what you want to store.

```
BOOL GetDiskFreeSpaceEx( LPCTSTR lpDirName,
PULARGE_INTEGER lpFreeBytesAvail,
PULARGE_INTEGER lpTotalNumOfBytes,
PULARGE_INTEGER lpTotalNumOfFreeBytes
);
```

The parameters for **GetDiskFreeSpaceEx** are as follows:

▼ *lpDirName* is an input parameter. This parameter points to a string that specifies any directory on the disk to return information about. Use NULL for the root of the current directory. You can use the UNC format for the directory name, if desired.

■ *lpFreeBytesAvail* is an output parameter. This parameter points to a variable representing the total number of free bytes on the disk that are available to the user associated with the calling thread.

■ *lpTotalNumOfBytes* is an output parameter. This parameter points to a variable that receives the total number of bytes on the disk that are available to the user associated with the calling thread.

▲ *lpTotalNumOfFreeBytes* is an output parameter. This parameter receives the total number of free bytes on the disk. It can be NULL.

GetDiskFreeSpaceEx returns nonzero if it succeeds and returns zero otherwise.

NEW IN WINDOWS 2000: In Windows 2000, the administrator can set quotas for specific users on a volume. If your Windows 2000 installation uses per-user quotas, the values for *lpFreeBytesAvailable* and *lpTotalNumberOfBytes* may be less than the total number of free bytes and total number of bytes on the disk.

If you want to show a list of available drives and let the user pick a drive, you can call **GetLogicalDriveStrings**, which shows the user the available root directories (such as C:\, D:\, ...). Once the user picks a drive, you can ensure that the drive is a valid drive for the application's purpose (you may not want to let the user pick a CD-ROM drive to write to) by calling **GetDriveType**. Once a valid drive has been picked, you can ensure that there is enough space on the drive by calling **GetDiskFreeSpace**.

TIP: Do not assume or hard-code filename lengths in your program. Use the *lpMaximumComponent-Length* parameter of **GetVolumeInformation**, which tells you the maximum filename length.

Directory Functions

The functions available for your applications related to directories are summarized in Table 4-3.

Function	Information Returned or Action Performed
CreateDirectory, CreateDirectoryEx	Creates new directories. You can specify a security descriptor. Directory names can use Unicode or Uniform Naming Convention (UNC) format. **CreateDirectoryEx** can use a directory template.
RemoveDirectory	Deletes existing directories. Directories should be empty, and the calling process must have delete access.

Table 4-3. Directory Functions

Function	Information Returned or Action Performed
GetCurrentDirectory	Retrieves the current directory (directory at the end of the active path) for the calling process as a fully qualified path.
SetCurrentDirectory	Changes the current directory for the current process. You can supply a relative path or a fully qualified path.
ReadDirectoryChangesW	Retrieves information about changes occurring within a directory you specify synchronously or asynchronously. Refer to "File System Notifications" later in this chapter.
GetSystemDirectory	Retrieves path to the Windows system directory.
GetWindowsDirectory	Retrieves path to the Windows directory.

Table 4-3. Directory Functions *(continued)*

Let's look at the prototype of one of the directory functions—**GetCurrentDirectory**.

```
DWORD GetCurrentDirectory( DWORD nBufLen,
                           LPTSTR lpBuf
                           );
```

The parameters for **GetCurrentDirectory** are as follows:

▼ *nBufLen* specifies the length of the buffer current directory string (in characters and including space for a terminating null character).

▲ *lpBuf* is a pointer to the buffer that holds the fully qualified path of the current directory string.

GetCurrentDirectory returns the number of characters written to the buffer if successful, and zero if it fails. If the failure is caused by insufficient buffer size to hold the results of the call, the return value specifies the required size of the buffer.

TIP: In instances where you do not know the buffer size (as in the case of *lpBuf* earlier) you can code zero for the buffer length parameter (*nBufLen* earlier). The function call will fail, but the return value will indicate the length of buffer required. You can then repeat your call using the correct buffer size.

File Functions

The common functions available for your application related to files are summarized in Table 4-4.

Function	Information Returned or Action Performed
AreFileApisANSI	Determines whether a set of Win32 file functions uses the American National Standards Institute (ANSI) or Original Equipment Manufacturer (OEM) character set *code page.* The function returns nonzero for the ANSI code page and zero for the OEM code page. You can set the code page using **SetFileApisToANSI** and **SetFileApisToOEM**.
CancelIO	Cancels all pending and in-progress overlapped I/O operations issued by the calling thread for a specified file handle.
CopyFile, CopyFileEx	Copies an existing file to a new file. You can choose to overwrite an existing file. File attributes are copied to the new file, but security attributes are not copied to the new file. **CopyFileEx** also preserves extended attributes, OLE structured storage, and NTFS alternate data streams.
CopyProgressRoutine	Application-defined callback routine that is called when a portion of a copy operation started by **CopyFileEx** is completed. You can use the callback routine to display a progress bar indicating copy progress.

Table 4-4. File Functions

Function	Information Returned or Action Performed
CreateFile	Creates or opens a file and returns a handle. Filenames can use Unicode or Uniform Naming Convention (UNC) format. You can use the attributes of an existing template file. **CreateFile** is also used to create pipes, mailslots, consoles, and so on.
CreateIOCompletionPort	Associates an instance of an opened file with an I/O completion port to let applications receive notification of asynchronous I/O completion.
DeleteFile	Deletes a file (that is not open or is not a memory-mapped file).
FileIOCompletionRoutine	Routine that is called when an asynchronous I/O function (such as **ReadFileEx**) is completed and the calling thread is waiting for an alert.
FindClose	Closes the search handle used by the **FindFirstFile** and **FindNextFile** functions.
FindFirstFile, FindFirstFileEx	Searches a directory for a file. Filenames can use Unicode or UNC format. The function returns a handle that can be used to find the next file that matches the same name criteria using **FindNextFile**. **FindFirstFile** uses filenames only. **FindFirstFileEx** uses filenames as well as attributes.
FindNextFile	Locates the next file that matches a given search criteria using the handle returned by **FindFirstFile** or **FindFirstFileEx**.
FlushFileBuffers	Writes all buffered data to the file and clears the buffers.
GetBinaryType	Determines if a file is executable and the appropriate subsystem (32-bit Windows, 16-bit Windows, OS/2, POSIX, and so on).

Table 4-4. File Functions *(continued)*

Function	Information Returned or Action Performed
GetFileAttributes, GetFileAttributesEx	Retrieves attributes (such as hidden, system, archive, compressed, and so on) for a specified file or directory. **GetFileAttributesEx** retrieves attribute information that is more than the FAT-style attribute information retrieved by **GetFileAttributes**.
GetFileInformationByHandle	Retrieves information about a specified file.
GetFileSize	Retrieves the uncompressed file size in bytes. (To get the compressed file size, use **GetCompressedFileSize**.)
GetFileType	Retrieves the file type, which could be FILE_TYPE_UNKNOWN (for an unknown file type), FILE_TYPE_DISK (for a disk file), FILE_TYPE_CHAR (for a character file such as an LPT device or a console), or FILE_TYPE_PIPE (for a named or anonymous pipe).
GetFullPathName	Retrieves the full path and filename by merging the name of the current drive and directory with the specified filename (but doesn't verify to see if the path is valid or if the file is actually present).
GetShortPathName	Obtains the short path form of a specified input path. You can obtain a file's long name from the short name by calling **FindFirstFile**.
LockFile, LockFileEx	Locks and prevents other processes from accessing a region or byte range in an open file.
MoveFile, MoveFileEx	Moves (renames) a file or directory. Renaming a directory renames all children. **MoveFileEx** adds other options including moving a file across volumes, delaying the move until reboot, and so on.

Table 4-4.   File Functions *(continued)*

Function	Information Returned or Action Performed
ReadFile, ReadFileEx	Reads data from a file synchronously or asynchronously. **ReadFileEx** performs only asynchronous reads and calls an application completion routine upon read completion.
SearchPath	Searches for the specified file.
SetEndOfFile	Truncates or extends a file by moving the end-of-file.
SetFileAttributes	Sets a file's attributes (such as Hidden, Normal, System, and Read-only).
SetFilePointer	Sets the file pointer forward or backward. Exercise caution if you use this function in a multithreaded application.
UnlockFile, UnlockFileEx	Unlocks a region or byte range of a file previously locked by **LockFile** or **LockFileEx**.
WriteFile, WriteFileEx	Writes data to a file synchronously or asynchronously. **WriteFileEx** performs only asynchronous writes and calls an application completion routine upon write completion.

Table 4-4.   File Functions *(continued)*

Let's look at the prototype of one of the file functions—**WriteFileEx**.

```
BOOL WriteFileEx( HANDLE hFile,
                  LPCVOID lpBuf,
                  DWORD nNumOfBytesToWrite,
                  LPOVERLAPPED lpOvrlap,
                  LPOVERLAPPED_COMPLETION_ROUTINE lpCompletionRoutine
                  );
```

The parameters for **WriteFileEx** are as follows:

▼   *hFile* is the file handle for a file opened (with the FILE_FLAG_OVERLAPPED and with GENERIC_WRITE access) by the **CreateFile** function or a socket handle returned by the *socket* or *accept* function.

- *lpBuf* points to the buffer containing the data to be written to the file.

- *nNumOfBytesToWrite* specifies the number of bytes to write to the file.

- *lpOvrlap* points to an **OVERLAPPED** (shown later in the chapter) data structure that supplies data to be used during the asynchronous write operation.

▲ *lpCompletionRoutine* points to your application completion routine that is called when the write operation is complete and the calling thread is in an alertable wait state (*fAlertable* flag set to TRUE for **SleepEx**, **WaitForSingleObjectEx**, or **WaitForMultipleObjectsEx** function).

WriteFileEx returns nonzero if successful, and zero if it fails.

Programming Notes

Let's take the example of reading data from disk, let the user make updates, and write the data back to the file. You call **CreateFile** to open the file. If it is a shared file and you want to prevent other accesses, you use **LockFile** to lock the file. You then call **ReadFile** as many times as you need to get the data from the file that you want to display to the user. When the user has completed the updates, you call **WriteFile** and **UnlockFile**. You can call the "Ex" version in the preceding calls where appropriate.

In the previous scenario, if you are unable to **CreateFile** because it doesn't exist, then the file could have been moved. You can give the user the option to search for the file using **SearchPath** and **FindNextFile**. If there are multiple files that match the search criteria provided by the user, you can get more details about the files using **GetFileSize**, **GetFileType**, and **GetFileInformationByHandle** to help the user pick the specific file.

Windows 2000 stores the long filenames on disk in Unicode. This means that the original long filename is always preserved, even if it contains extended characters, and regardless of the code page that is active during a disk read or write operation. The case of the filename is preserved, although the file system itself is not case sensitive.

MEMORY-MAPPED FILES

The use of memory-mapped files is a way of associating the contents of a file with a process's virtual memory through a file-mapping object. Although a memory-mapped file appears to the process using it to be resident in virtual memory, a memory-mapped file's contents are actually held in real memory associated with a file-mapping object. Thus, memory-mapping is a much faster way to access the file's contents compared with disk I/O. Since a file-mapping object can be shared between processes, memory-mapped files can also be used as shared memory between processes in Windows 2000 (remember that in Windows 2000, each process has its own address space, unlike the shared memory that is available in other Windows operating systems). The portion of a process's virtual address space that is mapped to the file's contents is called *file view*. Since a file view is part of the virtual memory, you can use read and write using pointers.

You can memory-map any file, including the system pagefile. The file-mapping object can be for all or any part of a file, and similarly the file view can be for all or any part of a file-mapping object. The capability to map only a portion of a file makes it easy to process very big files by mapping portions of the file at a time. Different processes can have different views, and a process can have multiple views. Windows 2000 ensures *coherence* between the different views (all the views display the same data even if a process updates the data in one view), except when the file is a remote file, or if you simultaneously update the file using views and APIs. For example, if you map a complete file and the size of the physical file grows after the mapping object has been created, the mapping object will no longer reflect the complete file. A process can access a file randomly or sequentially using a file mapping (by setting the pointer where you want).

Windows 2000 internally uses memory-mapped files to speed up the loading of EXE and DLL files. Just as you can use locking functions such as **LockFile** when you access files on disk, you can use the **VirtualProtect** function to control access to file view. Having looked at the characteristics of memory-mapped files, let's look at the programming aspects of memory-mapped files.

Programming Memory-Mapped Files

You can use the functions shown in Table 4-5 to program memory-mapped files.

Function	Information Returned or Action Performed
CreateFileMapping	Creates a file-mapping object for a file and optionally lets you name the file-mapping object.
FlushViewOfFile	Flushes the cached writes to the file.
MapViewOfFile, MapViewOfFileEx	Maps a view of a file into calling a process's address space. **MapViewOfFileEx** lets you pass a starting address for the map.
OpenFileMapping	Opens a named file-mapping object. Used by other processes to access a file-mapping object once it has been created.
UnmapViewOfFile	Unmaps a view created by **MapViewOfFile** or **MapViewOfFileEx**.

Table 4-5.   Memory-Mapped File Functions

Let's look at the prototype of one of the memory-mapped file functions—
CreateFileMapping.

```
HANDLE CreateFileMapping( HANDLE hFile,
                          LPSECURITY_ATTRIBUTES lpFileMappingAttributes,
                          DWORD flProtect,
                          DWORD dwMaxSizeHigh,
                          DWORD dwMaxSizeLow,
                          LPCTSTR lpName
);
```

The parameters of **CreateFileMapping** are as follows:

▼   *hFile* identifies the file for which a mapping object is to be created.
   lpFileMappingAttributes is a pointer to a **SECURITY_ATTRIBUTES** structure.
   If this parameter is NULL, the default security descriptor is used.

■   *flProtect* specifies the desired protection for the file view. The valid values
   for this parameter are PAGE_READONLY (for read-only access), PAGE_
   READWRITE (for read/write access), and PAGE_WRITECOPY (for
   copy-on-write access where a new copy of the page is created for a write).

■   *dwMaxSizeHigh* is the maximum size of the file-mapping object (the high-order
   32 bits).

■   *dwMaxSizeLow* is the maximum size of the file-mapping object (the low-order
   32 bits). Specify *dwMaxSizeLow* and *dwMaxSizeHigh* as zero to make the
   maximum size of the file-mapping object the same size as the file you are
   creating a mapping for.

▲   *lpName* is the name for the file-mapping object. Specifying NULL creates the
   file-mapping object without a name. Using a name of a file mapping that
   already exists causes the function to access the existing object.

CreateFileMapping returns a handle to the file-mapping object if it succeeds, and
NULL upon failure.

NEW IN WINDOWS 2000:   Windows NT used a flat 32-bit virtual addressing mechanism providing
applications with up to 2GB of virtual memory. While this memory size is enough for many applications,
some database and scientific applications need additional virtual memory. Windows 2000 supports
Very Large Memory (VLM), whereby 64-bit pointers are used to address memory, resulting in applications being able to address up to 28GB.

To use a memory-mapped file, you perform the following steps:

1. Create (or open) a file by use of **CreateFile**. If you want exclusive access to prevent others from using the file (for example, to preserve coherence), set the *dwShareMode* parameter of **CreateFile** to zero.

2. Create a file-mapping object using **CreateFileMapping**. **CreateFileMapping** will use the handle returned by **CreateFile** in step 1. You can name the file-mapping object using the *lpName* parameter of **CreateFileMapping** if the file-mapping object will be shared by use of its name.

3. Create a file view using **MapViewOfFile** or **MapViewOfFileEx** using the handle of the file-mapping object returned by **CreateFileMapping** in step 2. Keep track of the base address.

4. If the file-mapping object is to be shared by processes, the other processes can use the **OpenFileMapping** function using the name of the file-mapping object from step 2. Using a name is one of three ways to share a file-mapping object. The other ways you can share a file-mapping object are by duplicating a handle or by getting a handle at process creation time.

5. You read and write by dereferencing the pointer to the view(s). The data from the writes is normally cached to improve efficiency and save time, but you can cause the *dirty pages* (pages that have been modified since the file view was mapped) to be flushed using **FlushViewOfFile**.

6. Once you have finished using a view, you unmap it using **UnmapViewOfFile**. You pass the base address of the mapped view of a file that is to be unmapped. This base address value is returned by a previous call to the **MapViewOfFile** in step 3.

7. You close the file-mapping object using its handle (from step 2) in a call to **CloseHandle**.

FILE SYSTEM NOTIFICATIONS

We talked about showing the user a list of files to choose from (under "File Functions"). If you have displayed a list of files, the user can switch to another window and actually create a file or directory that invalidates the file list being displayed by your application. It

Note for UNIX Programmers

Most UNIX systems support memory-mapped files. If you have programmed using mmap in UNIX, then you can program memory-mapped file functions in Windows 2000 using **CreateFileMapping**, **MapViewOfFile**, and other functions as mentioned earlier.

would be nice for you to be able to detect file system changes and update your list. You can do this using file system notification functions. Windows 2000 provides the file system notification functions listed in Table 4-6.

You can use file system notifications in the following manner:

First, you use **FindFirstChangeNotification** to set up the triggers you want to watch for. The prototype for **FindFirstChangeNotification** is shown next:

```
HANDLE FindFirstChangeNotification( LPCTSTR lpPathName,
                                    BOOL bWatchSubtree,
```

Function	Information Returned or Action Performed
FindFirstChangeNotification	Creates a change notification handle and sets up initial change notification filter conditions. Filters can be change of a filename, a directory name, and so on.
FindNextChangeNotification	Signals a change notification handle the next time an appropriate change is detected.
FindCloseChangeNotification	Stops change notification handle monitoring.
ReadDirectoryChangesW	Retrieves information about changes occurring in a directory.
SignalObjectAndWait	Allows the caller to signal one object and wait for another object.
WaitForSingleObject, WaitForSingleObjectEx	Waits for an object to be signaled (or for a time-out). **WaitForSingleObjectEx** also waits for an I/O completion routine or *asynchronous procedure call (APC)* to be queued.
WaitForMultipleObjects, WaitForMultipleObjectsEx	Same as preceding, except that the wait is for multiple objects instead of one object.
MsgWaitForMultipleObjects, MsgWaitForMultipleObjectsEx	Waits for the specified objects to be in the signaled state. The objects can include different types of input event objects including mouse event, hot key event, and so on.

Table 4-6.   File System Notification Functions

```
                              DWORD  dwNotifyFilter
);
```

▼   The *lpPathName* parameter specifies the path of the directory to watch. Here the directory could be at any level (that is, it could be a subdirectory).

■   The *bWatchSubtree* parameter specifies whether the scope of the watch is limited to the directory (or subdirectory) specified, or whether the watch should include all levels starting with the directory (or subdirectory) specified and continuing down the tree hierarchy.

▲   The *dwNotifyFilter* parameter specifies the trigger conditions to watch out for. The values for this parameter are listed in Table 4-7.

Parameter Value	Triggered By
FILE_NOTIFY_CHANGE_FILE_NAME	A filename change within the watch scope—for example, when a file is created, moved (renamed), or deleted
FILE_NOTIFY_CHANGE_DIR_NAME	A directory name change within the watch scope—for example, when a directory is created, moved (renamed), or deleted
FILE_NOTIFY_CHANGE_ATTRIBUTES	A file attribute change within the watch scope—for example, from hidden to normal
FILE_NOTIFY_CHANGE_SIZE	A file size change for files within the watch scope
FILE_NOTIFY_CHANGE_LAST_WRITE	A change to the last write time of files within the watch scope
FILE_NOTIFY_CHANGE_SECURITY	A security descriptor change for files or directories within the watch scope

Table 4-7.   File or Directory Change Triggers

NOTE: The trigger occurs when the operating system detects the changes in the file system, which will be slightly delayed compared with when an application changes it (due to caching). Normally this delay is insignificantly small.

FindFirstChangeNotification returns a handle if successful, and INVALID_ HANDLE_VALUE if it fails.

Now that you have set up the triggers, you can detect if a file system change has happened by using one of the wait functions, such as **WaitForSingleObject**, whose prototype is shown next:

```
DWORD WaitForSingleObject( HANDLE hHandle,
                           DWORD dwMillisecs

);
```

▼ The *hHandle* parameter identifies the file system change notification object.

▲ The *dwMillisecs* parameter is the time-out interval, in milliseconds. Code zero to return immediately without waiting and INFINITE to wait until the object is signaled.

Once **WaitForSingleObject** returns, you can scan the directory for changes or call **ReadDirectoryChangesW** to get a list of the changes. You can use the changes to update your user interface, if appropriate. If you think there could have been further changes to the directory while you were performing the user interface update, then you can call **FindNextChangeNotification**, which will indicate if there have been changes to your triggers since the time of **FindFirstChangeNotification**. When you have finished processing, you call **FindCloseChangeNotification**. **WaitForSingleObject** returns a value that indicates the event that caused the function to return (for example, the state of the waited upon object or time-out is signaled if it succeeds and WAIT_FAILED if it fails).

ASYNCHRONOUS I/O

It is well known that of all the subsystems in a computer system, the I/O subsystem is the slowest. Reading and writing to disks, tapes, and CDs take a lot of time. (We are talking relative computer time here. A disk I/O may only take a few milliseconds, which is a lot less than the time for you to blink an eye, but milliseconds long compared with the microseconds or nanoseconds it takes to execute instructions or access real memory. If you have a 120 MHz Pentium, then its clock speed is 120×10^6 cycles/sec. In other words, the time for one cycle is 1/120 microsecond. Since each instruction takes only a few cycles, you can see that executing instructions is a lot faster than I/O access.)

Solutions to ensure that the central processing unit (CPU) isn't idle have included preemptive scheduling and multiprocessing. Windows 2000 preempts the thread requesting

I/O and schedules another thread. Another solution to the slow I/O problem is the use of memory-mapped files, covered earlier, where you substitute fast memory access for slow disk access. Yet another solution is *asynchronous I/O*. What if, instead of automatically scheduling *another* thread to execute, Windows 2000 lets *your own* thread that requested the I/O continue to do other things (presuming you have other things to do) and notifies your thread when the I/O is complete? Windows 2000 lets you do precisely that with its support for asynchronous I/O. Asynchronous I/O is also called *overlapped I/O*.

Let's start with the data structure that plays a central part in overlapped I/O—the **OVERLAPPED** structure shown next:

```
typedef struct _OVERLAPPED { // Overlapped Data Structure
                    DWORD   Internal;
                    DWORD   InternalHigh;
                    DWORD   Offset;
                    DWORD   OffsetHigh;
                    HANDLE  hEvent;
} OVERLAPPED;
```

▼ *Internal*, reserved for Windows 2000, specifies a system-dependent status when the **GetOverlappedResult** function returns without setting the extended error information to ERROR_IO_PENDING.

■ *InternalHigh*, reserved for Windows 2000, specifies the length of the data transferred when the **GetOverlappedResult** function returns TRUE.

■ *Offset* specifies the file position to start the transfer, which is a byte offset from the start of the file. You set this member before calling **ReadFile** or **WriteFile**.

■ *OffsetHigh* specifies the high word of the byte offset at which to start the transfer.

▲ *hEvent* is the event that is set to the signaled state when the transfer has been completed. You set this member before calling **ReadFile** or **WriteFile**.

To use overlapped I/O in your program, start with **CreateFile** and specify FILE_FLAG_OVERLAPPED for the *dwFlagsAndAttributes* parameter as shown in the prototype that follows:

```
HANDLE CreateFile(LPCTSTR lpFileName,
                    DWORD dwDesiredAccess,
                    DWORD dwShareMode,
                    LPSECURITY_ATTRIBUTES lpSecurityAttributes,
                    DWORD dwCreationDistribution,
                    DWORD dwFlagsAndAttributes,
                    HANDLE hTemplateFile
);
```

Let's look at the only parameter of interest for asynchronous I/O—the *dwFlagsAndAttributes* parameter—and the values you can specify that affect asynchronous I/O.

▼   FILE_FLAG_OVERLAPPED—I/O operations that take a significant amount of time return ERROR_IO_PENDING. When the operation is finished, the specified event is set to the signaled state. With this flag, the system does not maintain the file pointer. The file position must be passed as part of the *lpOverlapped* parameter to the **ReadFile** and **WriteFile** functions. This flag also enables more than one operation, such as simultaneous read and write, to be performed with the handle.

▲   FILE_FLAG_NO_BUFFERING—Opens the file with no intermediate buffering or caching. If you also specify FILE_FLAG_OVERLAPPED, then I/O operations do not use the synchronous operations of the memory manager, and thus some overhead is reduced. On the other hand, benefits of caching, such as delayed writes, are not available.

Once you have created or opened the file, you initialize the overlapped structure and specify the portion of the file you want to read using the *Offset* and *OffsetHigh* parameters described earlier. You then call **ReadFile** with the *lpOverlapped* parameter. Control will be immediately returned, and you can perform other functions. Once you are ready to check if the asynchronous I/O is complete, you can use the **WaitForSingleObject** function covered earlier in the chapter. When the I/O is complete, **WaitForSingleObject** returns. You can check the results of your read using the **GetOverlappedResult** function. You can use the **CancelIO** function to cancel an asynchronous I/O operation.

The console program that follows demonstrates asynchronous I/O. It creates a large stream of data, encrypts it, and saves it to a file. But instead of encrypting all the data and then writing to the file, it tries to encrypt blocks of data while the program is writing another encrypted block. Whenever I/O takes a long time to complete, the program proceeds to encrypt the next block of data. It displays a message on the console to indicate this. Since only a small amount of data is written by this program, it is difficult to simulate a long I/O operation that will take considerable time. For you to experiment, some of the data in the program is defined using **#define**, and you can vary these data parameters and try them out. In my local test, I was able to overlap I/O and encryption 10 to 15 times out of 200 I/O attempts. Of course, your results will vary depending on your computer configuration, other programs you are running, and so on.

```
#include <windows.h>
#include <iostream.h>

#define TOTAL_BUFFER_SIZE          200000
#define BYTES_PER_WRITE            100
#define SAMPLE_STRING_LENGTH       100
```

Instead of hard-coding the buffer size and number of bytes that are written to the disk in each block, these values are #defined.

```
void EncryptNextSegment();
char *pOutBuf;
```

For simplicity, the pointer to the buffer that is written out is defined to be global.

```
int main ()
{
    char *szString = "This is a long string. It will be encrypted and\
stored in the file. This string is 100 bytes long...";
    char *pStrTemp;
    char *pOutBufTemp;

    pOutBuf = new char[TOTAL_BUFFER_SIZE];
    pOutBufTemp = pOutBuf;
    // make repetitive copy of szString into pOutBuf
    for(int i = 0; i < TOTAL_BUFFER_SIZE/SAMPLE_STRING_LENGTH; i++)
    {
      pStrTemp = szString;
      for (int j = 0; j < SAMPLE_STRING_LENGTH; j++)
      {
      *pOutBufTemp++ = *pStrTemp++;
      }
    }
    HANDLE hFile = CreateFile ("a:Out.enc", GENERIC_WRITE, 0, NULL,
CREATE_ALWAYS, FILE_FLAG_OVERLAPPED, NULL);
    // Return code should be checked here.  But assume it is OK for this
    // sample.
    // Prepare to write data to the file.
```

A buffer is allocated from the heap, and the data is initialized. The file *a:Out.enc* is created. Drive A is used to attempt to slow down the I/O. Note that the FILE_FLAG_OVERLAPPED value is used while creating the file (by use of **CreateFile**).

```
    DWORD dwWrite;
    OVERLAPPED     ov;
    ov.Offset = 0;
    ov.OffsetHigh = 0;
    ov.hEvent = NULL;

    const int iTotalEncryptSegment = TOTAL_BUFFER_SIZE/BYTES_PER_WRITE;
    pOutBufTemp = pOutBuf;
    EncryptNextSegment();       // Encrypt first segment
```

The total number of blocks to be encrypted and written to the file is calculated, and the first block is encrypted.

```
for (int k = 0; k < iTotalEncryptSegment; k++)
    {
      BOOL       fWriteResult;

      fWriteResult = WriteFile(hFile, pOutBufTemp, BYTES_PER_WRITE,
                            NULL, &ov);
      for(;;)
      {
          DWORD dwResult = WaitForSingleObject(hFile, 20);
          if(dwResult == WAIT_TIMEOUT)
          {
          // The I/O is still going on - Proceed to encrypt the next block
                cout << "Proceed to encrypt while waiting for the IO\
to complete." << endl;
                EncryptNextSegment();
          }
          else if(dwResult == WAIT_OBJECT_0)
          {
              // Write is completed. Do at least one more encryption
              // if we did not time out the first time
                cout << "IO completed." << endl;
                EncryptNextSegment();
                break;
          }
          else if(dwResult == WAIT_FAILED)
          {
                cout << "WAIT_FAILED" << endl;
                break;
          }
      }

    }
```

The encrypted block is written to the file asynchronously. The program then goes into a loop, periodically checking to see if the I/O has been completed. If the I/O is still pending, it proceeds to encrypt the next block of data. If the I/O is completed, it still tries to encrypt one more block just in case the first try to check the I/O completion was successful without a wait. It breaks out of the *for* loop, proceeds to get the overlap I/O result, and writes the next block of data. When all the data is written, it closes the file.

```
    pOutBufTemp += BYTES_PER_WRITE;
    GetOverlappedResult(hFile, &ov, &dwWrite, TRUE);
    ov.Offset += dwWrite;
```

```
    }
    CloseHandle(hFile);
    return(1);
}
```

The function **EncryptNextSegment** does a trivial encryption, where it increments the character by one. So "A" is rotated to "B," "B" to "C," and so on. This is a simplified version of more complex rotation encryption algorithms. **EncryptNextSegment** remembers which block is to be encrypted, and if all the blocks are encrypted, it just returns without doing anything.

```
void EncryptNextSegment()
{
    // Remember which segment is to be encrypted
    static int iCurrentEncSegment = 0;
    char *pBuf;
    if (iCurrentEncSegment < TOTAL_BUFFER_SIZE/BYTES_PER_WRITE)
    {
      // We still have more data to encrypt
        pBuf = pOutBuf + iCurrentEncSegment*BYTES_PER_WRITE;
        for (int i = 0; i < BYTES_PER_WRITE; i++)
        {
//Rot 1 encryption. Just increase the value by 1. So 'A' will be 'B'
            *pBuf = *pBuf+1;

            pBuf++;
        }
        iCurrentEncSegment++;
    }
}
```

FILE ENCRYPTION

Encryption of files and directories is new to Windows 2000. Windows 2000 supports the Encrypted File System (EFS). EFS provides cryptographic protection of files on NTFS volumes. EFS encrypts individual files using a public-key system.

The following items cannot be encrypted:

▼ System files

■ System directories

▲ Root directories

If you are not sure if your file system supports encryption, you can determine that by calling the **GetVolumeInformation** function and examining the FILE_SUPPORTS_ENCRYPTION bit flag.

TIP: EFS encryption and NTFS file compression are mutually exclusive. You cannot compress an encrypted file. However, encrypted files tend to be compressed already, due to the nature of cryptographic algorithms. Sparse files (very large files without a lot of data) may be encrypted.

The APIs Windows 2000 provides to support encryption are summarized in Table 4-8. Before we venture into the next example, it is worth looking into building simple applications using Visual C++, since most of the sample applications are built this way. It is quite easy to create simple applications using Visual C++ and ClassWizard. To demonstrate the Encrypted File System, follow these steps to create a dialog-based application that accepts a filename and either encrypts, decrypts, or queries the encryption status of the file.

1. From Visual C++ Visual Studio create a new MFC AppWizard (exe) project.

2. In the AppWizard– Step 1, select the Dialog Based radio button to create a dialog-based application.

3. In Step 2 of 6 make sure just the About box and 3D Controls check boxes are selected, since we are not interested in other features.

The rest of the options can be left at their default values, and when the AppWizard is finished, it creates a project with all the files needed. The ResourceView will be brought up automatically, and you will be presented with a sample dialog. For our example, you need two entry fields, one where the user can enter the filename for the operation and the other to present the status of certain operations or information about the operations. It also needs five buttons, Browse… to bring up the file dialog, Encrypt to encrypt the specified file, Decrypt to decrypt the specified file, Query to query the encryption status of the specified file, and Cancel to close the application.

4. Using the Controls Palette, create these controls and place them in the dialog box.
   The initial dialog that is presented already has an OK button and a Cancel button, along with a static text control with "TODO: Place dialog controls here." as the text. These may be reused or deleted. The Layout menu can be used to arrange the layout for various controls. Each control's property, such as the control's ID, name, and style, can be set by right-clicking the control and selecting Properties in the pop-up menu. Of the two entry fields that we

Encryption API	Description and Usage Notes	Parameters
EncryptFile	This function encrypts a file or directory. All data streams in a file are encrypted. All new files created in an encrypted directory are encrypted. Exclusive access to the file being encrypted is required. If the file is compressed, **EncryptFile** will decompress the file before encrypting it.	Name of the file or directory
DecryptFile	This function decrypts a file or directory. Exclusive access to the file being decrypted is required.	Name of the file or directory
EncryptionDisable	This function disables or enables encryption of the indicated directory and the files in it without affecting encryption of subdirectories below the indicated directory. **EncryptionDisable** disables encryption of directories and files but does not affect the visibility of files that have the FILE_ATTRIBUTE_SYSTEM attribute set.	Name of the directory and an option (enable/disable)

Table 4-8. Encryption APIs, Description, and Parameters

created, we want one to accept the filename from the user and the other one to display the status of the operation. We want to present the status in a MultiLine Edit control, so there is no need to enable this control for the user's input. This read-only style as well as the multiline style can be set by selecting the Property menu item when you right-click the control.

5. After creating the controls, bring up the ClassWizard by right-clicking the dialog and selecting the ClassWizard menu item from the pop-up menu.

6. In the Memory Maps tab, indicate which messages you will be interested in. We want to be notified when any of the buttons are clicked. The action for the Cancel button is already handled by the default code, which is good enough for this application, since no cleanup is necessary.

7. In the Object IDs list box, select the various button's IDs, and for each button double-click the BN_CLICKED messages. This will bring up a dialog to enter a member function stub to be inserted in the code.
You have handled how to react to various user actions in the dialog box. You should now handle how to present information to the user. In this application, you can present information to the user in the filename field and the status multiline edit field. In both cases you need to modify these fields. The filename field is modified to include the name of the file that the user selects from the file dialog, and the status field is updated with the status of the operation.

8. To update these fields, you need to create two member variables. To do this, go to the Member Variables tab and double-click the filename control ID. This will bring up a dialog where you can specify the name and type of the variable. Since you need to access the control itself to set the filename or status, the category of the variable is selected to be Control.

9. Repeat the procedure for the status field. When the ClassWizard operation is completed, it generates the stub code to which functional code is added.

Let us now look at the next example, which allows the user to encrypt or decrypt a file or to query the encryption status of a file. This example application serves only as a sample, since Windows 2000 already includes a command called *cipher* to do what this example does. Still this example shows the usage of the encryption, decryption, and file encryption status APIs that can be used in your application. When executed, this example presents a dialog box to the user and accepts a filename. Alternatively, the file can be browsed using a file dialog. The buttons in the dialog then enable the user to encrypt, decrypt, or query the encryption status of the selected file. The results of the operation are displayed in the multiline edit field in the dialog box.

What follows is the code that was generated by the Visual C++ Wizard. The main program code is in the EncDec.cpp module and the associated EncDec.h header file, which defines the main application class. The class that handles the functioning of the dialog box is in the EncDecDlg.cpp module and the associated EncDecDlg.h header file, which defines the dialog class. Some essential sections of the header files and the code generated by the AppWizard and ClassWizard are shown here, since this is the first example dealing with GUIs. In future examples in the book, some of this generated code will not be shown, but if you need to look at the code, please check the CD-ROM that is provided with this book.

Shown here is the part of the EncDec.h header file that defines the **CEncDecApp** class:

```
//////////////////////////////////////////////////////////////////////

// CEncDecApp:
// See EncDec.cpp for the implementation of this class
//
class CEncDecApp : public CWinApp
{
public:
    CEncDecApp();

// Overrides
    // ClassWizard generated virtual function overrides
    //{{AFX_VIRTUAL(CEncDecApp)
    public:
    virtual BOOL InitInstance();
    //}}AFX_VIRTUAL

// Implementation

    //{{AFX_MSG(CEncDecApp)
    //}}AFX_MSG
    DECLARE_MESSAGE_MAP()
};
```

Shown here is the module code that implements the **CEncDecApp** class:

```
// EncDec.cpp : Defines the class behaviors for the application.

#include "stdafx.h"
#include "EncDec.h"
#include "EncDecDlg.h"

#ifdef _DEBUG
#define new DEBUG_NEW
#undef THIS_FILE
static char THIS_FILE[] = __FILE__;
#endif
```

```
/////////////////////////////////////////////////////////////////////
// CEncDecApp

BEGIN_MESSAGE_MAP(CEncDecApp, CWinApp)
    //{{AFX_MSG_MAP(CEncDecApp)
    // NOTE - the ClassWizard will add and remove mapping macros here.
    //    DO NOT EDIT what you see in these blocks of generated code!
    //}}AFX_MSG
    ON_COMMAND(ID_HELP, CWinApp::OnHelp)
END_MESSAGE_MAP()

/////////////////////////////////////////////////////////////////////
// CEncDecApp construction

CEncDecApp::CEncDecApp()
{
    // TODO: add construction code here,
    // Place all significant initialization in InitInstance
}

/////////////////////////////////////////////////////////////////////
// The one and only CEncDecApp object

CEncDecApp theApp;

/////////////////////////////////////////////////////////////////////
// CEncDecApp initialization

BOOL CEncDecApp::InitInstance()
{
    // Standard initialization

#ifdef _AFXDLL
    Enable3dControls();      // Call this when using MFC in a shared DLL
#else
    Enable3dControlsStatic();// Call this when linking to MFC statically
#endif
```

In the next few lines the application creates an instance of the application dialog box class and runs it by calling the **DoModal()** method. It ignores whether the OK button or the Cancel button was clicked.

```
    CEncDecDlg dlg;
    m_pMainWnd = &dlg;
```

```
    int nResponse = dlg.DoModal();
    if (nResponse == IDOK)
    {
        // TODO: Place code here to handle when the dialog is
        //  dismissed with OK
    }
    else if (nResponse == IDCANCEL)
    {
        // TODO: Place code here to handle when the dialog is
        //  dismissed with Cancel
    }

return FALSE;
}
```

Shown next is the dialog class code generated by the ClassWizard:

```
/////////////////////////////////////////////////////////////////////
// CEncDecDlg dialog

class CEncDecDlg : public CDialog
{

// Construction
public:
    CEncDecDlg(CWnd* pParent = NULL);    // standard constructor

// Dialog Data
    //{{AFX_DATA(CEncDecDlg)
    enum { IDD = IDD_ENCDEC_DIALOG };
```

The two member variables that were added for the filename entry field and the status multiline entry field are shown here:

```
    CEdit    m_FileName;
    CEdit    m_Status;
    //}}AFX_DATA

    // ClassWizard generated virtual function overrides
    //{{AFX_VIRTUAL(CEncDecDlg)
    protected:
    virtual void DoDataExchange(CDataExchange* pDX);
```

The dialog data exchange mechanism can be used to set and retrieve values to and from the dialog box controls. If the member variable data is set, then it is transferred to the control before it is displayed by the dialog data exchange mechanism. The mechanism also retrieves the values into the member variables when the OK button is clicked or the **UpdateData** API is called. The **UpdateData** API can also be used to set the value to the control. By overriding the **DoDataExchange** method, we get control during data update and can perform validation. A variety of DDX functions are available for various types of exchange.

```
    //}}AFX_VIRTUAL
// Implementation
protected:
    HICON m_hIcon;
```

Shown next are the definitions of various notification functions that were added using the ClassWizard. In a traditional window processing function, the messages are typically processed in a switch statement, but MFC provides a different means of doing this. It maintains a mapping of member functions to the messages and calls the appropriate member function to process the message. This mapping is called the message map and is typically declared by inserting the **DECLARE_MESSAGE_MAP** macro into the class definition. In conjunction with this, another set of macros, **BEGIN_MESSAGE_MAP** and **END_MESSAGE_MAP**, is used in the implementation of the class to define the message map. With this message map in place, MFC routes to the appropriate member function to handle the message. These macros are defined in AFXWIN.H:

```
    // Generated message map functions
    //{{AFX_MSG(CEncDecDlg)
    virtual BOOL OnInitDialog();
    afx_msg void OnSysCommand(UINT nID, LPARAM lParam);
    afx_msg void OnPaint();
    afx_msg HCURSOR OnQueryDragIcon();
    afx_msg void OnBrowse();
    afx_msg void OnDecrypt();
    afx_msg void OnEncrypt();
    afx_msg void OnQuery();
    //}}AFX_MSG
    DECLARE_MESSAGE_MAP()
};
```

The code for the **CEncDecDlg** class, which processes various user actions, follows:

```
// EncDecDlg.cpp : implementation file
//
#include "stdafx.h"
#include "EncDec.h"
#include "EncDecDlg.h"
```

```
///////////////////////////////////////////////////////////////
// CEncDecDlg dialog

CEncDecDlg::CEncDecDlg(CWnd* pParent /*=NULL*/)
    : CDialog(CEncDecDlg::IDD, pParent)
{
    //{{AFX_DATA_INIT(CEncDecDlg)
    //}}AFX_DATA_INIT
    m_hIcon = AfxGetApp()->LoadIcon(IDR_MAINFRAME);
}

void CEncDecDlg::DoDataExchange(CDataExchange* pDX)
{
    CDialog::DoDataExchange(pDX);
    //{{AFX_DATA_MAP(CEncDecDlg)
    DDX_Control(pDX, IDC_FILENAME, m_FileName);
    DDX_Control(pDX, IDC_STATUS, m_Status);
    //}}AFX_DATA_MAP
}

BEGIN_MESSAGE_MAP(CEncDecDlg, CDialog)
    //{{AFX_MSG_MAP(CEncDecDlg)
    ON_WM_SYSCOMMAND()
    ON_WM_PAINT()
    ON_WM_QUERYDRAGICON()
    ON_BN_CLICKED(IDC_BROWSE, OnBrowse)
    ON_BN_CLICKED(IDC_DECRYPT, OnDecrypt)
    ON_BN_CLICKED(IDC_ENCRYPT, OnEncrypt)
    ON_BN_CLICKED(IDC_QUERY, OnQuery)
    //}}AFX_MSG_MAP
END_MESSAGE_MAP()

///////////////////////////////////////////////////////////////
// CEncDecDlg message handlers

BOOL CEncDecDlg::OnInitDialog()
{
    CDialog::OnInitDialog();

    // Add "About..." menu item to system menu.

    // IDM_ABOUTBOX must be in the system command range.
    ASSERT((IDM_ABOUTBOX & 0xFFF0) == IDM_ABOUTBOX);
    ASSERT(IDM_ABOUTBOX < 0xF000);
```

```
        CMenu* pSysMenu = GetSystemMenu(FALSE);
        if (pSysMenu != NULL)
        {
            CString strAboutMenu;
            strAboutMenu.LoadString(IDS_ABOUTBOX);
            if (!strAboutMenu.IsEmpty())
            {
                pSysMenu->AppendMenu(MF_SEPARATOR);
                pSysMenu->AppendMenu(MF_STRING, IDM_ABOUTBOX,
                                strAboutMenu) ;
            }
        }

        // Set the icon for this dialog.  The framework does this
        // automatically
        //  when the application's main window is not a dialog
        SetIcon(m_hIcon, TRUE);            // Set big icon
        SetIcon(m_hIcon, FALSE);           // Set small icon

        // TODO: Add extra initialization here

        return TRUE;  // return TRUE  unless you set the focus to a control
}

void CEncDecDlg::OnSysCommand(UINT nID, LPARAM lParam)
{
    if ((nID & 0xFFF0) == IDM_ABOUTBOX)
    {
        CAboutDlg dlgAbout;
        dlgAbout.DoModal();
    }
    else
    {
        CDialog::OnSysCommand(nID, lParam);
    }
}

void CEncDecDlg::OnPaint()
{
    if (IsIconic())
    {
        CPaintDC dc(this); // device context for painting
        SendMessage(WM_ICONERASEBKGND, (WPARAM) dc.GetSafeHdc(), 0);
```

```
        // Center icon in client rectangle
        int cxIcon = GetSystemMetrics(SM_CXICON);
        int cyIcon = GetSystemMetrics(SM_CYICON);
        CRect rect;
        GetClientRect(&rect);
        int x = (rect.Width() - cxIcon + 1) / 2;
        int y = (rect.Height() - cyIcon + 1) / 2;

        // Draw the icon
        dc.DrawIcon(x, y, m_hIcon);
    }
    else
    {
        CDialog::OnPaint();
    }
}

// The system calls this to obtain the cursor to display while the user
//  drags the minimized window.
HCURSOR CEncDecDlg::OnQueryDragIcon()
{
    return (HCURSOR) m_hIcon;
}
```

The user can provide the filename either by typing the name in the entry field or by clicking the Browse… button. When the Browse… button is selected, the control is transferred to this member function, which displays the file dialog and updates the filename field.

```
void CEncDecDlg::OnBrowse()
{
    CString strPath("");
    CFileDialog m_File(TRUE, NULL, NULL, OFN_FILEMUSTEXIST);

    // TODO: Add your control notification handler code here
    if (m_File.DoModal() == IDOK)
    {
        strPath = m_File.GetPathName();
    }

    m_FileName.SetWindowText((LPCTSTR)strPath);
    m_Status.SetWindowText((LPCTSTR)"");//Clear the status
}
```

When the user clicks Decrypt, the **OnDecrypt** member function is called. This function gets the filename and calls the **DecryptFile** API to decrypt the file. The same API can also be used to decrypt the directory. This API requires exclusive access to the file and will fail if it is being accessed by another process. It is safe to call this API and pass a file that has already been decrypted or a file that was never encrypted. If this API fails, the extended error can be queried by calling the **GetLastError** API.

```
void CEncDecDlg::OnDecrypt()
{
    // TODO: Add your control notification handler code here
    CString strPath;
    m_FileName.GetWindowText(strPath);
    if (!strPath.IsEmpty())
    {
        if (DecryptFile((LPCTSTR)strPath, 0))
        {
            m_Status.SetWindowText((LPCTSTR)"File decrypted.");
        }
        else
        {
            // Use GetLastError to get extended error
            m_Status.SetWindowText((LPCTSTR)"Failed to decrypted.");
        }
    }
    else
    {
        m_Status.SetWindowText((LPCTSTR)"Filename is empty");
    }
}
```

When the user clicks Encrypt, the **OnEncrypt** member function is called. This function gets the filename and calls the **EncryptFile** API to encrypt the file. If a directory is specified instead of a file, the directory is encrypted and all the new files created in the directory will be encrypted. This API requires exclusive access to the file and will fail if that file is being accessed by another process. If the specified file is already encrypted, the API simply returns a success. It should be noted that system files, system directories, and root directories cannot be encrypted. If this API fails, the extended error can be queried by calling the **GetLastError** API.

```
void CEncDecDlg::OnEncrypt()
{
    // TODO: Add your control notification handler code here
    CString strPath;
    m_FileName.GetWindowText(strPath);
    if (!strPath.IsEmpty())
```

```
    {
        if (EncryptFile((LPCTSTR)strPath))
        {
            m_Status.SetWindowText((LPCTSTR)"File encrypted.");
        }
        else
        {
            // Use GetLastError to get extended error
            m_Status.SetWindowText((LPCTSTR)"Failed to encrypt.");
        }
    }
    else
    {
        m_Status.SetWindowText((LPCTSTR)"Filename is empty");
    }

}
```

When the user clicks the Query button, the **OnQuery** member function is called; it retrieves the filename, checks the encryption status of the file, and displays a message in the multiline edit field.

```
void CEncDecDlg::OnQuery()
{
    // TODO: Add your control notification handler code here
    CString strPath;
    DWORD   dwStatus;
    char    *pszMessage;
    m_FileName.GetWindowText(strPath);
    if (!strPath.IsEmpty())
    {
        if (FileEncryptionStatus((LPCTSTR)strPath, &dwStatus))
{
            switch (dwStatus)
            {
                case FILE_ENCRYPTABLE:
                    pszMessage = "The file can be encrypted.";
                break;

                case FILE_IS_ENCRYPTED:
                    pszMessage = "The file is encrypted.";
                break;
```

```
                 case FILE_SYSTEM_ATTR:
                     pszMessage = "The file cannot be encrypted because\
it is a system file.";
                     break;

                 case FILE_ROOT_DIR:
                     pszMessage = "The file cannot be encrypted because\
it is a root directory.";
                     break;

                 case FILE_SYSTEM_DIR:
                     pszMessage = "The file cannot be encrypted because\
it is a system directory.";
                     break;

                 case FILE_UNKNOWN:
                     pszMessage = "The file encryption status is\
unknown.  It may be encrypted.";
                     break;

                 case FILE_SYSTEM_NOT_SUPPORT:
                     pszMessage = "The file system does not support\
encryption.";
                     break;

                 case FILE_READ_ONLY:
                     pszMessage = "The file is a read only file.";
                     break;

                 default:
                     pszMessage = "Unknown error occurred";
                     break;
             }
             m_Status.SetWindowText((LPCTSTR)pszMessage);
         }
         else
         {
             // Use GetLastError to get extended error
             m_Status.SetWindowText((LPCTSTR)"Failed to query status.");
         }
     }
     else
     {
         m_Status.SetWindowText((LPCTSTR)"Filename is empty");
```

```
        }

}
```

Please make sure that this application is tried out on files or directories on Encrypted File System. When the file is encrypted, it is encrypted on behalf of the currently logged-on user, and it is automatically decrypted for that user. To try this example logon as one user, run this example, encrypt some text file, and log off. Log back on as a different user and display the file that was encrypted earlier.

RAID SUPPORT

You've probably noticed two things about disk drives. First, the prices keep falling, as with many other computer components. Second, occasionally you have problems. I don't necessarily mean a crash, but you have files that have to be recovered, you have bad disk sectors, and on occasion your computer won't boot up because the boot sector is damaged. The problems of getting a magnetic head so close to a disk while ensuring that the two don't actually touch each other (with at least one of them moving at a high speed) has been likened to flying a Boeing 747 just a few feet off the ground. I started my floppy disk backup seriously since I read that.

The first solution to the disk problems is backups and an uninterruptible power supply (UPS). A UPS is good, but it only takes care of disk problems attributable to power failures. Backups are good and if you have mission-critical data, you want to ensure that at least one copy of the backup is physically stored away from the building where the original is (in the event of a fire in the building). But backups are a separate step, and it typically takes time to locate and get at the backup data. There is another solution. If disk prices are cheap and one disk may have problems, why not write the same data to more than one disk at the same time? The data in one disk is like a backup to the data in another disk, and vice versa. Since the data is written to all the disks at the same time, there is no extra step involved. That is the idea behind using a Redundant Array of Inexpensive Disks (RAID) instead of just one disk.

Six levels of RAID are recognized, and these are summarized in Table 4-9.

Windows 2000 supports RAID in two ways—hardware and software:

▼ Hardware support for RAID disks

▲ Software support for RAID levels 0, 1, and 5

Using RAID is primarily the job of a system administrator. When the system administrator mirrors a partition, another partition with the same drive letter as the one being partitioned is created. All data written to one partition is also written to the other. As an advanced programmer, you ought to be familiar with RAID and its benefits.

RAID Level	Function
0	Striping. Data that is written to the disk is split and written (striped across) to multiple disks.
1	Mirroring and duplexing. All data written to one disk is duplicated (mirrored) in another disk.
2	Bit-level striping with error-correction code (ECC). This technique is proprietary, using multiple parity drives.
3	Byte-level striping, also with ECC for parity. This is similar to RAID 2, except that only one parity drive is used.
4	Block-level striping, with single-drive parity. Drives are not synchronized.
5	Block-level striping with parity information distributed across multiple drives.

Table 4-9.   RAID Levels and Functions

CONCLUSION

We looked at the characteristics of the different file systems supported by Windows 2000 including FAT and its variations, NTFS, HPFS, and CDFS. We looked at the programming functions provided by Windows 2000 for volumes, drives, directories, and files. We looked at some advanced file system features, such as asynchronous input/output and memory-mapped files. We also looked at how your program can be notified of changes in the file system. Finally, we briefly looked at the characteristics of RAID.

The first four chapters surveyed the major features of Windows 2000 from a programming perspective. We looked at 2000's architecture and related topics in Chapter 1. We looked at user interface–related topics in Chapter 2. We looked at communications-related topics in Chapter 3 and file-related topics in this chapter.

CHAPTER 5

Windows 2000 Enhancements for Programmers

W indows 2000 introduces many new capabilities as well as additional features for capabilities available in Windows NT 4.0. In this chapter, we will take a brief look at the new capabilities and additional features, focusing on those capabilities and features of special interest to developers. Some of the new capabilities such as Active Directory, Distributed interNet Applications Architecture (DNA), and advanced security features are really significant. While these capabilities are briefly discussed in this chapter, they are covered in detail later. Active Directory is covered in Chapter 10, DNA in Chapter 16, and security features in Chapter 22.

WHAT'S NEW IN WINDOWS 2000

We will cover the new capabilities and features of Windows 2000 using the same part breakdown adopted for the book. We will use the following categories:

▼   General capabilities and features

■   New capabilities and features in GUI and OS services

▲   New capabilities and features in Windows communications programming

Let's start with new capabilities and features that are common to all areas.

General Capabilities and Features

The Win32 APIs are common to all Windows technologies and have particular importance to the programmer. Let us start with enhancements to the Win32 APIs.

Win32 APIs

A complete list of new functions and interfaces is available in *Win32API.csv*, which is located on the Platform SDK CD-ROM. Probably the most important enhancement in this area lies in the preparatory steps for moving to a 64-bit environment. For Windows 2000, the definitions of the Win32 API elements have been updated with new Win64-compatible types. One of the major problems that Microsoft will face in going to the 64-bit environment is compatibility of existing applications, and to minimize this problem, Microsoft is providing details of data types that will be used in the 64-bit environment.

You should be aware of these types and use them to the extent possible, as it is likely that the applications you develop will still be running when the 64-bit environment is introduced. Since these new types are derived from the basic C-language integer and long types, you can use these data types in your current Win32-based application. When 64-bit Windows is available, you can recompile your current Win32 application as a Win64-based application.

These data types are broadly classified as follows:

▼   Fixed-precision data types

- ■ Pointer-precision types
- ▲ Specific-precision pointers

These types were added to *basetsd.h*. Appendix B contains a complete list of the data types.

Some specific API changes are listed in Table 5-1.

Security Enhancements

Windows 2000 includes a number of security-related capabilities such as certificate services, CryptoAPI, and Smartcard support. CryptoAPIs are introduced in this chapter. CryptoAPIs and Smartcards are covered in more detail in Chapter 22.

API Change	Impact
TranslateMessage and *wParam*	To support a new input method, Windows 2000 will pass back information in *wParam* for WM_KEYUP and the WM_KEYDOWN messages. For this passing to function properly, you need to pass *wParam* untouched to **TranslateMessage**.
DS_SHELLFONT	If you specify DS_SHELLFONT inside a dialog structure, you can change the font size but not the font face in Windows 2000. Windows 2000 uses Shell Dlg 2 as the font face.
Open File	If **OpenFile** doesn't find any files of the type you are looking for, it defaults to the My Documents folder, as a shortcut.
GetWindowsDirectory	If you're running on terminal server, you may get a system directory that's set up for a particular user instead of the real system directory. If you are running on terminal server and you want the actual system directory returned, call the new API **GetWindowsSystemDirectory**.

Table 5-1. Win32 API Changes in Windows 2000

Certificate Services   Certificate Services enables an organization to manage the issuing, renewal, and revocation of certificates without the need for the organization to rely upon external certification authorities. Certificate Services receives requests for new certificates over transports such as RPC or HTTP. It processes each request using custom or site-specific policies, sets optional properties for the certificate to be issued, and issues the certificate. Certificate Services publishes a signed certificate revocation list (CRL) on a regular basis. Certificate Services allows administrators to add elements to a CRL. You can use the interfaces supported by Certificate Services to create support for additional transports, policies, and certificate properties and formats.

The version of Certificate Services supported by Windows 2000 is Certificate Services 2.0. You can install Certificate Services using the Control Panel's Add/Remove Programs function.

CryptoAPIs   CryptoAPI enables you to add security based on cryptography to your applications. CryptoAPI includes functionality for you to add encryption/decryption of data, authentication using digital certificates, and encoding to/decoding from ASN.1 to your Win32 applications. CryptoAPI works with a number of cryptographic service providers that perform the actual cryptographic functions. This permits you to use the functions in CryptoAPI without knowing details of the underlying implementation.

Windows Installer

The Windows Installer enables your customers to efficiently install and configure your products and applications. The installer can also provide your product with new capabilities to advertise features without installing them, to install products on demand, and to add user customizations. The install on demand feature permits required features and components to be installed on the local hard drive as and when needed.

Windows Management Instrumentation (WMI)

WMI is the Microsoft implementation of Web-Based Enterprise Management (WBEM). WBEM is an industry initiative to develop a standard technology for accessing management information in an enterprise environment. Management information includes inventories of currently installed client applications, information on client status, the state of system memory, and so on. This information is represented using the Common Information Model (CIM) designed by the Distributed Management Task Force (DMTF).

New Capabilities and Features in GUI and OS Services

Part II of the book deals with GUI and OS services. In this section we will look at what's new in Windows 2000 in both of these areas.

New GUI Capabilities and Features

Windows 2000 adds support for multiple monitors, a feature that is supported by Windows 98 but not Windows NT. To support multiple monitors, you have to ensure that your application handles both negative coordinates and very large coordinates correctly.

This is because, if you have a multiple monitor set up and your primary monitor is to the right of your secondary monitor, the secondary monitor will be entirely in negative coordinate space. A non-multimonitor-aware application may move a window that should be shown fully visible on a secondary monitor to be shown entirely on the primary monitor because of the negative coordinates. A similar behavior could happen for high positive coordinates. To enable support for multiple monitors, you need to use the new system metrics available with Windows 2000 and you should test your applications specifically with multiple monitors.

One of the complaints against Windows operating systems is the number of system files. These seem to have grown significantly with each new version of Windows. Windows 2000 tries to address this. Many MS-DOS-related files that do not have a significant role will no longer show up when the user looks at files in the Windows Explorer. In addition, Windows 2000 has changed the file attributes of many system files and marked them as both "system" and "hidden." The consequence is that these files do not show up in Windows Explorer, even if you check "Show Hidden Files." If you want to see these files, you must click a new check box on the list of attributes for a folder. The older DOS files and the files marked "system" and "hidden" are still accessible through the other file access functions such as Open dialogs and the command line prompt.

New Common Controls   Windows 2000 supports a number of new common controls including ComboBoxEx, Date and Time Picker, Flat Scroll Bar, IP Address, Month Calendar, Pager, and Rebar. Refer to Chapter 7 for further details about these and other common controls.

Microsoft Agent   Microsoft Agent is a set of programmable software services that enables software developers and Web authors to incorporate a new form of user interaction, known as conversational interfaces. Microsoft Agent supports interactive animated characters that you can use to enhance your applications or Web pages. The Agent can help conduct a natural interactive conversation where the user can use voice commands (Microsoft Agent also includes optional support for speech recognition) to interact with your applications and your application can use characters that respond using synthesized speech, recorded audio, or text in a cartoon word balloon.

Microsoft Management Console (MMC)   The Microsoft Management Console is an extensible user interface. MMC provides an environment for running systems management applications. System Management applications should be structured as components called "snap-ins."

To assist you with writing COM-based snap-ins, Microsoft provides the MMC COM SDK.

Graphical Device Interface (GDI) Enhancements   GDI provides functions and data structures that an application can use to generate graphical output for devices such as displays, printers, and plotters. Using GDI functions, you can draw lines, curves, closed figures, paths, text, and bitmap images.

The enhancements to GDI include:

▼ *Alpha blending* Display bitmaps that have transparent or semitransparent pixels using **AlphaBlend**.

▲ *Smooth shading* Shade a region with a color gradient. Drawing on vertex and color information, GDI linearly interpolates the color of the inside of the region to achieve a gradient. Smooth shading uses the **GradientFill** function.

New OS Services Capabilities and Features

Windows 2000 includes a number of new capabilities and features related to OS services. As a result, we have added additional material to Chapters 9 and 10 related to OS services. In this section, we will summarize some of the new capabilities and features.

DLL Redirection DLLs with incorrect versions have been plaguing application developers to the extent that sometimes the phrase "DLL Hell" is used to refer to this problem. With Windows 2000, you can ensure that your application uses the correct version of a DLL by creating a *redirection file*. The redirection file is named by adding the suffix to your application name. For example, if your application's name is *yourapp.exe,* the redirection file is named *yourapp.exe.local.* You must install *yourapp.exe.local* in the same directory that contains *yourapp.exe.* You must also install the DLLs in the same directory. While the contents of the redirection file itself are ignored, its presence forces all DLLs in the application's directory to be loaded from that directory. The **LoadLibrary** and **LoadLibraryEx** functions change their search sequence if a redirection file is present. Additional details about DLL redirection can be found in Chapter 8.

Service Model Enhancements The service model has been enhanced in Windows 2000. Here are some of the new features:

▼ New service functions and structures have been introduced. These include **EnumServiceStatusEx**, **QueryServiceConfig2**, **ChangeServiceConfig2**, and **RegisterServiceCtrlHandlerEx**.

■ A better way to share service handlers is introduced. This sharing results in more efficient coding of your service applications.

■ Enhanced support is provided for extended control codes. This support makes it easier for you to develop well-behaved service applications.

▲ Enhanced support is provided for error handling. With expanded error handling capabilities, it is now easier to manage Windows services.

Job Objects A *job object* is a feature that allows groups of processes to be managed as a unit. Job objects control attributes of the processes associated with them. Operations performed on a job object affect all processes associated with that job object. You can name, secure, and share job objects.

The functions that you can use with job objects and associated description are summarized in Table 5-2.

Thread Pooling   You may have developed applications where you spawn a large number of threads although most of your threads are idle or in the sleeping state most of the time awaiting an event to occur. The task of creating and maintaining threads has an associated overhead, and some of the benefits of multithreading are offset by the overhead of a large number of relatively idle threads. Wouldn't it be great if there were a way to have a smaller number of active threads instead of a much larger number of idle threads and still accomplish all the functions? That is the idea behind thread pooling.

Job Object Function	Description
CreateJobObject	Create a job object. Creating a job object by itself does not associate any processes with that job object.
AssignProcessTo JobObject	Associate a process with a job object. Once a process is associated with a job object, the association cannot be broken. Child processes of a process associated with a job object are also associated, by default, with the same job object.
SetInformationJobObject	Set limits for a job object. The limits are applied to each associated process of the job object. Limits can be applied for process attributes such as process priority, working set size, and end-of-job time limit. If a process makes function calls to change the limits enforced by a job object, such calls are ignored.
QueryInformation JobObject	Retrieve basic accounting information for all associated processes, including terminated processes.
TerminateJobObject	Terminate all processes currently associated with a job object.

Table 5-2.   Job Object Functions and Associated Descriptions

With *thread pooling*, you get a pool of worker threads that are managed by the system. At least one thread monitors the status of all wait operations queued to the thread pool. When a wait operation has completed, a worker thread from the thread pool executes the corresponding callback function. To request that a work item be handled by a thread in the thread pool, call the **QueueUserWorkItem** function. You can use the **BindIoCompletionCallback** function to post asynchronous I/O operations. Upon completion of the I/O, the callback is executed by a thread pool thread.

New Capabilities and Features in Windows Communications Programming

Windows 2000 has a number of new communications programming–related capabilities and features. These are summarized in this section.

NetBIOS Changes

NetBIOS is no longer an integral part of Windows 2000 (unlike Windows NT), and it is possible for users to set up Windows 2000 systems without NetBIOS support. If you have communications applications that use NetBIOS APIs such as **NetServerEnum**, those applications will no longer work in Windows 2000 systems without NetBIOS support. You need to change the applications to make non-NetBIOS calls to accomplish the same function. In addition, you need to make sure there are new network *.inf* files for network drivers, transport drivers, and some network file print providers, to support Windows 2000 Plug and Play.

Asynchronous Remote Procedure Calls

Asynchronous Remote Procedure Call is a Microsoft extension to the traditional Remote Procedure Call (RPC) model as defined by the Open Software Foundation's Distributed Computing Environment (OSF-DCE). Asynchronous RPC, as its name suggests, differs from the traditional, synchronous RPC in that you do not wait for the call to be completed and get a return value. Instead, asynchronous RPC separates the call from its return value, and your call and return are no longer synchronous. Microsoft's extension is aimed at providing some benefits over and above the traditional synchronous model, including the following:

▼ Multiple outstanding calls are possible from a single-threaded client. In the traditional RPC model, you are blocked in a remote procedure call until the call returns, and hence it is not possible for you to have multiple outstanding calls.

■ Slow or delayed clients/servers. A client or a server that is slow does not tie up the call. Instead the client and/or the server works at its own pace. This is particularly useful when the load on the server varies and there could be extended periods of time when the client may have to wait for the server.

▲ Incremental data transfer. Since the call and the response are made asynchronously, both the client and the server can decide to send whatever amount of data they choose in each call. And the client or the server can in turn decide to wait for some or all of the increments to arrive before responding. This feature is particularly useful in transferring large amounts of data between the client and server, a process that, especially over slow links, historically has tied up both the client thread and the server manager thread for the duration of the transfer. With asynchronous RPC and pipes, data transfer can take place incrementally, and without blocking the client or server from performing other tasks.

To take advantage of asynchronous RPC mechanisms, you declare functions with the **ASYNC** attribute, which is new in Windows 2000. You make this declaration in an attribute configuration file (ACF), not an Interface Definition Language (IDL) file.

Opportunistic Locks

An *opportunistic lock* is a lock placed by a client on a file residing on a server. A client places an opportunistic lock so that it can cache data locally, leading to reduced network traffic and improved response time. Opportunistic locks coordinate data caching between servers and multiple clients so that the data in the server and the cached data in one or more clients is *coherent*. Keep in mind that the current implementation provides for a capability for servers to refuse granting of opportunistic locks.

Microsoft's implementation of opportunistic locks follows the Common Internet File System (CIFS) protocol. As of the writing of this book, this protocol is still in draft form and hence the protocol and Microsoft's implementation are subject to change. The CIFS protocol is an enhanced version of the Server Message Block (SMB) protocol.

Collaboration Data Objects (CDO)

CDO is a Component Object Model (COM) component designed to simplify writing programs that create or manipulate Internet messages. CDO provides COM classes that expose dual interfaces that you can use in applications written in languages supporting COM and automation, including Microsoft Visual Basic, Microsoft Visual C++, Microsoft Visual J++, and scripting languages such as Visual Basic, Scripting Edition. CDO supports creating and managing messages formatted and sent using Internet standards such as the Multipurpose Internet Mail Extensions (MIME) standard. CDO can also be used to implement SMTP/NNTP transport event sinks (sinks that can examine or modify the messages as they reach the particular service).

CDO implements version 2.0 of the Collaboration Data Objects API specification. The DLL that implements CDO is *Cdosys.dll*. In Windows 2000, CDO supports transmitting messages using both the SMTP and NNTP protocols, as well as through a local SMTP/NNTP service pickup directory. CDO is not based on the Messaging API (MAPI).

Extensible Authentication Protocol (EAP)

EAP is an extension to the Point-to-Point (PPP) protocol, providing a standard support mechanism for authentication schemes such as token cards, Kerberos, Public Key, and

S/Key. EAP is critical technology in implementing secure Virtual Private Networks (VPN) and protects VPNs against "brute force" attacks and password guessing.

EAP is an enhancement to existing authentication protocols such as Password Authentication Protocol (PAP) and Challenge Handshake Authentication Protocol (CHAP). EAP is fully supported on both the Windows 2000 Dial-Up Server and the Dial-Up Networking Client.

Internet Authentication Service (IAS)

IAS provides support for the Remote Authentication Dial-In User Service (RADIUS) protocol, in both the client and the server. IAS enables developers to implement session control and accounting plug-ins, add authorizations, or use network authentication methods for remote access. Although IAS has been available with Windows NT service pack 5, the Windows 2000 version of IAS supports authorization DLLs and the **RadiusExtensionProcessEx** API, which are not supported in Windows NT.

APPLICATION COMPATIBILITY

Because of the number of enhancements introduced in Windows 2000, you may find that your prior Windows application may not work or may work differently. Here, we will discuss some of the changes in Windows 2000 and how they may affect your existing application.

Operating System Version Number Check

You may have used **GetVersionEx** to check the version of the operating system before proceeding with the install of your application. Windows 2000 has a new major version number that may cause a problem if your code does not account for the possibility of a new (higher) version number. If you are changing your install code to accommodate the new version number, you may want to consider using **VerifyVersionInfo** instead. **VerifyVersionInfo** will check the major version, the minor version, and the service pack in a hierarchy. **VerifyVersionInfo** addresses the problem of checking for specific versions by returning TRUE when the current operating system can support the specific minimum version you need. If you still want to use **GetVersionEx**, then Windows 2000 has introduced a new structure, **OSVERSIONINFOEX**, that gives you a new field where service pack, major version, and minor version are provided as integers, which are easier to compare.

DLL Version Number Check

If you have been developing Windows applications for a while, you have invariably come across the situation where one DLL has been overlaid by another version of the DLL, leading to unwanted side effects. Microsoft's solution for Windows NT was to encourage application developers to use DLL version numbers while creating DLLs and to check the versions before install. Chapter 8 includes a programming example illustrating use of versioning for DLLs.

Windows 2000 includes some additional features to help with the problems of DLL versions. New Windows 2000 applications will be using Windows Installer, which always checks the version of a DLL for you, relieving you from having to do this yourself. Another feature that Windows 2000 introduces is "side-by-side" DLLs, which permit different applications to use different versions of the same DLL simultaneously and still peacefully coexist. To use this feature, you'll need to rename the DLL itself and also change any GUIDs in the DLL. Once a DLL is renamed, applications can install it into their own managed directories instead of installing it into the system directory. Additionally, the DLL is registered with a relative path pointing to your own local directory, instead of the system directory. **LoadLibrary** functionality has been changed to ensure that if an application has registered a DLL with a relative path, then that DLL is used (regardless of whether the system directory also has a copy of that DLL).

Windows File Protection Check

Windows 2000 uses a locking-down mechanism to prevent an application from changing one of the system files. In Windows 2000, if an application replaces one of the system files, Windows file protection mechanisms will kick in and restore the system file. In a future version of Windows Installer, the installer will not permit the replacement of system files. Windows 2000 includes two APIs—**SFCGetNextProtectedFile** and **SfcIsFileProtected**—to help you determine if file(s) are system protected files. **SFCGetNextProtectedFile** gives you a list of all files that are protected or could be protected. **SfcIsFileProtected** returns TRUE if a specified file (indicated by the full path name) is protected.

Component Check

If your application uses Windows components such as TAPI, MAPI, or DirectX, there are changes that could affect your application. Windows 2000 includes the latest version of TAPI (TAPI 3.0) and the latest version of DirectX (version 7). Some versions of Windows NT did not include DirectX. If you have code that presumes the absence of DirectX or presumes the levels of components, you need to change your code. In addition, Windows 2000 does not include MAPI by default (unlike Windows NT). If you use a component, you need to always check for its presence and its level. Do not make any assumptions based on such things as platform or components. Also do not assume the locations of components, such as by using hard-coded path names.

Application Location

I am sure you have noticed that even when you ask an application to be installed to a drive other than "C:", many applications normally copy some files to the Windows directory and/or one of its subdirectories, such as System32. The common result is that these directories end up having hundreds of files occupying a large amount of space and you cannot install any application in the "C:" drive for want of space. In addition, it is normally very difficult for a user to figure out which of the hundreds of files are no longer needed and can be deleted. The only solutions to this problem are either to buy uninstall utilities or, alternatively, to reinstall Windows. Microsoft wants to change this situation.

Windows 2000 supports a new API called **SHGetFolderPath**. This API returns the location of most folders that you would normally need in your application. The DLL that implements this API is *SHFolder.dll*. For example, the folder *My Documents* in Windows 9.*x* systems is the folder *%windir%\profiles\user\personal* (where *user* is the userid of the particular user using the system) in Windows NT, and it is the folder *Documents and Settings\user\My Documents* in Windows 2000. Your Windows 9.*x* or NT application that uses hard-coded path names may fail in Windows 2000.

The average path returned by Windows 2000 is about 60–70 characters, compared to 30–40 characters for Windows NT. If your application passes a short buffer to Windows NT, it may have a problem with Windows 2000.

Memory-Related Checks

Unlike Windows NT, Windows 2000 is strongly enforcing the rule that anything that is running in kernel mode cannot write to write-protected regions of the memory (without exception). Some applications, such as device drivers, may not work with Windows 2000 due to the strong enforcement. This does not mean that all device drivers written for Windows NT 4.0 will automatically fail if they violate the preceding rule. Windows 2000 accommodates existing applications in this respect. Windows 2000, however, will strictly enforce it for new Windows 2000 applications.

If you have made your applications run faster through using less memory (by tweaking the stack size for example), your application may crash in Windows 2000. This is because Windows 2000 uses much more stack space than Windows NT 4.0 and the combination of your application and Windows 2000 together is likely to run out of stack space a lot faster than your application in Windows NT.

Another memory-related compatibility area relates to heaps. In prior versions of Windows NT, when you freed a block, Windows NT would move that block to the unused block list (at the bottom of the list), and eventually it would filter up and be reused. Windows 2000 has changed this behavior. To speed things up, Windows 2000 attempts to keep you on the same page by caching the last blocks that your application used. In Windows 2000, when you free a block, the block effectively goes to the top of the list, and when you need another block, you're more likely to get the block back sooner than later. This has a lot of implications. If you access memory that you have freed, you may or may not get an access violation in Windows 2000. If you do not get an access violation, chances are that you are corrupting data without being aware that the data is getting corrupted. Also in Windows 2000, do not count on your pointer still being valid when you reallocate a block that is smaller than your original block.

CONCLUSION

In this chapter we looked a number of new capabilities and features of Windows 2000. Keep in mind that it is not meant to be a comprehensive list. Also, topics such as Active Directory and DNA are covered in detail in later chapters dedicated to those topics. This chapter also covers compatibility issues that your current applications may have when moving to Windows 2000.

PART II

Advanced GUI and OS Services Programming

CHAPTER 6

GDI Programming

Part I of this book laid the programming foundations. The remainder, Parts II through IV, will build on those foundations. Here in Part II we will look at one of the most important programming areas in Windows 2000—the user interface. Part III deals with communications programming, and Part IV covers multimedia and database programming.

In this chapter, we will look at graphics programming using the graphical device interface (GDI). Chapter 7 will focus on advanced user interface programming. Chapter 7 will look at an animation programming method that uses controls, as well as other advanced controls available in Windows 2000. Chapters 8 and 9 will cover advanced OS services such as dynamic link libraries (DLLs), Active Directory, Registry, and threads.

GDI BASICS

Windows 2000 includes a number of tools to aid graphics programming. We will review the basics briefly. By using the programming tools, you can draw regularly shaped objects, such as lines and circles, as well as irregularly shaped objects, such as irregular polygons. The programming tools include *pens* to draw lines, arcs, circles, ellipses, and so on. You can use *brushes* to fill in enclosed spaces. If you want to see a sample graphics program in action, check the paint accessory included with Windows.

The Graphics Coordinate System

Windows 2000 uses a graphics coordinate system to draw graphics. For example, if you draw a line, it is from the current coordinate of the cursor (the cursor is not visible, unlike with text) to the coordinate where the line terminates. When your program begins, the current cursor coordinate is set to (0,0). By default, (0,0) is the coordinate of the upper-left corner of the screen. You specify the drawing units (for example, the length of the line you want to draw) in *logical units.* By default, logical units are pixels. Remember, you can change the defaults for both the coordinate system and the logical units by using mapping modes (see the "Mapping Modes" section a bit later in this chapter).

Device Context

A *device context (DC)* is a structure that Windows maintains when it outputs information to a device or collects information about a device. The device could be a display, a printer, or a memory area. The DCs that access memory areas are also called *compatible DCs,* and the DCs used to collect information are also called *informational DCs.* The MFC library provides classes that support DCs. The MFC DC classes and their descriptions are summarized in Table 6-1.

MFC DC Class	Description
CDC	This is the base class for all DC classes such as CPaintDC, CMetafileDC, and so on.
CPaintDC	This class is derived from CDC. It performs CWnd::BeginPaint and constructs a CPaintDC object at construction time. It performs CWnd::EndPaint at destruction time. CPaintDC is typically used when you respond to the WM_PAINT message.
CMetaFileDC	This is used to create a CMetaFileDC object. A Windows metafile consists of GDI commands such as MoveTo and LineTo; it is an alternative way to reproduce images (compared with storing the whole image in a bitmap and reproducing the image).
CWindowDC	This is used to access the entire screen area (both client and nonclient areas) of a window. CWindowsDC calls GetWindowDC at construction time and ReleaseDC at destruction time.
CClientDC	This is used to access the client area of a window. CClientDC calls GetDC at construction time and ReleaseDC at destruction time.

Table 6-1.   MFC Library DC Classes

Output Mode

Windows copies the graphics output of your program as is and overwrites current window contents by default. However, you can AND, OR, or XOR your output with the current window contents by setting the appropriate mode. You can set the output mode using the **SetROP2** function. You can also choose the mode parameter values of **SetROP2**. The resulting colors when you subsequently use a pen or brush are shown in Table 6-2.

Mapping Modes

As mentioned earlier, the windows default is to map one logical unit to one pixel. You can change this mapping using the **SetMapMode** function. GDI uses the mapping mode to

Mode Parameter Value	Drawing Mode
R2_BLACK	Black
R2_COPYPEN	Output copied to the window, overwrites the current contents
R2_MASKNOTPEN	AND of the inverse of the pen color and the current screen color
R2_MASKPEN	AND of the pen color and the current screen color
R2_MASKPENNOT	AND of the pen color and the inverse of the current screen color
R2_MERGENOTPEN	OR of the inverse of the pen color and the current screen color
R2_MERGEPEN	OR of the pen color and the current screen color
R2_MERGEPENNOT	OR of the pen color and the inverse of the current screen color
R2_NOP	No effect
R2_NOT	Inverse of the current screen color
R2_NOTCOPYPEN	Inverse of the current pen color
R2_NOTMASKPEN	Inverse of R2_MASKPEN
R2_NOTMERGEPEN	Inverse of R2_MERGEPEN
R2_NOTXORPEN	Inverse of R2_XORPEN
R2_WHITE	White
R2_XORPEN	Exclusive-OR of pen color with the current screen color

Table 6-2. Parameter Values to Choose Output Modes

convert logical coordinates into the appropriate device coordinates. The mapping mode defines the unit of measure used to convert logical units to device units. It also defines the orientation of the device's X and Y axes. The **SetMapMode** function prototype is shown next.

```
virtual int SetMapMode(
HDC hdc
int nMapMode );
```

Here, *hdc* is the handle to the device context and *nMapMode* is the new mapping mode. The valid values of *nMapMode* and the resulting modes are summarized in Table 6-3.

Having covered some graphics programming basics, let's look at some of the graphics programming topics in depth. As an advanced Windows programmer, you probably are already familiar with regular graphics programming using pens to draw lines, arcs, ellipses, and so on, and the use of brushes to fill in enclosed areas. We will not go into the programming details here. However, the sample program in this chapter draws an irregular polygon, an ellipse, and a rectangle. You can follow the code to see how this is done. If you want to read more about these topics, please refer to *Windows 2000 Programming from the Ground Up,* by Herbert Schildt, published in 2000 by Osborne/McGraw-Hill.

FONTS

Our discussion of graphics would be incomplete without covering the topic of text. You invariably need text in most graphics for titles, descriptions, notes, and so on. As an advanced programmer, you may already be familiar with different programming aspects of displaying text, such as specifying the color of the text you display as well as setting the background color, specifying the exact portion of the screen where your text will be dis-

nMapMode Value	Mode
MM_ANISOTROPIC	Maps logical units to programmer-defined units with arbitrarily scaled axes. You can use SetWindowExtEx or SetViewportExtEx to specify the units, scaling, and so on.
MM_HIENGLISH	Maps each logical unit to 0.001 inch.
MM_HIMETRIC	Maps each logical unit to 0.01 millimeter.
MM_ISOTROPIC	Maps logical units to programmer-defined units with equal-scaled axes resulting in a 1:1 aspect ratio.
MM_LOMETRIC	Maps each logical unit to 0.1 millimeter.
MM_LOENGLISH	Maps each logical unit to 0.01 inch.
MM_TEXT	Maps each logical unit to one device pixel.
MM_TWIPS	Maps each logical unit to 1/20 of a printer's point, or approximately 1/1440 inch.

Table 6-3.   nMapMode Values and Resulting Modes

played using Windows coordinates and text metrics, setting the display mode, and so on. These topics will not be covered in this book. We will cover one key text aspect that can turn a simple-looking program into a professional-looking one—using font features. Windows 2000 provides multiple types of fonts and several built-in fonts within each type for your use. You can also create custom fonts. In the following sections, we will cover the different font types, how to choose a specific font, and creating custom fonts. A number of attributes are associated with fonts. Since many of the attributes are used in the rest of the chapter and examples, let us quickly review these terms in Table 6-4.

Attribute	Description
Character set	This identifies which of the different character sets (ANSI, UNICODE, OEM, Symbol, and so on) is used by the font. The examples in this chapter will use the standard Windows character set, which is based on the ANSI character set.
Typeface	This defines the shaping features, such as the line slopes, curves, and so on, that visually set one font apart from other fonts.
Style	This is the style of the font, such as bold, italics, or normal.
Weight	This is the thickness of the lines that make up the font. Windows NT supports several thickness levels.
Size	This is the size of a font measured in *points* (approximately 1/72 inch).
Font family	This is the family that a font belongs to. Windows NT supports the following font families: Decorative, Modern, Roman, Script, and Swiss.
Pitch	This is the width of each font character.
Proportional	The pitch of characters in the same font may vary; thus proportional fonts are also called *variable-pitch fonts*. For example, a "W" will not occupy the same width as an "I."
Nonproportional	This is the opposite of proportional. The pitch of all font characters is the same (also called *fixed-pitch* or *monospace*).
Serif	Serifs are the short lines found at the character endpoints (*sans serif* characters do not have a serif).

Table 6-4. Font Attributes

Raster, Vector, and TrueType Fonts

While the attributes listed in Table 6-4 deal with a font's appearance, it is left to the operating system to decide *how* to create and display or print a font. There are three types of fonts corresponding to three ways of creating and displaying a font. These are summarized in Table 6-5. Windows 2000 supports all three font types.

Font Type	Creation Method	Advantages/ Disadvantages	Typical Use
Raster font	This font type stores bitmaps for each font character, and displays or prints bitmaps.	No additional work is needed in displaying or printing. Scaling is a problem, since scaling bitmaps leads to loss of resolution.	This is used in displays and in printers supporting bitmaps.
Vector font	This font type stores the endpoints to the line segments that make up each glyph and draws the segments to display each character.	This type takes less space than raster fonts.	This is well suited to plotters.
TrueType font	This font type stores information about the lines and arcs that make up each glyph and drawing instructions for them.	This type scales well.	This is used in applications that need WYSIWYG (what you see is what you get).

Table 6-5.   Font Types and Characteristics

USING BUILT-IN FONTS

Windows 2000 includes six built-in or stock fonts as shown in Table 6-6.

As with all other Windows versions after Windows NT 3.0, Windows 2000 uses a variable-pitch system font. System fonts are an example of a *stock object*, which is an existing object that is ready for use in your GDI application. Other stock objects included with Windows 2000 are brushes, pens, and palettes.

NEW IN WINDOWS 2000:   Windows 2000 includes support for OpenType fonts. OpenType fonts are an extension of the TrueType font and are referred to as TrueType Open v.2.0 fonts, as they use the TrueType 'sfnt' font file format. Developed jointly by Microsoft and Adobe, OpenType fonts support PostScript font data and let the users install and use fonts, whether the fonts contain TrueType outlines or CFF (PostScript) outlines.

FONT PROGRAMMING EXAMPLE

Let's look at a sample program to illustrate the font-related concepts discussed so far. The program uses the **LOGFONT** structure. The **LOGFONT** structure defines the attributes of a font.

The **LOGFONT** structure has the following form:

```
typedef struct tagLOGFONT { /* lf */
    LONG Height;
    LONG Width;
    LONG Escapmnt;
    LONG Orient;
    LONG Weight;
    BYTE Italic;
    BYTE Underln;
    BYTE StrikeOut;
    BYTE CharSet;
    BYTE Outprecis;
    BYTE Clipprecis;
    BYTE Qual;
    BYTE PitchFam;
    CHAR TypeFaceName[LF_FACESIZE];
} LOGFONT;
```

Height is the height of the font in logical units. If *Height* is zero, a default size is used. If *Height* is nonzero, then Windows 2000 tries to locate a font that is as close in height as possible to the requested height without exceeding the requested height.

Font	Description
ANSI_FIXED_FONT	Monospace (fixed-pitch) font
ANSI_VAR_FONT	Proportional (variable-pitch) font
DEVICE_DEFAULT_FONT	Default device font, normally the system font
OEM_FIXED_FONT	OEM-defined font based on an OEM character set
SYSTEM_FONT	Proportional default font used by Windows NT for menus, dialog boxes, and so on
SYSTEM_FIXED_FONT	Font used by older versions of Windows (prior to Windows 3.0), included for compatibility purposes

Table 6-6.   Built-in Fonts in Windows 2000

Width is the width of the font in logical units. If *Width* is zero, then Windows picks a font that is closest to the requested width by comparing the digitization aspect ratio of available fonts to the aspect ratio of the device where the font will be used.

Using the *Escapmnt* parameter, you can output text at an any angle with reference to the X axis of the device where your text is displayed. Imagine a line that goes through the base of all the text characters you want to display. The *Escapmnt* parameter specifies the angle between this line and the X axis of the device. The angle is specified in tenths of a degree ("10" for 1 degree, "20" for 2 degrees, and so on) in a counterclockwise direction. For regular text display (where the text is horizontal), there is no angle and the *Escapmnt* parameter is 0. Specify 900 (90 degrees) for text going up, 2700 (270 degrees) for text going down, and so on.

Unlike *Escapmnt*, which specifies the angle for all the characters of the text you are displaying, *Orient* specifies the angle of individual text characters. *Orient* is also specified in tenths of a degree in a counterclockwise direction.

Weight specifies the font weight. You can either specify a number in the range 0 to 1000 or you can use predefined macros. Typical values are 400 for normal and 700 for bold. If you specify zero, it means that you want Windows 2000 to pick a default weight. The predefined macros you can use and their weight values are as follows:

Predefined Macro	Weight Value
FW_DONTCARE	0
FW_THIN	100
FW_EXTRALIGHT or FW_ULTRALIGHT	200

Predefined Macro	Weight Value
FW_LIGHT	300
FW_NORMAL or FW_REGULAR	400
FW_MEDIUM	500
FW_SEMIBOLD or FW_DEMIBOLD	600
FW_BOLD	700
FW_EXTRABOLD or FW_ULTRABOLD	800
FW_HEAVY or FW_BLACK	900

A nonzero value for *Italic* specifies an italic style. If you do not want the italic style, specify this parameter as zero.

A nonzero value for *Underln* creates an underlined font. If you do not want underlines, specify this parameter as zero.

A nonzero value for *StrikeOut* creates a strike-through font. If you do not want strike-through, specify this parameter as zero.

CharSet indicates the character set you want to use. Some commonly used values are predefined. ANSI_CHARSET is a common value. Other values that can be specified include DEFAULT_CHARSET, SYMBOL_CHARSET, OEM_CHARSET, and so on. If you specify DEFAULT_CHARSET, Windows 2000 picks a font based on the font's name (see discussion of *TypeFaceName,* later in this section) and size. If a font with the specified *TypeFaceName* does not exist, Windows 2000 will pick a font from any character set. You should be consistent between this parameter and the *TypeFaceName* parameter.

Outprecis is the desired output precision. Precision reflects how closely the selected font's characteristics should match the requested font characteristics such as height, width, and so on. The valid values for this parameter and their descriptions of how Windows 2000 maps the fonts are as follows:

Precision Value	Description
OUT_CHARACTER_PRECIS	Not used
OUT_DEFAULT_PRECIS	Uses the default way of mapping the closest font
OUT_DEVICE_PRECIS	Chooses a device font when there are multiple fonts with the same font name
OUT_OUTLINE_PRECIS	Chooses from TrueType (and other outline-based) fonts when there are multiple fonts with the same font name

Precision Value	Description
OUT_RASTER_PRECIS	Chooses a raster font when there are multiple fonts with the same font name
OUT_STRING_PRECIS	Value returned when raster fonts are enumerated
OUT_STROKE_PRECIS	Value returned when TrueType (and other outline-based) fonts or vector fonts are enumerated
OUT_TT_ONLY_PRECIS	Chooses a TrueType font (only) and uses the default mapping when no TrueType fonts are available
OUT_TT_PRECIS	Chooses a TrueType font when the system contains multiple fonts with the same name

Clipprecis specifies how each character that extends outside the clipping region is to be clipped (or truncated). The commonly used value for this parameter is CLIP_DEFAULT_PRECIS, which specifies the default clipping action. Other values for this parameter include CLIP_LH_ANGLES, which specifies whether the coordinate system orientation is left-handed or right-handed, and CLIP_EMBEDDED, which is specified when you're using embedded read-only fonts.

Qual determines how closely the logical font will match the actual physical fonts provided for the requested output device. The values you can specify and their descriptions are as follows:

Qual Value	Description
DEFAULT_QUALITY	This quality is a "don't care" (the font appearance is not significant).
DRAFT_QUALITY	This is draft quality level. Uses scaling for raster fonts where needed to match the required font characteristics. While this option permits more font choices, the quality of a scaled font may not be as good as a font that is not scaled, due to scaling distortions.
PROOF_QUALITY	This is the highest quality level. It does not use scaling and instead picks the font that matches the closest in size. This avoids scaling distortions.
ANTIALIASED_QUALITY	Font is antialiased if: • font supports it and • the size of the font is not too small or too large.
NONANTIALIASED_QUALITY	Font is not antialiased.

PitchFam specifies the OR values of the pitch and family of the font. For pitch, you can specify DEFAULT_PITCH (which uses the default of the family such as fixed pitch for MODERN), FIXED_PITCH, or VARIABLE_PITCH. If you specify a typeface (see following paragraph on *TypeFaceName*), then Windows 2000 attempts to use it if available. If the specific typeface is not available, the font family value will be used. The font family value is one of five families and a "don't care" as follows:

Font Family/Value	Description
FF_DECORATIVE	Fonts used for decorative purposes and old manuscripts, such as Old English
FF_MODERN	Fixed-pitch fonts, such as Courier
FF_ROMAN	Proportional fonts with serifs (short lines at the character endpoints), such as MS Serif
FF_SCRIPT	Fonts that mimic handwriting, such as Cursive
FF_SWISS	Proportional fonts without serifs, such as MS Sans Serif
FF_DONTCARE	Lets the system pick any font family

TypeFaceName is a pointer to the name of the typeface. When you specify a *TypeFaceName*, Windows 2000 will try to locate a font with the specified typeface name in the system where your application executes. You should be consistent between this parameter and the character set you specify. This name is limited to 32 characters. If you specify NULL for this parameter, Windows 2000 automatically selects the first font that matches the other font characteristics you specify.

Figure 6-1 shows the output from the *Font* sample program and illustrates a small font height and the bold style. Figure 6-2 shows output from the same program with a bigger font height and italic style.

The Font sample program shows how to enumerate all the fonts available in the system by use of **EnumFontFamiliesEx** and **EnumFontFamExProc**. It also shows how to manipulate dialog controls such as listbox, combobox, and editfield and how to set a font to a window by use of the **CFont** class and the **LOGFONT** structure. The sample is a dialog-based sample application that lists all available fonts in the system; when a font is selected, it displays the complete character set that is available for the selected font. It also displays sample text in the selected font in a multiline edit control. To display text in a font of your choice, select the font, the character set, and then the style. For example, Figure 6-3 shows the result of selecting the Monotype Corsiva font and normal style. The sample program also enables changing the font height and applying basic styles like normal, bold, or italic to the sample text in the selected font. The multiline edit control also accepts entered text, enabling you to try other text strings in the selected font, height, and style.

Like the earlier sample, this sample was created using AppWizard and ClassWizard in Visual C++. What follows is the header file that has the font dialog definition. Some

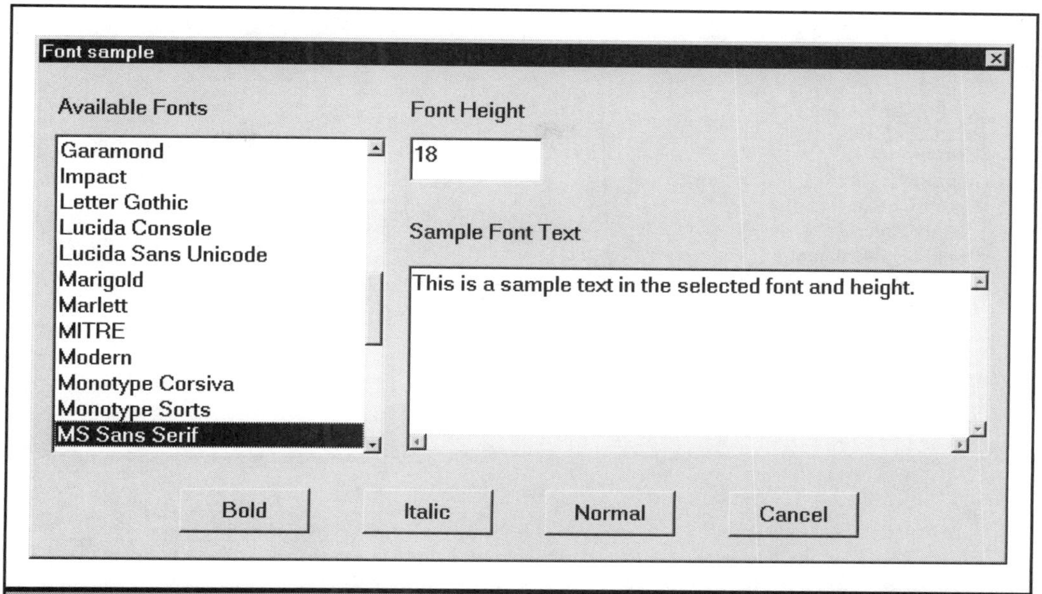

Figure 6-1.   Sample of small font and bold style

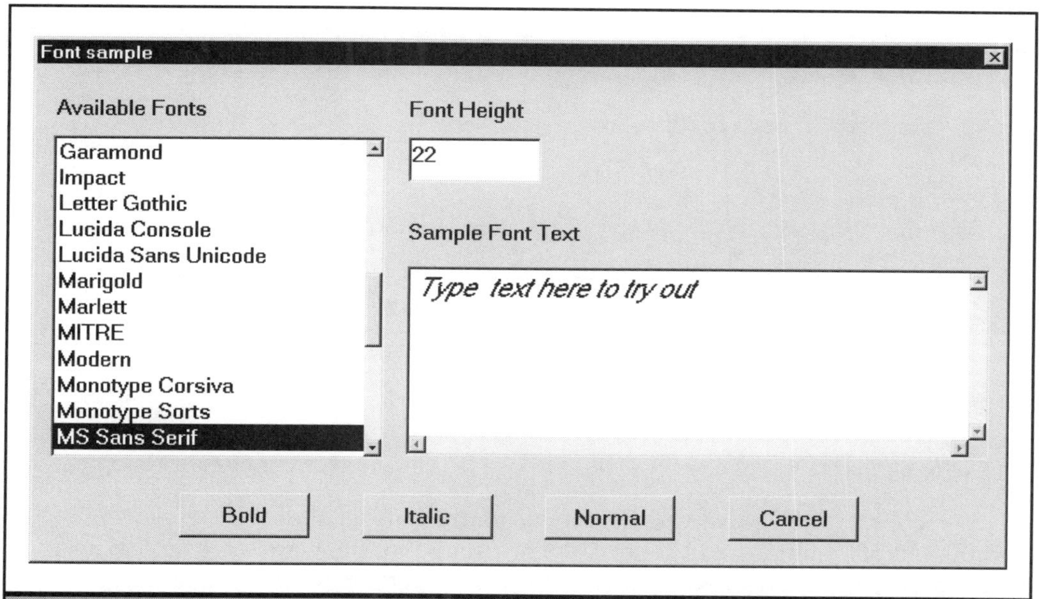

Figure 6-2.   Sample of large font and italic style

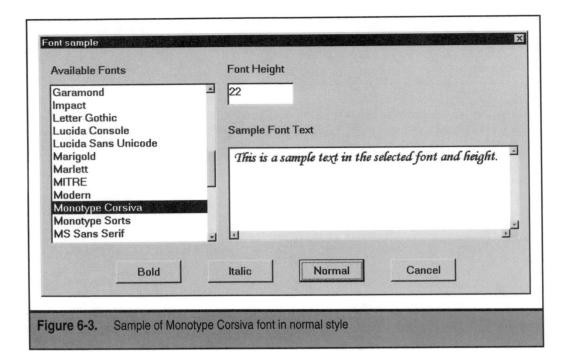

Figure 6-3.   Sample of Monotype Corsiva font in normal style

code of special interest is highlighted. The class defines some private member variables and functions to keep track of the selections and to update the font in the dialog box.

```
class CFontDlg : public CDialog
{
private:


        void CFontDlg::ChangeFont();
        int     iFontFeature;  // 0 = Normal, 1 = Bold, 2 = Italics
        CFont   *psaveFont;

// Construction
public:
    CFontDlg(CWnd* pParent = NULL);    // standard constructor
```

As the sample needs to access the control for the font list, the character set combo box, and the sample multiline edit control, the respective control classes are used as member variables. But it is not necessary to access the control for the font size, so an integer is used to retrieve the font size.

```
// Dialog Data
    //{{AFX_DATA(CFontDlg)
    enum { IDD = IDD_FONT_DIALOG };
    CListBox     m_FontList;
    CComboBox    m_CharSet;
    CEdit     m_SampleText;
    int          m_FontSize;
    //}}AFX_DATA

    // ClassWizard generated virtual function overrides
    //{{AFX_VIRTUAL(CFontDlg)
    protected:
    virtual void DoDataExchange(CDataExchange* pDX);      // DDX/DDV support
    //}}AFX_VIRTUAL

// Implementation
protected:
    HICON m_hIcon;

    // Generated message map functions
    //{{AFX_MSG(CFontDlg)
    virtual BOOL OnInitDialog();
    afx_msg void OnSysCommand(UINT nID, LPARAM lParam);
    afx_msg void OnPaint();
    afx_msg HCURSOR OnQueryDragIcon();
    afx_msg void OnBold();
    afx_msg void OnSelchangeFontlist();
    afx_msg void OnItalics();
    afx_msg void OnNormal();
    virtual void OnCancel();
    //}}AFX_MSG
    DECLARE_MESSAGE_MAP()
};
```

Shown next is the implementation of the font dialog sample. Some of the nonessential code is not shown; if you need it, you can find it on the CD-ROM.

```
// FontDlg.cpp : implementation file
//
#include "stdafx.h"
#include "Font.h"
#include "FontDlg.h"

#ifdef _DEBUG
```

```
#define new DEBUG_NEW
#undef THIS_FILE
static char THIS_FILE[] = __FILE__;
#endif
```

The **EnumFontFamiliesEx** callback functions are declared as follows:

```
int CALLBACK EnumFontsProcInsertFontName (LPENUMLOGFONTEX lpelfe,
NEWTEXTMETRICEX *lpntme, DWORD dwFontType, LONG lParam);
int CALLBACK EnumFontsProcInsertCharSet (LPENUMLOGFONTEX lpelfe,
NEWTEXTMETRICEX *lpntme, DWORD dwFontType, LONG lParam);
void ChangeFont();
/////////////////////////////////////////////////////////////////////
// CFontDlg dialog
CFontDlg::CFontDlg(CWnd* pParent /*=NULL*/)
    : CDialog(CFontDlg::IDD, pParent)
{
    //{{AFX_DATA_INIT(CFontDlg)
    m_FontSize = 0;
    //}}AFX_DATA_INIT
    // Note that LoadIcon does not require a subsequent DestroyIcon in Win32
    m_hIcon = AfxGetApp()->LoadIcon(IDR_MAINFRAME);
}

void CFontDlg::DoDataExchange(CDataExchange* pDX)
{
    CDialog::DoDataExchange(pDX);
    //{{AFX_DATA_MAP(CFontDlg)
    DDX_Control(pDX, IDC_FONTLIST, m_FontList);
    DDX_Control(pDX, IDC_CHARSET, m_CharSet);
    DDX_Control(pDX, IDC_SAMPLETEXT, m_SampleText);
    DDX_Text(pDX, IDC_FONTSIZE, m_FontSize);
    //}}AFX_DATA_MAP
}
```

The message map functions are declared next. Whenever the Bold, Italic, or Normal button is clicked, the application needs to be notified in order to update the sample text. The application requests notification when the font in the font list box is selected. When the font is selected, the application proceeds to find all the available character sets and populates the character set combo box:

```
BEGIN_MESSAGE_MAP(CFontDlg, CDialog)
    //{{AFX_MSG_MAP(CFontDlg)
    ON_WM_SYSCOMMAND()
    ON_WM_PAINT()
```

```
ON_WM_QUERYDRAGICON()
    ON_BN_CLICKED(IDC_BOLD, OnBold)
    ON_LBN_SELCHANGE(IDC_FONTLIST, OnSelchangeFontlist)
    ON_BN_CLICKED(IDC_ITALICS, OnItalics)
    ON_BN_CLICKED(IDC_NORMAL, OnNormal)
    //}}AFX_MSG_MAP
END_MESSAGE_MAP()

////////////////////////////////////////////////////////////////////
// CFontDlg message handlers

BOOL CFontDlg::OnInitDialog()
{
    CDialog::OnInitDialog();

    // Add "About..." menu item to system menu.

    // IDM_ABOUTBOX must be in the system command range.
    ASSERT((IDM_ABOUTBOX & 0xFFF0) == IDM_ABOUTBOX);
    ASSERT(IDM_ABOUTBOX < 0xF000);

    CMenu* pSysMenu = GetSystemMenu(FALSE);
    if (pSysMenu != NULL)
    {
        CString strAboutMenu;
        strAboutMenu.LoadString(IDS_ABOUTBOX);
        if (!strAboutMenu.IsEmpty())
        {
            pSysMenu->AppendMenu(MF_SEPARATOR);
            pSysMenu->AppendMenu(MF_STRING, IDM_ABOUTBOX, strAboutMenu);
        }
    }

    // Set the icon for this dialog.
    // The framework does this automatically
    //  when the application's main window is not a dialog
    SetIcon(m_hIcon, TRUE);              // Set big icon
    SetIcon(m_hIcon, FALSE);             // Set small icon
```

This code does the standard initialization for any dialog-based application. It updates the system menu to add an About… menu item and sets up the icon for the application. The application then initializes its variables and calls **EnumFontFamiliesEx** to enumerate the fonts. By controlling the font name and the character set in the **LOGFONT** structure, **EnumFontFamiliesEx** can be used to enumerate some or all of the fonts in the system.

Since this application needs to enumerate all possible fonts, it sets the font face name to null and requests the default character set. If instead a specific font is specified, then all character sets and styles in that font will be enumerated. If a specific character set is given, then all fonts in all styles for the given character set are enumerated.

Fonts are specific to a device context, hence a device context, window in this sample, is provided to the **EnumFontFamiliesEx** API. Applications that will use a printer to show the fonts available should use the printer device context. **EnumFontsProcInsertFontName** is the callback function; this function is called for every font that is available. If necessary, a parameter can be passed to the callback; this application uses this mechanism to pass the listbox member variable, which is used in the callback function to insert the available fonts into the list box.

```
CDC *hdc;
CFont     *defaultFont;
LOGFONT    lf;

CDialog::OnInitDialog();
psaveFont = NULL;
szInsertedFont[0] = '\0';

hdc = this->GetDC();

lf.lfFaceName[0] = '\0';
lf.lfCharSet = DEFAULT_CHARSET;
EnumFontFamiliesEx(hdc->GetSafeHdc(), &lf, (FONTENUMPROC)
EnumFontsProcInsertFontName, (LPARAM)&m_FontList, (DWORD)0);
    ReleaseDC(hdc);
```

The default font for the multiline edit field is queried, and that font is selected in the font list box. The application also sets the font height and triggers to update the character set combo box.

```
// Get the default font for the edit control
defaultFont = m_SampleText.GetFont();    // Get the pointer to the logfont
defaultFont->GetLogFont(&lf);    // Select the default font in the list box.
m_FontList.SelectString(0, lf.lfFaceName);
SetDlgItemInt(IDC_FONTSIZE, -lf.lfHeight, FALSE);
OnSelchangeFontlist();

m_SampleText.LimitText(256);
m_SampleText.SetWindowText((LPCTSTR)"This is a sample text in the selected
font and height.");

    return TRUE;  // return TRUE  unless you set the focus to a control
}

void CFontDlg::OnSysCommand(UINT nID, LPARAM lParam)
{
```

```
    if ((nID & 0xFFF0) == IDM_ABOUTBOX)
    {
        CAboutDlg dlgAbout;
        dlgAbout.DoModal();
    }
    else
    {
        CDialog::OnSysCommand(nID, lParam);
    }
}

// If you add a minimize button to your dialog, you will need the code below
//  to draw the icon.  For MFC applications using the document/view model,
//  this is automatically done for you by the framework.

void CFontDlg::OnPaint()
{
    if (IsIconic())
    {
        CPaintDC dc(this); // device context for painting

        SendMessage(WM_ICONERASEBKGND, (WPARAM) dc.GetSafeHdc(), 0);

        // Center icon in client rectangle
        int cxIcon = GetSystemMetrics(SM_CXICON);
        int cyIcon = GetSystemMetrics(SM_CYICON);
        CRect rect;
        GetClientRect(&rect);
        int x = (rect.Width() - cxIcon + 1) / 2;
        int y = (rect.Height() - cyIcon + 1) / 2;

        // Draw the icon
        dc.DrawIcon(x, y, m_hIcon);
    }
    else
    {
        CDialog::OnPaint();
    }
}

// The system calls this to obtain the cursor to display while the user drags
//  the minimized window.
HCURSOR CFontDlg::OnQueryDragIcon()
{
    return (HCURSOR) m_hIcon;
}


void CFontDlg::OnCancel()
```

```
{
    // TODO: Add extra cleanup here

    CDialog::OnCancel();
}
```

Shown next is the callback function that **EnumFontFamiliesEx** calls for every font that it finds in the system. The first parameter that this callback expects is a pointer to a **ENUMLOGFONTEX** structure (although in Windows 2000 this could also be a **ENUMLOGFONTEXDV** structure), which contains the information used to create the font. **ENUMLOGFONTEXDV** contains a **DESIGNVECTOR** structure in addition to the **ENUMLOGFONTEX** structure. If necessary, an application can use the **DESIGNVECTOR** structure to provide the axes of a multiple master OpenType font. The last parameter contains the listbox member variable passed when **EnumFont-FamiliesEx** was invoked. This is used to insert the font into the list box. Since all fonts are requested to be enumerated, this callback function is called for all styles and character sets for a given font. But the application wants to show only the fonts in the list box, so it filters the font names by remembering the previously inserted font. Another way to achieve this end is to check if the font name string already exists in the list box. This technique is used in the next callback function. By returning a nonzero value, the callback requests further enumeration of fonts if available:

```
char    szInsertedFont[LF_FACESIZE];   // Previously inserted font.
int CALLBACK EnumFontsProcInsertFontName (LPENUMLOGFONTEX lpelfe,
NEWTEXTMETRICEX *lpntme, DWORD dwFontType, LONG lParam)
{
        CListBox        *pLBox;
        LOGFONT         *lplf;

        lplf = &lpelfe->elfLogFont;
        pLBox = (CListBox *)lParam;
        if (strcmp(szInsertedFont, lplf->lfFaceName))
        {
            // Add this font to the list box.
            pLBox->AddString((LPCTSTR)lplf->lfFaceName);
            strcpy (szInsertedFont, lplf->lfFaceName);
        }
        return 1;

}
```

When a font is selected, the application needs to update the available character set for that font in the character set combo box. To do this, the application requests notification for any selection change in the font list box. When a selection is made, the **OnSelchangeFontList** member function that follows is called. This function gets the currently selected font and enumerates the available character set for that font. Notice that it sends the character set combo box member variable. This is retrieved in the callback function and used to insert the character set.

```
void CFontDlg::OnSelchangeFontlist()
{
    // TODO: Add your control notification handler code here
    // TODO: Add extra initialization here
    CDC       *hdc;
    LOGFONT lf;
    int       index;

    index = m_FontList.GetCurSel();
    m_FontList.GetText(index, lf.lfFaceName);
    m_CharSet.ResetContent();

    hdc = this->GetDC();

    lf.lfCharSet = DEFAULT_CHARSET;
    EnumFontFamiliesEx(hdc->GetSafeHdc(), &lf,
                       (FONTENUMPROC) EnumFontsProcInsertCharSet,
                       (LPARAM)&m_CharSet, (DWORD)0);
    ReleaseDC(hdc);
}
```

The callback function that processes the character set is shown next. This callback is similar to the callback function that was shown earlier. The character set is retrieved through the **LOGFONT** structure and used to insert the appropriate text in the character set combo box after making sure that it was not already inserted. Code to insert a few character sets is shown here. The code in the CD-ROM has the complete set of character sets:

```
int CALLBACK EnumFontsProcInsertCharSet (LPENUMLOGFONTEX lpelfe,
NEWTEXTMETRICEX *lpntme, DWORD dwFontType, LONG lParam)
{
        CComboBox        *pCBCharSet;
        LOGFONT           *lplf;
        short            sCharSet;
        int              index;
        pCBCharSet = (CComboBox *)lParam;


        lplf = &lpelfe->elfLogFont;
        sCharSet = (short) lplf->lfCharSet;
```

```
            switch(sCharSet)
            {
                case ANSI_CHARSET:
                    if (pCBCharSet->FindStringExact(-1, "ANSI" ) == CB_ERR)
                    {
                        index = pCBCharSet->AddString("ANSI");
                        if (index != LB_ERR)
                        {
                            pCBCharSet->SetItemData(index, ANSI_CHARSET);
                        }
                    }
                    break;
                case DEFAULT_CHARSET:
                    if (pCBCharSet->FindStringExact(-1, "Default" ) == CB_ERR)
                    {
                        index = pCBCharSet->AddString("Default");
                        if (index != LB_ERR)
                        {
                            pCBCharSet->SetItemData(index, DEFAULT_CHARSET);
                        }
                    }
                    break;
                case SYMBOL_CHARSET:
                    if (pCBCharSet->FindStringExact(-1, "Symbol" ) == CB_ERR)
                    {
                        index = pCBCharSet->AddString("Symbol");
                        if (index != LB_ERR)
                        {
                            pCBCharSet->SetItemData(index, SYMBOL_CHARSET);
                        }
                    }
                    break;
    ;
    ;
    ;      // See the complete code on the CD-ROM
    ;
    :

            }
            return 1;


    }
```

When the Bold, Normal, or Italics button is pressed, the application sets the appropriate font feature to the multiline edit control and redraws the sample text by calling the **ChangeFont** method:

```
void CFontDlg::OnBold()
{
    // TODO: Add your control notification handler code here
    iFontFeature = 1;
    ChangeFont ();

}


void CFontDlg::OnItalics()
{
    // TODO: Add your control notification handler code here
    iFontFeature = 2;
    ChangeFont ();

}

void CFontDlg::OnNormal()
{
    // TODO: Add your control notification handler code here
    iFontFeature = 3;
    ChangeFont ();

}


void CFontDlg::ChangeFont()
{
    char     newFace[LF_FACESIZE];
    int         index;
    int         iFontSize;
    CFont    *poldFont;
    CFont    *pnewFont;
    LOGFONT    lf;
```

The **CFont** class encapsulates a Windows GDI font and provides member functions for manipulating the font. The **LOGFONT** structure defines the attributes of a font.

A new **CFont** object is created, and the existing font attributes are collected. The new font and the new font height are substituted in the font attribute structure. The font style is changed in accordance with the user selection.

```
pnewFont = new CFont ();
memset (&lf, 0, sizeof(LOGFONT));
poldFont = m_SampleText.GetFont();
poldFont->GetLogFont(&lf);

index = m_FontList.GetCurSel();
m_FontList.GetText(index, newFace);

if ((index = m_CharSet.GetCurSel()) == CB_ERR)
{
    index = 0; // Assume the first Char Set
}

lf.lfCharSet = (BYTE) m_CharSet.GetItemData(index);

strcpy (lf.lfFaceName, newFace);
if (iFontFeature == 1)
{
lf.lfWeight = FW_BOLD;
lf.lfItalic = FALSE;
}
else if (iFontFeature == 2)
{
lf.lfWeight = FW_NORMAL;
lf.lfItalic = TRUE;
}
else
{
lf.lfWeight = FW_NORMAL;
lf.lfItalic = FALSE;
}
iFontSize = GetDlgItemInt(IDC_FONTSIZE, NULL, FALSE);
if (iFontSize <= 0)
    iFontSize = 10;
lf.lfHeight = -iFontSize;
pnewFont->CreateFontIndirect(&lf);
```

The new font is set to the multiline edit control. The **LOGFONT** structure has many more attributes that can be modified. The results can be viewed by making additional changes to other attributes.

Finally, the old font object is deleted, freeing up the resource.

```
m_SampleText.SetFont(pnewFont, TRUE);
if (psaveFont)
    delete psaveFont;
psaveFont = pnewFont;
}
```

The CD-ROM includes a sample application that uses **EnumFontFamilies**, which exhibits a slightly different behavior. Try this sample if you need more font programming examples.

Now let's take a look at some functions in Windows 2000 that let you manipulate the graphics you display. With these functions, you can rotate, translate, shear, reflect, and scale graphics. Windows calls these manipulations *world transforms.*

WORLD TRANSFORMS

To understand how to program world transforms, you should start by understanding coordinate spaces.

Coordinate Spaces

Windows 2000 defines four *coordinate spaces.* They are as follows:

▼ *World space* is used to perform world transformations.

■ *Page space* is logical coordinate space used by your program.

■ *Device space* allows translation to ensure that the origin of the device space maps to the proper location in physical device space.

▲ *Physical device space* is used to map to the physical device. This space uses physical coordinates.

The mapping of output (which is specified in logical units) to the physical units for the output device starts at page space unless you are using world transforms. If you are using world transforms, then the output mapping begins at world space. To use world transforms, you must do two things. First, you must enable Windows 2000's advanced graphics mode using the **SetGraphicsMode( )** function, whose prototype is shown here:

```
int SetGraphicsMode(HDC hdc,
                    int GraphMode);
```

Here, *hdc* is the handle to the device context, and *GraphMode* specifies the graphics mode to be set. It must be either GM_COMPATIBLE or GM_ADVANCED. The function returns the previous mode or zero on failure. To use **SetWorldTransform( )**, you must set the mode to GM_ADVANCED. The default is GM_COMPATIBLE.

Second, you specify world transforms using **SetWorldTransform( )** as shown in the next section.

TIP: Once you have set the mode to GM_ADVANCED and specified transformations using **SetWorldTransform( )**, you can return to the GM_COMPATIBLE mode only if you reset your transformations using **SetWorldTransform( )** or **ModifyWorldTransform( )**.

SetWorldTransform( )

SetWorldTransform( ) sets a two-dimensional linear transformation (such as rotation) between world space and page space for a given device context.

Its prototype is shown here:

```
BOOL SetWorldTransform(HDC hdc,
                       CONST XFORM *lpTrnsfrm);
```

Here, *hdc* is the handle to the device context, and *lpTrnsfrm* points to the **XFORM** structure (see next), which specifies the actual transformations. The function returns non-zero if successful and zero on failure.

Transformations are specified by use of an **XFORM** structure as follows:

```
typedef struct   tagXFORM
{
  FLOAT eM11;
  FLOAT eM12;
  FLOAT eM21;
  FLOAT eM22;
  FLOAT eDx;
  FLOAT eDy;
} XFORM;
```

The exact transformation that takes place is determined by the values you place in the matrix defined by **XFORM**. Let's see how each type of transformation can be achieved.

For any coordinate (x,y) in world space, the transformed coordinate in page space (x′,y′) is determined by the following algorithm:

```
x' = x * eM11 + y * eM21 + eDx,
y' = x * eM12 + y * eM22 + eDy,
```

where the transformation matrix is represented by the following:

```
| eM11 eM12  0 |
| eM21 eM22  0 |
| eDx  eDy   1 |
```

Transformations

Let's see how to perform each of the world transformations.

Translation   To translate output, specify the following:

Field	Value
eDx	X offset
eDy	Y offset

Rotation   To rotate output through an angle q, specify the following:

Field	Value
eM11	Cosine of q
eM12	Sine of q
eM21	Negative sine of q
eM22	Cosine of q

Scaling   To scale output, specify the following:

Field	Value
eM11	Horizontal scaling factor
eM12	Zero
eM21	Zero
eM22	Vertical scaling factor

Shearing   To shear output, specify the following:

Field	Value
eM11	Zero
eM12	Horizontal shear factor
eM21	Vertical shear factor
eM22	Zero

Reflection   To reflect output along the X axis, specify the following:

Field	Value
eM11	–1
eM12	Zero
eM21	Zero
eM22	1

To reflect output along the Y axis, specify the following:

Field	Value
eM11	1
eM12	Horizontal shear factor
eM21	Vertical shear factor
eM22	–1

To reflect output along both axes, specify the following:

Field	Value
eM11	–1
eM12	Horizontal shear factor
eM21	Vertical shear factor
eM22	–1

TIP: You can combine transformations. For example, you can combine rotation and translation. The screen shots in the next section show the results of combinations. You can achieve the same effect programmatically.

World Transformation Example

Figure 6-4 shows the window with three adjacent figures—an overlapping polygon, an ellipse, and a rectangle—when the sample program is executed. Figure 6-5 shows the effect of rotation, and Figure 6-6 shows the effect of translation. Figure 6-7 shows the effect of shearing, and Figure 6-8 shows the effect of combined shearing and rotation. Many more effects and combinations are possible. Try them on your own!

The *WrldXForm* sample program illustrates the world coordinate transformation. The sample displays an overlapping polygon (which appears like a five-pointed star), an

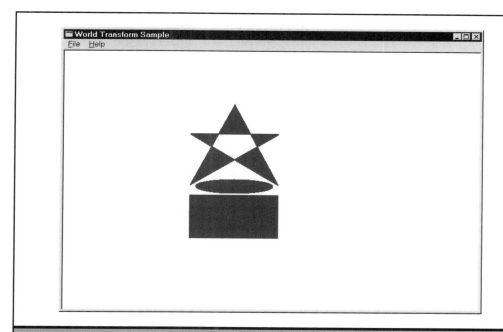

Figure 6-4.   World transformation example

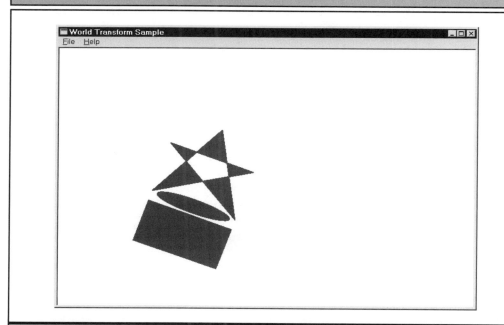

Figure 6-5.   World transformation example—rotation

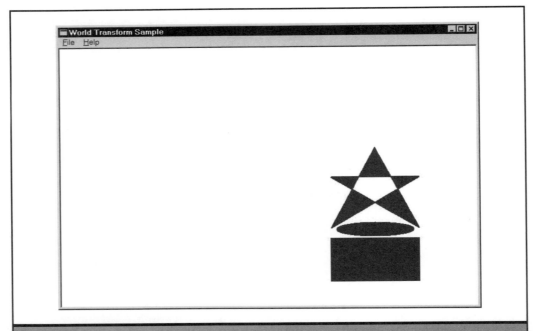

Figure 6-6.   World transformation example—translation

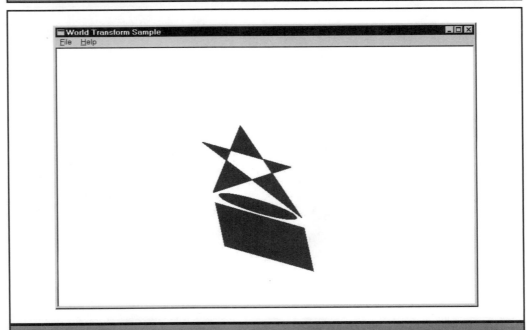

Figure 6-7.   World transformation example—shearing

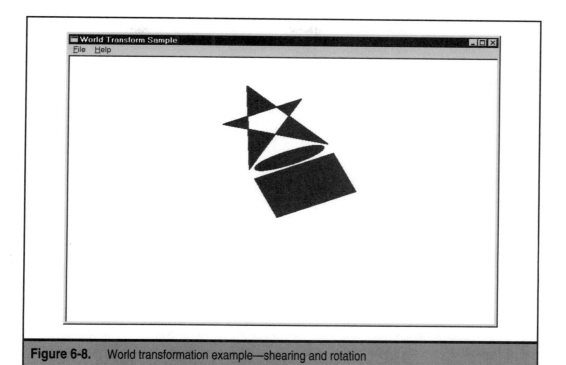

Figure 6-8.   World transformation example—shearing and rotation

ellipse, and a rectangle. Using menu selection and arrow keys, you can manipulate these graphic objects. The program shows the use of the **XFORM** structure and the **SetWorldTransform** API. The shell code for the second *Font* sample from the CD-ROM accompanying the book is taken as the basis for this sample. When the program is executed, it displays a window with these three graphic objects. From the File menu, you can select transformations such as Rotate, Translate, Shear, Reflect, and Scale. After being selected, the graphic objects can be manipulated with the arrow keys. Selecting Original from the File menu will initialize the graphic objects to their initial state. Some of the transformations can be combined. The objects could be translated to a different location and then their reflections taken. The code for this sample is shown later in this chapter.

The *Math.h* header file is included for the trigonometric functions. A set of transformations is defined with values ranging from 1 to 6. This is followed by the global variable **xForm**, which specifies a world space–to–page space transformation. Various functions in the program modify this structure, and the paint section of the code picks up the change and sets the world transform accordingly. Two variables maintain the state information of the current and previous transforms the user selected, and another variable keeps track of the incremental angle by which the graphic objects are rotated.

```
//****************************************************************
// This sample demonstrates the class/functions related to
// World Transform
//****************************************************************
// Wrldform.cpp

#include <afxwin.h>
#include <afxdlgs.h>
#include <math.h>
#include "Resource.h"

#define ORIGINAL    1
#define ROTATE      2
#define TRANSLATE   3
#define SHEAR       4
#define REFLECT     5
#define SCALE       6

XFORM   xForm;
int     iCurrentTransform;
int     iPreviousTransform;
short   sAngle;


// Define the application object class
class CApp : public CWinApp
{
public:
    virtual BOOL InitInstance ();
};
```

The **CWindow** class defines the application window and defines all the class member functions:

```
// Define the application's window class
class CWindow : public CFrameWnd
{
public:
    CWindow();
    afx_msg void OnPaint();
    afx_msg void OnKeyUp(UINT, UINT, UINT);
    afx_msg void OnAppAbout();
    afx_msg void OnOriginal();
    afx_msg void OnRotate();
    afx_msg void OnTranslate();
    afx_msg void OnShear();
    afx_msg void OnReflect();
    afx_msg void OnScale();
    afx_msg void OnExit();
```

```
        void UncheckMenu();
        void CheckMenu();
        DECLARE_MESSAGE_MAP()
};
```

The message map declares the action for various menu selections. It also declares a message map for the key-up message. Every time a key is pressed and released, this message is sent to the application. This message is used to manipulate the graphic objects.

```
/////////////////////////////////////////////////////////////////////////////
// CWindow

BEGIN_MESSAGE_MAP(CWindow, CFrameWnd)
    ON_WM_PAINT()
    ON_WM_KEYUP()
    ON_COMMAND(ID_APP_ABOUT, OnAppAbout)
    ON_COMMAND(IDM_ORIGINAL, OnOriginal)
    ON_COMMAND(IDM_ROTATE, OnRotate)
    ON_COMMAND(IDM_TRANSLATE, OnTranslate)
    ON_COMMAND(IDM_SHEAR, OnShear)
    ON_COMMAND(IDM_REFLECT, OnReflect)
    ON_COMMAND(IDM_SCALE, OnScale)
    ON_COMMAND(ID_APP_EXIT, OnExit)
END_MESSAGE_MAP()
```

During the construction of the **CWindow** object, the global variables are initialized to represent no transformation.

```
/////////////////////////////////////////////////////////////////////////////
// CWindow construction

CWindow::CWindow()
{
    LoadAccelTable(MAKEINTRESOURCE(IDR_MAINFRAME));
    Create( NULL, "World Transform Sample",
    WS_OVERLAPPEDWINDOW,
    rectDefault, NULL, MAKEINTRESOURCE(IDR_MAINFRAME) );
    xForm.eM11 = 1.0;
    xForm.eM12 = 0.0;
    xForm.eM21 = 0.0;
    xForm.eM22 = 1.0;
    xForm.eDx  = 0.0;
    xForm.eDy  = 0.0;
    iCurrentTransform = ORIGINAL;
    iPreviousTransform = ORIGINAL;
}


/////////////////////////////////////////////////////////////////////////////
// Create the application class object
```

```
CApp theApp;

//////////////////////////////////////////////////////////////////////
// Application initialization

BOOL CApp::InitInstance()
{

    m_pMainWnd = new CWindow();
    m_pMainWnd -> ShowWindow( m_nCmdShow );
    m_pMainWnd -> UpdateWindow();
    return TRUE;
}


//////////////////////////////////////////////////////////////////////
// CAboutDlg dialog triggered by About... menu item.

class CAboutDlg : public CDialog
{
public:
    CAboutDlg();

    enum { IDD = IDD_ABOUTBOX };
};

CAboutDlg::CAboutDlg() : CDialog(CAboutDlg::IDD)
{
}
// About... menu item command handler.
void CWindow::OnAppAbout()
{
    CAboutDlg aboutDlg;
    aboutDlg.DoModal();
}
```

OnPaint is called every time the window needs to be repainted. A **CPaintDC** object is created. This paint device context will perform the **BeginPaint( )** and **EndPaint( )** functions during construction and destruction, respectively. A red pen and a red brush are selected for drawing. The graphic mode is set to advanced graphics mode to allow world transformations. The mode must be GM_ADVANCED in order to perform world transformation. The **SetWorldTransform** function sets a two-dimensional linear transformation between world space and page space. We will be using this transformation for rotation, translation, shear, reflection, and scale by specifying appropriate values in the **XFORM** structure.

```
// Paint message handler
void CWindow::OnPaint()
{
```

```
CPaintDC dc(this);
// Change the pen and the brush
CPen pen(PS_SOLID, 2, RGB(255,0,0));
CBrush brush(RGB(255,0,0));
dc.SelectObject(&pen);
dc.SelectObject(&brush);

SetGraphicsMode(dc.GetSafeHdc(), GM_ADVANCED);
SetWorldTransform(dc.GetSafeHdc(), &xForm);
```

A *polygon* is a versatile function that can be used to construct various shapes such as a pentagon or star depending on how the points are connected. Here the polygon is used to construct a five-point star. The polygon fill mode is set to ALTERNATE, which, in fact, is the default mode. In the ALTERNATE mode, the system fills the area between odd-numbered and even-numbered polygon sides on each scan line. The other option is to set the mode to WINDING, where the system uses the direction in which the graphic object is drawn to determine whether to fill an area. The **Polygon( )** function draws the polygon according to the array of points passed to the function. The polygon is drawn by connecting all the points given. Notice that the order of selection of the points creates a five-point star. By changing the selection order of the points, you can change the shape of the polygon.

Following the five-point star, a rectangle and an ellipse are drawn. Also note that the objects are drawn with the same values every time. When the program is run, though the specified coordinate is the same, the graphic objects appear different depending on the transformation used.

```
CPoint a[5];
a[0] = CPoint(80,160);
a[1] = CPoint(160,10);
a[2] = CPoint(240,160);
a[3] = CPoint(80,40);
a[4] = CPoint(240,40);
dc.SetPolyFillMode(ALTERNATE);
dc.Polygon(a, 5);
dc.Rectangle(80,180,240,260);
dc.Ellipse(90,150,230,175);
}
```

As you know, every time a key is pressed and released, a key-up message is sent by the system. The **OnKeyUp** function is called every time this message is sent. This function ignores all keys except the arrow keys. Depending on the currently selected transform, the transform structure is updated and the window is forced to repaint.

For *rotation,* the LEFT ARROW and the RIGHT ARROW keys are ignored. When the UP ARROW or DOWN ARROW key is pressed, the graphic objects are rotated counter-clockwise or clockwise by 10 degrees. The check to see if the angle is between 0 and 360 degrees is just cosmetic and is not necessary trigonometrically. The eM11 and eM22 values in the transformation structure take the cosine of the angle of rotation. The eM12 value takes the sine of the angle, and eM21 takes the negative of the sine of the angle of rotation.

For *translation,* pressing the UP ARROW key decreases the y coordinate by 10, while pressing the DOWN ARROW key increases it by 10. The LEFT ARROW and RIGHT ARROW keys, respectively, decrease and increase the x coordinate by 10.

For *shear,* pressing the UP ARROW or DOWN ARROW key decreases or increases the proportionality constant along the y coordinate, and the LEFT ARROW or RIGHT ARROW key does the same along the x coordinate.

For *reflection,* pressing the UP ARROW or DOWN ARROW key reflects vertically, while the LEFT ARROW or RIGHT ARROW key reflects horizontally.

For *scale,* pressing the UP ARROW or RIGHT ARROW key increases the scale, while the DOWN ARROW or LEFT ARROW key decreases the scale. Scaling both x and y coordinates is done for visual effect, and they can both be independently scaled. Scaling is done at an increment of 0.1; when the scaling factor reaches 0, it is reset to 1.0.

```
void CWindow::OnKeyUp(UINT c, UINT repCount, UINT Flags)

{
    switch (c)
    {
        case VK_UP:
        {
            switch(iCurrentTransform)
            {
            case ROTATE:
                sAngle -= 10;
                if (sAngle < 0)
                    sAngle += 360;
                xForm.eM11 = (float) cos((sAngle*3.14159)/180.0);
                xForm.eM12 = (float) sin((sAngle*3.14159)/180.0);
                xForm.eM21 = (float) -sin((sAngle*3.14159)/180.0);
                xForm.eM22 = (float) cos((sAngle*3.14159)/180.0);

                break;
            case TRANSLATE:
                xForm.eDy -= (float)10.0;
                break;
            case SHEAR:
                xForm.eM21 -= (float)0.1;
                break;
            case REFLECT:
                xForm.eM22 = (float)-1.0;
                break;
            case SCALE:
                xForm.eM11 += (float)0.1;  // Remove this line for
                                           //disproportionate scaling
                xForm.eM22 += (float)0.1;
                break;
```

```
        }
Invalidate(TRUE);
}

break;
case VK_DOWN:
{
    switch(iCurrentTransform)
    {
    case ROTATE:
        sAngle += 10;
        if (sAngle > 360)
            sAngle -= 360;
        xForm.eM11 = (float) cos((sAngle*3.14159)/180.0);
        xForm.eM12 = (float) sin((sAngle*3.14159)/180.0);
        xForm.eM21 = (float) -sin((sAngle*3.14159)/180.0);
        xForm.eM22 = (float) cos((sAngle*3.14159)/180.0);

        break;
    case TRANSLATE:
        xForm.eDy += (float)10.0;
        break;
    case SHEAR:
        xForm.eM21 += (float)0.1;
        break;
    case REFLECT:
        xForm.eM22 = (float)1.0;     // Reset to original

        break;
    case SCALE:
        xForm.eM11 -= (float)0.1; // Remove this line for
                                  // disproportionate scaling
        xForm.eM22 -= (float)0.1;
        if(xForm.eM11 < 0.0)     // If scaling becomes negative reset
                                 // to original size
            xForm.eM11 = 1.0;
        if(xForm.eM22 < 0.0)
            xForm.eM22 = 1.0;
        break;
    }
Invalidate(TRUE);
}

break;
case VK_LEFT:
{
    switch(iCurrentTransform)
    {
    case ROTATE:
        break;
    case TRANSLATE:
```

```
                                xForm.eDx -= (float)10.0;
                                break;
                       case SHEAR:
                                xForm.eM12 += (float)0.1;
                                break;
                       case REFLECT:
                                xForm.eM11 = (float)-1.0;
                                break;
                       case SCALE:
                                xForm.eM22 -= (float)0.1; // Remove this line for
                                                          // disproportionate scaling
                                xForm.eM11 -= (float)0.1;
                                if(xForm.eM22 < 0.0)     // If scaling becomes negative reset
                                                          // to original size
                                       xForm.eM22 = 1.0;
                                if(xForm.eM11 < 0.0)
                                       xForm.eM11 = 1.0;

                                break;
                      }
                 Invalidate(TRUE);
                 }
                 break;
                 case VK_RIGHT:
                 {
                      switch(iCurrentTransform)
                      {
                      case ROTATE:
                           break;
                      case TRANSLATE:
                           xForm.eDx += (float)10.0;
                           break;
                      case SHEAR:
                           xForm.eM12 -= (float)0.1;
                           break;
                      case REFLECT:
                           xForm.eM11 = (float)1.0;     // Reset to original
                           break;
                      case SCALE:
                           xForm.eM22 += (float)0.1; // Remove this line for
                                                     //disproportionate
                                                     //scaling
                           xForm.eM11 += (float)0.1;
                           break;
                      }
                 Invalidate(TRUE);
                 }
                 break;
           }

      }
```

The following functions process the menu item commands. When the Original menu item is selected, the transform structure is reset and the global variables are set to their initial value. For all selections, the current and previous selections are stored in the global variable and the menu selections are visually indicated by unchecking and checking the menu items. This is done by calling the **UnCheckMenu( )** and **CheckMenu( )** functions.

```
// Handle the menu commands.
void CWindow::OnOriginal()
{
    sAngle = 0;
    xForm.eM11 = 1.0;
    xForm.eM12 = 0.0;
    xForm.eM21 = 0.0;
    xForm.eM22 = 1.0;
    xForm.eDx  = 0.0;
    xForm.eDy  = 0.0;
    iPreviousTransform = iCurrentTransform;
    iCurrentTransform = ORIGINAL;
    UncheckMenu();
    CheckMenu();
    Invalidate(TRUE);
}


void CWindow::OnRotate()
{
    iPreviousTransform = iCurrentTransform;
    iCurrentTransform = ROTATE;
    UncheckMenu();
    CheckMenu();
    Invalidate(TRUE);
}
void CWindow::OnTranslate()
{
    iPreviousTransform = iCurrentTransform;
    iCurrentTransform = TRANSLATE;
    UncheckMenu();
    CheckMenu();
    Invalidate(TRUE);
}
void CWindow::OnShear()
{
    iPreviousTransform = iCurrentTransform;
    iCurrentTransform = SHEAR;
    UncheckMenu();
    CheckMenu();
    Invalidate(TRUE);
}
```

```
void CWindow::OnReflect()
{
    iPreviousTransform = iCurrentTransform;
    iCurrentTransform = REFLECT;
    UncheckMenu();
    CheckMenu();
    Invalidate(TRUE);
}

void CWindow::OnScale()
{
    iPreviousTransform = iCurrentTransform;
    iCurrentTransform = SCALE;
    UncheckMenu();
    CheckMenu();
    Invalidate(TRUE);
}
```

UncheckMenu( ) removes the checkmark that appears against the menu item. It uses the previous transform state to determine which menu item needs to be unchecked. It then calls **CheckMenuItem( )** to remove the check. **CheckMenuItem( )** determines the menu item from the command. **CheckMenu( )** does the opposite—it checks the menu items.

```
void CWindow::UncheckMenu()
{
    CMenu    *Menu;

    Menu = GetMenu();
    switch(iPreviousTransform)
    {
        case ORIGINAL:
            Menu->CheckMenuItem(IDM_ORIGINAL, MF_BYCOMMAND | MF_UNCHECKED);
            break;
        case ROTATE:
            Menu->CheckMenuItem(IDM_ROTATE, MF_BYCOMMAND | MF_UNCHECKED);
            break;
        case TRANSLATE:
            Menu->CheckMenuItem(IDM_TRANSLATE, MF_BYCOMMAND | MF_UNCHECKED);
            break;
        case SHEAR:
            Menu->CheckMenuItem(IDM_SHEAR, MF_BYCOMMAND | MF_UNCHECKED);
            break;
        case REFLECT:
            Menu->CheckMenuItem(IDM_REFLECT, MF_BYCOMMAND | MF_UNCHECKED);
            break;
        case SCALE:
```

```
            Menu->CheckMenuItem(IDM_SCALE, MF_BYCOMMAND | MF_UNCHECKED);
            break;
    }
}

void CWindow::CheckMenu()
{
    CMenu    *Menu;

    Menu = GetMenu();
    switch(iCurrentTransform)
    {
        case ORIGINAL:
            Menu->CheckMenuItem(IDM_ORIGINAL, MF_BYCOMMAND | MF_CHECKED);
            break;
        case ROTATE:
            Menu->CheckMenuItem(IDM_ROTATE, MF_BYCOMMAND | MF_CHECKED);
            break;
        case TRANSLATE:
            Menu->CheckMenuItem(IDM_TRANSLATE, MF_BYCOMMAND | MF_CHECKED);
            break;
        case SHEAR:
            Menu->CheckMenuItem(IDM_SHEAR, MF_BYCOMMAND | MF_CHECKED);
            break;
        case REFLECT:
            Menu->CheckMenuItem(IDM_REFLECT, MF_BYCOMMAND | MF_CHECKED);
            break;
        case SCALE:
            Menu->CheckMenuItem(IDM_SCALE, MF_BYCOMMAND | MF_CHECKED);
            break;
    }

}

// On Exit handles the void
void CWindow::OnExit()
{
    DestroyWindow();
}
```

CONCLUSION

In this chapter, you looked at graphics programming in Windows 2000 using the GDI. Besides creating simple graphical objects such as circles, rectangles, and arcs, you can also use GDI for more complicated shapes such as irregular polygons, as illustrated in the example. You learned how to perform functions such as rotation on the graphical objects. You also looked at another area that you are likely to use—fonts. The programming sample uses one of the most important programming tools to add to your utility collection—a utility to figure out the available fonts in a computer. Tooltips will be covered in the next chapter (Chapter 7), but you got a preview of how you can use tooltips to add pizzazz to your user interface. You can have tooltips with static text as well as dynamically changing text as illustrated in the example.

CHAPTER 7

Common Controls

C hapter 2 covered some of the basics of programming for the Windows user interface. We looked at the menu, the dialog box, the message box, the scroll bar, and so on. In this chapter we will take a look at some *common* controls, such as the Animation control and HotKey control. Use of the common controls gives you the same benefits as using the standard (or basic) controls—it gives your program's user interface a consistent look, and you get a lot of built-in code that makes your programming task easier. Common controls also add pizzazz to your user interface. They give your user interface a professional look.

COMMON CONTROLS

Although common controls have been around since Windows NT 3.51, these controls have become really popular since Windows NT 4.0 got the Windows 95 user interface and it became clear that the common user interface would be carried forward in future versions such as Windows 98 and Windows 2000. Now you can develop an application using common controls that will work with all these operating systems. Maybe the commonality between Windows 95 and Windows NT led to the term "common" in "common controls," but the common controls are anything but common or ordinary. Programs developed using common controls will work only with Windows 95 or Windows NT/2000 (and not with prior versions such as 3.1). Windows 2000 provides a number of common controls. These controls, their function descriptions, and the associated classes are summarized in Table 7-1.

Control	Function Description	MFC Class/Usage Information
Animation control	Displays an audio video interleaved (AVI) file, without the sound	CAnimateCtrl
Drag list box	Allows dragging of items in a list box	*See List View control*
Header control	Displays column headings	CHeaderCtrl
HotKey control	Supports user-created hot keys	CHotKeyCtrl
Image list	Displays a list of graphical images	CImageList
List View control	Displays a list of icons and labels	CListCtrl

Table 7-1. Windows 2000 Common Controls, Function Descriptions, and Associated Classes

Control	Function Description	MFC Class/Usage Information
Progress control (also called *progress bar*)	Displays a visual indicator used to indicate the progress of a task	CProgressCtrl
Property Sheet	Displays a properties dialog box	CPropertySheet, CPropertyPage
Slider control (also called *trackbar*)	Displays a slider-based control	CSliderCtrl
Spin control	Displays a combination Edit box and Up-Down control	CSpinButtonCtrl. Newer versions of common controls call the combination an Up-Down control. *See the later entry "Up-Down control"*
Status window	Displays a horizontal bar that displays an application's status information	CStatusBarCtrl
Tab control	Displays a menu with tabs that can be selected	CTabCtrl
Toolbar control	Displays a menu of buttons that the user can select by clicking	CToolBarCtrl
Tooltip	Displays small pop-up windows that have text describing toolbar buttons	CToolTipCtrl
Tree View control	Displays a list of items in the form of a tree hierarchy	CTreeCtrl
Up-Down control	Displays up and down arrows (like a scroll bar without the middle portion—just the end arrows)	Most commonly used with a "buddy" control such as an edit box. *See the previous entry "Spin control"*
ComboBoxEx	Extension of the basic combo box control that includes support for item images	CComboBoxEx

Table 7-1. Windows 2000 Common Controls, Function Descriptions, and Associated Classes *(continued)*

Control	Function Description	MFC Class/Usage Information
Date and Time Picker (DTP) control	Simple interface to exchange date and time information with the user	CDateTimeCtrl
Flat Scroll Bar	Similar to a standard scroll bar except that its appearance can be customized to a greater extent	Call InitializeFlatSB. Use FlatSB_XXX functions instead of the standard scroll bar manipulation functions
IP Address control	Lets the user enter a numeric address in Internet Protocol (IP) format	To create an IP address control, call CreateWindowEx API using the class WC_IPADDRESS
Month Calendar	Lets the user select a date using a familiar calendar interface	CMonthCalCtrl
Pager	Allows the user to scroll to the window area that is not currently in view due to lack of display area	To create a Pager control, call CreateWindowEx API using the class WC_PAGESCROLLER
Rebar	Provides containers for child windows called *bands*. Each band can have any combination of a gripper bar, a bitmap, a text label, and a child window	To create a Pager control, call CreateWindowEx API using the class REBARCLASSNAME

Table 7-1. Windows 2000 Common Controls, Function Descriptions, and Associated Classes *(continued)*

It is beyond the scope of this book to discuss all the common controls. We will cover some of the important ones—Animation, HotKey, Spin, Progress, and Slider controls—in detail with programming examples. We will briefly cover the characteristics of some of the other common controls. The techniques you gather from the controls discussed here should enable you to program all the common controls.

Common controls are child windows, so the programming considerations of using child windows apply to common controls. Common controls are implemented as a controls library and are supplied with Windows 2000 as a DLL that you invoke. The DLL has the definitions of window classes and the window procedures that handle the window classes. The window procedures handle the control's details, such as the properties, appearance, and behavior of the control. You can vary the appearance and behavior of a control by the use of control styles included in the DLL.

PROGRAMMING COMMON CONTROLS USING APIs

You need to follow the steps listed here to include common controls in your program:

1. Include the standard header file *Commctrl.h* in your program.

2. Link the common controls library to your program. For Microsoft Visual C++, the common controls library is called *Comctl32.lib*. For other vendor compilers, check the vendor documentation. You may need to link this library manually once if it is not automatically linked.

3. Call **InitCommonControlsEx** to load the common controls library DLL.

4. Create a common control by passing the name of the control's window class as a parameter to the **CreateWindow** or **CreateWindowEx** function. Windows 2000: **CreateWindowEx** supports some additional parameters for Windows 2000 to support message-only windows and layered windows. Chapter 2 addressed some of the new functions. You can also specify the control's window class name in a dialog box template or call a control-specific API. The advantage of using **CreateWindowEx** is that it permits the use of extended style attributes. Examples of the extended style attributes include WS_EX_ACCEPTFILES, which specifies that a window created with this style accepts drag-drop files.

NOTE: New in Windows 2000: As mentioned in Chapter 2, Windows 2000 supports layered windows. This support is reflected in **CreateWindowEx** by some additional extended style attributes. These attributes include WS_EX_LAYERED to create a layered window.

While extended style attributes are supported using **CreateWindowEx**, there are built-in styles that can be used with many common controls. These styles are listed in Table 7-2. Keep in mind that not all of these styles apply to all the controls—some of these are default values for the controls, and use of some styles may override the use of other styles. (All styles listed here apply to header controls, toolbar controls, and status windows.)

5. Process messages from the controls such as **WM_COMMAND** or **WM_NOTIFY**.

6. Send messages to the controls using **SendMessage**.

Control Style	Description
CCS_ADJUSTABLE	This enables a toolbar's built-in customization features. The features include dragging buttons to move them to a new position or removing them from the toolbar. The features also include displaying the Customize Toolbar dialog box when the toolbar is double-clicked.
CCS_BOTTOM	This positions the control at the bottom of the client area of the parent window. The control's width is set to be the same as the parent window's width. Status windows have this style by default.
CCS_NODIVIDER	This prevents the drawing of a divider (two-pixel highlight) at the top of the control.
CCS_NOMOVEY	This prevents vertical movement of the control (the control can still be moved horizontally). The control is moved by a WM_SIZE message. Control movements are possible with this style only if CCS_NORESIZE is not used. Header windows include this style by default.
CCS_NOPARENTALIGN	This causes the control to be in its position even if the parent window is resized. If CCS_TOP or CCS_BOTTOM is also used, the height is adjusted to the default, but the position and width are unchanged.
CCS_NORESIZE	This causes the control to use the width and height specified in the control creation or sizing request, and to override the default width and height settings.
CCS_TOP	This positions the control at the top of the client area of the parent window. The control's width is set to be the same as the parent window's width. Toolbars include this style by default.

Table 7-2.   Control Styles and Their Descriptions

The following are new to Version 4.70 of common controls and are supported in Windows 2000

Control Style	Description
CCS_LEFT	This causes the control to be displayed (vertically) on the left side of the parent window.
CCS_NOMOVEX	This prevents horizontal movement of the control (the control can still be moved horizontally). The control is moved by a WM_SIZE message. Control movements are possible with this style only if CCS_NORESIZE is not used.
CCS_RIGHT	This causes the control to be displayed (vertically) on the right side of the parent window.
CCS_VERT	Causes the control to be displayed vertically.

Table 7-2.   Control Styles and Their Descriptions *(continued)*

The common control examples in this chapter use the MFC library. For common controls programming examples using APIs, see *Windows 2000 Programming from the Ground Up*, by Herbert Schildt (Osborne/McGraw-Hill, 2000).

PROGRAMMING COMMON CONTROLS USING THE MFC LIBRARY

You can include common controls in your MFC program by following these steps:

1. Create the control. You can do this by using the dialog editor or (in some cases) by hand.
2. Add a variable representing the control to the dialog class. Declare additional variables for handling I/O with the control as needed.
3. Initialize the control by use of **OnInitDialog** or dialog data exchange (DDX).
4. Send and receive messages from the control.
5. Perform cleanup activities such as destroying unnecessary objects and disposing of unwanted memory allocations (if needed).

This is the general sequence of steps. Let's look at some of the controls in detail. Keep in mind that the controls are not mutually exclusive, and you typically will use a combination of these controls to implement your user interface.

> **TIP:** Microsoft has been making ongoing enhancements to common controls. The enhancements are good for you as a programmer, as you have better control to use. On the down side, the enhancements typically cause the need to extend many of the structures. As a result, the sizes of the structures change between different versions of *Commctrl.h*. Since most of the common control structures take a structure size as one of the parameters, this can result in a message or function failure caused by size changes. To fix this, Microsoft added structure size constants to make it easy to target different versions of *Comctl32.dll*.

The programming example that we will cover later in the chapter combines a Spin control, a Slider, and a progress bar in a dialog box, as shown in Figure 7-1.

At times you will also find that the functions of the controls complement each other, and you can combine the working of the controls to make the user interface more intuitive. For example, the Edit box is typically combined with an *Up-Down control*. This is also called a *Spin control* and is covered later in the section on the Spin control. You can also combine a slider with an Up-Down control, and this is covered in the section on the Slider control.

ANIMATION CONTROL

An *Animation control* is a rectangular window that displays a video clip in audio video interleaved (AVI) format, which is the standard Windows video/audio format. An AVI clip is a series of bitmap frames. The Animation control displays the series of bitmap frames, adjusting the timing and position on the display. This creates an animation effect.

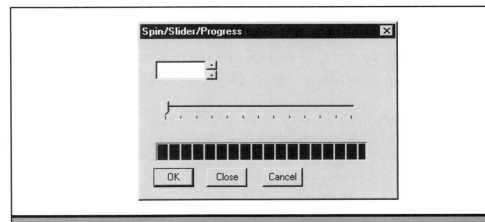

Figure 7-1.   Spin, Slider, and Progress controls in a dialog box

Use the Animation control when you are performing a lengthy operation and you want the user to see something other than an hourglass icon. You can also use the progress bar for this purpose. Examples of using the Animation control in Windows include when you copy a big file using the Explorer or when you do a search in Visual C++ and you see a rotating magnifying glass.

The Animation control does not support all the capabilities of the AVI format. Some of the capabilities of AVI that are not supported by the Animation control include the following:

▼ The Animation control does not support the audio stream in AVI.

■ There must be only one video stream with at least one frame.

■ There can be at most two streams in the file (normally a video stream and an audio stream, although the audio is not used).

■ The clip must be either uncompressed or compressed with RLE8 compression.

▲ The video stream cannot have palette changes.

The typical sequence of an instance of Animation control execution is as follows: First you create the Animation control using a dialog box template or the **Create** member function. Load the AVI clip by using the **Open** member function or **OnInitDialog**. Play the AVI clip using the **Play** member function. Alternatively, you can use the **OnInitDialog** for this purpose, or use the ACS_AUTOPLAY style for automatic playing of the animation. You can then use the **Close** member function, if required. Besides the ACS_AUTOPLAY style, the other styles you can use are ACS_CENTER, to center the control within the window, and ACS_TRANSPARENT, to use a transparent background instead of the background that is present in the AVI clip. The styles you can use with the Animation control are summarized in Table 7-3.

You can play all the frames in the AVI clip, or you can specify the number of frames you want the Animation control to play. You can also specify if you want to replay the animation and the number of times you want to replay it. One useful variation is to set the number of times to replay as –1, which replays the AVI clip forever. This feature is useful if you want an unattended demo of the Animation control—in a conference or before a presentation.

The AVI clip you want to animate can be included as a dialog resource by use of the dialog editor. If you are importing the AVI clip from another source, you can leave the AVI clip in its own file. You can create AVI files using the Aviedit sample application included with the Win32 SDK. The Aviedit application is rather rudimentary. If you have to program a lot with animations, then try a third-party tool such as Digital Video Producer to create AVI files.

Execution of the Animation control is asynchronous. When you can call the Animation control, Windows 2000 creates a separate thread, and your calling thread can perform other functions while the Animation control thread displays the animation.

When using **CAnimateCtrl**, you may have to ensure that you don't have memory leaks. A **CAnimateCtrl** object you create within a dialog box or from a dialog resource is

Style	Description
ACS_AUTOPLAY	This automatically starts playing as soon as the animation clip is opened.
ACS_CENTER	This centers the animation in the Animation control's window.
ACS_TIMER	This plays the clip without creating a thread (the default is to create a separate thread to play the AVI clip). To synchronize playback internally, the control uses a Win32 timer.
ACS_TRANSPARENT	This uses a transparent background rather than the background color in the animation clip.

Table 7-3. Animation Control Styles and Descriptions

automatically destroyed when the dialog box is closed. It is also automatically destroyed if you create the **CAnimateCtrl** object on the stack. If you create the **CAnimateCtrl** object on the heap by using the new function or if you derive a new class from **CAnimateCtrl** and allocate any memory in that class, then you have to manually destroy the **CAnimateCtrl** object and/or dispose of the memory allocations.

Animation Control Programming Example

The *Animate* sample program shows how to use the Animation control by use of the **CAnimateCtrl** MFC library class. The sample when run displays a window with a menu. Figures 7-2 through 7-4 show the AVI clip as it is being displayed. If Animate is selected from the File menu, a dialog panel with the Animation control is displayed. The AVI clip file is loaded and can be played by selecting the Play button. Selecting the Autoplay check box will make the AVI clip play automatically and continuously. This play can be stopped by clicking the Stop button. Choosing the Transparent check box will make the Animation control transparent. Clicking the Cancel button will close the dialog panel. The AVI file used in Figures 7-2 through 7-4 is the *dillo.avi* included with version 5 of Visual C++. You can use other AVI files as well.

This sample, like most of the others in this chapter, extends the second *Font* sample program available in the CD-ROM in Chapter 6. The main application code is simple and functionally minimal. It creates the main application by deriving from the CWinApp

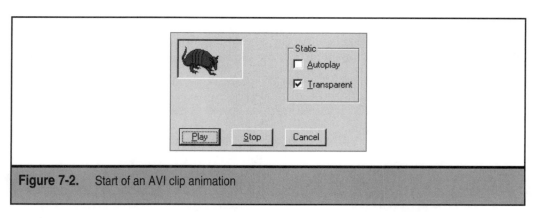

Figure 7-2. Start of an AVI clip animation

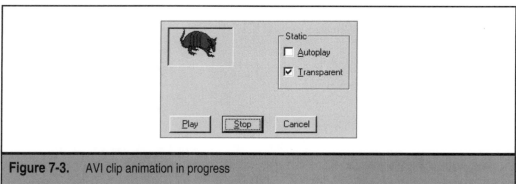

Figure 7-3. AVI clip animation in progress

Figure 7-4. AVI clip about to reverse direction

class that runs it. While the code on the CD-ROM also has the font enumeration, this section will only discuss the dialog that displays the animation control, which is triggered by selecting a menu item from the menu. For the sample a simple animation file is used.

```
#include <afxwin.h>
#include <afxdlgs.h>
#include <afxcmn.h>            // Header file for Common controls
#include <strstrea.h>
#include "FontDlg.h"
#include "AnimateDlg.h"
#include "resource.h"

// Define the application object class
class CApp : public CWinApp
{
public:
        virtual BOOL InitInstance ();
};

// Define the window class
class CWindow : public CFrameWnd
{
public:
    CWindow();
    afx_msg void OnAppAbout();
    afx_msg void OnFontDlg();
    afx_msg void OnAnimateDlg();
    afx_msg void OnExit();
    DECLARE_MESSAGE_MAP()
};

////////////////////////////////////////////////////////////////////////
// CWindow

BEGIN_MESSAGE_MAP(CWindow, CFrameWnd)
        ON_COMMAND(ID_APP_ABOUT, OnAppAbout)
        ON_COMMAND(ID_FONTDLG, OnFontDlg)
        ON_COMMAND(ID_ANIMATEDLG, OnAnimateDlg)
        ON_COMMAND(ID_APP_EXIT, OnExit)
END_MESSAGE_MAP()

////////////////////////////////////////////////////////////////////////
// CWindow construction

CWindow::CWindow()
{
     Create( NULL, "Control Sample",
     WS_OVERLAPPEDWINDOW,
     rectDefault, NULL, MAKEINTRESOURCE(IDR_MAINFRAME) );
}
```

```
///////////////////////////////////////////////////////////////////////
// The one and only CApp object

CApp theApp;

///////////////////////////////////////////////////////////////////////
// CApp initialization

BOOL CApp::InitInstance()
{
        m_pMainWnd = new CWindow();
        m_pMainWnd -> ShowWindow( m_nCmdShow );
        m_pMainWnd -> UpdateWindow();
        return TRUE;
}

///////////////////////////////////////////////////////////////////////
// CAboutDlg dialog used for App About

class CAboutDlg : public CDialog
{
public:
        CAboutDlg();
        enum { IDD = IDD_ABOUTBOX };
        protected:

};

CAboutDlg::CAboutDlg() : CDialog(CAboutDlg::IDD)
{
}

// App command to run the dialog
void CWindow::OnAppAbout()
{
        CAboutDlg aboutDlg;
        aboutDlg.DoModal();
}

///////////////////////////////////////////////////////////////////////
// CWindow commands
// App command to run the dialog

// Font Dialog selected
void CWindow::OnFontDlg()
{
        CFontDlg fontDlg(this);
        fontDlg.DoModal();
}
```

```
// Animate Dialog selected
void CWindow::OnAnimateDlg()
{
        CAnimateDlg animateDlg(this);
        animateDlg.DoModal();
}

// On Exit handles the void
void CWindow::OnExit()
{
        DestroyWindow();
}
```

Before we look into the source code that deals with the Animation control dialog box, consider the dialog resource:

```
IDD_ANIMATEDLG DIALOG DISCARDABLE  0, 0, 166, 95
STYLE DS_MODALFRAME | WS_POPUP | WS_CAPTION | WS_SYSMENU
CAPTION "Animate Control"
FONT 8, "MS Sans Serif"
BEGIN
    CONTROL         "Animate1",IDC_ANIMATE1,"SysAnimate32",WS_BORDER |
                    WS_TABSTOP,5,5,87,54
    CONTROL         "&Autoplay",IDC_AUTOPLAY,"Button",BS_AUTOCHECKBOX |
                    WS_TABSTOP,104,20,43,10
    CONTROL         "&Transparent",IDC_TRANSPARENT,"Button",BS_AUTOCHECKBOX |
                    WS_TABSTOP,104,36,54,10
    GROUPBOX        "Static",IDC_STATIC,99,8,61,48
    DEFPUSHBUTTON   "&Play",IDC_PLAY,7,77,35,14
    PUSHBUTTON      "Cancel",IDCANCEL,97,77,35,14
    PUSHBUTTON      "&Stop",IDC_STOP,52,77,35,14
END
```

The dialog box basically has an Animation control that in this case uses all the default styles for the Animation control. It has two check boxes, which are used to manipulate the style of the Animation control dynamically. It also has push buttons, one of which stops the animation. The resource file in addition has resource entries for menu items, icons, and so on.

Let's look at the dialog panel class code that handles the Animation control dialog box. As with many other sample programs, the template code was generated by use of the ClassWizard of Visual C++. There are advantages in doing this—not the least of which is that code generation through this method does not require you to memorize or refer to the manual for function prototypes.

```
// AnimateDlg.h : header file

/////////////////////////////////////////////////////////////////////
// CAnimateDlg dialog

class CAnimateDlg : public CDialog
{
private:
        CAnimateCtrl animateCtrl;
// Construction
public:
        CAnimateDlg(CWnd* pParent = NULL)
                : CDialog(IDD_ANIMATEDLG, pParent)
                                {}
// Implementation
protected:
        // Generated message map functions
        //{{AFX_MSG(CAnimateDlg)
        afx_msg void OnStop();
        afx_msg void OnPlay();
        afx_msg void OnAutoPlay();
        afx_msg void OnTransparent();
        virtual BOOL OnInitDialog();
        virtual void DoDataExchange(CDataExchange* pDX);        // DDX/DDV
        //}}AFX_MSG
        DECLARE_MESSAGE_MAP()
};
```

The **CAnimateDlg** class constructor constructs the Animate dialog box. A set of message map functions is also declared. The code for the class is discussed next.

```
// AnimateDlg.cpp : implementation file
//
#include <afxwin.h>
#include <afxdlgs.h>
#include <afxcmn.h>
#include "resource.h"
#include "AnimateDlg.h"
```

Note the inclusion of the common control header file *Afxcmn.h* and the **CAnimateDlg** class header file *AnimateDlg.h*.

```
BEGIN_MESSAGE_MAP(CAnimateDlg, CDialog)
        //{{AFX_MSG_MAP(CAnimateDlg)
        ON_BN_CLICKED(IDC_STOP, OnStop)
        ON_BN_CLICKED(IDC_PLAY, OnPlay)
        ON_BN_CLICKED(IDC_AUTOPLAY, OnAutoPlay)
        ON_BN_CLICKED(IDC_TRANSPARENT, OnTransparent)
        //}}AFX_MSG_MAP
END_MESSAGE_MAP()
```

The message map indicates that when the Stop button is clicked, the **OnStop** function is called; when the Play button is clicked, the **OnPlay** function is called; when the Autoplay check box is checked, the **OnAutoPlay** function is called; and when the Transparent check box is selected, the **OnTransparent** function is called.

```
///////////////////////////////////////////////////////////////////////
// CAnimateDlg message handlers

void CAnimateDlg::DoDataExchange(CDataExchange* pDX)
{
        CDialog::DoDataExchange(pDX);
        DDX_Control(pDX, IDC_ANIMATE1, animateCtrl);
}
```

The standard data exchange function called for the **CAnimateCtrl** class member **animateCtrl**.

```
BOOL CAnimateDlg::OnInitDialog()
{
        // TODO: Add extra initialization here
        CDialog::OnInitDialog();
        animateCtrl.Open("sample.avi");
        return TRUE;

}
```

After the dialog box is initialized, an AVI file is opened by use of the **Open** member function of the **CAnimateCtrl**. This opens the AVI file and displays the first frame. Notice that in the resource file we did not specify any style for the Animation control. Showing the first frame is the default behavior of this control. If the ACS_AUTOPLAY style was set during creation of the Animation control or specified in the resource file, then opening the AVI file will automatically start playing the AVI clip. You may change the resource file to include the ACS_AUTOPLAY style in the Animation control and try this out.

```
void CAnimateDlg::OnStop()
{
        // TODO: Add your control notification handler code here
        animateCtrl.Stop();
}
```

When the Stop button is clicked, the **OnStop** function is called, and it calls the **Stop** member function of the **CAnimateCtrl**.

```
void CAnimateDlg::OnPlay()
{
        animateCtrl.Play(0, (UINT)-1, (UINT)1);
}
```

When the Play button is clicked, the **OnPlay** function is called, and it calls the **Play** member function of **CAnimateCtrl**. Here it specifies the control to play from frame 0 to −1, where −1 indicates the last frame. If a different number were specified, the control would have played until that frame. The third parameter indicates the replay count, and here the control is requested to play once. A value of −1 would tell it to play indefinitely.

```
void CAnimateDlg::OnAutoPlay()
{
        DWORD   dwStyle;
        animateCtrl.Stop();
        animateCtrl.Close();
        dwStyle = animateCtrl.GetStyle();        // Get the current style
        if(dwStyle & ACS_AUTOPLAY) // Check current style and toggle it
            dwStyle &= ~ACS_AUTOPLAY;
        else
            dwStyle |= ACS_AUTOPLAY;
        SetWindowLong(animateCtrl.GetSafeHwnd(), GWL_STYLE, dwStyle);
        animateCtrl.Open("sample.avi");
}
```

When the Autoplay check box is clicked, the **OnAutoPlay** function is called. Here it stops the control in case the AVI clip is playing, gets the control's current style, toggles the style, and sets the style again. It then reopens the AVI clip. A similar style change is made when the Transparent check box is clicked. The code is shown next:

```
void CAnimateDlg::OnTransparent()
{
        DWORD   dwStyle;
        dwStyle = animateCtrl.GetStyle();        // Get the current style
        if(dwStyle & ACS_TRANSPARENT) // Check current style and toggle it
            dwStyle &= ~ACS_TRANSPARENT;
        else
            dwStyle |= ACS_TRANSPARENT;
        SetWindowLong(animateCtrl.GetSafeHwnd(), GWL_STYLE, dwStyle);
        animateCtrl.Open("sample.avi");
}
```

UP-DOWN CONTROL

An Up-Down control consists of two arrows pointing in opposite directions. One way to visualize an Up-Down control is to think of a scroll bar with just the arrows and no bar connecting them (see the following illustration). As noted earlier, an Up-Down control is commonly used with an edit box and in earlier versions of common controls, this combination was called a Spin control.

Although you can use an Up-Down control in a stand-alone manner, the more common use is with another control such as an Edit box. The Edit box is called the Up-Down control's *buddy window.* As mentioned, the combination of an Up-Down control and an Edit box is called a Spin control (see the following illustration).

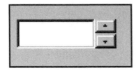

The Edit box contains a value, and clicking the arrows of the associated Up-Down control increments and decrements the value in the Edit box. The following illustration shows the results after the up arrow has been clicked and the Edit box has counted up to 45.

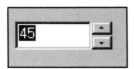

While the name suggests a vertical orientation for the Up-Down control, you can in fact give this control a horizontal orientation. In addition, you can position the control to the left of the Edit box if you choose. The following illustration shows the Up-Down control oriented horizontally and positioned to the left of the Edit box.

You can use the MFC class **CSpinButtonCtrl** to program a Spin control. **CSpinButtonCtrl** has several member functions that you can use to change the attributes of the Spin control. The attributes, their descriptions, and the member functions you can use to set the attributes are summarized in Table 7-4.

TIP: The default behavior of the Spin control is counterintuitive. The default maximum is 0, and the minimum is 100. Clicking the up arrow decreases the Edit box value, while clicking the down arrow increases it. You can change the range limits by using the **SetRange, SetRange32, GetRange, and GetRange32** member functions.

Attribute	Description	Member Functions
Acceleration	This adjusts the rate at which the position changes when the user holds down the arrow button.	SetAccel and GetAccel
Base	This changes the base to 10 or 16. Base is used to display the position in the caption of the buddy window.	GetBase and SetBase
Buddy Window	This dynamically queries or sets the buddy window.	GetBuddy and SetBuddy
Position	This queries and changes the position.	GetPos and SetPos
Range	This changes the maximum and minimum positions for the Spin control.	SetRange and GetRange
32-bit Range	Same as Range except that the range is a 32-bit range.	SetRange32 and GetRange32

Table 7-4.   Spin Control Attributes, Descriptions, and Associated Member Functions

You can also use styles to set the properties for a Spin control using the Styles tab of the Spin Properties dialog box in the dialog editor. The styles you can set and their descriptions are summarized in Table 7-5.

TIP: The AUTOBUDDY style automatically selects the previous window in Z order. So the order in which you specify the windows is important. Refer to the example for an illustration of this point.

Up-Down Control Programming Example

The *SpSlProg* sample program shows how to use the Spin Button control. If Spin Slider Progress is selected from the File menu, a dialog panel with a Spin control attached to an Edit control is displayed. Clicking the Spin control increments the count in the Edit control.

The main application code is still functionally minimal, with code added to handle the new menu item that will bring up the Spin Slider Progress dialog panel. These additional lines are shown in boldface. Although the code illustrates Slider and Progress controls,

Property	Meaning
Orientation	This sets the orientation of the control to be horizontal or vertical. Up-Down controls are vertical by default.
Alignment	This aligns the Up-Down control to the left or right of its buddy window. The width of the buddy window is adjusted to fit the Up-Down control.
Auto Buddy	This makes the buddy window the previous window in Z order.
No Thousands	This does not use the thousands separator (usually the comma) for buddy window displays.
Arrow Keys	This increments or decrements the Spin control value when the UP ARROW or DOWN ARROW key is pressed.
Set Buddy Integer	This automatically maintains synchronization between the value in the buddy window and the current position of the Up-Down control.
Wrap	This causes the position of the Up-Down control to "wrap around" when moved past an end. The default is to stop at the end.

Table 7-5.   Spin Control Properties and Descriptions

just look at the Spin control portions for this example. We will look at the other controls in the next two sections.

```cpp
// Controls.CPP
#include <afxwin.h>
#include <afxdlgs.h>
#include <afxcmn.h>                    // Header file for Common controls
#include <strstrea.h>
#include "FontDlg.h"
#include "AnimateDlg.h"
#include "HotKeyDlg.h"
#include "SpSlProgDlg.h"
#include "resource.h"


// Define the application object class
class CApp : public CWinApp
{
```

```cpp
public:
        virtual BOOL InitInstance ();
};

// Define the window class
class CWindow : public CFrameWnd
{
public:
    CWindow();
    afx_msg void OnAppAbout();
    afx_msg void OnFontDlg();
    afx_msg void OnAnimateDlg();
    afx_msg void OnHotKeyDlg();
    afx_msg void OnSpSlProgDlg();
    afx_msg void OnExit();
    afx_msg void OnSysCommand(UINT nID, LPARAM lParam);// Process the Hot Key
    DECLARE_MESSAGE_MAP()
};

/////////////////////////////////////////////////////////////////////////////
// CWindow
BEGIN_MESSAGE_MAP(CWindow, CFrameWnd)
        ON_COMMAND(ID_APP_ABOUT, OnAppAbout)
        ON_COMMAND(ID_FONTDLG, OnFontDlg)
        ON_COMMAND(ID_ANIMATEDLG, OnAnimateDlg)
        ON_COMMAND(ID_HOTKEYDLG, OnHotKeyDlg)
        ON_COMMAND(ID_SPSLPROGDLG, OnSpSlProgDlg)
        ON_COMMAND(ID_APP_EXIT, OnExit)
        ON_WM_SYSCOMMAND()
END_MESSAGE_MAP()

/////////////////////////////////////////////////////////////////////////////
// CWindow construction
CWindow::CWindow()
{
    LoadAccelTable(MAKEINTRESOURCE(IDR_MAINFRAME));
    Create( NULL, "Control Sample",
    WS_OVERLAPPEDWINDOW,
    rectDefault, NULL, MAKEINTRESOURCE(IDR_MAINFRAME) );
}

/////////////////////////////////////////////////////////////////////////////
// The one and only CApp object
CApp theApp;
/////////////////////////////////////////////////////////////////////////////
// CApp initialization
BOOL CApp::InitInstance()
{
```

```
        m_pMainWnd = new CWindow();
        m_pMainWnd -> ShowWindow( m_nCmdShow );
        m_pMainWnd -> UpdateWindow();
        return TRUE;
}
//////////////////////////////////////////////////////////////////////
// CAboutDlg dialog used for App About
class CAboutDlg : public CDialog
{
public:
        CAboutDlg();
        enum { IDD = IDD_ABOUTBOX };
        protected:
};

CAboutDlg::CAboutDlg() : CDialog(CAboutDlg::IDD)
{
}

// App command to run the dialog
void CWindow::OnAppAbout()
{
        CAboutDlg aboutDlg;
        aboutDlg.DoModal();
}


//////////////////////////////////////////////////////////////////////
// CWindow commands
// App command to run the dialog

// Font Dialog selected

void CWindow::OnFontDlg()
{
        CFontDlg fontDlg(this);
        fontDlg.DoModal();
}
// Animate Dialog selected
void CWindow::OnAnimateDlg()
{
        CAnimateDlg animateDlg(this);
        animateDlg.DoModal();
}
// HotKey Dialog selected
void CWindow::OnHotKeyDlg()
{
        CHotKeyDlg hotkeyDlg(this);
        hotkeyDlg.DoModal();
}
```

```
// Spin Slider Progress Dialog selected
void CWindow::OnSpSlProgDlg()
{
        CSpSlProgDlg spslprogDlg(this);
        spslprogDlg.DoModal();
}
// On Exit handles the void
void CWindow::OnExit()
{
        DestroyWindow();
}
void CWindow::OnSysCommand(UINT nID, LPARAM lParam)
{
    if (nID == SC_HOTKEY)
    {
        DestroyWindow();
    }
    else
    {   // Pass on all other messages to be processed.
        CWnd::OnSysCommand(nID, lParam);
    }
}
```

The dialog resource file for this sample is shown next. The style for the Spin control is set to be UDS_AUTOBUDDY. This will automatically select the previous window in the Z order as the control's buddy window. In the case of the dialog resource, it is the control that precedes the spin button in the tab order. So the position of the Edit control and the Spin control in the dialog resource is important. The other styles specify to wrap the position beyond the ending or beginning of the range (UDS_WRAP), not to inset thousand separators (UDS_NOTHOUSANDS), to set the text of the Edit control, and to enable the UP ARROW and DOWN ARROW keys to increment and decrement the spin position. The style for the Slider control is set to TBS_AUTOTICKS to display tick marks in the Slider control.

```
IDD_SPSLPROG  DIALOG DISCARDABLE  0, 0, 201, 118
STYLE DS_MODALFRAME | WS_POPUP | WS_CAPTION | WS_SYSMENU
CAPTION "Spin/Slider/Progress"
FONT 8, "MS Sans Serif"
BEGIN
/* Since we are using AUTOBUDDY for the spin control the order   */
/* of the next two controls is essential. The AUTOBUDDY style    */
/* automatically selects the previous window in Z_order. In the  */
/* case of dialog template it is the control that precedes the   */
/* spin button in the tab order.                                 */
    EDITTEXT        IDC_EDIT,12,16,40,14,ES_AUTOHSCROLL
    CONTROL         "Spin2",IDC_SPIN,"msctls_updown32",
                    UDS_WRAP | UDS_NOTHOUSANDS | UDS_SETBUDDYINT |
                    UDS_AUTOBUDDY | UDS_ARROWKEYS,52,16,10,14
    CONTROL         "Slider1",IDC_SLIDER,"msctls_trackbar32",TBS_AUTOTICKS |
```

```
                              WS_TABSTOP,12,45,162,17
        CONTROL               "Progress1",IDC_PROGRESS,"msctls_progress32",WS_BORDER,
                              12,77,167,14,WS_EX_RTLREADING
        DEFPUSHBUTTON         "OK",IDOK,10,96,32,14
        PUSHBUTTON            "Close",IDC_CLOSE,52,96,32,14
        PUSHBUTTON            "Cancel",IDCANCEL,96,96,32,14
END
```

The class created for this dialog is shown next. It has three members, which correspond to **CSpinButtonCtrl**, **CSliderCtrl**, and **CProgressCtrl**. For the Edit control a
CString member data is declared. It also declares the member functions **OnInitDialog**,
which is called when the dialog panel is initialized; **OnChangeEdit**, which is called when
the text in the Edit control changes; and **OnClose**, which is called when the Close button
is clicked. Since the Edit control is set as the buddy to the Spin control, its value in the Edit
control changes every time the Spin control is operated. This in turn will invoke the
OnChangeEdit function.

```
// SpSlProgDlg.h : header file
/////////////////////////////////////////////////////////////////////////
// CSpSlProgDlg dialog
class CSpSlProgDlg : public CDialog
{
// Construction
public:
        CSpSlProgDlg(CWnd* pParent = NULL);          // standard constructor
// Dialog Data
        //{{AFX_DATA(CSpSlProgDlg)
        CSpinButtonCtrl m_spin;
        CSliderCtrl     m_slider;
        CProgressCtrl   m_progress;
        CString m_buddyedit;
        //}}AFX_DATA

        // ClassWizard generated virtual function overrides
        //{{AFX_VIRTUAL(CSpSlProgDlg)
        protected:
        virtual void DoDataExchange(CDataExchange* pDX);
        //}}AFX_VIRTUAL

// Implementation
protected:
        // Generated message map functions
        //{{AFX_MSG(CSpSlProgDlg)
        virtual BOOL OnInitDialog();
        afx_msg void OnChangeEdit();
        afx_msg void OnClose();
        //}}AFX_MSG
        DECLARE_MESSAGE_MAP()
};
```

The implementation code for the dialog panel class discussed earlier follows:

```
// SpSlProgDlg.cpp : implementation file
//
#include <afxwin.h>
#include <afxdlgs.h>
#include <afxcmn.h>
#include "resource.h"
#include "SpSlProgDlg.h"
/////////////////////////////////////////////////////////////////////////////
// CSpSlProgDlg dialog

CSpSlProgDlg::CSpSlProgDlg(CWnd* pParent /*=NULL*/)
        : CDialog(IDD_SPSLPROG, pParent)
{
    //{{AFX_DATA_INIT(CSpSlProgDlg)
    m_buddyedit = _T("");
    //}}AFX_DATA_INIT
}

void CSpSlProgDlg::DoDataExchange(CDataExchange* pDX)
{
        CDialog::DoDataExchange(pDX);
        //{{AFX_DATA_MAP(CSpSlProgDlg)
        DDX_Control(pDX, IDC_SPIN, m_spin);
        DDX_Control(pDX, IDC_SLIDER, m_slider);
        DDX_Control(pDX, IDC_PROGRESS, m_progress);
        DDX_Text(pDX, IDC_EDIT, m_buddyedit);
        //}}AFX_DATA_MAP
}
```

Notice that the data exchange between the Edit control and the member variable is done at the text level here.

```
BEGIN_MESSAGE_MAP(CSpSlProgDlg, CDialog)
        //{{AFX_MSG_MAP(CSpSlProgDlg)
        ON_EN_CHANGE(IDC_EDIT, OnChangeEdit)
        ON_BN_CLICKED(IDC_CLOSE, OnClose)
        //}}AFX_MSG_MAP
END_MESSAGE_MAP()
```

The message map specifies that the **OnChangeEdit** function be called when the text in the Edit control changes, and that the **OnClose** function be called when the Close button is clicked.

```
/////////////////////////////////////////////////////////////////////////////
// CSpSlProgDlg message handlers

BOOL CSpSlProgDlg::OnInitDialog()
{
```

```
    CDialog::OnInitDialog();
    // TODO: Add extra initialization here
    // Modify the default Spin button control range from 0-100 to 0-120
    // The rate at which the button spins can also be
    // controlled by SetAccel method
    // When running this sample, keep the spin button
    // pressed and notice the slider
    // control's speed increasing after a few seconds.
    m_spin.SetRange(0, 120);      // Just set the range.
    m_slider.SetRange(0, 120, TRUE); // Set the slider range
    m_slider.SetTicFreq(10);      // Put a tick mark at every 10 ticks

    m_progress.SetRange(0, 100);// Range of the Progress indicator.
    m_progress.SetPos(100);      // Set the initial position.
    m_progress.SetStep(-1);      // Step increment every time StepIt is called.
    return TRUE;   // return TRUE unless you set the focus to a control
}
```

During initialization, the default Spin button control range is changed from 0–100 to 0–120. In Windows 2000, the Spin button range can be set to a 32-bit range using the **SetRange32** member function.

One of the interesting member functions that the Spin control provides is **SetAccel**. This function allows the user to set the rate of change at which the Spin control spins. This sample uses the default value. Another sample provided on the CD-ROM modifies the acceleration of the Spin control by defining a UDACCEL structure and setting the acceleration by calling the **SetAccel** member function. If the Spin control is kept selected when you're running the sample, the entry in the Edit control changes. This triggers the **OnChangeEdit** function, which reads the Spin control's position and sets the slider to reflect the position. As the Spin control is kept selected, the slider starts accelerating after a few seconds. This acceleration can be controlled by the **SetAccel** method of **CSpinButtonCtrl**.

```
void CSpSlProgDlg::OnChangeEdit()
{
    // TODO: Add your control notification handler code here
    int iCurrentPos;
    if (m_spin && m_slider) // Do not process before getting valid objects.
    {
        iCurrentPos = m_spin.GetPos();
        m_slider.SetPos(iCurrentPos);
    }
}

void CSpSlProgDlg::OnClose()
{
    // TODO: Add your control notification handler code here
    AfxMessageBox("Watch the Progress Control.\nIn ten seconds this
Spin/Slider/Progress dialog will close");
```

```
    for (int i = 0; i < 100; i++)
    {
        Sleep(100);
        m_progress.StepIt();
    }
    EndDialog(1);
}
```

TRACKBAR CONTROL

The *Trackbar control,* also called a *Slider control,* is a window that contains a slider and a track along which the slider can be dragged. You can click the slider indicator and drag it to set its position. The following illustration shows a Slider control.

A Trackbar control can also be associated with an Up-Down control, and the position of the slider can be controlled by use of the up and down arrows of the Up-Down control. Figures 7-5 through 7-7 show the position of the slider as it moves in relation to the Up-Down control. By default, the size of the slider is automatically determined by the system scroll bar width and is also limited by the size of the control.

You can control the appearance of a slider using styles. The common styles you can use with sliders are described in Table 7-6.

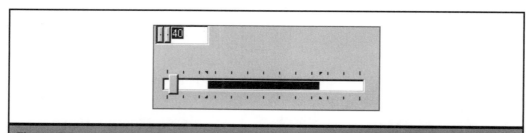

Figure 7-5.   Slider at the left position when the Up-Down control is set to a small value

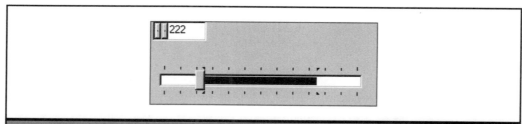

Figure 7-6.   Slider advances in response to changes in the Up-Down control

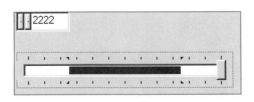

Figure 7-7.   Slider at the rightmost position when the Up-Down control is set to a large value

Trackbar Control Style	Description
TBS_HORZ	Slider is oriented horizontally (default).
TBS_VERT	Slider is oriented vertically.
TBS_AUTOTICKS	This automatically creates a slider with a tick mark for each increment in the slider's range of values (you can change the tick frequency with the TBM_SETTICFREQ message).
TBS_NOTICKS	Slider does not display tick marks.
TBS_BOTTOM or TBS_TOP	This displays the tick marks at the bottom or top of the slider (for horizontal orientation).
TBS_RIGHT or TBS_LEFT	This displays the tick marks at the left or right side of the slider (for vertical orientation).
TBS_BOTH	This displays tick marks on both sides of the slider (for any orientation).
TBS_ENABLESELRANGE	This displays a selection range within the slider. Range is set by use of the TBM_SETSEL message.
TBS_FIXEDLENGTH	This allows the size of the slider to be changed with the TBM_SETTHUMBLENGTH message.
TBS_NOTHUMB	This causes the trackbar control not to display a slider.
TBS_REVERSED	This is used for trackbars, where a smaller number indicates "higher" and a larger number indicates "lower." It is simply a label and has no effect on the control itself.
TBS_TOOLTIPS	This automatically creates a default tooltip control that displays the slider's current position.

Table 7-6.   Slider Control Styles

The Slider controls shown in Figures 7-5 through 7-8 have the selection range enabled. Note that the tick marks that correspond to the ends of the selection range change to triangles. This selection range-enabled slider is illustrated in the example that follows.

Trackbar Control Programming Example

The *SpSlProg* sample program also shows how to use the Slider control. When run, the sample displays a window with a menu. If Spin Slider Progress is selected from the File menu, a dialog panel with a Slider control is displayed. Clicking the Spin control arrows not only increments the count in the Edit control, but it also increments the Slider control.

The main application code is still functionally minimal, with code added to handle the new menu item that will bring up the Spin Slider Progress dialog panel. Lines that are of interest are shown in boldface. The dialog resource file for this sample is shown next. The style for the Slider control is set to TBS_AUTOTICKS. This style instructs the system to add tick marks to the Slider control automatically when the sample calls the **SetRange** member function.

```
IDD_SPSLPROG  DIALOG DISCARDABLE  0, 0, 201, 118
STYLE DS_MODALFRAME | WS_POPUP | WS_CAPTION | WS_SYSMENU
CAPTION "Spin/Slider/Progress"
FONT 8, "MS Sans Serif"
BEGIN
/* Since we are using AUTOBUDDY for the spin control the order    */
/* of the next two controls is essential. The AUTOBUDDY style     */
/* automatically selects the previous window in Z_order. In the   */
/* case of dialog template it is the control that precedes the    */
/* spin button in the tab order.                                  */
    EDITTEXT        IDC_EDIT,12,16,40,14,ES_AUTOHSCROLL
    CONTROL         "Spin2",IDC_SPIN,"msctls_updown32",
                    UDS_WRAP | UDS_NOTHOUSANDS | UDS_SETBUDDYINT |
                    UDS_AUTOBUDDY | UDS_ARROWKEYS,52,16,10,14
    CONTROL         "Slider1",IDC_SLIDER,"msctls_trackbar32",TBS_AUTOTICKS |
                    WS_TABSTOP,12,45,162,17
```

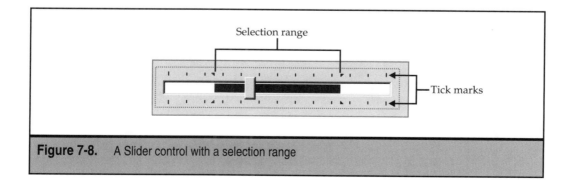

Figure 7-8.   A Slider control with a selection range

```
     CONTROL           "Progress1",IDC_PROGRESS,"msctls_progress32",WS_BORDER,
                       12,77,167,14,WS_EX_RTLREADING
     DEFPUSHBUTTON     "OK",IDOK,10,96,32,14
     PUSHBUTTON        "Close",IDC_CLOSE,52,96,32,14
     PUSHBUTTON        "Cancel",IDCANCEL,96,96,32,14
END
```

The class created for this dialog is shown next. It has three members, one each corresponding to **CSpinButtonCtrl**, **CSliderCtrl**, and **CProgressCtrl**. It also declares the member functions **OnInitDialog**, which is called when the dialog panel is initialized; **OnChangeEdit**, which is called when the text in the Edit control changes; and **OnClose**, which is called when the Close button is clicked.

```
// SpSlProgDlg.h : header file
//////////////////////////////////////////////////////////////////////////////
// CSpSlProgDlg dialog
class CSpSlProgDlg : public CDialog
{
// Construction
public:
       CSpSlProgDlg(CWnd* pParent = NULL);       // standard constructor
// Dialog Data
       //{{AFX_DATA(CSpSlProgDlg)
       CSpinButtonCtrl m_spin;
       CSliderCtrl     m_slider;
       CProgressCtrl   m_progress;
       CString m_buddyedit;
       //}}AFX_DATA

       // ClassWizard generated virtual function overrides
       //{{AFX_VIRTUAL(CSpSlProgDlg)
       protected:
       virtual void DoDataExchange(CDataExchange* pDX);// DDX/DDV support
       //}}AFX_VIRTUAL

// Implementation
protected:
       // Generated message map functions
       //{{AFX_MSG(CSpSlProgDlg)
       virtual BOOL OnInitDialog();
       afx_msg void OnChangeEdit();
       afx_msg void OnClose();
       //}}AFX_MSG
       DECLARE_MESSAGE_MAP()
};
```

The implementation code for the dialog panel class discussed earlier follows:

```
// SpSlProgDlg.cpp : implementation file
//
#include <afxwin.h>
#include <afxdlgs.h>
#include <afxcmn.h>
#include "resource.h"
#include "SpSlProgDlg.h"
/////////////////////////////////////////////////////////////////////////////
// CSpSlProgDlg dialog

CSpSlProgDlg::CSpSlProgDlg(CWnd* pParent /*=NULL*/)
        : CDialog(IDD_SPSLPROG, pParent)
{
    //{{AFX_DATA_INIT(CSpSlProgDlg)
    m_buddyedit = _T("");
    //}}AFX_DATA_INIT
}

void CSpSlProgDlg::DoDataExchange(CDataExchange* pDX)
{
        CDialog::DoDataExchange(pDX);
        //{{AFX_DATA_MAP(CSpSlProgDlg)
        DDX_Control(pDX, IDC_SPIN, m_spin);
        DDX_Control(pDX, IDC_SLIDER, m_slider);
        DDX_Control(pDX, IDC_PROGRESS, m_progress);
        DDX_Text(pDX, IDC_EDIT, m_buddyedit);
        //}}AFX_DATA_MAP
}
```

Notice that the data exchange between the Edit control and the member variable is done at the text level here.

```
BEGIN_MESSAGE_MAP(CSpSlProgDlg, CDialog)
        //{{AFX_MSG_MAP(CSpSlProgDlg)
        ON_EN_CHANGE(IDC_EDIT, OnChangeEdit)
        ON_BN_CLICKED(IDC_CLOSE, OnClose)
        //}}AFX_MSG_MAP
END_MESSAGE_MAP()


/////////////////////////////////////////////////////////////////////////////
// CSpSlProgDlg message handlers

BOOL CSpSlProgDlg::OnInitDialog()
{
    CDialog::OnInitDialog();
    // TODO: Add extra initialization here
    // Modify the default Spin button control range from 0-100 to 0-120
    // The rate at which the button spins can also be
```

```
    // controlled by SetAccel method
    // When running this sample, keep the spin button
    // pressed and notice the slider
    // control's speed increasing after a few seconds.
    m_spin.SetRange(0, 120);      // Just set the range.
    m_slider.SetRange(0, 120, TRUE); // Set the slider range
    m_slider.SetTicFreq(10);      // Put a tick mark at every 10 ticks

    m_progress.SetRange(0, 100);// Range of the Progress indicator.
    m_progress.SetPos(100);       // Set the initial position.
    m_progress.SetStep(-1);       // Step increment every time StepIt is called.
    return TRUE;   // return TRUE unless you set the focus to a control
}
```

During initialization the slider range is also set to 0–120. When the Up-Down control is used, the value in the buddy edit control changes and this triggers a call to the **OnChangeEdit** member function. The value is queried, and the slider's position is set to match it.

```
void CSpSlProgDlg::OnChangeEdit()
{

    int iCurrentPos;
    if (m_spin && m_slider) // Do not process before getting valid objects.
    {
        iCurrentPos = m_spin.GetPos();
        m_slider.SetPos(iCurrentPos);
    }
}


void CSpSlProgDlg::OnClose()
{
    // TODO: Add your control notification handler code here
    AfxMessageBox("Watch the Progress Control.\nIn ten seconds this
Spin/Slider/Progress dialog will close");
    for (int i = 0; i < 100; i++)
    {
        Sleep(100);
        m_progress.StepIt();
    }
    EndDialog(1);
}
```

When the Close button is clicked, a message box is displayed to notify the user of the pending action, which in this case is the closure of the dialog panel.

The CD-ROM contains additional samples that show a Slider control with TBS_BOTH and TBS_ENABLESELRANGE styles. TBS_BOTH instructs the control to place ticks marks on both sides, and TBS_ENABLESELRANGE displays a selection range that can be set by calling the **SetSelection** member function.

PROGRESS CONTROL

The *Progress control* is used to indicate the progress of a long operation where the user has to wait. It consists of a rectangle that is gradually filled, from left to right or right to left, with the system highlight color as the operation progresses. Figures 7-9 and 7-10 show the progress bar progressing from left to right. Figures 7-11 and 7-12 show a progress bar progressing from right to left. You can control the progress direction, as the example program illustrates. Keep in mind that with snapshots, it is difficult to show the progress direction. Execute the programs to see the progress direction.

The operation could be copying a big file or a computation-intensive function. You see this control a lot when you install software. The user gets a much better feeling watching a progress bar compared with staring at an hourglass icon for a long time. The control also assures the user that the operation has not gone into a loop.

Progress Control Programming Example

The *SpSlProg* sample program shows how to use the Progress control. The sample when run displays a window with a menu. If Spin Slider Progress is selected from the File menu, a dialog panel with a Progress control is displayed. Selecting the Close button displays a message box and starts a countdown to close the dialog panel. As it counts down, the progress indicator is updated.

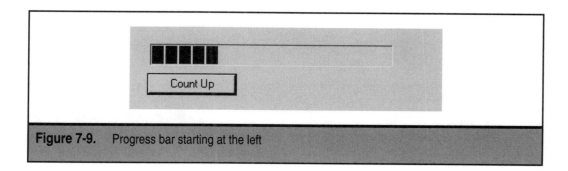

Figure 7-9. Progress bar starting at the left

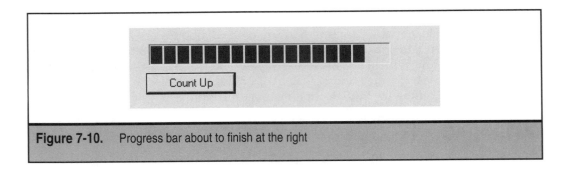

Figure 7-10.   Progress bar about to finish at the right

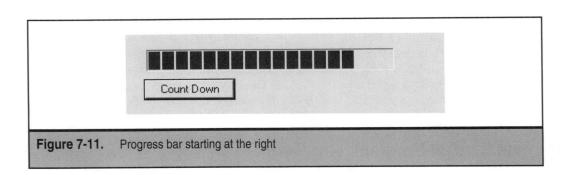

Figure 7-11.   Progress bar starting at the right

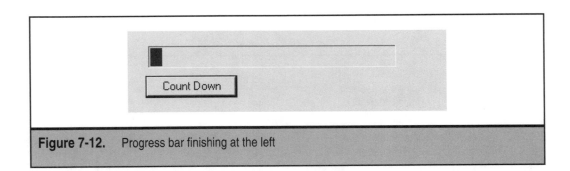

Figure 7-12.   Progress bar finishing at the left

The main application code is still functionally minimal, with code added to handle the new menu item that will bring up the Spin Slider Progress dialog panel. Lines that are of interest are shown in boldface.

The dialog resource file for this sample is shown next. It includes a simple Progress control.

```
IDD_SPSLPROG  DIALOG DISCARDABLE  0, 0, 201, 118
STYLE DS_MODALFRAME | WS_POPUP | WS_CAPTION | WS_SYSMENU
CAPTION "Spin/Slider/Progress"
FONT 8, "MS Sans Serif"
BEGIN
/* Since we are using AUTOBUDDY for the spin control the order   */
/* of the next two controls is essential. The AUTOBUDDY style    */
/* automatically selects the previous window in Z_order. In the  */
/* case of dialog template it is the control that precedes the   */
/* spin button in the tab order.                                 */
    EDITTEXT        IDC_EDIT,12,16,40,14,ES_AUTOHSCROLL
    CONTROL         "Spin2",IDC_SPIN,"msctls_updown32",
                    UDS_WRAP | UDS_NOTHOUSANDS | UDS_SETBUDDYINT |
                    UDS_AUTOBUDDY | UDS_ARROWKEYS,52,16,10,14
    CONTROL         "Slider1",IDC_SLIDER,"msctls_trackbar32",TBS_AUTOTICKS |
                    WS_TABSTOP,12,45,162,17
    CONTROL         "Progress1",IDC_PROGRESS,"msctls_progress32",WS_BORDER,
                    12,77,167,14,WS_EX_RTLREADING
    DEFPUSHBUTTON   "OK",IDOK,10,96,32,14
    PUSHBUTTON      "Close",IDC_CLOSE,52,96,32,14
    PUSHBUTTON      "Cancel",IDCANCEL,96,96,32,14
END


// SpSlProgDlg.h : header file
//////////////////////////////////////////////////////////////////////
// CSpSlProgDlg dialog
class CSpSlProgDlg : public CDialog
{
// Construction
public:
        CSpSlProgDlg(CWnd* pParent = NULL);       // standard constructor
// Dialog Data
        //{{AFX_DATA(CSpSlProgDlg)
        CSpinButtonCtrl m_spin;
        CSliderCtrl     m_slider;
```

```
                    CProgressCtrl    m_progress;
                    CString m_buddyedit;
                    //}}AFX_DATA

                    // ClassWizard generated virtual function overrides
                    //{{AFX_VIRTUAL(CSpSlProgDlg)
                    protected:
                    virtual void DoDataExchange(CDataExchange* pDX);// DDX/DDV support
                    //}}AFX_VIRTUAL

// Implementation
protected:
                    // Generated message map functions
                    //{{AFX_MSG(CSpSlProgDlg)
                    virtual BOOL OnInitDialog();
                    afx_msg void OnChangeEdit();
                    afx_msg void OnClose();
                    //}}AFX_MSG
                    DECLARE_MESSAGE_MAP()
};
```

The implementation code for the dialog panel class discussed earlier follows:

```
// SpSlProgDlg.cpp : implementation file
//
#include <afxwin.h>
#include <afxdlgs.h>
#include <afxcmn.h>
#include "resource.h"
#include "SpSlProgDlg.h"
/////////////////////////////////////////////////////////////////////////////
// CSpSlProgDlg dialog

CSpSlProgDlg::CSpSlProgDlg(CWnd* pParent /*=NULL*/)
        : CDialog(IDD_SPSLPROG, pParent)
{
    //{{AFX_DATA_INIT(CSpSlProgDlg)
    m_buddyedit = _T("");
    //}}AFX_DATA_INIT
}

void CSpSlProgDlg::DoDataExchange(CDataExchange* pDX)
{
        CDialog::DoDataExchange(pDX);
        //{{AFX_DATA_MAP(CSpSlProgDlg)
        DDX_Control(pDX, IDC_SPIN, m_spin);
        DDX_Control(pDX, IDC_SLIDER, m_slider);
        DDX_Control(pDX, IDC_PROGRESS, m_progress);
        DDX_Text(pDX, IDC_EDIT, m_buddyedit);
        //}}AFX_DATA_MAP
}
```

Notice that the data exchange between the Edit control and the member variable is done at the text level here.

```
BEGIN_MESSAGE_MAP(CSpSlProgDlg, CDialog)
        //{{AFX_MSG_MAP(CSpSlProgDlg)
        ON_EN_CHANGE(IDC_EDIT, OnChangeEdit)
        ON_BN_CLICKED(IDC_CLOSE, OnClose)
        //}}AFX_MSG_MAP
END_MESSAGE_MAP()

/////////////////////////////////////////////////////////////////////////////
// CSpSlProgDlg message handlers

BOOL CSpSlProgDlg::OnInitDialog()
{
    CDialog::OnInitDialog();

    // Modify the default Spin button control range from 0-100 to 0-120
    // The rate at which the button spins can also be
    // controlled by SetAccel method
    // When running this sample, keep the spin button
    // pressed and notice the slider
    // control's speed increasing after a few seconds.
    m_spin.SetRange(0, 120);    // Just set the range.
    m_slider.SetRange(0, 120, TRUE); // Set the slider range
    m_slider.SetTicFreq(10);    // Put a tick mark at every 10 ticks

    m_progress.SetRange(0, 100);// Range of the Progress indicator.
    m_progress.SetPos(100);     // Set the initial position.
    m_progress.SetStep(-1);     // Step increment every time StepIt is called.
    return TRUE;  // return TRUE unless you set the focus to a control
}
```

During initialization the initial position for the Progress control is set to 100, which is the maximum, and the step increment is set to –1. This would mean that the progress indicator will drop by 1 every time the Progress control is asked to step. It is being set to a negative range because the objective of the progress indicator is to visually show the countdown. Windows 2000 also allows the control to have a 32-bit range (by calling the **SetRange32** member function).

```
void CSpSlProgDlg::OnChangeEdit()
{
    // TODO: Add your control notification handler code here
    int iCurrentPos;
    if (m_spin && m_slider) // Do not process before getting valid objects.
    {
        iCurrentPos = m_spin.GetPos();
        m_slider.SetPos(iCurrentPos);
    }
}
```

```
void CSpSlProgDlg::OnClose()
{

    AfxMessageBox("Watch the Progress Control.\nIn ten seconds this
Spin/Slider/Progress dialog will close");
    for (int i = 0; i < 100; i++)
    {
        Sleep(100);
        m_progress.StepIt();
    }
    EndDialog(1);
}
```

When the Close button is clicked, a message box is displayed to notify the user of the pending action—which in this case is the closure of the dialog panel—and the progress indicator is stepped down after every 100 milliseconds. Notice that the progress indicator slides down because a negative value was set as the step value.

The sample discussed here shows a simple Progress control. The CD-ROM contains additional samples that show a progress in percent next to the Progress control. Windows 2000 also supports smooth filling, unlike the block filling, and vertical orientation of the control. These are enabled by providing the **PBS_SMOOTH** and **PBS_VERTICAL** styles either in the resource file or during creation of the control.

Though MFC does not provide a member function to set the bar and background color, these can still be changed by sending **PBM_SETBARCOLOR** and **PBM_SETBKCOLOR** messages to the control. One of the samples in the CD-ROM uses this feature.

HOTKEY CONTROL

Hot keys are key combinations that let the user bypass menus and directly invoke a window or function. A *HotKey control* aids in the setting up of hot keys. A HotKey control is a window that displays a text representation of the key combination the user types, such as SHIFT-CTRL-ALT. Figure 7-13 shows setting a hot key dialog box.

The control internally maintains the virtual key code for the hot key and a set of flags that represent the shift state. The HotKey control passes the key combination to your program so that you can set it. The scope of the hot key can be global, or it can be thread specific.

The typical sequence of a HotKey control execution is as follows: The control is created by use of a dialog box template (with **CHotKeyCtrl** in your dialog class) or by use of the **Create** member function to create the control as a child window. You can set a default value by calling the **SetHotKey** member function. You can prohibit certain shift states by calling **SetRules**. The user interacts with the HotKey control and selects a hot key combi-

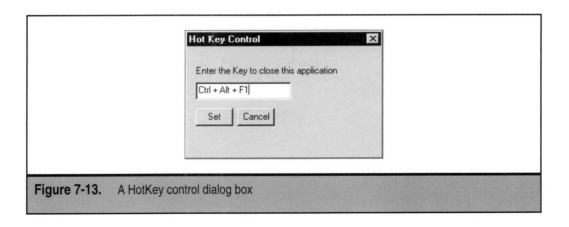

Figure 7-13. A HotKey control dialog box

nation. Use the **GetHotKey** member function to retrieve the virtual key and shift state values when your program is notified that the user has selected a hot key. You then set the hot key as a global hot key by sending a **WM_SETHOTKEY** message, or as a thread-specific hot key by calling the Windows function **RegisterHotKey**. You then terminate the dialog box with the user and perform any cleanups, such as destroying the HotKey control and associated object.

TIP: The HotKey control facilitates setting up the hot key but does not actually set the hot key. You have to programmatically set the hot key.

HotKey Control Progamming Example

The HotKey sample program shows how to use the HotKey control by use of the MFC library class **CHotKeyCtrl**. The sample when run displays a window with a menu. If the HotKey menu item is selected from the File menu, a dialog panel with a HotKey control is displayed. A hot key combination can be entered in the HotKey control. Clicking the Set button will set this hot key as the global hot key. The panel allows you to reset the hot key until the Cancel button is clicked. If the hot key is pressed after the panel is dismissed, the application terminates.

The main application code is still the same, with code added to handle the new menu item that will bring up the HotKey control dialog panel. The sample program shows the setting of a global hot key. When the hot key is pressed, the specified window, which in this case is the main window, receives a **WM_SYSCOMMAND** that specifies **SC_HOTKEY** as the type of command. Code is added in the main application code to handle this message. These additional lines are shown in boldface.

```
// Controls.CPP
#include <afxwin.h>
#include <afxdlgs.h>
#include <afxcmn.h>                    // Header file for Common controls
#include <strstrea.h>
#include "FontDlg.h"
#include "AnimateDlg.h"
#include "HotKeyDlg.h"
#include "resource.h"

// Define the application object class
class CApp : public CWinApp
{
public:
        virtual BOOL InitInstance ();
};

// Define the window class
class CWindow : public CFrameWnd
{
public:
    CWindow();
    afx_msg void OnAppAbout();
    afx_msg void OnFontDlg();
    afx_msg void OnAnimateDlg();
    afx_msg void OnHotKeyDlg();
    afx_msg void OnExit();
    // To Process the Hot Key
    afx_msg void OnSysCommand(UINT nID, LPARAM lParam);
    DECLARE_MESSAGE_MAP()
};

///////////////////////////////////////////////////////////////////////////
// CWindow

BEGIN_MESSAGE_MAP(CWindow, CFrameWnd)
        ON_COMMAND(ID_APP_ABOUT, OnAppAbout)
        ON_COMMAND(ID_FONTDLG, OnFontDlg)
        ON_COMMAND(ID_ANIMATEDLG, OnAnimateDlg)
        ON_COMMAND(ID_HOTKEYDLG, OnHotKeyDlg)
        ON_COMMAND(ID_APP_EXIT, OnExit)
        ON_WM_SYSCOMMAND()
END_MESSAGE_MAP()

///////////////////////////////////////////////////////////////////////////
// CWindow construction

CWindow::CWindow()
{
```

```
        LoadAccelTable(MAKEINTRESOURCE(IDR_MAINFRAME));
        Create( NULL, "Control Sample",
        WS_OVERLAPPEDWINDOW,
        rectDefault, NULL, MAKEINTRESOURCE(IDR_MAINFRAME) );
}


/////////////////////////////////////////////////////////////////////////
// The one and only CApp object

CApp theApp;


/////////////////////////////////////////////////////////////////////////
// CApp initialization
BOOL CApp::InitInstance()
{
        m_pMainWnd = new CWindow();
        m_pMainWnd -> ShowWindow( m_nCmdShow );
        m_pMainWnd -> UpdateWindow();
        return TRUE;
}


/////////////////////////////////////////////////////////////////////////
// CAboutDlg dialog used for App About

class CAboutDlg : public CDialog
{
public:
        CAboutDlg();

        enum { IDD = IDD_ABOUTBOX };

        protected:

};

CAboutDlg::CAboutDlg() : CDialog(CAboutDlg::IDD)
{
}


// App command to run the dialog
void CWindow::OnAppAbout()
{
        CAboutDlg aboutDlg;
        aboutDlg.DoModal();
}


/////////////////////////////////////////////////////////////////////////
// CWindow commands
```

```
// App command to run the dialog

// Font Dialog selected
void CWindow::OnFontDlg()
{
        CFontDlg fontDlg(this);
        fontDlg.DoModal();
}
// Animate Dialog selected
void CWindow::OnAnimateDlg()
{
        CAnimateDlg animateDlg(this);
        animateDlg.DoModal();
}
// HotKey Dialog selected

void CWindow::OnHotKeyDlg()
{
        CHotKeyDlg hotkeyDlg(this);
        hotkeyDlg.DoModal();
}
// On Exit handles the void
void CWindow::OnExit()
{
        DestroyWindow();
}


void CWindow::OnSysCommand(UINT nID, LPARAM lParam)
{
    if (nID == SC_HOTKEY)
    {
        DestroyWindow();
    }
    else
    {   // Pass on all other messages to be processed.
        CWnd::OnSysCommand(nID, lParam);
    }
}
```

When the window receives a **WM_SYSCOMMAND** message, the **OnSysCommand** member function is called. If the command is **SC_HOTKEY**, it terminates the application. If needed, any other action could have been performed here. The dialog resource for the HotKey dialog panel is given next. No special style has been included for the HotKey control.

```
IDD_HOTKEYDLG  DIALOG DISCARDABLE  0, 0, 162, 88
STYLE DS_MODALFRAME | WS_POPUP | WS_CAPTION | WS_SYSMENU
CAPTION "Hot Key Control"
FONT 8, "MS Sans Serif"
```

```
BEGIN
    LTEXT       "Enter the Key to close this application",IDC_STATIC,7,15,135,8
    CONTROL         "Hotkey1",IDC_HOTKEY,"msctls_hotkey32",WS_BORDER |
                    WS_TABSTOP,7,28,80,14
    PUSHBUTTON      "Set",IDC_SETHOTKEY,7,49,31,14
    PUSHBUTTON      "Cancel",IDCANCEL,42,49,31,14
END
```

The dialog panel class maintains a pointer to the parent window's class handle, which is passed to the class during construction. This is used to send the **WM_SETHOTKEY**, which should be sent to the main window. It also has a **CHotKeyCtrl** member that corresponds to the HotKey control in the dialog box. The inline constructor code takes the parent window pointer and initializes the local member. It also declares the member functions **OnInitDialog** and **OnSet**. **OnInitDialog** is called when the dialog is initialized. The **OnSet** function is called when the Set button in the dialog panel is clicked.

```
// HotKeyDlg.h : header file
//
/////////////////////////////////////////////////////////////////////
// CHotKeyDlg dialog
class CHotKeyDlg : public CDialog
{
private:
        CWnd        *m_parent;
        CHotKeyCtrl hotkeyCtrl;

// Construction
public:
        CHotKeyDlg(CWnd* pParent = NULL)
                : CDialog(IDD_HOTKEYDLG, pParent)
                        {m_parent = pParent;}
        virtual void DoDataExchange(CDataExchange* pDX);
protected:
        // Generated message map functions
        //{{AFX_MSG(CHotKeyDlg)
        afx_msg void OnSet();
        virtual BOOL OnInitDialog();
        //}}AFX_MSG
        DECLARE_MESSAGE_MAP()
};


// AnimateDlg.cpp : implementation file
//
#include <afxwin.h>
#include <afxdlgs.h>
#include <afxcmn.h>
#include "resource.h"
#include "HotKeyDlg.h"
```

```
BEGIN_MESSAGE_MAP(CHotKeyDlg, CDialog)
        //{{AFX_MSG_MAP(CHotKeyDlg)
        ON_BN_CLICKED(IDC_SETHOTKEY, OnSet)
        //}}AFX_MSG_MAP
END_MESSAGE_MAP()
```

The message map specifies that the **OnSet** function should be called when the Set button is clicked. Next follows the standard data exchange function:

```
/////////////////////////////////////////////////////////////////////
// CHotKeyDlg message handlers
void CHotKeyDlg::DoDataExchange(CDataExchange* pDX)
{
        CDialog::DoDataExchange(pDX);
        DDX_Control(pDX, IDC_HOTKEY, hotkeyCtrl);
}


BOOL CHotKeyDlg::OnInitDialog()
{
    CDialog::OnInitDialog();
    // Make Alt+ key combination invalid. Modify Alt+ to Ctrl+ hot key.
    hotkeyCtrl.SetRules((WORD)(HKCOMB_A),
                        (WORD)(HKCOMB_C));
    return TRUE;  // return TRUE unless you set the focus to a control
                        // EXCEPTION: OCX Property Pages should return FALSE
}
```

The HotKey control enables you to specify invalid key combinations. It can be a combination of ALT, CTRL, CTRL-ALT, SHIFT, SHIFT-ALT, SHIFT-CTRL, or SHIFT-CTRL-ALT. It also allows you to specify the key combination to use when the user enters an invalid combination. During initialization, the ALT key is defined to be invalid and is modified by the CTRL key. When a user enters an invalid key combination as defined in this function, the system uses the OR operator to combine the keys entered by the user with the flags specified as the second parameter here.

```
void CHotKeyDlg::OnSet()
{
        // TODO: Add your control notification handler code here
    WORD wKeyAndShift;
    // Get the hot key set in the HotKey control
    wKeyAndShift = (WORD)hotkeyCtrl.GetHotKey();
    // Set the hot key. It should be set to a nonchild window.
    // In our case it is being set to the main window.
    m_parent->SendMessage (WM_SETHOTKEY, wKeyAndShift);
}
```

When the user clicks the Set button, this function is called. It gets the hot key from the HotKey control and gives it to the main window by sending the **WM_SETHOTKEY** message. This hot key should be given to a nonchild window. In this case it is given to the main window.

TOOLBAR CONTROL

A *toolbar* is a bar that contains icons representing menu choices that the user can select by clicking an icon. Using the toolbar to perform a menu selection is faster than navigating through layers of menus. In addition, it is easier for most users to recognize an icon than to remember the name of the menu selection, or on what menu or submenu the selection is listed. Typically the toolbar appears just below an application's menu bar, although the toolbar can be free-floating as well. An application can support multiple toolbars. Microsoft Office products such as Word and PowerPoint and developer products such as the Developer Studio support multiple toolbars and provide functions to let the user customize the toolbars. The user can select which toolbars he or she wants displayed. The user can also select the icons for each of the toolbars. In your program, you have to decide to what extent you want to provide customization features. The buttons on a toolbar can display a bitmap, a string, or both. A toolbar's height is determined by the height of the buttons, and its width is adjusted to be the same as that of the parent window's client area by default.

The MFC library provides two classes to create toolbars—**CToolBar** and **CToolBarCtrl**. **CToolBar** is a superset of **CToolBarCtrl**. However, if you don't need the added functionality of **CToolBar**, then **CToolBarCtrl** is preferable, as it results in a smaller executable. **CToolBarCtrl** objects use multiple data structures, and you must set up the following data structures before invoking **CToolBarCtrl**:

▼   A list of button image bitmaps

■   A list of strings for button labels

▲   A list of **TBBUTTON** structures to associate an image bitmap and/or a label with the position, style, state, and command ID of the button

TIP: Remember that when you access the individual elements in these data structures, the index starts with zero. For example, in the bitmaps' data structure, the first bitmap has an index of zero, the second bitmap has an index of one, and so on.

One way you can create a bitmap is by using the Image Editor in the Developer Studio. All the buttons you want on the toolbar are contained in the bitmap. Figure 7-14

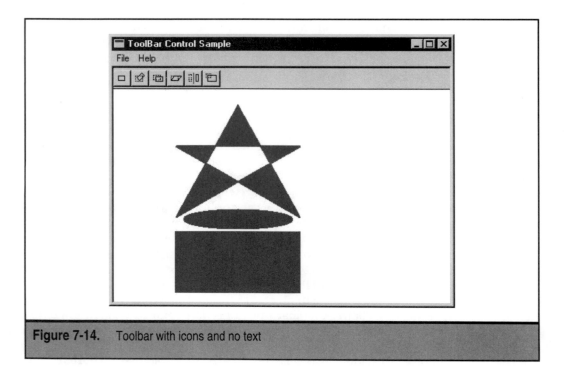

Figure 7-14.   Toolbar with icons and no text

shows a toolbar with icons. Figure 7-15 shows the same toolbar with icons and text and Shear selected. Figure 7-16 shows the same toolbar with icons and text and Scale selected.

Toolbar Control Programming Example

The sample program shown next takes the *WrldXForm* sample from Chapter 6 and extends it to have a toolbar by use of the **CToolBarCtrl** MFC library class. **CToolBarCtrl** provides the functionality of Windows 2000's toolbar common control. The *WrldXForm* sample draws a graphic object and allows the user to choose from a menu of transforms. This sample extends that same functionality to the toolbar.

A command toolbar class, **CCmdToolBar**, is derived from **CToolBarCtrl**. The class header file is shown next. The number of buttons in the toolbar and the pointer to the toolbar button structure are declared as private members. Since additional initialization and termination need to be done during the creation and destruction of the toolbar control, the **Create** method is overridden and a destructor is defined.

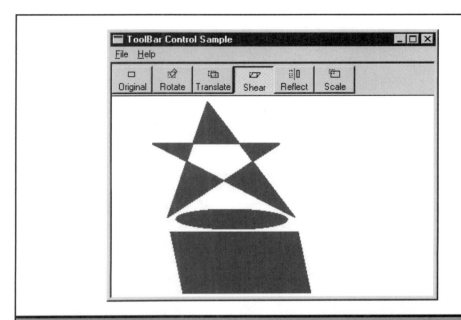

Figure 7-15.   Toolbar with icons and text

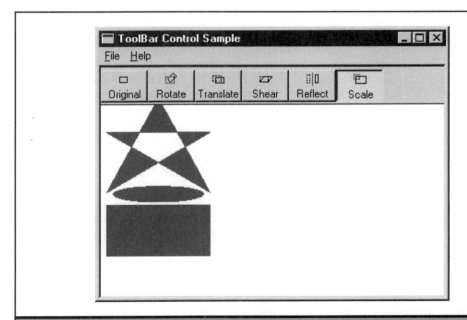

Figure 7-16.   Toolbar with icons and text indicating a different selection

```
// CmdToolBar.h : header file
class CCmdToolBar : public CToolBarCtrl
{
private:
    int         m_nButtonCount;
    TBBUTTON    *m_pTBButtons;

// Construction
public:
    CCmdToolBar();

// ClassWizard generated virtual function overrides
//{{AFX_VIRTUAL(CCmdToolBar)
public:
    virtual BOOL Create( DWORD dwStyle, const RECT& rect, CWnd* pParentWnd, UINT
nID);
    //}}AFX_VIRTUAL
// Implementation
public:
    ~CCmdToolBar();
protected:
    DECLARE_MESSAGE_MAP()
};
```

The implementation file for the **CCmdToolBarCtrl** class is shown next. By design the sample application needs a toolbar with six buttons, one for each transform. A bitmap for this toolbar is created. An easy way to create this toolbar bitmap is through Visual C++ Developer Studio. This toolbar bitmap resource is added to the resource file. During the creation of the toolbar control, the toolbar bitmap is added by calling the **AddBitmap** function, and six toolbar button structures are allocated. For each toolbar button the state, style, bitmap, and command are initialized. The state of the button is set to be enabled, which will activate the button for user action. While the enabled state might be a logical state in this application, other applications may not need to enable the buttons. A typical example is the initial state of the Paste toolbar button, which will not be enabled if the Clipboard is empty. The state of the button can be queried by calling the **GetState** function, and changed by calling the **SetState** function. The style of the button is set to TBSTYLE_BUTTON, TBSTYLE_CHECK, and TBSTYLE_CHECKGROUP. TBSTYLE_BUTTON creates a standard push button. TBSTYLE_CHECK creates the button that toggles between the pressed and unpressed states each time the user clicks it. Since only one transform can be active at a given time, all the buttons are given the TBSTYLE_CHECKGROUP style, which will release a button when another button gets pressed in the group. The command ID for each button is set to the command that the button would generate when it is pressed. The bitmap for the button is determined using the index of the bitmap in the toolbar bitmap, that was added to the control earlier. After the toolbar button structures are created, they are added to the control by calling the **AddButtons** function. This will take the number of buttons to be added and the button structure.

```
// CmdToolBar.cpp : implementation file
#include <afxcmn.h>
#include <afxpriv.h>
#include "Resource.h"
#include "CmdToolBar.h"
/////////////////////////////////////////////////////////////////////
// CCmdToolBar

CCmdToolBar::CCmdToolBar() : m_pTBButtons(NULL)
{
}

CCmdToolBar::~CCmdToolBar()
{
    if (m_pTBButtons)
        delete []m_pTBButtons;
}

BEGIN_MESSAGE_MAP(CCmdToolBar, CToolBarCtrl)
    //{{AFX_MSG_MAP(CCmdToolBar)
    //}}AFX_MSG_MAP
END_MESSAGE_MAP()

BOOL CCmdToolBar::Create(DWORD dwStyle, const RECT& rect, CWnd* pParentWnd,
                         UINT nID )
{
    BOOL bRet = CToolBarCtrl::Create(dwStyle, rect, pParentWnd, nID);
    m_nButtonCount = 6;
    AddBitmap(m_nButtonCount,IDR_CMDTOOLBAR);
    m_pTBButtons = new TBBUTTON[m_nButtonCount];

    for (int i = 0; i < m_nButtonCount; i++)
    {
        m_pTBButtons[i].fsState = TBSTATE_ENABLED;
        m_pTBButtons[i].fsStyle = TBSTYLE_BUTTON | TBSTYLE_CHECK |
                                  TBSTYLE_CHECKGROUP;
        m_pTBButtons[i].dwData = 0;
        m_pTBButtons[i].iBitmap = i;
        m_pTBButtons[i].idCommand = i + IDM_ORIGINAL;
    }
    AddButtons(m_nButtonCount,&m_pTBButtons[0]);
    return bRet;
}
```

The main application code is shown next. This code is similar to that discussed earlier for *Wrldxform.cpp.* Some of the unchanged code has not been shown here. The changes made in order to add the toolbar are highlighted. As was done for other common controls, the *Afxcmn.h* header file is included along with the *Cmdtoolbar.h,* which has the

CCmdToolBar class definitions. A private member data to correspond to the toolbar control is added in the **CWindow** class.

```cpp
// WRLDXFORM.CPP
#include <afxwin.h>
#include <afxdlgs.h>
#include <afxcmn.h>
#include <math.h>
#include "Resource.h"
#include "CmdToolBar.h"

#define ORIGINAL     1
#define ROTATE       2
#define TRANSLATE    3
#define SHEAR        4
#define REFLECT      5
#define SCALE        6

XFORM    xForm;
int      iCurrentTransform;
int      iPreviousTransform;
short    sAngle;

// Define the application object class
class CApp : public CWinApp
{
public:
    virtual BOOL InitInstance ();
};
// Define the window class
class CWindow : public CFrameWnd
{
private:
    CCmdToolBar m_cmdtoolbar;
public:
    CWindow();
    afx_msg void OnPaint();
    afx_msg void OnSize(UINT, INT, INT);
    afx_msg void OnKeyUp(UINT, UINT, UINT);
    afx_msg void OnAppAbout();
    afx_msg void OnOriginal();
    afx_msg void OnRotate();
    afx_msg void OnTranslate();
    afx_msg void OnShear();
    afx_msg void OnReflect();
    afx_msg void OnScale();
    afx_msg void OnExit();
    void UncheckMenu();
    void CheckMenu();
```

```
    DECLARE_MESSAGE_MAP()
};

//////////////////////////////////////////////////////////////////////////
// CWindow

BEGIN_MESSAGE_MAP(CWindow, CFrameWnd)
    ON_WM_PAINT()
    ON_WM_SIZE()
    ON_WM_KEYUP()
    ON_COMMAND(ID_APP_ABOUT, OnAppAbout)
    ON_COMMAND(IDM_ORIGINAL, OnOriginal)
    ON_COMMAND(IDM_ROTATE, OnRotate)
    ON_COMMAND(IDM_TRANSLATE, OnTranslate)
    ON_COMMAND(IDM_SHEAR, OnShear)
    ON_COMMAND(IDM_REFLECT, OnReflect)
    ON_COMMAND(IDM_SCALE, OnScale)
    ON_COMMAND(ID_APP_EXIT, OnExit)
END_MESSAGE_MAP()

//////////////////////////////////////////////////////////////////////////
// CWindow construction

CWindow::CWindow()
{
    LoadAccelTable(MAKEINTRESOURCE(IDR_MAINFRAME));
    Create( NULL, "ToolBar Control Sample",
    WS_OVERLAPPEDWINDOW,
    rectDefault, NULL, MAKEINTRESOURCE(IDR_MAINFRAME) );
    xForm.eM11 = 1.0;
    xForm.eM12 = 0.0;
    xForm.eM21 = 0.0;
    xForm.eM22 = 1.0;
    xForm.eDx  = 0.0;
    xForm.eDy  = 0.0;
    iCurrentTransform = ORIGINAL;
    iPreviousTransform = ORIGINAL;
```

The toolbar control is created by calling the **Create** method and passing the style, position, parent, and control ID. The toolbar control automatically sets the size and position of the toolbar window. The height is based on the height of the buttons in the toolbar. The width is the same as the width of the parent window's client area. Where the toolbar control is positioned is determined by the style CCS_TOP or CCS_BOTTOM, which places the control either at the top or bottom of the client area, respectively.

```
    m_cmdtoolbar.Create(WS_BORDER | WS_VISIBLE | WS_CHILD
            | CCS_TOP, CRect(0,0,0,0),this, IDR_CMDTOOLBAR);
    m_cmdtoolbar.AutoSize();
```

```
}

CApp theApp;

BOOL CApp::InitInstance()
{
    m_pMainWnd = new CWindow();
    m_pMainWnd -> ShowWindow( m_nCmdShow );
    m_pMainWnd -> UpdateWindow();
    return TRUE;
}

// Paint the window
void CWindow::OnPaint()
{
    CPaintDC dc(this);
    // Change the pen and the brush
    CPen pen(PS_SOLID, 2, RGB(255,0,0));
    CBrush brush(RGB(255,0,0));
    dc.SelectObject(&pen);
    dc.SelectObject(&brush);

    SetGraphicsMode(dc.GetSafeHdc(), GM_ADVANCED);
    SetWorldTransform(dc.GetSafeHdc(), &xForm);
    // Create the polygon

    CPoint a[5];
    a[0] = CPoint(80,200);
    a[1] = CPoint(160,50);
    a[2] = CPoint(240,200);
    a[3] = CPoint(80,105);
    a[4] = CPoint(240,105);
    dc.SetPolyFillMode(ALTERNATE);
    dc.Polygon(a, 5);
    dc.Rectangle(80,220,240,300);
    dc.Ellipse(90,190,230,215);

}
```

Whenever the window is resized, the toolbar should also be resized. To react to the change in size, the **WM_SIZE** message is handled through the **OnSize** function. The message map indicates this with the ON_WM_SIZE macro. This function checks to see that the window is minimized and resets the size of the toolbar control to fit to the new window size by calling the **AutoSize** method.

```
void CWindow::OnSize(UINT Type, INT x, INT y )
{
    if (Type != SIZE_MINIMIZED)
        m_cmdtoolbar.AutoSize();
}
```

The application allows you to select the transformation by means of a menu, an accelerator key, or the toolbar button. When the selection is made through the toolbar control button, the selection is depicted by a pressed button. To simulate this when the selection is made through the menu, the **CheckButton** function is called when processing the appropriate menu command. The command identifier and the checked state (TRUE) are passed to the **CheckButton** function.

```
void CWindow::OnOriginal()
{
    sAngle = 0;
    xForm.eM11 = 1.0;
    xForm.eM12 = 0.0;
    xForm.eM21 = 0.0;
    xForm.eM22 = 1.0;
    xForm.eDx  = 0.0;
    xForm.eDy  = 0.0;
    iPreviousTransform = iCurrentTransform;
    iCurrentTransform = ORIGINAL;
    UncheckMenu();
    CheckMenu();
    m_cmdtoolbar.CheckButton(IDM_ORIGINAL, TRUE);
    Invalidate(TRUE);
}
void CWindow::OnRotate()
{
    iPreviousTransform = iCurrentTransform;
    iCurrentTransform = ROTATE;
    UncheckMenu();
    CheckMenu();
    m_cmdtoolbar.CheckButton(IDM_ROTATE, TRUE);
}
```

Sometimes it is clearer to show text below the toolbar buttons (called *button labels*), particularly when the meaning of the bitmaps is not obvious. This text can easily be added by providing the text to appear below the bitmap in the toolbar button structure. Do not confuse button labels with tooltips. Button labels, when included, are always present. Tooltips are shown only when the mouse pointer pauses over the button bitmap. Also, the available space for button labels is somewhat restricted compared to tooltips.

The **Create** function is modified to add this feature, and the change is highlighted in the code that follows. A buffer that contains an array of characters, which has the text that appears underneath the toolbar bitmap, is declared. The address of this string is given to **AddStrings**, which returns an integer that is given to the toolbar button structure.

```
BOOL CCmdToolBar::Create(DWORD dwStyle, const RECT& rect, CWnd* pParentWnd,
                         UINT nID )
{
    char ToolBarText[6][12] = {"Original\0", "Rotate\0", "Translate\0",
                               "Shear\0", "Reflect\0", "Scale\0"};
    BOOL bRet = CToolBarCtrl::Create(dwStyle, rect, pParentWnd, nID);
    m_nButtonCount = 6;
    AddBitmap(m_nButtonCount,IDR_CMDTOOLBAR);
    m_pTBButtons = new TBBUTTON[m_nButtonCount];

    for (int i = 0; i < m_nButtonCount; i++)
    {

        m_pTBButtons[i].iString = AddStrings(ToolBarText[i]);
        m_pTBButtons[i].fsState = TBSTATE_ENABLED;
        m_pTBButtons[i].fsStyle = TBSTYLE_BUTTON | TBSTYLE_CHECK |
                                  TBSTYLE_CHECKGROUP;
        m_pTBButtons[i].dwData = 0;
        m_pTBButtons[i].iBitmap = i;
        m_pTBButtons[i].idCommand = i + IDM_ORIGINAL;
    }
    AddButtons(m_nButtonCount,&m_pTBButtons[0]);
    return bRet;
}
```

Tooltips

A *tooltip* is a small text window that pops up when the mouse pointer pauses for about a second on a toolbar button (unless the mouse pointer was moved directly after displaying the tooltip of another button). The tooltip disappears when the mouse pointer is moved off the button. The text window typically displays a short description of the button. Tooltips enhance the user friendliness of your program, particularly if you opt to use a lot of icons that the users of your program may be unfamiliar with. To be consistent with Windows programming style, you may not want to wait for one second in your program, if the cursor was moved directly after displaying the tooltip of another button in the toolbar.

Tooltips can display static text windows, or you can dynamically change the text in the tooltip window according to the cursor position or selection. Figure 7-17 shows an example of a tooltip with static text. Figures 7-18 and 7-19 show examples of tooltips where the text changes dynamically according to the cursor position or selection.

Tooltips for the buttons in the toolbar control can be added as follows: The toolbar control is created with the TBSTYLE_TOOLTIPS style. This style lets the toolbar create

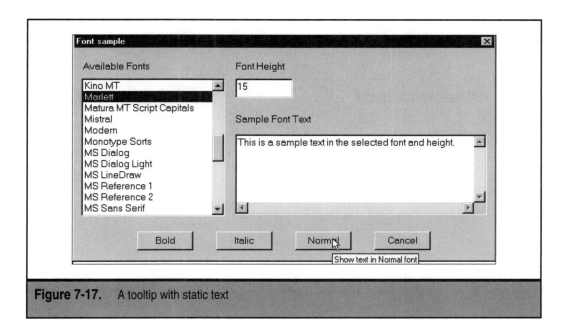

Figure 7-17.   A tooltip with static text

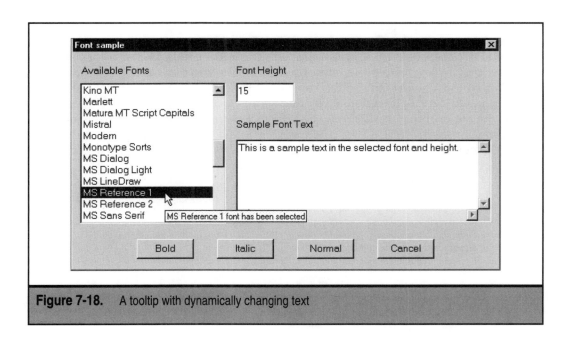

Figure 7-18.   A tooltip with dynamically changing text

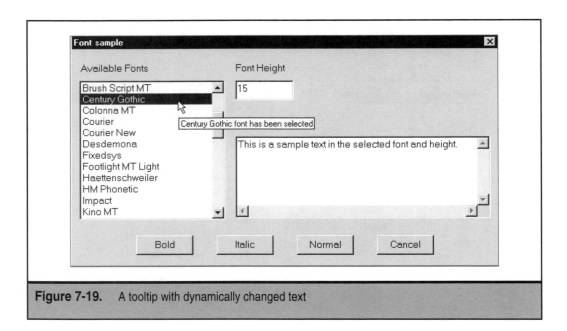

Figure 7-19. A tooltip with dynamically changed text

and manage a tooltip control. After this style is specified, the window should handle the tooltip notification message. The ON_NOTIFY_RANGE message macro is used to process the tooltip notification. The TTN_NEEDTEXT notification code is associated with the **WM_NOTIFY** message. Thus, when the tooltip control needs to display a tooltip, it would request the text from the window by sending a notification message. This message is handled by the function **OnToolBarToolTip** as indicated in the ON_NOTIFY_RANGE macro. Since the control ID generated by the notification message is not guaranteed to be unique, the range of control ID should be set to between zero and the toolbar control ID. Depending on the control ID specified in the notification message header structure **NMHDR**, the tooltip text is given to the tooltip control, which then displays it. Sections of the code added in *Wrldxform.cpp* to handle tooltips are highlighted next.

```
// Define the window class
class CWindow : public CFrameWnd
{
private:
        CCmdToolBar m_cmdtoolbar;
public:
    CWindow();
    afx_msg void OnPaint();
    afx_msg void OnSize(UINT, INT, INT);
    afx_msg void OnKeyUp(UINT, UINT, UINT);
    afx_msg void OnAppAbout();
    afx_msg void OnOriginal();
```

```
    afx_msg void OnRotate();
    afx_msg void OnTranslate();
    afx_msg void OnShear();
    afx_msg void OnReflect();
    afx_msg void OnScale();
    afx_msg void OnToolBarToolTip(UINT nID, NMHDR * pNotifyStruct,
                                  LRESULT * lResult);
    afx_msg void OnExit();
    void UncheckMenu();
    void CheckMenu();
    DECLARE_MESSAGE_MAP()
};


// CWindow
BEGIN_MESSAGE_MAP(CWindow, CFrameWnd)
    ON_WM_PAINT()
    ON_WM_SIZE()
    ON_WM_KEYUP()
    ON_COMMAND(ID_APP_ABOUT, OnAppAbout)
    ON_COMMAND(IDM_ORIGINAL, OnOriginal)
    ON_COMMAND(IDM_ROTATE, OnRotate)
    ON_COMMAND(IDM_TRANSLATE, OnTranslate)
    ON_COMMAND(IDM_SHEAR, OnShear)
    ON_COMMAND(IDM_REFLECT, OnReflect)
    ON_COMMAND(IDM_SCALE, OnScale)
    ON_COMMAND(ID_APP_EXIT, OnExit)
    ON_NOTIFY_RANGE( TTN_NEEDTEXT, 0, IDR_CMDTOOLBAR, OnToolBarToolTip)
END_MESSAGE_MAP()

//////////////////////////////////////////////////////////////////////
// CWindow construction
CWindow::CWindow()
{
    LoadAccelTable(MAKEINTRESOURCE(IDR_MAINFRAME));
    Create( NULL, "ToolBar Control Sample",
    WS_OVERLAPPEDWINDOW,
    rectDefault, NULL, MAKEINTRESOURCE(IDR_MAINFRAME) );
    xForm.eM11 = 1.0;
    xForm.eM12 = 0.0;
    xForm.eM21 = 0.0;
    xForm.eM22 = 1.0;
    xForm.eDx  = 0.0;
    xForm.eDy  = 0.0;
    iCurrentTransform = ORIGINAL;
    iPreviousTransform = ORIGINAL;

        m_cmdtoolbar.Create(WS_BORDER | WS_VISIBLE | WS_CHILD
                    | CCS_TOP | CCS_ADJUSTABLE | TBSTYLE_TOOLTIPS,
            CRect(0,0,0,0),this, IDR_CMDTOOLBAR);
```

```
            m_cmdtoolbar.AutoSize();

}


void CWindow::OnToolBarToolTip(UINT nID, NMHDR * pNotifyStruct,
                               LRESULT * lResult )
{
    switch (pNotifyStruct->idFrom)
    {
    case IDM_ORIGINAL:
        ((TOOLTIPTEXT *)pNotifyStruct)->lpszText = "Original - Return to initial
                                                    settings";
        break;
    case IDM_ROTATE:
        ((TOOLTIPTEXT *)pNotifyStruct)->lpszText = "Rotate - Use Up/Down arrow
                                                    keys to rotate";
        break;
    case IDM_TRANSLATE:
        ((TOOLTIPTEXT *)pNotifyStruct)->lpszText = "Translate - Use
                                                    Up/Down/Left/Right arrow
                                                    keys to translate";
        break;
    case IDM_SHEAR:
        ((TOOLTIPTEXT *)pNotifyStruct)->lpszText = "Shear - Use
                                                    Up/Down/Left/Right arrow
                                                    keys to shear";
        break;
    case IDM_REFLECT:
        ((TOOLTIPTEXT *)pNotifyStruct)->lpszText = "Refelect - Use
                                                    Up/Down/Left/Right arrow
                                                    keys to reflect";
        break;
    case IDM_SCALE:
        ((TOOLTIPTEXT *)pNotifyStruct)->lpszText = "Scale - Use
                                                    Up/Down/Left/Right arrow
                                                    keys to scale";
        break;
    }

}
```

You can add *tooltips* to make the program easier to use and to make it look more professional. An enhanced version of the font enumeration program including the tooltips is shown next. Previous Figures 7-17, 7-18, and 7-19 illustrate adding tooltips. You can add tooltips to many Windows user-interface components using the technique illustrated in the example to come.

The functioning of the tooltip control is shown by modifying the second Font sample program that was mentioned earlier. The function of the Font sample program remains the same, except that it now shows tooltips for all the controls in the dialog box. When the cursor is moved over various controls, tooltip text appears. The tooltip text is static for all controls except the Font list box, where the tooltip changes every time a new font is selected from the list box. Only the changes made to the Font sample program are highlighted here. The **CToolTipCtrl** class, which encapsulates the functionality of a tooltip control, is used in the sample program.

Shown next is the header file for the **CFontDlg** class. *Afxcmn.h,* the header file that defines **CToolTipCtrl**, is included. **CToolTipCtrl** member data is added to correspond to the tooltip control, and two member functions to show the tooltip are also added.

```
// FontDlg.h : header file
/////////////////////////////////////////////////////////////////////
// CFontDlg dialog
#include <afxcmn.h>
#include "Resource.h"

class CFontDlg : public CDialog
{
private:
        int       iFontFeature;   // 0 = Normal, 1 = Bold, 2 = Italics
        CFont     *psaveFont;
        CWnd      *pParentWnd;
        CListBox  m_ListBox;
        CEdit     m_MLE;
        CEdit     m_FontHeight;
        CToolTipCtrl m_ToolTips;

         void ChangeFont();
// Implementation
protected:
        // Generated message map functions
        virtual BOOL OnInitDialog();
        afx_msg void OnBold();
        afx_msg void OnItalic();
        afx_msg void OnNormal();
        virtual void DoDataExchange(CDataExchange* pDX);        // DDX/DDV
        virtual BOOL PreTranslateMessage(MSG* pMsg);
        BOOL OnToolTipNotify ( UINT id, NMHDR * pTTTStruct, LRESULT * pResult );
// Construction
public:
        CFontDlg(CWnd* pParent)
                : CDialog(IDD_FONTDLG, pParent)
                { pParentWnd = pParent;}
        ~CFontDlg();
DECLARE_MESSAGE_MAP()
};
```

The code that handles the Font dialog box is shown next. This code is similar to the font sample that was discussed earlier, and the changes made to add a tooltip are highlighted. To show the tooltip, a **CToolTipCtrl** is created and various tools are added. The **PreTranslateMessage** method is handled, and information is relayed to the tooltip control to show the tooltip text. If the tooltip text is dynamic, then the **TTN_NEEDTEXT** notification message is handled.

```
//********************************************************************
// This sample demonstrates the class/functions related to
// Fonts.  This module implements the font dialog class.
// FontDlg.cpp : implementation file

#include <afxwin.h>
#include <afxdlgs.h>
#include <afxcmn.h>
#include "FontDlg.h"
#include "Resource.h"

// Function declaration for EnumFontFamilies callback
int  CALLBACK EnumFontsProc(LPLOGFONT, LPTEXTMETRIC, DWORD, LONG) ;

BEGIN_MESSAGE_MAP(CFontDlg, CDialog)
        //{{AFX_MSG_MAP(CFontDlg)
        ON_BN_CLICKED(IDC_BOLD, OnBold)
        ON_BN_CLICKED(IDC_ITALIC, OnItalic)
        ON_BN_CLICKED(IDC_NORMAL, OnNormal)
        ON_NOTIFY_EX(TTN_NEEDTEXT, 0, OnToolTipNotify)
        //}}AFX_MSG_MAP
END_MESSAGE_MAP()
```

As part of enabling the tooltips, the **TTN_NEEDTEXT** message is handled by adding an entry in the message map. The ID of the tooltip is always 0. You'll see later in the code that the tooltip text for the list box control is requested by the system from the application. The system requests the tooltip text by sending this notification message. The system would call **OnToolTipNotify** to get the text.

```
/////////////////////////////////////////////////////////////////////
// CFontDlg message handlers

void CFontDlg::DoDataExchange(CDataExchange* pDX)
{
        CDialog::DoDataExchange(pDX);
        DDX_Control(pDX, IDC_FONTLIST, m_ListBox );
        DDX_Control(pDX, IDC_FONTHEIGHT, m_FontHeight);
        DDX_Control(pDX, IDC_MLE, m_MLE);
}
/////////////////////////////////////////////////////////////////////
// CFontDlg dialog

int CALLBACK EnumFontsProc (LPLOGFONT lplf, LPTEXTMETRIC lptm, DWORD dwStyle,
```

```
                          LONG lParam)
{
        CListBox        *pLBox;
        pLBox = (CListBox *)lParam;
        pLBox->AddString((LPCTSTR)lplf->lfFaceName);
        return 1;
}


/////////////////////////////////////////////////////////////////////////
// CFontDlg message handlers
BOOL CFontDlg::OnInitDialog()
{
    CDC *hdc;
    CFont    *defaultFont;
    LOGFONT lf;

    CDialog::OnInitDialog();
    psaveFont = NULL;
```

In the next section **CToolTipCtrl** is created, and the tools are added to the tooltip control. For all controls except the list box, static text is used for the tooltip. For the list box tooltip, the goal is to show which font has been selected. Since this is dynamic text, the value LPSTR_TEXTCALLBACK is given. When the mouse pointer moves over the list box control, a **TTN_NEEDTEXT** notification message is sent to the parent of the list box control window. The handling of this message will be discussed later in this chapter. The delay between the time the mouse pointer moves over the control and the time the tooltip text appears can be set by calling the **SetDelayTime** member function. It is set to 50 milliseconds here. The default is 500 milliseconds. The length of time to display the tool text can be controlled by sending a **TTM_SETDELAYTIME** message to the tooltip control and specifying the delay time in milliseconds. Here it is set to SHRT_MAX milliseconds, which is approximately 33 seconds. Since **CToolTipCtrl** is derived from **CWnd** class, the member functions of **CWnd** can be used to change other attributes of the tooltip text and window like font, color, and so on.

```
m_ToolTips.Create(this);
        m_ToolTips.AddTool (&m_FontHeight, "Type in the font height");
        m_ToolTips.AddTool (&m_ListBox,  LPSTR_TEXTCALLBACK);
        m_ToolTips.AddTool (&m_MLE, "You may type your own text");
        m_ToolTips.AddTool (GetDlgItem(IDC_BOLD), "Show text in Bold font");
        m_ToolTips.AddTool (GetDlgItem(IDC_ITALIC), "Show text in Italic font");
        m_ToolTips.AddTool (GetDlgItem(IDC_NORMAL), "Show text in Normal font");
        m_ToolTips.AddTool (GetDlgItem(IDCANCEL), "Close the dialog box");
        m_ToolTips.SetDelayTime(50);
        m_ToolTips.SendMessage(TTM_SETDELAYTIME, TTDT_AUTOPOP, SHRT_MAX);

        hdc = pParentWnd->GetDC();
        EnumFontFamilies(hdc->GetSafeHdc(), (LPSTR)NULL,
                        (FONTENUMPROC) EnumFontsProc, (LONG)&m_ListBox);
```

```
        ReleaseDC(hdc);

        defaultFont = m_MLE.GetFont();  // Get the default font for the edit
                                        // control
        defaultFont->GetLogFont(&lf);   // Get the pointer to the logfont
        m_ListBox.SelectString(0, lf.lfFaceName); // Select the default font in
                                                  // the list box.
        SetDlgItemInt(IDC_FONTHEIGHT, -lf.lfHeight, FALSE);
        m_MLE.LimitText(256);
        m_MLE.SetWindowText((LPCTSTR)"This is sample text in the selected font
                                     and height.");
    return TRUE;  // return TRUE unless you set the focus to a control
}
```

When the tooltip for the list box is needed, a **TTN_NEEDTEXT** notification message is sent. It is handled by the **OnToolTipNotify** function shown next. The first parameter, *id*, is the control ID associated with the **WM_NOTIFY** message; since this ID is not unique, it is not used. The ID is taken from the NMHDR structure. If it is a handle to the window, the control is queried by calling the **GetDlgCtrlID** function and passing the handle to the window. Given this control ID, the tooltip text is decided. In this example we have only one control that would request the tooltip. So this text is created by finding out which font has been selected and appending a textual string. Either the pointer to the string can be sent in *lpszText*, or the string can be copied in *szText*—provided it can fit in 80 bytes. Since in this example the text will be less than 80 bytes, it is copied in the *szText* buffer.

```
BOOL CFontDlg::OnToolTipNotify ( UINT id, NMHDR * pNMHDR, LRESULT * pResult )
{
TOOLTIPTEXT *pTTT = (TOOLTIPTEXT *) pNMHDR;

   UINT nID =pNMHDR->idFrom;
   if ((pTTT->uFlags & TTF_IDISHWND))
     {
     nID = ::GetDlgCtrlID((HWND)nID);
     if(nID)
      {
      char     szFontFace[80];
      int index = m_ListBox.GetCurSel();
      m_ListBox.GetText(index, szFontFace);
      strcat (szFontFace, " font has been selected");
      pTTT->lpszText = szFontFace;
      return (TRUE);
      }
     }
return (FALSE);
}
```

Finally, the **PreTranslateMessage** method overrides the default handling. The **RelayEvent** method of the tooltip control is called to handle mouse button moves (up, down, dragging). This method triggers the display of the tooltips for the control. If the tooltip control already has the tooltip text, it will display; if not, it will send a notification message.

```
BOOL CFontDlg::PreTranslateMessage(MSG * pMsg)
{
  switch(pMsg->message)
  {
    case WM_LBUTTONDOWN:
    case WM_RBUTTONDOWN:
    case WM_MBUTTONDOWN:
    case WM_LBUTTONUP:
    case WM_MBUTTONUP:
    case WM_RBUTTONUP:
    case WM_MOUSEMOVE:
        m_ToolTips.RelayEvent(pMsg);
        break;
  }
  return CDialog::PreTranslateMessage(pMsg);
}


void CFontDlg::ChangeFont()
{
        char    newFace[LF_FACESIZE];
        int     index;
        int     iFontSize;
        CFont   *poldFont;
        CFont   *pnewFont;
        LOGFONT lf;

        pnewFont = new CFont ();
        memset (&lf, 0, sizeof(LOGFONT));
        poldFont = m_MLE.GetFont();
        poldFont->GetLogFont(&lf);

        index = m_ListBox.GetCurSel();
        m_ListBox.GetText(index, newFace);

        strcpy (lf.lfFaceName, newFace);
        if (iFontFeature == 1)
        {
        lf.lfWeight = FW_BOLD;
        lf.lfItalic = FALSE;
        }
```

```
      else if (iFontFeature == 2)
      {
      lf.lfWeight = FW_NORMAL;
      lf.lfItalic = TRUE;
      }
      else
      {
      lf.lfWeight = FW_NORMAL;
      lf.lfItalic = FALSE;
      }
      iFontSize = GetDlgItemInt(IDC_FONTHEIGHT, NULL, FALSE);
      if (iFontSize <= 0)
            iFontSize = 10;
      lf.lfHeight = -iFontSize;
      pnewFont->CreateFontIndirect(&lf);

      m_MLE.SetFont(pnewFont, TRUE);
      if (psaveFont)
            delete psaveFont;
      psaveFont = pnewFont;

}

void CFontDlg::OnBold()
{
      iFontFeature = 1;
      ChangeFont ();
}

void CFontDlg::OnItalic()
{
      iFontFeature = 2;
      ChangeFont ();
}

void CFontDlg::OnNormal()
{
      iFontFeature = 3;
      ChangeFont ();
}


CFontDlg::~CFontDlg()
{
      delete psaveFont;
}
```

PROPERTY SHEETS

A *property sheet* allows the user to view and update properties associated with an item. A property sheet is used when an item's properties won't fit in one dialog box. In this case, you can use a series of dialog boxes, with each dialog box containing logically related properties. Each dialog box is a page or sheet of the item's properties and is identified and selected by a tab associated with it. A sample property sheet is shown in Figure 7-20.

You can consider a property sheet as being a collection of one or more child windows, each window being a modeless dialog box. That is, each page in a property sheet is defined by a dialog box template, and interaction with the page is handled by a dialog function. Each dialog box template is specified in your application's resource file.

All property sheets contain the OK and Cancel buttons at a minimum. Usually a third button, Apply, is also included. Depending on your application, a Help button may also be included. Keep in mind that the individual pages are just part of the overall property sheet. Items in one page of the property sheet may be related to items on another page, and the item settings on one page may affect another. Thus, you use the OK, Cancel, and Apply buttons at the overall property sheet level and not at the individual page level.

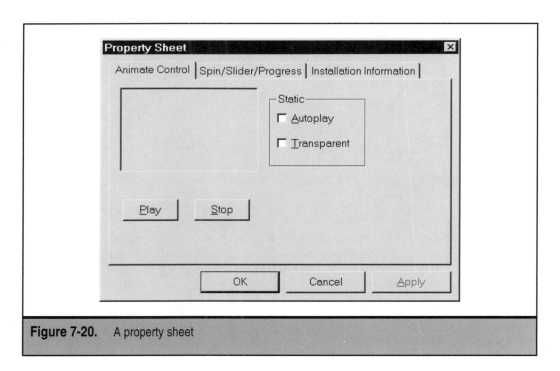

Figure 7-20. A property sheet

The dialog boxes that constitute the property sheet pages are part of the Property Sheet control. The Property Sheet control manages interaction with and between the individual pages. As a general rule, each dialog box function responds to its own controls in the normal fashion. That is, the individual controls that make up each page are handled in the standard way by the page's dialog box function. However, each page must also respond to messages generated by the enclosing property sheet.

A Property Sheet Programming Example

The *PropSheet* sample program shows how to use the property sheet by use of the **CPropertySheet** and **CPropertyPage** MFC library classes. The sample also shows how easy it is to convert a set of individual dialog boxes into property pages in a property sheet dialog box. To this end it takes the samples discussed earlier, *Animate* and *SpSlProg*, and a third dialog box as pages in a property sheet dialog box. When the program is run and the Property Sheet menu item is selected from the File menu, the property sheet dialog box with three tabs is displayed. When the information in the third dialog box is changed, the Apply button is enabled. When the OK button is clicked, a message box is displayed indicating the selection made in the third page.

The main program closely follows the structure discussed in earlier examples. Shown next is the code in the main section that is executed when the Property Sheet menu item is selected.

```
////////////////////////////////////////////////////////////
// CWindow commands
// App command to run the dialog

// Property Sheet Dialog selected
void CWindow::OnPropShDlg()
{
        CPropShDlg propshDlg("Property Sheet", this);
        propshDlg.DoModal();
}
```

Some trivial changes have been made to the *Animate* and *SpSlProg* dialog resources to suit this example. A third dialog box resource has been added, and this resource is shown next. This dialog box will form the third and last page of the property sheet. This page is a simple page that obtains path, drive, and version information selected by means of radio buttons.

```
IDD_INSTALLINFO DIALOG DISCARDABLE 0, 0, 185, 92
STYLE DS_MODALFRAME | WS_POPUP | WS_VISIBLE | WS_CAPTION | WS_SYSMENU
CAPTION "Installation Information"
FONT 8, "MS Sans Serif"
BEGIN
    LTEXT    "Path",IDC_STATIC,7,16,16,8
```

```
    LTEXT    "Drive",IDC_STATIC,7,32,18,8
    EDITTEXT IDC_PATH,35,13,40,14,ES_AUTOHSCROLL
    EDITTEXT IDC_DRIVE,36,31,40,14,ES_AUTOHSCROLL
    GROUPBOX "Version",IDC_STATIC,93,7,64,54
    CONTROL  "Win95",IDC_95,"Button",BS_AUTORADIOBUTTON,102,18,39,10
    CONTROL  "Win NT",IDC_NT,"Button",BS_AUTORADIOBUTTON,102,30,41,10
END
```

The dialog captions appear as the default tab text for individual tabs. The code for the individual property page is very similar to the dialog box code that was discussed earlier. The difference is that instead of deriving the dialog from the **CDialog** class, the property pages are derived from **CPropertyPage**. The code for the last property page is shown next. As before, this code was generated with the aid of ClassWizard. The only thing to note here is that **CInstalInfoDlg** is derived from **CPropertyPage** instead of the usual **CDialog**.

```
// InstalInfoDlg.h : header file
//
// CInstalInfoDlg dialog
class CInstalInfoDlg : public CPropertyPage
{
        DECLARE_DYNCREATE(CInstalInfoDlg)
// Construction
public:
        CInstalInfoDlg();
        ~CInstalInfoDlg();

// Dialog Data
        //{{AFX_DATA(CInstalInfoDlg)
        enum { IDD = IDD_INSTALLINFO };
        CString m_drive;
        CString m_path;
        int     m_version;        // 0-Win95, 1 = WinNT
        //}}AFX_DATA
// Overrides
        // ClassWizard generate virtual function overrides
        //{{AFX_VIRTUAL(CInstalInfoDlg)
        public:
        virtual BOOL OnApply();
        protected:
        virtual void DoDataExchange(CDataExchange* pDX);// DDX/DDV support
        //}}AFX_VIRTUAL

// Implementation
protected:
        // Generated message map functions
        //{{AFX_MSG(CInstalInfoDlg)
        afx_msg void OnPathChange();
        afx_msg void OnNt();
```

```
        afx_msg void On95();
        //}}AFX_MSG
        DECLARE_MESSAGE_MAP()
};
```

The code that implements the **CInstalInfoDlg** class is shown next:

```
// InstalInfoDlg.cpp : implementation file
//
#include <afxwin.h>
#include <afxdlgs.h>
#include <afxcmn.h>
#include "resource.h"
#include "InstalInfoDlg.h"
////
// CInstalInfoDlg property page

IMPLEMENT_DYNCREATE(CInstalInfoDlg, CPropertyPage)

CInstalInfoDlg::CInstalInfoDlg() : CPropertyPage(CInstalInfoDlg::IDD)
{
        //{{AFX_DATA_INIT(CInstalInfoDlg)
        m_drive = _T("");
        m_path = _T("");
        m_version = 0;
        //}}AFX_DATA_INIT
}
```

Apart from loading the resource, the constructor does some initialization of the member variables.

```
CInstalInfoDlg::~CInstalInfoDlg()
{
}

void CInstalInfoDlg::DoDataExchange(CDataExchange* pDX)
{
        CPropertyPage::DoDataExchange(pDX);
        //{{AFX_DATA_MAP(CInstalInfoDlg)
        DDX_Text(pDX, IDC_DRIVE, m_drive);
        DDV_MaxChars(pDX, m_drive, 1);
        DDX_Text(pDX, IDC_PATH, m_path);
        DDV_MaxChars(pDX, m_path, 32);
        //}}AFX_DATA_MAP
}
```

Unlike in earlier samples, the dialog data exchange is done at the text level, and dialog data validation is done for both Edit controls for the number of characters that can be entered. Here the Drive Edit control is set to accept only one character, and the Path Edit control is set to accept 32 characters.

```
BEGIN_MESSAGE_MAP(CInstalInfoDlg, CPropertyPage)
        //{{AFX_MSG_MAP(CInstalInfoDlg)
        ON_EN_CHANGE(IDC_PATH, OnPathChange)
        ON_BN_CLICKED(IDC_NT, OnNt)
        ON_BN_CLICKED(IDC_95, On95)
        //}}AFX_MSG_MAP
END_MESSAGE_MAP()
///////////////////////////////////////////////////////////////////////////
// CInstalInfoDlg message handlers

void CInstalInfoDlg::OnPathChange()
{
        // TODO: Add your control notification handler code here
        SetModified(TRUE);    // This page has been modified
}

void CInstalInfoDlg::OnNt()
{
        // TODO: Add your control notification handler code here
        m_version = 1;
        SetModified(TRUE);    // This page has been modified
}

void CInstalInfoDlg::On95()
{
        // TODO: Add your control notification handler code here
        m_version = 0;
        SetModified(TRUE);    // This page has been modified
}
```

The property sheet has OK, Cancel, and Apply buttons. It is the responsibility of the individual property page to inform the property sheet whether data inside the page has changed. When a property page becomes "dirty" (the user has made changes to the property page), it can indicate this fact to the property sheet by calling the **SetModified** member function and passing a value of TRUE. In the code earlier, whenever the Path, Drive, or Version radio buttons are changed, it indicates that the page has become dirty by calling **SetModified**.

The **OnApply** member function, which is overridden here, is called by the framework when the user chooses the OK or Apply button. When these buttons are clicked, the **OnApply** method is called only for those pages that are dirty. Again a page can indicate that it is dirty by calling the **SetModified** member function and passing a value of TRUE. In the code next, it displays a message box indicating the selection made in the page and resets the dirty page by calling **SetModified** and passing a value of FALSE. It also returns TRUE to accept changes. Return FALSE to prevent changes from taking effect.

```
BOOL CInstalInfoDlg::OnApply()
{
        // TODO: Add your specialized code here and/or call the base class
        // UpdateData() would have been called automatically by the framework
        CString     message;
        message = m_drive + ":\\" + m_path;
        if (m_version == 1)
        {
            message = "NT Version to be installed at " + message;
        }
        else
        {
            message = "Win95 Version to be installed at " + message;
        }
        AfxMessageBox(message);
        SetModified(FALSE);
        return CPropertyPage::OnApply();
}
```

So far the property page has been discussed. Shown next is the code for the Property Sheet dialog box, which derives from **CPropertySheet**. For each page in the property sheet a member variable is defined that corresponds to the respective dialog class.

```
//////////////////////////////////////////////////////////////////
// CPropShDlg

#include "AnimateDlg.h"
#include "SpSlProgDlg.h"
#include "InstalInfoDlg.h"

class CPropShDlg : public CPropertySheet
{
        DECLARE_DYNAMIC(CPropShDlg)

// Construction
public:
        CPropShDlg(LPCTSTR pszCaption, CWnd* pParentWnd = NULL,
                UINT iSelectPage = 0);

// Attributes
public:

        CAnimateDlg         m_animatedlg;
        CSpSlProgDlg      m_spslprogdlg;
        CInstalInfoDlg      m_installinfodlg;

// Operations
public:
```

```
// Overrides
        // ClassWizard generated virtual function overrides
        //{{AFX_VIRTUAL(CPropShDlg)
        //}}AFX_VIRTUAL

// Implementation
public:
        virtual ~CPropShDlg();
        virtual BOOL OnInitDialog();
        virtual void OnOK();

// Generated message map functions
protected:

        DECLARE_MESSAGE_MAP()
};
```

The code that implements this class is shown next. During construction of the class, the three pages are added to the property sheet by use of the **AddPage** method. Though it is defaulted here to the first page, the property sheet can be initialized such that any page is seen on top when the property sheet is shown.

```
// PropShDlg.cpp : implementation file
//
#include <afxwin.h>
#include <afxdlgs.h>
#include <afxcmn.h>
#include "resource.h"
#include "PropShDlg.h"


/////////////////////////////////////////////////////////////////////////
// CPropShDlg

IMPLEMENT_DYNAMIC(CPropShDlg, CPropertySheet)

CPropShDlg::CPropShDlg(LPCTSTR pszCaption, CWnd* pParentWnd, UINT iSelectPage)
        :CPropertySheet(pszCaption, pParentWnd, iSelectPage)
{
        AddPage(&m_animatedlg);
        AddPage(&m_spslprogdlg);
        AddPage(&m_installinfodlg);
}

CPropShDlg::~CPropShDlg()
{
}


BEGIN_MESSAGE_MAP(CPropShDlg, CPropertySheet)
```

```
        //{{AFX_MSG_MAP(CPropShDlg)
        //}}AFX_MSG_MAP
END_MESSAGE_MAP()

/////////////////////////////////////////////////////////////////////////
// CPropShDlg message handlers

BOOL CPropShDlg::OnInitDialog()
{
        return CPropertySheet::OnInitDialog();
}

void CPropShDlg::OnOK()
{
    AfxMessageBox("The results are ");
}
```

Many software installation programs display a series of dialog panels one after the other within the same dialog frame, giving the user the ability to go to a previous page or to proceed to the next page. This is accomplished through the Property Sheet dialog box by setting it to wizard mode. Call **SetWizardMode** before calling **DoModal**. The buttons that appear can also be customized by calling **SetWizardButtons**. Notice that when running in wizard mode, **DoModal** will return ID_WIZFINISH if the user closes with the Finish button or IDCANCEL.

TREE VIEW CONTROL

Tree View controls use a tree structure to display information. For example, the file list used by Windows NT's Explorer is an example of a Tree View control. Because trees imply a hierarchy, Tree View controls are typically used to display hierarchical information. They support a large number of different options. Each item in the tree can have associated images (bitmaps) or text that is displayed to the user when the Tree View control is displayed (see Figure 7-21).

The Tree View control uses the **TVINSERTSTRUCT** (formerly the **TV_INSERTSTRUCT**) and **TVITEM** (formerly the **TV_ITEM**) data structures shown next. These structures are used in the example.

```
typedef struct tagTVINSERTSTRUCT {
    HTREEITEM hParent;
    HTREEITEM hInsertAfter;
#if (_WIN32_IE >= 0x0400)
    union
    {
        TVITEMEX itemex;
        TVITEM item;
    } DUMMYUNIONNAME;
#else
```

```
      TVITEM item;
#endif
} TVINSERTSTRUCT, FAR *LPTVINSERTSTRUCT;



typedef struct tagTVITEM{
    UINT        mask;
    HTREEITEM   hItem;
    UINT        state;
    UINT        stateMask;
    LPTSTR      pszText;
    int         cchTextMax;
    int         iImage;
    int         iSelectedImage;
    int         cChildren;
    LPARAM      lParam;
} TVITEM, FAR *LPTVITEM;
```

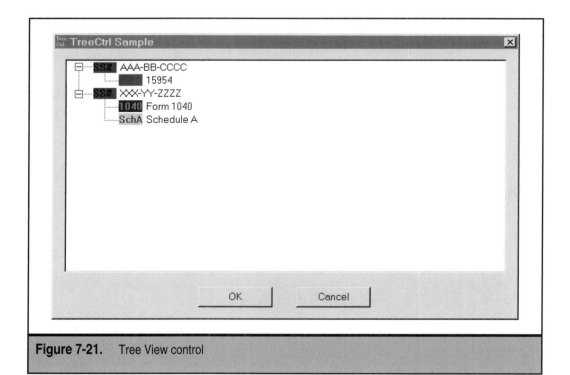

Figure 7-21.   Tree View control

Here, the values in *mask* determine which of the other members of **TV_ITEM** contain valid data when this structure receives information from the Tree View control.

The values that it may contain are shown here:

Mask Value	Meaning
TVIF_HANDLE	*hItem* contains data
TVIF_STATE	*state* and *stateMask* contain data
TVIF_TEXT	*PszText* and *cchTextMax* contain data
TVIF_IMAGE	*IImage* contains data
TVIF_SELECTEDIMAGE	*ISelectedImage* contains data
TVIF_CHILDREN	*CChildren* contains data
TVIF_LPARAM	*LParam* contains data

The *state* member contains the state of the Tree View control. Here are some common tree *state* values:

State Value	Meaning
TVIS_DROPHILITED	The item is highlighted as the target of drag/drop operation.
TVIS_EXPANDED	The branch descending from the item is fully expanded (applies to parent items only).
TVIS_EXPANDEDONCE	The branch descending from the item is expanded one (or more) levels (applies to parent items only).
TVIS_SELECTED	The item is selected.

The *stateMask* variable determines which tab state to set or obtain. It will also be one or more of the preceding values.

When an item is being inserted into the tree, *pszText* points to the string that will be displayed in the tree. When information about an item is being obtained, *pszText* must point to an array that will receive its text. In this case, the value of *cchTextMax* specifies the size of the array pointed to by *pszText*. Otherwise, *cchTextMax* is ignored.

If there is an image list associated with the Tree View control, then *iImage* will contain the index of the image associated with the item when it is not selected. *iImageSelected* contains the index of the image used by the item when it is selected.

cChildren will contain 1 if the item has child items and zero if it does not.

lParam contains application-defined data.

A Tree View Control Programming Example

The TreeCtrl sample program shows how to use the Tree View control by use of the **CTreeCtrl** MFC library class. The sample is a dialog-based application that displays a dialog box with a Tree View control inside. It takes a tax filing example, where it displays two tax filers—one filing a 1040EZ and the other filing the long form 1040 and a Schedule A form. Each person is identified by his or her social security number. When the application starts, it displays two icons—one for each taxpayer. They are identified by their social security numbers. When these icons are expanded by clicking them, they show their respective tax returns. These icons can also be opened by double-clicking, which then displays the details of the icons selected. For example, if the 1040EZ icon were opened, it would show the details of the 1040EZ form, and so on. Changes could be made to the forms and saved.

This hierarchical structure exists in many business applications. For instance, it could be employed in user administration in a LAN environment, where users and groups could be represented this way, or an organization chart could be represented this way.

The template code for this sample was generated by use of AppWizard and ClassWizard. The main application code is slightly different from the earlier samples that we saw. Here the dialog box containing the Tree View control is created and assigned as the main window for the application. The main application class header file and the class implementation code are shown next. You can ignore some of the details that were added by the AppWizard.

```
// TreeCtrl.h : main header file for the TREECTRL application
//
#ifndef __AFXWIN_H__
    #error include 'stdafx.h' before including this file for PCH
#endif
#include "resource.h"        // main symbols
/////////////////////////////////////////////////////////////////////////
// CApp:
// See TreeCtrl.cpp for the implementation of this class
//
class CApp : public CWinApp
{
public:
    CApp();
// Overrides
    // ClassWizard generated virtual function overrides
    //{{AFX_VIRTUAL(CApp)
    public:
    virtual BOOL InitInstance();
    //}}AFX_VIRTUAL
```

```
// Implementation
    //{{AFX_MSG(CApp)
        // NOTE-the ClassWizard will add and remove member functions here.
        //      DO NOT EDIT what you see in these blocks of generated code!
    //}}AFX_MSG
    DECLARE_MESSAGE_MAP()
};

// TreeCtrl.cpp : Defines the class behaviors for the application.
//
#include "stdafx.h"
#include "TreeCtrl.h"
#include "TreeCtrlDlg.h"

#ifdef _DEBUG
#define new DEBUG_NEW
#undef THIS_FILE
static char THIS_FILE[] = __FILE__;
#endif

/////////////////////////////////////////////////////////////////////////////
// CApp

BEGIN_MESSAGE_MAP(CApp, CWinApp)
    //{{AFX_MSG_MAP(CApp)
        // NOTE-the ClassWizard will add and remove mapping macros here.
        //      DO NOT EDIT what you see in these blocks of generated code!
    //}}AFX_MSG
    ON_COMMAND(ID_HELP, CWinApp::OnHelp)
END_MESSAGE_MAP()

/////////////////////////////////////////////////////////////////////////////
// CApp construction

CApp::CApp()
{
    // TODO: add construction code here,
    // Place all significant initialization in InitInstance
}

/////////////////////////////////////////////////////////////////////////////
// The one and only CApp object

CApp theApp;

/////////////////////////////////////////////////////////////////////////////
// CApp initialization

BOOL CApp::InitInstance()
```

```
{
    // Standard initialization
    // If you are not using these features and wish to reduce the size
    //  of your final executable, you should remove from the following
    //  the specific initialization routines you do not need.

#ifdef _AFXDLL
    Enable3dControls();             // Call this when using MFC in a shared DLL
#else
    Enable3dControlsStatic();       // Call this when linking to MFC statically
#endif

    CTreeCtrlDlg dlg;
    m_pMainWnd = &dlg;
    int nResponse = dlg.DoModal();
```

The code creates the Tree View control dialog box and assigns it as the application's main window. It then runs the dialog modally. In this sample it does not do much when the dialog box is closed. But if, for example, the data were loaded from a database, then you may want to commit the data to the database, depending on what the user selected in the dialog box.

```
if (nResponse == IDOK)
    {
        // TODO: Place code here to handle when the dialog is
        //  dismissed with OK
    }
    else if (nResponse == IDCANCEL)
    {
        // TODO: Place code here to handle when the dialog is
        //  dismissed with Cancel
    }

    // Since the dialog has been closed, return FALSE so that we exit the
    //  application, rather than start the application's message pump.
    return FALSE;
}
```

The dialog resource for the dialog box is given next. Notice that the style of the Tree View control is specified right in the resource. It indicates that the Tree View control has lines linking the child items to the parent items, has lines linking child items to the root of the hierarchy, and adds a button to the left of each parent item. These styles can be modified and rebuilt. These styles can also be set dynamically.

```
IDD_TREECTRL_DIALOG DIALOGEX 0, 0, 311, 185
STYLE DS_MODALFRAME | WS_POPUP | WS_VISIBLE | WS_CAPTION | WS_SYSMENU
EXSTYLE WS_EX_APPWINDOW
CAPTION "TreeCtrl Sample"
FONT 8, "MS Sans Serif", 0, 0, 0x1
```

```
BEGIN
    DEFPUSHBUTTON       "OK",IDOK,97,164,50,14
    PUSHBUTTON          "Cancel",IDCANCEL,163,164,50,14
    CONTROL             "Tree1",IDC_TREE,"SysTreeView32",WS_BORDER | WS_TABSTOP |
                        TVS_HASLINES | TVS_LINESATROOT | TVS_HASBUTTONS |
                        TVS_DISABLEDRAGDROP, 7,7,297,147
END
```

The **CTreeCtrlDlg** class declaration is shown next. This is similar to samples that were seen earlier.

```cpp
// TreeCtrlDlg.h : header file
//
/////////////////////////////////////////////////////////////////////////////
// CTreeCtrlDlg dialog
class CTreeCtrlDlg : public CDialog
{
// Construction
public:
    CTreeCtrlDlg(CWnd* pParent = NULL);    // standard constructor

// Dialog Data
    //{{AFX_DATA(CTreeCtrlDlg)
    enum { IDD = IDD_TREECTRL_DIALOG };
    CTreeCtrl    m_treectrl;
    //}}AFX_DATA

    // ClassWizard generated virtual function overrides
    //{{AFX_VIRTUAL(CTreeCtrlDlg)
    protected:
    virtual void DoDataExchange(CDataExchange* pDX);// DDX/DDV support
    //}}AFX_VIRTUAL

// Implementation
protected:
    HICON m_hIcon;

    // Generated message map functions
    //{{AFX_MSG(CTreeCtrlDlg)
    virtual BOOL OnInitDialog();
    afx_msg void OnSysCommand(UINT nID, LPARAM lParam);
    afx_msg void OnPaint();
    afx_msg HCURSOR OnQueryDragIcon();
    afx_msg void OnDblclkTree(NMHDR* pNMHDR, LRESULT* pResult);
    afx_msg void OnDestroy();
    void FreeItem(HTREEITEM hTVItem);
    //}}AFX_MSG
    DECLARE_MESSAGE_MAP()
private:
```

```
        void AddDataToTree(HTREEITEM hParent, int iType, char * pszText,
        LPARAM lpItemData, HTREEITEM *it);
};
```

The code for the **CTreeCtrlDlg** is shown next. The initial section of the code deals with information needed in the rest of the code, including the **#defines**, the processing of the About box, and so on.

```
// TreeCtrlDlg.cpp : implementation file
//
#include "stdafx.h"
#include "TreeCtrl.h"
#include "TreeCtrlDlg.h"
#include "resource.h"
#include "TaxData.h"
#include "TaxPayer.h"
#include "Tax1040.h"
#include "EZ1040.h"
#include "SchA.h"

#ifdef _DEBUG
#define new DEBUG_NEW
#undef THIS_FILE
static char THIS_FILE[] = __FILE__;
#endif


#define BASE_BITMAP_ID   IDB_BITMAP1
#define TAXPAYER    0
#define FORMSTD     1
#define FORMSCHA    2
#define FORMEZ      3


///////////////////////////////////////////////////////////////////////
// CAboutDlg dialog used for App About

class CAboutDlg : public CDialog
{
public:
        CAboutDlg();

// Dialog Data
        //{{AFX_DATA(CAboutDlg)
        enum { IDD = IDD_ABOUTBOX };
        //}}AFX_DATA

        // ClassWizard generated virtual function overrides
        //{{AFX_VIRTUAL(CAboutDlg)
        protected:
```

```
        virtual void DoDataExchange(CDataExchange* pDX);// DDX/DDV support
        //}}AFX_VIRTUAL

// Implementation
protected:
        //{{AFX_MSG(CAboutDlg)
        //}}AFX_MSG
        DECLARE_MESSAGE_MAP()
};

CAboutDlg::CAboutDlg() : CDialog(CAboutDlg::IDD)
{
        //{{AFX_DATA_INIT(CAboutDlg)
        //}}AFX_DATA_INIT
}

void CAboutDlg::DoDataExchange(CDataExchange* pDX)
{
        CDialog::DoDataExchange(pDX);
        //{{AFX_DATA_MAP(CAboutDlg)
        //}}AFX_DATA_MAP
}

BEGIN_MESSAGE_MAP(CAboutDlg, CDialog)
        //{{AFX_MSG_MAP(CAboutDlg)
                // No message handlers
        //}}AFX_MSG_MAP
END_MESSAGE_MAP()

/////////////////////////////////////////////////////////////////////////
// CTreeCtrlDlg dialog

CTreeCtrlDlg::CTreeCtrlDlg(CWnd* pParent /*=NULL*/)
        : CDialog(CTreeCtrlDlg::IDD, pParent)
{
        //{{AFX_DATA_INIT(CTreeCtrlDlg)
        // NOTE: the ClassWizard will add member initialization here
        //}}AFX_DATA_INIT
        // Note that LoadIcon does not require a subsequent
        // DestroyIcon in Win32
        m_hIcon = AfxGetApp()->LoadIcon(IDR_MAINFRAME);
}


void CTreeCtrlDlg::DoDataExchange(CDataExchange* pDX)
{
        CDialog::DoDataExchange(pDX);
        //{{AFX_DATA_MAP(CTreeCtrlDlg)
        DDX_Control(pDX, IDC_TREE, m_treectrl);
        //}}AFX_DATA_MAP
```

```
}

BEGIN_MESSAGE_MAP(CTreeCtrlDlg, CDialog)
        //{{AFX_MSG_MAP(CTreeCtrlDlg)
        ON_WM_SYSCOMMAND()
        ON_WM_PAINT()
        ON_WM_QUERYDRAGICON()
        ON_NOTIFY(NM_DBLCLK, IDC_TREE, OnDblclkTree)
        ON_WM_DESTROY()
    //}}AFX_MSG_MAP
END_MESSAGE_MAP()


//////////////////////////////////////////////////////////////////////
// CTreeCtrlDlg message handlers
```

The code that follows does the initialization on the **CTreeCtrlDlg** dialog box. Since this sample is a dialog-based application, the About menu item is added to the system menu. The advantage of code generation by use of AppWizard is that the code is automatically generated for the user.

During initialization the program creates various objects that are to be placed in the Tree View control. In this sample these objects are created and given to the Tree View control. In practical applications these objects would likely be queried from a database and created. Five objects of four kinds are created, and their data is initialized.

```
BOOL CTreeCtrlDlg::OnInitDialog()
{
        CDialog::OnInitDialog();

        // Add "About..." menu item to system menu.
        // IDM_ABOUTBOX must be in the system command range.
        ASSERT((IDM_ABOUTBOX & 0xFFF0) == IDM_ABOUTBOX);
        ASSERT(IDM_ABOUTBOX < 0xF000);

        CMenu* pSysMenu = GetSystemMenu(FALSE);
        CString strAboutMenu;
        strAboutMenu.LoadString(IDS_ABOUTBOX);
        if (!strAboutMenu.IsEmpty())
        {
                pSysMenu->AppendMenu(MF_SEPARATOR);
                pSysMenu->AppendMenu(MF_STRING, IDM_ABOUTBOX, strAboutMenu);
        }

        // Set the icon for this dialog.
        // The framework does this automatically
        //  when the application's main window is not a dialog
        SetIcon(m_hIcon, TRUE);                 // Set big icon
        SetIcon(m_hIcon, FALSE);                // Set small icon

        // TODO: Add extra initialization here
```

This program defines a set of structures to maintain the information about individual taxpayers and individual forms. **TaxPayerStruct** has information about the taxpayer's name and social security number. **EZStruct** has information filed in the 1040EZ form, **StdStruct** has information filed in the standard 1040 tax form, and **SchAStruct** has information filed in the Schedule A form.

```
// Set up taxpayers data.
PTaxPayerStruct pJohn, pKate;
PEZStruct        pJohnEZ;
PStdStruct        pKateStd;
PSchAStruct        pKateSchA;

pJohn = new TaxPayerStruct;
pKate = new TaxPayerStruct;
pJohnEZ = new EZStruct;
pKateStd = new StdStruct;
pKateSchA = new SchAStruct;

strcpy(pJohn->szName, "John");
strcpy(pJohn->szSSN, "AAA-BB-CCCC");
strcpy(pJohnEZ->szTotalIncome, "49875");
strcpy(pJohnEZ->szTotalTax, "15954");
strcpy(pKate->szName, "Kate");
strcpy(pKate->szSSN, "XXX-YY-ZZZZ");
strcpy(pKateStd->szTotalIncome, "64851");
strcpy(pKateStd->szTotalDeduction, "14175");
strcpy(pKateStd->szTotalTax, "13169");
strcpy(pKateSchA->szRealEstateDeduction, "9175");
strcpy(pKateSchA->szOtherDeductions, "5000");
```

Every tree view item can be associated with two images, one for the selected state and the other for the regular state. These images are loaded and added to an image list, and the image list is given to the Tree View control. The indices of the images in this image list can later be referenced when a tree view item is inserted into the Tree View control. In this sample the same image is used for both selected state and regular state. The tree view items are added to the Tree View control by use of the **AddDataToTree** function. The individual tax returns are added as children of the respective taxpayer.

```
// Set up the Tree View control related data
CImageList        *pImageList;
CBitmap        bitmap;
pImageList = new CImageList();
pImageList->Create(32, 16, TRUE, 4, 2);
// Load the bitmaps into the imagelist.
for (int  i = 0; i<4; i++)
{
        bitmap.LoadBitmap(BASE_BITMAP_ID + i);
        pImageList->Add(&bitmap, (COLORREF)0xFFFFFF);
```

```
                bitmap.DeleteObject();
        }
        m_treectrl.SetImageList(pImageList, TVSIL_NORMAL);

// Start inserting the taxpayers and their info in the Tree View control.
        HTREEITEM hTreeItem, hParentItem;
```

To each tree view item, 32-bit application-defined data can be attached inside the tree view item's attribute structure **TVITEM**. This data can be used by the application for its own advantage. In this sample the data associated with each object is in a structure, and a pointer to this structure, essentially data associated with an individual tree view item, is stored in the 32-bit application-defined data. This 32-bit data will be retrieved later by getting the item's attribute and then used to get information about the object itself.

```
        AddDataToTree(NULL, TAXPAYER, pJohn->szSSN,
                    (LPARAM)pJohn, &hTreeItem);
        hParentItem = hTreeItem;
        AddDataToTree(hParentItem, FORMEZ, pJohnEZ->szTotalTax,
                    (LPARAM)pJohnEZ, &hTreeItem);
        AddDataToTree(NULL, TAXPAYER, pKate->szSSN,
                    (LPARAM)pKate, &hTreeItem);
        hParentItem = hTreeItem;
        AddDataToTree(hParentItem, FORMSTD, "Form 1040", (LPARAM)pKateStd,
                    &hTreeItem);
        AddDataToTree(hParentItem, FORMSCHA, "Schedule A", (LPARAM)pKateSchA,
                    &hTreeItem);
        return TRUE; // return TRUE unless you set the focus to a control
}


void CTreeCtrlDlg::OnSysCommand(UINT nID, LPARAM lParam)
{
        if ((nID & 0xFFF0) == IDM_ABOUTBOX)
        {
                CAboutDlg dlgAbout;
                dlgAbout.DoModal();
        }
        else
        {
                CDialog::OnSysCommand(nID, lParam);
        }
}


// If you add a minimize button to your dialog, you will need the code below
//  to draw the icon.  For MFC applications using the document/view model,
//  this is automatically done for you by the framework.

void CTreeCtrlDlg::OnPaint()
{
        if (IsIconic())
```

```
        {
                CPaintDC dc(this); // device context for painting

                SendMessage(WM_ICONERASEBKGND, (WPARAM) dc.GetSafeHdc(), 0);

                // Center icon in client rectangle
                int cxIcon = GetSystemMetrics(SM_CXICON);
                int cyIcon = GetSystemMetrics(SM_CYICON);
                CRect rect;
                GetClientRect(&rect);
                int x = (rect.Width()-cxIcon + 1) / 2;
                int y = (rect.Height()-cyIcon + 1) / 2;

                // Draw the icon
                dc.DrawIcon(x, y, m_hIcon);
        }
        else
        {
                CDialog::OnPaint();
        }
}


// The system calls this to obtain the cursor to display
// while the user drags the minimized window.
HCURSOR CTreeCtrlDlg::OnQueryDragIcon()
{
        return (HCURSOR) m_hIcon;
}
```

The functions **OnSysCommand**, **OnPaint**, and **OnQueryDragIcon** are generated by the AppWizard and would meet the needs of this sample. When the user double-clicks the tree view item, the details of the item are displayed in a dialog box. The dialog box allows the user to change the information and save it. The double-click is processed by the following section of code. The selected Tree View item is queried, and the type of item is identified from its image information. From the Tree View item's attribute the application data is retrieved and passed on to the respective dialog boxes. The code dealing with these dialog boxes shows how this data is used.

```
void CTreeCtrlDlg::OnDblclkTree(NMHDR* pNMHDR, LRESULT* pResult)
{
        // TODO: Add your control notification handler code here
        HTREEITEM    hSelectedItem;
        hSelectedItem = m_treectrl.GetSelectedItem();

        TVITEM    tvItem;
        tvItem.hItem = hSelectedItem;
        tvItem.mask = TVIF_HANDLE | TVIF_IMAGE | TVIF_PARAM;
        m_treectrl.GetItem(&tvItem);
```

```
switch (tvItem.iImage)
{
case TAXPAYER:
    {
        // Do other processing if needed.
        PTaxPayerStruct pTaxPayer = (PTaxPayerStruct) tvItem.lParam;
        TaxPayer     tp(NULL, pTaxPayer);
```

The dialog box is created and is run modally. When the dialog box terminates, the information on the screen is updated to reflect any change that the user would have made. Similar processing is done for all the other types of tree view items.

```
        if(tp.DoModal() == IDOK)
        {
            m_treectrl.SetItem(hSelectedItem, TVIF_TEXT,
                            pTaxPayer->szSSN,0,0,0,0,0);
        }
    }
    break;

case FORMSTD:
    {
        // Do other processing if needed.
        PStdStruct pStd = (PStdStruct) tvItem.lParam;
        Tax1040    tp(NULL, pStd);
        tp.DoModal();
    }
    break;

case FORMSCHA:
    {
        // Do other processing if needed.
        PSchAStruct pSchA = (PSchAStruct) tvItem.lParam;
        SchA     tp(NULL, pSchA);
        tp.DoModal();
    }
    break;

case FORMEZ:
    {
        // Do other processing if needed.
        PEZStruct pEZ = (PEZStruct) tvItem.lParam;
        EZ1040    tp(NULL, pEZ);
        tp.DoModal();
    }
    break;

}
```

```
        *pResult = 1;
}
```

Notice that the value pointed to by **pResult** is set to 1. This specifies to the MFC library class that the message has been processed and nothing else needs to be done. Returning a zero will cause the MFC library class to process the message, yielding a result similar to that obtained by clicking the buttons on the left of the root items.

To add an item to a Tree View control, a **TVINSERTSTRUCT** is created and the three pieces of information that it needs—the parent to this item, the order of insertion, and the item's attribute in **TVITEM**—are supplied. Given the item type, the image for the item and its image when selected are set. In this case both are assumed to be the same image. The parent for this item is set, and the order of insertion is indicated to be TVI_SORT, sorted order. Other possible orders are TVI_FIRST, which inserts the item at the beginning of the list, and TVI_LAST, which inserts the item at the end of the list. The item's attribute should be set in a **TVITEM** structure. The text to appear at the bottom of the item image and application-specific data are set. The **InsertItem** method inserts the tree view item into the Tree View control.

```
void CTreeCtrlDlg::AddDataToTree(HTREEITEM hParent, int iType, char * pszText,
LPARAM lpItemData, HTREEITEM *it)
{
    TVINSERTSTRUCT tvistruct;
    if (iType == TAXPAYER)
    {
        tvistruct.item.iImage = 0;
        tvistruct.item.iSelectedImage = 0;
    }
    else if (iType == FORMSTD)
    {
        tvistruct.item.iImage = 1;
        tvistruct.item.iSelectedImage = 1;
    }
    else if (iType == FORMSCHA)
    {
        tvistruct.item.iImage = 2;
        tvistruct.item.iSelectedImage = 2;
    }
    else if (iType == FORMEZ)
    {
        tvistruct.item.iImage = 3;
        tvistruct.item.iSelectedImage = 3;
    }
    tvistruct.hParent = hParent;
    tvistruct.hInsertAfter = TVI_SORT;
    tvistruct.item.pszText = pszText;
    tvistruct.item.mask = TVIF_IMAGE | TVIF_SELECTEDIMAGE | TVIF_TEXT |
                          TVIF_PARAM;
    tvistruct.item.lParam = lpItemData;
```

```
    *it = m_treectrl.InsertItem (&tvistruct);
}


void CTreeCtrlDlg::OnDestroy()
{
    CDialog::OnDestroy();

    // TODO: Add your message handler code here
    CImageList    *pImageList;
    pImageList = m_treectrl.GetImageList(TVSIL_NORMAL);
    delete pImageList;
    HTREEITEM    hTVItemRoot, hTVItemChild;
    hTVItemRoot = m_treectrl.GetRootItem();

    do
    {
        FreeItem(hTVItemRoot);
        if (m_treectrl.ItemHasChildren(hTVItemRoot))
        {
            hTVItemChild = m_treectrl.GetChildItem(hTVItemRoot);
            do
            {
                FreeItem(hTVItemChild);
            } while(hTVItemChild = m_treectrl.GetNextSiblingItem(hTVItemChild));
        }
    } while (hTVItemRoot = m_treectrl.GetNextSiblingItem(hTVItemRoot));

}
```

Notice that during creation of tree view items, memory was allocated to hold information about the taxpayer and the individual tax forms. We also allocated resources for the bitmap. These resources have to be freed when the application terminates. This is done when the **CTreeCtrlDlg** class is destroyed. The code starts from the root, and for every item at the root level, it frees the resources associated with the root item and proceeds until all the resources for all its second-level children are freed. It assumes that there are only two levels. It uses the **FreeItem** member functions to free a given Tree View item.

```
void CTreeCtrlDlg::FreeItem (HTREEITEM hTVItem)
{
    TVITEM    tvItem;
    tvItem.hItem = hTVItem;
    tvItem.mask = TVIF_HANDLE | TVIF_IMAGE | TVIF_PARAM;
    m_treectrl.GetItem(&tvItem);
    switch (tvItem.iImage)
    {
    case TAXPAYER:
        {
            // Do other processing if needed.
            PTaxPayerStruct pTaxPayer = (PTaxPayerStruct) tvItem.lParam;
```

```
                delete pTaxPayer;
        }
        break;

    case FORMSTD:
        {
            // Do other processing if needed.
            PStdStruct pStd = (PStdStruct) tvItem.lParam;
            delete pStd;
        }
        break;
    case FORMSCHA:
        {
            // Do other processing if needed.
            PSchAStruct pSchA = (PSchAStruct) tvItem.lParam;
            delete pSchA;
        }
        break;
    case FORMEZ:
        {
            // Do other processing if needed.
            PEZStruct pEZ = (PEZStruct) tvItem.lParam;
            delete pEZ;
        }
        break;
    }

}
```

The code that actually processes the dialog box when the user double-clicks the tax-payer item is shown next. This is standard dialog box processing, except that during construction of the dialog, the information associated with the item is passed and is saved in a private member data. The code for processing the 1040, EZ, and SchA items is similar to this.

```
#if !defined(AFX_TAXPAYER_H__16A0A280_B455_11D0_9768_0004ACB5DCC1__INCLUDED_)
#define AFX_TAXPAYER_H__16A0A280_B455_11D0_9768_0004ACB5DCC1__INCLUDED_

#if _MSC_VER >= 1000
#pragma once
#endif // _MSC_VER >= 1000
// TaxPayer.h : header file
//


/////////////////////////////////////////////////////////////////////////
// TaxPayer dialog

class TaxPayer : public CDialog
```

```
{
// Construction
public:
        TaxPayer(CWnd* pParent = NULL, PTaxPayerStruct pData = NULL);    //
standard constructor

// Dialog Data
        //{{AFX_DATA(TaxPayer)
        enum { IDD = IDD_TAXPAYER };
        CEdit   m_ssno;
        CEdit   m_name;
        //}}AFX_DATA

// Overrides
        // ClassWizard generated virtual function overrides
        //{{AFX_VIRTUAL(TaxPayer)
        protected:
        virtual void DoDataExchange(CDataExchange* pDX);// DDX/DDV support
        //}}AFX_VIRTUAL

// Implementation
protected:

        // Generated message map functions
        //{{AFX_MSG(TaxPayer)
        virtual BOOL OnInitDialog();
        virtual void OnOK();
        //}}AFX_MSG
        DECLARE_MESSAGE_MAP()
private:
        PTaxPayerStruct pTaxPayerData;
};

//{{AFX_INSERT_LOCATION}}

#endif //

// TaxPayer.cpp : implementation file
//

#include "stdafx.h"
#include "treectrl.h"
#include "TaxData.h"
#include "TaxPayer.h"

#ifdef _DEBUG
#define new DEBUG_NEW
#undef THIS_FILE
static char THIS_FILE[] = __FILE__;
```

```
#endif

///////////////////////////////////////////////////////////////////////
// TaxPayer dialog

TaxPayer::TaxPayer(CWnd* pParent /*=NULL*/, PTaxPayerStruct pData)
        : CDialog(TaxPayer::IDD, pParent)
{
        //{{AFX_DATA_INIT(TaxPayer)
        //}}AFX_DATA_INIT
        pTaxPayerData = pData;
}

void TaxPayer::DoDataExchange(CDataExchange* pDX)
{
        CDialog::DoDataExchange(pDX);
        //{{AFX_DATA_MAP(TaxPayer)
        DDX_Control(pDX, IDC_SSNO, m_ssno);
        DDX_Control(pDX, IDC_NAME, m_name);
        //}}AFX_DATA_MAP
}


BEGIN_MESSAGE_MAP(TaxPayer, CDialog)
        //{{AFX_MSG_MAP(TaxPayer)
        //}}AFX_MSG_MAP
END_MESSAGE_MAP()

///////////////////////////////////////////////////////////////////////
// TaxPayer message handlers

BOOL TaxPayer::OnInitDialog()
{
        CDialog::OnInitDialog();

        // TODO: Add extra initialization here
        m_ssno.SetWindowText(pTaxPayerData->szSSN);
        m_name.SetWindowText(pTaxPayerData->szName);
        return TRUE;  // return TRUE unless you set the focus to a control
                      // EXCEPTION: OCX Property Pages should return FALSE
}

void TaxPayer::OnOK()
{
        // TODO: Add extra validation here
        CDialog::OnOK();
        m_name.GetWindowText(pTaxPayerData->szName, 16+1);
        m_ssno.GetWindowText(pTaxPayerData->szSSN, 11+1);


}
```

LIST VIEW CONTROL

A List View control lets you show a list of items in different ways, such as using small icons, large icons, lists, and so on, as shown in Figures 7-22 through 7-25.

The List View control uses a number of data structures, but two of the important ones are the **LVCOLUMN** (formerly **LV_COLUMN**) structure and the **LV_ITEM** structure. These structures are used in the example program. Let's look at these data structures.

The **LVCOLUMN** structure contains information about a column in a List View control. This structure is also used to receive information about a column.

```
typedef struct _LVCOLUMN { UINT mask;
    int fmt;
    int cx;
    LPTSTR pszText;
    int cchTextMax;
    int iSubItem;

#if (_WIN32_IE >= 0x0300)

int iImage;

int iOrder;

    #endif
} LVCOLUMN, FAR *LPLVCOLUMN;
```

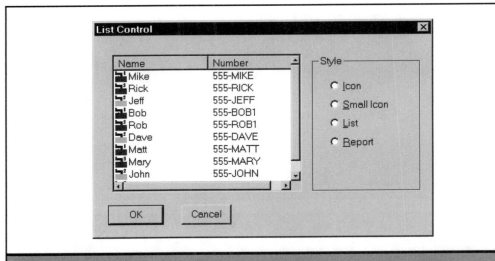

Figure 7-22. A List View control listing data in report format

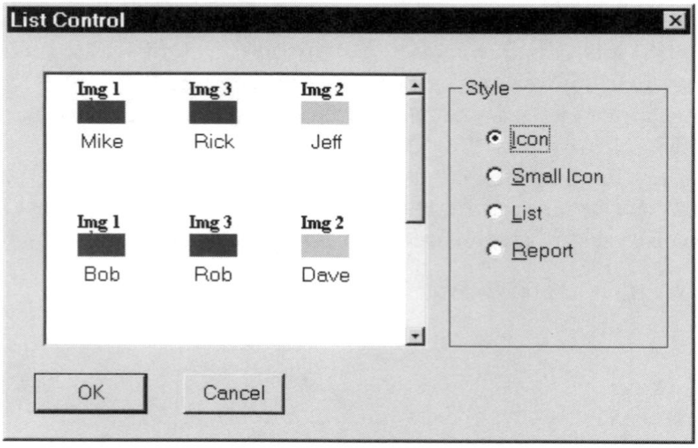

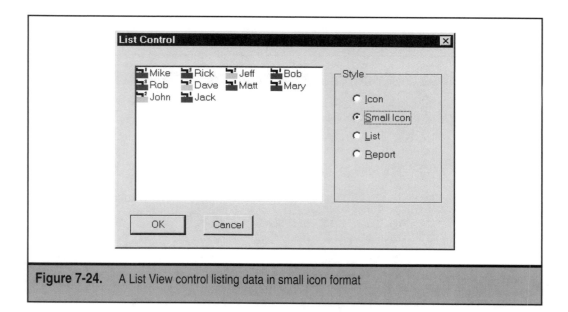

Figure 7-23.   A List View control listing data in (regular) icon format

Figure 7-24.   A List View control listing data in small icon format

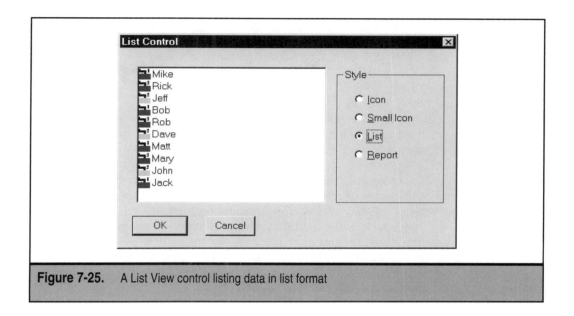

Figure 7-25.   A List View control listing data in list format

mask specifies which members of this structure contain valid information, as shown in the table that follows:

Mask Value	Description
LVCF_FMT	The *fmt* member is valid.
LVCF_SUBITEM	The *iSubItem* member is valid.
LVCF_TEXT	The *pszText* member is valid.
LVCF_WIDTH	The *cx* member is valid.

Starting with version 4.7 (see Chapter 5 for more details on the different versions of common control and shell DLLs), two new mask values have been introduced. These are LVCF_IMAGE, which specifies that the *iImage* member is valid, and LVCF_ORDER, which specifies that the *iOrder* member is valid.

fmt specifies the alignment of the column heading and the subitem text in all columns except the leftmost column in a List View control, which must be left-aligned. The values and description for *fmt* are as follows:

Fmt V alue	Description
LVCFMT_CENTER	Text is centered.
LVCFMT_LEFT	Text is left-aligned.
LVCFMT_RIGHT	Text is right-aligned.

Starting with version 4.7, new *fmt* values have been introduced. These are LVCFMT_BITMAP_ON_RIGHT, which specifies that the bitmap appears to the right of text, LVCFMT_COL_HAS_IMAGES, which specifies that the header item contains an image in the image list, and LVCFMT_IMAGE, which specifies that the item displays an image from an image list.

cx specifies the width, in pixels, of the column.

pszText is a pointer to the column heading if the structure contains information about a column. If the structure is receiving information about a column, this member specifies the address of the buffer that receives the column heading.

cchTextMax specifies the size, in characters, of the buffer pointed to by the *pszText* member. If the structure is not receiving information about a column, this member is ignored.

iSubItem specifies the index of the subitem associated with a column.

Starting with version 4.7, new fields were introduced for LVCOLUMN. These are *iImage* and *iOrder*. *iImage* specifies the index of an image within the image list. The specified image will appear within the column. *IOrder* specifies the column offset. Column offset is in left-to-right order. For example, zero indicates the leftmost column.

List View Control Programming Example

The *ListCtrl* sample program shows how to use the List View control by use of the MFC library class **CListCtrl**. When the sample is run, it displays a window with a menu. If List Control is selected from the File menu, a dialog box with the list control is displayed. The list control has two columns and displays ten different entries. The style of the List View control can be changed by selecting various radio buttons shown in the Style Group box.

This sample extends the Spin/Slider/Progress control sample. The main application code is shown next. It is similar to the earlier samples, and it would suffice to look at the boldface code.

```
//*****************************************************************
// This sample demonstrates the class/functions related to
// Common controls.
//*****************************************************************
// Controls.CPP

#include <afxwin.h>
#include <afxdlgs.h>
#include <afxcmn.h>                    // Header file for Common controls
#include <strstrea.h>
#include "FontDlg.h"
#include "AnimateDlg.h"
#include "HotKeyDlg.h"
#include "SpSlProgDlg.h"
#include "ListCtrlDlg.h"
#include "resource.h"
```

```
// Define the application object class
class CApp : public CWinApp
{
public:
        virtual BOOL InitInstance ();
};
// Define the window class
class CWindow : public CFrameWnd
{
public:
    CWindow();
    afx_msg void OnAppAbout();
    afx_msg void OnFontDlg();
    afx_msg void OnAnimateDlg();
    afx_msg void OnHotKeyDlg();
    afx_msg void OnSpSlProgDlg();
    afx_msg void OnListCtrlDlg();
    afx_msg void OnExit();
    afx_msg void OnSysCommand(UINT nID, LPARAM lParam);//Process the Hot Key
    DECLARE_MESSAGE_MAP()
};
/////////////////////////////////////////////////////////////////////////////
// CWindow
BEGIN_MESSAGE_MAP(CWindow, CFrameWnd)
        ON_COMMAND(ID_APP_ABOUT, OnAppAbout)
        ON_COMMAND(ID_FONTDLG, OnFontDlg)
        ON_COMMAND(ID_ANIMATEDLG, OnAnimateDlg)
        ON_COMMAND(ID_HOTKEYDLG, OnHotKeyDlg)
        ON_COMMAND(ID_SPSLPROGDLG, OnSpSlProgDlg)
        ON_COMMAND(ID_LISTCTRLDLG, OnListCtrlDlg)
        ON_COMMAND(ID_APP_EXIT, OnExit)
        ON_WM_SYSCOMMAND()
END_MESSAGE_MAP()
/////////////////////////////////////////////////////////////////////////////
// CWindow construction
CWindow::CWindow()
{
    LoadAccelTable(MAKEINTRESOURCE(IDR_MAINFRAME));
    Create( NULL, "Control Sample",
    WS_OVERLAPPEDWINDOW,
    rectDefault, NULL, MAKEINTRESOURCE(IDR_MAINFRAME) );
}
/////////////////////////////////////////////////////////////////////////////
// The one and only CApp object

CApp theApp;

/////////////////////////////////////////////////////////////////////////////
```

```
// CApp initialization

BOOL CApp::InitInstance()
{
        m_pMainWnd = new CWindow();
        m_pMainWnd -> ShowWindow( m_nCmdShow );
        m_pMainWnd -> UpdateWindow();
        return TRUE;
}


///////////////////////////////////////////////////////////////////////////
// CAboutDlg dialog used for App About

class CAboutDlg : public CDialog
{
public:
        CAboutDlg();
        enum { IDD = IDD_ABOUTBOX };
        protected:
};

CAboutDlg::CAboutDlg() : CDialog(CAboutDlg::IDD)
{
}
// App command to run the dialog
void CWindow::OnAppAbout()
{
        CAboutDlg aboutDlg;
        aboutDlg.DoModal();
}
// Code to process other menu items…

// ListControl Dialog selected

void CWindow::OnListCtrlDlg()
{
        CListCtrlDlg listctrlDlg(this);
        listctrlDlg.DoModal();
}

// On Exit handles the void
void CWindow::OnExit()
{
        DestroyWindow();
}
```

The items shown inside the List View control have icons associated with them. These icons and the resource for the List Control dialog box are shown next. Three icons are defined; these icons will be reused for the items inserted into the List View control. The style

LVS_REPORT specifies a report view for the List View control, and the style LVS_AUTOARRANGE specifies that the icons are automatically kept arranged in icon and small icon view. Some of the other styles will be dynamically changed.

```
LANGUAGE LANG_NEUTRAL, SUBLANG_NEUTRAL
/////////////////////////////////////////////////////////////////////////////
// Icon
// Icon with lowest ID value placed first to ensure application icon
// remains consistent on all systems.
IDR_MAINFRAME           ICON    DISCARDABLE     "Control.ico"
IDI_IMG1                ICON    DISCARDABLE     "Img1.ico"
IDI_IMG2                ICON    DISCARDABLE     "Img2.ico"
IDI_IMG3                ICON    DISCARDABLE     "Img3.ico"

IDD_LISTCTRLDLG DIALOG DISCARDABLE  0, 0, 229, 140
STYLE DS_MODALFRAME | WS_POPUP | WS_CAPTION | WS_SYSMENU
CAPTION "List Control"
FONT 8, "MS Sans Serif"
BEGIN
    CONTROL         "List1",IDC_LISTCTRL,"SysListView32",LVS_REPORT |
                    LVS_AUTOARRANGE | WS_BORDER | WS_TABSTOP,12,13,129,96
    GROUPBOX        "Static",IDC_STATIC,148,14,74,95
    CONTROL         "&Icon",IDC_ICONVIEW,"Button",BS_AUTORADIOBUTTON,160,31,
                    47,10
    CONTROL         "&Small Icon",IDC_SMALLICON,"Button",BS_AUTORADIOBUTTON,
                    160,44,47,10
    CONTROL         "&List",IDC_LIST,"Button",BS_AUTORADIOBUTTON,160,57,47,
                    10
    CONTROL         "&Report",IDC_REPORT,"Button",BS_AUTORADIOBUTTON,160,70,
                    47,10
    DEFPUSHBUTTON   "OK",IDOK,9,118,38,14
    PUSHBUTTON      "Cancel",IDCANCEL,59,118,34,14
END
```

The **CListCtrlDlg** class declaration is shown next. A **CListCtrl** member is defined for the list control in the dialog box. Pointers to two **CImageListobjects** are also defined. The image list for the full-sized icons and a separate image list contain smaller versions of the same icons for use in other views. Member functions **OnInitDialog**, **OnIconView**, **OnSmallIconView**, **OnListView**, and **OnReportView** are declared. These functions are tied to the button-click event on the radio button through the message map. A private function, **InsertOneItem**, which is used to add one item at a time to the List View control, is also declared. A destructor is also defined, since the resource allocated for the image list should be released. This image list resource is freed in the destructor.

```
// ListCtrlDlg.h : header file
/////////////////////////////////////////////////////////////////////
// CListCtrlDlg dialog
```

```
class CListCtrlDlg : public CDialog
{
// Construction
public:
        CListCtrlDlg(CWnd* pParent = NULL);    // standard constructor
        ~CListCtrlDlg();
// Dialog Data
        //{{AFX_DATA(CListCtrlDlg)
        enum { IDD = IDD_LISTCTRLDLG };
        CListCtrl        m_listctrl;
        CImageList       *m_pimagelist;
        CImageList       *m_psmallimagelist;
        //}}AFX_DATA
// Overrides
        // ClassWizard generated virtual function overrides
        //{{AFX_VIRTUAL(CListCtrlDlg)
        protected:
        virtual void DoDataExchange(CDataExchange* pDX);// DDX/DDV support
        //}}AFX_VIRTUAL
// Implementation
protected:
        // Generated message map functions
        //{{AFX_MSG(CListCtrlDlg)
        virtual BOOL OnInitDialog();
        afx_msg void OnIconView();
        afx_msg void OnSmallIconView();
        afx_msg void OnListView();
        afx_msg void OnReportView();
        //}}AFX_MSG
        DECLARE_MESSAGE_MAP()
private:
        void InsertOneItem(short sItemNumber, char *szName, char *szNumber,
                        short sImage);
};
```

The code that implements the **CListCtrlDlg** is shown next. The class constructor just initializes the member variables. The DDX is used to update the data between the control and the **CListCtrl** member variable in the class. The message map specifies what function is to be called when the radio buttons are clicked.

```
// ListCtrlDlg.cpp : implementation file
//
#include <afxwin.h>
#include <afxdlgs.h>
#include <afxcmn.h>
#include "resource.h"
#include "ListCtrlDlg.h"
///////////////////////////////////////////////////////////////////////////
// CListCtrlDlg dialog
```

```
CListCtrlDlg::CListCtrlDlg(CWnd* pParent /*=NULL*/)
        : CDialog(CListCtrlDlg::IDD, pParent)
{
        //{{AFX_DATA_INIT(CListCtrlDlg)
                // NOTE: the ClassWizard will add member initialization here
        //}}AFX_DATA_INIT
        m_pimagelist = NULL;
        m_psmallimagelist = NULL;
}
void CListCtrlDlg::DoDataExchange(CDataExchange* pDX)
{
        CDialog::DoDataExchange(pDX);
        //{{AFX_DATA_MAP(CListCtrlDlg)
        DDX_Control(pDX, IDC_LISTCTRL, m_listctrl);
        //}}AFX_DATA_MAP
}
BEGIN_MESSAGE_MAP(CListCtrlDlg, CDialog)
        //{{AFX_MSG_MAP(CListCtrlDlg)
        ON_BN_CLICKED(IDC_ICONVIEW, OnIconView)
        ON_BN_CLICKED(IDC_SMALLICON, OnSmallIconView)
        ON_BN_CLICKED(IDC_LIST, OnListView)
        ON_BN_CLICKED(IDC_REPORT, OnReportView)
        //}}AFX_MSG_MAP
END_MESSAGE_MAP()
```

During the dialog box initialization, the List View control is populated with items. For this sample ten items are inserted. In a real application the data to be inserted inside the List View control can be queried during this initialization process and inserted. Before inserting the items, two image lists are created and assigned to the List View control by use of the **SetImageList** function. The List View control displays names and phone numbers. Therefore two columns are needed. To insert a column, a **LV_COLUMN** structure is created. The width of each column is half the size of the control. The columns are headed "Name" and "Number." **InsertColumn** inserts the column.

```
//////////////////////////////////////////////////////////////////////////
// CListCtrlDlg message handlers
BOOL CListCtrlDlg::OnInitDialog()
{
        CWinApp *pApp;
        LVCOLUMN lvcolumn;
        CDialog::OnInitDialog();

        char Name[10][10] = {"Jack", "John", "Mary", "Matt", "Dave", "Rob",
                        "Bob", "Jeff", "Rick", "Mike"};
        char Number[10][10] = {"555-JACK", "555-JOHN","555-MARY",
                        "555-MATT","555-DAVE", "555-ROB1",
                        "555-BOB1", "555-JEFF","555-RICK",
                        "555-MIKE"};
        // TODO: Add extra initialization here
```

```
pApp = (CWinApp *)AfxGetApp();
m_pimagelist = new CImageList();
m_psmallimagelist = new CImageList();
m_pimagelist->Create(32, 32, TRUE, 3, 3);
m_psmallimagelist->Create(16, 16, TRUE, 3, 3);
m_pimagelist->Add(pApp->LoadIcon(IDI_IMG1));
m_pimagelist->Add(pApp->LoadIcon(IDI_IMG2));
m_pimagelist->Add(pApp->LoadIcon(IDI_IMG3));
m_psmallimagelist->Add(pApp->LoadIcon(IDI_IMG1));
m_psmallimagelist->Add(pApp->LoadIcon(IDI_IMG2));
m_psmallimagelist->Add(pApp->LoadIcon(IDI_IMG3));

m_listctrl.SetImageList(m_pimagelist, LVSIL_NORMAL);
m_listctrl.SetImageList(m_psmallimagelist, LVSIL_SMALL);

CRect rect;
m_listctrl.GetWindowRect(&rect);  // Get the size of the List control

// Create two columns.

lvcolumn.mask = LVCF_FMT | LVCF_SUBITEM | LVCF_TEXT | LVCF_WIDTH;
lvcolumn.fmt = LVCFMT_LEFT;//Other possible formats are LVCFMT_CENTER
// & LVCFMT_RIGHT
lvcolumn.cx = rect.Width()/2;   // Occupy half the width

lvcolumn.pszText = "Name";
lvcolumn.iSubItem = 1;
m_listctrl.InsertColumn(1, &lvcolumn);

lvcolumn.pszText = "Number";
lvcolumn.iSubItem = 2;
m_listctrl.InsertColumn(2, &lvcolumn);


for (int j = 0; j < 10; j++)
{
    InsertOneItem(j, Name[j], Number[j], j%3);
}

return TRUE;  // return TRUE unless you set the focus to a control
              // EXCEPTION: OCX Property Pages should return FALSE
}
```

The resource allocated for the **CImageList** is released when the **CListCtrlDlg** class is destroyed.

```
CListCtrlDlg::~CListCtrlDlg()
{
    // Delete the memory allocated
```

```
        delete m_pimagelist;
        delete m_psmallimagelist;
}
```

The next four member functions modify the style of the List View control when the user changes the styles by clicking the radio button. The list control style is stored in a 32-bit value at a specified offset into the extra window memory of the window. This is retrieved by calling **GetWindowLong**. The least significant two bits store the style, which specifies whether the style of the List View control is icon, small icon, list, or report. The current style of the List View control is checked to make sure that the style's setting is not set redundantly. If style needs to be set, the appropriate bit is set and the style is updated by calling **SetWindowLong**.

```
void CListCtrlDlg::OnIconView()
{
    long    lStyle;
    short   sStyle;

    lStyle = GetWindowLong(m_listctrl.m_hWnd, GWL_STYLE);
    sStyle = lStyle & LVS_TYPEMASK;
    if (!(sStyle == LVS_ICON))
    {
        lStyle &= ~0x00000003;      //Reset the view mode bits
        lStyle |= LVS_ICON;         //Set the new view mode
    }
    SetWindowLong(m_listctrl.m_hWnd, GWL_STYLE, lStyle);

}
void CListCtrlDlg::OnSmallIconView()
{
    long    lStyle;
    short   sStyle;

    lStyle = GetWindowLong(m_listctrl.m_hWnd, GWL_STYLE);
    sStyle = lStyle & LVS_TYPEMASK;
    if (!(sStyle == LVS_SMALLICON))
    {
        lStyle &= ~0x00000003;//Reset the view mode bits
        lStyle |= LVS_SMALLICON;        // Set the new view mode
    }
    SetWindowLong(m_listctrl.m_hWnd, GWL_STYLE, lStyle);

}
void CListCtrlDlg::OnListView()
{
    long    lStyle;
    short   sStyle;

    lStyle = GetWindowLong(m_listctrl.m_hWnd, GWL_STYLE);
```

```
    sStyle = lStyle & LVS_TYPEMASK;
    if (!(sStyle == LVS_LIST))
    {
        lStyle &= ~0x00000003;      //Reset the view mode bits
        lStyle |= LVS_LIST;         //Set the new view mode
    }
    SetWindowLong(m_listctrl.m_hWnd, GWL_STYLE, lStyle);

}
void CListCtrlDlg::OnReportView()
{
    long    lStyle;
    short   sStyle;

    lStyle = GetWindowLong(m_listctrl.m_hWnd, GWL_STYLE);
    sStyle = lStyle & LVS_TYPEMASK;
    if (!(sStyle == LVS_REPORT))
    {
        lStyle &= ~0x00000003;      //Reset the view mode bits
        lStyle |= LVS_REPORT;       //Set the new view mode
    }
    SetWindowLong(m_listctrl.m_hWnd, GWL_STYLE, lStyle);

}
```

The next function is a helper function that inserts one item into the List View control.

```
void CListCtrlDlg::InsertOneItem(short sItemNumber, char *szName, char *szNumber,
short sImage)
{
        int inewitem;
        LVITEM lvitem;

        lvitem.mask = LVIF_TEXT|LVIF_IMAGE;
        lvitem.iItem =   0;
        lvitem.iSubItem = 0;
        lvitem.pszText = szName;
        lvitem.iImage = sImage;
        inewitem = m_listctrl.InsertItem(&lvitem);

        lvitem.mask = LVIF_TEXT;
        lvitem.iItem =   0;
        lvitem.iSubItem = 1;
        lvitem.pszText = szNumber;
        m_listctrl.SetItem(&lvitem);

}
```

NEW COMMON CONTROLS IN WINDOWS 2000

Windows 2000 supports a number of common controls not supported in Windows NT 4.0. These include ComboBoxEx, Date and Time picker, Flat Scroll Bar, IP Address, Month Calendar, Pager, and Rebar. A description of these controls and a brief usage note is included in Table 7-1.

We will look at programming examples for two of these controls—the Date and Time picker control and Month Calendar control. In addition to the controls themselves, Windows 2000 also supports custom draw, which is a service provided by many common controls to allow an application greater flexibility in customizing a control's appearance.

Custom Draw

Custom draw is implemented in version 4.70 and later of *Comctl32.dll*. Common controls that support custom draw send NM_CUSTOMDRAW notifications (as **WM_NOTIFY** Messages) at specific stages during drawing operations. These notifications describe drawing operations that apply to the entire control as well as drawing operations specific to items within the control. Your application can use custom draw notifications for your own custom processing such as changing the font used to display items or manually drawing an item without performing a complete owner draw. The return values your application sends in response to these notifications determine the control's behavior.

The *lParam* parameter of a custom draw notification contains the address of an **NMCUSTOMDRAW** structure (or a control-specific structure that contains an **NMCUSTOMDRAW** structure as its first member). The **dwDrawStage** member of the **NMCUSTOMDRAW** structure conatins a value that represents the *draw stage*. There are four basic draw stages: before the paint cycle begins, after the paint cycle is complete, before the erase cycle begins, and after the erase cycle is complete. In response to the custom draw notifications at the different stages, you can perform a number of different activities such as:

▼   Respond to the notification

■   Request item-specific notifications (for draw stages of specific items)

■   Draw the item yourself

▲   Change fonts and colors

Now, let us look at the Date and Time picker control in more detail.

Date and Time Picker Control

Date and Time picker controls are implemented in version 4.70 and later of *Comctl32.dll*. A Date and Time picker control makes it possible to use a simple interface that the user is already likely to be familiar with.

You can utilize the Date and Time picker control using the MFC class **CDateTimeCtrl**. You can also use the **CreateWindowEx** API and specify DATETIMEPICK_CLASS as the window class, after which you register this class by calling the **InitCommonControlsEx** function. The class is registered when the Date and Time picker class is loaded from the common control DLL. The programming example discussed a bit later in this chapter uses the MFC class **CDateTimeCtrl**.

Format Strings

A DTP control relies on a format string to determine how it will display the date and time fields. A format string consists of a series of elements. Each element represents a specific piece of date/time information. The elements are displayed in the order they appear in the format string. The element "dd" represents a two-digit day, "hh" represents a two-digit hour (in 12-hour format), "HH" represents a two-digit hour (in 24-hour format), and "yyyy" represents the year in four-digit year format. For example, to display the current date with the format Sunday Jun 25, 2000, the format string is 'dddd MMM dd', 'yyyy'. To simplify programming, there are three predefined date formats and one predefined time format. You can choose a predefined format by selecting the appropriate window style as shown here:

Style	Output
DTS_LONGDATEFORMAT	"Sunday, June 25, 2000"
DTS_SHORTDATEFORMAT	"6/25/00"
DTS_SHORTDATECENTURYFORMAT	"6/25/2000"
DTS_TIMEFORMAT	"4:49:42 PM"

The programming example shown next uses the DTS_TIMEFORMAT style. If the preset formats do not meet your requirements, you can create a custom format by defining your own format string. Creating custom formats provides complete control for you in the display and formatting of the date and time fields. You can include body text as well as callback fields (for requesting information from the user) in your custom format. After you create a string, you assign it to the DTP control with a DTM_SETFORMAT message.

Programming Example for the Date and Time Picker Control

Figures 7-26 and 7-27 show the output of the following programming sample.

The next sample shows the usage of the Date and Time picker control using the MFC class **CDateTimeCtrl**. It reuses and modifies another sample that will be discussed in Chapter 9. It is a simple reminder application that reminds the user at a selected time. To display the time this sample uses a **CDateTimeCtrl** control. When the sample is initialized, it leaves the control with no time restriction, and every time the user changes the time, it checks if the changed time is a future time. If the user selects a past time, it

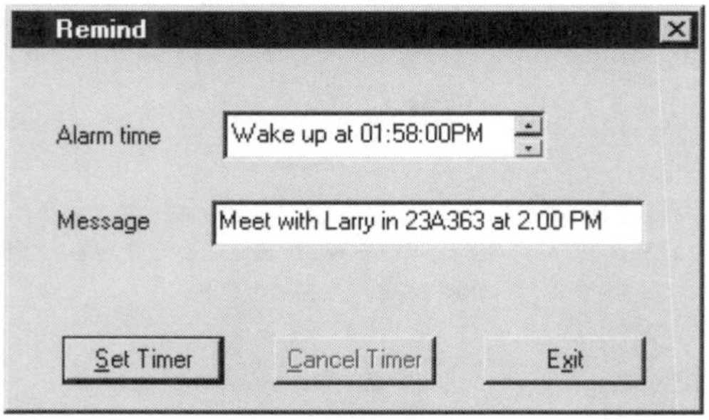

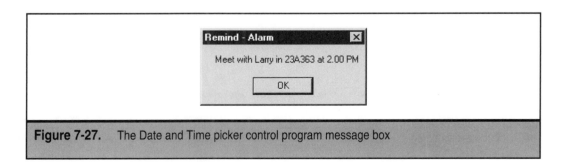

Figure 7-26.   The Date and Time picker control program dialog

displays a message indicating that only a future time can be picked and resets the range of the control from the current time till the end of that day. The discussion here covers only the code related to the Date and Time picker control and not the actual mechanism of the time, which will be discussed in Chapter 9. This is a dialog-based application, and the main code that brings up this dialog is not shown here. Shown first is the resource file with the Date and Time picker control. Notice the styles used for this control. The control is used to select the time to wake up, so the style of the control is set to DTS_TIMEFORMAT. When DTS_TIMEFORMAT is selected, the spin control is required, and the style DTS_UPDOWN places a spin button control to the right of the Date and Time picker control. This control can be used to change the time. In the resource file given next, the DTS_TIMEFORMAT is missing, and a style of value 0x8 appears instead. If you look at the *CommCtrl.h* header file, you can see that the DTS_TIMEFORMAT is defined as 0x9. The Visual Studio resource editor, which was used to generate this resource file, places a DTS_UPDOWN (0x1) and 0x8 ORed together to create the DTS_TIMEFORMAT (0x9) style.

Figure 7-27.   The Date and Time picker control program message box

```
IDD_REMIND_DIALOG DIALOGEX 0, 0, 212, 105
STYLE DS_MODALFRAME | WS_POPUP | WS_VISIBLE | WS_CAPTION | WS_SYSMENU
EXSTYLE WS_EX_APPWINDOW
CAPTION "Remind"
FONT 8, "MS Sans Serif"
BEGIN
    CONTROL         "DateTimePicker1",IDC_DATETIMEPICKER,"SysDateTimePick32",
                    DTS_RIGHTALIGN | DTS_UPDOWN | DTS_APPCANPARSE |
                    WS_TABSTOP | 0x8,65,18,100,15
    EDITTEXT        IDC_MESSAGE,62,44,134,14,ES_AUTOHSCROLL
    DEFPUSHBUTTON   "&Set Timer",IDOK,16,84,50,14
    PUSHBUTTON      "&Cancel Timer",IDC_CANCEL_TIMER,81,84,50,14
    PUSHBUTTON      "E&xit",IDCANCEL,146,84,50,14
    LTEXT           "Alarm time",IDC_STATIC,14,21,44,8
    LTEXT           "Message",IDC_STATIC,14,46,44,8
END
```

Shown next is the class definition for the dialog box. Notice the member variable of type **CDateTimeCtrl** defined for the Date and Time picker control:

```
// RemindDlg.h : header file
//

#if !defined(AFX_REMINDDLG_H)
#define AFX_REMINDDLG_H

#if _MSC_VER >= 1000
#pragma once
#endif // _MSC_VER >= 1000

// CRemindDlg dialog

class CRemindDlg : public CDialog
{
// Construction
public:
    CRemindDlg(CWnd* pParent = NULL);
// Dialog Data
    //{{AFX_DATA(CRemindDlg)
    enum { IDD = IDD_REMIND_DIALOG };
    CDateTimeCtrl    m_datetime;
    CString     m_message;
    //}}AFX_DATA

    // ClassWizard generated virtual function overrides
    //{{AFX_VIRTUAL(CRemindDlg)
    protected:
    virtual void DoDataExchange(CDataExchange* pDX);
    //}}AFX_VIRTUAL
```

```
// Implementation
protected:
    HICON m_hIcon;

    // Generated message map functions
    //{{AFX_MSG(CRemindDlg)
    virtual BOOL OnInitDialog();
    afx_msg void OnSysCommand(UINT nID, LPARAM lParam);
    afx_msg void OnPaint();
    afx_msg HCURSOR OnQueryDragIcon();
    afx_msg void OnSetTimer();
    afx_msg void OnCancelTimer();
    afx_msg void OnExit();
    afx_msg void OnAlarm();
    afx_msg void OnDatetimechangeDatetimepicker(NMHDR* pNMHDR, LRESULT* pResult);
    //}}AFX_MSG
    DECLARE_MESSAGE_MAP()
};

#endif // !defined(AFX_REMINDDLG_H)
```

The code that processes the dialog is shown next. While most of the code deals with the timer, the code that is of interest is shown in boldface.

```
// RemindDlg.cpp : implementation file
//
#define _WIN32_WINNT 0x400

#include "stdafx.h"
#include "Remind.h"
#include "RemindDlg.h"

#ifdef _DEBUG
#define new DEBUG_NEW
#undef THIS_FILE
static char THIS_FILE[] = __FILE__;
#endif


#define WM_USER_ALARM   WM_USER+200
UINT TimerThread(LPVOID);

typedef struct _TIMERINFO {
    HWND     hDialogHandle;
    LARGE_INTEGER   li;
} TIMERINFO;

HANDLE  hWaitableTimer;
```

```
CString AlarmMessage;
HANDLE  hTimerThread;
TIMERINFO    *ptinfo;
BOOL    bTimerExists;

//////////////////////////////////////////////////////////////////////////
// CRemindDlg dialog

CRemindDlg::CRemindDlg(CWnd* pParent /*=NULL*/)
        : CDialog(CRemindDlg::IDD, pParent)
{
        //{{AFX_DATA_INIT(CRemindDlg)
        m_message = _T("");
        //}}AFX_DATA_INIT
        m_hIcon = AfxGetApp()->LoadIcon(IDR_MAINFRAME);
}

void CRemindDlg::DoDataExchange(CDataExchange* pDX)
{
        CDialog::DoDataExchange(pDX);
        //{{AFX_DATA_MAP(CRemindDlg)
        DDX_Control(pDX, IDC_DATETIMEPICKER, m_datetime);
        DDX_Text(pDX, IDC_MESSAGE, m_message);
    //}}AFX_DATA_MAP
}

BEGIN_MESSAGE_MAP(CRemindDlg, CDialog)
        //{{AFX_MSG_MAP(CRemindDlg)
        ON_WM_SYSCOMMAND()
        ON_WM_PAINT()
        ON_WM_QUERYDRAGICON()
        ON_BN_CLICKED(IDOK, OnSetTimer)
        ON_BN_CLICKED(IDC_CANCEL_TIMER, OnCancelTimer)
        ON_BN_CLICKED(IDCANCEL, OnExit)
        ON_MESSAGE(WM_USER_ALARM, OnAlarm)
        ON_NOTIFY(DTN_DATETIMECHANGE, IDC_DATETIMEPICKER,
OnDatetimechangeDatetimepicker)
    //}}AFX_MSG_MAP
END_MESSAGE_MAP()
```

The message map requests control any time the Date and Time picker control changes. This is requested so that the program can make sure that the time specified is a future time. The sample when executed will allow the user to type in any time value, but after the user first enters a past time, it will then prevent the user from entering a past time again. For example, suppose the current time when the program is executed is 07:45:45PM. The program will allow the user to type 05 in the hour field. Because 05:45:45PM is a past time, the program will then impose a restriction such that the user can no longer type 05 in the hour field but can only type a value for a time in the future.

```
////////////////////////////////////////////////////////////////////////
// CRemindDlg message handlers

BOOL CRemindDlg::OnInitDialog()
{
    CDialog::OnInitDialog();

    // Add "About..." menu item to system menu.

    // IDM_ABOUTBOX must be in the system command range.
    ASSERT((IDM_ABOUTBOX & 0xFFF0) == IDM_ABOUTBOX);
    ASSERT(IDM_ABOUTBOX < 0xF000);

    CMenu* pSysMenu = GetSystemMenu(FALSE);
    if (pSysMenu != NULL)
    {
        CString strAboutMenu;
        strAboutMenu.LoadString(IDS_ABOUTBOX);
        if (!strAboutMenu.IsEmpty())
        {
            pSysMenu->AppendMenu(MF_SEPARATOR);
            pSysMenu->AppendMenu(MF_STRING, IDM_ABOUTBOX, strAboutMenu);
        }
    }

    // Set the icon for this dialog.  The framework does this automatically
    //  when the application's main window is not a dialog
    SetIcon(m_hIcon, TRUE);                 // Set big icon
    SetIcon(m_hIcon, FALSE);                // Set small icon

    // TODO: Add extra initialization here


    SYSTEMTIME  systemTime;
    GetLocalTime(&systemTime);
    m_datetime.SetFormat(_T("'Wake up at 'hh':'mm':'sstt"));
    m_datetime.SetTime(&systemTime);

    hWaitableTimer = CreateWaitableTimer(NULL, 1, NULL);
    // Gray the Cancel Timer button
    GetDlgItem(IDC_CANCEL_TIMER)->EnableWindow(FALSE);
    return TRUE;
}
```

The format of the time is set by calling the **SetFormat** member function. Given the variety of formatting strings available, the control can be made very versatile to suit the application's needs.

```
void CRemindDlg::OnSysCommand(UINT nID, LPARAM lParam)
{
    if ((nID & 0xFFF0) == IDM_ABOUTBOX)
    {
        CAboutDlg dlgAbout;
        dlgAbout.DoModal();
    }
    else
    {
        CDialog::OnSysCommand(nID, lParam);
    }
}

// If you add a minimize button to your dialog, you will need the code below
//  to draw the icon.  For MFC applications using the document/view model,
//  this is automatically done for you by the framework.

void CRemindDlg::OnPaint()
{
    if (IsIconic())
    {
        CPaintDC dc(this); // device context for painting

        SendMessage(WM_ICONERASEBKGND, (WPARAM) dc.GetSafeHdc(), 0);

        // Center icon in client rectangle
        int cxIcon = GetSystemMetrics(SM_CXICON);
        int cyIcon = GetSystemMetrics(SM_CYICON);
        CRect rect;
        GetClientRect(&rect);
        int x = (rect.Width() - cxIcon + 1) / 2;
        int y = (rect.Height() - cyIcon + 1) / 2;

        // Draw the icon
        dc.DrawIcon(x, y, m_hIcon);
    }
    else
    {
        CDialog::OnPaint();
    }
}

// The system calls this to obtain the cursor to display while the user drags
//  the minimized window.
HCURSOR CRemindDlg::OnQueryDragIcon()
```

```
{
    return (HCURSOR) m_hIcon;
}

void CRemindDlg::OnSetTimer()
{
        // TODO: Add your control notification handler code here
    SYSTEMTIME   systemTime;
    FILETIME     localfileTime;
    FILETIME     duefileTime;
    LARGE_INTEGER   largeInt;

    UpdateData();

    ptinfo = new TIMERINFO;
    AlarmMessage = m_message;

    GetLocalTime(&systemTime);
    m_datetime.GetTime(&systemTime);
    systemTime.wSecond = 0;     // On the second
    systemTime.wMilliseconds = 0;  // On the millisec

    SystemTimeToFileTime(&systemTime, &localfileTime);
    LocalFileTimeToFileTime(&localfileTime, &duefileTime);
    largeInt.LowPart = duefileTime.dwLowDateTime;
    largeInt.HighPart = duefileTime.dwHighDateTime;

    ptinfo->li = largeInt;
    ptinfo->hDialogHandle = GetSafeHwnd();
    hTimerThread = AfxBeginThread(TimerThread, ptinfo);

    // Gray the Set Time button and enable the Cancel Timer button
    GetDlgItem(IDOK)->EnableWindow(FALSE);
    GetDlgItem(IDC_CANCEL_TIMER)->EnableWindow(TRUE);
    ShowWindow(SW_MINIMIZE);
}

void CRemindDlg::OnCancelTimer()
{
        // TODO: Add your control notification handler code here
    if (bTimerExists)
    {   // Clean up allocated data and thread
        CancelWaitableTimer(hWaitableTimer);
        TerminateThread(hTimerThread, 0);
        delete ptinfo;
        ptinfo = NULL;
        bTimerExists = FALSE;

        // Gray the Cancel Time button and enable the Set Timer button
```

```
        GetDlgItem(IDOK)->EnableWindow(TRUE);
        GetDlgItem(IDC_CANCEL_TIMER)->EnableWindow(FALSE);
    }
}


void CRemindDlg::OnExit()
{
    // TODO: Add extra cleanup here
    if (ptinfo)
    {
        delete ptinfo;
    }
    CDialog::OnCancel();
}


void CRemindDlg::OnAlarm()
{
        // TODO: Add your control notification handler code here
    ShowWindow(SW_RESTORE);
    // include your own music here
    Beep(2000,70);
    Sleep(200);
    Beep(2000,70);
    Sleep(200);
    Beep(2000,70);
    Sleep(500);
    Beep(2000,500);
    MessageBox(AlarmMessage, "Remind - Alarm");

    // Gray the Cancel Time button and enable the Set Timer button
    GetDlgItem(IDOK)->EnableWindow(TRUE);
    GetDlgItem(IDC_CANCEL_TIMER)->EnableWindow(FALSE);
    if (ptinfo) // Free memory
    {
        delete ptinfo;
        ptinfo = NULL;
    }
}
```

The next member function is invoked whenever the user changes the time in the Date and Time picker control. The time change is picked up from the notification message checked against the current time. If the selected time is past, then a message is displayed and the Date and Time picker control is reset to the time range from the current time till the end of the day. This is set using the **SetRange** member function. From now on, the user cannot pick a past time.

```
void CRemindDlg::OnDatetimechangeDatetimepicker(NMHDR* pNMHDR, LRESULT* pResult)
{
    // TODO: Add your control notification handler code here
```

```
        CTime currentTime, selectedTime;
        LPNMDATETIMECHANGE pDTChange = (LPNMDATETIMECHANGE)pNMHDR;

        DWORD dwRet = m_datetime.GetTime(selectedTime);
        currentTime =   CTime::GetCurrentTime();
        if (dwRet == GDT_VALID)
        {
            if (selectedTime < currentTime)
            {
                CString meridian;
                if (currentTime.GetHour() >= 12)
                {
                    meridian = "PM";
                }
                else
                {
                    meridian = "AM";
                }
                CString message = "The time should be in future.  Resetting the \
time from " + currentTime.Format("%I:%M:%S ") + meridian+ " now till end \
of day.";
                MessageBox(message);
                pDTChange->st.wHour = 23;
                pDTChange->st.wMinute = 59;
                pDTChange->st.wSecond = 59;
                pDTChange->st.wMilliseconds = 0;
                CTime *newTimeTime = new CTime (pDTChange->st);
                m_datetime.SetRange(&currentTime, newTimeTime);
                m_datetime.SetTime(&currentTime);
                delete newTimeTime;
            }
        }
        *pResult = 0;
}


UINT TimerThread(LPVOID alarmTime)
{
    TIMERINFO       *ptinfo;
    ptinfo = (TIMERINFO *)alarmTime;
    bTimerExists = SetWaitableTimer (hWaitableTimer, &ptinfo->li,
                                0 , NULL, NULL, 0);
    if (WaitForSingleObject(hWaitableTimer, INFINITE) == WAIT_TIMEOUT)
    {
        // You may change INFINITE to a value and
        // optionally act when it times out.
        // Since the wait is currently INFINITE no action is needed.
    }
```

```
    else
    {
      PostMessage(ptinfo->hDialogHandle, WM_USER_ALARM, 0 ,0); // Post Message
    }
    bTimerExists = FALSE;
    return 0;
}
```

Month Calendar Control

The Month Calendar control is implemented in version 4.70 and later of *Comctl32.dll*. The Adjust Date/Time function (normally found in the bottom-right corner) is an example of setting the month using a calendar format that the Month Calendar control provides. Some of the ways in which this control makes it easy for the user to pick the month and date include:

▼ Display of the day that corresponds to a date

■ Display of week numbers

▲ Scrolling backward or forward between months

You can utilize the Month Calendar control using the MFC class **CMonthCalCtrl**. You can also use the **CreateWindowEx** API and specify MONTHCAL_CLASS as the window class, after which you register this class by calling the **InitCommonControlsEx** function. The class is registered when the Date and Time picker class is loaded from the common control DLL. The programming example discussed later in this chapter uses the MFC class **CDateTimeCtrl**.

Month Calendar Control Programming Example

Figures 7-28 through 7-33 show the output of the programming example.

The next sample shows the functioning of a Month Calendar control using the MFC wrapper **CMonthCalCtrl**. It is a dialog-based application, which displays a Month Calendar control, three radio buttons, and a status area that displays the various activities that go on as the user interacts with the sample. Shown next is the resource file for the dialog box. MCS_DAYSTATE style is specific to the Month Calendar control. By specifying this style, the application is notified with a MCN_GETDAYSTATE message by the Month Calendar control to request information about which days should be displayed in bold. This way the application can control which days should be shown in bold. The MCS_MULTISELECT style allows the user to select a range of dates, and MCN_NOTODAY tells the control not to display today's date at the bottom of the control. There are two other styles: MCS_NOTODAYCIRCLE, which draws a circle around the "today" date, and MCS_WEEKNUMBERS, which displays the week numbers available for use with the control. These are set and reset dynamically in the sample application.

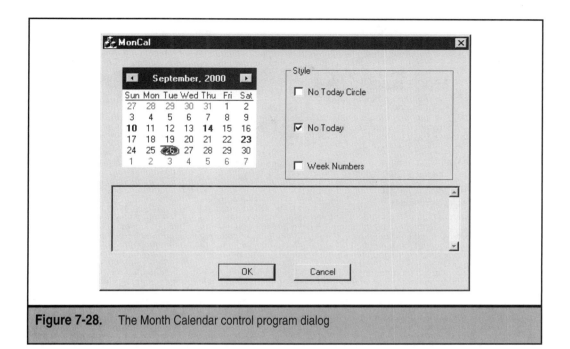

Figure 7-28. The Month Calendar control program dialog

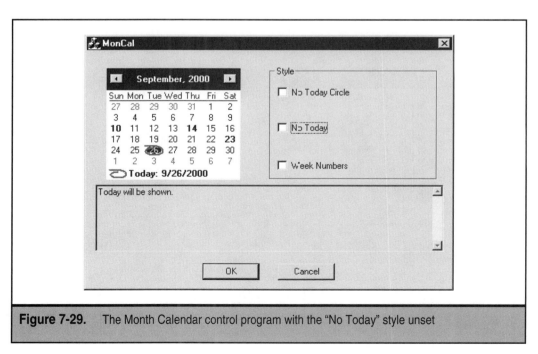

Figure 7-29. The Month Calendar control program with the "No Today" style unset

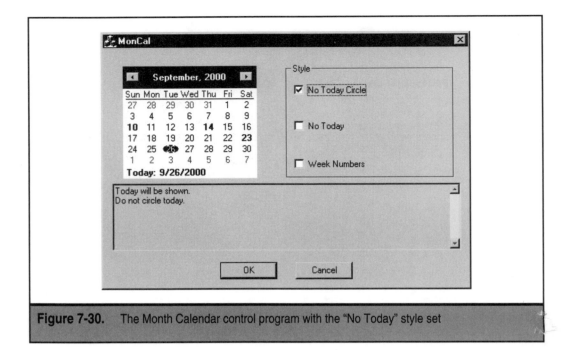

Figure 7-30.   The Month Calendar control program with the "No Today" style set

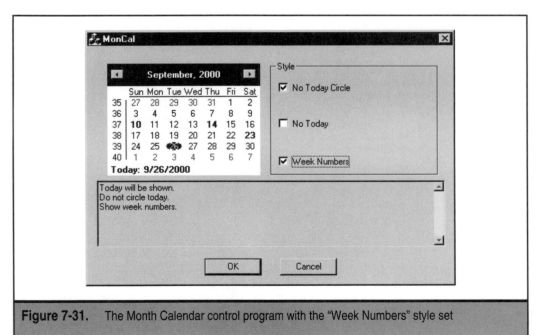

Figure 7-31.   The Month Calendar control program with the "Week Numbers" style set

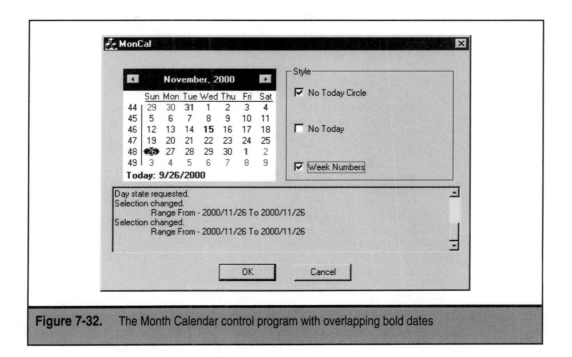

Figure 7-32. The Month Calendar control program with overlapping bold dates

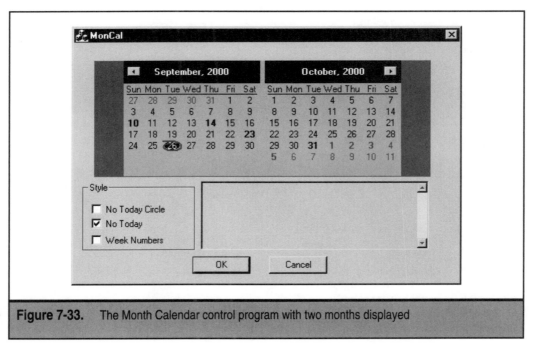

Figure 7-33. The Month Calendar control program with two months displayed

```
IDD_MONCAL_DIALOG DIALOGEX 0, 0, 320, 200
STYLE DS_MODALFRAME | WS_POPUP | WS_VISIBLE | WS_CAPTION | WS_SYSMENU
EXSTYLE WS_EX_APPWINDOW
CAPTION "MonCal"
FONT 8, "MS Sans Serif"
BEGIN
    CONTROL         "MonthCalendar1",IDC_MONTHCALENDAR,"SysMonthCal32",
                    MCS_DAYSTATE | MCS_MULTISELECT | MCS_NOTODAY |
                    WS_TABSTOP,17,15,117,84
    GROUPBOX        "Style",IDC_STATIC,160,13,147,96
    CONTROL         "No Today Circle",IDC_NOTODAYCIRCLE,"Button",
                    BS_AUTOCHECKBOX | WS_TABSTOP,167,30,136,10
    CONTROL         "No Today",IDC_NOTODAY,"Button",BS_AUTOCHECKBOX |
                    WS_TABSTOP,167,60,136,10
    CONTROL         "Week Numbers",IDC_WEEKNUMBERS,"Button",BS_AUTOCHECKBOX |
                    WS_TABSTOP,167,92,136,10
    EDITTEXT        IDC_NOTIFICATION,8,113,305,56,ES_MULTILINE |
                    ES_AUTOVSCROLL | ES_AUTOHSCROLL | ES_READONLY |
                    ES_WANTRETURN | WS_VSCROLL
    DEFPUSHBUTTON   "OK",IDOK,102,179,50,14
    PUSHBUTTON      "Cancel",IDCANCEL,168,179,50,14
END
```

Shown next is the header file for the dialog box class in the application. Notice the **CMonthCalCtrl** member variable. Other code of interest is shown in bold.

```
// MonCalDlg.h : header file

#if !defined(AFX_MONCALDLG_H)
#define AFX_MONCALDLG_H

#if _MSC_VER > 1000
#pragma once
#endif // _MSC_VER > 1000

// CMonCalDlg dialog

class CMonCalDlg : public CDialog
{
// Construction
public:
    CMonCalDlg(CWnd* pParent = NULL);

// Dialog Data
    //{{AFX_DATA(CMonCalDlg)
    enum { IDD = IDD_MONCAL_DIALOG };
    CEdit    m_notification;
    CMonthCalCtrl    m_moncal;
```

```
    BOOL    m_notoday;
    BOOL    m_notodaycircle;
    BOOL    m_weeknumbers;
    //}}AFX_DATA

    // ClassWizard generated virtual function overrides
    //{{AFX_VIRTUAL(CMonCalDlg)
    protected:
    virtual void DoDataExchange(CDataExchange* pDX);    // DDX/DDV support
    //}}AFX_VIRTUAL

// Implementation
protected:
    HICON m_hIcon;

    // Generated message map functions
    //{{AFX_MSG(CMonCalDlg)
    virtual BOOL OnInitDialog();
    afx_msg void OnPaint();
    afx_msg HCURSOR OnQueryDragIcon();
    afx_msg void OnNotoday();
    afx_msg void OnNotodaycircle();
    afx_msg void OnWeeknumbers();
    afx_msg void OnGetdaystateMonthcalendar(NMHDR* pNMHDR, LRESULT* pResult);
    afx_msg void OnSelchangeMonthcalendar(NMHDR* pNMHDR, LRESULT* pResult);
    afx_msg void OnSelectMonthcalendar(NMHDR* pNMHDR, LRESULT* pResult);
    virtual void OnOK();
    //}}AFX_MSG
    DECLARE_MESSAGE_MAP()
};

#endif // !defined(AFX_MONCALDLG_H)
```

The code that processes the dialog box is shown next. As the user navigates through the calendar, the application is notified and is requested for days in a month, which should be shown in bold. For convenience, a static array of bold dates is used. When the application is notified, the months are given as a 1-based index where 1 is January and 12 is December. For convenience, the **bolddays** array has an extra element, the zeroth element, which is ignored. For certain reasons, the bold days are selected according to a variety of orders, including the beginning of the month, the middle of the month, and the end of the month. These reasons will be discussed later.

```
// MonCalDlg.cpp : implementation file

#include "stdafx.h"
#include "MonCal.h"
#include "MonCalDlg.h"

#ifdef _DEBUG
```

```
#define new DEBUG_NEW
#undef THIS_FILE
static char THIS_FILE[] = __FILE__;
#endif

MONTHDAYSTATE    bolddays[13] = {
                        0x00000000,
                        0x02000001, // 1st, 26th
                        0x00002000, // 14th
                        0x00010000, // 17th
                        0x08800000, // 24th, 28th
                        0x00040000, // 19th
                        0x00800000, // 24th
                        0x00000008, // 4th
                        0x00000800, // 12th
                        0x00402200, // 10th, 14th, 23rd
                        0x40000000, // 31st
                        0x00004000, // 15th
                        0x01000001  // 1st, 25th
                        };


// CMonCalDlg dialog

CMonCalDlg::CMonCalDlg(CWnd* pParent /*=NULL*/)
    : CDialog(CMonCalDlg::IDD, pParent)
{
    //{{AFX_DATA_INIT(CMonCalDlg)
    m_notoday = FALSE;
    m_notodaycircle = FALSE;
    m_weeknumbers = FALSE;
    //}}AFX_DATA_INIT
    // Note that LoadIcon does not require a subsequent DestroyIcon in Win32
    m_hIcon = AfxGetApp()->LoadIcon(IDR_MAINFRAME);
}

void CMonCalDlg::DoDataExchange(CDataExchange* pDX)
{
    CDialog::DoDataExchange(pDX);
    //{{AFX_DATA_MAP(CMonCalDlg)
    DDX_Control(pDX, IDC_NOTIFICATION, m_notification);
    DDX_Control(pDX, IDC_MONTHCALENDAR, m_moncal);
    DDX_Check(pDX, IDC_NOTODAY, m_notoday);
    DDX_Check(pDX, IDC_NOTODAYCIRCLE, m_notodaycircle);
    DDX_Check(pDX, IDC_WEEKNUMBERS, m_weeknumbers);
    //}}AFX_DATA_MAP
}
```

This application wants to be notified when a calendar selection changes, when a date is selected, or whenever day states are to be shown. It also wants to be notified when the user changes the style of the Month Calendar control. These notification requests are defined in the following message map:

```
BEGIN_MESSAGE_MAP(CMonCalDlg, CDialog)
    //{{AFX_MSG_MAP(CMonCalDlg)
    ON_WM_PAINT()
    ON_WM_QUERYDRAGICON()
    ON_BN_CLICKED(IDC_NOTODAY, OnNotoday)
    ON_BN_CLICKED(IDC_NOTODAYCIRCLE, OnNotodaycircle)
    ON_BN_CLICKED(IDC_WEEKNUMBERS, OnWeeknumbers)
    ON_NOTIFY(MCN_GETDAYSTATE, IDC_MONTHCALENDAR, OnGetdaystateMonthcalendar)
    ON_NOTIFY(MCN_SELCHANGE, IDC_MONTHCALENDAR, OnSelchangeMonthcalendar)
    ON_NOTIFY(MCN_SELECT, IDC_MONTHCALENDAR, OnSelectMonthcalendar)
    //}}AFX_MSG_MAP
END_MESSAGE_MAP()
```

During initialization, the application gets the styles of the month calendar control using the **GetStyle** method and updates the style check boxes appropriately.

```
// CMonCalDlg message handlers
BOOL CMonCalDlg::OnInitDialog()
{
    CDialog::OnInitDialog();

    // Set the icon for this dialog.  The framework does this automatically
    //  when the application's main window is not a dialog
    SetIcon(m_hIcon, TRUE);            // Set big icon
    SetIcon(m_hIcon, FALSE);           // Set small icon

    // TODO: Add extra initialization here
    DWORD    dwStyle;
    dwStyle = m_moncal.GetStyle();     // Get the current style
    if (dwStyle & MCS_NOTODAY)
    {
        m_notoday = TRUE;
    }
    if (dwStyle & MCS_NOTODAYCIRCLE)
    {
        m_notodaycircle = TRUE;
    }
    if (dwStyle & MCS_WEEKNUMBERS)
    {
        m_weeknumbers = TRUE;
    }
```

The application wants to set the current day selection to today. However, the current date cannot be set if the Month Calendar control has a style MCS_MULTISELECT.

The sample code available in the CD-ROM can be used to experiment with this setting. (A better alternative to **#if**, is to check the style, queried earlier and then set it. Refer to the code in the **OnOK** processing.) Finally it calls the **SizeMinReq** member function to display just one month. The most common use of the Month Calendar control requires it to show only one month. However, this control can be used to show more than one month. The number of months shown depends on the size of the control. But if your code calls the **SizeMinReq** member function, the control ignores its size and shows just one month. The CD-ROM has another variation of this sample that shows two months; the **SetMinReq** call is missing in that sample.

```
#if 0 // If the calendar does not have MCS_MULTISELECT style
      // you can initialize the current date.
    SYSTEMTIME selTime;
    memset(&selTime, 0, sizeof(selTime));
    // Set our date
    selTime.wYear = 1994;
    selTime.wMonth = 4;
    selTime.wDay = 28;
    m_moncal.SetCurSel(&selTime);
#endif
    m_moncal.SizeMinReq();
    UpdateData(FALSE);
    return TRUE;  // return TRUE  unless you set the focus to a control
}


// If you add a minimize button to your dialog, you will need the code below
//  to draw the icon.  For MFC applications using the document/view model,
//  this is automatically done for you by the framework.

void CMonCalDlg::OnPaint()
{
    if (IsIconic())
    {
        CPaintDC dc(this); // device context for painting

        SendMessage(WM_ICONERASEBKGND, (WPARAM) dc.GetSafeHdc(), 0);

        // Center icon in client rectangle
        int cxIcon = GetSystemMetrics(SM_CXICON);
        int cyIcon = GetSystemMetrics(SM_CYICON);
        CRect rect;
        GetClientRect(&rect);
        int x = (rect.Width() - cxIcon + 1) / 2;
        int y = (rect.Height() - cyIcon + 1) / 2;

        // Draw the icon
        dc.DrawIcon(x, y, m_hIcon);
    }
```

```
        else
        {
            CDialog::OnPaint();
        }
}

// The system calls this to obtain the cursor to display while the user drags
//    the minimized window.
HCURSOR CMonCalDlg::OnQueryDragIcon()
{
    return (HCURSOR) m_hIcon;
}
```

The next three member functions process the user action to set/unset the styles that relate to MCS_NOTODAY, MCS_NOTODAYCIRCLE, MCS_WEEKNUMBERS. In each case the status window is updated as to what is being done to the control.

```
void CMonCalDlg::OnNotoday()
{
    DWORD    dwStyle;
    TCHAR    *message;
    dwStyle = m_moncal.GetStyle();
    if(dwStyle & MCS_NOTODAY) // Check current style and toggle it
    {
        dwStyle &= ~MCS_NOTODAY;
        message = "Today will be shown.\r\n";
    }
    else
    {
        dwStyle |= MCS_NOTODAY;
        message = "Today will not be shown.\r\n";
    }
    SetWindowLong(m_moncal.GetSafeHwnd(), GWL_STYLE, dwStyle);
    m_moncal.SizeMinReq();
    m_notification.SetSel(-1,0);
    m_notification.ReplaceSel(message);
}

void CMonCalDlg::OnNotodaycircle()
{
    DWORD    dwStyle;
    TCHAR    *message;
    dwStyle = m_moncal.GetStyle();
    if(dwStyle & MCS_NOTODAYCIRCLE) // Check current style and toggle it
    {
        dwStyle &= ~MCS_NOTODAYCIRCLE;
        message = "Circle today.\r\n";
    }
    else
```

```
    {
        dwStyle |= MCS_NOTODAYCIRCLE;
        message = "Do not circle today.\r\n";
    }
    SetWindowLong(m_moncal.GetSafeHwnd(), GWL_STYLE, dwStyle);
    m_moncal.SizeMinReq();
    m_notification.SetSel(-1,0);
    m_notification.ReplaceSel(message);
}

void CMonCalDlg::OnWeeknumbers()
{
    DWORD   dwStyle;
    TCHAR   *message;
    dwStyle = m_moncal.GetStyle();
    if(dwStyle & MCS_WEEKNUMBERS) // Check current style and toggle it
    {
        dwStyle &= ~MCS_WEEKNUMBERS;
        message = "Remove week numbers.\r\n";
    }
    else
    {
        dwStyle |= MCS_WEEKNUMBERS;
        message = "Show week numbers.\r\n";
    }
    SetWindowLong(m_moncal.GetSafeHwnd(), GWL_STYLE, dwStyle);
    m_moncal.SizeMinReq();
    m_notification.SetSel(-1,0);
    m_notification.ReplaceSel(message);
}
```

Perhaps the most frequently customized feature of the Month Calendar control is its capacity to show certain dates in the calendar in bold. For example, an application may want to show the holidays. The month calendar control provides a mechanism that allows the application to tell which dates should be shown in bold. To do this the control should have the MCS_DAYSTATE style set and and should be enabled to process the notification of the MCN_GETDAYSTATE message. In this sample the member function **OnGetdaystateMonthcalendar** gets called when the control needs the day state.

A Month Calendar control displays 42 days in each month's display. Thus each month's display includes an overlap with dates from the previous and next months. Given this fact, whenever the Month Calendar control requests the day state, it requests two more months' worth of day states than whatever is visible. For example, if the control is large enough to display four months at a time, then it will request six months' worth of day states. These six months are the four visible months plus the month previous to the first visible month and the month next to the last visible month. Even though the days in the previous month and next month are grayed, they still have the day state set. The days chosen to be shown in bold in the **bolddays** array are random for this reason.

The notification message header data provided during MCN_GETDAYSTATE notification is of type **LPNMDAYSTATE**. The **cDayState** member in this structure indicates the number of day states elements in the array pointed by **prgDayState**. The application should fill the array pointed by **prgDayState** with **cDayState** months' worth of day states. If the application calls the **SizeMinReq** member function, then **cDayState** cannot be larger than 3, since calling **SizeMinReg** would allow the control to display only one month. **cDayState** is the sum of visible months plus 2. Since this sample displays one month, it proceeds to fill three elements.

The day state is provided using a variable of type **MONTHDAYSTATE,** which essentially is a DWORD. It is bit field, and when a bit is set, it indicates a date that should be shown in bold. Bit 1 represents day 1, and bit 31 represents day 31. A popular macro to show a given date in bold is shown here:

```
#define BOLDDAY(ds,iDay) if(iDay>0 && iDay<32) (ds)|=(0x00000001<<(iDay-1))
```

These day states should be set in the array pointed by **prgDayState** member.

```
void CMonCalDlg::OnGetdaystateMonthcalendar(NMHDR* pNMHDR, LRESULT* pResult)
{
    if ((void *)m_notification != NULL)
    {
        m_notification.SetSel(-1,0);
        m_notification.ReplaceSel("Day state requested.\r\n");
    }
    LPNMDAYSTATE pNMDayState;
    pNMDayState = (LPNMDAYSTATE) pNMHDR;

    INT cDayState;

    cDayState = pNMDayState->cDayState;
    WORD startMonth;
    SHORT indexOne;
    SHORT indexTwo;
    SHORT indexThree;

    startMonth = (pNMDayState->stStart).wMonth;

    if (startMonth == 11)
    {
        indexOne = 11;
        indexTwo = 12;
        indexThree = 1;
    }
    else if (startMonth == 12)
    {
        indexOne = 12;
        indexTwo = 1;
        indexThree = 2;
```

```
    }
    else
    {
        indexOne = startMonth;
        indexTwo = startMonth+1;
        indexThree = startMonth+2;
    }

    MONTHDAYSTATE *pMDS;
    pMDS = pNMDayState->prgDayState;

    *pMDS++ = bolddays[indexOne];
    *(pMDS++) = bolddays[indexTwo];
    *pMDS = bolddays[indexThree];
    *pResult = 0;
}
```

The next two member functions process the MCN_SELCHANGE and MCN_SELECT messages for selection change and selection notification. The application is provided with the start date and the end date, which the application can process.

```
void CMonCalDlg::OnSelchangeMonthcalendar(NMHDR* pNMHDR, LRESULT* pResult)
{
    TCHAR    message[256];
    LPNMSELCHANGE pNMSelChange;
    pNMSelChange = (LPNMSELCHANGE) pNMHDR;

    wsprintf (message, "Selection changed.\r\n\tRange From -\
%d/%d/%d To %d/%d/%d\r\n",
                pNMSelChange->stSelStart.wYear,
                pNMSelChange->stSelStart.wMonth,
                pNMSelChange->stSelStart.wDay,
                pNMSelChange->stSelEnd.wYear,
                pNMSelChange->stSelEnd.wMonth,
                pNMSelChange->stSelEnd.wDay);
    m_notification.SetSel(-1,0);
    m_notification.ReplaceSel(message);

    *pResult = 0;
}

void CMonCalDlg::OnSelectMonthcalendar(NMHDR* pNMHDR, LRESULT* pResult)
{
    TCHAR    message[256];
    LPNMSELCHANGE pNMSelChange;
    pNMSelChange = (LPNMSELCHANGE) pNMHDR;
```

```
        wsprintf (message, "Selection.\r\n\tRange From - %d/%d/%d\
  To %d/%d/%d\r\n",
                pNMSelChange->stSelStart.wYear,
                pNMSelChange->stSelStart.wMonth,
                pNMSelChange->stSelStart.wDay,
                pNMSelChange->stSelEnd.wYear,
                pNMSelChange->stSelEnd.wMonth,
                pNMSelChange->stSelEnd.wDay);
    m_notification.SetSel(-1,0);
    m_notification.ReplaceSel(message);

    *pResult = 0;
}
```

When the user closes the application by clicking OK, it checks if the style is not MCS_MULTISELECT and displays the currently selected date.

```
void CMonCalDlg::OnOK()
{
    DWORD dwStyle;

    dwStyle = m_moncal.GetStyle();
    if(!(dwStyle & MCS_MULTISELECT))
    {
        TCHAR message[256];
        SYSTEMTIME selTime;
        memset(&selTime, 0, sizeof(selTime));
        m_moncal.GetCurSel(&selTime);
        wsprintf (message, "Selected date is: %d/%d/%d", selTime.wYear,
selTime.wMonth, selTime.wDay);
        MessageBox(message);
    }
    CDialog::OnOK();
}
```

There are other member functions available in the **CMonthCalCtrl** to get and set a variety of attributes such as the color of the first day of the week. By default the first day of the week is set according to the locale, and in most cases this should suffice.

CONCLUSION

In this chapter, we examined common controls. Common controls make your user interface look professional, and you will most certainly be using common controls in your business applications. We looked at programming examples of the Animation control, the HotKey control, the Spin control, the Slider control, the Progress control, the List View control, and the Tree View control, as well as two of the controls introduced with version 4.70 of common controls and supported in Windows 2000—the Date and Time picker control and the Month Calendar control. As mentioned earlier, it is not possible to cover all the common controls here. But using the examples shown, you should be able to use the other common controls.

Although Windows 2000 has a variety of common controls, there are times when you need more powerful user interfaces. In such cases, you can extend the available controls. The CD-ROM has one such extended control (in Chapter 7 on the CD), which extends the List control to behave like a form with a prompt date in the left column and a date entry in the right column.

So far in this part, we have looked at graphics programming and using common controls. These user interface topics give you a good set of programs and techniques to use in your own user interface programming.

CHAPTER 8

Windows 2000 Dynamic Link Libraries (DLLs)

A *dynamic link library* is a library of functions or resources. The process of creating the DLL is very similar to that of creating a Windows application. The functions are invoked by applications or other DLLs. DLLs are an integral part of Windows 2000 programming, and using DLLs is an important tool in the repertoire of Windows NT programmers. DLLs have been available in prior versions of Windows—you may have programmed DLLs with Win16. But don't skip this chapter because of your 16-bit DLL experience, since there are significant differences between Win32 DLLs and Win16 DLLs. We will cover the differences in this chapter.

We will start with the need for DLLs and compare the development of DLLs and of applications. Developing DLLs is very similar to developing applications, with minor differences in linking and execution. You can invoke a DLL for execution in two ways. We will see how you can make functions in a DLL available for invocation by applications. We will explore the concept of DLL versions and how you can use versions to ensure that the right version of the DLL is loaded.

Note for UNIX Programmers

If you have used shared libraries that support dynamic linking/loading, then Windows NT DLLs are conceptually the same.

WHY DLLs

If you are developing a Windows application, then using DLLs is not mandatory, although you are likely to find that any nontrivial system using Windows applications will use DLLs. There are good reasons to use DLLs. Windows 2000 itself uses a large number of DLLs internally. You may be familiar with many of these DLLs. Table 8-1 lists some of these DLLs and the functions performed by them.

One of the advantages of using DLLs is that DLLs enable you to group commonly used functions into a unit that can be invoked by a number of different applications. In the course of developing a large software system, after high-level design and before coding, you will allocate the overall system functions into code modules. During this allocation, you will identify a number of common functions that are useful throughout the overall system. DLLs are a handy way to group these functions. You will typically end up with a number of DLLs, with each DLL containing related functions, data, and/or resources. Any application in the system can invoke the functionality in the DLL and thus does not have to repeat the DLL functionality. Allocating the common functions to DLLs also helps to contain any changes required in the common functions to the DLLs, and to ensure that the rest of the applications in the system are not affected. For example, in a financial system, calculating interest needs to be performed in different parts of the system. Isolating the interest calculation code to a DLL makes it easy to compute interest differ-

DLL	Function
Kernel32.dll	Kernel functions, such as functions for managing processes, memory, and so on
Gdi32.dll	Graphics functions, such as drawing geometrical shapes, filling the shapes, and so on
Olesvr32.dll	OLE server functions (32 bit)
Shell32.dll	Shell functions supporting 32-bit shell APIs
User32.dll	User interface functions, such as managing windows and handling messages

Table 8-1.   Windows 2000 DLLs and Their Functions

ently (for example, to use a different compounding method). Later in this chapter we will look at an example where calculating interest is one of the functions in a DLL.

Another advantage of DLLs lies in software packaging and distribution. In software development, you will invariably have portions of the overall software that are applicable only to certain customers. Thus, it is beneficial to isolate the portions that are customer-specific to DLLs, and to organize the rest of the system as one or more EXEs applicable to all customers. Appendix A contains a simple example that lets users key in their name and then redisplay the name keyed in. The example is designed to let users using different languages, such as French and German, see dialog boxes that are in their own language. The names are input with keyboards supporting their language. In this case, there is one EXE and the language-specific resources are contained within DLLs. Such an approach permits shipping the main EXE and appropriate language-specific DLLs to each country. If you want to add an additional language, you just add the DLLs for it (which does not affect the existing users). The same is true if you want to drop the support for a language. Thus, you can add new resources, functions, and so on to a DLL, and the new DLLs will work with the existing applications so long as the EXE-to-DLL interface does not change.

Yet another advantage of DLLs is run-time memory savings. Once a DLL has been loaded, further requests to load the DLL by other threads in the same process do not cause additional copies of the DLL to be loaded. Windows recognizes that the DLL has already been loaded and keeps a count of the number of threads using the DLL by means of a *usage count*. Loading a DLL only once saves memory. In addition, the DLL can be loaded when needed. The initial memory to be allocated to the EXE that invokes the DLL is less than the memory that would need to be allocated if the DLL were part of the EXE.

Finally, splitting the overall system functions into EXEs and DLLs permits simultaneous development of DLLs and the EXEs.

The benefits of using DLLs are not free. Once you split the functions that are in an EXE into an EXE and a DLL, you have introduced an interface (that between the EXE and the DLL). Interfaces between applications are one of the trouble spots in a software system. Any large software system is like a chain of links. The individual programs make up the software system chain, and the adage "A chain is as strong as its weakest link" translates into "The software system is as error free as its interfaces." Quite often the individual programs that make up a software system work fine, but the system as a whole does not. Invariably the first set of error reports from a system test almost exclusively contains interface errors.

A related problem with DLLs is one of version control. DLLs can be changed without changing the invoking EXE or DLL. This is true only as long as the interface does not change. If the interface changes and the invoking EXE or DLL has to change, we may have situations where the invoking EXE or DLL will work correctly only if the correct version of the invoked DLL is available (and not any older version). If you are in programming, you are bound to come across "Murphy's law." In this case, Murphy's law states that the EXE will somehow find the wrong versions of the DLL. One of the most common questions support teams and help desks face deals with versions. It is not uncommon in many development efforts to repeat program builds because the wrong version was picked up during the build. Software configuration control systems try to maintain version control. You can also use the version feature of DLLs to keep track of DLL versions. This is covered in an example later in this chapter.

Another simple problem is that although you can create a DLL with Visual C++, you can create the EXE with another tool, for example, a regular C compiler. In this case, you have to watch out for name mangling. *Name mangling* refers to the fact that C++ compilers alter the names of functions they export, and as a result a calling application using an unmangled name may not be able to find the function in the DLL. Name mangling is covered later in this chapter.

COMPARING DLL AND APPLICATION DEVELOPMENT

The development of DLLs up to the compilation stage is the same as that of a Windows application. You write the DLL code and compile the code just as you would with any Windows application.

At the linking stage, you have to indicate to the linkage editor that you are link-editing a DLL and not an application. The typical linkage editor options for a DLL are /dll, /nologo, and /subsystem:windows. The "/dll" indicates to the linkage editor that you are link-editing a DLL. You can also check the Win32 DLL box in the Developer Studio as a type of application.

In the execution stage, you manually start an application for execution by double-clicking an icon associated with the application's EXE file (you can also key in the application's name at a command prompt). The DLL does not execute in a stand-alone manner, unlike the application. Instead it is invoked for execution by an application or by another DLL. DLLs can be specified to be invoked during link-edit time or at run time. Invoking DLLs is covered later in the chapter.

Typically, DLLs do not handle end-user interfaces. One of the consequences is that DLLs cannot use the About option under Help to display information about the DLL itself. EXEs that handle end-user interfaces use the About option under Help to display messages about the EXE itself, such as its version information, copyright information, and so on. However, you can use a DLL's version-control resource file for this purpose, and this is illustrated in an example later in this chapter.

WIN16 AND WIN32 DLL DIFFERENCES

As mentioned in the beginning of the chapter, there are significant differences between Win16 DLLs and Win32 DLLs. These differences are summarized in Table 8-2.

If you are migrating old 16-bit DLLs to 32-bit DLLs in Windows 2000, then you have to take care of references to **LibMain**, **WEP**, **GetModuleUsage**, and so on by replacing obsolete references with equivalent current ones.

Win16 DLL	Win32 DLL
Once the DLL is loaded, all executing applications can access all functions in the DLL.	The DLL is process-specific, and only the threads of the process that loads the DLL can access the DLL functions by default.
The DLL allocates and uses its own memory.	The DLL allocates from the memory space of the process.
GetModuleUsage provides the current usage count for the DLL.	GetModuleUsage is not supported. You can check if a DLL is loaded using GetModuleHandle.
The return value when a DLL is not loaded is a number that indicates the reason for the error.	The return value is NULL. Use GET_LAST_ERROR to find the reason.
LibMain is called when a DLL is initialized.	DllMain is called as the entry and exit routine.
There is no concept of threads in Win16.	DllMain is called for the process loading the DLL as well as when individual threads are created in the process after the DLL is loaded.

Table 8-2.   Win16 and Win32 DLL Differences

INVOKING AND FREEING DLLs

As mentioned earlier, DLLs can be specified to be invoked during link-edit time or at run time. Let's look at each of the methods in detail.

At link-edit time, you specify the DLL functions that an application can call in the DLL's LIB file that is passed to the linkage editor. The linkage editor includes the name of the DLL in the calling application's EXE file. At run time, Windows looks for the required DLLs when it loads the application's EXE file and performs a number of steps related to the invocation of the DLL as shown under "Steps in Invoking a DLL." The usage count of a DLL included at link-edit time is automatically set to 1 at run time. In addition, if the same DLL is loaded again at run time by another thread in the process, then the usage count is incremented.

Alternatively, you can invoke a DLL at run time by using **LoadLibrary** or **LoadLibraryEx**. Both specify the name of the DLL to be loaded. **LoadLibraryEx** supports two additional parameters, one of which (see the HANDLE *hFl* parameter in the prototype next) must be NULL. The other parameter (*dwFlgs*) lets you include some options to override the default Windows behavior as mentioned under "Steps in Invoking a DLL." If the *dwFlgs* parameter is zero, **LoadLibrary** and **LoadLibraryEx** behave identically. We will cover these options in this section.

TIP: If you use the Visual C++ compiler support for thread-local variables (**_declspec(*thread*)**), you will not be able to load the DLL explicitly using **LoadLibrary** or **LoadLibraryEx**. If you want to load your DLL explicitly, you must use the thread local storage functions instead of **_declspec(*thread*)**.

The prototype for **LoadLibraryEx** is shown here:

```
HMODULE LoadLibraryEx( LPCTSTR lpLibFlNam,
                       HANDLE hFl,
                       DWORD dwFlgs
    );
```

Here, *lpLibFlNam* is a pointer to a string that contains the filename of an executable module. The executable module can be either a DLL file or an EXE file. The filename can be just the filename, or it can include a path name. If the path name is specified and the LOAD_WITH_ALTERED_SEARCH_PATH value is specified for *dwFlgs*, then Windows tries to load the executable using the path name. If the executable is not found in the directory pointed to by the path name or in one of the other directories Windows uses to locate a DLL (see "Library Search Order" next), **LoadLibraryEx** returns NULL.

If the path name is not specified and the filename does not have an extension, then ".DLL" is automatically appended to the filename (unless the filename ends with a period).

If the path name is not specified or the LOAD_WITH_ALTERED_SEARCH_PATH value is not specified for *dwFlgs*, then Windows 2000 uses a specific search order (see "Library Search Order" next).

hFl is reserved and must be NULL.

dwFlgs can contain valid combinations of LOAD_LIBRARY_AS_DATAFILE, LOAD_ WITH_ALTERED_SEARCH_PATH, and DONT_RESOLVE_DLL_REFERENCES.

LOAD_LIBRARY_AS_DATAFILE, as its name implies, just causes Windows 2000 to load the DLL as a data file and not perform some of the steps that are normally done when a DLL is loaded (see steps 4 through 6 in "Steps in Invoking a DLL" later in this chapter). This option is normally used to load a DLL to access resources and messages (but not functions) from the DLL.

DONT_RESOLVE_DLL_REFERENCES is similar to LOAD_LIBRARY_AS_ DATAFILE in that it also causes Windows 2000 to just load the DLL and not perform other steps (see steps 4 through 6 in "Steps in Invoking a DLL" later in this chapter) that Windows 2000 normally performs. In particular, Windows 2000 does not call the entry point function that performs initialization steps associated with the DLL.

Both **LoadLibrary** and **LoadLibraryEx** return the handle to the loaded DLL if successful and NULL otherwise.

NEW IN WINDOWS 2000:   In Windows 2000, if a path is specified and a redirection file is associated with the application, the **LoadLibraryEx** function searches for the module in the application directory. If the module exists in the application directory, **LoadLibraryEx** ignores the path specification and loads the module from the application directory. If the module does not exist in the application directory, the function loads the module from the specified directory.

You can free a DLL you invoked by using **FreeLibrary**, whose prototype is shown next:

```
BOOL FreeLibrary( HMODULE hLibMod
    );
```

Here, *hLibMod* contains the handle that was returned by **LoadLibrary**/**LoadLibraryEx** or **GetModuleHandle**.

FreeLibrary returns nonzero if successful, and zero otherwise.

Windows 2000 decrements the usage count in response to the **FreeLibrary** call. If the usage count is zero, then the DLL is unmapped from the process's address space. Windows 2000 also invokes your DLL exit routine.

In instances when you create a thread within the invoked DLL and want to unload the DLL and terminate the thread, you must use the **FreeLibraryAndExitThread** function instead of **FreeLibrary**. This is because when you call **FreeLibrary** in the DLL, the DLL immediately gets unmapped and the rest of the DLL code (including the **ExitThread**) is no longer available. **FreeLibraryAndExitThread** also decrements the usage count, but it has no return values. (The absence of return values is normally not a problem, since no real exceptions are expected in **FreeLibraryAndExitThread**. The only real exception you can have is that the handle of the DLL you passed is invalid, and **FreeLibraryAndExitThread** ignores invalid handles—you are freeing the DLL anyway and an invalid handle suggests that the DLL is probably already free.)

TIP: Both **GetModuleHandle** and **LoadLibraryEx** return handles that can be used subsequently by the same functions, such as **GetProcAddress**, **FreeLibrary**, and **LoadResource**. However, there is a difference. **LoadLibraryEx** maps a module into the address space of the calling process if the module is not already mapped, and it increments the module's usage count. **GetModuleHandle** returns the handle to a mapped module without incrementing its usage count. Therefore, since the usage count is used in **FreeLibraryEx** to determine whether to unmap the function from the address space of the process, use care when using a handle returned by **GetModuleHandle** in a call to **FreeLibraryEx**, because doing so can cause a dynamic link library (DLL) module to be unmapped prematurely.

Library Search Order

Windows searches various libraries in the following sequence to locate the DLL to load:

1. The directory that contains the EXE file of the application (which is loading the DLL) or the directory specified in the *lpLibFlNam* parameter (you must also specify *LOAD_WITH_ALTERED_SEARCH_PATH* for *dwFlgs*).

2. The current directory of the process.

3. The 32-bit Windows System Directory, which is SYSTEM32 by default. (The user can override the default. You can obtain the current Windows System Directory by using the **GetSystemDirectory** function.)

4. The 16-bit Windows System Directory (which is SYSTEM by default).

5. The Windows Directory.

6. The directories contained in the PATH environment variable.

KnownDLLs

Windows 2000 has a Registry entry called KnownDLLs that affects the search order of the DLL. In order to improve performance, some commonly used DLLs such as the system DLLs are preloaded when the system is started. The DLLs that are to be loaded at the system start time are specified in the Registry entry called KnownDLLs. When a program runs, the system determines which DLLs that program will use. This search order was mentioned earlier. If a KnownDLL's Registry entry is present, however, this search order is altered, and it also depends on whether the DLL is a 16-bit DLL or a 32-bit DLL. For 16-bit DLLs, the KnownDLL's Registry appears in the HKEY_LOCAL_MACHINE\ System\CurrentControlSet\Control\WOW key, and for the 32-bit DLL it appears in HKEY_LOCAL_MACHINES\System\CurrentControlSet\Control\Session Manager. The 16-bit DLL entry affects both the implicitly and explicitly loaded DLLs. If the KnownDLLs Registry entry is set, WOW only looks in the \WINNT\SYSTEM32 directory for the DLL, and if it cannot find the DLL, it will fail, even though the DLL may be located at other locations mentioned earlier. You may recall from Chapter 1 that WOW, which stands for Win16-on-Win32, is the mechanism used to run 16-bit Windows 3.1 applications on 32-bit operating systems such as Windows 2000. The 32-bit KnownDLLs entry affects only the implicitly loaded DLLs. For 32-bit KnownDLLs, the search order is altered, starting with the \WINNT\SYSTEM32 directory. However, the search order is not changed for explicitly loaded DLLs.

Note that a DLL is treated as *KnownDLL* if another DLL from the KnownDLLs entry implicitly loads it. For example if *foo.dll* uses a function in *foobar.dll* and if *foo.dll* is a *KnownDLL*, then *foobar.dll* is also treated as a *KnownDLL*. This has an interesting side effect. Most of the KnownDLLs are system DLLs, and these system DLLs typically link to *msvcrt.dll* implicitly; therefore the system treats *msvcrt.dll* as a *KnownDLL*.

STEPS IN INVOKING A DLL

When you invoke a DLL, Windows, by default, performs the following steps. (You can change some of this behavior by using the options for the *dwFlgs* parameter as mentioned earlier.)

1. Windows checks to see if the DLL has already been loaded or mapped into the address space of the process.

2. If the DLL is not currently loaded, Windows loads the DLL into the address space of the invoking process and sets the usage count to 1.

3. If the DLL is currently loaded, then Windows does not load the DLL again. Windows just increments the usage count for the DLL by 1 (see the Tip that follows). The rest of the steps listed apply only when a DLL is being loaded for the first time.

4. Windows also checks to see if additional DLLs are invoked by the DLL being loaded and recursively invokes the other DLLs as well.

5. Windows prepares the DLL for execution by performing such functions as assigning page attributes.

6. Windows calls the entry point function to initialize the DLL. DLL entry and exit functions are covered in more detail in the next section.

TIP: Keep in mind that in Windows 2000, DLLs are process specific. If process X and process Y invoke the same DLL, two usage counts are established—one for process X, and one for process Y. Incrementing and decrementing are on a per-process basis. Thus, if the usage count for the DLL goes to zero in process X, the DLL will be unmapped for the address space of process X, but this has no effect on the DLL or its usage count in process Y.

DLL ENTRY/EXIT FUNCTIONS

You can have an entry/exit function for your DLL, although it is not mandatory. (There is a default entry/exit routine that just returns TRUE regardless of the purpose for which it is called.) It is one function that is called for both entry and exit. The entry/exit function is called when the DLL is being mapped and unmapped to a process. The function also is called when a thread is created or terminated. This function is typically made up of different parts, each of which handles one reason for which the function is called. The entry/exit function could use the following prototype:

```
BOOL WINAPI DllMain(
HANDLE hinst,
DWORD dwcallpurpose,
LPVOID lpvResvd,
);
```

Here, *hinst* is the handle to the DLL. This value is the base address of the DLL. The HINSTANCE of a DLL is the same as the HMODULE of the DLL. Thus, hinstDLL can be used in calls to, for instance, the **GetModuleFileName** function and other functions that require a module handle.

lpvResvd is reserved.

dwcallpurpose identifies the purpose of the call to the function. The valid values for *dwcallpurpose* and their descriptions are summarized as follows:

DLL_PROCESS_ATTACH	The DLL is being mapped to the current process address space. This call is made only when the usage count is 1. You can use the part of the entry/exit function dealing with DLL_PROCESS_ATTACH to perform process-specific DLL initialization, such as allocating heap memory, and so on.
DLL_THREAD_ATTACH	The entry/exit function is called because the process is creating a new thread (after the DLL has already been mapped into the process's address space). Windows creates a primary thread when it creates the process. During the process creation, the entry/exit function was called with DLL_PROCESS_ATTACH. The entry/exit function is not called again for the primary thread with DLL_THREAD_ATTACH. In addition, Windows 2000 does not retroactively call the entry/exit function for threads that may already be running when the DLL is mapped (using LoadLibrary). You can use the part of the entry/exit routine dealing with DLL_THREAD_ATTACH to perform thread-specific initialization, such as allocating memory for a thread local storage (TLS) slot.

DLL_THREAD_DETACH   The entry/exit function is called as a result of a thread terminating. You can use the part of the entry/exit routine dealing with DLL_THREAD_DETACH to perform thread-relative cleanup functions, such as freeing memory allocated to a TLS slot.

DLL_PROCESS_DETACH   The DLL is being unmapped from the address space of the calling process. You can use the part of the entry/ exit routine dealing with DLL_PROCESS_DETACH to perform process-relative cleanup functions such as freeing heap memory, and so on.

TIP: Although there appears to be a sequence (Attach Process, Attach Thread, Detach Thread, Detach Process) for calling the entry/exit routine, do not count on this sequence to happen all the time. One reason is that if there is only one thread (a very common situation), the entry/exit routine will not be called with DLL_THREAD_ATTACH. Another reason is that if any thread calls **Terminate_thread**, or worse yet, calls **Terminate_process**, the entry/exit function is not called. Finally, the timing of starting the thread and loading the DLL is important. The entry/exit routines are not called for the threads that have already started when the DLL is loaded.

EXPORTING AND IMPORTING FUNCTIONS AND VARIABLES WITH DLLs

While the purpose of creating DLLs is to provide a common library of functions, resources, and data variables, you still have to perform work in addition to invoking the DLL. This is because none of the functions, data variables, and so on within a DLL is available to a calling EXE or another DLL by default. The functions and data variables have to be exported from the DLL. You can then specify (as shown in the example that follows) how to "import" the exported functions and data in an EXE or calling DLL. You can export functions and data using module definition files or by using **dllexport**. Using **dllexport** is a newer and better method, and this is the method used in the following example. You can import functions and data using **dllimport**, or you can use the C **extern** keyword. The example uses **dllimport**.

TIP: You have to watch out for name mangling when you export a DLL created with a Visual C++ compiler and try to use a function in the DLL from an EXE created using non-C++ compilers or C++ compilers from other vendors. When a function is exported, Visual C++ mangles the name by prefixing the function name with an underscore (_) and suffixing the function name with the @ symbol and a number that represents the total number of bytes of the function's parameters. One way of taking care of name mangling is by using a module definition file with an EXPORTS section. Refer to KB article Q126845 for more detail on name mangling.

DLL PROGRAMMING EXAMPLE FOR EXPORT/IMPORT

Exporting a function and a variable in a DLL and importing a function and a variable in an EXE are shown in the following example. The example consists of a DLL that has a function that calculates simple interest given the principal and the period. The interest rate is initialized during DLL initialization. The function and the interest rate variable are exported. An EXE prompts the user for the principal and period, and calculates the interest rate. After two iterations, it prompts for a new interest rate and modifies the interest rate stored in the interest rate variable, which is also exported.

The symbols that need to be exported can be exported by use of a module definition file. Using a module definition file, or DEF file, can be cumbersome. Newer compilers provide a better means of exporting symbols. Visual C++ and Borland C++ compilers have defined **dllexport** and **dllimport** as extended keywords. These keywords are combined with another keyword, **__declspec**, to export or import symbols. The sample uses this method. The header file for the DLL is shown next:

```
// CalcInterest.h
#ifdef __cplusplus
extern "C" {
#endif

#ifdef DLLBUILD
// export the function
float __declspec(dllexport) CalcInterest(float flPrincipal, int iYear);
#else
// import the function
float __declspec(dllimport) CalcInterest(float flPrincipal, int iYear);
#endif

#ifdef __cplusplus
}
#endif
```

As the same header file is used in both the DLL and the EXE, a conditional compile is done for DLL and EXE. Using the "C" linkage specification prevents the name mangling of the symbol. The DLL code is shown next:

```
//CalcInterest.c
#define DLLBUILD    // Trigger for dll export in the header file
#include "CalcInterest.h"

float __declspec(dllexport) flInterestRate;

BOOL WINAPI DllMain(HINSTANCE hInstance, DWORD dwReason, LPVOID lpReserved)
{
```

```
    if (dwReason == DLL_PROCESS_ATTACH)
    {
        flInterestRate = 5.0;
    }
    else if (dwReason == DLL_PROCESS_DETACH)
    {
        flInterestRate = 0.0;
    }
    else if (dwReason == DLL_THREAD_DETACH)
    {
    }
    else if (dwReason == DLL_THREAD_DETACH)
    {
    }
    return 1;   // Return TRUE if successful
}


float CalcInterest(float flPrincipal, int iYear)
{
    return ((float)((flPrincipal * (float)iYear * flInterestRate)/ 100.0));
}
```

The code for the DLL shown here is compiled and linked to produce a DLL named *CalcIntDll.dll*. The program that uses this DLL is shown next. Notice that after two iterations the interest rate is changed, and the rest of the interest calculation will be based on the new interest rate:

```
// Interest.Cpp
#include <iostream.h>
#include "CalcInterest.h"
extern "C" {
extern float __declspec(dllimport) flInterestRate;
}
void main ()
{
    float   flP;
    int     iY;
    float   flInterest;

    for (int i =0; i<4; i++)
    {
        cout << "Enter the Principal: ";
        cin >> flP;
        cout << "Enter number of years: ";
        cin >> iY;
```

```
        cout << "Interest Rate is " << flInterestRate << endl;
        flInterest = CalcInterest(flP, iY);

        cout << "The interest is: " << flInterest << endl;

        if (i == 1)
        {
            cout << "Now change the interest rate. Enter the new \
interest rate:";
            cin >> flInterestRate;
        }
    }
}
```

The program that follows changes the interest rate that is stored in the DLL. While running the preceding program, notice that the change in the interest rate by this program has no effect on the other program. This is because the DLL is loaded in the address space of the calling process instead of in a global address space.

```
//  ChangeInt.Cpp
#include <iostream.h>
#include "CalcInterest.h"
extern "C" {
extern float __declspec(dllimport) flInterestRate;
}
void main ()

{
    char c;
    cout << "The interest rate will be changed in the DLL.\n";
    cout << "But this will not affect the other executable using \
            the CalcIntDll.dll.\n";
    cout << "\nEnter the new interest rate: ";
    cin >> flInterestRate;
    cout << "The interest rate has been changed.\n";
    cout << "Type any character and press enter to continue.";
    cin >> c;
}
```

A PROGRAMMING EXAMPLE TO LOAD A DLL

As mentioned earlier in the chapter, you can specify that a DLL is to be loaded either at link-edit time or at run time. The following example shows how the same DLL that was loaded at link-edit time can be loaded at run time.

In the previous example, the function that calculates the interest was *linked* to the executable by use of the DLL's export library. When the executable is loaded, the system also loads the DLL that this executable uses. This is called *load-time dynamic linking*. It is also possible to defer this DLL loading at load time by use of *run-time dynamic linking*. The next sample performs the same function as earlier, but it loads the DLL dynamically, uses the function, and frees the DLL.

This is achieved by the **LoadLibrary**, **GetProcAddress**, and **FreeLibrary** APIs. The DLL name is provided to the **LoadLibrary** API, which loads the DLL and returns a handle to the library. The address of the function, **CalcInterest**, that is needed from the library can then be retrieved by providing the library handle and the function name to the **GetProcAddress** API. Note that the function name is case sensitive, and only functions that are exported can be retrieved. The library is finally freed by calling the **FreeLibrary** API and passing in the library handle.

NEW IN WINDOWS 2000:   One of the dilemmas application developers face when a future version of the product is released is how to deal with earlier versions of the DLLs. They want to make sure their new version of the application uses the new DLLs shipped with the product rather than the older versions of the DLLs that have the same name. With Windows 2000, you can address this issue by creating a *redirection file*. A redirection file for an application is a file with the same name as the application plus an additional extension, *local*. For example, if the application is *CalcIntLoadLib.exe*, the redirection file is a file with the name *CalcIntLoadLib.exe.local*. The system ignores the contents of the redirection file, but its presence forces all DLLs in the application's directory to be loaded from that directory. As noted earlier, the **LoadLibrary** and **LoadLibraryEx** functions change their search sequence if a redirection file is present, ignoring the path specified in the API.

```
#include <iostream.h>
#include <windows.h>
#include "CalcInterest.h"

void main ()
{
    float    flP;
    int      iY;
    float    flInterest;

    HMODULE hLoadLib;
    float (*CalcIntFunc)(float, int);


    hLoadLib = LoadLibrary("CalcIntDll.dll");
    if (!hLoadLib)
    {
        cout << "Cannot load CalcIntDll.dll";
```

```
            return;
    }
    CalcIntFunc = (float (*)(float, int)) GetProcAddress(hLoadLib,
                                           "CalcInterest");

    cout << "Enter the Principal: ";
    cin >> flP;
    cout << "Enter number of years: ";
    cin >> iY;

    flInterest = (*CalcIntFunc) (flP, iY);

    cout << "The interest is: " << flInterest << endl;

    FreeLibrary(hLoadLib);
}
```

The next sample shows a DLL exporting a class:

```
//  CalcIntClass.h
#ifdef DLLBUILD
#define DLLClass __declspec(dllexport)
#else
#define DLLClass __declspec(dllimport)
#endif

class DLLClass CCalcInterest
{
private:
    float   flInterestRate;

public:
    CCalcInterest();
    float getInterestRate();
    float getInterest(float flP, int iY);

};

//  CalcIntClass.Cpp
#define DLLBUILD    // trigger class export
#include <iostream.h>
#include "CalcIntClass.h"

CCalcInterest::CCalcInterest()
{
```

```
        flInterestRate = 5.0;
}


float CCalcInterest::getInterestRate()
{
return (flInterestRate);
}


float CCalcInterest::getInterest(float flPrincipal, int iYear)
{
return ((float)((flPrincipal * (float)iYear * flInterestRate)/100.0));
}


// ClassCalcInt.cpp
#include <iostream.h>
#include "CalcIntClass.h"
void main ()
{
    CCalcInterest    intCalc;
    float    flP;
    float    flI;
    int      iY;
    cout << "Enter the Principal: ";
    cin >> flP;
    cout << "Enter number of years: ";
    cin >> iY;
    cout << "Interest Rate is " << intCalc.getInterestRate() << endl;
    flI = intCalc.getInterest(flP, iY);
    cout << "The interest is: " << flI << endl;
}
```

DLL VERSION CONTROL

As mentioned earlier in the chapter, one of the disadvantages of DLLs is that you have to ensure that the correct version of the DLL is used when an EXE or DLL invokes it. Version information could be a hierarchy that includes a company name, a product name, the specific version and/or release of the product, and so on. Windows 2000 lets you attach a version resource to an executable or DLL. You can use the built-in functions in Microsoft Developer Studio to attach a version resource. Windows 2000 also provides functions to query the version-control information. The following example illustrates DLL version control.

A DLL PROGRAMMING EXAMPLE FOR VERSION CONTROL

One of the resources that can be attached to a dynamic link library or an executable is a version resource. Information like the company name, product name, version, and so on can be specified in the version resource. These version-control resources can be queried by use of version-control functions provided by Windows 2000. The sample checks if the DLL is of the correct version; if not, it terminates. An easy way to add the version-control resource is through Developer Studio. However, the version-control information can also be created with an editor and linked to the DLL or EXE. The DLL code is shown next. This code is compiled, and a DLL by name *CalcInterestDLL.dll* is created. The code is available from the CD-ROM in the *DLLVersion* subdirectory.

```c
// CalcInterest.c
#define DLLBUILD    // Trigger for dll export in the header file
#include "CalcInterest.h"
float __declspec(dllexport) flInterestRate = 5.0;
float CalcInterest(float flPrincipal, int iYear)
{
    return ((float)((flPrincipal * (float)iYear * flInterestRate)/100.0));
}


// CalcInterest.h
#ifdef __cplusplus
extern "C" {
#endif

#ifdef DLLBUILD
// export the function
float __declspec(dllexport) CalcInterest(float flPrincipal, int iYear);
#else
// import the function
float __declspec(dllimport) CalcInterest(float flPrincipal, int iYear);
#endif

#ifdef __cplusplus
}
#endif
```

The version-control resource file for this DLL is shown next. This file was generated by use of the Visual C++ Developer Studio. The product version is set to 2, 1, 2, 3. Other information such as file version, operating system, file type (application, DLL, device driver, font), and type of build (debug or nondebug, prerelease, special build) can also be specified. This can be a good place to put the copyright information, company information, and product name.

```
// CalcInterest.rc
/////////////////////////////////////////////////////////////////////
//
// Version
//

VS_VERSION_INFO VERSIONINFO
 FILEVERSION 1,2,3,4
 PRODUCTVERSION 2,1,2,3
 FILEFLAGSMASK 0x3fL
#ifdef _DEBUG
 FILEFLAGS 0x21L
#else
 FILEFLAGS 0x20L
#endif
 FILEOS 0x40004L
 FILETYPE 0x2L
 FILESUBTYPE 0x0L
BEGIN
    BLOCK "StringFileInfo"
    BEGIN
        BLOCK "040904b0"
        BEGIN
            VALUE "CompanyName", "Osborne\0"
            VALUE "FileDescription", "Interest Calculator DLL\0"
            VALUE "FileVersion", "1, 2, 3, 4\0"
            VALUE "InternalName", "CalcInterest\0"
            VALUE "LegalCopyright", "Copyright © 1997\0"
            VALUE "OriginalFilename", "CalcInterest.dll\0"
            VALUE "ProductName", "Osborne Interest Calculator\0"
            VALUE "ProductVersion", "2, 1, 2, 3\0"
            VALUE "SpecialBuild", "7525\0"
        END
    END
    BLOCK "VarFileInfo"
    BEGIN
        VALUE "Translation", 0x409, 1200
    END
END
```

The code that reads this version-control information is shown next. First, the program checks if the version information of the DLL can be queried, and if available, it obtains the size in bytes of version information. This is done by calling the **GetFileVersionInfoSize** function. The DLL name is given to the function, and if version information is available, it returns the size in bytes of that information. A buffer to retrieve the version information is allocated, and the information is retrieved by calling the **GetFileVersionInfo** function. From this information in the buffer, various individual items are queried by calling the **VerQueryValue** function. The \StringFile Info\040904b0 signifies the block that needs to be read. The value 040904b0 is essentially the hex representation of sublanguage, language, and code page information. "04" is the SUBLANG_ENGLISH_USA, "09" is the LANG_ENGLISH, and the rest is the code page information. The program checks if the DLL version is 2, 1, 2, 3 and if it's not, it terminates. This version-related library is available in the *Version.lib* library.

```cpp
// Interest.cpp
#include <iostream.h>
#include <windows.h>
#include "CalcInterest.h"

extern "C" {
extern float __declspec(dllimport) flInterestRate;
}

void main ()

{
    float   flP;
    int     iY;
    float   flInterest;

    DWORD   dwVersionInfoLen;
    LPSTR   lpVersion;
    DWORD   dwVersionHandle;
    UINT    uVersionLen;
    BOOL    bRetCode;
    char    szDLLName[20];


    strcpy(szDLLName, "CalcInterestDLL.dll");

    dwVersionInfoLen = GetFileVersionInfoSize(szDLLName, &dwVersionHandle);
    if (dwVersionInfoLen)
    {
        LPSTR   lpstrVersionInfo;
```

```
        lpstrVersionInfo = (LPSTR)new char[dwVersionInfoLen];
        GetFileVersionInfo(szDLLName, dwVersionHandle, dwVersionInfoLen,
                        lpstrVersionInfo);

        bRetCode = VerQueryValue((LPVOID)lpstrVersionInfo,
                        TEXT("\\StringFileInfo\\040904b0\\ProductVersion"),
                        (LPVOID *)&lpVersion, &uVersionLen);

        if(bRetCode && !strcmp(lpVersion, "2, 1, 2, 3"))
        {
            for (int i =0; i<4; i++)
            {
                cout << "Enter the Principal: ";
                cin >> flP;
                cout << "Enter number of years: ";
                cin >> iY;

                cout << "Interest Rate is " << flInterestRate << endl;
                flInterest = CalcInterest(flP, iY);

                cout << "The interest is: " << flInterest << endl;

                if (i == 1)
                {
                    cout << "Now change the interest rate.  Enter the new \
                            interest rate: ";
                    cin >> flInterestRate;
                }
            }
        }
        else
        {
            cout << "Incorrect DLL. Program terminated.\n";
        }

        delete [] lpstrVersionInfo;
    }
    else
    {
        cout << "Incorrect DLL. Program terminated.\n";
    }
}
```

CONCLUSION

In this chapter, we looked at an important tool for Windows 2000 programmers—using a DLL. We considered why DLLs are needed as well as the advantages and disadvantages of using DLLs. We compared DLLs and applications. We examined examples of exporting functions from a DLL and importing them into other executables. We also looked at the two ways of invoking a DLL and looked at a sample that illustrated them. Finally, we looked at how to use the version-control information with a DLL.

In the next chapter, we will continue our discussion of OS services and look at threads, interprocess communication mechanisms, and so on.

CHAPTER 9

Advanced OS Services

As a Windows programmer, you have already used basic operating system services such as memory allocation, message processing, and so on. While these services are common in all Windows environments, Windows 2000 also includes some advanced services such as multithreading and communication between threads. As an advanced Windows 2000 programmer, you should be aware of these important programming tools, which are covered in this chapter.

We will start with how to create and terminate processes. Next we will look at one of the important programming tools that Windows 2000 provides—threads. We will discuss how and when to create threads, and the safe and not so safe ways to terminate threads. Then we will cover how thread priorities work and how you can adjust them. Next we will discuss guidelines on when to use a thread. We will also cover thread local storage and end the chapter by covering the different communications mechanisms available for communicating between threads.

Before we begin, let's clarify what the different "multi" things in Windows 2000 are, since we will be discussing one of them here. Windows 2000 is a multitasking, multithreading operating system that supports symmetric multiprocessing (SMP) on multiple processors, but it is not a multiuser operating system (at least not the way UNIX and mainframe operating systems are).

Multitasking is the ability to run more than one program (or task) at the same time by sharing the CPU among the different tasks. This feature has been part of Windows since its first release. Multitasking is also sometimes referred to as "multiprocessing" (the "process" in multiprocessing refers to a program process, not a CPU processor).

A *process* is an instance of an application that is scheduled for execution. This doesn't mean that the process is the actual unit of execution, as we will see later. It just means that rather than just residing on the disk, your application now has an instance that is known to the operating system and has resources allocated to it. A process is made up of at least one thread, called the *primary* or *main thread.* A process (the primary thread) or a thread created by the primary thread can create more threads. There is no hierarchy among threads as there is between a process and its threads. (Terminating a process terminates the threads of that process, whereas terminating a thread does not terminate the threads created by that thread.) In Windows 2000, it is the threads of a process that are executed. A multithreading operating system is one that supports a process having multiple threads. Windows 2000 is a multitasking, multithreading operating system. By contrast, Windows 3.1 is a multitasking but not a multithreading operating system.

NEW IN WINDOWS 2000:   Windows 2000 introduces a new object called the *job object.* A job object allows groups of processes to be managed as a unit based on factors such as processor usage; it also provides an easy way to control attributes of all processes associated with the job object. **CreateJobObject** creates a job object (without processes). You can associate processes with a job object using **AssignProcessToJobObject**. By default, child processes of a process that is associated with a job are also associated with the same job. A job object can enforce limits on each associated process, such as the working set size, process priority, end-of-job time limit, etc., using **SetInformationJobObject**. You can terminate all processes associated with a job object using **TerminateJobObject**.

An operating system can also recognize and take advantage of multiple CPUs that may be present on a machine. It can treat all installed processors the same (*symmetric multiprocessing*) or reserve one for the operating system itself and use other CPUs for application programs (*asymmetric multiprocessing*). Again, Windows 2000 supports SMP, and Windows 95 does not.

There is one important difference between Windows 2000 and operating systems such as UNIX and mainframe operating systems. The difference is the concept of who a user is. In UNIX and mainframe operating systems, the user is typically the human being who can log in from a *terminal*. The operating system maintains a list of valid users and logs in those users to let them use the system. Windows 2000 is a client/server operating system. To such an operating system, the users are clients requesting services from the operating system. The fact that a client may be a computer with a human being as its user is incidental to the operating system itself. In this sense, Windows 2000 is not a "multiuser" system. Citrix systems licensed Windows 2000 source code and added multiuser features to enable Windows 2000 to perform multiuser functions the way other operating systems do. Microsoft recently licensed these multiuser enhancements from Citrix and may provide the multiuser capabilities in future versions of Windows 2000.

CREATING AND TERMINATING PROCESSES

As mentioned earlier, even though Windows 2000 executes threads, threads belong to a process. Let's start with processes. Here "process" refers to the program process. As mentioned earlier, a process is an executing instance of an application program. An executing instance has memory and other resources assigned to it. You can start a process either manually or programmatically. You manually start a process when you start an application in Windows 2000. There are different ways to start an application. You can start an application by double-clicking the program entry in Windows 2000 Explorer or (if you have included it) from the Start menu or the program's icon on the desktop. You can also use the DOS method of keying in the program name at the command prompt. Regardless of how you start an application, Windows 2000 creates a process for your application. A process has its own 4GB address space, by default.

Note for UNIX Programmers

Creating a process from another process is conceptually similar between UNIX and Windows 2000, although there are a lot of differences in detail. To create a process, you *fork* and *exec* in UNIX, whereas you **CreateProcess** in Windows 2000. However, Windows 2000 does not automatically establish a parent-child relationship, unlike UNIX. There are also differences between UNIX and Windows 2000 in what is passed to the created processes.

You can programmatically create a process using **CreateProcess**, whose prototype is as follows:

```
BOOL CreateProcess( LPCTSTR lpAppNam,
                    LPTSTR lpCmdLine,
                    LPSECURITY_ATTRIBUTES lpProcAttr,
                    LPSECURITY_ATTRIBUTES lpThreadAttr,
                    BOOL bInhHandls,
                    DWORD dwCreatFlgs,
                    LPVOID lpEnv,
                    LPCTSTR lpCurrDir,
                    LPSTARTUPINFO lpStrtInfo,
                    LPPROCESS_INFORMATION lpProcInfo
);
```

where the parameters are as follows:

lpAppNam points to the program to be executed and contains the fully or partially qualified path name of the executable. You can specify this parameter as NULL, in which case the *lpCmdLine* parameter must contain the name of the program. For 16-bit applications, you *should* specify the program name in *lpCmdLine* and specify NULL for *lpAppNam*. If you want to pass parameters to the program through the command line (which can retrieve the passed parameters using **GetCommandLine** or argc/argv), specify the program name in *lpAppNam* and the command-line parameters in *lpCmdLine*. If you do not specify a fully qualified path name, Windows 2000 searches for the program to be executed in different directories in the following order:

1. The directory where your application resides
2. The directory of the parent process
3. The 32-bit Windows system directory (which typically is SYSTEM32)
4. The 16-bit Windows system directory (which typically is SYSTEM)
5. The Windows directory
6. The directories listed in the PATH environment variable

lpProcAttr points to a **SECURITY_ATTRIBUTES** structure. You can use the structure to specify security attributes (such as whether another child process can inherit object handles). If *lpProcAttr* is NULL, a default security descriptor is used.

lpThreadAttr is exactly similar to *lpProcAttr,* except that it deals with thread security instead of process security. *lpThreadAttr* points to a **SECURITY_ATTRIBUTES** structure. You can use the structure to specify security attributes (such as whether another child process can inherit object handles). If *lpThreadAttr* is NULL, a default security descriptor is used.

bInhHandls is a Boolean parameter to specify whether the new process being created can inherit handles of the calling process.

dwCreatFlgs specifies flags relating to the priority of the process being created, as shown in the table that follows.

Flag Value	Description
CREATE_DEFAULT _ERROR_MODE	This flag overrides the default that the newly created process inherits from the error mode of the calling process.
CREATE_NEW _CONSOLE	This flag, which is mutually exclusive with the DETACHED_PROCESS flag, lets the newly created process have its own console, instead of inheriting the console of the calling process.
CREATE_NEW _PROCESS_GROUP	The newly created process is the root process of a new process group.
CREATE_SEPARATE _WOW_VDM	Processes of 16-bit Windows-based applications run in their own private virtual DOS machine (VDM). This overrides the default of a shared VDM.
CREATE_SHARED _WOW_VDM	This flag overrides the DefaultSeparateVDM switch (which runs applications in separate VDMs) and runs the new process in the shared virtual DOS machine.
CREATE _SUSPENDED	The primary thread of the new process is created in a suspended state (and is not scheduled for execution until a ResumeThread is issued—see the ResumeThread discussion in the section "Thread Priority Classes and Levels" later in this chapter).
CREATE_UNICODE _ENVIRONMENT	The environment block uses Unicode characters if set, and ANSI characters otherwise.
DEBUG_PROCESS	The calling process is notified of all debug events in the created process.
DEBUG_ONLY_THIS _PROCESS	This is set to debug the calling process using the created process' debugger.
DETACHED _PROCESS	The newly created process does not get the default console and has to allocate one if it needs a console. This flag is mutually exclusive with the CREATE_ NEW_CONSOLE flag.

New for Windows 2000

CREATE_BREAKAWAY_ FROM_JOB	Change the default so that the child processes of a process (that is associated with a job) are not associated with the job.
CREATE_FORCE_DOS	Force the application to run as an MS-DOS-based application (rather than as an OS/2-based application). This flag is valid only for 16-bit bound applications.
CREATE_NO_WINDOW	Force the console application to run without a console window. This flag is valid only when starting a console application.

You can also set the priority class for the newly created process using dwCreation Flags. The priority class, which can be one of the values shown in Table 9-1, determines a range of priority levels. For example, for the NORMAL_PRIORITY_CLASS, the priority for a "lowest" level thread is 6. The highest priority for a "highest" level thread is 10 (for an average value of 8). Thread priority levels are covered in the section "Thread Priority Classes and Levels" later in this chapter.

lpEnv is a pointer to an environment block. Specifying NULL for this parameter causes the new process to use the environment of the calling process.

lpCurrDir is a pointer to a string that specifies the current drive and directory for the newly created process. Specifying NULL for this parameter causes the newly created process to have the same current drive and directory as that of the calling process.

Priority Class	Description
HIGH_PRIORITY_CLASS	This is used for tasks that require very high priority, such as tasks that handle user interfaces. The average priority level is 13.
IDLE_PRIORITY_CLASS	This is used for low-priority tasks that need to run only when the system is idle (for example, screen savers). The average priority level is 4. This priority class is assigned to the created process if the calling process has this priority class.
NORMAL_PRIORITY _CLASS	This is used normally for most tasks. The average priority level is 8.
REALTIME_PRIORITY _CLASS	This is used for tasks that need the highest possible priority. Be careful with this, since a thread with this priority class is scheduled for execution even ahead of Windows NT's own tasks. The average priority level is 24.
New for Windows 2000	
ABOVE_NORMAL_PRIORITY_ CLASS	Indicates a process that has a priority level that is in between that of NORMAL_PRIORITY_ CLASS and HIGH_PRIORITY_CLASS.
BELOW_NORMAL_PRIORITY_ CLASS	Indicates a process that has a priority level that is in between that of NORMAL_PRIORITY_ CLASS and IDLE_PRIORITY_CLASS.

Table 9-1. Priority Classes and Descriptions

lpStrtInfo is a pointer to a **STARTUPINFO** structure. The **STARTUPINFO** structure specifies the properties of the main window for a GUI process such as the window title, or the console for a Console process.

lpProcInfo is a pointer to a **PROCESS_INFORMATION** structure. Windows 2000 fills the **PROCESS_INFORMATION** structure with information such as the handle and ID for a newly created process and its primary thread.

CreateProcess returns nonzero if successful and zero otherwise.

You can use **CreateProcess** to invoke another application if the functions you want already exist in the other application. If you are developing a new application and you want split functions, you can use threads.

You can terminate a process in three ways.

First, you can call **ExitProcess**, whose prototype is shown here:

```
VOID ExitProcess( UINT uExitCode
);
```

ExitProcess is a clean way to terminate a process and all the threads of the process and is the preferred way to terminate a process. Windows 2000 performs the following cleanup actions in response to **ExitProcess**:

▼ The entry-point functions of all attached dynamic link libraries (DLLs) are called with an indication that the process is detaching.

■ Object handles opened by the process are closed.

■ The threads in the process are terminated.

■ Threads waiting for this process or any of its threads to terminate are released (the states of the process and all its threads are set to the Signaled state).

▲ Process termination status changes from STILL_ACTIVE to the exit value.

Second, a process can also be terminated by calling **TerminateProcess**, whose prototype is shown here:

```
BOOL TerminateProcess( HANDLE hProcess,
                       UINT uExitCd
);
```

where *hProcess* is the process handle, and *uExitCd* is the process's exit code. **TerminateProcess** returns nonzero when successful and zero otherwise.

Unlike **ExitProcess**, **TerminateProcess** does not call the entry-point functions of attached DLLs. Accordingly, the processing in the entry point functions is skipped, and this in turn may lead to unpredictable consequences and loss of data integrity.

A third way that processes are terminated is when all the threads in a process are terminated. The threads in a process could be terminated by **ExitThread** or **TerminateThread**. Terminating threads is covered in the section "Thread Programming with the Win32 API" later in this chapter.

Before we move on to threads and how to write multithreaded programs, let's examine the need for multithreading. If your application has only one thread and that thread has to wait for an event such as an I/O completion, then your thread will not execute until the event it is waiting for has completed. On the other hand, if your application has more than one thread, then while one of your application's threads is waiting, other threads of your application can execute. Thus, developing your application as a multithreaded application improves the overall throughput of your application, besides potentially improving processor utilization. The results will be even more significant when there is more than one processor on the system. In this case, two or more threads of your application could actually be executing in parallel.

This does not mean that you should divide your application into a large number of threads. Having multiple threads may imply the need for more communication between threads, so the complexity increases. In addition, Windows 2000 has to keep track of more threads, and more threads need more system resources. Thus, deciding how many threads to have and what the threads will do is as much an art as it is a science. You need to balance the cost of having additional threads with the potential benefits. There is no set formula that will specify if, when, and how many threads should be used in a given situation.

TIP: Do not conclude that you should think of multithreading your application only if you are running your application on systems with multiple processors. If your application would benefit from multithreading, go ahead with multithreading. There will be some benefits even on single-processor systems. Also, with the falling prices of processors, multiprocessor systems are becoming more common, and your application will transparently be able to take advantage of multiple processors if it is multithreaded and runs on a system with multiple processors.

THREAD BASICS

As mentioned earlier, a process is made up of one or more threads. In Windows 2000, a process has memory and other resources, but it does not execute by itself. Rather, it is the threads in the process that are scheduled for execution. A process must have at least one thread. When you create a process, one thread is also created for the process. This thread is called the primary thread. The primary thread can create other threads. Threads created by the *primary thread* can also create threads.

Windows 2000 schedules threads for execution using the priority of threads. Each thread has a *priority class.* A priority class has multiple priority levels within it. Thread priority is covered later, in the section "Thread Priority Classes and Levels." When Windows 2000 wants to schedule a thread for execution, it schedules the next highest priority thread that is ready for execution (that is, the thread is in a ready state—thread states are covered later). If multiple threads are available with the same priority, Windows 2000 schedules the threads with the same priority in a round-robin fashion. In addition, when a low-priority thread is executing and a higher-priority thread becomes ready for execution, Windows 2000 preempts the low-priority thread and schedules the higher-priority thread. You may wonder if a low-priority thread will ever be executed if there are always higher-priority threads around. Windows 2000 ensures that low-priority threads are executed by incrementing the priority of low-priority threads if the threads have not executed in a while.

A thread that is ready to be executed is in a *ready state*. The different states a thread can be in are summarized in Table 9-2.

Actually, there is another state value that happens rarely. The state value is 7 and the state is Unknown.

The life of a thread in the system starts with Initialized and ends at Terminated. In the interim, it goes through repetitive cycles of the Ready, Standby, Running, Waiting, and/or Transition states.

You have three options if you want to work with threads in Microsoft Windows 2000:

1. You can use C library multithreading functions.
2. You can use Win32 APIs such as **CreateThread**.
3. You can use MFC classes such as **CWinThread**.

We will not cover option 1 in this chapter. We will cover option 2 briefly, including the relevant APIs. We also will cover option 3 and include code samples using it.

Thread State Value	Description	Comment
0	Initialized	The thread is now a valid thread in the system.
1	Ready	The thread is ready for execution (usually when what the thread was waiting for is now available).
2	Running	The thread is currently executing in a processor.
3	Standby	The thread is about to start execution in a processor.
4	Terminated	The thread has completed execution.
5	Waiting	The thread is waiting for events such as I/O completion.
6	Transition	The thread is waiting for resources (other than the processor).

Table 9-2.   Thread State Values and Descriptions

THREAD PROGRAMMING WITH THE WIN32 API

We will look at the Win32 API method in this section. For creating and terminating threads using MFC, see the next section, "Thread Programming with MFC." You can create a thread using the **CreateThread** API, whose prototype is shown here:

```
HANDLE CreateThread( LPSECURITY_ATTRIBUTES lpThreadAttr,
                     DWORD dwStakSz,
                     LPTHREAD_START_ROUTINE lpStrtAddr,
                     LPVOID lpParm,
                     DWORD dwCreatFlgs,
                     LPDWORD lpThreadId
);
```

where the parameters are as follows:

lpThreadAttr points to a **SECURITY_ATTRIBUTES** structure. Specifying NULL for this parameter causes a default security descriptor to be used.

dwStakSz is the thread stack size in bytes. The thread stack is part of the process address space. Specifying zero causes the thread stack size to be the same as that of the primary thread of the process.

lpStrtAddr is the starting address of the new thread.

lpParm is a parameter that can be passed to the thread.

dwCreatFlgs is a flag to specify if the thread is to be created in a suspended state or whether it can execute right after creation.

lpThreadId is a pointer to the thread identifier that is returned when the thread is successfully created.

CreateThread returns the handle to the created thread when successful and NULL otherwise.

As with processes, you can terminate threads in three ways.

First, you can call **ExitThread**, whose prototype is shown here:

```
VOID ExitThread (DWORD dwExitCd
);
```

where *dwExitCd* is the thread's exit code (which can be retrieved using the **GetExit CodeThread** function). **ExitThread** does not return a value. Windows 2000 performs the following cleanup actions in response to **ExitThread**:

▼　The thread's stack is deallocated.

■　The entry-point function of all attached dynamic link libraries (DLLs) is called with an indication that the thread is detaching.

■　The process that created the thread is terminated if the current thread is the last thread of the process.

■ Threads waiting for this thread to terminate are released (the state of the thread is changed to Signaled).

▲ Thread termination status changes from STILL_ACTIVE to the exit code.

Second, you can call **TerminateThread**, whose prototype is shown here:

```
BOOL TerminateThread( HANDLE hThread,
                      DWORD dwExitCd
);
```

where *hThread* is the thread handle, and *dwExitCd* is the thread's exit code (which can be retrieved using the **GetExitCodeThread** function). **TerminateThread** returns nonzero when successful and zero otherwise.

Unlike **ExitThread**, **TerminateThread** does not deallocate the thread's stack and does not call the entry-point functions of attached DLLs. Thus the processing in the entry-point functions is skipped, and this may lead to unpredictable consequences and loss of data integrity.

Third, a thread (actually all the threads of a process) is terminated if the process is terminated.

TIP: You can also use C run-time functions for thread management. Don't mix and match C functions and Win32 functions. For example, don't try to terminate a thread using **ExitThread** if you are using C functions such as **_beginthread**.

THREAD PROGRAMMING WITH MFC

Threads in MFC applications are represented by **CWinThread** objects, which you can create by calling **AfxBeginThread**. Creating and managing threads through Win32 APIs are relatively simpler than through **CWinThread** objects. The sample that follows creates threads using the **CWinThread** method by calling the **AfxBeginThread** API. In MFC applications all threads should be created through the **CWinThread** method to make your MFC application thread safe. The thread local data that is used by the framework to maintain thread-specific information is managed by **CWinThread** objects. Since **CWinThread** handles the thread local data, any thread that uses the MFC must be created by the MFC through the **CWinThread** method. This may sound complicated, but it is straightforward to do this in most cases. All that has to be done in an MFC application is to create threads by calling **AfxBeginThread**.

Though threads are not distinguished at the Win32 API level, they are distinguished at the MFC level. MFC distinguishes two types of threads. Threads that generally handle user input and respond to events and user-generated messages are called *user-interface* threads, and those that do not have any interaction with the user interface are called *worker* threads. User-interface threads handle *message pumps* (a message pump is a program loop that retrieves messages from a thread's message queue, translates them, and dispatches them), while worker threads do not handle message pumps. The primary thread that is automatically created when you start an MFC application is a user-interface thread. You create user-interface and worker threads using **AfxBeginThread**. This is illustrated in the example that follows. The prototype for **AfxBeginThread** is shown here:

```
CWinThread *AfxBeginThread (AFX_THREADPROC ThreadProc,
                            LPVOID Parm,

                            int Prty = THREAD_PRIORITY_NORMAL,
                            UINT StakSz = 0,
                            DWORD CreatFlgs = 0,
                            LPSECURITY_ATTRIBUTES
                            SecAttr = NULL );
```

where the parameters are defined as follows:

ThreadProc is a thread function that has the prototype

```
UINT ThreadProc(LPVOID tpparm)
```

A thread starts and terminates its execution in the thread function. The thread function is defined in the process that is creating the thread.

Parm is a parameter you can pass to the thread function.

Prty is the priority level you want for the thread being created, which must be one of the values listed in Table 9-3. You can specify zero for this parameter, in which case the priority of the created thread becomes the same as that of the creating thread.

Base Priority	Priority Class of Process	Priority Level of Thread
1	IDLE_PRIORITY_CLASS	THREAD_PRIORITY_IDLE
1	BELOW_NORMAL_PRIORITY_CLASS	THREAD_PRIORITY_IDLE
1	NORMAL_PRIORITY_CLASS	THREAD_PRIORITY_IDLE
1	ABOVE_NORMAL_PRIORITY_CLASS	THREAD_PRIORITY_IDLE
1	HIGH_PRIORITY_CLASS	THREAD_PRIORITY_IDLE
2	IDLE_PRIORITY_CLASS	THREAD_PRIORITY_LOWEST
3	IDLE_PRIORITY_CLASS	THREAD_PRIORITY_BELOW_NORMAL

Table 9-3. Base Priority Related to Priority Classes and Priority Levels

Base Priority	Priority Class of Process	Priority Level of Thread
4	IDLE_PRIORITY_CLASS	THREAD_PRIORITY_NORMAL
4	BELOW_NORMAL_PRIORITY_CLASS	THREAD_PRIORITY_LOWEST
5	IDLE_PRIORITY_CLASS	THREAD_PRIORITY_ABOVE_NORMAL
5	BELOW_NORMAL_PRIORITY_CLASS	THREAD_PRIORITY_BELOW_NORMAL
5	Background NORMAL_PRIORITY_CLASS	THREAD_PRIORITY_LOWEST
6	IDLE_PRIORITY_CLASS	THREAD_PRIORITY_HIGHEST
6	BELOW_NORMAL_PRIORITY_CLASS	THREAD_PRIORITY_NORMAL
6	Background NORMAL_PRIORITY_CLASS	THREAD_PRIORITY_BELOW_NORMAL
7	BELOW_NORMAL_PRIORITY_CLASS	THREAD_PRIORITY_ABOVE_NORMAL
7	Background NORMAL_PRIORITY_CLASS	THREAD_PRIORITY_NORMAL
7	Foreground NORMAL_PRIORITY_CLASS	THREAD_PRIORITY_LOWEST
8	BELOW_NORMAL_PRIORITY_CLASS	THREAD_PRIORITY_HIGHEST
8	NORMAL_PRIORITY_CLASS	THREAD_PRIORITY_ABOVE_NORMAL
8	Foreground NORMAL_PRIORITY_CLASS	THREAD_PRIORITY_BELOW_NORMAL
8	ABOVE_NORMAL_PRIORITY_CLASS	THREAD_PRIORITY_LOWEST
9	NORMAL_PRIORITY_CLASS	THREAD_PRIORITY_HIGHEST
9	Foreground NORMAL_PRIORITY_CLASS	THREAD_PRIORITY_NORMAL

Table 9-3.   Base Priority Related to Priority Classes and Priority Levels *(continued)*

Base Priority	Priority Class of Process	Priority Level of Thread
9	ABOVE_NORMAL_PRIORITY_CLASS	THREAD_PRIORITY_BELOW_NORMAL
10	Foreground NORMAL_PRIORITY_CLASS	THREAD_PRIORITY_ABOVE_NORMAL
10	ABOVE_NORMAL_PRIORITY_CLASS	THREAD_PRIORITY_NORMAL
11	Foreground NORMAL_PRIORITY_CLASS	THREAD_PRIORITY_HIGHEST
11	ABOVE_NORMAL_PRIORITY_CLASS	THREAD_PRIORITY_ABOVE_NORMAL
11	HIGH_PRIORITY_CLASS	THREAD_PRIORITY_LOWEST
12	ABOVE_NORMAL_PRIORITY_CLASS	THREAD_PRIORITY_HIGHEST
12	HIGH_PRIORITY_CLASS	THREAD_PRIORITY_BELOW_NORMAL
13	HIGH_PRIORITY_CLASS	THREAD_PRIORITY_NORMAL
14	HIGH_PRIORITY_CLASS	THREAD_PRIORITY_ABOVE_NORMAL
15	HIGH_PRIORITY_CLASS	THREAD_PRIORITY_HIGHEST
15	HIGH_PRIORITY_CLASS	THREAD_PRIORITY_TIME_CRITICAL
15	IDLE_PRIORITY_CLASS	THREAD_PRIORITY_TIME_CRITICAL
15	BELOW_NORMAL_PRIORITY_CLASS	THREAD_PRIORITY_TIME_CRITICAL
15	NORMAL_PRIORITY_CLASS	THREAD_PRIORITY_TIME_CRITICAL
15	ABOVE_NORMAL_PRIORITY_CLASS	THREAD_PRIORITY_TIME_CRITICAL
16	REALTIME_PRIORITY_CLASS	THREAD_PRIORITY_IDLE
17	REALTIME_PRIORITY_CLASS	-7

Table 9-3. Base Priority Related to Priority Classes and Priority Levels *(continued)*

Base Priority	Priority Class of Process	Priority Level of Thread
18	REALTIME_PRIORITY_CLASS	-6
19	REALTIME_PRIORITY_CLASS	-5
20	REALTIME_PRIORITY_CLASS	-4
21	REALTIME_PRIORITY_CLASS	-3
22	REALTIME_PRIORITY_CLASS	THREAD_PRIORITY_LOWEST
23	REALTIME_PRIORITY_CLASS	THREAD_PRIORITY_BELOW_ NORMAL
24	REALTIME_PRIORITY_CLASS	THREAD_PRIORITY_NORMAL
25	REALTIME_PRIORITY_CLASS	THREAD_PRIORITY_ABOVE_ NORMAL
26	REALTIME_PRIORITY_CLASS	THREAD_PRIORITY_HIGHEST
27	REALTIME_PRIORITY_CLASS	3
28	REALTIME_PRIORITY_CLASS	4
29	REALTIME_PRIORITY_CLASS	5
30	REALTIME_PRIORITY_CLASS	6
31	REALTIME_PRIORITY_CLASS	THREAD_PRIORITY_TIME_ CRITICAL

Note: Priority levels -7, -6, -5, -4, -3, 3, 4, 5, and 6 are supported only on Windows 2000. Table reprinted with permission from Microsoft.

Table 9-3. Base Priority Related to Priority Classes and Priority Levels *(continued)*

StakSz is the stack size in bytes for the thread being created. The thread stack is part of the process address space. You can specify zero for this parameter, in which case the stack size of the created thread becomes the same as that of the creating thread.

CreatFlgs specifies if the thread is to be created in a suspended state (use CREATE_ SUSPEND) or whether it can execute right after creation (use zero).

SecAttr points to a **SECURITY_ATTRIBUTES** structure. Specifying NULL for this parameter causes the security attributes of the created thread to be the same as those of the creating thread.

AfxBeginThread returns a pointer to the newly created thread if successful and zero otherwise. You will use this pointer for subsequent processing involving the newly created thread.

The thread terminates in one of two ways. The thread automatically terminates when *ThreadProc* completes. At times, you may know within the thread that you can terminate the thread processing. At any point, a thread can terminate itself by calling **AfxEndThread**. The prototype of **AfxEndThread** is shown here:

```
void AfxEndThread( UINT ExitCd );
```

where *ExitCd* is the exit code.

PROGRAMMING EXAMPLE FOR CREATING THREADS

The *Threads* sample program demonstrates the creation of threads using the **AfxBeginThread** API. When run, the program will display a window, and a new thread can be created by selecting New Thread from the File menu. This will create a thread that will run a color ribbon across the window. Notice that while one ribbon runs across the window, more threads can be created.

The code for the *Threads* sample is shown next. The main application class is similar to other samples discussed earlier. The frame window class is derived from **CFrameWnd**. The method that is used to draw the ribbon will draw it in a compatible device context and then **BitBlt** while processing the **WM_PAINT** message. Appropriate members are defined in the frame window class. When the user selects New Thread from the File menu, **OnNewThread** is called. It creates the thread by calling **AfxBeginThread** and passing the controlling function for the worker thread.

```
#include <afxwin.h>
#include "Resource.h"

UINT RibbonThread(LPVOID);
COLORREF GetRibbonColor(int);


#define RIBBONWIDTH        50
#define RIBBONSEPARATION   10
COLORREF GetRibbonColor(int);

int iWidth, iHeight;    // Screen size
int iThreadInstance;    // Instance of the thread
// Define the application object class
class CApp : public CWinApp
{
public:
    virtual BOOL InitInstance ();
};
```

The frame window class definition and the message map follow.

```
// The frame window class
class CThreadWindow : public CFrameWnd
{
public:
    CDC m_memDC;
    CBitmap m_bmp;
    CBrush m_bkbrush;

    CThreadWindow();
    afx_msg void OnAppAbout();
    afx_msg void OnPaint();
    afx_msg void OnNewThread();
    afx_msg void OnExit();
    DECLARE_MESSAGE_MAP()
};


/////////////////////////////////////////////////////////////////////
// CThreadWindow

BEGIN_MESSAGE_MAP(CThreadWindow, CFrameWnd)
    ON_WM_PAINT()
    ON_COMMAND(ID_APP_ABOUT, OnAppAbout)
    ON_COMMAND(IDM_NEWTHREAD, OnNewThread)
    ON_COMMAND(ID_APP_EXIT, OnExit)
END_MESSAGE_MAP()


/////////////////////////////////////////////////////////////////////
// CThreadWindow construction

CThreadWindow::CThreadWindow()
{
    LoadAccelTable(MAKEINTRESOURCE(IDR_MAINFRAME));
    Create( NULL, "Threads Sample",
            WS_OVERLAPPEDWINDOW,
            rectDefault, NULL, MAKEINTRESOURCE(IDR_MAINFRAME) );

    iWidth = GetSystemMetrics(SM_CXSCREEN);
    iHeight = GetSystemMetrics(SM_CYSCREEN);
```

The thread that draws the ribbon does so indirectly. The ribbon is first drawn in a memory device context. Then it is bit-block transferred by the main application thread when processing the paint message. To achieve this, a compatible device context and a compatible bitmap are created, selected, and cleared.

```
    // create a compatible background window for the thread
    // and clear the background to white.
    CClientDC  DC(this);
    m_memDC.CreateCompatibleDC(&DC);
    m_bmp.CreateCompatibleBitmap(&DC, iWidth, iHeight);
    m_memDC.SelectObject(&m_bmp);
    m_bkbrush.CreateStockObject(WHITE_BRUSH);
    m_memDC.SelectObject(&m_bkbrush);
    m_memDC.PatBlt(0, 0, iWidth, iHeight, PATCOPY);
}


//////////////////////////////////////////////////////////////////////
// The CApp object

CApp theApp;

//////////////////////////////////////////////////////////////////////
// CApp initialization

BOOL CApp::InitInstance()
{
    m_pMainWnd = new CThreadWindow();
    m_pMainWnd -> ShowWindow( m_nCmdShow );
    m_pMainWnd -> UpdateWindow();
    return TRUE;
}


//////////////////////////////////////////////////////////////////////
// CAboutDlg dialog used for App About

class CAboutDlg : public CDialog
{
public:
    CAboutDlg();

    enum { IDD = IDD_ABOUTBOX };
};

CAboutDlg::CAboutDlg() : CDialog(CAboutDlg::IDD)
{
}
```

```
// App command to run the dialog
void CThreadWindow::OnAppAbout()
{
    CAboutDlg aboutDlg;
    aboutDlg.DoModal();
}


// Handle exposures
void CThreadWindow::OnPaint()
{
    CPaintDC dc(this);
    dc.BitBlt(0, 0, iWidth, iHeight, &m_memDC, 0, 0, SRCCOPY);
}


void CThreadWindow::OnNewThread()
{
    AfxBeginThread(RibbonThread, this);
}


// On Exit processing
void CThreadWindow::OnExit()
{
    DestroyWindow();
}
```

Shown next is the thread function of the worker thread that was created earlier. When the thread was created, a pointer to the frame window object was passed. This pointer is passed to the function as a parameter. Though the MFC objects created by one thread cannot be used by another thread, in general it is okay to call the inline functions in the MFC objects. The color of the ribbon is decided, and a small filled rectangle is drawn. The drawing of the rectangle proceeds in a loop, sleeping a fixed amount of time at the beginning of each loop.

```
UINT RibbonThread(LPVOID ThreadWindow)
{
    int iX1, iY1, iX2, iY2;
    int yOffset;
    COLORREF  c;
    RECT   rect;

    iThreadInstance++;
    CThreadWindow *pTW = (CThreadWindow *) ThreadWindow;
```

```
    iX1= iY1 = iX2 = iY2 = 0;

    yOffset = (iThreadInstance-1)*(RIBBONWIDTH+RIBBONSEPARATION);
    c = GetRibbonColor(iThreadInstance);
    CBrush Brush(c);
    for(int i=1; i<500; i++)
    {
        Sleep(50);
        iX1 = (i-1)*2;
        iY1 = yOffset;
        iX2 = i*2;
        iY2 = iY1+RIBBONWIDTH;

        rect.left = (long) iX1;
        rect.top = (long) iY1;
        rect.right = (long) iX2;
        rect.bottom = (long) iY2;

        pTW->m_memDC.FillRect(&rect, &Brush);
        pTW->InvalidateRect(&rect);
    }
  return 0;
}


COLORREF GetRibbonColor(int i)
{
    COLORREF c;
    switch(i%8)
    {
    case 0:
        c = RGB(0xFF, 0, 0);
        break;
    case 1:
        c = RGB(0, 0xFF, 0);
        break;
    case 2:
        c = RGB(0,0,0xFF);
        break;
    case 3:
        c = RGB(0xFF, 0xFF, 0);
        break;
    case 4:
```

```
        c = RGB(0xFF, 0, 0xFF);
        break;
    case 5:
        c = RGB(0x77, 0x77, 0x77);
        break;
    case 6:
        c = RGB(0xFF, 0x77, 0);
        break;
    case 7:
        c = RGB(0, 0xFF, 0x77);
        break;
    }
    return (c);
}
```

The sleep time can be increased to make the ribbon run slower. While running the program, notice that the menu bar and the rest of the application window are active and respond to user interaction. If, instead of the creating thread, the **RibbonThread** function were directly called, the whole application would hang without responding to the user action until the entire loop completed. More than one thread can be started, and all the ribbons are drawn simultaneously. As each thread gets a slice of CPU time, a section of the ribbon is drawn.

THREAD PRIORITY CLASSES AND LEVELS

As mentioned earlier, each thread has a priority class. Priority classes are subdivided into priority levels. There are four priority classes: HIGH_PRIORITY, IDLE_PRIORITY, NORMAL_PRIORITY, and REALTIME_PRIORITY.

NEW IN WINDOWS 2000: Windows 2000 includes two additional priority classes—ABOVE_ NORMAL_PRIORITY_CLASS and BELOW_NORMAL_PRIORITY_CLASS.

For a description of these priority classes and the average priority value for each class, see Table 9-1. Within each priority class, there are seven levels. When a thread is initialized, it is given a *base priority* based on its priority class and priority level as shown in Table 9-3.

As shown in the table, each thread will have a base priority from 1 through 31. The higher the number, the bigger the priority. Even when priorities are changed automatically by Windows 2000, the 1 through 31 range still holds.

You can use the **GetPriorityClass** function to get the current priority class of the process. You can use the **SetPriorityClass** function to set the priority class of a process. You can use the **GetThreadPriority** function to get the current priority level of a thread. You can use the **SetThreadPriority** function to set the priority level of a thread.

The prototype for **GetPriorityClass** is

```
DWORD GetPriorityClass(HANDLE hProcess);
```

and the prototype for **SetPriorityClass** is

```
BOOL SetPriorityClass( HANDLE hProcess,
                       DWORD dwPrtyCls
);
```

The priority class returned by **GetPriorityClass** and the priority specified in *dwPrtyCls* for **SetPriorityClass** is one of the values listed in Table 9-1. *hProcess* is the process's handle.

The prototype for **GetThreadPriority** is

```
int GetThreadPriority( );
```

and the prototype for **SetThreadPriority** is

```
BOOL SetThreadPriority( int nPrty );
```

The priority level returned by **GetThreadPriority** and the priority level specified in *nPrty* for **SetThreadPriority** are values from Table 9-3. Unlike **GetPriorityClass** and **SetPriorityClass**, which are API functions and need a handle, **GetThreadPriority** and **SetThreadPriority** are **CWinThread** member functions.

TIP: Remember, there is no free lunch here. The benefits of executing with increased priority for your thread(s) comes at the expense of the other applications' threads. If users notice a significant performance degradation in other applications after they install your application, they are not likely to accept your application.

Besides using the priority-related functions in the preceding paragraph, you can also suspend and resume the execution of a thread using the **SuspendThread** and **ResumeThread** member functions.

Each thread has a count used with these functions. **SuspendThread** increments the count, while **ResumeThread** decrements the count. The count is zero, by default, when the thread is created (unless the thread was created with the CREATE_SUSPENDED flag). When the thread's count is zero and you call **SuspendThread**, Windows 2000 increments the count to 1 and suspends the thread. Subsequently when you call **ResumeThread**, the count goes back to zero and the thread resumes. The thread will not be scheduled for execution as long as the count is nonzero.

The prototype for **SuspendThread** is

```
DWORD SuspendThread( );
```

and the prototype for **ResumeThread** is

```
DWORD ResumeThread( );
```

Both **ResumeThread** and **SuspendThread** return the thread's previous suspend count if successful and –1 otherwise.

For a programming example using thread priority, see the example under "Critical Sections," later in this chapter.

TIP: Keep in mind that when a thread resumes as a result of **ResumeThread**, it resumes at the starting point of its code, although it may have been at another point in the code when it was suspended (by use of **SuspendThread**).

STATIC AND DYNAMIC THREAD LOCAL STORAGE

Thread local storage (TLS) is a mechanism to allocate memory for storing thread-specific data. Only the thread that owns the TLS can access the data in the TLS. You can allocate and use TLS dynamically using APIs such as **TlsAlloc**, **TlsGetValue**, **TlsSetValue**, and **TlsFree**. The TLS APIs and their descriptions are summarized next.

TLS API	Description
TlsAlloc	Allocates a TLS index that is used on subsequent TLS-related calls
TlsGetValue	Retrieves the TLS slot data given a TLS index
TlsSetValue	Stores TLS slot data for a given TLS index
TlsFree	Frees a TLS index

You can also allocate and use TLS in a static manner using an extended storage class modifier called *thread* as shown in the following example:

```
typedef _declspec (thread) TLStor;
TLStor char x;
```

You can have both dynamic and static TLS allocated to your application.

PROCESS AND THREAD SYNCHRONIZATION

While multithreading solves some issues and improves some aspects of your application, it also introduces new issues that you need to handle in your program.

Note for UNIX Programmers

Most UNIX systems provide synchronization mechanisms similar to the ones provided by Windows 2000. If you have programmed using these mechanisms, the concepts and semantics are the same. Of course, there are syntax differences.

Let's first understand the need for synchronization using a real-life example. There are many bridges where the number of lanes on the bridge is less than the number of lanes leading up to it. In a very simple example, there may be only one lane on the bridge, while there may be multiple lanes leading up to the bridge. Signals are typically used to ensure that only the automobiles on one lane at a time are allowed access to the bridge. Automobiles in other lanes wait for access to the bridge if they arrive when the bridge is already being used. In a computer version of this example, the bridge is a resource. The automobiles are threads. The signals are synchronization objects. When one of your application threads wants to use a resource, it must synchronize its access with other threads using synchronization objects.

Since all the threads of your application work together in performing the functions in your application, quite often there is a need for the threads to synchronize their actions. Windows 2000 provides a number of *synchronization objects* such as semaphores, mutexes, and critical sections, and these are summarized in Table 9-4.

Synchronization Object	Description
Event	One or more threads can wait for an event object. An event object notifies waiting threads when the event occurs.
Mutex	This enables threads to take turns by forcing each thread to own the mutex object. The mutex object can be owned by only one thread at a time.
Semaphore	This restricts the number of threads that can access a shared resource.
Timer	This waits for a specific time and notifies waiting threads.
Critical section	This allows only one thread at a time to access a resource such as common data or a section of code.

Table 9-4.　Synchronization Objects and Descriptions

Critical Sections

Critical sections serialize the access of multiple threads to a common resource or to a portion of code by allowing access to only one thread at a time. Critical sections are fast relative to other synchronization objects such as mutexes, but a critical section can be used only for the threads within a process. You can use a critical section by creating a variable of type **CSingleLock** or **CMultiLock** in your resource's access member function. You then call the lock object's **Lock** member function. If the resource is not being used, your thread gains access. If the resource is being used, your thread waits (until it either gains access or times out). You unlock (and release the resource if you gained access) using the **Unlock** member function. The APIs you can use with critical sections are summarized in the following table:

Critical Section APIs	Description
InitializeCriticalSection	This initializes a critical section object prior to using other critical section APIs listed in this table.
EnterCriticalSection	This causes the calling thread to wait to own the critical section object and returns when the calling thread gets ownership.
TryEnterCriticalSection	This is the same as EnterCriticalSection, except that this API does not wait.
DeleteCriticalSection	This releases the system resources used by a critical section object. The critical section object should not be owned by any thread.
LeaveCriticalSection	This releases ownership of a critical section object.

In addition to the APIs just listed, there are two other critical section APIs: **InitializeCriticalSectionAndSpinCount**, which initializes a critical section object and sets its spin count, and **SetCriticalSectionSpinCount**, which sets the spin count for an existing critical section that may be provided in a future release of Windows 2000.

A programming sample illustrating thread priority and the use of critical sections is shown here. This sample shows how to suspend, resume, and change the priority of a thread. This sample and the next two samples use trains as an example. When the threads are started, two small rectangular blocks (representing two trains traveling), each in a different color, travel across the screen from left to right. Through menu pull-downs or accelerator keys, these trains could be stopped or resumed or their speed could be altered. This is achieved by changing the priority of the threads or suspending and resuming the threads that draw the train. Figure 9-1 shows the trains starting. Figure 9-2 shows the top train (thread) suspended. Figure 9-3 shows the top train moving slower than the bottom train due to reduced thread priority.

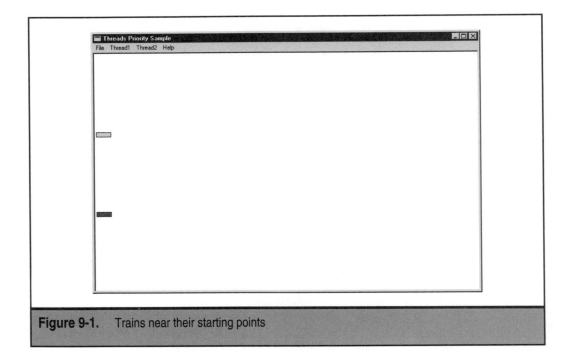

Figure 9-1.   Trains near their starting points

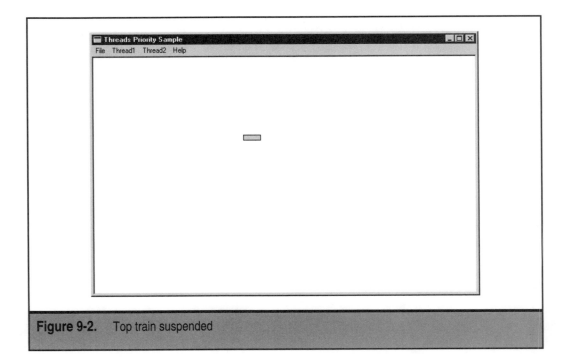

Figure 9-2.   Top train suspended

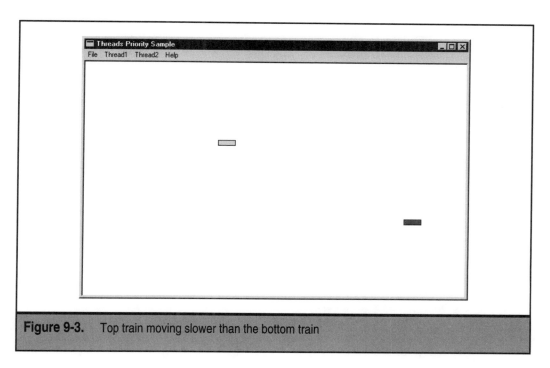

Figure 9-3.   Top train moving slower than the bottom train

Unlike the earlier sample, the trains are user-interface threads that are derived from **CWinThread**, and they serialize drawing the train by using critical sections. The sample is made up of two C++ modules—one the main application processing the user commands and the other dealing with the user-interface thread. The main module that handles the user command is shown next. This is very similar to other samples discussed earlier. The pointers to the two thread objects that represent the trains are held globally for simplicity. The message map shows the functions called for various menu selections.

```
#include <afxwin.h>
#include "Resource.h"
#include "TrainThread.h"


CTrainThread  *Thread1;   // Pointer to two threads
CTrainThread  *Thread2;

// Define the application object class
class CApp : public CWinApp
{
public:
    virtual BOOL InitInstance ();
    virtual BOOL ExitInstance ();
};
// The frame window class
```

```
class CThreadWindow : public CFrameWnd
{
public:
    CClientDC    *m_pDC;
public:
    CThreadWindow();
    ~CThreadWindow();
    afx_msg void OnAppAbout();
    afx_msg void OnNewThread();
    afx_msg void OnT1Suspend();
    afx_msg void OnT1Resume();
    afx_msg void OnT1TimeCritical();
    afx_msg void OnT1Highest();
    afx_msg void OnT1AboveNormal();
    afx_msg void OnT1Normal();
    afx_msg void OnT1BelowNormal();
    afx_msg void OnT1Lowest();
    afx_msg void OnT1Idle();
    afx_msg void OnT2Suspend();
    afx_msg void OnT2Resume();
    afx_msg void OnT2TimeCritical();
    afx_msg void OnT2Highest();
    afx_msg void OnT2AboveNormal();
    afx_msg void OnT2Normal();
    afx_msg void OnT2BelowNormal();
    afx_msg void OnT2Lowest();
    afx_msg void OnT2Idle();
    afx_msg void OnExit();
    DECLARE_MESSAGE_MAP()
};

// CThreadWindow message map
BEGIN_MESSAGE_MAP(CThreadWindow, CFrameWnd)
    ON_COMMAND(ID_APP_ABOUT, OnAppAbout)
    ON_COMMAND(IDM_NEWTHREAD,              OnNewThread)
    ON_COMMAND(IDM_T1_SUSPEND,            OnT1Suspend)
    ON_COMMAND(IDM_T1_RESUME,             OnT1Resume)
    ON_COMMAND(IDM_T1_PRIORITY_CRITICAL,   OnT1TimeCritical)
    ON_COMMAND(IDM_T1_PRIORITY_HIGHEST,    OnT1Highest)
    ON_COMMAND(IDM_T1_PRIORITY_ABOVENORMAL,OnT1AboveNormal)
    ON_COMMAND(IDM_T1_PRIORITY_NORMAL,    OnT1Normal)

    ON_COMMAND(IDM_T1_PRIORITY_BELOWNORMAL,OnT1BelowNormal)
    ON_COMMAND(IDM_T1_PRIORITY_LOWEST,    OnT1Lowest)
```

```
        ON_COMMAND(IDM_T1_PRIORITY_IDLE,        OnT1Idle)
        ON_COMMAND(IDM_T2_SUSPEND,              OnT2Suspend)
        ON_COMMAND(IDM_T2_RESUME,               OnT2Resume)
        ON_COMMAND(IDM_T2_PRIORITY_CRITICAL,    OnT2TimeCritical)
        ON_COMMAND(IDM_T2_PRIORITY_HIGHEST,     OnT2Highest)
        ON_COMMAND(IDM_T2_PRIORITY_ABOVENORMAL,OnT2AboveNormal)
        ON_COMMAND(IDM_T2_PRIORITY_NORMAL,      OnT2Normal)
        ON_COMMAND(IDM_T2_PRIORITY_BELOWNORMAL,OnT2BelowNormal)
        ON_COMMAND(IDM_T2_PRIORITY_LOWEST,      OnT2Lowest)
        ON_COMMAND(IDM_T2_PRIORITY_IDLE,        OnT2Idle)
    ON_COMMAND(ID_APP_EXIT, OnExit)
END_MESSAGE_MAP()

// CThreadWindow constructor
CThreadWindow::CThreadWindow()
{
    LoadAccelTable(MAKEINTRESOURCE(IDR_MAINFRAME));
    Create( NULL, "Threads Priority Sample",
            WS_OVERLAPPEDWINDOW,
            rectDefault, NULL, MAKEINTRESOURCE(IDR_MAINFRAME) );
    m_pDC = new CClientDC(this);
    Thread2 = NULL;
    Thread1 = NULL;
}
```

The resource associated with the thread objects, if they exist, are freed when the user-interface thread is deleted.

```
CThreadWindow::~CThreadWindow()
{
    //  free the thread resource.
    if (Thread2)
    {
        delete Thread2;
    }
    if (Thread1)
    {
        delete Thread1;
    }
    delete m_pDC;
}

// The Main appplication CApp object

CApp theApp;
```

When the threads are created, they use the same device context to render the train. Since they share the same device context, this resource should be serialized. A critical section object is used to serialize the access to the device context while rendering. This critical section object should be initialized before using it. Once initialized, the threads of the process can **EnterCriticalSection** and **LeaveCriticalSection** using that object. The initialization of the critical section object is done when the application is started, and it is deleted when the application exits.

```
// The Main application class initialization
BOOL CApp::InitInstance()
{
    InitializeCriticalSection(&CTrainThread::m_cs);
    m_pMainWnd = new CThreadWindow();
    m_pMainWnd -> ShowWindow( m_nCmdShow );
    m_pMainWnd -> UpdateWindow();
    return TRUE;
}

int CApp::ExitInstance()
{
    DeleteCriticalSection(&CTrainThread::m_cs);
    return CWinApp::ExitInstance();
}

// CAboutDlg dialog used for App About
class CAboutDlg : public CDialog
{
public:
    CAboutDlg();
    enum { IDD = IDD_ABOUTBOX };
};

CAboutDlg::CAboutDlg() : CDialog(CAboutDlg::IDD)
{
}

// App command to run the dialog
void CThreadWindow::OnAppAbout()
{
    CAboutDlg aboutDlg;
    aboutDlg.DoModal();
}
```

When the user starts the new threads, the old thread objects are deleted if they exist, new thread objects are allocated, and threads are created. The constructor of the thread takes the pointer to the frame window object and the handle to the device context, and it tracks where the train runs. MFC maintains a list of all GDI objects on a per-thread basis. Thus, the CDC object in the main application thread cannot be directly used. Instead, the handle to the device context is passed, which can then be converted to an MFC object. This is done in the code that handles the train thread, which will be seen later.

```
void CThreadWindow::OnNewThread()
{
    if (Thread2)
    {
        delete Thread2;
    }
    if (Thread1)
    {
        delete Thread1;
    }
    Thread1 = new CTrainThread(this, m_pDC->GetSafeHdc(), UPPER_TRAIN);
    Thread2 = new CTrainThread(this, m_pDC->GetSafeHdc(), LOWER_TRAIN);

    Thread1->CreateThread();
    Thread2->CreateThread();
}

// On Exit handles the void
void CThreadWindow::OnExit()
{
    DestroyWindow();
}
```

The rest of the code deals with processing user commands for suspending, resuming, and altering the priorities of the threads. These are done by use of the **SuspendThread**, **ResumeThread**, and **SetThreadPriority** member functions of **CWinThread**.

```
void CThreadWindow::OnT1Suspend()
{
  Thread1->SuspendThread();
}
void CThreadWindow::OnT1Resume()
{
  Thread1->ResumeThread();
}
void CThreadWindow::OnT1TimeCritical()
{
  Thread1->SetThreadPriority(THREAD_PRIORITY_TIME_CRITICAL);
  Beep(300,30);
}
void CThreadWindow::OnT1Highest()
{
```

```
  Thread1->SetThreadPriority(THREAD_PRIORITY_HIGHEST);
  Beep(300,30);
}
void CThreadWindow::OnT1AboveNormal()
{
  Thread1->SetThreadPriority(THREAD_PRIORITY_ABOVE_NORMAL);
  Beep(300,30);
}
void CThreadWindow::OnT1Normal()
{
  Thread1->SetThreadPriority(THREAD_PRIORITY_NORMAL);
  Beep(300,30);
}
void CThreadWindow::OnT1BelowNormal()
{
  Thread1->SetThreadPriority(THREAD_PRIORITY_BELOW_NORMAL);
  Beep(300,30);
}
void CThreadWindow::OnT1Lowest()
{
  Thread1->SetThreadPriority(THREAD_PRIORITY_LOWEST);
  Beep(300,30);
}
void CThreadWindow::OnT1Idle()
{
  Thread1->SetThreadPriority(THREAD_PRIORITY_IDLE);
  Beep(300,30);
}
void CThreadWindow::OnT2Suspend()
{
  Thread2->SuspendThread();
}
void CThreadWindow::OnT2Resume()
{
  Thread2->ResumeThread();
}
void CThreadWindow::OnT2TimeCritical()
{
  Thread2->SetThreadPriority(THREAD_PRIORITY_TIME_CRITICAL);
  Beep(300,30);
}
void CThreadWindow::OnT2Highest()
{
  Thread2->SetThreadPriority(THREAD_PRIORITY_HIGHEST);
  Beep(300,30);
}
void CThreadWindow::OnT2AboveNormal()
{
  Thread2->SetThreadPriority(THREAD_PRIORITY_ABOVE_NORMAL);
  Beep(300,30);
```

```
}
void CThreadWindow::OnT2Normal()
{
  Thread2->SetThreadPriority(THREAD_PRIORITY_NORMAL);
  Beep(300,30);
}
void CThreadWindow::OnT2BelowNormal()
{
  Thread2->SetThreadPriority(THREAD_PRIORITY_BELOW_NORMAL);
  Beep(300,30);
}
void CThreadWindow::OnT2Lowest()
{
  Thread2->SetThreadPriority(THREAD_PRIORITY_LOWEST);
  Beep(300,30);
}
void CThreadWindow::OnT2Idle()
{
  Thread2->SetThreadPriority(THREAD_PRIORITY_IDLE);
  Beep(300,30);
}
```

The resource file for this sample is shown next.

```
//Microsoft Developer Studio generated resource script.
//
#include "afxres.h"
#include "resource.h"
LANGUAGE LANG_NEUTRAL, SUBLANG_NEUTRAL
/////////////////////////////////////////////////////////////////////////
//
// Icon
//

// Icon with lowest ID value placed first to ensure application icon
// remains consistent on all systems.
IDR_MAINFRAME            ICON    DISCARDABLE     "Threads.ico"


/////////////////////////////////////////////////////////////////////////
//
// Menu
//

IDR_MAINFRAME MENU PRELOAD DISCARDABLE
BEGIN
    POPUP "&File"
    BEGIN
        MENUITEM "&New Threads\tCtrl+T",        IDM_NEWTHREAD
        MENUITEM SEPARATOR
        MENUITEM "E&xit",                       ID_APP_EXIT
```

```
        END
        POPUP "&Thread1"
        BEGIN
            MENUITEM "&Suspend\tCtrl+S",                 IDM_T1_SUSPEND
            MENUITEM "&Resume\tCtrl+R",                  IDM_T1_RESUME
            POPUP "&Priority"
            BEGIN
                MENUITEM "&Time Critical\tCtrl+1",       IDM_T1_PRIORITY_CRITICAL
                MENUITEM "&Highest\tCtrl+2",             IDM_T1_PRIORITY_HIGHEST
                MENUITEM "&Above Normal\tCtrl+3",        IDM_T1_PRIORITY_ABOVENORMAL

                MENUITEM "&Normal\tCtrl+4",              IDM_T1_PRIORITY_NORMAL
                MENUITEM "&Below Normal\tCtrl+5",        IDM_T1_PRIORITY_BELOWNORMAL
                MENUITEM "&Lowest\tCtrl+6",              IDM_T1_PRIORITY_LOWEST
                MENUITEM "&Idle\tCtrl+7",                IDM_T1_PRIORITY_IDLE
            END
        END
        POPUP "&Thread2"
        BEGIN
            MENUITEM "&Suspend\tAlt+S",                  IDM_T2_SUSPEND
            MENUITEM "&Resume\tAlt+R",                   IDM_T2_RESUME
            POPUP "&Priority"
            BEGIN
                MENUITEM "&Time Critical\tAlt+1",        IDM_T2_PRIORITY_CRITICAL
                MENUITEM "&Highest\tAlt+2",              IDM_T2_PRIORITY_HIGHEST
                MENUITEM "&Above Normal\tAlt+3",         IDM_T2_PRIORITY_ABOVENORMAL
                MENUITEM "&Normal\tAlt+4",               IDM_T2_PRIORITY_NORMAL
                MENUITEM "&Below Normal\tAlt+5",         IDM_T2_PRIORITY_BELOWNORMAL
                MENUITEM "&Lowest\tAlt+6",               IDM_T2_PRIORITY_LOWEST
                MENUITEM "&Idle\tAlt+7",                 IDM_T2_PRIORITY_IDLE
            END
        END
        POPUP "&Help"
        BEGIN
            MENUITEM "&About...",                        ID_APP_ABOUT
        END
END


/////////////////////////////////////////////////////////////////
//
// Accelerator
//

IDR_MAINFRAME ACCELERATORS PRELOAD MOVEABLE PURE
BEGIN
    "T",            IDM_NEWTHREAD,              VIRTKEY, CONTROL
    "S",            IDM_T1_SUSPEND,             VIRTKEY, CONTROL
    "R",            IDM_T1_RESUME,              VIRTKEY, CONTROL
```

```
    "1",              IDM_T1_PRIORITY_CRITICAL,       VIRTKEY, CONTROL

    "2",              IDM_T1_PRIORITY_HIGHEST,        VIRTKEY, CONTROL
    "3",              IDM_T1_PRIORITY_ABOVENORMAL,    VIRTKEY, CONTROL
    "4",              IDM_T1_PRIORITY_NORMAL,         VIRTKEY, CONTROL
    "5",              IDM_T1_PRIORITY_BELOWNORMAL,    VIRTKEY, CONTROL
    "6",              IDM_T1_PRIORITY_LOWEST,         VIRTKEY, CONTROL
    "7",              IDM_T1_PRIORITY_IDLE,           VIRTKEY, CONTROL
    "S",              IDM_T2_SUSPEND,                 VIRTKEY, ALT
    "R",              IDM_T2_RESUME,                  VIRTKEY, ALT
    "1",              IDM_T2_PRIORITY_CRITICAL,       VIRTKEY, ALT
    "2",              IDM_T2_PRIORITY_HIGHEST,        VIRTKEY, ALT
    "3",              IDM_T2_PRIORITY_ABOVENORMAL,    VIRTKEY, ALT
    "4",              IDM_T2_PRIORITY_NORMAL,         VIRTKEY, ALT
    "5",              IDM_T2_PRIORITY_BELOWNORMAL,    VIRTKEY, ALT
    "6",              IDM_T2_PRIORITY_LOWEST,         VIRTKEY, ALT
    "7",              IDM_T2_PRIORITY_IDLE,           VIRTKEY, ALT
END


/////////////////////////////////////////////////////////////////
//
// Dialog
//

IDD_ABOUTBOX DIALOG DISCARDABLE  0, 0, 217, 55
STYLE DS_MODALFRAME | WS_POPUP | WS_CAPTION | WS_SYSMENU
CAPTION "About Threads"
FONT 8, "MS Sans Serif"
BEGIN
    ICON            IDR_MAINFRAME,IDC_STATIC,11,17,21,20
    LTEXT           "Threads-Priority sample",IDC_STATIC,40,10,119,8,SS_NOPREFIX
    LTEXT           "Copyright © 1997",IDC_STATIC,40,25,119,8
    DEFPUSHBUTTON   "OK",IDOK,178,7,32,14,WS_GROUP
END
```

The header file and implementation file for the **CTrainThread** user-interface thread are shown next. A user-interface thread is commonly used to handle user input and respond to user events independent of other threads that might be running in the current process. All user-interface threads are derived from **CWinThread** and must declare and implement this class using the DECLARE_DYNCREATE and IMPLEMENT_DYNCREATE macros. The classes derived from **CWinThread** must override the **InitInstance** method and may optionally override other methods. In this sample the **InitInstance** and **ExitInstance** methods are overridden.

```
class CTrainThread : public CWinThread
{
public:
    DECLARE_DYNAMIC(CTrainThread)
```

```
        CTrainThread(CWnd* pWnd, HDC hDC, short sDirection);
public:
    short    m_position;
    short    m_trainmoves;
    HDC m_hDC;
    HBRUSH m_hBrush;
    HBRUSH m_hWbrush;
    CDC m_dc;
    CBrush m_brush;
    CBrush m_wbrush;
    CRect m_clientsize;
    CRect m_rectPosition;

    static CRITICAL_SECTION m_csGDILock;

public:
    void MoveTrain();

protected:
    virtual BOOL InitInstance();
    virtual int ExitInstance();
    DECLARE_MESSAGE_MAP()
};
```

The implementation file for **CTrainThread** is shown next.

```
#include <afxwin.h>
#include "TrainThread.h"

#define TRAINLENGTH     30
#define TRAINWIDTH      10
#define TRAINSTEPSIZE   3

// CTrainThread—Implementation file
CRITICAL_SECTION CTrainThread::m_cs;
IMPLEMENT_DYNAMIC(CTrainThread, CWinThread)
BEGIN_MESSAGE_MAP(CTrainThread, CWinThread)
        //{{AFX_MSG_MAP(CTrainThread)
                // NOTE-the ClassWizard will add and remove mapping macros here.
        //}}AFX_MSG_MAP
END_MESSAGE_MAP()
```

As mentioned earlier, the GDI objects cannot be passed between threads, so the handle to the device context is passed to the thread during thread creation. This is maintained as a member variable and is later used in **InitInstance** to attach to a CDC object. When the thread is created, the color and the location of the thread are initialized in accordance with the position of the train. The width of the screen is determined to calculate the position of the train and the number of moves it has to make to go across the window.

```
CTrainThread::CTrainThread(CWnd* pWnd, HDC hDC, short sPosition)
{
    CBrush  brush;
    CBrush  Whitebrush;

    m_bAutoDelete = FALSE;
    m_pMainWnd = pWnd;
    m_pMainWnd->GetClientRect(&m_clientsize);
    m_hDC = hDC;
    m_position = sPosition;

    Whitebrush.CreateSolidBrush(RGB(0xFF, 0xFF,0xFF));
    m_hWbrush = (HBRUSH)Whitebrush.Detach();

    if (m_position == UPPER_TRAIN)
    {
        brush.CreateSolidBrush(RGB(0x00, 0xFF,0x00));
        m_rectPosition.SetRect(0, m_clientsize.Height()/3,
                            0+TRAINLENGTH,
                            (m_clientsize.Height()/3)+TRAINWIDTH);
    }
    else
    {
        brush.CreateSolidBrush(RGB(0xFF, 0x00,0x00));
        m_rectPosition.SetRect(0, m_clientsize.Height()*2/3,
                            0+TRAINLENGTH,
                            (m_clientsize.Height()*2/3)+TRAINWIDTH);
    }
    m_trainmoves = (short)(m_clientsize.Width()/TRAINSTEPSIZE);
    m_hBrush = (HBRUSH)brush.Detach();
}


BOOL CTrainThread::InitInstance()
{
    m_wbrush.Attach(m_hWbrush);
    m_brush.Attach(m_hBrush);
    m_dc.Attach(m_hDC);
    for (int j = 0; j<m_trainmoves; j++)
    {
        for (unsigned int k =0; k<200000;k++);
        MoveTrain();
    }
    // Destination reached.  Beep
    Beep(1000,200);
    // thread cleanup
    m_dc.Detach();
    return FALSE;
}
```

```
int CTrainThread::ExitInstance()
{
    return (0);
}
```

The **MoveTrain** method moves the rectangular color block by redrawing one new color block and clearing the old color block. This simulates the train movement. The same device context is used by both threads for rendering. The thread currently rendering in the device context enters a critical section to prevent the other thread from rendering.

```
void CTrainThread::MoveTrain()
{

    CRect OldRect;
    OldRect = m_rectPosition;

    m_rectPosition.OffsetRect(TRAINSTEPSIZE,0);
    EnterCriticalSection(&CTrainThread::m_cs);
    {
        CBrush* oldbrush;
        CPen*   oldPen;
// Draw the new position of the train
        oldbrush = m_dc.SelectObject(&m_brush);
        m_dc.Rectangle(m_rectPosition);
        m_dc.SelectObject(oldbrush);

// Clear the old position of the train
        oldbrush = m_dc.SelectObject(&m_wbrush);
        oldPen = (CPen*) m_dc.SelectStockObject(WHITE_PEN);
        OldRect.OffsetRect(TRAINSTEPSIZE-TRAINLENGTH, 0);
        m_dc.Rectangle(OldRect);
        m_dc.SelectObject(oldbrush);
        m_dc.SelectObject(oldPen);
        GdiFlush();
    }
    LeaveCriticalSection(&CTrainThread::m_cs);
}
```

When you're trying the example, it is better to create a debug version of the program, since the looping that simulates the work in the thread will be more manageable that way. Also try it with the window maximized to give more room for the train movement. After you start the trains, the priority of the train, actually the thread, can be altered and the change observed. The trains can be suspended and resumed. Notice that if the train is suspended twice, then it has to be resumed twice before it starts moving again. This is because each thread has a suspend count, and if the suspend count is greater than zero, the thread is suspended. Every time **SuspendThread** is called, the suspend count is incremented once, and every time **ResumeThread** is called, the suspend thread count is decremented once.

> ***TIP:***   MFC maintains a list of all GDI objects on a per-thread basis.

Mutexes

A *mutex* is very similar to a critical section, except that a mutex can be used across processes. One way in which you can use a mutex is by creating a variable of type **CSingleLock** or **CMultiLock** in your resource's access member function. You then call the lock object's **Lock** member function. If the resource is not being used, your thread gains access. If the resource is being used, your thread waits (until it either gains access or it times out). You unlock (and release the resource if you gained access) using the **Unlock** member function. The APIs you can use with mutex objects are summarized in the following table:

Mutex APIs	Description
ReleaseMutex	This releases ownership of the specified mutex object. It is used when the owning thread has finished using the resource controlled by the mutex.
CreateMutex	This creates a mutex object.
OpenMutex	This enables synchronization across multiple processes by returning the handle of a mutex object that has already been created (using CreateMutex).

As an exercise, try rewriting the critical section example using a mutex.

Events

An *event* is a synchronization object, which (like other synchronization objects) has two states, signaled and nonsignaled. Events are typically used to synchronize thread execution. When Thread A has to wait for Thread B, it waits for Thread B to signal an event. Windows 2000 does not schedule Thread A for execution until Thread B signals the event and changes the state of the event to Signaled. Windows 2000 now schedules Thread A for execution. The APIs you can use with event objects are summarized in the table here:

Event APIs	Description
SetEvent	This sets the state of the event object to Signaled.
CreateEvent	This creates an event object.
ResetEvent	This resets the state of the event object to Nonsignaled.

Event APIs	Description
OpenEvent	This enables multiple processes to use an event object by returning the handle of an existing event object.
PulseEvent	This sets the state of the specified event object to Signaled and then resets it to Nonsignaled. It is used for releasing waiting threads.

The *ThreadEvent* sample takes the Thread Priority sample and uses Event to synchronize the two threads. In the *ThreadPriority* sample the two trains were running from left to right across the screen. In this sample one train runs from west to east, and the other train runs from north to south. When the train running from north to south (NSTrain) comes to the center of the screen, it waits for the other train to cross. The west to east train (WETrain) signals the NSTrain after it crosses the center of the screen. After receiving the signal, the NSTrain proceeds south. The NSTrain does not wait indefinitely. If for some reason the WETrain gets stuck before reaching the center, the NSTrain will still proceed south after waiting for a while. Synchronization, in this multithreaded example, is implemented using events. Most of the code is the same or similar to the Thread Priority sample, and the differences are highlighted and discussed next. Shots of the screens you get when the event sample program is executed are shown in Figures 9-4 through 9-6. Figure 9-4 shows the two trains close to their starting positions. Figure 9-5 shows the trains about to cross paths. Figure 9-6 shows the trains after they have crossed.

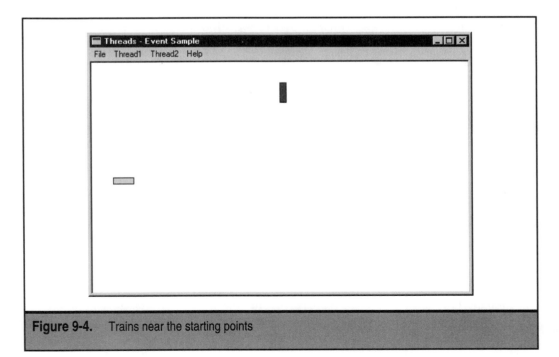

Figure 9-4.   Trains near the starting points

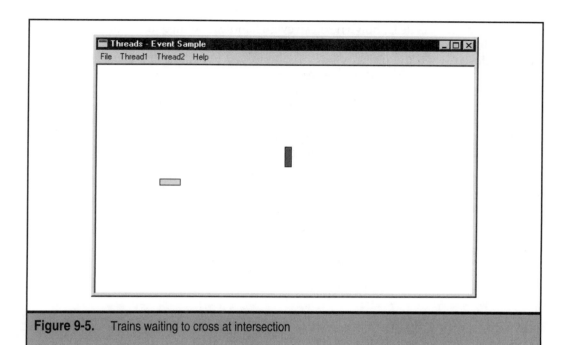

Figure 9-5.   Trains waiting to cross at intersection

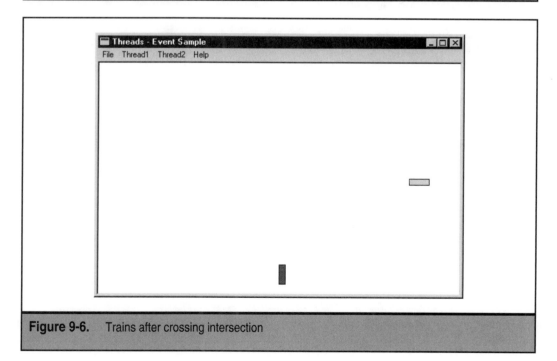

Figure 9-6.   Trains after crossing intersection

The *Threads.Cpp* code is shown next. An event handle is defined in the global space, and the event is created when the frame window is created by calling the **CreateEvent** API. This event is closed when the frame window is destroyed by calling the **CloseHandle** API. When the threads are created, the event is reset by calling **ResetEvent** API. Thus, any thread waiting for this event would be blocked until the event is set. The rest of the code that deals with this event is in the *TrainThread.Cpp* module. Notice that the priority of the threads can be altered, or the threads can be suspended and resumed as in the *ThreadPriority* example. The rest of the code has no significant changes. The resource file is not shown here, since it changes very little.

```
#include <afxwin.h>
#include "Resource.h"
#include "TrainThread.h"

CTrainThread  *ThreadWE;    // Pointer to two threads
CTrainThread  *ThreadNS;
HANDLE  hEventGreenLight;   // Signal light event handle

// Define the application object class
class CApp : public CWinApp
{
public:
    virtual BOOL InitInstance ();
    virtual BOOL ExitInstance ();
};
// The frame window class
class CThreadWindow : public CFrameWnd
{

public:
    CClientDC   *m_pDC;
public:
    CThreadWindow ();
    ~CThreadWindow ();
    afx_msg void OnAppAbout ();
    afx_msg void OnNewThread ();
    afx_msg void OnT1Suspend ();
    afx_msg void OnT1Resume ();
    afx_msg void OnT1TimeCritical ();
    afx_msg void OnT1Highest ();
    afx_msg void OnT1AboveNormal ();
    afx_msg void OnT1Normal ();
    afx_msg void OnT1BelowNormal ();
    afx_msg void OnT1Lowest ();
    afx_msg void OnT1Idle ();
    afx_msg void OnT2Suspend ();
    afx_msg void OnT2Resume ();
    afx_msg void OnT2TimeCritical ();
```

```
        afx_msg void OnT2Highest();
        afx_msg void OnT2AboveNormal();
        afx_msg void OnT2Normal();
        afx_msg void OnT2BelowNormal();
        afx_msg void OnT2Lowest();
        afx_msg void OnT2Idle();
        afx_msg void OnExit();
        DECLARE_MESSAGE_MAP()
};


// CThreadWindow

BEGIN_MESSAGE_MAP(CThreadWindow, CFrameWnd)
    ON_COMMAND(ID_APP_ABOUT, OnAppAbout)
    ON_COMMAND(IDM_NEWTHREAD,              OnNewThread)
    ON_COMMAND(IDM_T1_SUSPEND,             OnT1Suspend)
    ON_COMMAND(IDM_T1_RESUME,              OnT1Resume)
    ON_COMMAND(IDM_T1_PRIORITY_CRITICAL,   OnT1TimeCritical)
    ON_COMMAND(IDM_T1_PRIORITY_HIGHEST,    OnT1Highest)
    ON_COMMAND(IDM_T1_PRIORITY_ABOVENORMAL,OnT1AboveNormal)

    ON_COMMAND(IDM_T1_PRIORITY_NORMAL,     OnT1Normal)
    ON_COMMAND(IDM_T1_PRIORITY_BELOWNORMAL,OnT1BelowNormal)
    ON_COMMAND(IDM_T1_PRIORITY_LOWEST,     OnT1Lowest)
    ON_COMMAND(IDM_T1_PRIORITY_IDLE,       OnT1Idle)
    ON_COMMAND(IDM_T2_SUSPEND,             OnT2Suspend)
    ON_COMMAND(IDM_T2_RESUME,              OnT2Resume)
    ON_COMMAND(IDM_T2_PRIORITY_CRITICAL,   OnT2TimeCritical)
    ON_COMMAND(IDM_T2_PRIORITY_HIGHEST,    OnT2Highest)
    ON_COMMAND(IDM_T2_PRIORITY_ABOVENORMAL,OnT2AboveNormal)
    ON_COMMAND(IDM_T2_PRIORITY_NORMAL,     OnT2Normal)
    ON_COMMAND(IDM_T2_PRIORITY_BELOWNORMAL,OnT2BelowNormal)
    ON_COMMAND(IDM_T2_PRIORITY_LOWEST,     OnT2Lowest)
    ON_COMMAND(IDM_T2_PRIORITY_IDLE,       OnT2Idle)
    ON_COMMAND(ID_APP_EXIT, OnExit)
END_MESSAGE_MAP()

// CThreadWindow constructor and destructor

CThreadWindow::CThreadWindow()
{
    LoadAccelTable(MAKEINTRESOURCE(IDR_MAINFRAME));
    Create( NULL, "Threads-Event Sample",
            WS_OVERLAPPEDWINDOW,
            rectDefault, NULL, MAKEINTRESOURCE(IDR_MAINFRAME) );

    m_pDC = new CClientDC(this);
    hEventGreenLight = CreateEvent(NULL, TRUE, FALSE, NULL);
    ThreadNS = NULL;
```

```
        ThreadWE = NULL;
}

CThreadWindow::~CThreadWindow()
{
    // Close the handle and free the thread resource.
    CloseHandle(hEventGreenLight);
    if (ThreadNS)
    {
        delete ThreadNS;
    }
    if (ThreadWE)
    {

        delete ThreadWE;
    }

    delete m_pDC;
}

// The CApp object

CApp theApp;

// CApp initialization

BOOL CApp::InitInstance()
{
    InitializeCriticalSection(&CTrainThread::m_cs);
    m_pMainWnd = new CThreadWindow();
    m_pMainWnd -> ShowWindow( m_nCmdShow );
    m_pMainWnd -> UpdateWindow();
    return TRUE;
}

int CApp::ExitInstance()
{
    DeleteCriticalSection(&CTrainThread::m_cs);

        return CWinApp::ExitInstance();
}

// CAboutDlg dialog used for App About box
class CAboutDlg : public CDialog
{
public:
    CAboutDlg();
    enum { IDD = IDD_ABOUTBOX };
};
```

```
CAboutDlg::CAboutDlg()  :  CDialog(CAboutDlg::IDD)
{
}

// App command to run the dialog
void CThreadWindow::OnAppAbout()
{

    CAboutDlg aboutDlg;
    aboutDlg.DoModal();
}


void CThreadWindow::OnNewThread()
{
    if (ThreadNS)
    {
        delete ThreadNS;
    }
    if (ThreadWE)
    {
        delete ThreadWE;
    }

    ResetEvent(hEventGreenLight);

    ThreadWE = new CTrainThread(this, m_pDC->GetSafeHdc(),
                               DIRECTION_WEST_TO_EAST);
    ThreadNS = new CTrainThread(this, m_pDC->GetSafeHdc(),
                               DIRECTION_NORTH_TO_SOUTH);
    ThreadWE->CreateThread();
    ThreadNS->CreateThread();
}


// On Exit handling function
void CThreadWindow::OnExit()
{
    DestroyWindow();
}
```

The **CTrainThread** class header file is shown next. There is no significant change here when compared with the *ThreadPriority* sample.

```
// TrainThread.h : The Train thread header file for
// the ThreadEvent sample application

#define DIRECTION_WEST_TO_EAST 1
#define DIRECTION_NORTH_TO_SOUTH 2
```

```
class CTrainThread : public CWinThread
{
public:
    DECLARE_DYNAMIC(CTrainThread)
    CTrainThread(CWnd* pWnd, HDC hDC, short sDirection);

// Attributes
public:
    short    m_direction;       // W-E or N-S train direction
    short    m_trainmoves;
    HDC m_hDC;
    HBRUSH m_hBrush;
    HBRUSH m_hWbrush;
    CDC m_dc;
    CBrush m_brush;
    CBrush m_wbrush;
    CRect m_clientsize;
    CRect m_rectPosition;

    static CRITICAL_SECTION m_cs;

public:
    virtual ~CTrainThread();
    void MoveTrain();

protected:
    virtual BOOL InitInstance();
    DECLARE_MESSAGE_MAP()
};
```

The code that handles the execution of the thread is shown next. The significant code is in the **InitInstance** section of the code.

```
#include <afxwin.h>
#include "TrainThread.h"


#define TRAINLENGTH     30
#define TRAINWIDTH      10
#define TRAINSTEPSIZE   30
#define SLEEPTIME       200

// CTrainThread—Implementation file

CRITICAL_SECTION CTrainThread::m_cs;

IMPLEMENT_DYNAMIC(CTrainThread, CWinThread)

BEGIN_MESSAGE_MAP(CTrainThread, CWinThread)
```

```
        //{{AFX_MSG_MAP(CTrainThread)
        // NOTE-the ClassWizard will add and remove mapping macros here.
        //}}AFX_MSG_MAP
END_MESSAGE_MAP()

CTrainThread::CTrainThread(CWnd* pWnd, HDC hDC, short sDirection)
{
    CBrush  brush;
    CBrush  Whitebrush;

    m_bAutoDelete = FALSE;
    m_pMainWnd = pWnd;
    m_pMainWnd->GetClientRect(&m_clientsize);
    m_hDC = hDC;
    m_direction = sDirection;

    Whitebrush.CreateSolidBrush(RGB(0xFF, 0xFF,0xFF));
    m_hWbrush = (HBRUSH)Whitebrush.Detach();

    if (m_direction == DIRECTION_WEST_TO_EAST)
    {
        brush.CreateSolidBrush(RGB(0x00, 0xFF,0x00));
        m_rectPosition.SetRect(0, m_clientsize.Height()/2,
                            0+TRAINLENGTH,
                            (m_clientsize.Height()/2)+TRAINWIDTH);

        m_trainmoves = (short)(m_clientsize.Width()/TRAINLENGTH);
    }
    else
    {
        brush.CreateSolidBrush(RGB(0xFF, 0x00,0x00));
        m_rectPosition.SetRect((m_clientsize.Width()/2),0,
                            (m_clientsize.Width()/2)+TRAINWIDTH,
                            0+TRAINLENGTH);
        m_trainmoves = (short)(m_clientsize.Height()/TRAINLENGTH);
    }

    m_hBrush = (HBRUSH)brush.Detach();
}
```

When the thread is executed, the thread that represents NSTrain moves to a point just above the center of the screen and then waits for the event by calling the **WaitForSingleObject** API. However, it does not wait indefinitely. It waits for the amount of time it would take for the other train to go across the screen. The thread representing the WETrain signals the event just after passing the center of the screen. It beeps after setting the signal. When WETrain signals, this will trigger the NSTrain, which will be waiting to proceed. When the sample is run, the trains can be seen going from north to south and west to east. The NSTrain will wait for a beep and then proceed south. If the WETrain is suspended, the NSTrain, which is waiting, will proceed after a while.

```
BOOL CTrainThread::InitInstance()
{

    extern HANDLE    hEventGreenLight;
    m_wbrush.Attach(m_hWbrush);
    m_brush.Attach(m_hBrush);
    m_dc.Attach(m_hDC);


    // Move the train until it reaches the signal light
    for (int j = 0; j<m_trainmoves; j++)
    {
        Sleep(SLEEPTIME);
        if ((m_direction == DIRECTION_NORTH_TO_SOUTH) &&
            (j == (m_trainmoves/2-1)) )
        {   // North South train waits at the center till the West East train
            // passes OR times out.
            WaitForSingleObject(hEventGreenLight, SLEEPTIME*m_trainmoves);
        }

        if ((m_direction == DIRECTION_WEST_TO_EAST) &&
            (j == (m_trainmoves/2 + 1)) )
        {   // West East train signals the North South train after it passes the
            // center
            Beep(1000,70);
            SetEvent(hEventGreenLight);
        }
          MoveTrain();
    }
        // Destination reached.  Beep
    Beep(1000,200);
    // thread cleanup
    m_dc.Detach();

    // avoid entering standard message loop by returning FALSE
    return FALSE;
}

CTrainThread::~CTrainThread()
{
}

void CTrainThread::MoveTrain()
{

    CRect OldRect;
    OldRect = m_rectPosition;
```

```
    if (m_direction == DIRECTION_WEST_TO_EAST)
    {
        m_rectPosition.OffsetRect(TRAINSTEPSIZE,0);
    }
    else
    {
        m_rectPosition.OffsetRect(0,TRAINSTEPSIZE);
    }

    EnterCriticalSection(&CTrainThread::m_cs);
    {
        CBrush* oldbrush;

        CPen*   oldPen;
// Draw the new position of the train
        oldbrush = m_dc.SelectObject(&m_brush);
        m_dc.Rectangle(m_rectPosition);
        m_dc.SelectObject(oldbrush);

// Clear the old position of the train
        oldbrush = m_dc.SelectObject(&m_wbrush);
        oldPen = (CPen*) m_dc.SelectStockObject(WHITE_PEN);
        m_dc.Rectangle(OldRect);
        m_dc.SelectObject(oldbrush);
        m_dc.SelectObject(oldPen);

        GdiFlush();
    }
    LeaveCriticalSection(&CTrainThread::m_cs);
}
```

Another example that uses events for synchronization is covered in the next chapter during the discussion of Named Pipes.

Semaphores

Semaphores are used to control access to a resource by a certain number of threads (as opposed to critical sections, which let only one thread access a resource or section of code). A semaphore has a *resource counter*. Every thread that wants to access the resource controlled by the semaphore waits for the semaphore, and the resource counter is decremented by 1. If the counter is zero, then there are no more resources, and future requests to access the resource wait. When a thread finishes using the resource, it releases the semaphore, which increments the resource counter. The following APIs are used with semaphores:

Semaphore-Related APIs	Description
CreateSemaphore	Creates a semaphore and sets its resource count
OpenSemaphore	Opens an existing semaphore

Semaphore-Related APIs	Description
ReleaseSemaphore	Releases a semaphore and increments its resource count
WaitForSingleObject	Waits for a semaphore (or any object)
CloseHandle	Closes handle and releases resources

The *ThreadSem* sample shows the use of semaphores by simulating two trains traveling in different directions competing for a single track on a bridge. There are two train tracks running left to right, with a bridge one-third of the way through. Though there is one track for each direction, there is only one track for both directions on the bridge. Trains crossing the bridge share this one track resource on the bridge. The train coming to the bridge first uses the track on the bridge, while the train coming later waits until the track is available. To implement this scenario, the program uses threads for each train, and the single-track bridge is protected by a semaphore. When the program is run and the threads are started, two trains can be seen, one moving left to right on the upper track, and the other moving right to left on the lower track. When they each travel one-third of the way, the train coming first uses the bridge, while the other train waits on the other side of the bridge. After the first train crosses over the bridge, the next train uses the bridge. The priority of each train can be controlled as before, and the trains can be suspended and resumed. The screen shots of the trains as they start, as they are waiting to

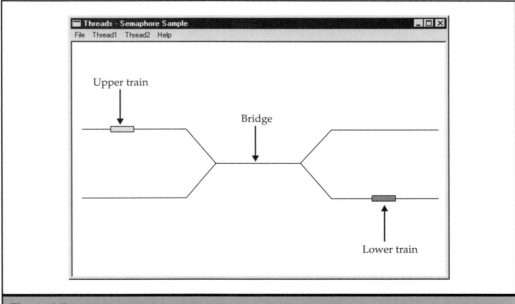

Figure 9-7. Trains near their starting points

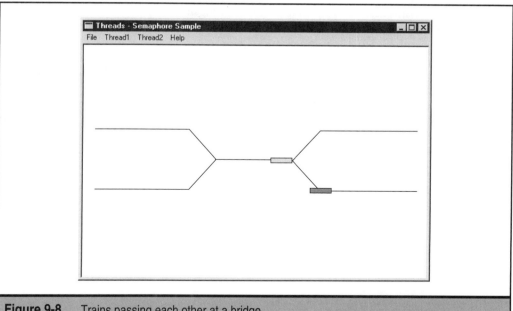

Figure 9-8. Trains passing each other at a bridge

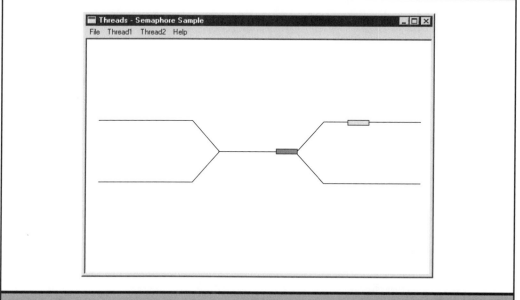

Figure 9-9. Trains after passing at the bridge

cross at a bridge, and after they cross are shown in Figures 9-7, 9-8, and 9-9, respectively. The bridge is not shown in the figure, but when you execute the program, you will see that the trains come close to each other and then move apart.

The main application code, shown next, is similar to the code discussed earlier. The changes made are in the semaphore area and are highlighted. A semaphore handle is defined in the global space, and the semaphore is created during the creation of the application frame window by calling the **CreateSemaphore** API. Since there is only one resource to control (one track on the bridge), the maximum resource count is set to 1. The track is available, so the initial count is also set to 1. When the application is closed, the semaphore is also closed by calling the **CloseHandle** API. The rest of the code and the resource file have little significant change.

```
#include <afxwin.h>
#include "Resource.h"
#include "TrainThread.h"

CTrainThread  *TrainThread1;     // Pointer to two threads
CTrainThread  *TrainThread2;
HANDLE  hSemaphore;              // Train track availability semaphore.

// Define the application object class
class CApp : public CWinApp
{
public:
    virtual BOOL InitInstance ();
    virtual BOOL ExitInstance ();
};

// The window class
class CThreadWindow : public CFrameWnd
{
public:
    CClientDC   *m_pDC;
public:
    CThreadWindow ();
    ~CThreadWindow ();
    afx_msg void OnAppAbout ();
    afx_msg void OnNewThread ();
    afx_msg void OnT1Suspend ();
    afx_msg void OnT1Resume ();
    afx_msg void OnT1TimeCritical ();
    afx_msg void OnT1Highest ();
    afx_msg void OnT1AboveNormal ();
    afx_msg void OnT1Normal ();
    afx_msg void OnT1BelowNormal ();
    afx_msg void OnT1Lowest ();
    afx_msg void OnT1Idle ();
    afx_msg void OnT2Suspend ();
    afx_msg void OnT2Resume ();
```

```
        afx_msg void OnT2TimeCritical();
        afx_msg void OnT2Highest();
        afx_msg void OnT2AboveNormal();
        afx_msg void OnT2Normal();
        afx_msg void OnT2BelowNormal();
        afx_msg void OnT2Lowest();
        afx_msg void OnT2Idle();
        afx_msg void OnExit();
        DECLARE_MESSAGE_MAP()
    };

    // CThreadWindow

    BEGIN_MESSAGE_MAP(CThreadWindow, CFrameWnd)
        ON_COMMAND(ID_APP_ABOUT, OnAppAbout)
        ON_COMMAND(IDM_NEWTHREAD,                 OnNewThread)
        ON_COMMAND(IDM_T1_SUSPEND,                OnT1Suspend)
        ON_COMMAND(IDM_T1_RESUME,                 OnT1Resume)
        ON_COMMAND(IDM_T1_PRIORITY_CRITICAL,      OnT1TimeCritical)
        ON_COMMAND(IDM_T1_PRIORITY_HIGHEST,       OnT1Highest)
        ON_COMMAND(IDM_T1_PRIORITY_ABOVENORMAL,   OnT1AboveNormal)
        ON_COMMAND(IDM_T1_PRIORITY_NORMAL,        OnT1Normal)
        ON_COMMAND(IDM_T1_PRIORITY_BELOWNORMAL,   OnT1BelowNormal)

        ON_COMMAND(IDM_T1_PRIORITY_LOWEST,        OnT1Lowest)
        ON_COMMAND(IDM_T1_PRIORITY_IDLE,          OnT1Idle)
        ON_COMMAND(IDM_T2_SUSPEND,                OnT2Suspend)
        ON_COMMAND(IDM_T2_RESUME,                 OnT2Resume)
        ON_COMMAND(IDM_T2_PRIORITY_CRITICAL,      OnT2TimeCritical)
        ON_COMMAND(IDM_T2_PRIORITY_HIGHEST,       OnT2Highest)
        ON_COMMAND(IDM_T2_PRIORITY_ABOVENORMAL,   OnT2AboveNormal)
        ON_COMMAND(IDM_T2_PRIORITY_NORMAL,        OnT2Normal)
        ON_COMMAND(IDM_T2_PRIORITY_BELOWNORMAL,   OnT2BelowNormal)
        ON_COMMAND(IDM_T2_PRIORITY_LOWEST,        OnT2Lowest)
        ON_COMMAND(IDM_T2_PRIORITY_IDLE,          OnT2Idle)
        ON_COMMAND(ID_APP_EXIT, OnExit)
    END_MESSAGE_MAP()

    // CThreadWindow constructor and destructor
    CThreadWindow::CThreadWindow()
    {
        LoadAccelTable(MAKEINTRESOURCE(IDR_MAINFRAME));
        Create( NULL, "Threads—Semaphore Sample",
                WS_OVERLAPPEDWINDOW,
                rectDefault, NULL, MAKEINTRESOURCE(IDR_MAINFRAME) );
        m_pDC = new CClientDC(this);
        hSemaphore = CreateSemaphore(NULL, 1, 1, NULL);
        TrainThread2 = NULL;
        TrainThread1 = NULL;
```

```
}
CThreadWindow::~CThreadWindow()
{
    // Close the handle and free the thread resource.

    CloseHandle(hSemaphore);
    if (TrainThread2)
    {
        delete TrainThread2;
    }
    if (TrainThread1)
    {
        delete TrainThread1;
    }
    delete m_pDC;
}
// The CApp object
CApp theApp;

BOOL CApp::InitInstance()
{
    InitializeCriticalSection(&CTrainThread::m_csGDILock);
    m_pMainWnd = new CThreadWindow();
    m_pMainWnd -> ShowWindow( m_nCmdShow );
    m_pMainWnd -> UpdateWindow();
    return TRUE;
}
int CApp::ExitInstance()
{
    DeleteCriticalSection(&CTrainThread::m_csGDILock);
    return CWinApp::ExitInstance();
}
// CAboutDlg dialog used for Application About box
class CAboutDlg : public CDialog
{
public:
    CAboutDlg();
    enum { IDD = IDD_ABOUTBOX };
};

CAboutDlg::CAboutDlg() : CDialog(CAboutDlg::IDD)
{
}

// App command to run the dialog
void CThreadWindow::OnAppAbout()
{
    CAboutDlg aboutDlg;
    aboutDlg.DoModal();
```

```
}
void CThreadWindow::OnNewThread()
{
    if (TrainThread2)
    {
        delete TrainThread2;
    }
    if (TrainThread1)
    {
        delete TrainThread1;
    }
    TrainThread1 = new CTrainThread(this, m_pDC->GetSafeHdc(), TRAIN_NO_1);
    TrainThread2 = new CTrainThread(this, m_pDC->GetSafeHdc(), TRAIN_NO_2);

    TrainThread1->CreateThread();
    TrainThread2->CreateThread();
}

// OnExit handles Exit command
void CThreadWindow::OnExit()
{
    DestroyWindow();
}
```

The *TrainThread* header file, shown next, has no significant change.

```
#define TRAIN_NO_1  1
#define TRAIN_NO_2  2
class CTrainThread : public CWinThread
{
public:
    DECLARE_DYNAMIC(CTrainThread)
    CTrainThread(CWnd* pWnd, HDC hDC, short sTrainNo);

// Attributes
public:
    short   m_train;
    short   m_trainmoves;
    HDC     m_hDC;
    HBRUSH  m_hBrush;
    HBRUSH  m_hWbrush;
    CDC     m_dc;
    CBrush  m_brush;
    CBrush  m_wbrush;
    CRect   m_clientsize;
    CRect   m_rectPosition;
    CRect   m_oldRect;

    static CRITICAL_SECTION m_csGDILock;
```

```
public:
    virtual ~CTrainThread();
    void MoveTrain(short);

protected:
    virtual BOOL InitInstance();
    DECLARE_MESSAGE_MAP()
};
```

The thread function is shown next.

```
#include <afxwin.h>
#include "TrainThread.h"


#define TRAINLENGTH      30
#define TRAINWIDTH       10
#define TRAINSTEPSIZE    30
#define SLEEPTIME        200
#define SINGLETRACKSECTION   2
#define MULTITRACKSECTION    1
// CTrainThread-Implementation file

CRITICAL_SECTION CTrainThread::m_csGDILock;
IMPLEMENT_DYNAMIC(CTrainThread, CWinThread)
BEGIN_MESSAGE_MAP(CTrainThread, CWinThread)
    //{{AFX_MSG_MAP(CTrainThread)
    // NOTE—the ClassWizard will add and remove mapping macros here.
    //}}AFX_MSG_MAP
END_MESSAGE_MAP()

CTrainThread::CTrainThread(CWnd* pWnd, HDC hDC, short sTrainNo)
{
    CBrush  brush;
    CBrush  Whitebrush;

    m_bAutoDelete = FALSE;
    m_pMainWnd = pWnd;
    m_pMainWnd->GetClientRect(&m_clientsize);
    m_hDC = hDC;
    m_train = sTrainNo;

    Whitebrush.CreateSolidBrush(RGB(0xFF, 0xFF,0xFF));
    m_hWbrush = (HBRUSH)Whitebrush.Detach();

    if (m_train == TRAIN_NO_1)
    {
        brush.CreateSolidBrush(RGB(0x00, 0xFF,0x00));
        m_rectPosition.SetRect(0, m_clientsize.Height()/3,
```

```
                                    0+TRAINLENGTH,
                                    (m_clientsize.Height()/3)+TRAINWIDTH);
    }
    else

    {
        brush.CreateSolidBrush(RGB(0xFF, 0x00,0x00));
        m_rectPosition.SetRect(m_clientsize.Width(), m_clientsize.Height()*2/3,
                        m_clientsize.Width()-TRAINLENGTH,
                        (m_clientsize.Height()*2/3)+TRAINWIDTH);
    }

    m_trainmoves = (short)(m_clientsize.Width()/TRAINLENGTH);
    m_hBrush = (HBRUSH)brush.Detach();
}
```

The **InitInstance** function controls the movement of the thread. When the train has moved one-third of the way, it will have reached the bridge. The thread (and hence the train) waits for the semaphore using the **WaitForSingelObject** API and proceeds when the semaphore is acquired. Notice that it waits indefinitely, as makes sense in this situation. After crossing the bridge, it releases the semaphore by calling the **ReleaseSemaphore** API, thereby indicating the release of the resource. Since only one count of the resource was released, the release count is set to 1 in the **ReleaseSemaphore** API. Waiting for a semaphore indefinitely is the common cause of deadlocks in multithreading programs. You can simulate this deadlock situation by suspending the thread whose train is on the bridge.

```
BOOL CTrainThread::InitInstance()
{
    extern HANDLE   hSemaphore;
    m_wbrush.Attach(m_hWbrush);
    m_brush.Attach(m_hBrush);
    m_dc.Attach(m_hDC);

    // Move the train until it reaches the single track section which is 1/3
    // way through
    for (int j = 0; j<m_trainmoves/3; j++)
    {
        Sleep(SLEEPTIME);
        MoveTrain(MULTITRACKSECTION);
        m_oldRect = m_rectPosition;
    }
    WaitForSingleObject(hSemaphore, INFINITE);
    // Move the train in the single track section
    if(m_train == TRAIN_NO_1)
    {
        m_rectPosition.OffsetRect(TRAINSTEPSIZE,m_clientsize.Height()/6);
    }
    else
```

```
    {
        m_rectPosition.OffsetRect(TRAINSTEPSIZE,-m_clientsize.Height()/6);
    }
    for (j = 0; j<m_trainmoves/3; j++)
    {
        Sleep(SLEEPTIME);
        MoveTrain(SINGLETRACKSECTION);
        m_oldRect = m_rectPosition;
    }


            // Off the single track section. Release the Semaphore and put back in
            // the original track
    ReleaseSemaphore(hSemaphore, 1, NULL);
    if(m_train == TRAIN_NO_1)
    {
        m_rectPosition.OffsetRect(TRAINSTEPSIZE,-m_clientsize.Height()/6);
    }
    else
    {
        m_rectPosition.OffsetRect(TRAINSTEPSIZE, m_clientsize.Height()/6);
    }
    for (j = 0; j<m_trainmoves/3; j++)
    {
        Sleep(SLEEPTIME);
        MoveTrain(MULTITRACKSECTION);
        m_oldRect = m_rectPosition;
    }
    // Destination reached.  Beep
    Beep(1000,200);
    // thread cleanup
    m_dc.Detach();

    return FALSE;    // return false to prevent entering the message loop
}


CTrainThread::~CTrainThread()
{
}

void CTrainThread::MoveTrain(short Track)
{
    if (m_train == TRAIN_NO_1)
    {
        m_rectPosition.OffsetRect(TRAINSTEPSIZE,0);
    }
    else
    {
        m_rectPosition.OffsetRect(-TRAINSTEPSIZE,0);
```

```
   }

   EnterCriticalSection(&CTrainThread::m_csGDILock);
   {
      CBrush* oldbrush;
      CPen*   oldPen;
// Draw the new position of the train
      oldbrush = m_dc.SelectObject(&m_brush);
      m_dc.Rectangle(m_rectPosition);
      m_dc.SelectObject(oldbrush);

// Clear the old position of the train
      oldbrush = m_dc.SelectObject(&m_wbrush);
      oldPen = (CPen*) m_dc.SelectStockObject(WHITE_PEN);
      m_dc.Rectangle(m_oldRect);
      m_dc.SelectObject(oldbrush);
      m_dc.SelectObject(oldPen);

      GdiFlush();
   }
   LeaveCriticalSection(&CTrainThread::m_csGDILock);
}
```

Assume that there are more than two tracks on either side of the bridge and that there are two tracks on the bridge. This sample can be easily modified to simulate such a situation. When creating the semaphore, the maximum count will be set to 2, and the initial count will also be set to 2. The graphic rendering of the train should also be adjusted for additional tracks.

Waitable Timers

Many events happen according to the time of day. Customer service lines typically start at a given time. When a number of activities have to be started in a synchronous manner based on a single occurrence such as a specific time of day, a *waitable timer* could be used. You can start a waitable timer thread, which will use a timer to release all the other threads. The APIs you can use with a waitable timer are summarized in the table that follows. The sample uses all of these APIs except **OpenWaitableTimer**.

Waitable Timer APIs	Description
CancelWaitableTimer	This cancels the request to the waitable timer and sets the timer to the inactive state.
CreateWaitableTimer	This creates a waitable timer.
SetWaitableTimer	This sets the waitable timer by specifying the time at which the timer will be activated (or set to Signaled state).

Waitable Timer APIs	Description
OpenWaitableTimer	This enables multiple processes to wait for the same waitable timer. One process uses CreateWaitableTimer, and the other processes get a handle to the waitable timer using OpenWaitableTimer.

The *Remind* sample program is a simple reminder that accepts a notification time and a message. When the time comes, it displays a message box with the given message. After setting the reminder, it minimizes itself and also allows the user to cancel the reminder. For simplicity, the reminder can be set for the given day. However, it can be modified to accommodate future dates.

The following figures illustrate this example. Figure 9-10 shows the initial menu that lets you specify the time when you want to be reminded and a brief description. Figure 9-11 shows the message box displayed when the timer goes off. Figure 9-12 shows how you can cancel the timer that has been set. Note that the Cancel Timer button, which was grayed out in Figure 9-10, is now enabled. The Set Timer button, which was enabled in Figure 9-10, is now grayed out.

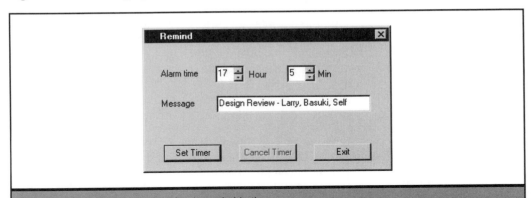

Figure 9-8.   Setting the time for the waitable timer

Figure 9-9.   The message box displayed when the waitable timer goes off

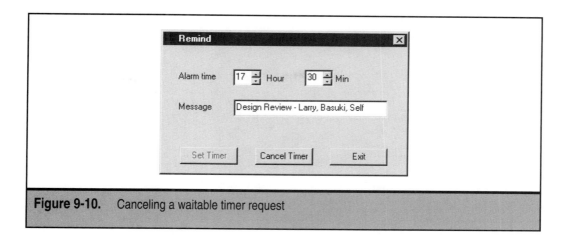

Figure 9-10. Canceling a waitable timer request

This sample uses the waitable timer available in Windows 2000 to set the timer. A separate thread sets the timer and waits for its expiration. Once the timer has expired, the waitable timer posts a message to the main program to display a message. The various APIs used are **CreateWaitableTimer**, **SetWaitableTimer**, and **CancelWaitableTimer**.

The sample is a dialog-based application and was created using the Visual C++ App Wizard. The **CRemindDlg** class is shown next; there is nothing unusual in the class.

```
#if !defined(AFX_REMINDDLG_H__68C4EAF6_E1DA_11D0_977C_0004ACB5DCC1__INCLUDED_)
#define AFX_REMINDDLG_H__68C4EAF6_E1DA_11D0_977C_0004ACB5DCC1__INCLUDED_

#if _MSC_VER >= 1000
#pragma once
#endif // _MSC_VER >= 1000

/////////////////////////////////////////////////////////////////////

// CRemindDlg dialog

class CRemindDlg : public CDialog
{
// Construction
public:
    CRemindDlg(CWnd* pParent = NULL);    // standard constructor

// Dialog Data
    //{{AFX_DATA(CRemindDlg)
    enum { IDD = IDD_REMIND_DIALOG };
    CSpinButtonCtrl    m_spinmin;
    CSpinButtonCtrl    m_spinhour;
    CString    m_edithour;
```

```
    CString     m_editmin;
    CString     m_message;
    //}}AFX_DATA

    // ClassWizard generated virtual function overrides
    //{{AFX_VIRTUAL(CRemindDlg)
    protected:
    virtual void DoDataExchange(CDataExchange* pDX);     // DDX/DDV support
    //}}AFX_VIRTUAL

// Implementation
protected:
    HICON m_hIcon;

    // Generated message map functions
    //{{AFX_MSG(CRemindDlg)
    virtual BOOL OnInitDialog();
    afx_msg void OnSysCommand(UINT nID, LPARAM lParam);
    afx_msg void OnPaint();
    afx_msg HCURSOR OnQueryDragIcon();
    afx_msg void OnSetTimer();
    afx_msg void OnCancelTimer();
    afx_msg void OnExit();
    afx_msg void OnAlarm();
    //}}AFX_MSG
    DECLARE_MESSAGE_MAP()
};

//{{AFX_INSERT_LOCATION}}

#endif //
!defined(AFX_REMINDDLG_H__68C4EAF6_E1DA_11D0_977C_0004ACB5DCC1__INCLUDED_)
```

The **RemindDlg** class implementation file is shown next. Note the definition of _WIN32_WINNT_, which is required to include appropriate header files dealing with waitable timer APIs. A user-defined message is defined to communicate between the waitable timer thread and the application. The **TIMERINFO** structure is defined and used to pass information from the main thread to the timer thread. The due time and the application dialog window handle are passed to the thread through the **TIMERINFO** structure. For simplicity, the handles to the waitable timer, to the timer thread, and to the message to display when the alarm goes off are defined in the global space. The message map indicates the functions to be called for various messages. The relevant code is highlighted for quick browsing.

```
// RemindDlg.cpp : implementation file
//
#define _WIN32_WINNT 0x400
```

```
#include "stdafx.h"
#include "Remind.h"
#include "RemindDlg.h"// RemindDlg.h : header file
//

#ifdef _DEBUG
#define new DEBUG_NEW
#undef THIS_FILE
static char THIS_FILE[] = __FILE__;
#endif


#define WM_USER_ALARM   WM_USER+200
UINT TimerThread(LPVOID);

typedef struct _TIMERINFO {
    HWND      hDialogHandle;
    LARGE_INTEGER   li;
} TIMERINFO;

HANDLE  hWaitableTimer;
CString AlarmMessage;
HANDLE  hTimerThread;
TIMERINFO    *ptinfo;
BOOL    bTimerExists;
//////////////////////////////////////////////////////////////////////
// CAboutDlg dialog used for App About

class CAboutDlg : public CDialog
{
public:

        CAboutDlg();

// Dialog Data
        //{{AFX_DATA(CAboutDlg)
        enum { IDD = IDD_ABOUTBOX };
        //}}AFX_DATA

        // ClassWizard generated virtual function overrides
        //{{AFX_VIRTUAL(CAboutDlg)
        protected:
        virtual void DoDataExchange(CDataExchange* pDX);    // DDX/DDV support
        //}}AFX_VIRTUAL

// Implementation
protected:
        //{{AFX_MSG(CAboutDlg)
        //}}AFX_MSG
```

```
            DECLARE_MESSAGE_MAP()
};

CAboutDlg::CAboutDlg()  : CDialog(CAboutDlg::IDD)
{
        //{{AFX_DATA_INIT(CAboutDlg)
        //}}AFX_DATA_INIT
}

void CAboutDlg::DoDataExchange(CDataExchange* pDX)
{
        CDialog::DoDataExchange(pDX);
        //{{AFX_DATA_MAP(CAboutDlg)
        //}}AFX_DATA_MAP
}

BEGIN_MESSAGE_MAP(CAboutDlg, CDialog)
        //{{AFX_MSG_MAP(CAboutDlg)
                // No message handlers
        //}}AFX_MSG_MAP
END_MESSAGE_MAP()

/////////////////////////////////////////////////////////////////////
// CRemindDlg dialog

CRemindDlg::CRemindDlg(CWnd* pParent /*=NULL*/)

        : CDialog(CRemindDlg::IDD, pParent)
{
        //{{AFX_DATA_INIT(CRemindDlg)
        m_edithour = _T("");
        m_editmin = _T("");
        m_message = _T("");
        //}}AFX_DATA_INIT
        // Note that LoadIcon does not require a subsequent DestroyIcon in Win32
        m_hIcon = AfxGetApp()->LoadIcon(IDR_MAINFRAME);
}

void CRemindDlg::DoDataExchange(CDataExchange* pDX)
{
        CDialog::DoDataExchange(pDX);
        //{{AFX_DATA_MAP(CRemindDlg)
        DDX_Control(pDX, IDC_SPINMINUTE, m_spinmin);
        DDX_Control(pDX, IDC_SPINHOUR, m_spinhour);
        DDX_Text(pDX, IDC_HOUR, m_edithour);
        DDX_Text(pDX, IDC_MINUTE, m_editmin);
        DDX_Text(pDX, IDC_MESSAGE, m_message);
        //}}AFX_DATA_MAP
}
```

```
BEGIN_MESSAGE_MAP(CRemindDlg, CDialog)
        //{{AFX_MSG_MAP(CRemindDlg)
        ON_WM_SYSCOMMAND()
        ON_WM_PAINT()
        ON_WM_QUERYDRAGICON()
        ON_BN_CLICKED(IDOK, OnSetTimer)
        ON_BN_CLICKED(IDCANCEL, OnExit)
        ON_BN_CLICKED(IDC_CANCEL_TIMER, OnCancelTimer)
        ON_MESSAGE(WM_USER_ALARM, OnAlarm)
        //}}AFX_MSG_MAP
END_MESSAGE_MAP()
```

When the dialog box is initialized, the spin controls are initialized with the relevant range of hour and minute. The hour is set from the current hour onward. The waitable timer is created by calling the **CreateWaitableTimer** API, and the handle is stored for future use. Since the timer is a local timer, a NULL is passed as the name of the timer. This sample conveniently leaves the responsibility of closing the waitable timer handle to the system, which closes the handle when the program terminates. The Cancel Timer button is grayed, since it is not valid to operate yet.

```
//////////////////////////////////////////////////////////////////////
// CRemindDlg message handlers

BOOL CRemindDlg::OnInitDialog()
{
    CDialog::OnInitDialog();

    // Add "About..." menu item to system menu.

    // IDM_ABOUTBOX must be in the system command range.
    ASSERT((IDM_ABOUTBOX & 0xFFF0) == IDM_ABOUTBOX);
    ASSERT(IDM_ABOUTBOX < 0xF000);

    CMenu* pSysMenu = GetSystemMenu(FALSE);
    if (pSysMenu != NULL)
    {
        CString strAboutMenu;
        strAboutMenu.LoadString(IDS_ABOUTBOX);
        if (!strAboutMenu.IsEmpty())
        {
            pSysMenu->AppendMenu(MF_SEPARATOR);
            pSysMenu->AppendMenu(MF_STRING, IDM_ABOUTBOX, strAboutMenu);
        }
    }

    // Set the icon for this dialog.  The framework does this automatically
    //  when the application's main window is not a dialog
    SetIcon(m_hIcon, TRUE);                    // Set big icon
```

```
    SetIcon(m_hIcon, FALSE);                    // Set small icon

    // TODO: Add extra initialization here
    SYSTEMTIME  systemTime;
    GetLocalTime(&systemTime);
    m_spinhour.SetRange(systemTime.wHour, 23);  // Hour range : Current hour-23
    m_spinmin.SetRange(0, 59);   // Min 0—59
    hWaitableTimer = CreateWaitableTimer(NULL, 1, NULL);

    // Gray the Cancel Timer button
    GetDlgItem(IDC_CANCEL_TIMER)->EnableWindow(FALSE);
    return TRUE;   // return TRUE unless you set the focus to a control
}

void CRemindDlg::OnSysCommand(UINT nID, LPARAM lParam)
{
    if ((nID & 0xFFF0) == IDM_ABOUTBOX)
    {
        CAboutDlg dlgAbout;
        dlgAbout.DoModal();
    }
    else
    {
        CDialog::OnSysCommand(nID, lParam);
    }
}

// If you add a minimize button to your dialog, you will need the code below
//  to draw the icon. For MFC applications using the document/view model,
//  this is automatically done for you by the framework.

void CRemindDlg::OnPaint()

{
    if (IsIconic())
    {
        CPaintDC dc(this); // device context for painting

        SendMessage(WM_ICONERASEBKGND, (WPARAM) dc.GetSafeHdc(), 0);

        // Center icon in client rectangle
        int cxIcon = GetSystemMetrics(SM_CXICON);
        int cyIcon = GetSystemMetrics(SM_CYICON);
        CRect rect;
        GetClientRect(&rect);
        int x = (rect.Width()—cxIcon + 1) / 2;
        int y = (rect.Height()—cyIcon + 1) / 2;

        // Draw the icon
        dc.DrawIcon(x, y, m_hIcon);
```

```
        }
        else
        {
            CDialog::OnPaint();
        }
}


// The system calls this to obtain the cursor to display while the user drags
//  the minimized window.
HCURSOR CRemindDlg::OnQueryDragIcon()
{
    return (HCURSOR) m_hIcon;
}
```

When the user sets the timer, the local time is queried (as the hour and minute) and is overlaid on the system time. When the waitable timer is set, the time when the timer is to be set to the Signaled state (or in other words, the *due time*) is given in a LARGE_INTEGER format. To convert to this format, the local time is first converted to FILETIME format by calling the **SystemTimeToFileTime** API. Since the due time given to the **SetWaitableTimer** function is based on the system time, the local time in the FILETIME format is converted to the system time in FILETIME format by calling the **LocalFileTimeToFileTime** API. The resulting FILETIME is then copied to the LARGE_INTERGER format. The due time and the dialog window handle are then moved to the **TIMERINFO** structure. A worker thread is created, and the data is passed to the thread. The thread function will be seen later. The Cancel Timer button is enabled, the Set Timer button is disabled, and the dialog window is minimized.

```
void CRemindDlg::OnSetTimer()
{
        // TODO: Add your control notification handler code here
    int iHour;
    int iMin;
    SYSTEMTIME    systemTime;
    FILETIME      localfileTime;
    FILETIME      duefileTime;
    LARGE_INTEGER    largeInt;

    UpdateData();

    ptinfo = new TIMERINFO;
    iHour = m_spinhour.GetPos();
    iMin = m_spinmin.GetPos();
    AlarmMessage = m_message;

    GetLocalTime(&systemTime);
    systemTime.wSecond = 0;       // On the second
    systemTime.wMilliseconds = 0;   // On the millisec
    systemTime.wMinute = iMin;   // At the given minute
    systemTime.wHour = iHour;    // At the given hour
```

```
SystemTimeToFileTime(&systemTime, &localfileTime);
LocalFileTimeToFileTime(&localfileTime, &duefileTime);
largeInt.LowPart = duefileTime.dwLowDateTime;
largeInt.HighPart = duefileTime.dwHighDateTime;

ptinfo->li = largeInt;
ptinfo->hDialogHandle = GetSafeHwnd();
hTimerThread = AfxBeginThread(TimerThread, ptinfo);

// Gray the Set Time button and enable the Cancel Timer button
GetDlgItem(IDOK)->EnableWindow(FALSE);
GetDlgItem(IDC_CANCEL_TIMER)->EnableWindow(TRUE);
ShowWindow(SW_MINIMIZE);
}
```

When the user cancels the pending reminder, the **CancelWaitableTimer** API is called to cancel the timer. The **CancelWaitableTimer** function sets the specified waitable timer to the inactive state. Note that the function does not change the signaled state of the timer. Thus, the thread that will be waiting for this timer will wait forever, or until the timer is activated and its state is set to Signaled state. In this sample, the thread is terminated by calling **TerminateThread** API, and the memory allocated for the information passed to the thread is freed.

```
void CRemindDlg::OnCancelTimer()
{
        // TODO: Add your control notification handler code here
    if (bTimerExists)
    {   // Clean up allocated data and thread
        CancelWaitableTimer(hWaitableTimer);
        TerminateThread(hTimerThread, 0);
        delete ptinfo;
        ptinfo = NULL;
        bTimerExists = FALSE;

        // Gray the Cancel Time button and enable the Set Timer button
        GetDlgItem(IDOK)->EnableWindow(TRUE);
        GetDlgItem(IDC_CANCEL_TIMER)->EnableWindow(FALSE);
    }
}

void CRemindDlg::OnExit()
{
        // TODO: Add extra cleanup here
    if (ptinfo)
    {
        delete ptinfo;
    }
    CDialog::OnCancel();
}
```

When the timer goes off, the timer thread that was created sends a user message to the application. The application beeps and puts a message box with the reminder message text. To improve this sample, a WAV file may be played here and some animation may be shown.

```
void CRemindDlg::OnAlarm()
{
        // TODO: Add your control notification handler code here
    ShowWindow(SW_RESTORE);
    // include your own music here
    Beep(300,70);
    Sleep(100);
    Beep(300,70);
    Sleep(100);
    Beep(300,70);
    Sleep(100);
    Beep(300,500);
    MessageBox(AlarmMessage, "Remind—Alarm");

    // Gray the Cancel Time button and enable the Set Timer button
    GetDlgItem(IDOK)->EnableWindow(TRUE);
    GetDlgItem(IDC_CANCEL_TIMER)->EnableWindow(FALSE);
    if (ptinfo) // Free memory
    {
        delete ptinfo;
        ptinfo = NULL;
    }
}
```

The thread function is shown next. It receives the due time parameter passed to the thread when the thread is started. This due time is used to call the **SetWaitableTimer** API. This sample does not use the periodic timer and completion routine. The sample can be extended to provide a snooze facility, in which case a value can be specified for the periodic timer. Note that if a completion routine is provided, then the thread should be in an alertable state. If the thread is not in an alertable state, the completion routine is skipped. The thread in the sample is not in an alertable state. APIs such as **WaitForSingleObjectEx** can be used instead.

```
UINT TimerThread(LPVOID alarmTime)
{
    TIMERINFO       *ptinfo;
    ptinfo = (TIMERINFO *)alarmTime;
    bTimerExists = SetWaitableTimer (hWaitableTimer, &ptinfo->li, 0 , NULL,
                            NULL, 0);
    if (WaitForSingleObject(hWaitableTimer, INFINITE) == WAIT_TIMEOUT)
    {
        // You may change INFINITE to a value and
        // optionally act when it times out.
        // Since the wait is currently INFINITE no need for any action.
```

```
    }
    else
    {
      PostMessage(ptinfo->hDialogHandle, WM_USER_ALARM, 0 ,0); // Post Message
    }
    bTimerExists = FALSE;
    return 0;
}
```

The resource file that is relevant to the sample is shown next.

```
IDD_REMIND_DIALOG DIALOGEX 0, 0, 212, 105
STYLE DS_MODALFRAME | WS_POPUP | WS_VISIBLE | WS_CAPTION | WS_SYSMENU
EXSTYLE WS_EX_APPWINDOW
CAPTION "Remind"
FONT 8, "MS Sans Serif"
BEGIN
    LTEXT           "Alarm time",IDC_STATIC,14,21,44,8
    EDITTEXT        IDC_HOUR,61,19,25,14,ES_AUTOHSCROLL
    CONTROL         "Spin1",IDC_SPINHOUR,"msctls_updown32",UDS_WRAP |
                    UDS_SETBUDDYINT | UDS_ALIGNRIGHT | UDS_AUTOBUDDY |
                    UDS_ARROWKEYS,86,19,10,14
    LTEXT           "Hour",IDC_STATIC,90,22,16,8
    EDITTEXT        IDC_MINUTE,123,19,25,14,ES_AUTOHSCROLL
    CONTROL         "Spin2",IDC_SPINMINUTE,"msctls_updown32",UDS_WRAP |
                    UDS_SETBUDDYINT | UDS_ALIGNRIGHT | UDS_AUTOBUDDY |
                    UDS_ARROWKEYS,147,19,10,14
    LTEXT           "Min",IDC_STATIC,150,22,12,8
    LTEXT           "Message",IDC_STATIC,14,46,44,8
    EDITTEXT        IDC_MESSAGE,62,44,134,14,ES_AUTOHSCROLL
    DEFPUSHBUTTON   "&Set Timer",IDOK,16,84,50,14
    PUSHBUTTON      "&Cancel Timer",IDC_CANCEL_TIMER,81,84,50,14
    PUSHBUTTON      "E&xit",IDCANCEL,146,84,50,14
END
```

For an example of using critical sections, please refer to the earlier example on thread priority under "Critical Sections."

Note that there are other means of synchronizing threads. For example, you can use **SuspendThread** and **ResumeThread** as a synchronization mechanism. You can start worker threads using the CREATE_SUSPENDED flag in your primary user-interface thread, and you can **ResumeThread** for the worker threads when appropriate. You may want to start multiple worker threads for different distinct functions using this technique. Based on user action of type of job, you can adjust the thread attributes such as priority when starting the worker threads. A printing job or virus scanning program may be run in a thread with lower priority.

You can also use the **Sleep/SleepEx** and **SwitchToThread** functions. You can think of **Sleep/SleepEx** as a way for a thread to synchronize with itself after an elapsed time interval. **Sleep/SleepEx** and **SwitchToThread** give up the use of the processor.

THREAD POOLING

Threads, when they were first introduced, were viewed as the one solution to make Windows applications really efficient. While creating efficient applications is possible with threads, it soon became evident that using threads does have some side effects that have to be addressed. One of the side effects is that creating, destroying, and managing threads does involve execution overhead, which takes away some of the efficiencies of multithreading. Another side effect is that programming multithreaded applications tended to be more complex. The complexity is due to two reasons. First, programmers have to handle the creation, destruction, and management of threads. Second, since threads within an application typically perform related actions, they need to be synchronized using the synchronization primitives provided by Windows. Synchronization primitives were covered in the last chapter. Windows 2000 attempts to reduce the amount of work you need to do as a programmer to use threads by providing *thread pooling* functions.

In the *Threads* sample that was discussed in the last chapter, every time the user wanted a ribbon, a new thread is created and the ribbon was drawn. Every time a thread is created, there is an overhead in creating the thread and executing the code in that thread's context. The performance of the *Threads* example could have been improved by creating a pool of threads and each thread waiting for the user to tell it to draw the ribbon. But that would have substantially added code to the example for dispatching the work and synchronizing. While this code overhead cannot be justified for this simple example, it could be justified for a real client/server application where performance is more important than amount of code required to write. With thread pooling, Windows 2000 offers a general-purpose solution to manage a pool of threads. And the best part is that there is not much effort involved to utilize this.

Just as there are instances in which threads are appropriate to use, there are also instances when thread pooling is appropriate. Applications that have threads that spend a lot of time in the sleeping state waiting for an event and applications that periodically poll for a change or update status information are examples of instances where thread pooling is appropriate.

The typical way in which a thread pool is used is as follows: At least one thread monitors the status of all wait operations queued to the thread pool. When a wait operation has completed, a worker thread from the thread pool executes the corresponding callback function. You can use the **BindIoCompletionCallback** function to post asynchronous I/O operations. Upon I/O completion, the callback is executed by a thread pool thread. Besides the wait operation completion, you can also queue work items that are not related to a wait operation to the thread pool. You can queue work by calling the **QueueUserWorkItem** function. Keep in mind, though, that there is no way to cancel a work item after it has been queued.

The thread pool is created the first time you call **QueueUserWorkItem** or **BindIoCompletionCallback**, or when a callback function is queued. There is no preset limit to the number of threads that you can create in the thread pool (limited only by available memory). Each thread in the thread uses the default stack size and runs at the default priority.

PROGRAMMING EXAMPLE TO ILLUSTRATE THREAD POOLING

The next example illustrates the use of the thread pooling functions available in Windows 2000. The code shown here takes the *Threads* sample and converts it to utilize the thread pooling functions. The changes to the code are highlighted. You will notice that changes are very few. To start with, the **#define** tells the compiler that the environment is Windows 2000 by setting the value of _WIN32_WINNT to 0x0500. This is important, since the thread pooling function is available only in Windows 2000 and not on Windows NT. The signature of the thread function is changed to match what is needed for the asynchronous queuing function of thread pooling. The ribbon width and separation between ribbons are changed to accommodate more ribbons in the screen. Beyond this, the only code change required for this sample to use thread pooling is in the **OnNewThread** function. Some of the irrelevant code is not shown here.

```
// Threads.cpp
#define _WIN32_WINNT 0x0500
#include <afxwin.h>
#include "Resource.h"

DWORD WINAPI RibbonThread(LPVOID);
COLORREF GetRibbonColor(int);


#define RIBBONWIDTH          15
#define RIBBONSEPARATION      3
COLORREF GetRibbonColor(int);

int iWidth, iHeight;     // Screen size
int iThreadInstance;
// Define the application object class
class CApp : public CWinApp
{
public:
    virtual BOOL InitInstance ();
};

// The window class
class CThreadWindow : public CFrameWnd
{
public:
    CDC m_memDC;
    CBitmap m_bmp;
    CBrush m_bkbrush;

    CThreadWindow();
    afx_msg void OnAppAbout();
    afx_msg void OnPaint();
    afx_msg void OnNewThread();
```

```
    afx_msg void OnExit();
    DECLARE_MESSAGE_MAP()
};

/////////////////////////////////////////////////////////////////////////
// CThreadWindow

BEGIN_MESSAGE_MAP(CThreadWindow, CFrameWnd)
    ON_WM_PAINT()
    ON_COMMAND(ID_APP_ABOUT, OnAppAbout)
    ON_COMMAND(IDM_NEWTHREAD, OnNewThread)
    ON_COMMAND(ID_APP_EXIT, OnExit)
END_MESSAGE_MAP()

/////////////////////////////////////////////////////////////////////////
// CThreadWindow construction

CThreadWindow::CThreadWindow()
{
    LoadAccelTable(MAKEINTRESOURCE(IDR_MAINFRAME));
    Create( NULL, "Threads Sample",
            WS_OVERLAPPEDWINDOW,
            rectDefault, NULL, MAKEINTRESOURCE(IDR_MAINFRAME) );

    iWidth = GetSystemMetrics(SM_CXSCREEN);
    iHeight = GetSystemMetrics(SM_CYSCREEN);

    // create a compatible background window for the thread
    // and clear the background to white.
    CClientDC  DC(this);
    m_memDC.CreateCompatibleDC(&DC);
    m_bmp.CreateCompatibleBitmap(&DC, iWidth, iHeight);
    m_memDC.SelectObject(&m_bmp);
    m_bkbrush.CreateStockObject(WHITE_BRUSH);
    m_memDC.SelectObject(&m_bkbrush);
    m_memDC.PatBlt(0, 0, iWidth, iHeight, PATCOPY);
}

/////////////////////////////////////////////////////////////////////////
// The CApp object

CApp theApp;

/////////////////////////////////////////////////////////////////////////
// CApp initialization

BOOL CApp::InitInstance()
{
    m_pMainWnd = new CThreadWindow();
    m_pMainWnd -> ShowWindow( m_nCmdShow );
```

```
        m_pMainWnd -> UpdateWindow();
        return TRUE;
}
// Handle exposures
void CThreadWindow::OnPaint()
{
        CPaintDC dc(this);

        dc.BitBlt(0, 0, iWidth, iHeight, &m_memDC, 0, 0, SRCCOPY);
}


void CThreadWindow::OnNewThread()
{
        QueueUserWorkItem(RibbonThread, this, WT_EXECUTEDEFAULT);
        // Comment the line before and uncomment
        // the next line to see the difference.
//      QueueUserWorkItem(RibbonThread, this, WT_EXECUTELONGFUNCTION);
}
```

Every time the user presses CTRL+T or selects New Thread from the File menu, **OnNewThread** gets called. This function does nothing but queue a work item to a thread in the thread pool. A *work item* is a unit of work or code, like the **RibbonThread** in this sample, that gets executed in a thread. The context is some data that we as application writers know how to interpret. The system does not interpret that data but simply passes it to the thread function. Note that we did not create a thread ourselves by calling either **CreateThread** or **AfxBeginThread**. The system creates a pool of threads, and when a work item is queued, it basically hands over the work item to one of the threads. The biggest advantage here is that the system maintains and manages the pool of threads, creating new ones when necessary and reusing old ones if available.

The last parameter tells the system how to queue the thread. Since the sample here does not perform any asynchronous I/O, it passes **WT_EXECUTEDEFAULT**, which causes the system to queue the thread function to a non-I/O thread. In general, the thread pool contains a few threads ready to perform the work item. If the number of work items exceeds the number of available threads in the pool, the work item in general waits for a thread to become available. Thus if the thread pool contains two threads, then the third work item that arrives waits for one of the currently executing work items to be completed before executing it. If each of the work items takes a long time to complete, then the third work item takes a long time before executing. You can see that the efficiency of the system suffers because of this. The problem is that the system has no clue how long the work item would take to complete. It is the responsibility of the application writer to indicate to the system if the work item would take a long time to complete. This is indicated by passing the **WT_EXECUTELONGFUNCTION**. This said, the system also monitors the pending load and automatically increases the number of threads in the thread pool. So if you are certain that the work item would take a long time to complete, then this flag needs to be passed. While we can keep talking about this function, it is easier to experiment with the code by running the application and seeing its behavior.

After starting the program, start two threads by pressing the accelerator CTRL+T. For the first few initiations (two in this case), you can start seeing the thread ribbon being drawn, indicating that the work item started to run. But after a few initiations (the first two in this case), the ribbons are not drawn, indicating that even though the work item is queued, it does not get executed. But if you keep pressing a few more CTRL+Ts (before the first ribbon ends), another thread (the third in this case) will soon be added. This happens because the system monitors the load and decides to add another (third) thread to the thread pool. Wait till all the ribbons are completed. Then press CTRL+T again repeatedly and you will notice that this time one additional thread starts right away, additional to when the program was initially started. This is because we now have one additional thread in the thread pool. Now wait till all the ribbons are drawn and keep waiting for a few seconds or minutes. During this time, when the application is idle for a given threshold period, the number of threads in the thread pool reverts to the original number of threads. If you now start the threads, the application behavior will revert to the original behavior, where the first few threads will start right away and the next invocation will delay until one of the ribbons completes its task.

Another way of experimenting with this is by using the *pstat* command, available in the resource kit, and the *time* command. Create a batch file that has the following commands:

```
REM pstatdump.bat
time >> out.txt < cr
pstat -s | find "Threads" >> out.txt
REM " " >> out.txt
REM " " >> out.txt
pstatdump
```

Here, *cr* is an empty file with just a carriage return and a line feed. This file feeds input to the new time that the *time* command prompts. As you can see, the batch file recursively checks the process status of the *Threads* program. Each time it checks, it also writes out the system time. Shown next is sample output in the *out.txt* file for one execution. Notice the count in the threads column (**Thd**) for each output of the pstat command. When the threads were not initiated, the number of threads that the *Threads* process had is one. As the program is loaded for more ribbon requests by pressing CTRL+T, the number of threads increases. When the system is ideal, not doing any work, it reverts back to the original number of threads, the three threads that it started with when queuing the first work item. For brevity, some of the lines of the output are edited.

User Time	Kernel Time	Ws	Faults	Commit	Pri	Hnd	**Thd**	Pid	Name
The current time is: 18:43:58.90									
0:00:00.020	0:00:00.110	1344	333	244	8	16	1	656	Threads.exe
The current time is: 18:44:00.39									
0:00:00.020	0:00:00.120	1344	333	244	8	16	1	656	Threads.exe
The current time is: 18:44:01.50									
0:00:00.020	0:00:00.150	1352	335	244	8	16	1	656	Threads.exe
The current time is: 18:44:02.51									
0:00:00.030	0:00:00.150	1388	344	268	8	20	3	656	Threads.exe

```
The current time is: 18:44:03.54
     0:00:00.030    0:00:00.150   1388        344     268   8    20    3 656 Threads.exe
The current time is: 18:44:04.58
     0:00:00.040    0:00:00.160   1396        346     280   8    21    4 656 Threads.exe
     :
     :
The current time is: 18:44:14.06
     0:00:00.060    0:00:00.190   1396        346     280   8    21    4 656 Threads.exe
The current time is: 18:44:15.17
     0:00:00.060    0:00:00.190   1408        349     296   8    22    5 656 Threads.exe
     :
     :
The current time is: 18:44:21.55
     0:00:00.090    0:00:00.260   1420        352     296   8    22    5 656 Threads.exe
The current time is: 18:44:22.63
     0:00:00.090    0:00:00.270   1428        354     308   8    23    6 656 Threads.exe
     :
     :
The current time is: 18:44:56.29
     0:00:00.220    0:00:00.460   1432        355     308   8    23    6 656 Threads.exe
The current time is: 18:45:38.00
     0:00:00.220    0:00:00.470   1424        357     284   8    21    4 656 Threads.exe
The current time is: 18:45:39.07
     0:00:00.220    0:00:00.470   1424        357     284   8    21    4 656 Threads.exe
The current time is: 18:45:40.08
     0:00:00.220    0:00:00.470   1424        357     284   8    21    4 656 Threads.exe
The current time is: 18:45:41.13
     0:00:00.220    0:00:00.470   1412        357     268   8    20    3 656 Threads.exe
```

Another experiment that can be tried out is to change the flag that is passed in the **QueueUserWorkItem** call to **WT_EXECUTELONGFUNCTION** indicating that the work item would take a long time to complete. With this change, it may be noticed that there is no delay in starting the thread. This is because the system now knows that the work item would take a long time to complete and hence starts a thread for every invocation of the work item.

The rest of the program has no change.

```
// On Exit handles the void
void CThreadWindow::OnExit()
{
    DestroyWindow();
}


DWORD WINAPI RibbonThread(LPVOID ThreadWindow)
{
    int iX1, iY1, iX2, iY2;
    int yOffset;
```

```
    COLORREF   c;
    RECT   rect;

    iThreadInstance++;

    CThreadWindow *pTW = (CThreadWindow *) ThreadWindow;

    iX1= iY1 = iX2 = iY2 = 0;

    yOffset = (iThreadInstance-1)*(RIBBONWIDTH+RIBBONSEPARATION);
    c = GetRibbonColor(iThreadInstance);
    CBrush Brush(c);
    for(int i=1; i<300; i++)
    {
        Sleep(50);
        iX1 = (i-1)*2;
        iY1 = yOffset;
        iX2 = i*2;
        iY2 = iY1+RIBBONWIDTH;

        rect.left = (long) iX1;
        rect.top = (long) iY1;
        rect.right = (long) iX2;
        rect.bottom = (long) iY2;

        pTW->m_memDC.FillRect(&rect, &Brush);
        pTW->InvalidateRect(&rect);
    }
    Beep(1000,70);
  return 0;
}
```

PROGRAMMING EXAMPLE TO ILLUSTRATE THREAD POOLING AND WAITABLE TIMERS

Earlier we saw the use of the waitable timer. If the application has multiple time-triggered tasks, then it can use one or more waitable timers. However, using multiple waitable timers may not be efficient in some situations, and the code complexity of managing one waitable timer for multiple time-triggered tasks is not pleasant. Windows 2000 solves this problem by managing it with the thread pool functions. The next example uses two timers, one to wake up after a given time delay, and the other to start beeping before the alarm goes off. With this example, the user can set a time delay when the alarm should go off. Fifteen seconds before the alarm goes off, the program will start beeping, initially at a rate of one beep for every two seconds, and then after five beeps the frequency increases at the rate of one beep for every second. This continues for another five beeps and then the frequency increases to one beep for every 350 milliseconds until the timer goes off.

The code for the preceding example is shown next. Some of the code that is irrelevant for the discussion is not shown here. The complete code is available on the CD-ROM. Notice the WIN32_WINNT definition. Thread pooling is only available in Windows 2000 and not in Windows NT.

```cpp
// RemindDlg.cpp : implementation file
#define _WIN32_WINNT 0x500
#include "stdafx.h"
#include "Remind.h"
#include "RemindDlg.h"

#ifdef _DEBUG
#define new DEBUG_NEW
#undef THIS_FILE
static char THIS_FILE[] = __FILE__;
#endif
```

These user-defined windows messages are used to communicate to the main program from the timer thread functions.

```cpp
#define WM_USER_CANCELBEEP    WM_USER+200
#define WM_USER_ENABLEBUTTON WM_USER+201

VOID CALLBACK TimerThread(PVOID pvContext, BOOLEAN TimerOrWaitFired);
VOID CALLBACK BeeperThread(PVOID pvContext, BOOLEAN TimerOrWaitFired);

HANDLE   hRemindTimer;
HANDLE   hTimerQueue;
HANDLE   hBeeperTimer;
CString AlarmMessage;
INT      iBeepCounter;

// CRemindDlg dialog

CRemindDlg::CRemindDlg(CWnd* pParent /*=NULL*/)
        : CDialog(CRemindDlg::IDD, pParent)
{
        //{{AFX_DATA_INIT(CRemindDlg)
        m_editsec = _T("");
        m_message = _T("");
        //}}AFX_DATA_INIT
        m_hIcon = AfxGetApp()->LoadIcon(IDR_MAINFRAME);
}
```

```
void CRemindDlg::DoDataExchange(CDataExchange* pDX)
{
        CDialog::DoDataExchange(pDX);
        //{{AFX_DATA_MAP(CRemindDlg)
        DDX_Control(pDX, IDC_SPINSEC, m_spinsec);
        DDX_Text(pDX, IDC_SEC, m_editsec);
        DDX_Text(pDX, IDC_MESSAGE, m_message);
        //}}AFX_DATA_MAP
}


BEGIN_MESSAGE_MAP(CRemindDlg, CDialog)
        //{{AFX_MSG_MAP(CRemindDlg)
        ON_WM_SYSCOMMAND()
        ON_WM_PAINT()
        ON_WM_QUERYDRAGICON()
        ON_BN_CLICKED(IDOK, OnSetTimer)
        ON_BN_CLICKED(IDCANCEL, OnExit)
        ON_MESSAGE(WM_USER_CANCELBEEP, OnCancelBeep)
        ON_MESSAGE(WM_USER_ENABLEBUTTON, OnEnableButton)
        //}}AFX_MSG_MAP
END_MESSAGE_MAP()
```

The message handlers for the user-defined messages are included in the preceding code in the message map.

```
// CRemindDlg message handlers
BOOL CRemindDlg::OnInitDialog()
{
    CDialog::OnInitDialog();

    // Add "About..." menu item to system menu.
    // IDM_ABOUTBOX must be in the system command range.
    ASSERT((IDM_ABOUTBOX & 0xFFF0) == IDM_ABOUTBOX);
    ASSERT(IDM_ABOUTBOX < 0xF000);

    CMenu* pSysMenu = GetSystemMenu(FALSE);
    if (pSysMenu != NULL)
    {
        CString strAboutMenu;
        strAboutMenu.LoadString(IDS_ABOUTBOX);
        if (!strAboutMenu.IsEmpty())
        {
            pSysMenu->AppendMenu(MF_SEPARATOR);
            pSysMenu->AppendMenu(MF_STRING, IDM_ABOUTBOX, strAboutMenu);
```

```
        }
    }

    SetIcon(m_hIcon, TRUE);                 // Set big icon
    SetIcon(m_hIcon, FALSE);                // Set small icon

    m_spinsec.SetRange(20, 1000);   // Min 20 Secs and max 1000 secs
    hTimerQueue = CreateTimerQueue();
    return TRUE;
}
```

To start using timer-queue timers, a timer queue should first be created. Calling the **CreateTimerQueue** function creates a timer queue. The handle to the timer queue is returned and is used in other timer queue–related functions. The code also sets the minimum and maximum delays before the timer can wake up.

```
void CRemindDlg::OnSysCommand(UINT nID, LPARAM lParam)
{
    if ((nID & 0xFFF0) == IDM_ABOUTBOX)
    {
        CAboutDlg dlgAbout;
        dlgAbout.DoModal();
    }
    else
    {
        CDialog::OnSysCommand(nID, lParam);
    }
}


void CRemindDlg::OnPaint()
{
    if (IsIconic())
    {
        CPaintDC dc(this); // device context for painting
        SendMessage(WM_ICONERASEBKGND, (WPARAM) dc.GetSafeHdc(), 0);
        // Center icon in client rectangle
        int cxIcon = GetSystemMetrics(SM_CXICON);
        int cyIcon = GetSystemMetrics(SM_CYICON);
        CRect rect;
        GetClientRect(&rect);
        int x = (rect.Width() - cxIcon + 1) / 2;
        int y = (rect.Height() - cyIcon + 1) / 2;
        // Draw the icon
        dc.DrawIcon(x, y, m_hIcon);
    }
```

```
    else
    {
        CDialog::OnPaint();
    }
}


HCURSOR CRemindDlg::OnQueryDragIcon()
{
    return (HCURSOR) m_hIcon;
}
```

When the user clicks on the Set Timer button, the flow comes to the **OnSetTimer**. The delay time and the message are picked up to set the timer. Two timers are then created: one to wake up after the requested delay, and the other to wake up 15 seconds before the alarm and to beep to signal the upcoming alarm. The **CreateTimerQueueTimer** API is used to create a timer-queue timer. The handle to the timer queue created earlier during the dialog box initialization is used to create the timers. Alternatively, to use the default timer queue, a NULL can be passed. The callback function and the data to the callback function are also passed to the API. The first timer communicates with the dialog box to stop the beeping timer and to enable dialog box buttons by means of a windows message. Hence the dialog box window handle is passed as the parameter. This data could be any user data, and the data is passed to the thread function when the timer expires. The next parameter is the time in milliseconds when the timer should expire or, in other words, when the timer's state should be set to the signaled state. Following this parameter, the period in milliseconds is specified. If this parameter is not zero, then the timer is *periodic*, which indicates that the timer should be set to signaled state repeatedly after the specified time. In the code that follows, for the second timer that is created, this parameter is set to 2000, indicating that the timer will first be set to a signaled state 15 seconds prior to the alarm time, after which it will repeatedly be signaled every two seconds. If this parameter is zero, then the timer is signaled once. In a periodic timer, the callback function is called every time the period elapses whether or not the previously queued callback function has finished executing.

Every time the timer is set to the signaled state, the callback function is called by the system. The last parameter is a flag that tells the function how the work item should be queued when the timer is signaled. When the timer's state is set to signaled, the callback function is called and it is executed. Specifying WT_EXECUTEDEFAULT means that the callback function will be executed in a non-I/O component thread. If the callback function is to wait in an alertable state, then the WT_EXECUTEINIOTHREAD flag should be used. If the callback function will take a long time to complete, then the WT_EXECUTELONGFUNCTION flag should be used. The overhead involved in the creation of a thread can be avoided by using WT_EXECUTEINTIMERTHREAD where the callback function gets executed in the same thread in which the timers are managed. Since the callback function is processed in the same thread in which the timers are managed, great caution should be used in using this flag. A callback function that takes a long time to complete, or one that blocks, will cripple the timer queue.

After setting the alarm, the code minimizes that application.

```
void CRemindDlg::OnSetTimer()
{
    int iSec;
    iBeepCounter = 0;
    UpdateData();

    iSec = m_spinsec.GetPos();
    AlarmMessage = m_message;

    CreateTimerQueueTimer (&hRemindTimer, hTimerQueue,
                           (WAITORTIMERCALLBACK)TimerThread,
                           GetSafeHwnd(), iSec*1000,
                           0, WT_EXECUTEDEFAULT);
    CreateTimerQueueTimer (&hBeeperTimer, hTimerQueue,
                           (WAITORTIMERCALLBACK )BeeperThread, NULL,
                           ((iSec*1000) - 15000), 2000, WT_EXECUTEDEFAULT);

    // Gray the Set Time button and enable the Cancel Timer button
    GetDlgItem(IDOK)->EnableWindow(FALSE);
    ShowWindow(SW_MINIMIZE);
}
```

When the timer goes off, it sends a message to stop the beeping timer. This message is processed by the **OnCancelBeep** function that follows. Every timer, including the ones that are signaled once, should be deleted by calling the **DeleteTimerQueueTimer** function. To delete a timer, the handle to the timer queue, the handle to the timer, and optionally a handle to an event are passed. If a handle to an event is passed, then the event is signaled when the function is successful and all callback functions have completed. A value of INVALID_HANDLE_VALUE can also be passed for this parameter; in this case the DeleteTimerQueueTimer blocks until all queued work items for the timer have been completed. As with any event, great care should be given not to create a deadlock situation. For example, it is possible to get into a deadlock situation when deleting two timers in each other's callback functions or doing a blocking delete of a timer in its own timer callback. In the former case, each timer's delete function is waiting for the other timer's callback function to complete! In the latter case, the delete function is waiting for the callback to complete, but the callback will never get a chance to complete, since the delete functions will not yield! Yet another situation where a deadlock can occur is when the callback function is executed in the timer component's thread (WT_EXECUTEINTIMERTHREAD flag) and the callback function deletes another timer. When the timer is deleted, a notification is sent to the timer component's thread. Since this callback is waiting for the timer to be deleted and the timer is not getting deleted because the timer component's thread does not get a chance to delete, a deadlock occurs.

```
void CRemindDlg::OnCancelBeep()
{
    if (!DeleteTimerQueueTimer (hTimerQueue, hBeeperTimer,
        INVALID_HANDLE_VALUE))
    {
        DWORD rc;
        char szMessage[1024];
        rc = GetLastError();
        FormatMessage(FORMAT_MESSAGE_FROM_SYSTEM, NULL, rc, 0, szMessage,
                      1024, NULL);
        MessageBox(szMessage, "Error");
    }
}
```

After sounding the alarm in the **TimerThread** callback function, this function sends a message to the application to prepare itself for the next alarm. Notice that the nonperiodic alarm timer has not yet been deleted; it is deleted here.

```
void CRemindDlg::OnEnableButton()
{
    GetDlgItem(IDOK)->EnableWindow(TRUE);
    if (!DeleteTimerQueueTimer (hTimerQueue, hRemindTimer,
        INVALID_HANDLE_VALUE))
    {
        DWORD rc;
        char szMessage[1024];
        rc = GetLastError();
        FormatMessage(FORMAT_MESSAGE_FROM_SYSTEM, NULL, rc, 0, szMessage,
                      1024, NULL);
        MessageBox(szMessage, "Error");
    }
}
```

When the application no longer has a need for the timer queue, it can be deleted by calling the **DeleteTimerQueueEx** function. This function cancels and deletes all the pending timers in the queue and then deletes the timer queue. The handle to the timer queue is passed in as well as an event handle, which if valid is signaled when the timer queue is deleted. Alternatively, a value ID INVALID_HANDLE_VALUE can be passed for the event handle, in which case the function blocks until the queue is deleted. A recipe for deadlock is to do a blocking delete of the timer queue in a timer callback function.

```
void CRemindDlg::OnExit()
{
        // TODO: Add extra cleanup here
    DeleteTimerQueueEx(hTimerQueue, INVALID_HANDLE_VALUE);
```

```
        CDialog::OnCancel();
}

VOID CALLBACK TimerThread(PVOID pvContext, BOOLEAN TimerOrWaitFired)
{
    SendMessage((HWND)pvContext, WM_USER_CANCELBEEP, 0 ,0);
    Beep(300,70);
    Sleep(100);
    Beep(300,70);
    Sleep(100);
    Beep(300,70);
    Sleep(100);
    Beep(300,500);
    AfxMessageBox(AlarmMessage);
    PostMessage((HWND)pvContext, WM_USER_ENABLEBUTTON, 0 ,0);
}
```

The alarm timer thread callback code shown here sends a message to cancel the beeping timer, displays a message, and posts a message to enable the application for the next use of the alarm. The beeping timer callback function code is shown next. The beeping starts at a frequency of one beep every two seconds, and the frequency of the beep as well as the tone increases after five beeps. The alarm turns off after 15 seconds. This change in the timer is done by calling the **ChangeTimerQueueTimer** function and altering the due time and the period.

```
VOID CALLBACK BeeperThread(PVOID pvContext, BOOLEAN TimerOrWaitFired)
{
    DWORD iFreq;
    iBeepCounter++;
    if (iBeepCounter >= 10)
    {
        iFreq = 1000;
        ChangeTimerQueueTimer (hTimerQueue, hBeeperTimer, 350, 350);
    }
    else if (iBeepCounter >= 5)
    {
        iFreq = 500;
        ChangeTimerQueueTimer (hTimerQueue, hBeeperTimer, 1000, 1000);
    }
    else
    {
        iFreq = 300;
    }
    Beep(iFreq,50);
```

PIPES

Pipes are used for communication between processes. The underlying mechanism that pipes use is a section of shared memory. One process writes information to the pipe (shared memory) using a write handle, then the other process reads the information from the pipe (shared memory) using a read handle.

Let's briefly review some pipes-related terminology. The process that creates a pipe is the *pipe server*. A process that connects to a pipe is a *pipe client*. Pipes can support one-way or duplex communication. A one-way pipe allows a process at one end to write to the pipe, and allows another process accessing the pipe from the other end to read from the pipe. A duplex pipe allows a process to read and write from its end of the pipe. There are two types of pipes: named pipes and unnamed pipes. Unnamed pipes are also called anonymous pipes. Anonymous pipes are used for related processes to communicate with each other. Typically, the anonymous pipe is used for redirecting the standard input or output of a child process so that it can communicate with its parent process. Since the anonymous pipe is a one-way pipe, you must create two anonymous pipes to exchange data in both directions between two processes. Named pipes are used to transfer data between unrelated processes and between processes on different computers. Typically, a named-pipe server process creates a named pipe with a unique name. The named-pipe client uses the name assigned by the pipe-server process. The pipe name could be a well-known name already known to both the server and the client, or alternatively, the server could pass the pipe name to the client. The client uses the pipe name to open its end of the pipe. The server can specify access restrictions that the client will have to follow in accessing the pipe.

The functions used with pipes are summarized in Table 9-5.

Using Anonymous Pipes

You can create an anonymous pipe using the **CreatePipe** function. **CreatePipe** returns two handles: a read handle that has read-only access to the pipe and a write handle that has write-only access to the pipe. To read from the pipe, use the pipe's read handle and call the **ReadFile** function. **ReadFile** returns when another process writes to the pipe or an error occurs. To write to the pipe, use the pipe's write handle and call the **WriteFile** function. The **WriteFile** call does not return until it has written the specified number of bytes to the pipe or an error occurs.

The pipe server, which is responsible for the creation of the handles, typically passes the handles to another process through inheritance if it is a child process or through some form of interprocess communication (such as DDE or shared memory) if it is an unrelated process. Although anonymous pipes are in general unnamed, Windows 2000 implements anonymous pipes using a named pipe with a unique name, which makes it possible for you to pass a handle to an anonymous pipe to a function that requires a handle to a named pipe. You can close anonymous pipe handles using the **CloseHandle** function. All anonymous pipe handles are also closed when the process terminates. An anonymous pipe exists until all pipe's handles, both read and write, have been closed.

Pipe Functions	Description
CreateNamedPipe	Creates an instance of a named pipe and returns a handle. This handle is required for all subsequent pipe operations on that named pipe. This function is used to create the first instance of a specific named pipe along with the pipe's basic attributes, as well as to create a new instance of an existing named pipe.
ConnectNamedPipe	Enables a named pipe server process to wait for a client process to connect to an instance of a named pipe. If the specified pipe instance was previously connected to another client process, the server process must first call DisconnectNamedPipe to disconnect the handle from the previous client before the handle can be connected to a new client.
CallNamedPipe	Connects to a pipe, reads and writes using the pipe, and then closes the pipe. This function waits for an instance of the pipe if one is not available. CallNamedPipe will fail if the pipe is a byte-type pipe.
TransactNamedPipe	Combination of the read and write functions using the specified named pipe in one call.
DisconnectNamedPipe	Disconnects the server end of a named pipe (from a client process).
GetNamedPipeHandleState	Retrieves information about the state of specified named pipe including the number of current instances of the named pipe.
GetNamedPipeInfo	Retrieves information about the specified named pipe such as whether the handle is the client end or server end of the pipe and whether the pipe is a byte pipe or message pipe.
PeekNamedPipe	Copies data from a named or anonymous pipe into a buffer without removing it from the pipe.
SetNamedPipeHandleState	Sets the read mode and the blocking mode of the specified named pipe.
WaitNamedPipe	Waits until either a time-out interval elapses or an instance of the specified named pipe is available for a connection.
CreatePipe	Creates an anonymous pipe.

Table 9-5.   Pipe Functions and Descriptions

You can control access to an anonymous pipe using Windows 2000 security functions. As with other Windows functions, access control is implemented using a security descriptor. The security descriptor controls access for both the read and write functions of the anonymous pipe. You can specify a security descriptor for an anonymous pipe when you call the **CreatePipe** function. Call the **GetSecurityInfo** function to retrieve a pipe's security descriptor and the **SetSecurityInfo** function to change a pipe's security descriptor.

Asynchronous (overlapped) read and write operations (those provided by the **ReadFileEx** and **WriteFileEx** functions) are not supported by anonymous pipes. By the same token, the *lpOverLapped* parameter of **ReadFile** and **WriteFile** is ignored when these functions are used with anonymous pipes.

PROGRAMMING EXAMPLE FOR ANONYMOUS PIPES

Shown next is an example of the use of an anonymous pipe. The example consists of two programs: one is a server, which broadcasts messages entered by the user, and the other is a client, which reads the broadcast message and displays it in a dialog box. The server program when started creates an anonymous pipe and spawns the client program. Before starting the client program, the server program changes the client program's standard input handle to be the same as the anonymous pipe's read handle. The client program reads the data from the standard input and displays it.

The application class of the server program is shown next.

```
// PipeServ.cpp
#include "stdafx.h"
#include "PipeServ.h"
#include "PipeServDlg.h"


#ifdef _DEBUG
#define new DEBUG_NEW
#undef THIS_FILE
static char THIS_FILE[] = __FILE__;
#endif


// CPipeServApp


BEGIN_MESSAGE_MAP(CPipeServApp, CWinApp)
    //{{AFX_MSG_MAP(CPipeServApp)
    // NOTE - the ClassWizard will add and remove mapping macros here.
    //    DO NOT EDIT what you see in these blocks of generated code!
    //}}AFX_MSG
    ON_COMMAND(ID_HELP, CWinApp::OnHelp)
END_MESSAGE_MAP()


// CPipeServApp construction
```

```
CPipeServApp::CPipeServApp()
{
    // TODO: add construction code here,
    // Place all significant initialization in InitInstance
}
// The one and only CPipeServApp object

CPipeServApp theApp;

// CPipeServApp initialization

BOOL CPipeServApp::InitInstance()
{
#ifdef _AFXDLL
    Enable3dControls();
#else
    Enable3dControlsStatic();
#endif
```

Pipes are nothing but sections of shared memory where processes exchange data. Pipes when created can be either named or unnamed. An unnamed pipe, which is called an anonymous pipe, as implemented in Windows 2000 is essentially a restricted named pipe with a unique name. It is a one-way pipe, which transfers data in one direction. Such pipes can exist only on a local machine and cannot be used to communicate over a network. The **CreatePipe** function creates an anonymous pipe and returns two handles to the process. One handle is to write to the pipe, and the other to read from it. If the server needs to communicate with another process, it needs to pass one of these handles to the client. This can be done by any means of sharing data between programs such as a shared file or a DDE conversation. The method employed in this sample is to change the standard input handle of the client program to be the pipe's read handle. Thus when the client program starts reading data from the standard input, it will be actually reading from the pipe. By default, these handles cannot be inherited by the child process, and in order for the child process to inherit these handles, a security attribute with **bInheritHandle** set to TRUE is passed to the **CreatePipe** function. An instance of the server dialog box is created, and the pipe handles are set. It can be seen later that these handles are used to write data that is to be sent to the client and to set the client program's input handle when the client program process is created.

By setting the **bInheritHandle** flag to TRUE, the program allows all handles to be inherited by the child process, including the anonymous pipe's write handle. It is generally advisable to let only specific handles be inherited by the child process. If not, the handles may stay around even after the parent program terminates. This sample server when terminated also terminates the client program. So this problem is solved here. However, if your program follows a different logic, in which the child program stays around, then a handle that is not intended to be inherited should be duplicated by calling the **DuplicateHandle** API and changing its inheritance attribute.

```
HANDLE hRead;
HANDLE hWrite;
SECURITY_ATTRIBUTES secAttr;

secAttr.nLength = sizeof(SECURITY_ATTRIBUTES);
secAttr.lpSecurityDescriptor = NULL;
secAttr.bInheritHandle = TRUE;

if (!CreatePipe (&hRead, &hWrite, &secAttr, 0))
{
    AfxMessageBox("Could not create the pipe");
    return FALSE;;
}

CPipeServDlg dlg;
dlg.SetReadHandle(hRead);
dlg.SetWriteHandle(hWrite);

m_pMainWnd = &dlg;
int nResponse = dlg.DoModal();
if (nResponse == IDOK)
{
    // TODO: Place code here to handle when the dialog is
    //  dismissed with OK
}
else if (nResponse == IDCANCEL)
{
    // TODO: Place code here to handle when the dialog is
    //  dismissed with Cancel
}
return FALSE;
}
```

Shown next is the dialog box code, which interfaces with the user to send data to the client program. The application class shown earlier sets the anonymous pipe handles:

```
// PipeServDlg.cpp : implementation file
#include "stdafx.h"
#include "PipeServ.h"
#include "PipeServDlg.h"
```

```
#ifdef _DEBUG
#define new DEBUG_NEW
#undef THIS_FILE
static char THIS_FILE[] = __FILE__;
#endif

// CPipeServDlg dialog

CPipeServDlg::CPipeServDlg(CWnd* pParent /*=NULL*/)
    : CDialog(CPipeServDlg::IDD, pParent)
{
    //{{AFX_DATA_INIT(CPipeServDlg)
    m_pipedata = _T("");
    //}}AFX_DATA_INIT
    m_hIcon = AfxGetApp()->LoadIcon(IDR_MAINFRAME);
}

void CPipeServDlg::DoDataExchange(CDataExchange* pDX)
{
    CDialog::DoDataExchange(pDX);
    //{{AFX_DATA_MAP(CPipeServDlg)
    DDX_Text(pDX, IDC_EDIT, m_pipedata);
    //}}AFX_DATA_MAP
}

BEGIN_MESSAGE_MAP(CPipeServDlg, CDialog)
    //{{AFX_MSG_MAP(CPipeServDlg)
    ON_WM_PAINT()
    ON_WM_QUERYDRAGICON()
    ON_BN_CLICKED(IDOK, OnSend)
    ON_BN_CLICKED(IDCANCEL, OnExit)
    //}}AFX_MSG_MAP
END_MESSAGE_MAP()
```

// CPipeServDlg message handlers

The client program is spawned during the dialog box initialization; before this happens, the standard input for the spawned program is set to the anonymous pipe's read handle. This spawned client process is made to inherit this handle. Thus when the client program reads data from the standard input handle, it actually reads data from the anonymous pipe. Note the hard-coded path of the client program that is spawned. When you copy the code from the CD-ROM and try it out, make sure you update the path where the client program resides.

```
BOOL CPipeServDlg::OnInitDialog()
{
    CDialog::OnInitDialog();
    // Set the icon for this dialog.  The framework does this automatically
    //   when the application's main window is not a dialog
    SetIcon(m_hIcon, TRUE);            // Set big icon
    SetIcon(m_hIcon, FALSE);           // Set small icon

    // TODO: Add extra initialization here
    STARTUPINFO startupInfo;
    PROCESS_INFORMATION processInfo;
    memset (&startupInfo, 0, sizeof(STARTUPINFO));
    startupInfo.cb = sizeof(STARTUPINFO);
    startupInfo.dwFlags = STARTF_USESTDHANDLES;
    startupInfo.hStdInput=hRead;

    if (!CreateProcess(

                "e:/book/Ch10/AnonPipe/Client/Release/PipeClient.exe",
            NULL, NULL, NULL, TRUE, 0, NULL, NULL, &startupInfo,
            &processInfo))
    {
        DWORD rc;
        char szMessage[1024];
        rc = GetLastError();
        FormatMessage(FORMAT_MESSAGE_FROM_SYSTEM, NULL, rc, 0,
                    szMessage, 1024, NULL);
        MessageBox(szMessage, "Error");
        EndDialog(0);
    }
    return TRUE;
}

void CPipeServDlg::OnPaint()
{
    if (IsIconic())
    {
        CPaintDC dc(this); // device context for painting
        SendMessage(WM_ICONERASEBKGND, (WPARAM) dc.GetSafeHdc(), 0);
        // Center icon in client rectangle
        int cxIcon = GetSystemMetrics(SM_CXICON);
        int cyIcon = GetSystemMetrics(SM_CYICON);
        CRect rect;
        GetClientRect(&rect);
        int x = (rect.Width() - cxIcon + 1) / 2;
        int y = (rect.Height() - cyIcon + 1) / 2;

        // Draw the icon
        dc.DrawIcon(x, y, m_hIcon);
```

```
        }
        else
        {
            CDialog::OnPaint();
        }
    }
    //   the minimized window.
    HCURSOR CPipeServDlg::OnQueryDragIcon()
    {
        return (HCURSOR) m_hIcon;
    }
```

The next two functions process the Send and Exit buttons in the dialog box. When the user clicks on the Send button, the data is collected and is written to the anonymous pipe using the **WriteFile** API. If any error occurs while writing the data, the server terminates after sending a termination signal to the client. The code can discriminate the error and send the termination signal only if the anonymous pipe is not broken or closed by checking to see if the error is **ERROR_BROKEN_PIPE** or **ERROR_NO_DATA**.

When the user closes the server by clicking on the Exit button, the **OnExit** function is called. This function sends a carriage return/line feed string, which the client interprets as an instruction to terminate itself.

```
void CPipeServDlg::OnSend()
{
    DWORD dwBytesWritten;
    UpdateData();
    if (!WriteFile(hWrite, m_pipedata,
        m_pipedata.GetLength(),&dwBytesWritten, NULL))
    {
        DWORD rc;
        char szMessage[1024];
        rc = GetLastError();
        FormatMessage(FORMAT_MESSAGE_FROM_SYSTEM, NULL, rc, 0,
                    szMessage, 1024, NULL);
        MessageBox(szMessage, "Error");
        WriteFile(hWrite, "\r\n", 2,&dwBytesWritten, NULL);
        EndDialog(TRUE);
    }
    else
    {
        m_pipedata="";
        UpdateData(FALSE);
    }
}


void CPipeServDlg::OnExit()
{
    // TODO: Add your control notification handler code here
```

```
    DWORD dwBytesWritten;
    WriteFile(hWrite, "\r\n", 2,&dwBytesWritten, NULL);
    EndDialog(TRUE);
}

void CPipeServDlg::SetReadHandle(HANDLE hr)
{
    hRead = hr;
}

void CPipeServDlg::SetWriteHandle(HANDLE hw)
{
    hWrite = hw;
}
```

Shown next is the part of the client application code that reads the data sent by the server application. The application class that puts up this client dialog box is not shown, since it is pretty much boilerplate code. The code is available on the CD-ROM accompanying this book. When the dialog box is created, the client starts a thread that reads data that the server sends; every time it sees data, it sends the data read from the anonymous pipe to the dialog box to display it. When fewer than three bytes of data are sent, the application is terminated.

```
// PipeClientDlg.cpp : implementation file
//

#include "stdafx.h"
#include "PipeClient.h"
#include "PipeClientDlg.h"

#ifdef _DEBUG
#define new DEBUG_NEW
#undef THIS_FILE
static char THIS_FILE[] = __FILE__;
#endif

#define BUFFER_SIZE 256
```

The two user messages that the thread sends to the dialog box are defined next:

```
#define WM_USER_UPDATEDATA    WM_USER+200
#define WM_USER_EXIT          WM_USER+201

UINT ReadServerData( LPVOID hWnd);

// CPipeClientDlg dialog

CPipeClientDlg::CPipeClientDlg(CWnd* pParent /*=NULL*/)
    : CDialog(CPipeClientDlg::IDD, pParent)
```

```
{
    //{{AFX_DATA_INIT(CPipeClientDlg)
    m_pipedata = _T("");
    //}}AFX_DATA_INIT
    // Note that LoadIcon does not require a subsequent DestroyIcon in Win32
    m_hIcon = AfxGetApp()->LoadIcon(IDR_MAINFRAME);
}

void CPipeClientDlg::DoDataExchange(CDataExchange* pDX)
{
    CDialog::DoDataExchange(pDX);
    //{{AFX_DATA_MAP(CPipeClientDlg)
    DDX_Text(pDX, IDC_EDIT, m_pipedata);
    //}}AFX_DATA_MAP
}

BEGIN_MESSAGE_MAP(CPipeClientDlg, CDialog)
    //{{AFX_MSG_MAP(CPipeClientDlg)
    ON_WM_PAINT()
    ON_WM_QUERYDRAGICON()
    ON_MESSAGE(WM_USER_UPDATEDATA, OnUpdateData)
    ON_MESSAGE(WM_USER_EXIT, OnExit)
    //}}AFX_MSG_MAP
END_MESSAGE_MAP()

// CPipeClientDlg message handlers

BOOL CPipeClientDlg::OnInitDialog()
{
    CDialog::OnInitDialog();

    // Set the icon for this dialog.  The framework does this automatically
    //  when the application's main window is not a dialog
    SetIcon(m_hIcon, TRUE);            // Set big icon
    SetIcon(m_hIcon, FALSE);           // Set small icon
```

During initialization, a thread that reads the data sent by the server program is started. The thread function is **ReadServerData**:

```
    AfxBeginThread(ReadServerData, GetSafeHwnd());

    return TRUE;  // return TRUE  unless you set the focus to a control
}

// If you add a minimize button to your dialog, you will need the code below
//  to draw the icon.  For MFC applications using the document/view model,
//  this is automatically done for you by the framework.

void CPipeClientDlg::OnPaint()
{
```

```
    if (IsIconic())
    {
        CPaintDC dc(this); // device context for painting

        SendMessage(WM_ICONERASEBKGND, (WPARAM) dc.GetSafeHdc(), 0);

        // Center icon in client rectangle
        int cxIcon = GetSystemMetrics(SM_CXICON);
        int cyIcon = GetSystemMetrics(SM_CYICON);
        CRect rect;
        GetClientRect(&rect);
        int x = (rect.Width() - cxIcon + 1) / 2;
        int y = (rect.Height() - cyIcon + 1) / 2;

        // Draw the icon
        dc.DrawIcon(x, y, m_hIcon);
    }
    else
    {
        CDialog::OnPaint();
    }
}

// The system calls this to obtain the cursor to display while
// the user drags the minimized window.
HCURSOR CPipeClientDlg::OnQueryDragIcon()
{
    return (HCURSOR) m_hIcon;
}
```

When the thread receives the data, it sends the data to be displayed in the dialog box by sending a message, which is processed by the **OnUpdateData** function. The data to be displayed is sent in lParam.

```
LRESULT CPipeClientDlg::OnUpdateData(WPARAM wParam, LPARAM lParam)
{
    m_pipedata = (LPSTR)lParam;
    UpdateData(FALSE);
    return 0;
}
```

When the thread receives less than three bytes, it instructs the dialog box to close by sending a message, which is processed by **OnExit** function.

```
LRESULT CPipeClientDlg::OnExit(WPARAM wParam, LPARAM lParam)
{
    CDialog::EndDialog(IDOK);
    return 0;
}
```

The thread function **ReadServerData** reads the data sent by the server from the standard input. It may be recalled that the server reset the client's standard input handle to be the anonymous pipe's read handle. If it successfully reads and if the data is more than two bytes, it posts a message with the data it received to the dialog box, which then displays the data.

```
UINT ReadServerData( LPVOID hWnd)
{
    HANDLE hRead = GetStdHandle(STD_INPUT_HANDLE);
    BOOL    rc;
    DWORD dwBytesRead = 3;
    char * szBuf = new char [BUFFER_SIZE];
    while (dwBytesRead > 2)
    {
        dwBytesRead = 0;
        rc = ReadFile (hRead, szBuf, BUFFER_SIZE, &dwBytesRead, NULL);
        if (rc == FALSE)
            break;
        if (dwBytesRead)
        {
            szBuf[dwBytesRead] = 0;
            SendMessage((HWND)hWnd, WM_USER_UPDATEDATA,
                        NULL, (LPARAM)szBuf);
        }
    }
    delete [] szBuf;
    PostMessage((HWND)hWnd, WM_USER_EXIT, NULL, NULL);
    return 0;
}
```

PROGRAMMING EXAMPLE TO ILLUSTRATE USE OF NAMED PIPES

Shown next is an example of the use of named pipes. The sample consists of two programs, a server and a client, which send and receive text messages to each other. When the server program is started, it creates two named pipes and waits for a client to connect. When the client is also started, the server then enables the user to send and receive text messages. When the client terminates, the server detects the fact and terminates itself. The client terminates when there is no server on the other end to communicate. The programs use events for synchronization. Only the relevant code is shown and discussed here. The complete code and project are available on the CD-ROM accompanying this book.

The advantage of the named pipes over the anonymous pipes is that they are more versatile. Unlike anonymous pipes, named pipes can exchange data in both directions on a single pipe. Named pipes can exchange data to another process across the network. The main application class of the server program is shown next.

```
// PipeServ.cpp
#include "stdafx.h"
#include "PipeServ.h"
#include "PipeServDlg.h"

#ifdef _DEBUG
#define new DEBUG_NEW
#undef THIS_FILE
static char THIS_FILE[] = __FILE__;
#endif

#define BUFFER_SIZE 512

// CPipeServApp

BEGIN_MESSAGE_MAP(CPipeServApp, CWinApp)
    //{{AFX_MSG_MAP(CPipeServApp)
        // NOTE - the ClassWizard will add and remove mapping macros here.
        //     DO NOT EDIT what you see in these blocks of generated code!
    //}}AFX_MSG
    ON_COMMAND(ID_HELP, CWinApp::OnHelp)
END_MESSAGE_MAP()

// CPipeServApp construction

CPipeServApp::CPipeServApp()
{
    // TODO: add construction code here,
    // Place all significant initialization in InitInstance
}

// The one and only CPipeServApp object

CPipeServApp theApp;

// CPipeServApp initialization

BOOL CPipeServApp::InitInstance()
{
    // Standard initialization
    // If you are not using these features and wish to reduce the size
    //  of your final executable, you should remove from the following
    //  the specific initialization routines you do not need.

#ifdef _AFXDLL
    Enable3dControls();
#else
    Enable3dControlsStatic();
#endif
```

When the server is started, it creates two named pipes in order to simultaneously send and receive data to and from the client. The **CreateNamedPipe** API is used to create the named pipes. This API creates an instance of a named pipe and returns the handle, which is used in subsequent APIs to operate on that pipe. This API can be used either to create the first instance or to create a new instance of an existing named pipe. The pipe name and the necessary attributes for the pipe are passed to the API. The pipe name should be of the form \\.\pipe*pipename*, where *pipename* is the name of the pipe. The complete pipe name string can be up to 256 characters long. When a named pipe is created, it is always created on the local machine even though it can be accessed by another client from a remote machine. Since one pipe is used only for reading and the other for writing, the pipes' open mode is set to **PIPE_ACCESS_INBOUND** and **PIPE_ACCESS_OUTBOUND** respectively. The mode can also be set to **PIPE_ACCESS_DUPLEX**, in which case the pipe is bidirectional. This parameter can also include either **FILE_FLAG_WRITE_THROUGH** or **FILE_FLAG_OVERLAPPED**. When data sent through the pipe goes to a remote machine, the data is buffered to improve efficiency. The system buffers the data and sends them as a single unit. The **FILE_FLAG_WRITE_THROUGH** disables this buffering. Since any I/O can be a source of performance bottleneck, the read/write operation is improved with overlapping I/O, which was discussed in an earlier chapter. Specifying the **FILE_FLAG_OVERLAPPED** flag allows read/write operations on the pipe to be overlapped.

The next parameter specifies the type and the read and wait modes of the pipe handle. The type specifies how the data is written to the pipe. With the mode set to **PIPE_TYPE_BYTE**, the data is written as a stream of bytes and the application reads a stream of bytes. While this may be useful in certain circumstances, it puts the burden on the application to separate out the messages if the data has multiple messages. To let the system handle this, the **PIPE_TYPE_MESSAGE** flag can be used. This would cause the system to add appropriate headers to each message such that the read command will automatically stop when it reaches the end of the message. The equivalent read mode is flagged by **PIPE_READMODE_BYTE** and **PIPE_READMODE_MESSAGE**. Although these flags can be combined, the application cannot read the data in message mode when the pipe has a type **PIPE_TYPE_BYTE**. However, when the type is **PIPE_TYPE_MESSAGE**, the data can be read in byte mode.

Apart from the type and read mode, yet another mode relates to how the API should behave when operating on the pipe with data. There may be situations when an application should wait until data is read or written. At times, the application may decide to proceed when it can read or write data from or to the pipe. This flag, **PIPE_WAIT** or **PIPE_NOWAIT**, governs this behavior. By default, the wait mode is attributed to the pipe. With the wait mode specified, the read operation on the pipe waits until the API can read some data from the pipe. If data is not available, the read operation will wait for another application to write data to the pipe and return with the data. Similarly the write operation will return only after writing the data to the pipe. If the pipe is full with data, the write operation will wait until another application reads the data from the pipe and empties it for the new data to be written. If the pipe is created with **PIPE_NOWAIT**, then the read/write operation will return right away without waiting for the data to be available or without waiting until the empty buffer becomes available. This flag also affects the **ConnectNamedPipe** API. If wait mode is set, then **ConnectNamedPipe** waits until a client connects to the pipe. If not, it returns without the wait.

The next parameter tells the system how many instances of the pipe are to be created such that multiple clients can connect to them. Even though the same pipe name is used in later calls, the system will return a different handle and a different channel is created for communication. This parameter indicates the maximum number of instances that can be created for a pipe with the given name. The value can be anything in the range 1 through **PIPE_UNLIMITED_INSTANCES**. The latter value does not indicate an upper limit but is constrained by the system resource.

The next two parameters specify the initial allocation of the buffer sizes for the input and output buffer. This value is really a suggested value; the actual size of buffer allocated is governed by either the system default, the system minimum, the system maximum, or the user-specified value rounded to the next allocation boundary.

The next parameter is the default time-out value in milliseconds, which indicates how long a client should wait before timing out when the client issues a **WaitNamedPipe** and specifies a **NMPWAIT_USE_DEFAULT** value for time-out.

The last parameter is a pointer to a security attribute structure, **SECURITY_ ATTRIBUTES**, and specifies what type of security should be given to the pipe. This determines if the child processes can inherit the pipe handle. If the value specified is null, then the handle cannot be inherited.

In the sample here, once the pipes are created successfully, the handles are picked up and passed on to the server dialog box such that the dialog box can use them to send and receive data to and from the client application.

```
HANDLE hINPipe = INVALID_HANDLE_VALUE;
HANDLE hONPipe = INVALID_HANDLE_VALUE;

hINPipe = CreateNamedPipe("\\\\.\\pipe\\IChat", PIPE_ACCESS_INBOUND,
                         PIPE_TYPE_MESSAGE |
                         PIPE_READMODE_MESSAGE |
                         PIPE_WAIT,
                         PIPE_UNLIMITED_INSTANCES,
                         BUFFER_SIZE, BUFFER_SIZE,
                         INFINITE,
                         NULL);
hONPipe = CreateNamedPipe("\\\\.\\pipe\\OChat", PIPE_ACCESS_OUTBOUND,
                         PIPE_TYPE_MESSAGE |
                         PIPE_READMODE_MESSAGE |
                         PIPE_WAIT,
                         PIPE_UNLIMITED_INSTANCES,
                         BUFFER_SIZE, BUFFER_SIZE,
                         INFINITE,
                         NULL);

if (hINPipe != INVALID_HANDLE_VALUE && hONPipe != INVALID_HANDLE_VALUE)
{
    CPipeServDlg dlg;
```

```
        m_pMainWnd = &dlg;
        dlg.SetIPipeHandle(hINPipe);
        dlg.SetOPipeHandle(hONPipe);
        int nResponse = dlg.DoModal();
        if (nResponse == IDOK)
        {
            // TODO: Place code here to handle when the dialog is
            //  dismissed with OK
        }
        else if (nResponse == IDCANCEL)
        {
            // TODO: Place code here to handle when the dialog is
            //  dismissed with Cancel
        }
    }
    if (hINPipe == INVALID_HANDLE_VALUE )
    {
        AfxMessageBox ("Error creating inbound named pipe");
    }
    if (hONPipe == INVALID_HANDLE_VALUE )
    {
        AfxMessageBox ("Error creating outbound named pipe");
    }
    if (hINPipe != INVALID_HANDLE_VALUE )
    {
        // Destroy the pipe
        CloseHandle(hINPipe);
    }

    if (hONPipe != INVALID_HANDLE_VALUE )
    {
        // Destroy the pipe
        CloseHandle(hONPipe);
    }

    return FALSE;
}
```

When the pipes are no longer needed, calling the **CloseHandle** API closes them.

Shown next is the class definition of the server dialog box. It is a standard class definition generated using the ClassWizard; the relevant code is shown in boldface:

```
// PipeServDlg.h : header file
#if !defined(AFX_PIPESERVDLG_H)
#define AFX_PIPESERVDLG_H

#if _MSC_VER > 1000
#pragma once
#endif // _MSC_VER > 1000

// CPipeServDlg dialog
```

```
class CPipeServDlg : public CDialog
{
// Construction
public:
    CPipeServDlg(CWnd* pParent = NULL);    // standard constructor
    void SetIPipeHandle (HANDLE hHandle);
    void SetOPipeHandle (HANDLE hHandle);

// Dialog Data
    //{{AFX_DATA(CPipeServDlg)
    enum { IDD = IDD_PIPESERV_DIALOG };
    CEdit    m_rcvdmsg;
    CString    m_sendmsg;
    //}}AFX_DATA

    // ClassWizard generated virtual function overrides
    //{{AFX_VIRTUAL(CPipeServDlg)
    protected:
    virtual void DoDataExchange(CDataExchange* pDX);    // DDX/DDV support
    //}}AFX_VIRTUAL

// Implementation
protected:
    HICON m_hIcon;

    // Generated message map functions
    //{{AFX_MSG(CPipeServDlg)
    virtual BOOL OnInitDialog();
    afx_msg void OnPaint();
    afx_msg HCURSOR OnQueryDragIcon();
    afx_msg void OnSend();
    afx_msg LRESULT OnUpdateRecvData(WPARAM wParam, LPARAM lParam);
    afx_msg LRESULT OnClearSendData(WPARAM wParam, LPARAM lParam);
    afx_msg LRESULT OnEnableSendButton(WPARAM wParam, LPARAM lParam);
    virtual void OnCancel();
    //}}AFX_MSG
    DECLARE_MESSAGE_MAP()
private:
    HANDLE    hINPipe;
    HANDLE    hONPipe;
    HANDLE    hIEvent;
    HANDLE    hOEvent;
    HANDLE    ThreadReadClient;
    HANDLE    ThreadWriteClient;
    HANDLE    ThreadClientIConnect;
    HANDLE    ThreadClientOConnect;

};
#endif // !defined(AFX_PIPESERVDLG_H)
```

Shown next is the server dialog box code. During the dialog initialization, three threads are started: two to signal when the client establishes the connection and one to listen and read the data that is sent by the client. When the server reads the data sent by the client, it does a blocking read. The server should not perform a blocking read operation until the client has established a connection. This is the reason for the two other threads, which signal when the client establishes the connection. The thread that reads the data from the client and the thread that sends the data to the client wait for a signal to make sure that the client has established the connection. When the user types in some data and sends it, a thread is created to perform the write operation. All four threads that are created communicate with the dialog box class using messages.

```
// PipeServDlg.cpp

#include "stdafx.h"
#include "PipeServ.h"
#include "PipeServDlg.h"

#ifdef _DEBUG
#define new DEBUG_NEW
#undef THIS_FILE
static char THIS_FILE[] = __FILE__;
#endif

#define BUFFER_SIZE 512

#define WM_USER_UPDATE_RECV_DATA    WM_USER+200
#define WM_USER_CLEAR_SEND_DATA     WM_USER+201
#define WM_USER_ENABLE_SEND_BUTTON  WM_USER+202
#define WM_USER_TERMINATE_APP       WM_USER+203
```

The messages defined here update the dialog box with the data received from the client, clear the text that the user typed in the dialog box to send to the client, enable the Send button in the dialog box when the client establishes a connection, and terminate the application respectively. A structure is defined next to pass the information to the threads when the threads are created. This information consists of pipe handles, events, a dialog window handle, and character string data.

```
struct ThreadData {
    HANDLE  hINPipe;
    HANDLE  hONPipe;
    HANDLE  hIEvent;
    HANDLE  hOEvent;
    HWND    hWnd;
    CString data;
};
```

```
LONG   ReadClientData( LPVOID pTD );
LONG   WriteClientData( LPVOID pTD );
LONG   WaitForClientIConnect(LPVOID pTD);
LONG   WaitForClientOConnect(LPVOID pTD);

// CPipeServDlg dialog

CPipeServDlg::CPipeServDlg(CWnd* pParent /*=NULL*/)
    : CDialog(CPipeServDlg::IDD, pParent)
{
    //{{AFX_DATA_INIT(CPipeServDlg)
    m_sendmsg = _T("");
    //}}AFX_DATA_INIT
    m_hIcon = AfxGetApp()->LoadIcon(IDR_MAINFRAME);
}

void CPipeServDlg::DoDataExchange(CDataExchange* pDX)
{
    CDialog::DoDataExchange(pDX);
    //{{AFX_DATA_MAP(CPipeServDlg)
    DDX_Control(pDX, IDC_RECEIVEDMSG, m_rcvdmsg);
    DDX_Text(pDX, IDC_SENDMSG, m_sendmsg);
    //}}AFX_DATA_MAP
}

BEGIN_MESSAGE_MAP(CPipeServDlg, CDialog)
    //{{AFX_MSG_MAP(CPipeServDlg)
    ON_WM_PAINT()
    ON_WM_QUERYDRAGICON()
    ON_BN_CLICKED(IDOK, OnSend)
    ON_MESSAGE(WM_USER_UPDATE_RECV_DATA, OnUpdateRecvData)
    ON_MESSAGE(WM_USER_CLEAR_SEND_DATA, OnClearSendData)
    ON_MESSAGE(WM_USER_ENABLE_SEND_BUTTON, OnEnableSendButton)
    ON_MESSAGE(WM_USER_TERMINATE_APP, OnCancel)
    //}}AFX_MSG_MAP
END_MESSAGE_MAP()

// CPipeServDlg message handlers

BOOL CPipeServDlg::OnInitDialog()
{
    CDialog::OnInitDialog();

    // Set the icon for this dialog.  The framework does this automatically
    //  when the application's main window is not a dialog
    SetIcon(m_hIcon, TRUE);              // Set big icon
    SetIcon(m_hIcon, FALSE);             // Set small icon
    GetDlgItem(IDOK)->EnableWindow(FALSE);
```

Two events are created that are used for synchronization. Three threads are created to wait for the client's connection and the client's data. These thread functions are discussed later.

```
hIEvent = CreateEvent(NULL, TRUE, FALSE, NULL);
hOEvent = CreateEvent(NULL, TRUE, FALSE, NULL);

ThreadData *td1 = new ThreadData;
ThreadData *td2 = new ThreadData;
ThreadData *td3 = new ThreadData;
td1->hINPipe = td2->hINPipe = td3->hINPipe = hINPipe;
td1->hONPipe = td2->hONPipe = td3->hONPipe = hONPipe;
td1->hIEvent = td2->hIEvent = td3->hIEvent = hIEvent;
td1->hOEvent = td2->hOEvent = td3->hOEvent = hOEvent;
td1->hWnd = td2->hWnd = td3->hWnd = GetSafeHwnd();
td1->data = td2->data = td3->data = "";

DWORD dwThreadClientIConnect,
      dwThreadClientOConnect,
      dwThreadReadClient;

ThreadClientIConnect = CreateThread (NULL, 0,
                       (LPTHREAD_START_ROUTINE)WaitForClientIConnect,
                       (LPVOID)td1, 0, &dwThreadClientIConnect);
ThreadClientOConnect = CreateThread (NULL, 0,
                       (LPTHREAD_START_ROUTINE)WaitForClientOConnect,
                       (LPVOID)td2, 0, &dwThreadClientOConnect);
ThreadReadClient = CreateThread (NULL, 0,
                   (LPTHREAD_START_ROUTINE)ReadClientData,
                   (LPVOID)td3, 0, &dwThreadReadClient);

    return TRUE;
}

void CPipeServDlg::OnPaint()
{
    if (IsIconic())
    {
        CPaintDC dc(this); // device context for painting
        SendMessage(WM_ICONERASEBKGND, (WPARAM) dc.GetSafeHdc(), 0);
        // Center icon in client rectangle
        int cxIcon = GetSystemMetrics(SM_CXICON);
        int cyIcon = GetSystemMetrics(SM_CYICON);
        CRect rect;
        GetClientRect(&rect);
        int x = (rect.Width() - cxIcon + 1) / 2;
```

```
        int y = (rect.Height() - cyIcon + 1) / 2;
        // Draw the icon
        dc.DrawIcon(x, y, m_hIcon);
    }
    else
    {
        CDialog::OnPaint();
    }
}
//  the minimized window.
HCURSOR CPipeServDlg::OnQueryDragIcon()
{
    return (HCURSOR) m_hIcon;
}
```

When the user enters some data and clicks the Send button, the **OnSend** function is called. This function collects the user's data and sends it to the client. A thread is created to send the data. This thread function is discussed later.

```
void CPipeServDlg::OnSend()
{
    ThreadData *td = new ThreadData;

    UpdateData();

    td->hONPipe = hONPipe;
    td->hOEvent = hOEvent;
    td->hWnd = GetSafeHwnd();
    td->data = m_sendmsg;

    DWORD dwThreadWriteClient;
    ThreadWriteClient = CreateThread (NULL, 0,
                        (LPTHREAD_START_ROUTINE)WriteClientData,
                        (LPVOID)td, 0, &dwThreadWriteClient);
}
```

When the server is closed, it terminates the threads, closing all the event handles and the pipe handles. Note that before closing the named pipes, the server calls the **DisconnectNamedPipe** API to disconnect its end of the named pipe instance from the client. When the pipe is disconnected, the data that is not yet read by the client is discarded. So if the server cares not to discard the data, it should call **FlushFileBuffers** to make sure that all the data is not discarded. **FlushFileBuffers** waits until the data is retrieved by the client, thereby making sure that the data is not discarded. In our sample, however, it is irrelevant, since the buffer is flushed soon after it is written. This is shown later in the **WriteClientData** function.

Since this sample essentially terminates after disconnecting the pipe, it closes the pipe by calling the **CloseHandle** API. However, an application can reuse the same pipe if it does not close it by reissuing the **ConnectNamedPipe** call.

```
void CPipeServDlg::OnCancel()
{
    // TODO: Add extra cleanup here
    TerminateThread (ThreadReadClient, -1);
    TerminateThread (ThreadWriteClient, -1);
    TerminateThread (ThreadClientIConnect, -1);
    TerminateThread (ThreadClientOConnect, -1);
    DisconnectNamedPipe(hINPipe);
    DisconnectNamedPipe(hONPipe);
    CloseHandle(hIEvent);
    CloseHandle(hOEvent);
    CloseHandle(hINPipe);
    CloseHandle(hONPipe);
    CDialog::OnCancel();
}
```

When the server receives the message from the client, a thread collects the data and passes it to the server dialog box using a message, which is processed by the next function, **OnUpdateRecvData**. After the data is sent to the client, the code clears the data entered by the user by sending a message that is processed by **OnClearSendData**.

```
LRESULT CPipeServDlg::OnUpdateRecvData(WPARAM wParam, LPARAM lParam)
{
    char szAppendBuf[BUFFER_SIZE + 10];
    sprintf(szAppendBuf, "%s\r\n", (LPCTSTR)lParam);
    m_rcvdmsg.SetSel(-1, 0);
    m_rcvdmsg.ReplaceSel(szAppendBuf);
    return 0;
}


LRESULT CPipeServDlg::OnClearSendData(WPARAM wParam, LPARAM lParam)
{
    m_sendmsg = "";
    UpdateData(FALSE);
    return 0;
}
```

This sample enables the Send button in the dialog box only after establishing a connection with the client. To enable the Send button, the thread that is creating the connection to the outbound pipe sends a message when the connection is established.

```
LRESULT CPipeServDlg::OnEnableSendButton(WPARAM wParam, LPARAM lParam)
{
    GetDlgItem(IDOK)->EnableWindow(TRUE);
    return 0;
}


void CPipeServDlg::SetIPipeHandle(HANDLE hHandle)
{
    hINPipe = hHandle;
}


void CPipeServDlg::SetOPipeHandle(HANDLE hHandle)
{
    hONPipe = hHandle;
}
```

The purpose of the next two thread functions is to detect if the client connected to the other end of the pipe. This is done using the **ConnectNamedPipe** API. There is a need to synchronize between a client and a server to establish a proper connection. Writing to a pipe where no one listens at the other end would cause loss of data. In order to achieve this synchronization, two APIs are available to be used. On the server side, the application can use **ConnectNamedPipe**, and on the client side, it can use **WaitNamedPipe**. When the server creates a named pipe, it needs to know when the client connects to an instance of the named pipe. **ConnectNamePipe** can be used to wait for a client to connect. Since the pipes were not created with **FILE_FLAG_OVERLAPPED**, the second parameter used here in the API is NULL. If the pipe was created with the overlapped mode enabled, then a valid overlapped structure should be passed. When the API succeeds, it returns zero. However, if the client had connected to the pipe even before this API is called, then it will return a nonzero return code with the error code ERROR_PIPE_CONNECTED. Notice here that the code considers the connection successful even if it gets ERROR_PIPE_CONNECTED as the error code. When a connection is established in the case of the inbound pipe and the outbound pipe, events are set. This triggers other threads, which may be waiting for the connection to be established. The thread waiting for the outbound connection to be established also sends a message to the dialog box to enable the Send button on the dialog box.

```
LONG  WaitForClientIConnect(LPVOID pTD)
{
    BOOL rc;
    ThreadData *td = (ThreadData *)pTD;

    HANDLE hINPipe = td->hINPipe;
    HANDLE hIEvent = td->hIEvent;
```

```
    rc = ConnectNamedPipe(hINPipe, NULL);
    if (rc != 0 || GetLastError() == ERROR_PIPE_CONNECTED)
    {
        SetEvent(hIEvent);
    }
    delete td;
    return 0;
}

LONG  WaitForClientOConnect(LPVOID pTD)
{
    BOOL rc;
    ThreadData *td = (ThreadData *)pTD;

    HANDLE hONPipe = td->hONPipe;
    HANDLE hOEvent = td->hOEvent;
    HWND hWnd = td->hWnd;

    rc = ConnectNamedPipe(hONPipe, NULL);
    if (rc != 0 || GetLastError() == ERROR_PIPE_CONNECTED)
    {
        SetEvent(hOEvent);
    }
    SendMessage((HWND)hWnd, WM_USER_ENABLE_SEND_BUTTON, NULL, NULL);
    delete td;
    return 0;
}
```

To receive data from the client, the server initiates a thread and goes into an infinite loop waiting and reading data from the pipe. Before getting into a loop to read the data, the server needs to make sure that a connection has been established with the client. For this, the thread waits on the event by calling **WaitForSingleObject**. Recall that this event is set in the **WaitForClientIConnect** thread function earlier. To read the data from the pipe, the **ReadFile** API is called. This API reads the data from the inbound named pipe and returns after reading the data. The buffer into which the data is to be read and the number of bytes to be read are passed to the API. If more data is available than what is requested, the API will read part of the data available and return a failure. **GetLastError** in this case would return an error code of **ERROR_MORE_DATA**. Calling **ReadFile** again would return the rest of the data. This sample uses a buffer of 512 bytes and assumes that data overflow will not occur there by ignoring this error situation. Since this pipe was not created as an overlapped pipe, the overlapped parameter is set to NULL.

The data that is read is sent to the dialog box class by sending a message and passing in the data. The main dialog box processing code displays the data received in the dialog box.

When an error occurs during reading, an error message is displayed and the server is terminated by sending a termination message to the dialog box.

```
LONG   ReadClientData( LPVOID pTD)
{
    ThreadData *td = (ThreadData *)pTD;
    HANDLE hINPipe = td->hINPipe;
    HANDLE hIEvent = td->hIEvent;
    HWND hWnd = td->hWnd;

    BOOL    rc;
    char * szBuf = new char [BUFFER_SIZE];
    DWORD dwBytesRead;
    DWORD dwRC;

    WaitForSingleObject(hIEvent,  INFINITE);
    while (TRUE)
    {
        dwBytesRead = 0;
        rc = ReadFile (hINPipe, szBuf, BUFFER_SIZE, &dwBytesRead, NULL);
        dwRC = GetLastError();
        if (dwBytesRead)
        {
            szBuf[dwBytesRead] = 0;
            SendMessage((HWND)hWnd, WM_USER_UPDATE_RECV_DATA,
                        NULL, (LPARAM)szBuf);
        }
        if (dwRC != ERROR_SUCCESS)
        {
            char szErrorMsg[1024];
            FormatMessage(FORMAT_MESSAGE_FROM_SYSTEM, NULL, dwRC,
                        0, szErrorMsg, 1024, NULL);
            AfxMessageBox(szErrorMsg);
            break;
        }
    }

    delete [] szBuf;
    delete td;
    PostMessage((HWND)hWnd, WM_USER_TERMINATE_APP, NULL, NULL);
    return 0;
}
```

When the user types in some data and clicks on the Send button, the data is written to the outbound pipe by the thread function shown next. This function first makes sure that the client is listening to the outbound pipe before writing the data to the pipe. Actually, this check is not needed, since the Send button in the dialog box would not have been enabled if the connection was not established. It then calls the **WriteFile** API to write the data to the pipe. As in the case of the read, since the mode of the outbound pipe is wait mode, this API will return when it completes writing all the data. The function also calls **FlushFileBuffers** to flush out any data that may be held in the system buffer. This thread function also sends a message to the dialog box to clear the outbound data area in the dialog box. For every message, a new thread is created to send the message.

```
LONG  WriteClientData( LPVOID pTD)
{
    DWORD dwBytesWritten = 0;
    BOOL    rc;
    ThreadData *td = (ThreadData *)pTD;

    HANDLE hONPipe = td->hONPipe;
    HWND hWnd = td->hWnd;
    HANDLE hOEvent = td->hOEvent;
    CString Clientdata = td->data;

    WaitForSingleObject(hOEvent,  INFINITE);
    rc = WriteFile (hONPipe, (LPCVOID)((LPCTSTR)(td->data)),
                    (td->data).GetLength(), &dwBytesWritten, NULL);
    if (!rc)
    {
        DWORD dwRC;
        char szErrorMsg[1024];
        dwRC = GetLastError();
        FormatMessage(FORMAT_MESSAGE_FROM_SYSTEM, NULL, dwRC,
                      0, szErrorMsg, 1024, NULL);
        AfxMessageBox(szErrorMsg);
    }
    SendMessage((HWND)hWnd, WM_USER_CLEAR_SEND_DATA, NULL, NULL);
    FlushFileBuffers(hONPipe);
    delete td;
    return 0;
}
```

The client application, which receives the data from the server and responds to the server through a pipe, is shown next. There is no additional code in the main application class, and hence it is not shown here. The dialog box class definition is shown here; the code of interest is shown in boldface.

```
// PipeClientDlg.h

#if !defined(AFX_PIPECLIENTDLG_H)
#define AFX_PIPECLIENTDLG_H

#if _MSC_VER > 1000
#pragma once
#endif // _MSC_VER > 1000


// CPipeClientDlg dialog

class CPipeClientDlg : public CDialog
{
// Construction
public:
    CPipeClientDlg(CWnd* pParent = NULL);    // standard constructor

// Dialog Data
    //{{AFX_DATA(CPipeClientDlg)
    enum { IDD = IDD_PIPECLIENT_DIALOG };
    CEdit    m_rcvdmsg;
    CString    m_sendmsg;
    //}}AFX_DATA

    // ClassWizard generated virtual function overrides
    //{{AFX_VIRTUAL(CPipeClientDlg)
    protected:
    virtual void DoDataExchange(CDataExchange* pDX);    // DDX/DDV support
    //}}AFX_VIRTUAL

// Implementation
protected:
    HICON m_hIcon;

    // Generated message map functions
    //{{AFX_MSG(CPipeClientDlg)
    virtual BOOL OnInitDialog();
    afx_msg void OnPaint();
    afx_msg HCURSOR OnQueryDragIcon();
    afx_msg void OnSend();
    virtual void OnCancel();
    afx_msg LRESULT OnUpdateRecvData(WPARAM wParam, LPARAM lParam);
    afx_msg void OnSetIPipeHandle(WPARAM wParam, LPARAM lParam);
    afx_msg void OnSetOPipeHandle(WPARAM wParam, LPARAM lParam);
    afx_msg LRESULT OnGetIPipeHandle(WPARAM wParam, LPARAM lParam);
    afx_msg LRESULT OnGetOPipeHandle(WPARAM wParam, LPARAM lParam);
    afx_msg LRESULT OnClearSendData(WPARAM wParam, LPARAM lParam);
    //}}AFX_MSG
```

```
    DECLARE_MESSAGE_MAP()
private:
    HANDLE   hINPipe;
    HANDLE   hONPipe;
    HANDLE   hIEvent;
    HANDLE   hOEvent;
    HANDLE   ThreadReadServer;
    HANDLE   ThreadWriteServer;
    HANDLE   ThreadServerIConnect;
    HANDLE   ThreadServerOConnect;
};

//{{AFX_INSERT_LOCATION}}
// Microsoft Visual C++ will insert additional declarations immediately before the
previous line.

#endif // !defined(AFX_PIPECLIENTDLG_H)
```

The implementation of the client dialog box class is shown next. The functioning of the client dialog box is very similar to that of the server. When started, it tries to establish connections to the server's inbound and outbound pipes. Once the connections are established, it sends and receives data through these pipes. Events are used to synchronize the reading and writing of data from and to the pipe with the availability of the connection to the pipe. A range of user-defined messages are used to communicate to the dialog box from the threads.

```
// PipeClientDlg.cpp

#include "stdafx.h"
#include "PipeClient.h"
#include "PipeClientDlg.h"

#ifdef _DEBUG
#define new DEBUG_NEW
#undef THIS_FILE
static char THIS_FILE[] = __FILE__;
#endif

#define BUFFER_SIZE 512

#define WM_USER_UPDATE_RECV_DATA      WM_USER+200
#define WM_USER_SET_IPIPE_HANDLE      WM_USER+201
#define WM_USER_SET_OPIPE_HANDLE      WM_USER+202
#define WM_USER_GET_IPIPE_HANDLE      WM_USER+203
#define WM_USER_GET_OPIPE_HANDLE      WM_USER+204
#define WM_USER_CLEAR_SEND_DATA       WM_USER+205
#define WM_USER_TERMINATE_APP         WM_USER+206

struct ThreadData {
```

```
        HANDLE   hINPipe;
        HANDLE   hONPipe;
        HANDLE   hIEvent;
        HANDLE   hOEvent;
        HWND     hWnd;
        CString data;
    };


LONG ReadServerData( LPVOID pTD);
LONG WriteServerData( LPVOID pTD);
LONG WaitForServerIConnect( LPVOID pTD);
LONG WaitForServerOConnect( LPVOID pTD);

// CPipeClientDlg dialog

CPipeClientDlg::CPipeClientDlg(CWnd* pParent /*=NULL*/)
    : CDialog(CPipeClientDlg::IDD, pParent)
{
    //{{AFX_DATA_INIT(CPipeClientDlg)
    m_sendmsg = _T("");
    //}}AFX_DATA_INIT
    // Note that LoadIcon does not require a subsequent DestroyIcon in Win32
    m_hIcon = AfxGetApp()->LoadIcon(IDR_MAINFRAME);
}


void CPipeClientDlg::DoDataExchange(CDataExchange* pDX)
{
    CDialog::DoDataExchange(pDX);
    //{{AFX_DATA_MAP(CPipeClientDlg)
    DDX_Control(pDX, IDC_RECEIVEDMSG, m_rcvdmsg);
    DDX_Text(pDX, IDC_SENDMSG, m_sendmsg);
    //}}AFX_DATA_MAP
}


BEGIN_MESSAGE_MAP(CPipeClientDlg, CDialog)
    //{{AFX_MSG_MAP(CPipeClientDlg)
    ON_WM_PAINT()
    ON_WM_QUERYDRAGICON()
    ON_BN_CLICKED(IDOK, OnSend)
    ON_MESSAGE(WM_USER_UPDATE_RECV_DATA, OnUpdateRecvData)
    ON_MESSAGE(WM_USER_SET_IPIPE_HANDLE, OnSetIPipeHandle)
    ON_MESSAGE(WM_USER_SET_OPIPE_HANDLE, OnSetOPipeHandle)
    ON_MESSAGE(WM_USER_GET_IPIPE_HANDLE, OnGetIPipeHandle)
    ON_MESSAGE(WM_USER_GET_OPIPE_HANDLE, OnGetOPipeHandle)
    ON_MESSAGE(WM_USER_CLEAR_SEND_DATA, OnClearSendData)
    ON_MESSAGE(WM_USER_TERMINATE_APP, OnCancel)
    //}}AFX_MSG_MAP
END_MESSAGE_MAP()
```

During initialization, two events are created. Three threads are also created, and these events are passed to these threads. Two threads wait till they establish a connection with the inbound and outbound thread, and the third thread reads data from the server and sends the data received to the dialog box to be displayed.

```
// CPipeClientDlg message handlers
BOOL CPipeClientDlg::OnInitDialog()
{
    CDialog::OnInitDialog();

    // Set the icon for this dialog.  The framework does this automatically
    //  when the application's main window is not a dialog
    SetIcon(m_hIcon, TRUE);            // Set big icon
    SetIcon(m_hIcon, FALSE);           // Set small icon

    GetDlgItem(IDOK)->EnableWindow(FALSE);
    hIEvent = CreateEvent(NULL, TRUE, FALSE, NULL);
    hOEvent = CreateEvent(NULL, TRUE, FALSE, NULL);
    hINPipe = INVALID_HANDLE_VALUE;
    hONPipe = INVALID_HANDLE_VALUE;
    ThreadData *td1 = new ThreadData;
    ThreadData *td2 = new ThreadData;
    ThreadData *td3 = new ThreadData;
    td1->hINPipe = td2->hINPipe = td3->hINPipe = hINPipe;
    td1->hONPipe = td2->hONPipe = td3->hONPipe = hONPipe;
    td1->hIEvent = td2->hIEvent = td3->hIEvent = hIEvent;
    td1->hOEvent = td2->hOEvent = td3->hOEvent = hOEvent;
    td1->hWnd = td2->hWnd = td3->hWnd = GetSafeHwnd();
    td1->data = td2->data = td3->data = "";

    DWORD dwThreadServerIConnect,
          dwThreadServerOConnect,
          dwThreadReadServer;
    ThreadServerIConnect = CreateThread (NULL, 0,
                        (LPTHREAD_START_ROUTINE)WaitForServerIConnect,
                        (LPVOID)td1, 0, &dwThreadServerIConnect);
    ThreadServerOConnect = CreateThread (NULL, 0,
                        (LPTHREAD_START_ROUTINE)WaitForServerOConnect,
                        (LPVOID)td2, 0, &dwThreadServerOConnect);
    ThreadReadServer = CreateThread (NULL, 0,
                        (LPTHREAD_START_ROUTINE)ReadServerData,
                        (LPVOID)td3, 0, &dwThreadReadServer);
    return TRUE;
}

void CPipeClientDlg::OnPaint()
```

```
{
    if (IsIconic())
    {
        CPaintDC dc(this); // device context for painting

        SendMessage(WM_ICONERASEBKGND, (WPARAM) dc.GetSafeHdc(), 0);
        // Center icon in client rectangle
        int cxIcon = GetSystemMetrics(SM_CXICON);
        int cyIcon = GetSystemMetrics(SM_CYICON);
        CRect rect;
        GetClientRect(&rect);
        int x = (rect.Width() - cxIcon + 1) / 2;
        int y = (rect.Height() - cyIcon + 1) / 2;

        // Draw the icon
        dc.DrawIcon(x, y, m_hIcon);
    }
    else
    {
        CDialog::OnPaint();
    }
}

HCURSOR CPipeClientDlg::OnQueryDragIcon()
{
    return (HCURSOR) m_hIcon;
}
```

When the user types in some data and clicks on the Send button, the **OnSend** function is called. It creates a thread and passes on the data entered by the user. The thread function writes this data to the outbound pipe, which is then picked up by the server application.

```
void CPipeClientDlg::OnSend()
{
    ThreadData *td = new ThreadData;
    UpdateData();

    td->hONPipe = hONPipe;
    td->hOEvent = hOEvent;
    td->hWnd = GetSafeHwnd();
    td->data = m_sendmsg;

    DWORD dwThreadWriteServer;
    ThreadWriteServer = CreateThread (NULL, 0,
                     (LPTHREAD_START_ROUTINE)WriteServerData, (LPVOID)td,
                      0, &dwThreadWriteServer);

}
```

When the thread that is listening to the inbound pipe receives any data, it reads the data and sends it to the dialog box to be displayed to the user. This is handled by the **OnUpdateRecvData** function shown next.

```
LRESULT CPipeClientDlg::OnUpdateRecvData(WPARAM wParam, LPARAM lParam)
{
    char szAppendBuf[BUFFER_SIZE + 10];
    sprintf(szAppendBuf, "%s\r\n", (LPCTSTR)lParam);
    m_rcvdmsg.SetSel(-1, 0);
    m_rcvdmsg.ReplaceSel(szAppendBuf);
    return 0;
}
```

The next four functions are helper functions for setting and retrieving the inbound and outbound pipe handles. They are followed by another helper function that clears the data that has been sent to the server.

```
void CPipeClientDlg::OnSetIPipeHandle(WPARAM wParam, LPARAM lParam)
{
    hINPipe = (HANDLE)lParam;
}
void CPipeClientDlg::OnSetOPipeHandle(WPARAM wParam, LPARAM lParam)
{
    hONPipe = (HANDLE)lParam;
    GetDlgItem(IDOK)->EnableWindow(TRUE);
}

LRESULT CPipeClientDlg::OnGetIPipeHandle(WPARAM wParam, LPARAM lParam)
{
    return ((LRESULT)hINPipe);
}

LRESULT CPipeClientDlg::OnGetOPipeHandle(WPARAM wParam, LPARAM lParam)
{
    return ((LRESULT)hONPipe);
}

LRESULT CPipeClientDlg::OnClearSendData(WPARAM wParam, LPARAM lParam)
{
    m_sendmsg = "";
    UpdateData(FALSE);
    return 0;
}
```

When the client terminates, the threads are terminated. The events that were created are closed. Notice that unlike the server, the client just closes the pipe handle, whereas the server disconnects its end of the named pipe from the client. Even though the client end of the named pipe is closed, when the server calls **DisconnectNamedPipe**, the client should still call **CloseHandle** to close the named pipe.

```
void CPipeClientDlg::OnCancel()
{
    // TODO: Add extra cleanup here
    TerminateThread (ThreadReadServer, -1);
    TerminateThread (ThreadWriteServer, -1);
    TerminateThread (ThreadServerIConnect, -1);
    TerminateThread (ThreadServerOConnect, -1);
    CloseHandle(hIEvent);
    CloseHandle(hOEvent);
    CloseHandle(hINPipe);
    CloseHandle(hONPipe);
    CDialog::OnCancel();
}
```

The next two thread functions wait to establish a connection with the server; once the pipe is available, they get access to the pipe by calling **CreateFile** and getting the pipe handle. The client should use the **WaitNamedPipe** API to wait for a specific instance of the named pipe to be available for connection. The first parameter specifies the pipe name, and the second parameter specifies a period beyond which the API returns if the connection is not available. In this sample, there is one client and one server, and so the API waits forever by specifying **NMPWAIT_WAIT_FOREVER**. The client always expects to get a connection since the design of the application accommodates it. The server also terminates when the client terminates. However, the sample could have been designed differently, such that the server did not terminate when the client terminated; in that case, when two servers were started, the second client would wait until the first client terminated. The API returns immediately if it cannot find any instances of the named pipe. This can be illustrated by starting the client program without the server program running. However, the error checking in this sample is done by assuming that a connection is available and creating the connection. If a connection is really not available, it fails with an invalid handle error.

Once the named pipe is available for connection, calling the **CreateFile** API opens it and the handle is used for future conversation with the server. Notice that the name of the pipe that is used for reading by the client is the name of the pipe that the server uses for writing.

If a successful connection is established, the threads set the events, which are used by other threads to wait on before reading and writing to the pipes. An error during the operation terminates the client by sending a termination message to the dialog box. In this situation, there is no connection to the pipe, but the **OnCancel** function still incorrectly closes the handle that is not valid! To avoid this, the handles could have been initialized as invalid handles, and functions could check that a handle is valid before closing it.

```
LONG WaitForServerIConnect(LPVOID pTD)
{
    HANDLE hINPipe;
    ThreadData *td = (ThreadData *)pTD;

    HANDLE hIEvent = td->hIEvent;
    HWND hWnd = td->hWnd;
    WaitNamedPipe ("\\\\.\\pipe\\OChat", NMPWAIT_WAIT_FOREVER);
    hINPipe = CreateFile("\\\\.\\pipe\\OChat",
                    GENERIC_READ, 0, NULL,
                    OPEN_EXISTING, 0, NULL);

    if (hINPipe != INVALID_HANDLE_VALUE)
    {
        SendMessage(hWnd, WM_USER_SET_IPIPE_HANDLE, NULL, (LPARAM)hINPipe);
        SetEvent(hIEvent);
    }
    else
    {
        char szErrorMsg[1024];
        DWORD dwRC = GetLastError();
        FormatMessage(FORMAT_MESSAGE_FROM_SYSTEM, NULL, dwRC, 0,
                    szErrorMsg, 1024, NULL);
        AfxMessageBox(szErrorMsg);
        AfxMessageBox("Invalid pipe handle.  Terminating application");
        PostMessage(hWnd, WM_USER_TERMINATE_APP, NULL, NULL);
    }
    delete td;
    return 0;
}

LONG WaitForServerOConnect(LPVOID pTD)
{
    HANDLE hONPipe;
    ThreadData *td = (ThreadData *)pTD;

    HANDLE hOEvent = td->hOEvent;
    HWND hWnd = td->hWnd;
    WaitNamedPipe ("\\\\.\\pipe\\IChat", NMPWAIT_WAIT_FOREVER);
    hONPipe = CreateFile("\\\\.\\pipe\\IChat",
                    GENERIC_WRITE, 0, NULL,
                    OPEN_EXISTING, 0, NULL);

    if (hONPipe != INVALID_HANDLE_VALUE)
    {
        SendMessage(hWnd, WM_USER_SET_OPIPE_HANDLE, NULL, (LPARAM)hONPipe);
```

```
            SetEvent(hOEvent);
    }
    else
    {
        char szErrorMsg[1024];
        DWORD dwRC = GetLastError();
        FormatMessage(FORMAT_MESSAGE_FROM_SYSTEM, NULL, dwRC, 0,
                      szErrorMsg, 1024, NULL);
        AfxMessageBox(szErrorMsg);
        AfxMessageBox("Invalid pipe handle.  Terminating application");
        PostMessage(hWnd, WM_USER_TERMINATE_APP, NULL, NULL);
    }
    delete td;
    return 0;
}
```

The next two thread functions are very similar to the server thread functions that read and write data to the pipe. The only noticeable difference is that the functions here request the pipe handle by sending a message to the dialog box.

```
LONG ReadServerData( LPVOID pTD)
{
    ThreadData *td = (ThreadData *)pTD;
    HANDLE hINPipe;
    HWND hWnd = td->hWnd;
    HANDLE hIEvent = td->hIEvent;

    BOOL    rc;
    char * szBuf = new char [BUFFER_SIZE];
    DWORD dwBytesRead;
    DWORD dwRC;

    WaitForSingleObject(hIEvent,  INFINITE);
    hINPipe = (HANDLE)SendMessage(hWnd, WM_USER_GET_IPIPE_HANDLE,
                                  NULL, NULL);
    while (TRUE)
    {
        dwBytesRead = 0;
        rc = ReadFile (hINPipe, szBuf, BUFFER_SIZE, &dwBytesRead, NULL);
        dwRC = GetLastError();
        if (dwBytesRead)
        {
            szBuf[dwBytesRead] = 0;
            SendMessage(hWnd, WM_USER_UPDATE_RECV_DATA,
                        NULL, (LPARAM)szBuf);
        }
        if (dwRC != ERROR_SUCCESS)
        {
            char szErrorMsg[1024];
```

```
                    FormatMessage(FORMAT_MESSAGE_FROM_SYSTEM, NULL, dwRC, 0,
                               szErrorMsg, 1024, NULL);
                    AfxMessageBox(szErrorMsg);
                    AfxMessageBox("Server seems to have terminated");
                    break;
            }
        }

    delete [] szBuf;
    delete td;
    PostMessage((HWND)hWnd, WM_USER_TERMINATE_APP, NULL, NULL);
    return 0;
}

LONG WriteServerData( LPVOID pTD)
{
    DWORD dwBytesWritten = 0;
    BOOL    rc;
    ThreadData *td = (ThreadData *)pTD;

    HANDLE hONPipe;
    HWND hWnd = td->hWnd;
    HANDLE hOEvent = td->hOEvent;
    CString Serverdata = td->data;

    WaitForSingleObject(hOEvent,  INFINITE);
    hONPipe = (HANDLE)SendMessage(hWnd, WM_USER_GET_OPIPE_HANDLE,
                                   NULL, NULL);
    rc = WriteFile (hONPipe, (LPCVOID)((LPCTSTR)Serverdata),
                    Serverdata.GetLength(), &dwBytesWritten, NULL);
    if (!rc)
    {
        DWORD dwRC;
        char szErrorMsg[1024];
        dwRC = GetLastError();
        FormatMessage(FORMAT_MESSAGE_FROM_SYSTEM, NULL, dwRC, 0,
                      szErrorMsg, 1024, NULL);
        AfxMessageBox(szErrorMsg);
    }
    SendMessage((HWND)hWnd, WM_USER_CLEAR_SEND_DATA, NULL, NULL);
    FlushFileBuffers(hONPipe);
    delete td;
    return 0;
}
```

CONCLUSION

In this chapter we looked at how to create and terminate processes. Then we looked at one of the important programming tools that Windows 2000 provides to improve the efficiency of your application as well as processor usage—threads. We discussed how and when to create threads and the safe (and not so safe) ways of terminating threads. We covered how thread priorities work and how you can adjust them. We covered guidelines on when to use a thread. We covered thread local storage and the different communications mechanisms available for communicating between threads. We covered thread pooling and how it can be applied in programming with threads. We also covered named and anonymous pipes and illustrated both with programming examples.

In the next chapter we'll look at one of the most significant enhancements in Windows 2000 compared to Windows NT: Active Directory.

CHAPTER 10

Active Directory

Active Directory is one of the hot new technologies in Windows 2000. A *directory* in the computer context means the same as in any other context, such as a phone directory. Just as a phone directory lists phone numbers and some associated data, the directory in the computer context stores information about objects and associated data. The objects include files, users, printers, applications, databases, and so on. A directory in the computer context is not really new. We have had a directory of files for a long time. With the advent of the distributed computing and the Internet, the objects could be located anywhere on the network. Users like to access the objects in the same transparent and simple manner as they would local objects such as files on the local hard drive. The mechanism that makes this possible is the Active Directory. Of course, Microsoft is not the only vendor offering directory solutions. Novell, for instance, has a directory offering called Novell Directory Service (NDS).

Directory Concepts and Terminology

The term *directory service* is commonly used in conjunction with a directory. A directory service includes the directory itself and the services that make the directory information available to users. As mentioned earlier, an object is something concrete that is present somewhere in the network and needs to be located using the directory. Objects have attributes. Attributes describe the object.

A *container* holds a group of objects and other containers. Containers, like objects, have attributes and are part of the Active Directory. However, unlike an object, a container is not by itself something concrete such as a file or a user. Examples of containers include file directories and domains. A *tree* is used in the context of an Active Directory to describe a hierarchy of objects and containers. A tree shows how objects are connected or the path from one object to another. Containers are nodes in the tree, and objects are the endpoints. A *contiguous subtree* is any unbroken path in the tree, including all members of any container in that path. A *forest* is a set of one or more trees that do not form a contiguous name space. Unlike a tree, a forest does not need a separate and unique name (a forest can exist as a set of cross-reference objects and trust relationships known to the member trees). A *site* is a location in a network that contains Active Directory servers.

Every object in an Active Directory has two ways to locate the object—a *distinguished name (DN)* and a *relative distinguished name (RDN)*. A DN identifies the domain that holds the object and the complete path through the container hierarchy by which to locate the object. An RDN is that part of the DN that refers to the object itself.

The Active Directory is made up of one or more *naming contexts* or *partitions*. A naming context is any contiguous subtree of the directory. Naming contexts are the unit of replication. Replication is the technique whereby copies of a directory are available at different points in a network. Replication makes the directory available to more users as well and provides an alternate in event of failure. In the Active Directory, a single server always holds at least three naming contexts—the schema, the configuration, and one or more user naming contexts.

The functions that can be performed with a directory service include enforcement of security using an object's security attributes by administrators, distribution of a directory across computers, replication of a directory to improve availability and fault tolerance, and partitioning of a directory into multiple stores to improve scalability.

Active Directory Architecture

We will describe the architecture of the Active Directory in terms of its different components:

▼ Directory system agent

■ Data model and schema

■ Administration model

■ Global catalog

▲ Active directory security

Directory System Agent

The *directory system agent (DSA)* provides clients access to the Active Directory contents. The mechanisms clients use to access the directory depend on the type of client.

▼ LDAP clients connect to the DSA using the LDAP protocol. Active Directory supports LDAP 3.0 and LDAP 2.0. Windows 2000/98/95 Active Directory clients use LDAP 3.0 to connect to the DSA.

■ MAPI clients (e.g., Microsoft Exchange) connect to the DSA using the MAPI remote procedure call interface.

■ Older versions of Windows NT clients use the Security Account Manager (SAM) interface to connect to the DSA.

▲ Active Directory DSAs connect to each other using a proprietary remote procedure call interface to perform functions such as replication.

Data Model and Schema

The Active Directory data model is based on the X.500 data model. The directory holds objects of different types. These objects are described by attributes. At the heart of the Active Directory is the Active Directory Schema, which describes all the object classes that can be stored in the Active Directory. For each object class, the schema defines the mandatory attributes that an instance of the class must have, any additional optional attributes the instance may have, and the object class that can be a parent of the object class. Unlike with some other directories, the Active Directory schema is implemented as a set of object class instances that are themselves stored in the directory.

Storing the object class instances in the Directory permits applications to query objects in the Directory. In addition, applications can dynamically update the Active Directory schema by creating or modifying the schema objects stored in the directory. Applications can extend the schema with new attributes and classes and use such extensions immediately.

Extending the Schema   As mentioned previously, you can extend the schema by adding new attributes as well as adding new object classes. You add an attribute by specifying a name, specifying a unique Object Identifier (OID), specifying what kind of data the attribute can hold, and including optional range limits. When you define an attribute, you have the option of creating an index for that attribute. In deciding if you want an index, keep in mind that the traditional space versus performance tradeoffs apply. Indexes take up space in the directory and impact performance when objects are inserted, but they help with faster retrieval of data. Thus, you should define indexes when they are used often and when the values of the attribute are highly unique. The Active Directory schema can be updated dynamically, which means that the updates you perform programmatically are immediately available for use without your having to stop and restart the Active Directory.

Administration Model

Administering the Active Directory is very similar to other Windows administration tasks such as system administration and network administration. Administration of the Active Directory can be performed only by users authorized to perform such administrative tasks.

The Active Directory Administrator need not be one single individual. Administrative tasks can be delegated to other users. Any user can be authorized by a higher authority to perform a specified set of actions on a specified set of object classes and objects within an identified subtree of the directory. Since the Active Directory can be distributed, delegation of administration makes it easy to administer a directory that is spread out geographically. Delegation of administration also allows fine-grained control over who can do what. Keep in mind that delegation of authority does not mean that the delegated user automatically gets elevated privileges.

Global Catalog

A common way to look for an object in the Active Directory is to use the object's *distinguished name (DN)*. The DN includes not only the name itself but additional details to locate a replica of the partition in the Active Directory that holds the object. However, when the user or application does not know the DN of the target object or which partition might contain the object, the *global catalog (GC)* allows users and applications to find objects in an Active Directory domain tree using one or more attributes of the target object.

The GC contains a partial replica of every naming context in the directory including the schema and configuration naming contexts. The GC holds a replica of every object in Active Directory but with a subset of the attributes, those that are most frequently used in search operations, such as a user's last name, and those attributes required to locate a full replica of the object. The GC allows users to quickly find objects of interest without knowing what domain holds them and without requiring a contiguous extended name space in the enterprise.

The GC is built automatically by the Active Directory replication system. The replication topology for the GC is generated automatically. The properties replicated into the GC include a base set defined by Microsoft as well as additional properties specified by administrators.

Active Directory Security

Active Directory is an integral part of the Windows 2000 security infrastructure. Each directory object has its own security descriptor containing security information that protects the object. The security descriptor, among other things, can contain a discretionary access-control list (DACL). A DACL contains a list of access-control entries (ACEs). Each ACE allows or denies a set of access rights to a user or group. For those users who are allowed access, the ACE specifies what type of access will be granted. The ACE also specifies whether the access control settings can be propagated from an object to any of its children. The system validates any attempt to access an object or attribute in Active Directory by checking the access permissions allowed by the ACE. This protection mechanism includes the schema objects as well. In particular, access validation routines ensure that only authorized users alter the schema.

The sequence of steps to manage access controls over an ADSI object involves the following:

▼   Obtain the security descriptor for the object.

■   Retrieve an ACL from the security descriptor.

▲   Use the ACEs in the ACL.

Next, let's look at ADSI functions and interfaces.

ADSI FUNCTIONS AND INTERFACES

The Active Directory Service Interfaces (ADSI) are basically a set of COM interfaces. ADSI interfaces are used to access the capabilities of directory services from different network providers. The ADSI pull together a single set of directory service interfaces for managing network resources in a distributed computing environment. Thus, there is overlap between the functionality of ADSI interfaces and existing network management functions. In fact, if you are programming for Active Directory, you may be able to call certain ADSI interface methods to achieve the same functionality you can achieve by calling certain network management functions. For example, **NetGroup** and **IADsGroup** provide equivalent functionality. The same is true for **NetServer** and **IADsComputer** as well as **NetShare** and **IADsFileShare**.

ADSI interfaces can be categorized as shown in Table 10-1.

ADSI Interface Category	Description
Core	Core interfaces provide the basic object management functions of ADSI objects such as providing an entry point into a directory store, loading properties into the property cache, and committing changes to the underlying directory.
Schema	Schema interfaces provide methods for managing and extending the directory schema.
Property Cache	Property Cache interfaces define methods for manipulating properties in the property cache.
Persistent Object	Persistent Object interfaces manipulate persistent data in the name space of the underlying directory service. These interfaces are used to provide access to persistent data of an object such as user accounts, file shares, organizational hierarchies, and job listings in a print queue.
Dynamic Object	Dynamic Object interfaces are used to work with dynamic data in a directory service. These interfaces are used by directory objects that are not represented in the underlying directory service to handle dynamic information such as commands issued over a network.
Security	Security interfaces allow an ADSI client to establish its credentials to a server and use security features such as the access control list and security descriptors.
Non-Automation	Non-Automation interfaces allow non-automation clients, such as C++ applications, low-overhead access to directory objects by providing *VTable* access to methods for managing and searching directory service objects.
Extension	Extension interfaces allow ADSI clients to extend the functionality of existing ADSI classes to offer customized solutions.
Utility	Utility interfaces provide advanced helper functions for managing ADSI objects.
Data Type	Data Type interfaces provide methods to access ADSI data types.

Table 10-1.   ADSI Interface Categories and Descriptions

Many ADSI interfaces are designed to support client access through Automation and non-Automation. For this reason, there are dual interfaces for client access—through both **IUnknown** and **IDispatch** interfaces. If you are writing a non-automation client in C/C++, you will resolve method invocation directly, using the **IUnknown**::*QueryInterface,* and call the method directly. Let us look at some of these categories in more detail.

Core Interfaces

ADSI core interfaces are the following:

▼ **IADs**

■ **IADsContainer**

■ **IADsNamespaces**

▲ **IADsOpenDSObject**

The **IADs** interface defines basic object features including properties and methods for all ADSI objects including users, computers, services, file systems, and so on. Every ADSI object must support this interface. This interface ensures that ADSI objects provide network administrators and directory service providers with a simple and consistent representation of various underlying directory services. The directory services include identifying objects by name or class, identifying the object's container that manages the object's creation and deletion, retrieving the object's schema definition, loading an object's attributes to the property cache, and committing changes to the persistent directory store. This interface supports a number of methods, including the IUnknown method **QueryInterface**, IDispatch methods **GetTypeInfo** and **GetIDsOfNames**, and IADs property methods **get_Name**, **get_Class**, and **get_GUID** as shown in Figure   .

The **IADsContainer** interface enables an ADSI container object, such as the namespace object, to create, delete, and manage contained ADSI objects. You can recursively use this interface to navigate down a hierarchy tree of objects. For example, you can use this interface on an object to query the children of that object. You can then use this interface to query each of the child objects to query their children and so on. You know if you have reached a leaf node (an object without a child) if the **IADsContainer** interface is not supported. Although you can query the **IADsContainer** interface to determine if an object is a container or not, a much simpler way is to invoke the **IADsClass::get_Container** method on the object's schema class object. This method returns TRUE if the object is a container, FALSE otherwise. The interfaces supported by an ADSI container object are shown in Figure 10-2.

A namespace object is a top-level container that is equivalent to the root node of a directory tree. The **IADsNamespaces** interface is implemented in namespace objects. This interface is used to manage namespace objects. You can use this to get and set the *DefaultContainer* property. This property holds the path to a container object. This interface supports the IUnknown methods **QueryInterface**, **AddRef**, and **Release** and **IADsNamespaces** property methods **get/put_DefaultContainer**.

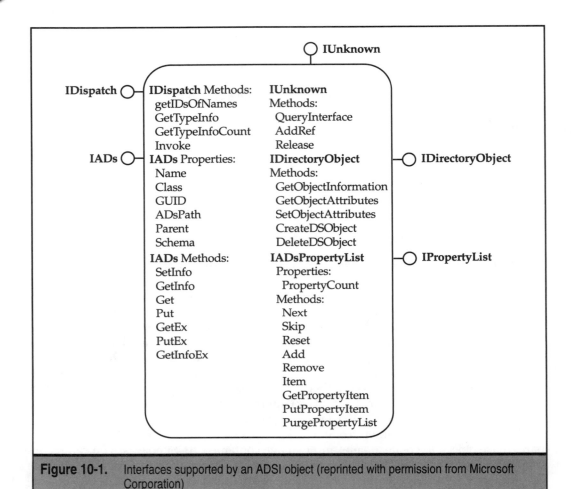

Figure 10-1.   Interfaces supported by an ADSI object (reprinted with permission from Microsoft Corporation)

The **IADsOpenDSObject** interface provides a security context for binding to an Active Directory object. For example, a security context is required when specifying credentials of a client. ADSI maintains the security context in its cache throughout the connection within a process. Once authenticated, the supplied user credentials are applied to all subsequent actions performed on this object and its children. The user credentials are also applied to binding to different objects as well, provided that the binding takes place within the same connection and process. You can get the cache handle by calling the **OpenDSObject** method of this interface. Keep in mind that when you release the cache handle, the security context is also released as well. **OpenDSObject** also provides you the ability to encrypt the data exchange over the network between your application and the directory server.

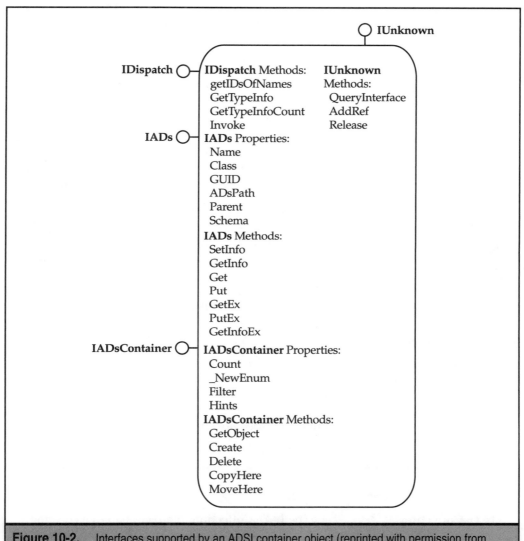

Figure 10-2.   Interfaces supported by an ADSI container object (reprinted with permission from Microsoft Corporation)

Schema Interfaces

The schema interfaces are the following:

▼ **IADsClass**

■ **IADsProperty**

▲ **IADsSyntax**

The **IADsClass** interface manages the schema class objects. This interface is complex compared to the other ADSI interfaces. This interface supports a number of methods including the **IUnknown** method **QueryInterface**, **IDispatch** methods **GetTypeInfo** and **GetIDsOfNames**, and **IADsClass** property methods **get_PrimaryInterface**, **get/put_CLSID**, and **get/put_OID**.

The **IADsProperty** interface manages the attribute definition, such as that for an object attribute. You can use the **IADsProperty** interface's methods to add new attributes and property objects to a provider-specific implementation.

You can use the **IADsSyntax** interface to process the property values of an instance of an ADSI schema class object. This interface supports a number of methods including the **IUnknown** method **QueryInterface**, **IDispatch** methods **GetTypeInfoCount** and **GetIDsOfNames**, and **IADsSyntax** property methods **get/put_OleAutoDataType**.

Persistent Object Interfaces

As mentioned earlier, persistent object interfaces manipulate persistent data in the name space of the underlying directory service. These interfaces are used to provide access to persistent data of an object such as user accounts, file shares, organizational hierarchies, and job listings in a print queue.

There are a number of these interfaces; they are summarized in Table 10-2.

Persistent Object Interface	Description
IADsCollection	The **IADsCollection** interface enables its hosting ADSI object to define and manage an arbitrary set of named data elements for a directory service. Of the ADSI system providers, only the WinNT and NWCOMPAT providers support this interface to handle active file service sessions, resources, and print jobs.

Table 10-2. Persistent Object Interfaces

Persistent Object Interface	Description
IADsComputer	The **IADsComputer** interface represents and manages any computer, including servers, clients, etc. Using the properties of this interface, you can access the information about the computer such as the operating system, the make and model, the processor, the computer identifier, or its network addresses.
IADsDomain	The **IADsDomain** interface represents a network domain and can be used to manage the accounts on the domain. Using this interface, you can examine whether the domain is actually a Workgroup, specify how frequently a user must change her password, etc. **IADsDomain** is a dual interface that inherits from **IADs**. For the WinNT provider supplied by Microsoft, this interface is implemented on the WinNTDomain object.
IADsFileService	The **IADsFileService** interface represents file services supported in the directory service. Using this interface, you can discover and change the maximum number of users simultaneously running a file service. **IADsFileService** is a dual interface that inherits from **IADsService**. For the WinNT provider supplied by Microsoft, this interface is implemented on the WinNTService object.
IADsFileShare	The **IADsFileShare** interface represents a published file share across the network. The **IADsFileShare** interface is a dual interface that inherits from **IADs**.
IADsGroup	The **IADsGroup** interface represents and manages group membership information in a directory service. Using this interface, you can retrieve member objects, test if a given object belongs to the group, and add/remove an object to/from the group. **IADsGroup** is a dual interface that inherits from **IADs**.

Table 10-2.   Persistent Object Interfaces (continued)

Persistent Object Interface	Description
IADsLocality	A directory service can provide hierarchical groupings of the directory entries by country, locality, organization, or organization unit. The **IADsLocality** interface represents the geographical location, or region, of a directory entity. Using this, you can organize by locality (region). This interface is similar to the **IADsO** interface (listed later in this table), which manages organization, and the **IADsOU** interface (listed later in this table), which manages the organization unit. **IADsLocality** is a dual interface that inherits from **IADs**.
IADsMembers	The **IADsMembers** interface is used to manage a collection of ADSI objects belonging to a group. You can use this interface to support group membership for individual accounts. **IADsMembers** is a dual interface.
IADsO	The **IADsO** interface represents and manages the organization of a directory entity. Using this, you can organize by organization. This interface is similar to the **IADsLocality** interface (listed earlier in this table), which manages locality, and the **IADsOU** interface (listed next in this table), which manages the organization unit. **IADsO** is a dual interface that inherits from **IADs**.
IADsOU	The **IADsOU** interface represents and manages the organizational unit of a directory entity. Using this, you can organize by organizational unit. This interface is similar to the **IADsLocality** interface (listed earlier in this table), which manages locality, and the **IADsO** interface (listed in the preceding row in this table), which manages the organization unit. **IADsOU** is a dual interface that inherits from **IADs**.

Table 10-2.   Persistent Object Interfaces *(continued)*

Persistent Object Interface	Description
IADsPrintjob	The **IADsPrintJob** interface represents a print job that gets created in the print queue when a user submits a request to a printer to print a document. Using this interface, you can get information about the print job such as the printer that will print the document, who submitted the document, the time it was submitted, and the number of pages. **IADsPrintJob** is a dual interface that inherits from **IADs**.
IADsPrintQueue	The **IADsPrintQueue** interface represents a printer on a network. Using this interface, you can get information about the printer including the printer model, its physical location, the network address, etc. You can also use this interface to browse through a collection of print jobs in the print queue. **IADsPrintQueue** is a dual interface that inherits from **IADs**.
IADsService	The **IADsService** interface maintains information about system services running on a host computer. The information about any system service includes the path to the executable file on the host computer, the type of the service, other services required to run a particular service, etc. Services include the Microsoft Fax Service, Routing and Remote Access Service, etc. **IADsService** is a dual interface that inherits from **IADs**.
IADsUser	The **IADsUser** interface represents and manages an end-user account on a network. Using this interface, you can access and manipulate the information about an end-user account including names of the user, telephone numbers, job title, etc. Using this interface, you can also determine the group association of the user and set/change the user password. **IADsUser** is a dual interface that inherits from **IADs**.

Table 10-2.   Persistent Object Interfaces *(continued)*

Dynamic Object

Dynamic information is information that has a relatively short life, such as commands issued over a network or status of print jobs. Due to the short life, these objects are not represented in a persistent manner in the underlying directory service. Dynamic Object interfaces are used to work with such dynamic data.

There are a number of these interfaces; they are summarized in Table 10-3.

Dynamic Object Interfaces	Description
IADsComputerOperations	The **IADsComputerOperations** interface provides methods for performing remote system administration. Using this interface, you can retrieve the status of a computer. You can also enable remote shutdown. **IADsComputerOperations** is a dual interface that inherits from **IADs**.
IADsFileServiceOperations	The **IADsFileServiceOperations** interface extends the functionality of the **IADsServiceOperations** interface, for managing the file service across a network. Using this interface, you can maintain and manage open resources and active sessions of the file service. **IADsFileService Operations** is a dual interface that inherits from **IADsServiceOperations**.
IADsPrintQueueOperations	The **IADsPrintQueueOperations** interface manages a network printer. You can use this interface to retrieve all print jobs submitted to a print queue, to suspend and resume the print queue, and to remove all print jobs from the print queue. **IADsPrintQueueOperations** is a dual interface that inherits from **IADs**.

Table 10-3. Dynamic Object Interfaces

Dynamic Object Interfaces	Description
IADsFileService	The **IADsFileService** interface represents file services supported in the directory service. Using this interface, you can discover and change the maximum number of users simultaneously running a file service. **IADsFileService** is a dual interface that inherits from **IADsService**. For the WinNT provider supplied by Microsoft, this interface is implemented on the WinNTService object.
IADsResource	An open resource is a folder or a subfolder on a public share point on a target computer when the folder or a subfolder has been opened by a remote user. ADSI represents an open resource with a resource object. The **IADsResource** interface implemented for the resource object manages the open resource for a file service across a network. **IADsResource** is a dual interface that inherits from **IADs**.
IADsServiceOperations	The **IADsServiceOperations** interface manages system services installed on a computer. Using this interface, you can start, pause, and stop a system service, change the password, and examine the status of a given service across a network. **IADsServiceOperations** is a dual interface that inherits from **IADs**.

Table 10-3.   Dynamic Object Interfaces *(continued)*

Dynamic Object Interfaces	Description
IADsSession	The **IADsSession** interface represents an active session for file service across a network. An active session is established between a remote user and a machine when the remote user opens resources on that machine. The remote user can open more than one resource in a single active session. Using this interface, you can examine session-specific information such as the user who is using the session, the computer that is being used, and the length of time that the user has been logged on for the current session.
IADsMembers	The **IADsMembers** interface is used to manage a collection of ADSI objects belonging to a group. You can use this interface to support group membership for individual accounts. **IADsMembers** is a dual interface.

Table 10-3.   Dynamic Object Interfaces *(continued)*

Security Interfaces

Security interfaces allow an ADSI client to establish its credentials to a server and use security features such as the access control list and security descriptors. The security interfaces are:

▼ **IADsAccessControlEntry**

■ **IADsAccessControlList**

▲ **IADsSecurityDescriptor**

The **IADsAccessControlEntry** interface enables directory clients to access and manipulate individual ACEs (see ACEs earlier in this chapter under "Active Directory Security") of the owning object. An object can have a number of ACEs, one for each client or a group of clients. ACEs are maintained in an access-control list (ACL), which implements the **IADsAccessControlList** interface. To access the ACL, you must obtain the object's security descriptor that implements the **IADsSecurityDescriptor** interface.

To make any new or modified ACEs persistent, you need to do the following:

▼   Add the ACEs to the ACL.

■   Assign the ACL to the security descriptor.

▲   Commit the security descriptor to the directory store.

The **IADsAccessControlList** interface manages individual ACEs. Access control implementation is provider-specific. Among the providers supplied by Microsoft, currently, only the LDAP provider supports access controls. Using the **IADsAccessControlList** interface, you can retrieve and enumerate ACEs, add new entries, or remove current ones.

The **IADsSecurityDescriptor** interface provides access to security descriptor object properties. Using this interface, you can examine and change the access controls to a directory service object as well as make copies of a security descriptor.

Non-Automation Interfaces

ADSI includes automation and non-automation interfaces. Non-automation interface methods are enabled by means of a direct on-the-wire protocol and are executed as soon as they are called. Properties are not cached using the ADSI property cache. Automation interface methods are invoked in batch, and the properties are cached in the ADSI property cache. Non-automation clients can call the methods of non-automation interfaces such as **IDirectoryObject** to optimize performance and take full advantage of native directory service interfaces. Automation clients cannot use **IDirectoryObject**. Instead, they should use the **IADs** interface.

The programming samples in this chapter use non-automation interfaces. The non-automation interfaces are:

▼   **IDirectoryObject**

▲   **IDirectorySearch**

The **IDirectoryObject** interface provides non-automation clients with direct access to directory service objects. Instead of the properties supported by the **IADs** interface, **IDirectoryObject** provides methods that support a subset of an object's properties and provides access to its attributes. Using this interface, you can get or set any number of object attributes with one method call. Of the Microsoft-supplied providers, only the LDAP provider supports this interface. The **IDirectoryObject** interface is a pure COM interface.

The **IDirectorySearch** interface provides non-automation clients methods to perform queries on the underlying directory. This interface has a low overhead. Of the Microsoft-supplied providers, only the LDAP provider supports this interface. The **IDirectorySearch** interface is a pure COM interface.

PROGRAMMING LANGUAGE SUPPORT

You can write ADSI client applications in a number of different ways including Visual Basic, C/C++, VBScript, Microsoft JScript, or as a Web application using Active Server Pages. The client could be automation or non-automation applications. Figure 10-3 depicts how the different applications use the ADSI interfaces.

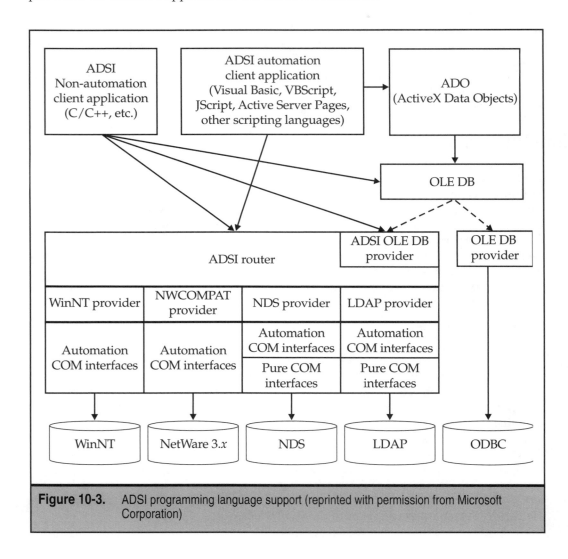

Figure 10-3.   ADSI programming language support (reprinted with permission from Microsoft Corporation)

As shown in the figure, ADSI defines interfaces and objects accessible from automation clients written in languages such as Microsoft Visual Basic, and Microsoft Visual Basic Scripting Edition (VBScript), and Java, as well as non-automation clients written in languages such as C and C++. For integration with OLE DB applications, ADSI supplies an OLE DB provider. The OLE DB provider supports a subset of the OLE DB query interfaces and provides read-only access to Active Directory. Internet applications can use scripting in Active Server Pages (*.asp*) files to create and manipulate ADSI objects on the server and display the results in a Web page.

ACTIVE DIRECTORY USES

There are a variety of uses for Active Directory. It is conceivable that server applications can advertise themselves as available to client applications, which may then connect to them. Clients can query the directory and locate server applications to serve their requirements. Security products can use Active Directory to store and retrieve a user's digital certificates. It is also used for storing domain, group, and user information. ADSI provides a single, consistent, open set of interfaces independent of the underlying directories and thus enables the use of multiple directories.

Extending Active Directory Functionality Using Providers

ADSI is extensible, and directory providers, software vendors, and end users can extend ADSI with new objects and functions. The actual implementation is transparent to you as the developer of a directory-based application, since the interface to your application remains the same, as shown in Figure 10-4.

File Sharing

You can publish any shared network folder, such as a distributed file system (DFS) folder, in Active Directory. Keep in mind, however, that creating a shared folder in Active Directory by itself does not automatically share the folder. To create a shared folder, first share the folder, and then publish it in Active Directory.

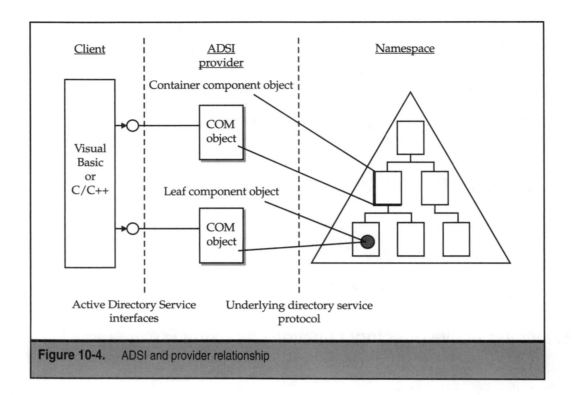

Figure 10-4.   ADSI and provider relationship

PROGRAMMING EXAMPLES USING THE ACTIVE DIRECTORY

Three sample applications that are shown here intend to show the general concept of managing objects in the Active Directory. They are, therefore, kept simple, and are also intended to be able to run in any Windows 2000 environment from a machine attached to a domain. The first one adds a domain user to the domain and modifies the user's properties. The second sample queries a domain user's properties, and the last one deletes a user in the domain.

Shown next is the sample that will create a user. The project is created using Visual Studio as a Win32 Console Application. In order to run this application, the user needs to be logged onto a domain and should have administrative privileges in order to create users. When the application is started, it will prompt for the container path name where the user is to be created. A container path of the form

```
LDAP://CN=Users,DC=ns10,DC=bethesda,DC=ibm,DC=com
```

can be entered where *DC* is your domain controller. The code also prompts for a user name and SAM Account Name. A name is given for each prompt, and the user will be created.

Active Directory uses Unicode strings, and hence the definition of UNICODE in the code as well as the inclusion of the wide character string functions header file, *wchar.h*. The Active Directory interfaces are defined through the master include file *activeds.h*. This is included in all the Active Directory client applications. After compilation, during the link step, the application is also linked with two active directory libraries, *activeds.lib* and *adsiid.lib*. In order to handle the Unicode strings more easily, this sample, as well as the next two, use **wmain** instead of **main**. By doing this, conversion between multibyte to wide characters can be avoided.

```
#define UNICODE
#define _WIN32_DCOM

#include <windows.h>
#include <wchar.h>
#include <activeds.h>

void wmain (int argc, wchar_t *argv[])
{

    HRESULT     hr;
    WCHAR pwLdap[256];
    WCHAR pwUser[64];
    WCHAR pwSAMName[32];
    WCHAR pwCN[128];
    IDirectoryObject *pDirContainer = NULL;

    wprintf (L"\nEnter the container path name where the new \
                user is created: ");
    wscanf (L"%ls",pwLdap);
    wprintf (L"\nEnter the user name: ");
    wscanf (L"%ls", pwUser);
    wsprintfW (pwCN, L"CN=%s", pwUser);
    wprintf (L"\nEnter the SAM-Account-Name: ");
    wscanf (L"%ls", pwSAMName);

    CoInitializeEx(NULL,COINIT_APARTMENTTHREADED);
```

We will be the COM library to access the ADSI, and so the COM library is initialized by calling **CoInitializeEx**. The first thing that needs to be done prior to accessing the Active Directory object is to bind to the object. Binding to an Active Directory object allows the application to then navigate through the object and manage it. There are two ways to bind to the Active Directory object. An application can use the **ADsGetObject** ADSI function to bind to an Active Directory object on behalf of the current user who is running the application. Alternatively, if an application would like to pass on new credentials for binding to an object, it can use the **ADsOpenObject** ADSI function. To bind to an object, a path name is used. This ADsPath consists of a provider and the path to the object. The ADSI provider for the Windows 2000 Active Directory is LDAP. This provider name is case sensitive and is followed by "*://*". The rest of the syntax depends on the individual providers. Examples of providers are WinNT for communicating with Windows NT 4.0 Primary Domain Controllers and Backup Domain Controllers, NDS for Novell Directory Services servers, and NWCOMPAT for accessing Novell NetWare servers. The provider is followed by the hostname, port number, and DN of the object. A sample pathname string is shown here:

```
LDAP://mydomain.mycompany.com:389/CN=Users,DC=ns10,DC=bethesda,DC=ibm,DC=com
```

or

```
LDAP://CN=Users,DC=ns10,DC=bethesda,DC=ibm,DC=com
```

If a hostname is not provided, it will bind to the container that contains the domain object that is currently logged on. Along with the AdsPath, the interface ID for the requested interface is passed. In order to add a user object to the directory, the **IDirectoryObject** interface is requested. The **IDirectoryObject** interface gives access to the directory service objects. Once we get access to this interface, methods are available in the interface to create a new directory object. A pointer to hold the interface is also passed in. Upon successful completion of this function, an interface pointer is returned and methods can be invoked on that interface. To create a user object, other interfaces such as **IADs** can also be used. However, the non-automation interface, **IDirectoryObject**, is optimized for performance. Properties manipulated using this interface are not cached, unlike those in the automation interfaces. Luckily, this sample is a non-automation client, thus enabling us to use the **IDirectoryObject** interface.

The **ADsGetObject** ADSI function, as well as other ADSI functions, returns the standard **HRESULT** return value. It returns S_OK when successful. The error values are typically of the format 0x00005xxx, 0x80005xxx for generic ADSI errors and 0x8007xxxx for Win32 error codes for ADSI.

```
do
{
    hr = ADsGetObject(pwLdap, IID_IDirectoryObject,
                      (void **)&pDirContainer);
    if (FAILED(hr))
```

```
{
    wprintf (L"Failed to bind to the object. HR = %x", hr);
    break;
}
```

After binding to the object, the next step is to create a user object in the directory. This sample uses the **CreateDSObject** method to create the user object as the child object of the directory. An array of attributes or properties is passed, and these attributes are set to the newly created user object. A user object has many properties that can be set. This sample sets a minimum number of properties that are required to create the user object. These are the common name of the user object and the **sAMAccountName**. Please refer to the SDK for a complete set of properties. The properties set by this sample are **objectClass** and **sAMAccountName**. This will create a user object but leaves the account disabled; the user cannot log on using this ID. The properties array is an array of ADS_ATTR_INFO structures, with each structure representing one property.

```
ADSVALUE      sAMValue;
ADSVALUE      classValue;

sAMValue.dwType = ADSTYPE_CASE_IGNORE_STRING;
sAMValue.CaseIgnoreString = pwSAMName;

classValue.dwType = ADSTYPE_CASE_IGNORE_STRING;
classValue.CaseIgnoreString = L"User";

ADS_ATTR_INFO adsAttrInfo[] = {
    { L"objectClass", ADS_ATTR_UPDATE,
        ADSTYPE_CASE_IGNORE_STRING, &classValue, 1},
    { L"sAMAccountName", ADS_ATTR_UPDATE,
        ADSTYPE_CASE_IGNORE_STRING, &sAMValue, 1},
};

LPDISPATCH  pDispatch = NULL;
hr = pDirContainer->CreateDSObject(pwCN, adsAttrInfo,
                                    2, &pDispatch);
if (FAILED (hr))
{
    wprintf (L"Failed creating the user. HR = %x", hr);
    break;
}
else
{
    wprintf (L"Successfully created the user.");
```

```
        }
        IADsUser *pUser = NULL;
```

By default, the user object is created with the account disabled. This will prevent the user from logging on. Though these properties can be set during creation, this sample shows how to reset the properties by accessing the **IADsUser** interface and resetting the properties. The **IADsUser** interface is specifically designed to manage the user account object. It inherits from the **IADs** interface and exposes methods that can be used to get/put various user properties. The **put_AccountDisabled** method is used to enable the account. When a property is set, it is cached locally, and to propagate this property to the underlying data store, it should be flushed by calling the **SetInfo** method. **SetInfo** saves the cached properties to the data store. Since this saving causes a trip to the network, it has a performance hit, and it will be wise to call this method once after setting all the properties for a user object.

```
        hr = pDispatch->QueryInterface(IID_IADsUser, (void **)&pUser);
        if (FAILED (hr))
        {
            wprintf (L"Could not change the user properties. HR = %x", hr);
        }
        else
        {
            hr = pUser->put_AccountDisabled(false);
            hr = pUser->SetInfo();
            wprintf (L"User account enabled.");
        }
```

Like any other OLE interface objects, the interface objects are released after use.

```
        if (pDispatch)
            pDispatch->Release();
        pDispatch = NULL;
        if (pUser)
            pUser->Release();
        pUser = NULL;
    } while (0);
    CoUninitialize();
}
```

The next sample queries a user from the Windows 2000 Active Directory and displays some of the user's properties. This sample, like the earlier one, is created using Visual Studio as a Win32 Console Application. Having created the project, we update it to link with ADSI-related libraries.

```
#define UNICODE
#define _WIN32_DCOM

#include <windows.h>
#include <wchar.h>
#include <activeds.h>

void DisplayUserInfo (IADsUser *pUser);
void DispBool (WCHAR *str, VARIANT_BOOL vBool);
void DispBStr (WCHAR *str, BSTR bstr);
void DispDate (WCHAR *str, DATE date);
void DispError (WCHAR *str, HRESULT hr);

void wmain (int argc, wchar_t *argv[])
{

    HRESULT     hr;
    WCHAR pwUser[64];
    IADs *pObject = NULL;
    IADs *pUserObject = NULL;
    IADsUser *pUser = NULL;
    IDirectorySearch *pDS = NULL;
    VARIANT var;
    WCHAR     pwBindPath[MAX_PATH];

    wprintf (L"\nEnter the user name: ");
    wscanf (L"%ls", pwUser);

    CoInitializeEx(NULL,COINIT_APARTMENTTHREADED);
```

Every domain controller has a top-level object. This top-level object is represented by a unique entry called RootDSE. This RootDSE stores information related to the connected domain controller. It provides information related to the directory server, its capabilities, the LDAP version the server supports, various naming contexts that exist under this root, and so on. Essentially, the RootDSE can be considered to contain the table of contents for the domain controller. In order to search for a user object in the directory, the application should first bind to the object from where to search. This sample binds to the RootDSE and then opens the **defaultNamingContext**, which is the distinguished name of the domain directory.

In the earlier sample, the application bound to the object by calling the **ADsGetObject** ADSI function. Here it uses the **ADsOpenObject** ADSI function. Being passed NULL for user name and password, as well as the ADS_SECURE_AUTHENTICATION flag, the function uses the security context of the calling thread, which in this case is the currently logged on user. The code binds to the RootDSE object in order to query the

defaultNamingContext. From the **IADs** interface the **defaultNamingContext** is retrieved using the **Get** method. Once we have the **defaultNamingContext**, the application binds to the domain root and gets the **IDirectorySearch** interface. The
IDirectorySearch interface provides a high-level and low-overhead non-automation interface for querying data of a directory.

```
do
{
    if (FAILED (hr = ADsOpenObject (L"LDAP://rootDSE", NULL, NULL,
                                    ADS_SECURE_AUTHENTICATION,
                                    IID_IADs,
                                    (void **)&pObject)))
    {
        wprintf (L"Failed to bind to the domain. HR = %x", hr);
        break;
    }
    if (FAILED(hr = pObject->Get(L"defaultNamingContext", &var)))
    {
        wprintf (L"Failed to get the default naming context. HR = %x",
                hr);
        break;
    }
    wcscpy(pwBindPath, L"LDAP://");
    wcscat(pwBindPath, var.bstrVal);

    if (FAILED(hr = ADsOpenObject(pwBindPath, NULL, NULL,
                        ADS_SECURE_AUTHENTICATION, IID_IDirectorySearch,
                        (void **)&pDS)))
    {
        wprintf (L"Failed to bind to %ls. HR = %x", pwBindPath, hr);
        break;
    }
```

Once we have the directory search interface, we are ready to search by some search filter. ADSI supports two types of search filters. The search filters can be provided either using
SQL dialect or using LDAP dialect. The SQL dialect query is the typical SQL query that is
used in the database environment. The LDAP dialect query is based on RFC 2254, and the
search filters are specified by Unicode strings. A few samples of the search filter are:

```
(objectClass=*)
```

This indicates all objects.

```
(&(objectCategory=person)(objectClass=user))
```

This indicates all users in the directory.

```
(&(objectCategory=person)(objectClass=user)(giveName=John)(sn=Z*))
```

This indicates all users whose given name is John and whose surname starts with Z.

```
(&(objectCategory=person)(objectClass=user)(sn=Z*)
        (|(st=Maryland)(st=Virginia)))
```

This indicates all users whose surname starts with Z in the state of Maryland or Virginia.

The search filter in this sample looks for all users with a user-specified cn in the object category person and object class user. To search for users, the query should contain both object category and object class. Since the computer object is a subclass of user, by specifying just the objectClass as user (objectClass=user), we arrange that the search will return both the user and the computer with the given cn. Furthermore, the object category of the user is *not* user but person. Therefore, a search containing just the object category as user (objectCategory=user) will not return any user.

This sample creates a search filter that is of the format (&(objectCategory=person) (objectClass=user) (cn=<*name*>)), where *name* is the user-specified name.

```
WCHAR    pwSearchFilter[MAX_PATH*2];
wcscpy(pwSearchFilter,
        L"(&(objectCategory=person)(objectClass=user)(cn=");
wcscat(pwSearchFilter, pwUser);
wcscat(pwSearchFilter, L"))");
```

The **ExecuteSearch** method of the directory search interface is used to search the directory for the user. Along with the search criteria, an array of attribute names for which the data is requested as part of the search is passed. Since this sample turns around and binds to the user object, it just needs the AdsPath. The number of attributes in the attribute array is also passed. Upon successful completion, the **ExecuteSearch** method returns a handle to the search context. This search handle can be used in other **IDirectorySearch** methods to examine and navigate through the search results.

```
ADS_SEARCH_HANDLE hSearch;
WCHAR    *pwAttr[1] = {L"ADsPath"};

if (FAILED (hr = pDS->ExecuteSearch(pwSearchFilter, pwAttr,
                                      1, &hSearch)))
{
    wprintf (L"Search failed. HR = %x", hr);
    break;
}
```

Once the search is executed and a search handle is retrieved, the **GetNextRow** method is used to navigate through the search results. This method moves the search handle to the next row in the search results. If this is the first time it is called, then it calls the **GetFirstRow** method underneath the covers. If there is a need to go to the previous row in the application, then the results can be optionally cached to scroll backward using the **GetPreviousRow** method. If, however, the ADSI provider does not provide cursor support, this method will fail. By default the results are cached, but this and other search preferences can be set by calling the **SetSearchPreference** method before executing the search.

```
if (pDS->GetNextRow(hSearch)   == S_ADS_NOMORE_ROWS)
{
    wprintf (L"User not found.");
    break;
}
```

After moving to the row of interest, in this sample the first row, the attribute of interest, AdsPath, is retrieved by calling the **GetColumn** method. The method allocates memory for the data that needs to be freed by calling **FreeColumn.** Once we have the ADsPath for the user, the sample binds to that object and later queries the **IADsUser** interface.

```
ADS_SEARCH_COLUMN    searchColumn;
hr = pDS->GetColumn(hSearch, pwAttr[0], &searchColumn);
WCHAR pwADsPath [MAX_PATH];
wcscpy (pwADsPath, searchColumn.pADsValues->CaseIgnoreString);

if (FAILED(hr = ADsOpenObject (pwADsPath, NULL, NULL,
                   ADS_SECURE_AUTHENTICATION,
                   IID_IADs, (void **) &pUserObject)))
{
    wprintf (L"Bind to user object failed. HR = %x", hr);
    break;
}
pDS->FreeColumn(&searchColumn);
pDS->CloseSearchHandle(hSearch);
```

During the process, **ExecuteSearch** resources are allocated that are freed by calling **CloseSearchHandle**. This closes the search handle and frees all the resources associated with the search handle. For every search handle that was returned by **ExecuteSearch**, the application should call **CloseSearchHandle** to free the resources.

```
if (FAILED(hr = pUserObject->QueryInterface(IID_IADsUser,
                              (void **)&pUser)))
    {
```

```
                wprintf (L"Failed to access user info. HR = %x", hr);
                break;
        }
```

With the user object retrieved, a helper function, **DisplayUserInfo**, is called to display the information about the user.

```
        DisplayUserInfo(pUser);
    } while (0);

    if (pObject)
        pObject->Release();
    if (pUserObject)
        pUserObject->Release();
    if (pDS)
        pDS->Release();
    if (pUser)
        pUser->Release();
    CoUninitialize();
}
```

A wide variety of information regarding the user can be retrieved using the **IADsPath** interface. For brevity, however, this sample just queries a few attributes and displays them.

```
void DisplayUserInfo (IADsUser *pUser)
{
    BSTR bstr;
    VARIANT_BOOL vBool;
    HRESULT hr;
    DATE date;


    if (FAILED(hr = pUser->get_FirstName(&bstr)))
    {
        DispError (L"First Name", hr);
    }
    else
    {
        DispBStr (L"First Name", bstr);
    }
```

```
if (FAILED(hr = pUser->get_LastName(&bstr)))
{
    DispError (L"Last Name", hr);
}
else
{
    DispBStr (L"Last Name", bstr);
}

if (FAILED(hr = pUser->get_AccountDisabled(&vBool)))
{
    DispError (L"AccountDisabled", hr);
}
else
{
    DispBool (L"AccountDisabled", vBool);
}

if (FAILED(hr = pUser->get_IsAccountLocked(&vBool)))
{
    DispError (L"IsAccountLocked", hr);
}
else
{
    DispBool (L"IsAccountLocked", vBool);
}

if (FAILED(hr = pUser->get_LastLogin(&date)))
{
    DispError (L"LastLogin", hr);
}
else
{
    DispDate (L"LastLogin", date);
}

if (FAILED(hr = pUser->get_LastFailedLogin(&date)))
{
    DispError (L"LastFailedLogin", hr);
}
else
{
    DispDate (L"LastFailedLogin", date);
}
```

```
        if (FAILED(hr = pUser->get_PasswordLastChanged(&date)))
        {
            DispError (L"PasswordLastChange", hr);
        }
        else
        {
            DispDate (L"PasswordLastChange", date);
        }

        if (FAILED(hr = pUser->get_PasswordExpirationDate(&date)))
        {
            DispError (L"PasswordExpirationDate", hr);
        }
        else
        {
            DispDate (L"PasswordExpirationDate", date);
        }
}

void DispBool (WCHAR *str, VARIANT_BOOL vBool)
{
    if (vBool)
    {
        wprintf (L"%s property is TRUE\n", str);
    }
    else
    {
        wprintf (L"%s property is FALSE\n", str);
    }
}

void DispBStr (WCHAR *str, BSTR bstr)
{
    wprintf (L"%ls: %ls\n", str, bstr);
    SysFreeString (bstr);
}

void DispDate (WCHAR *str, DATE date)
{
    VARIANT var;
    var.vt = VT_DATE;
    var.date = date;
    VariantChangeType (&var, &var, VARIANT_NOVALUEPROP, VT_BSTR);
```

```
      wprintf (L"%ls: %s\n", str, var.bstrVal);
}

void DispError (WCHAR *str, HRESULT hr)
{
    if (hr == E_ADS_PROPERTY_NOT_FOUND)
        wprintf (L"%s property not found.\n", str);
    else
        wprintf (L"Error retrieving %s property. Error = %x\n", str, hr);
}
```

The last sample deletes the user from the Active Directory. This sample is very similar to the first sample that was discussed earlier. The user is prompted for the directory path and the cn of the user to be deleted from the directory. After binding to the user object and retrieving the **IdirectoryObject**, **DeleteDSObject** is called to delete the user object. When the application is started, it will prompt for the container pathname where the user is to be created. A container path of the form

```
LDAP://CN=Users,DC=ns10,DC=bethesda,DC=ibm,DC=com
```

can be entered, where *DC* is your domain controller. It then prompts for the user's common name. With this data, the application queries and deletes the user object with the given common name.

```
#define UNICODE
#define _WIN32_DCOM

#include <windows.h>
#include <wchar.h>
#include <activeds.h>

void wmain (int argc, wchar_t *argv[])
{
    HRESULT     hr;
    WCHAR pwLdap[256];
    WCHAR pwUser[64];
    WCHAR pwCN[128];
    IDirectoryObject *pDirContainer = NULL;
```

```
wprintf(L"\nEnter the container path name where the user is deleted: ");
wscanf (L"%ls",pwLdap);
wprintf (L"\nEnter the user name: ");
wscanf (L"%ls", pwUser);
wsprintfW (pwCN, L"CN=%s", pwUser);

CoInitializeEx(NULL,COINIT_APARTMENTTHREADED);

do
{
    hr = ADsGetObject(pwLdap, IID_IDirectoryObject,
                       (void **)&pDirContainer);
    if (FAILED(hr))
    {
        wprintf (L"Failed to bind to the user object. HR = %x", hr);
        break;
    }
    hr = pDirContainer->DeleteDSObject(pwCN);
    if (FAILED (hr))
    {
        wprintf (L"Failed creating the user. HR = %x", hr);
    }
    else
    {
        wprintf (L"Successfully created the user.");
    }
} while (0);
CoUninitialize();
}
```

CONCLUSION

This chapter covered one of the most important new topics in Windows 2000—the Active Directory. It is important to keep in mind that the Active Directory is a vast area, and it is not possible to do full justice to this topic in just one chapter.

CHAPTER 11

Registry Programming

Ever since Microsoft moved all those *ini* settings of Windows 3.*x* to the Registry, the role of the Registry has been steadily increasing as a central repository of configuration information for all applications. In the process of setting up a Registry, the role of updating configuration information has also shifted from the end user (who was expected to update the *ini* settings) to you, the application developer. You are expected to provide an install program that automatically creates the Registry entries when your application is installed and delete those entries when your application is uninstalled.

INTRODUCTION TO THE REGISTRY

The Windows 2000 Registry is the repository that stores information about the computer's configuration. The information contained in the Registry includes:

▼ User profiles

■ Hardware information including ports usage

■ Applications installed on the computer

■ Document types that each application can create

▲ Property settings for folders and program icons

The Registry is a heavily used database. Most Windows operations refer to the values in the Registry.

STRUCTURE OF THE REGISTRY

The Registry is organized hierarchically as a tree consisting of subtrees, keys, subkeys, and entries. A subtree is a part of the overall tree that groups together related Registry keys. There are five subtrees through which all Registry keys, subkeys, and assigned values are accessed; these subtrees are listed in Table 11-1. Each node in the tree is called a *key*. Each key can contain both subkeys and data values (or neither). The data values can be of different types, including binary, string, link, and so on.

At the next level of the hierarchy, each of these subtrees contain keys. For example, the HKEY_LOCAL_MACHINE subtree contains the five keys listed in Table 11-2.

Subtree	Description
HKEY_CURRENT_USER	Root of the user's profile (configuration) information for the user currently logged on. User profile information includes the user's folders, screen colors, and Control Panel settings.
HKEY_USERS	Root of all user profiles on the computer. HKEY_CURRENT_USER is an alias for a key in the HKEY_USERS subtree.
HKEY_LOCAL_MACHINE	Configuration information of the computer that contains the Registry. This configuration information applies to all users defined for the computer.
HKEY_CLASSES_ROOT	Data that associates file types with programs that handle those data types and configuration data for COM objects.
HKEY_CURRENT_CONFIG	Information about the hardware profile used by the local computer at system startup.

Table 11-1.   Registry Subtrees and Associated Descriptions

Key	Description
HARDWARE	Descriptions of the physical hardware in the computer. Device drivers used by the hardware. Mappings and associated data to link kernel-mode drivers with user-mode code.
SAM	Security information for user accounts. Security information for group accounts.
SECURITY	Local security policy, such as specific user rights.
SOFTWARE	Software installed on each computer.
SYSTEM	Controls systemwide functions including: System startup Device driver loading Windows 2000 services Operating system behavior

Table 11-2.   Keys under HKEY_LOCAL_MACHINE

REGISTRY FEATURES

The Registry has a number of features: storage space, Registry hives, and others. Let us look at these in some detail.

Storage Space

Registry data is stored in the *paged pool.* The storage space occupied by the Registry is related to the amount of the paged pool space in the system. Windows 2000 typically sets the size of the paged pool to be approximately equal to the amount of physical memory on the computer, and it sets the maximum size of the Registry to be approximately 33 percent of the value of the paged pool. However, Windows 2000 attempts to set a minimum Registry size of 4MB and a maximum equal to 80 percent of the paged pool space. Both the Registry size limit and the paged pool space limit are themselves stored in the Registry. The **RegistrySizeLimit** Registry key value establishes the maximum amount of space that can be consumed by Registry data. The paged pool size is determined by the **PagedPoolSize** Registry key value. To ensure that a user can always start the system and edit the Registry, Windows 2000 does not subject the Registry to the limit set in **RegistrySizeLimit** until after the first successful loading of a user profile.

Windows 2000 does not impose any technical limits on the type and size of data an application can store in the Registry. However, there are some guidelines to follow that will help you develop an efficient Registry application. These guidelines are:

▼ Do not store executable binary code in the Registry.

■ Use the Registry to store configuration and initialization data.

■ If you have a large amount of data (more than half a kilobyte) and/or if you have multiple occurrences of data, try to store the data in a file and use the filename in the Registry.

■ Where applicable, store groups of data as one entity rather than using multiple Registry entries for each individual portion of data within the group. You will save on the amount of key space used in the Registry.

▲ Consider storing data in binary form if you have mixed data types.

Registry Hives

A *hive* is a group of keys, subkeys, and values in the Registry that has a set of supporting files. The supporting files contain backups of the data in the hive. Windows 2000 automatically retrieves data from these supporting files in the setup phase of the Windows boot process. Conversely, Windows 2000 automatically writes the hive data to the supporting files during shutdown. You can also retrieve or back up hive data manually using the Import and Export options under the File menu item of the Registry Editor (*Regedit.exe*).

Predefined Keys

An application must open a key before it can add data. To open a key, however, an application must supply a handle to another key in the Registry that is already open. The obvious question is, how does the first key get opened? Windows 2000 opens it. Windows 2000 defines standard handles that are always open. Your application can use these predefined handles as entry points to the Registry. Predefined keys exist at multiple levels of the Registry hierarchy. At the root level, there are two predefined keys: HKEY_LOCAL_MACHINE and HKEY_USERS. At the next level down, the available keys include HKEY_CURRENT_CONFIG (a subkey of HKEY_LOCAL_MACHINE) and HKEY_CURRENT_USER (a subkey of HKEY_USERS).

Your applications that add data to the Registry should always work within the framework of predefined keys. This is to facilitate administrative tools finding and using the data you have added.

Registry Data Categories

The two primary data categories in the Registry are the user and the computer. When you add data to the Registry, add computer-related data under the HKEY_LOCAL_MACHINE key and user-related data under the HKEY_CURRENT_USER key.

Registry Functions

Windows 2000 provides a number of functions to help you program the Registry. These functions and associated descriptions are listed in Table 11-3.

Function	Description
RegCloseKey	Releases a handle to the specified Registry key. Remember that the Registry may not be immediately updated after this function call due to caching. If you need immediate updates, use **RegFlushKey**.
RegConnectRegistry	Establishes a connection to a predefined Registry handle on a remote computer. The Registry handle used depends on the operating system of the remote computer. If the remote computer is running Windows NT/Windows 2000 HKEY_PERFORMANCE_DATA.

Table 11-3.   Registry Functions and Associated Descriptions

Function	Description
RegCreateKeyEx	Creates the specified Registry key. If the key already exists, this function opens it.
RegDeleteKey	Deletes a subkey. The subkey to be deleted must be empty (that is it must not have subkeys or values).
RegDeleteValue	Removes a named value from the specified Registry key. To use this function, you must have opened the specified Registry key with KEY_SET_VALUE or KEY_WRITE access.
RegDisablePredefinedCache	Disables the predefined Registry handle table of **HKEY_CURRENT_USER** for the specified process. If you access **HKEY_CURRENT_USER** after calling this function, Windows 2000 will cause open and close operations to be performed on HKEY_USERS\SID_of_current_process.
RegEnumKeyEx	Enumerates subkeys of the specified open Registry key. To enumerate subkeys, you must first call the **RegEnumKeyEx** function with the *dwIndex* parameter set to zero. After the first call, increment the *dwIndex* parameter and call **RegEnumKeyEx** repeatedly until there are no more subkeys. When using this function, you must ensure that you do not call any Registry functions that might change the key being enumerated.
RegEnumValue	Enumerates the values for the specified open Registry key. The specified Registry key must have been opened with KEY_QUERY_VALUE access. To enumerate all values, you must first set *dwIndex* to zero and then increment it by one in the same manner as **RegEnumKeyEx**.

Table 11-3.   Registry Functions and Associated Descriptions *(continued)*

Function	Description
RegFlushKey	Writes all the attributes of the specified open Registry key into the Registry. You should call **RegFlushKey** only if you need to be absolutely certain that Registry changes are propagated to disk. In general, you should call **RegCloseKey**.
RegGetKeySecurity	Retrieves a copy of the security descriptor protecting the specified open Registry key. To read the owner, group, or DACL values from the key's security descriptor, your calling process must have been granted READ_CONTROL access when the handle was opened.
RegLoadKey	Creates a subkey under **HKEY_USERS** or **HKEY_LOCAL_MACHINE** and stores registration information from a specified file into that subkey. Your calling process must have the SE_RESTORE_NAME privilege to be able to successfully use this function.
RegNotifyChangeKeyValue	Notifies the caller about changes to the attributes or contents of a specified Registry key. You cannot use this function with remote handles. This function also does not notify you if the specified Registry key is deleted.
RegOpenCurrentUser	Retrieves a handle to the **HKEY_CURRENT_ USER** key for the user the current thread is impersonating. Note that the **HKEY_ CURRENT_USER** key is cached for all threads in a process. If your process impersonates multiple users, **RegOpenCurrentUser** allows the threads to access the appropriate key.

Table 11-3.   Registry Functions and Associated Descriptions *(continued)*

Function	Description
RegOpenKeyEx	Opens the specified Registry key. Make sure that you specify the appropriate access rights required based on further operations you intend to perform on the Registry.
RegOpenUserClassesRoot	Retrieves a handle to the **HKEY_CLASSES_ROOT** key for the specified user. This function returns the merged class values from the local machine hive and the user hive. You can use this function for non-interactive users. For example, a server component could use this function to retrieve the information for a client. However, the user's profile must have been loaded before a call to this function. You can load profiles of non-interactive users using **LoadUserProfile**.
RegOverridePredefKey	Maps a predefined Registry key to a specified Registry key. This function is intended for software installation programs that want to inspect and modify Registry updates that may be performed by DLL components prior to the actual updates to the Registry.
RegQueryInfoKey	Retrieves information about the specified Registry key. The specified Registry key must have been opened with KEY_QUERY_VALUE or KEY_READ access.
RegQueryMultipleValues	Allows an application to query one or more values of a static or dynamic key. You can use this function to query a remote computer.
RegQueryValueEx	Retrieves the type and data for a specified value name associated with an open Registry key. The specified Registry key must have been opened with KEY_QUERY_VALUE or KEY_READ access.

Table 11-3.   Registry Functions and Associated Descriptions *(continued)*

Function	Description
RegReplaceKey	Replaces the file that is currently backing a Registry key and all its subkeys with another file. When the system is started the next time, the key and subkeys will have the values stored in the new file.
RegRestoreKey	Reads the Registry information in a specified file and copies it over the specified key. This function will fail if any subkeys of the specified key are open or if the calling process does not have the SE_RESTORE_NAME privilege.
RegSaveKey	Saves the specified key and all of its subkeys and values to a new file. This function saves only nonvolatile keys. You can use the file created by this function in subsequent calls to the **RegLoadKey**, **RegReplaceKey**, or **RegRestoreKey** functions.
RegSetKeySecurity	Sets the security of an open Registry key. Make sure that you close the open key to ensure that the changes take effect the next time the key is accessed.
RegSetValueEx	Sets the data and type of a specified value under a Registry key. The specified key identified must have been opened with KEY_SET_VALUE access.
RegUnLoadKey	Unloads the specified Registry key and its subkeys from the Registry. The calling process must have the SE_RESTORE_NAME privilege. This function removes a hive from the Registry but does not modify the file that has the Registry information.

Table 11-3.   Registry Functions and Associated Descriptions *(continued)*

Measuring Performance Data Using the Registry

Every software component creates keys for its objects and counters when it is installed. The components subsequently write counter data as they execute. Such counter data provide valuable insights into the software component's performance. You can access the performance data for the software components by calling Registry functions with the key HKEY_PEFORMANCE_DATA. Although you access this data as you would access any other Registry data, keep in mind that the performance data is not actually stored in the Registry itself. Instead, calling the Registry functions with the HKEY_PEFORMANCE_DATA key causes the system to collect the data from the appropriate system object managers.

NEW IN WINDOWS 2000: Class registration and file extension information is stored in Windows 2000 under both the HKEY_LOCAL_MACHINE key and the HKEY_CURRENT_USER key. Unlike in Windows NT 4.0, where the HKEY_CLASSES_ROOT key is an alias for the HKEY_LOCAL_MACHINE\Software\Classes key, HKEY_CLASSES_ROOT provides a merged view of the information in HKEY_LOCAL_MACHINE\Software\Classes and HKEY_CURRENT_USER\Software\Classes.

CLEANING THE REGISTRY

As mentioned earlier, application developers are expected to delete the Registry entries created by an application when that application is uninstalled. This does not always happen for a number of reasons. Sometimes, the application developer does not provide an uninstall routine or the user uses the standard Windows uninstall mechanism, which may not always delete all the entries. In many systems the size of the Registry tends to increase with time due to these additional entries. Microsoft provides a free utility called *RegClean* to remedy this problem.

TIP: Always back up the Registry before you update it using your application or manually using a Registry editor, as there is always a possibility that you may have difficulty booting up your system afterward. RegClean 4.1 will cause an access violation when run on Windows 2000 systems. You need RegClean version 4.1a.

Backing Up and Restoring the Registry

When you develop applications that update information in the Registry, you often need utilities to back up and restore the information in the Registry. Windows 2000 provides Registry functions to save part of the Registry in a file and then load the contents of the file back into the Registry. A Registry file is also useful when you are manipulating a large amount of data, when you are adding many entries to the Registry, or when the data is transitory and must be loaded and then unloaded again.

To save a key and its subkeys and values to a Registry file, call the **RegSaveKey** function. To write the Registry file back to the Registry, call the **RegLoadKey**, **RegReplaceKey**, or **RegRestoreKey** function.

SECURITY ASPECTS OF REGISTRY KEYS AND FILES

Windows 2000 security features enable you to control access to Registry keys. You can specify a security descriptor for a Registry key when you call the **RegCreateKeyEx** function. To get or set the security descriptor of a Registry key, call the **GetNamedSecurityInfo**, **SetNamedSecurityInfo**, **GetSecurityInfo**, or **SetSecurityInfo** function. Once the security descriptor is set, Windows 2000 checks the requested access rights against the key's security descriptor when you call the **RegOpenKeyEx** function. The valid access rights for Registry keys include the DELETE, READ_CONTROL, WRITE_DAC, and WRITE_OWNER standard access rights. Registry keys do not support the SYNCHRONIZE standard access right.

A SAMPLE APPLICATION TO QUERY AND MODIFY THE REGISTRY

The discussion that follows describes a sample application that opens, queries, and modifies certain Registry entries. Programmers who work in certain UNIX shell environments love the ability to type the TAB key and let the shell complete the filename or the directory name. Though not set by default, the same feature is also available in the Windows 2000 environment. A feature that annoys the power programmers in the Windows environment is the time it takes for the cascaded menu to appear. The sample application modifies the Registry entries such that the user can specify the delay before which the cascaded menu is shown, press the TAB key to complete the filename or directory, or preset the autologon information. You can also have a notice appear before the user is allowed to enter the system.

Registry modification will typically be done by applications to save and restore user- and/or application-specific information when the application is started or terminated. For example, an application may find the data file it needs by looking at a Registry hive, querying the information, and using it. It may also look at a Registry setting to find out what version of a certain software package is used, since most software uses the Registry to save information about an installed application. Thus a typical application uses the Registry somewhat differently from the sample, although nowadays Registry tools such as an application called *tweaki* do perform similar functions.

The sample application is a dialog-based stand-alone application that displays a dialog box; gets user input such as the menu delay, logon details, and command completion settings; and writes them to the Registry. The project is created using Visual Studio and by selecting an MFC AppWizard (exe)–type project. A dialog-based application is created for this sample. Figure 11-1 shows the opening dialog for this application, the code for which is shown as follows.

```
#include "stdafx.h"
#include "RegMod.h"
#include "RegModDlg.h"

#ifdef _DEBUG
#define new DEBUG_NEW
#undef THIS_FILE
static char THIS_FILE[] = __FILE__;
#endif
```

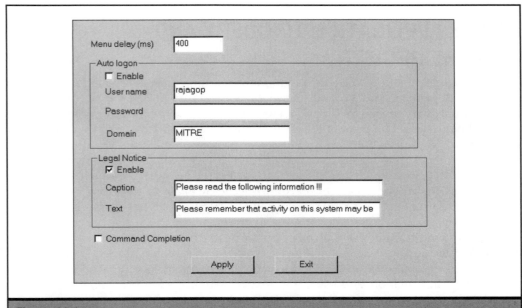

Figure 11-1. The Registry Mod application dialog

Shown next are the constructor and the data exchange methods. All the dialog box data are initialized during the construction of the class:

```
/////////////////////////////////////////////////////////////////
// CRegModDlg dialog

CRegModDlg::CRegModDlg(CWnd* pParent /*=NULL*/)
    : CDialog(CRegModDlg::IDD, pParent)
{
    //{{AFX_DATA_INIT(CRegModDlg)
    m_menudelay = _T("");
    m_autologon = FALSE;
    m_domain = _T("");
    m_username = _T("");
    m_password = _T("");
    m_legalnotice = FALSE;
    m_legal_caption = _T("");
    m_legal_text = _T("");
    m_command_complete = FALSE;
    //}}AFX_DATA_INIT
    m_hIcon = AfxGetApp()->LoadIcon(IDR_MAINFRAME);
}


void CRegModDlg::DoDataExchange(CDataExchange* pDX)
{
    CDialog::DoDataExchange(pDX);
    //{{AFX_DATA_MAP(CRegModDlg)
    DDX_Check(pDX, IDC_AUTOLOGON, m_autologon);
    DDX_Check(pDX, IDC_COMMAND_COMPLETE, m_command_complete);
    DDX_Text(pDX, IDC_DOMAIN, m_domain);
    DDX_Text(pDX, IDC_LEGAL_CAPTION, m_legal_caption);
    DDX_Text(pDX, IDC_LEGAL_TEXT, m_legal_text);
    DDX_Text(pDX, IDC_PASSWORD, m_password);
    DDX_Text(pDX, IDC_USERNAME, m_username);
    DDX_Check(pDX, IDC_LEGALNOTICE, m_legalnotice);
    DDX_Text(pDX, IDC_MENUDELAY, m_menudelay);
    //}}AFX_DATA_MAP
}
```

The message map indicates that the application is interested in processing when the *Autologon* and *Legal notice* check boxes are toggled. The application needs to disable the entry field whose data are not required if autologon is switched off or the legal notice is not required. It also requests notification when the Apply button is clicked.

```
BEGIN_MESSAGE_MAP(CRegModDlg, CDialog)
    //{{AFX_MSG_MAP(CRegModDlg)
    ON_WM_SYSCOMMAND()
    ON_WM_PAINT()
    ON_WM_QUERYDRAGICON()
    ON_BN_CLICKED(IDC_AUTOLOGON, OnAutologon)
    ON_BN_CLICKED(IDC_APPLY, OnApply)
    ON_BN_CLICKED(IDC_LEGALNOTICE, OnLegalnotice)
    //}}AFX_MSG_MAP
END_MESSAGE_MAP()


/////////////////////////////////////////////////////////////
// CRegModDlg message handlers

BOOL CRegModDlg::OnInitDialog()
{
    CDialog::OnInitDialog();
    // Add "About..." menu item to system menu.
    // IDM_ABOUTBOX must be in the system command range.
    ASSERT((IDM_ABOUTBOX & 0xFFF0) == IDM_ABOUTBOX);
    ASSERT(IDM_ABOUTBOX < 0xF000);
    CMenu* pSysMenu = GetSystemMenu(FALSE);
    if (pSysMenu != NULL)
    {
        CString strAboutMenu;
        strAboutMenu.LoadString(IDS_ABOUTBOX);
        if (!strAboutMenu.IsEmpty())
        {
            pSysMenu->AppendMenu(MF_SEPARATOR);
            pSysMenu->AppendMenu(MF_STRING, IDM_ABOUTBOX, strAboutMenu);
        }
    }

    SetIcon(m_hIcon, TRUE);         // Set big icon
    SetIcon(m_hIcon, FALSE);        // Set small icon
```

Being a dialog-based application, the sample has an About box in the system menu, and the preceding code adds this menu entry. The code that processes the selection of this About menu entry is not shown here. Before manipulating the Registry entry, you must first open it. After manipulating the Registry entry, you should close it. To open the key, call **RegOpenKeyEx**. **RegOpenKeyEx** takes a currently opened key or a predefined handle. This application needs to open the HKEY_CURRENT_USER\Control Panel\Desktop key; thus it uses the predefined handle HKEY_CURRENT_USER to open the subkey Control Panel\Desktop. Since the application needs to query the key, it requests the KEY_QUERY_VALUE permission. If the call is successful, the handle to the key is returned in the hKey variable. The API returns a return code that should be processed. This sample assumes success in the API.

Once the key handle is retrieved, the data and the type of the value, in this case *MenuShowDelay*, are queried by calling the **RegQueryValueEx** API. A buffer of size 1,024 is passed in the API. While the size of the data for this value is known and the allocated buffer is enough to hold it, this may not be the case for all data. If the data size is not known, the **RegQueryInfoKey** API can be used to get more information about the data, and an appropriate buffer can be allocated before querying the value. For efficiency, the size of the data should be limited to less than one or two kilobytes. If an application needs to store more data, then it should store that data in a file and keep the reference to that file in the Registry. After the value is queried, the key is closed by calling the **RegCloseKey** API.

```
HKEY hKey = NULL;
DWORD dwType;
TCHAR szData[1024];
DWORD dwBufSize;

// Set the Menu Delay
RegOpenKeyEx(HKEY_CURRENT_USER,
             _T("Control Panel\\Desktop"),
             0,
             KEY_QUERY_VALUE,
             &hKey);
dwBufSize = 1024;
RegQueryValueEx(hKey, _T("MenuShowDelay"),
                NULL, &dwType, (LPBYTE)szData, &dwBufSize);
m_menudelay = szData;
RegCloseKey(hKey);

// Set the autologon values
RegOpenKeyEx(HKEY_LOCAL_MACHINE,
             _T("Software\\Microsoft\\Windows NT\\CurrentVersion\\Winlogon"),
             0,
             KEY_QUERY_VALUE,
             &hKey);
dwBufSize = 1024;
RegQueryValueEx(hKey, _T("DefaultDomainName"),
                NULL, &dwType, (LPBYTE)szData, &dwBufSize);
```

```
if (dwBufSize)
{
    m_domain = szData;
}
else
{
    m_domain = "";
}
dwBufSize = 1024;
RegQueryValueEx(hKey, _T("DefaultUserName"),
                NULL, &dwType, (LPBYTE)szData, &dwBufSize);
if (dwBufSize)
{
    m_username = szData;
}
else
{
    m_username = "";
}
dwBufSize = 1024;
RegQueryValueEx(hKey, _T("DefaultPassword"),
                NULL, &dwType, (LPBYTE)szData, &dwBufSize);
if (dwBufSize)
{
    m_password = szData;
}
else
{
    m_password = "";
}
dwBufSize = 1024;
RegQueryValueEx(hKey, _T("AutoAdminLogon"),
                NULL, &dwType, (LPBYTE)szData, &dwBufSize);

if(strcmp(szData, "0"))
{
    m_autologon=TRUE;
}

// Set Legal notice
dwBufSize = 1024;
RegQueryValueEx(hKey, _T("LegalNoticeCaption"),
                NULL, &dwType, (LPBYTE)szData, &dwBufSize);
if (dwBufSize)
{
```

```
        m_legal_caption = szData;
    }
    else
    {
        m_legal_caption = "";
    }
    dwBufSize = 1024;
    RegQueryValueEx(hKey, _T("LegalNoticeText"),
                    NULL, &dwType, (LPBYTE)szData, &dwBufSize);
    if (dwBufSize)
    {
        m_legal_text = szData;
    }
    else
    {
        m_legal_text = "";
    }
    if (m_legal_caption.GetLength() && m_legal_text.GetLength())
    {
        m_legalnotice = TRUE;
    }

    RegCloseKey(hKey);

    // Set command completion
    RegOpenKeyEx(HKEY_CURRENT_USER,
                _T("Software\\Microsoft\\Command Processor"),
                0,
                KEY_QUERY_VALUE,
                &hKey);
    dwBufSize = 1024;
    RegQueryValueEx(hKey, _T("CompletionChar"),
                    NULL,
                    &dwType,
                    (LPBYTE)szData,
                    &dwBufSize);
    if (*szData == 9)
    {
        m_command_complete = TRUE;
    }

    RegCloseKey(hKey);
    UpdateData(FALSE);
    return TRUE;
}
```

The next two methods are usability-related methods that enable or disable the entry fields related to autologon and the legal notice:

```
void CRegModDlg::OnAutologon()
{
    // TODO: Add your control notification handler code here
    UpdateData();
    if (m_autologon)
    {
        GetDlgItem(IDC_STATIC_USERNAME)->EnableWindow(TRUE);
        GetDlgItem(IDC_STATIC_PASSWORD)->EnableWindow(TRUE);
        GetDlgItem(IDC_STATIC_DOMAIN)->EnableWindow(TRUE);
        GetDlgItem(IDC_USERNAME)->EnableWindow(TRUE);
        GetDlgItem(IDC_PASSWORD)->EnableWindow(TRUE);
        GetDlgItem(IDC_DOMAIN)->EnableWindow(TRUE);
    }
    else
    {
        GetDlgItem(IDC_STATIC_USERNAME)->EnableWindow(FALSE);
        GetDlgItem(IDC_STATIC_PASSWORD)->EnableWindow(FALSE);
        GetDlgItem(IDC_STATIC_DOMAIN)->EnableWindow(FALSE);
        GetDlgItem(IDC_USERNAME)->EnableWindow(FALSE);
        GetDlgItem(IDC_PASSWORD)->EnableWindow(FALSE);
        GetDlgItem(IDC_DOMAIN)->EnableWindow(FALSE);
    }

}

void CRegModDlg::OnLegalnotice()
{
    // TODO: Add your control notification handler code here
    UpdateData();
    if (m_legalnotice)
    {
        GetDlgItem(IDC_STATIC_CAPTION)->EnableWindow(TRUE);
        GetDlgItem(IDC_STATIC_TEXT)->EnableWindow(TRUE);
        GetDlgItem(IDC_LEGAL_CAPTION)->EnableWindow(TRUE);
        GetDlgItem(IDC_LEGAL_TEXT)->EnableWindow(TRUE);
    }
    else
    {
        GetDlgItem(IDC_STATIC_CAPTION)->EnableWindow(FALSE);
        GetDlgItem(IDC_STATIC_TEXT)->EnableWindow(FALSE);
        GetDlgItem(IDC_LEGAL_CAPTION)->EnableWindow(FALSE);
        GetDlgItem(IDC_LEGAL_TEXT)->EnableWindow(FALSE);
    }

}
```

When the user clicks the Apply button, the method that follows gets called. It does some basic checking to make sure that if the user enabled either autologon or the legal notice in the dialog box, then the relevant information to implement them is also specified. It then opens the key and sets the data by calling the **RegSetValueEx** API, after which it closes the key. The data for menu delay is provided in milliseconds, and the TAB key (ASCII value 0x9) is used for command completion.

```
void CRegModDlg::OnApply()
{
    // TODO: Add your control notification handler code here
    HKEY hKeyCmdProc = NULL;
    HKEY hKeyWinLogon = NULL;
    HKEY hKeyDesktop = NULL;
    LONG lRet;
    DWORD dwType;
    TCHAR szData[1024];
    DWORD dwBufSize = 1024;
    UpdateData();

    // Check if all data is given
    if (m_legalnotice)
    {
        if ((strlen(m_legal_caption)==0) &&
            (strlen(m_legal_text)==0))
        {
            MessageBox((LPCTSTR)"Provide both legal text caption and text or\\
                    uncheck the checkbox.", (LPCTSTR)"Error", MB_OK);
            return;
        }
    }
    if (m_autologon)
    {
        if ((strlen(m_username)==0) ||
            (strlen(m_password)==0) ||
            (strlen(m_domain) == 0)
            )
        {
            MessageBox((LPCTSTR)"Provide logon information or uncheck the\\
                    checkbox", (LPCTSTR)"Error", MB_OK);
            return;
        }
    }

    if ((lRet = RegOpenKeyEx(HKEY_CURRENT_USER,
                        _T("Control Panel\\Desktop"),
                        0,
                        KEY_QUERY_VALUE | KEY_SET_VALUE,
                        &hKeyDesktop)) == ERROR_SUCCESS)
    {
```

```
        dwType = REG_SZ;
        RegSetValueEx(hKeyDesktop, _T("MenuShowDelay"),
                        NULL, dwType,
                        (unsigned char *)(LPCTSTR)m_menudelay,
                        m_menudelay.GetLength());
        RegCloseKey (hKeyDesktop);
}

if ((lRet = RegOpenKeyEx(HKEY_LOCAL_MACHINE,
        _T("Software\\Microsoft\\Windows NT\\CurrentVersion\\Winlogon"),
        0,
        KEY_QUERY_VALUE | KEY_SET_VALUE,
        &hKeyWinLogon)) == ERROR_SUCCESS)
{
    if (m_autologon)
    {

        dwType = REG_SZ;
        RegSetValueEx(hKeyWinLogon, _T("DefaultDomainName"),
                        NULL, dwType, (unsigned char *)(LPCTSTR)m_domain,
                        m_domain.GetLength());
        RegSetValueEx(hKeyWinLogon, _T("DefaultUserName"),
                        NULL, dwType, (unsigned char *)(LPCTSTR)m_username,
                        m_username.GetLength());
        RegSetValueEx(hKeyWinLogon, _T("DefaultPassword"),
                        NULL, dwType, (unsigned char *)(LPCTSTR)m_password,
                        m_password.GetLength());
        RegSetValueEx(hKeyWinLogon, _T("AutoAdminLogon"),
                        NULL, dwType, (unsigned char *)"1", 1);

    }
    else
    {
        dwType = REG_SZ;
        RegSetValueEx(hKeyWinLogon, _T("DefaultPassword"),
                        NULL, dwType, (unsigned char *)"", 0);
        RegSetValueEx(hKeyWinLogon, _T("AutoAdminLogon"),
                        NULL, dwType, (unsigned char *)"0", 1);

    }
    if (m_legalnotice)
    {
        dwType = REG_SZ;
        RegSetValueEx(hKeyWinLogon, _T("LegalNoticeCaption"),
                        NULL, dwType,
                        (unsigned char *)(LPCTSTR)m_legal_caption,
                        m_legal_caption.GetLength());
        RegSetValueEx(hKeyWinLogon, _T("LegalNoticeText"),
                        NULL, dwType, (unsigned char *)(LPCTSTR)m_legal_text,
                        m_legal_text.GetLength());
```

```
        }
        else
        {
            dwType = REG_SZ;
            RegSetValueEx(hKeyWinLogon, _T("LegalNoticeCaption"),
                          NULL, dwType, (unsigned char *)"", 0);
            RegSetValueEx(hKeyWinLogon, _T("LegalNoticeText"),
                          NULL, dwType, (unsigned char *)"", 0);
        }
        RegCloseKey (hKeyWinLogon);
    }

    if ((lRet = RegOpenKeyEx(HKEY_CURRENT_USER,
                             _T("Software\\Microsoft\\Command Processor"),
                             0,
                             KEY_QUERY_VALUE | KEY_SET_VALUE,
                             &hKeyCmdProc)) == ERROR_SUCCESS)
    {
        if (m_command_complete)
        {
            dwType = REG_DWORD;
            szData[0] = 9;
            szData[1] = 0;
            szData[2] = 0;
            szData[3] = 0;
            RegSetValueEx(hKeyCmdProc, _T("CompletionChar"),
                          NULL,
                          dwType,
                          (LPBYTE)szData,
                          4);
        }
        else
        {
            dwType = REG_DWORD;
            szData[0] = 0;
            szData[1] = 0;
            szData[2] = 0;
            szData[3] = 0;
            RegSetValueEx(hKeyCmdProc, _T("CompletionChar"),
                          NULL,
                          dwType,
                          (LPBYTE)szData,
                          4);
        }
        RegCloseKey (hKeyCmdProc);
    }
}
```

In the preceding sample, it was shown how to open a query set and close a Registry key. The next sample application shows how to enumerate the Registry entries. When run, it enumerates all the keys under HKEY_CURRENT_USER/Software and displays them along with their data. The sample recursively calls the same functions until there are no more subkeys; at each level, if there are key values, it displays their data. For simplicity, this sample takes a short cut by assuming that the data length does not exceed one kilobyte. While it is generally safe to assume that the data does not exceed one kilobyte, this fact is not guaranteed; you will read later in this chapter how to dynamically allocate a buffer of the correct size.

Before the key is enumerated, it is opened and permission to query and enumerate subkeys is requested. Having obtained the handle to the key, the program calls the **EnumOneLevel** function to enumerate that and print the values at that level.

```
#include "stdafx.h"
void EnumOneLevel(HKEY hLevelKey, TCHAR *szCurLevel, int iLeadingSpaces);

int main(int argc, char* argv[])
{
    LONG lRet;
    HKEY hKeySoftware;
    DWORD dwClassLen = MAX_PATH;
    DWORD dwSubKeySize = MAX_PATH;

    lRet = RegOpenKeyEx(HKEY_CURRENT_USER,
                        "Software",
                        0,
                        KEY_QUERY_VALUE | KEY_ENUMERATE_SUB_KEYS,
                        &hKeySoftware);
    EnumOneLevel (hKeySoftware, "HKEY_CURRENT_USER\\Software", 0);
    return 0;
}
```

When the next function, **EnumOneLevel**, is called to enumerate one level of the key, it retrieves the information about the specified key by calling the **RegQueryInfoKey** API, which returns a range of information about the key, including the number of subkeys if available, the maximum length of the subkey names, the number of values associated with this key, the longest length of the subkey data values, the key's security information, and the last modified time. The return code of this API can be checked for errors.

If there are more subkeys, the sample calls the same function recursively until it exhausts all the subkeys. For each level, it checks if there are any values available for the key; if so, the values are retrieved by calling the **RegEnumValue** API. One modification that can be made here is to dynamically allocate the buffer to receive the data for the value. Before calling the **RegEnumValue** API, the **RegQueryInfoKey** API can be called to determine the size of the buffer and allocate it dynamically. This dynamically allocated buffer can then be used in the **RegEnumValue** API. While this is guaranteed to handle any size buffer, the application incurs the cost of allocating memory dynamically. A compromise to this approach could be to use a stack-allocated array of sufficient size, say, one or two kilobytes for most queries, and to dynamically allocate buffer space only for data larger than the static buffer. This can be achieved by looking for the error code from **RegEnumValue**, which returns ERROR_MORE_DATA when the given buffer size is not big enough for the data.

```
void EnumOneLevel(HKEY hLevelKey, TCHAR *szCurLevel, int iLeadingSpaces)
{
    LONG lRet;
    DWORD dwKeyIndex;
    HKEY hSubKey;
    TCHAR szClassName[MAX_PATH];
    DWORD dwClassLen = MAX_PATH;
    TCHAR szSubKeyName[MAX_PATH];
    DWORD dwSubKeySize = MAX_PATH;
    DWORD dwNumofSubKeys;
    DWORD dwMaxSubKeyLen;
    DWORD dwMaxClassLen;
    DWORD dwNumofValues;
    DWORD dwMaxValueNameLen;
    DWORD dwMaxValueDataLen;
    DWORD dwSecDesc;
    FILETIME  ftLastWriteTime;

    lRet = RegQueryInfoKey (hLevelKey, szClassName, &dwClassLen, NULL,
             &dwNumofSubKeys, &dwMaxSubKeyLen, &dwMaxClassLen, &dwNumofValues,
             &dwMaxValueNameLen, &dwMaxValueDataLen, &dwSecDesc,
             &ftLastWriteTime);

    if (dwNumofSubKeys)
    {
        for (dwKeyIndex = 0, lRet = ERROR_SUCCESS;
            dwKeyIndex < dwNumofSubKeys;
            dwKeyIndex++)
        {
            dwSubKeySize = MAX_PATH;
            lRet = RegEnumKeyEx(hLevelKey, dwKeyIndex,
                        szSubKeyName,
                        &dwSubKeySize, NULL,
                        szClassName, &dwClassLen,
                        &ftLastWriteTime);
            for (int j=0; j < iLeadingSpaces; j++)
            {
                cout << " ";
            }
            cout << "\\" << szSubKeyName << endl;
```

```
            if ((lRet = RegOpenKeyEx(hLevelKey, szSubKeyName, 0,
                            KEY_QUERY_VALUE |
                            KEY_ENUMERATE_SUB_KEYS,
                            &hSubKey)) == ERROR_SUCCESS)
            {
                EnumOneLevel(hSubKey, szSubKeyName,
                        strlen(szSubKeyName)+iLeadingSpaces+1);
            }
        }
    }
}
else if (dwNumofValues)
{   // Enumerate all values
    DWORD dwValueIndex;
    DWORD valueLen;
    DWORD dwType;
    BYTE bData[1024];
    DWORD cbData = 1024;;
    TCHAR *valueName = new TCHAR [1024];

    for (dwValueIndex = 0, lRet = ERROR_SUCCESS;
        dwValueIndex < dwNumofValues;
        dwValueIndex++)
    {
        valueLen = 1024;
        cbData = 1024;
        lRet = RegEnumValue (hLevelKey, dwValueIndex,
                        valueName, &valueLen,
                        NULL, &dwType, bData, &cbData);

        for (int j=0; j < iLeadingSpaces; j++)
        {
            cout << " ";
        }
```

RegEnumValue returns the type of data stored in the value that is used here to display the data. The code for displaying the popular types **REG_SZ**, **REG_DWORD**, and **REG_BINARY** is shown here:

```
            switch(dwType)
            {
            case REG_SZ:
                cout << "\\" << valueName << "[REG_SZ]"<< "=[" << bData \\
                    << "]"<< endl;
                break;

            case REG_DWORD:
                cout << "\\" << valueName <<"[REG_DWORD]"  << "=["
                    << setw(2) << hex << "0x"
```

```
                << (int)bData[3] << (int)bData[2]
                << (int)bData[1] << (int)bData[0]
                << "]"<< endl;
        break;

    case REG_BINARY:

        if (cbData > 0)
        {
            cout << "\\" << valueName <<"[REG_BINARY (" \\
                << setw(4) << dec
                << cbData << " bytes)]"
                << "=[" ;

            for (DWORD k=0; k < cbData; k++)
            {
                cout << setw(2) << hex << (int)bData[k];
            }
            cout << "]" << endl;
        }
        else
        {
            cout << "\\" << valueName << "[BINARY]" \\
                <<"=[" << "NONE" << "]"<< endl;
        }
        break;
        :
        :
        :
        :
        :
    }
  }
 }
 return;
}
```

The next sample shows how to save and restore the Registry key. It should be noted that manipulating the Registry is like playing with fire. You need to use the utmost caution before you change any Registry key. This is particularly true when restoring the key. So to play it safe, a sample subkey with the name *OMH* is created under HKEY_CURRENT_USER\\Software using the **regedt32** program. A few levels of other subkeys and values are created in this subkey before running the next sample.

Here again a project is created using Visual Studio. The type of project that is used for this sample is an MFC AppWizard (exe). A dialog-based application is created.

Figure 11-2 shows the window displayed when this application is executed.

In order to save the Registry key, the process should have the SE_BACKUP_NAME privilege. To restore the key, the process should have the SE_RESTORE_NAME privilege. Here are some brief comments on privileges: The system produces an access token for the user when the user logs on. This access token contains the list of privileges that the user has, which include all this user's account has been granted plus any that are granted to the group to which the user belongs to. In order to perform a task, not only should the user have the privilege, but the privilege should be enabled as well. Most privileges are disabled by default. To enable the privilege, the access token associated with this process is opened by calling the **OpenProcessToken** API. Though the string constants for various privileges, such as SE_BACKUP_NAME for file backup, are the same on all Windows 2000 machines, the functions that adjust the privileges in an access token use a 64-bit value of type **LUID** to uniquely identify the privileges. It should be noted that this value may be different on two different systems or change during a reboot. In order to get the LUID, the **LookupPrivilegeName** API is used, and to enable the privilege, the **AdjustTokenPrivileges** API is called. After the privilege is enabled, the Registry key is saved by calling the **RegSaveKey** API. If the file to which the Registry key is saved exists, then the API will fail, indicating that the file already exists. If the application does not

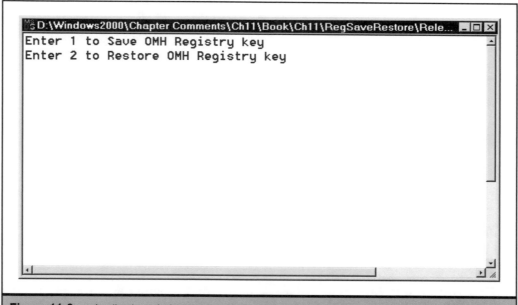

Figure 11-2. Application window to save and restore Registry keys

specify the path for the file, the file is created in the current directory (if the Registry key is for the local machine) and in the %systemroot%\system32 directory (if the key is for the remote machine).

```
#include "stdafx.h"

#define OMH_SAVE     1
#define OMH_RESTORE  2

int main(int argc, char* argv[])
{
    LONG lRet;
    HANDLE hProcessToken;
    TOKEN_PRIVILEGES tp;
    LUID luidBackup;
    LUID luidRestore;

    HKEY hKeyOMH = NULL;
    int iSelection = 0;
    TCHAR szMessage[1024];

    do
    {
        cout << "Enter 1 to Save OMH Registry key" << endl;
        cout << "Enter 2 to Restore OMH Registry key" << endl;
        cin >> iSelection;
        if (iSelection == OMH_SAVE)
        {
            // Enable backup privilege.
            lRet = OpenProcessToken(GetCurrentProcess(),
                                TOKEN_ADJUST_PRIVILEGES |
                                TOKEN_QUERY,
                                &hProcessToken);
            lRet = LookupPrivilegeValue( NULL, SE_BACKUP_NAME,
                                    &luidBackup );
            tp.PrivilegeCount = 1;
            tp.Privileges[0].Luid = luidBackup;
            tp.Privileges[0].Attributes = SE_PRIVILEGE_ENABLED;
            lRet = AdjustTokenPrivileges(hProcessToken, FALSE,
                                    &tp,
                                    sizeof(TOKEN_PRIVILEGES),
                                    NULL, NULL );
            lRet = RegOpenKeyEx(HKEY_CURRENT_USER,
                            "Software\\OMH",
```

```
                                   0,
                                   KEY_QUERY_VALUE | KEY_SET_VALUE,
                                   &hKeyOMH);
            if ((lRet = RegSaveKey(hKeyOMH, (LPCTSTR)".\\OMH",
                                NULL)) !=
                                ERROR_SUCCESS)
{
            FormatMessage(FORMAT_MESSAGE_FROM_SYSTEM, NULL,lRet, 0,
                          szMessage, 1024, NULL);
            cout << endl << szMessage << endl;
}
// Disable backup privilege.
lRet = AdjustTokenPrivileges(hProcessToken, TRUE, &tp,
                                sizeof(TOKEN_PRIVILEGES),
                                NULL, NULL);
lRet = RegCloseKey(hKeyOMH);
break;
        }
```

To restore the key from a file, the privileges are first enabled and the **RegRestoreKey**
API is called. This will restore all the keys and values from the file to the Registry. If any of
the subkeys of the key that is to be restored open, then the restore will fail. The
RegRestoreKey API will replace all the keys and values below the specified key with
new keys and values from the file.

```
            else if (iSelection == OMH_RESTORE)
            {
            // Enable backup privilege.
            lRet = OpenProcessToken(GetCurrentProcess(),
                                TOKEN_ADJUST_PRIVILEGES |
                                TOKEN_QUERY,
                                &hProcessToken);
            lRet = LookupPrivilegeValue( NULL,
                                SE_RESTORE_NAME,
                                &luidRestore );
            tp.PrivilegeCount = 1;
            tp.Privileges[0].Luid = luidRestore;
            tp.Privileges[0].Attributes = SE_PRIVILEGE_ENABLED;
            lRet = AdjustTokenPrivileges(hProcessToken, FALSE,
                                &tp,
                                sizeof(TOKEN_PRIVILEGES),
                                NULL, NULL );
            // Restore the key
            lRet = RegOpenKeyEx(HKEY_CURRENT_USER,
```

```
                               "Software\\OMH",
                               0,
                               KEY_ALL_ACCESS,
                               &hKeyOMH);

        if ( (lRet = RegRestoreKey(hKeyOMH, ".\\OMH",
                                REG_OPTION_NON_VOLATILE)))
        {
            FormatMessage(FORMAT_MESSAGE_FROM_SYSTEM, NULL,
                            lRet, 0,
                            szMessage, 1024, NULL);
            cout << endl << szMessage << endl;
        }
        lRet = AdjustTokenPrivileges(hProcessToken, TRUE, &tp,
                                sizeof(TOKEN_PRIVILEGES),
                                NULL, NULL);
        lRet = RegCloseKey(hKeyOMH);
        break;
    }
    else
    {
        cout << endl << "Invalid entry.  Please select again."
            << endl;
    }
} while (1);
return 0;
}
```

After the operation is completed, the privileges are reset and the key is closed.

CONCLUSION

In this chapter, we covered the Windows 2000 Registry, its features, and the functions you can use to update the Registry. We also looked at sample programs to enumerate Registry values and to set and restore Registry values. In the next chapter, we will begin to look at two of the exciting fundamental technologies underlying Windows 2000—OLE and ActiveX.

PART III

Windows 2000 Communications Programming

CHAPTER 12

Introduction to OLE and ActiveX

Continuing our communications focus, let's look at an important Windows technology—OLE (object linking and embedding). OLE is based on the Component Object Model (COM). One important aspect of OLE, OLE custom controls, has advanced significantly since the introduction of OLE and is now called ActiveX controls. As an advanced Windows 2000 programmer, you can expect to spend a lot of your programming effort in OLE and ActiveX. The interest in these COM-based technologies has grown, partly because Microsoft is facing intense competition in this area and is aggressively trying to establish OLE, ActiveX, and COM. HP and Compaq are among the vendors who plan to include support for COM in their own operating systems. Once you master COM and COM-based technologies, you may be able to develop applications in other environments besides Windows 2000.

The primary significance of COM and the technologies based on it, OLE and ActiveX, is not the features, such as including a spreadsheet in a Word document transparently or the ability to download and execute a control in a browser. The more important underlying phenomenon is the transition of Windows from an API-driven operating system (from an application development perspective) to an object-oriented operating system. Windows programming can be viewed as a three-step evolution—API, MFC, and OLE/ActiveX. The MFC library was a small step over APIs, but the programming benefits of masking the details and programming at a higher level are already apparent in the MFC library. OLE and ActiveX are a much bigger step and take programming to a still higher level. The transition is by no means complete. But the trend is evident.

In this chapter, we will briefly review the basics of OLE and ActiveX and the programming aspects of OLE and ActiveX controls. We will look at how OLE 2 attempts to address the problems of OLE 1. In the next two chapters, we will cover programming examples involving OLE and ActiveX.

OLE 2 BASICS

OLE started with the need to create documents that matched the real world. Within the computer world, we make a distinction between a word processing document, a spreadsheet, a graphic, or a multimedia object and have separate applications to deal with them. But more often than not, all the objects coexist as part of regular business communications. The term *compound document* denotes this coexistence of objects, and OLE started as the means for the different applications to individually deal with portions of the compound document. OLE performed this through object linking or object embedding. We will not go into the basics of OLE 1.0 here. Chapter 1 has a brief review of OLE. This chapter also presumes that you are familiar with OLE terminology such as an OLE *item* or *object* (a graphic, spreadsheet, and so on), an OLE *container* (the client that contains the different objects), an OLE *miniserver* (edits only embedded items), an OLE *full server* (edits embedded and linked items), and an OLE *automation server* (see "OLE Automation" later in this chapter). What we will note here are some of the limitations of OLE 1.0 and how these are addressed in OLE 2.0.

The primary advantage of object linking is that changes to the linked object are automatically reflected in the compound document that the object belongs to. The primary problem is that links get broken. Embedding an object ensures that the object cannot get lost, but in the process sacrifices the advantage of automatic updates. Another problem with OLE 1.0 relates to the end-user interface. When the user edits a linked or embedded object, the corresponding application takes over the existing user interface, including the menus, toolbars, and so on, and in the process takes a long time (in most environments).

OLE 2.0 has attempted to provide solutions to the problems of OLE 1.0, but it has also expanded beyond compound documents. It has become the basis for component software-based Windows programming and includes features such as reusable custom controls, in-place activation, OLE automation, enhanced linking, and drag-and-drop. Let's briefly review these concepts. Of these, two features are probably the most significant. One that has taken on a life of its own is the custom controls (ActiveX controls), and this is covered starting with the section "ActiveX Basics" later in this chapter. The other is OLE automation, which is covered starting with the section "OLE Automation" also later in this chapter.

In-Place Activation or Visual Editing

When you edit an embedded object, the complete application associated with the object is loaded and control is transferred to the application to edit the embedded object. This has two problems. First, it takes a long time to load the application and the whole object. This problem is somewhat alleviated by use of *structured storage*, which allows an application to read and write portions of an object instead of the whole object (see "Structured Storage" next in this chapter). Second, the user does not get the feeling that he or she is editing one document using one editor. The user is very aware that the application has been switched. For example, in OLE 1.0, if you wanted to insert a PowerPoint slide in a Word document, the PowerPoint application was started with its own window, menu, and toolbars. The heading for the slide was "Slide in Document2."

In-place activation addresses this problem. When an embedded object is edited, the application that handles the embedded object is activated in-place (rather than in a separate window), and most of the user interface elements of the original application (such as menus, toolbars, and palettes) are supplanted by those of the application handling the embedded object. Figure 12-1 shows that when you insert an Excel worksheet, a separate window is not created (actually the OLE 2 specification gives a choice between in-place activation and opening a separate window). Instead, the Excel menu and toolbars supplant Word's menu and toolbars, but the heading is still the Word heading "Document2." In addition, in-place activation also ensures that depending on where the cursor is in the compound document, the appropriate pop-up menu will be displayed.

Structured Storage

As mentioned earlier, when you double-click an OLE object in a container, the OLE server for the object and the entire object are loaded, which takes considerable time. The entire object is also saved when changes are made to the object.

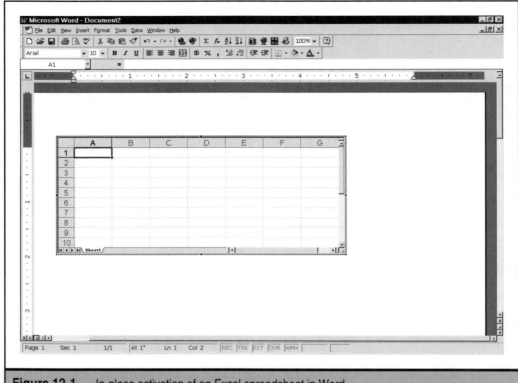

Figure 12-1. In-place activation of an Excel spreadsheet in Word

To understand some of the persistent storage features supported by COM, let's start with a word processor. A word processor like Word will store the changes you make to the word processing document separate from the document itself. This makes it easy for Word to support functions such as Undo, and it is also easy to support the option of letting the user discard all changes to a document in an editing session. Applying this analogy, COM makes it easy for your OLE application to store updates separate from the object (and thus save time compared with updating the whole object). OLE provides structured storage called *compound files*. Compound files support storage and stream objects.

TIP: Do not confuse "compound files" with the similar-sounding "compound documents." Compound documents contain types of objects, while compound files are one way of storing compound documents.

Storage and stream objects are conceptually equivalent to directories and files, respectively. *Storage objects,* like directories, contain other (child) storage objects and stream objects. *Stream objects* store your application's data.

You can perform updates to the storage/stream objects in one of two modes—direct or transaction mode. In *transaction mode,* updates are buffered until they are committed or reverted. You can use transaction mode to provide your user the option to cancel all updates and revert the object to its original state. Updates in *direct mode* are immediately applied to the object being updated.

The storage and stream objects are accessed by use of the **IStorage** and **IStream** interfaces, respectively. The **IStorage** interface creates and manages structured storage objects. It contains root storage objects, child storage objects, and stream objects and methods for managing these objects. These methods provide functions to create, open, copy, move, rename, and so on the objects contained in the storage object. **IStorage** interface methods are summarized in Table 12-1.

IStorage Method	Description
CreateStream	This creates/opens a stream object within the storage object. You can replace an existing stream by another with the same name using this method.
OpenStream	This opens an existing stream object within the storage object. You can specify permissions for the stream object, which must be stricter than (and constrained by) that of the parent storage object that the stream belongs to.
CreateStorage	This creates/opens a storage object within another storage object. The new storage object is nested within the other storage object.
OpenStorage	This opens an existing storage object.
CopyTo	This copies the contents of one storage object into another. Nested objects within the storage object are also copied. Contents of stream objects are replaced while copying, whereas contents of storage objects are added to.
MoveElementTo	This moves a substorage or stream object from this storage object to another storage object. You can set a flag value in this method to copy instead of move. You can also rename an element.

Table 12-1. IStorage Methods and Descriptions

IStorage Method	Description
Commit	This commits known changes for a transacted storage object to the next higher level. If the commit is done at the root storage object level, the changes are committed at the device level. Changes in currently opened nested elements are not committed. For a direct mode root storage object, changes in memory buffers are flushed.
Revert	This discards uncommitted changes to a transacted storage object. Committed changes from nested elements that have not been propagated to the next higher level are also discarded. If this method is used for a root storage object without a prior commit, then all changes by the object and nested elements are discarded, and the object reverts to its former state before the transaction. This method has no effect on directed mode storage objects.
EnumElements	This returns a handle to an enumerator object that implements the standard IEnumSTATSTG interface. Use this method to enumerate the storage and stream objects within this storage object.
DestroyElement	This deletes a substorage or stream element. Call the Commit method after a call to this method for a transacted object to commit the change.
RenameElement	This renames a substorage or stream object. The substorage or stream object cannot be open. Call the Commit method after a call to this method for a transacted object to commit the change.
SetElementTimes	This sets time statistics such as modification, access, and creation times of a storage element. A statistic is set only if supported by the underlying file system and is ignored otherwise. Specify NULL if you do not want to change an existing value.
SetClass	This assigns a class identifier (CLSID) to this storage object. A CLSID is a unique global 128-bit identifier.

Table 12-1.   IStorage Methods and Descriptions *(continued)*

IStorage Method	Description
SetStateBits	This is reserved (stores up to 32 bits of storage object state information).
Stat	This retrieves the STATSTG structure, which contains statistical information about the current storage. It is used in conjunction with EnumElements (see EnumElements in this table).

Table 12-1   IStorage Methods and Descriptions *(continued)*

You release the **IStorage** pointers when processing is complete to deallocate memory used by the storage object. At times, you may need to serialize the access to a storage object. You can serialize access using the **IPersistStorage** interface. The methods of the **IStorage** interface handle the management of objects. The methods to actually read and write data are part of the **IStream** interface.

The **IStream** interface contains methods for seeking, reading, and writing data as summarized in Table 12-2.

An important feature of storage and stream objects is that they are sharable across processes (an **IStorage** or **IStream** instance pointer can be marshaled to another process). Nested objects (for example, an Excel worksheet within a PowerPoint slide within a Word document) are easily implemented as nested storage objects.

Moniker

Another problem with OLE 1 is that of broken links. In OLE 1, when an OLE container links to another object, the linked-to object resides outside the OLE container in its own file. The filename of the object (including the path) is the link to the object. Thus, if the file is moved to another directory or to another computer, the link is broken.

OLE 2 attempts to solve this problem (to a large extent) through a *moniker*, which is a referencing mechanism to locate objects. OLE 2 stores the absolute path as in OLE 1, but it also stores a relative path. The *relative path* of an object is the path as it relates to the current location of the container and is typically the difference in the path (as opposed to the *absolute path*, which starts with a drive letter and has all the directories leading up to the object). The relative path is searched first, and if the link could not be established, the absolute path is searched. When an OLE object and its container are moved to another

IStream Method	Description
Read	This reads a specified number of bytes from the stream object into memory starting at the current seek pointer and increments the seek pointer. You can get the actual number of bytes read (the actual bytes read may be different from the requested number, in case there is not enough data left in the stream, or if there is an error).
Write	This writes a specified number of bytes into the stream object starting at the current seek pointer and increments the seek pointer. It optionally returns the actual number of bytes written (which may be zero if the data couldn't be written for any reason). If the amount of data to be written exceeds the available space in the stream, the stream is automatically extended.
Seek	This changes the seek pointer to a new location or returns the current location of the seek pointer. The new location can be specified as an offset relative to the beginning of the stream, the end of the stream, or the current seek pointer. You will get an error for seeking before the start of the stream but not after the end (the position beyond the end will be used to extend the stream for write requests with data that exceeds the available space in the stream).
SetSize	This allocates contiguous space for stream objects. For a new stream object, the space is allocated. For an existing stream object, the current size is truncated or extended to match the specified size. The seek pointer is unaffected.
CopyTo	This copies the data from a portion of a stream or the complete stream to another stream and adjusts the seek pointers in both streams.
Commit	This commits changes to a stream object opened in transacted mode to the next higher level. Note: OLE compound file implementation does not support transacted mode processing of streams.
Revert	This discards uncommitted changes to a transacted mode stream (changes since the last commit). This method has no effect on directed mode streams or on OLE compound file implementation (since commits are not supported, there is nothing to revert).

Table 12-2. IStream Methods and Descriptions

IStream Method	Description
LockRegion	This restricts access to a specified range of bytes in the stream for read, write, or exclusive access. The locked region must be unlocked (see UnlockRegion next) before releasing the stream. This method depends on the underlying file system for support. Compound files do not support this method.
UnlockRegion	This unlocks the range of bytes locked by LockRegion. Compound files do not support this method.
Stat	This retrieves the STATSTG structure, which contains statistical information about the current stream. This is used in conjunction with EnumElements (see the EnumElements method in Table 12-1).
Clone	This clones an existing stream object (creates a new stream object that references the same data as the existing stream). The cloned stream object has a new seek pointer (separate from the pointer of the existing stream) whose initial setting is the value of the seek pointer of the existing stream at cloning time.

Table 12-2.   IStream Methods and Descriptions *(continued)*

subdirectory or another drive (even a network drive) while maintaining the relative path, the link will break in OLE 1, but not in OLE 2. When only the container is moved, the relative path may change, but the linked object can still be found if its absolute path is not changed. Thus, the addition of the relative path in OLE 2 significantly reduced the possibility of broken links. Note, however, that a link may still be broken if the *linked object* is moved, and its relative path with the container is also changed. So far in this discussion monikers were used in the context of identifying any object that is stored in its own file. Such a moniker is called a *file moniker*. But there are other types of monikers such as *item moniker* (a moniker used to identify an object contained in another object), *composite moniker* (a moniker that is a composite of other monikers), and so on.

Drag-and-Drop

Your OLE application can be made really user friendly by providing support for OLE drag-and-drop functionality. OLE drag-and-drop is conceptually similar to transferring data between documents (or even within the same document) using the cut and paste functions and the Clipboard. However, OLE drag-and-drop is faster and easier because the menu bar is not used. In OLE drag-and-drop, you highlight the drag-and-drop source (the portion of the document you want to copy) and while keeping the left mouse button pressed, drag the highlighted selection to the drag-and-drop target and release the left mouse button. Both the source and target must be open and visible (at least partially) on the desktop for the drag-and-drop operation to be successful. The actual data transfer mechanism used by OLE is called *uniform data transfer*.

The source of drag-and-drop could be non-OLE applications. You can get source data from applications that do not support compound documents (or customize standard OLE drag-and-drop behavior). The programming details for implementing drag-and-drop are similar for both container and server applications. In most cases OLE takes care of deleting the data involved in the drag-and-drop operation after the drag-and-drop operation is complete. OLE drag-and-drop is covered in more detail in Chapter 13.

Binding

OLE 1 supported only one form of binding, called the VTable binding. OLE 2 supports additional forms of binding such as

▼ Early binding

■ Late binding

▲ ID binding

Early binding, also called *VTable (or VTBL) binding,* allows an ActiveX client to call a method or property access function directly. This binding tends to be faster than the other two forms of binding. Early binding does not require the object whose methods are being accessed to implement the **IDispatch** interface. Early binding also does not use dispatch identifiers (DISPIDs) and generates code to call the object's methods or properties through the object's VTable.

Late binding is performed by use of the **IDispatch** interface. The methods of the **IDispatch** interface are summarized in Table 12-3. This is the slowest of the three options. Typically, two calls are made at run time. The first call is used to find the DISPID (see **GetIDsOfNames** in Table 12-3), and the second call invokes the method using the DISPID. No compile-time checks are made, and there is no need for type libraries. Of course, besides the process being slow, you may get run-time errors, for example, if the name is not found.

ID binding established the DISPID-name equivalence at compile time by use of a type library. As a result, at run time you need only one call (invoke) instead of the two calls required for late binding. Thus, ID binding is faster compared with late binding, and name-not-found errors are caught at compile time rather than at run time.

Besides the previous enhancements, OLE 2 also removes the restriction that an embedded or linked object must fit in one contiguous region. Instead the embedded object can occupy noncontiguous regions within the container. OLE 2 also allows embedded text to be searched and edited by the container application.

IDispatch Member Function	Description
GetIDsOfNames	This maps method, property, and parameter names into a corresponding set of integer dispatch identifiers (DISPIDs). The DISPIDs are used by the Invoke member function.
GetTypeInfo	This retrieves the type information for interfaces supported by an OLE server.
GetTypeInfoCount	This retrieves the number of type information interfaces that an OLE server supports. The returned value is 1 if the server supports a type information interface and zero otherwise. However, the OLE server may still be programmable through IDispatch without the type information.
Invoke	This provides access to properties and methods exposed by an object. As an alternative, you may use the CreateStdDispatch and DispInvoke functions.

Table 12-3.   IDispatch Member Functions and Descriptions

OLE AUTOMATION

Another important programming concept associated with OLE that you should be familiar with is OLE Automation (or simply automation). *OLE Automation* is the mechanism by which one application (an OLE Automation client or automation controller) can invoke programmable objects of another application (an OLE Automation Server). This process involves the application that owns the programmable objects to expose the programming objects (properties and methods) it is designed to expose to client applications.

You can create a skeleton OLE Automation Server using the AppWizard, and enhance it to suit your needs. Before an Automation client can invoke the Automation Server, the Automation Server must be registered in the system Registry. (OLE uses the information in the Registry to present the user with a list of OLE objects that can be inserted when the user wants to insert a new object.)

The principal communication mechanism between an OLE client and an OLE Automation Server is the **IDispatch** interface. Access using **IDispatch** is a *late binding* access, since the connection between the OLE client and the OLE Automation Server occurs at run time (not when the OLE client is link-edited). OLE 2 also supports calling an object's methods using a table (early binding). The member functions of the **IDispatch** interface and their descriptions are summarized in Table 12-3.

TIP: An OLE Automation Server need not necessarily be an OLE object server as well, although it is possible to make the same application an OLE Automation Server and an OLE object server.

OLE PROGRAMMING ASPECTS

As mentioned earlier, OLE is based on COM, and this means that an OLE-compatible application should follow the COM rules for functions and interfaces. Many interfaces are available for OLE applications, and many OLE applications use only a small subset of the interfaces. The one interface all OLE applications should implement is the **IUnknown** interface, which is like an entry point for all other interfaces. In fact, it includes the **QueryInterface** function that provides the list of the other interfaces available.

OLE and MFC

The MFC library provides classes to support OLE. These classes can be classified by the type of OLE component (such as Base, Client, Server, and so on) the class supports. Table 12-4 summarizes the common OLE MFC library classes and their types.

There are also portions of OLE that are not partially or fully supported by the MFC library. For example, the MFC library implements only creation support for compound files and does not provide mechanisms for the programmer to invoke interfaces such as **IMoniker** using the MFC library.

TIP: It is important to distinguish between MFC library classes and OLE interfaces. COM defines a base class, the **IUnknown**, from which all COM-compatible classes are derived. In OLE, all classes derived from **IUnknown** are interfaces, which are just protocol definitions without any implementation. While sometimes the **IUnknown** interface is referred to as a C++ class, it is important to note that COM is not language specific. The "I" in **IUnknown** or **IDispatch** stands for "Interface."

ACTIVEX BASICS

ActiveX controls are an outgrowth of OLE custom controls. An ActiveX control is a COM object, the same as an OLE control. The primary difference, though, is that an ActiveX control is required to implement only the **IUnknown** interface, whereas an OLE control is required to implement many more interfaces. Although ActiveX controls typically implement more than just the **IUnknown** interface, removing mandatory support makes it possible to create ActiveX controls that are relatively small.

While it is common for an ActiveX control to have its own window, it is possible to have windowless ActiveX controls. You can make your ActiveX control use windowless activation, by including the windowless Activate flag in **COleControl::GetControlFlags**. A windowless control uses the window services of its container. An ActiveX control is in either an active state or an inactive state. Controls in the active state typically have a window, and

Class Name	Class Type	Description
COleDocument	Base	This is the base class for OLE documents. This class is derived from CDocument.
COleLinkingDoc	Base	This is the base class for OLE documents that support linking to the embedded items.
CDocItem	Base	This is the base class for OLE document items. Multiple CDocItems are treated as representations of OLE items by COleDocument.
COleClientItem	Client	This class defines the container interface to OLE items.
COleObjectFactory	Server	This class implements the OLE object factory. This class creates OLE objects such as server documents and OLE automation objects.
COleServerDoc	Server	This is the base class for OLE server documents. An OLE server document contains COleServerItem objects.
COleServerItem	Server	This class provides the server interface to OLE items.
COleTemplate Server	Server	This class is typically used to implement an OLE full server. Your application needs one COleTemplateServer object for each type of server document (spreadsheet, database, and so on) it supports.
COleIPFrameWnd	In-place Frame Window	This class handles control bars within the container application's window to support in-place editing.
COleException	Exception	This class has a data member that has a status code from operations. Typically, AfxThrowOleException is called to create a COleException object and throw an exception.

Table 12-4.   MFC OLE Classes, Types, and Descriptions

Class Name	Class Type	Description
COleDataSource	Data	This class is used as a data source by an application to provide data for Clipboard and drag-and-drop operations. COleClientItem and COleServerItem classes also create OLE data sources implicitly.
COleDataObject	Data	This class is used to retrieve data filled by other applications using data sources (for example retrieving data from a clipboard).
COleStreamFile	Data	This class is derived from CFile. An object of this class represents a stream of compound file data. This class enables MFC serialization to use OLE structured storage.

Table 12-4.   MFC OLE Classes, Types, and Descriptions *(continued)*

controls in the inactive state do not have a window. Even if a control has a window, you can cause a control to remain inactive until it needs to be activated (for example, when the user tabs to the control)—omit the control's OLEMISC_ ACTIVATEWHENVISIBLE flag (this is automatic if you use the ControlWizard to create the ActiveX control with the Activate When Visible option turned off). An inactive control can be the target of an OLE drag-and-drop operation. You can subclass a common control to create an ActiveX control. Common controls are covered in Chapter 7.

In-Process and Out-of-Process Servers

In-process servers are servers where the server code executes in the same process address space as that of the client that invoked the server. By contrast, servers are *out-of-process* when the server code executes in a process address space other than the client. This process address space could be on the same computer or on another computer. Sometimes the out-of-process server is also called a local server or a remote server, depending on whether the server executes on the same computer where the client code executes (in a different process space) or on a remote computer. In-process servers are typically implemented as DLLs, while local servers are commonly implemented as EXEs. Remote servers can either be EXEs or DLLs.

ActiveX controls are usually in-process servers. This is primarily because you can create one entity that handles user interface and additional server logic in-process, which makes it easy for distribution and licensing. In addition, an in-process server loads faster than an out-of-process server implemented as an EXE. The major downside to an in-process server is that it is a DLL and has the problems of DLLs, such as message handling. DLLs are covered in Chapter 9. Also, the code that contains the in-process server as an embedded DLL is usually longer than code that uses out-of-process servers.

Location Transparency

One of the benefits of the COM is that whether the servers are in-process or out-of-process, the interface to the COM object remains the same. If you are writing client code, then your calls interface with the actual COM object if in-process or to a *proxy object* if out-of-process. If you are writing server code, then the interface is likewise to the actual object if in-process or to a *stub object*. COM provides RPC mechanisms for the stub object and proxy object to communicate. This communication is transparent to your application. Thus, the location of the object is transparent to your application. For performance reasons, it is possible to override the default behavior by use of *custom marshaling* (custom marshaling refers to the overriding of the internal **Imarshal** interface used by COM when an object does not provide an **Imarshal** interface).

ActiveX Controls as Connectable Objects

Most ActiveX controls are connectable objects. A *connectable object* is one that supports outgoing interfaces (an *outgoing interface* is the opposite of the traditional incoming interface, where a client invokes an OLE server through one of its incoming interfaces). For the OLE server object to have an outgoing interface to the client, the client uses a *sink object* (the sink object's members are called by the OLE server), and it is the pointer to the sink that is used for the outgoing interface. The connectable object-related interfaces and their methods are summarized in Table 12-5.

Connectable Object Interface	Description
IConnectionPoint	Supports connection points for connectable objects
IConnectionPointContainer	Indicates the existence of the outgoing interfaces
IEnumConnectionPoints	Enumerates connection points
IEnumConnections	Enumerates all the supported connections for each outgoing interface

Table 12-5. Connectable Object Interfaces and Descriptions

The common methods used by the connection point interfaces listed in Table 12-5 are summarized in Table 12-6.

ActiveX Control Properties and Methods

An ActiveX control communicates with its container using events. An ActiveX control container interacts with the control using properties and methods. The methods can be stock methods or custom methods. Stock methods are similar to OLE automation methods. The properties associated with ActiveX controls are summarized in Table 12-7.

PROGRAMMING ACTIVEX CLIENTS

You can use the **IDispatch** interface discussed earlier in this chapter to create ActiveX clients as illustrated by the following steps:

1. Initialize OLE. You can do this using the **OleInitialize** API function.

2. Create an instance of the object you want to access using **CoCreateInstance**. The object's ActiveX component creates the object. **CoCreateInstance** creates an instance of the class represented by the specified CLSID and returns a pointer to the object's **IUnknown** interface. **CoCreateInstance** is a component object API function.

3. You can check if the object has implemented the **IDispatch** interface and get a pointer to the interface using the **IUnknown** interface's **QueryInterface**, which checks whether **IDispatch** has been implemented for the object. If so, it returns a pointer to the **IDispatch** implementation.

4. You can access and use the methods and properties of the object being accessed in one of three ways—early binding, late binding, or ID binding. (See "Binding" earlier in this chapter.)

5. Terminate the object by invoking the appropriate method in its **IDispatch** interface, or by releasing all references to the object. You can use **IUnknown's Release** method to decrement the reference count for the **IUnknown** or **IDispatch** object.

6. Uninitialize OLE using the OLE API function **OleUninitialize**.

As mentioned earlier, an ActiveX control is required to support only the **IUnknown** interface. Removing mandatory support makes it possible to create ActiveX controls that are relatively small. This opens up a particularly interesting possibility, where you can download an ActiveX control to enhance the functionality of a Web page. The relatively small size of an ActiveX control is an important factor here.

This functionality of ActiveX controls resembles that of Java applets for Java-enabled Web browsers. As is to be expected, there is a lot of competition in this area.

Connection Point Interface Methods	Description
GetConnectionInterface	Retrieves the IID (globally unique identifier) of the connection point interface
GetConnectionPointContainer	Retrieves an interface pointer to the connectable object
Advise	Establishes a connection between the connection point and the caller's sink
unAdvise	Terminates a connection previously established by Advise
EnumConnections	Creates an enumerator object to loop through the current connections for a connection point
FindConnectionPoint	Retrieves an interface pointer to the connection point supporting the specified IID

Table 12-6.   Connection Point Interfaces and Descriptions

Properties	Description
Stock	These are properties that have already been implemented and are ready to use, such as the control's foreground and background colors, caption, and so on.
Ambient	These are properties of the container that a control can use to make the control's appearance the same as that of the container. For example, a control can display text using the same font as that of the container.
Custom	These are properties you develop that are unique for each application.
Extended	These are properties implemented by the container on behalf of the control at run time, such as the control's position.
Advanced	These are properties with advanced functions related to properties, such as making properties read-only or write-only.

Table 12-7.   ActiveX Control Properties and Descriptions

CONCLUSION

In this chapter, we reviewed the basics of OLE and ActiveX and the programming aspects of OLE and ActiveX controls. We looked at how OLE 2 attempts to address the problems of OLE 1. In the next two chapters, we will cover programming examples involving OLE and ActiveX.

CHAPTER 13

Using OLE

L et's build on the introduction to OLE in the previous chapter and look at some programming examples. We will look at OLE Automation Servers and illustrate developing an OLE Automation Server using a programming example. In the example, we will also discuss how to make an OLE Automation Server a stand-alone application. Next we will look at OLE Automation clients and illustrate developing an OLE Automation client using a programming example. This example will access the OLE Automation Server mentioned in Chapter 12. Finally we will take a closer look at a significant OLE user interface enhancement—OLE drag-and-drop—including a programming example that illustrates OLE drag-and-drop.

COM ENHANCEMENTS IN WINDOWS 2000

As mentioned in the previous chapter, the underlying object model that supports OLE and ActiveX is COM. Windows 2000 adds some significant functionality to COM in respects summarized here:

▼ Windows 2000 integrates the functions in MTS (Microsoft Transaction Service) within the COM model.

■ A new utility apartment, called the *thread-neutral apartment (TNA),* has been added. TNA allows an object to be accessed by any thread in the process, and thread-neutral objects can safely hold object references between method calls. Classes indicate that they want to run in TNA by specifying **ThreadingModel= Neutral** in the Registry. TNA is likely to be the preferred threading model for most components that do not have a user interface.

■ COM components can now control concurrent access without requiring a thread switch and Windows message queue for serialization. If you have used a single-threaded apartment for serialization, a better method now would be to use **ThreadingModel=Neutral** and **Synchronization=Required**.

■ There were instances when it was dangerous to use critical sections or semaphores while waiting for an executive object to be signaled, due to the possibility of causing a deadlock. One example of this is when you have a single-threaded apartment (STA) that uses a message pump to service incoming calls and you are concerned about using blocking system calls. Windows 2000 introduces the **CoWaitForMultipleHandles** API to solve this problem. If you call this API from a single-threaded apartment, **CoWaitFor MultipleHandles** enters the COM modal loop, and the thread's message loop will continue to dispatch messages using the thread's message filter. If you call this API from a multithreaded apartment (MTA), **CoWaitForMultipleHandles** calls the Win32 function **WaitForMultipleObjects**.

■   It is now easy to have nonblocking invocation by decoupling the thread
that issues a method call from the thread that performs the operation.
Nonblocking invocation is specified by annotating the interface in IDL
using the [*async_uuid*] attribute.

▲   COM now supports a limited number of pipes designed to facilitate bulk
data transfer within a method call.

OLE AUTOMATION

OLE Automation is a mechanism for one application to implement a functionality and to
let other applications use that functionality. For example, let's say that you want to write
an application that includes these steps: access some data from a database, create a
spreadsheet using the data, create a graph with the output of the spreadsheet, and include the graph in a report and print it. You can, of course, do all these steps manually using the set of office products from Microsoft such as Microsoft Access, Microsoft Excel,
and so on, or use other vendors' equivalent products.

If you want to perform these steps to be implemented within an application, you can
do it in two ways. You can write the application from scratch and write all the code for ex-
tracting the data, performing the spreadsheet manipulation, and so on. But wouldn't it be
a lot simpler if you could access the necessary functionalities of the other applications,
and all you had to do was to invoke these functionalities? That is the idea behind OLE Automation. Automation is not restricted to shrink-wrapped applications such as Microsoft
Word or Excel. When you develop your business applications, you can make them OLE
Automation Servers and make some functionality available for other applications to invoke. Thus, an organization can significantly enhance code reuse and cut down new development by using OLE Automation. The application that provides the functionality for
other applications to invoke is called the *OLE Automation Server,* and the application that
invokes the functionality is typically the *OLE Automation client.*

OLE Automation Server

The client and the server can be on the same machine or on different machines connected
by a network. When the client and the server are on the same machine, the server can be
in-process, if the server is implemented as a DLL that runs in the client's address space, or
out-of-process, if the server executes in an address space different from that of the client.
Should you set up your OLE Automation in-process or out-of-process?

If your OLE Automation client is using products such as Word or Excel, then you do
not have a choice and the server is out-of-process. If you are developing an OLE Automation Server, keep the following points in mind in choosing between in-process and
out-of-process servers. It is faster to pass parameters between an OLE Automation client
and an in-process server compared with an out-of-process server. However, each client
of an in-process server has a copy of the server in its address space, whereas only one
copy is kept in memory for an out-of-process server.

OLE Automation Server and Client Communication

Communication between OLE Automation Server and client is implemented according to whether the server is an in-process server or an out-of-process server.

In an in-process server, since the OLE Automation Server and client share an address space, the in-process server can directly access reference parameters passed by the client, and the server's methods can use the client's stack.

In an out-of-process server, but within the same computer, the previously mentioned direct access facilitated by the client memory space is not feasible. In this case, OLE copies the data for passed parameters into the out-of-process OLE server's address space and makes a copy of the pointer to the original data. The OLE server method uses the copy pointer to modify the data in the server's address space. When the method ends, the modified data that needs to be copied back is copied back into the OLE client's address space. This method of parameter data transfer is called *marshaling*. The copying and passing of data is accomplished automatically and transparently by OLE using a *proxy* in the client process and a *stub* in the server process. The proxy and stub handle the marshaling and unmarshaling of parameters.

In an out-of-process server on a different computer than the client's computer, marshaling and unmarshaling are accomplished by use of an extended proxy/stub mechanism that uses remote procedure calls (RPCs) for communication between the proxy and the stub, and another OLE component called the Automation Manager is used. The proxy in the client process uses RPC to communicate with a stub in the Automation Manager, and a proxy within the Automation Manager communicates with the stub in the server.

GUIDs

Code reuse facilitated by automation is good, but there are some problems that must be solved. Within an organization, it may be possible to have unique names for classes and interfaces. But there is no simple way to achieve uniqueness across different vendor products. If two vendors come up with the same names for classes/interfaces, there should be a way to let both vendor implementations coexist. The way is to assign a *globally unique identifier (GUID)* to classes and interfaces. Microsoft includes utilities such as *UUIDGEN*, which generates a unique identifier that, practically, will not be duplicated. Although it is theoretically possible to produce duplicate IDs, inclusion of the time and the address of the machine (the address of the machine's network interface card) as part of the ID ensures nonduplication of IDs (including those produced on the same machine at different times or different machines at the same time).

PROGRAMMING EXAMPLE
FOR AN OLE AUTOMATION SERVER

The sample program shown here is an OLE Automation Server program. It is a simple mortgage calculator that is created as a stand-alone application and to which OLE Automation is added later. Since the program is a stand-alone application, loan details, such as the loan amount, interest rate, and period of loan, can be given by selecting a menu item. The monthly payment can be computed and displayed by selecting another menu item. Later a set of properties and methods is added to the program to make it an OLE Automation Server. This server will then be used by an OLE Automation client that will be created as part of the next sample program.

The simplest way to create the OLE Automation Server and client is by using MFC AppWizard. The steps to create the Automation Server application using MFC AppWizard are detailed next:

1. Create a new MFC AppWizard (exe) project by selecting New from the File menu.

2. Give the project name as **MortCalc**.

3. In MFC AppWizard—Step 1, select Single Document.

4. Click Next in the dialog box, and accept defaults in the Step 2 dialog box.

5. In the Step 3 dialog box, check the Automation check box.

6. In the Step 4 dialog box, click Advanced to specify advanced options.

7. Change the default **MortCa** to **MortCalc** in File New Name and File Type Name. The name given as the File Type Name (MortCalc Document) is used as the long name of the Automation object when used in the Automation client. Default values are accepted in the Window Style tab.

8. Accept default values in the next two steps, and click Finish followed by OK to create all the necessary files and open the project.

The information related to the mortgage calculation is stored in the **CMortCalcDoc** class. Thus, the loan amount *(flLoan)*, interest rate *(flRate)*, loan period in months *(iNumofPayments)*, and monthly payments *(flMonthlyPayment)* are declared as protected member variables in the *Mortcalcdoc.h* header file. The loan amount, interest rate, and monthly payment are declared as *float*, and the loan period is declared as *int*. Also declared are three member functions: **SetLoanData**, to set the loan amount, interest rate, and number of years to repay the loan; **Compute**, to calculate the monthly payment; and **GetLoanData**, to return all information about the loan, including the loan amount, rate, period, and monthly payment.

For this application to be a stand-alone application, there must be a way to input the loan details. This is done by use of a dialog box. So the next step is to create a dialog box to enter loan details. Figure 13-1 shows the initial dialog box displayed when the application is started.

1. Select the ResourceView tab in the workspace window, and insert the dialog box by clicking the right mouse button on the dialog folder and selecting Insert Dialog.

2. Create a dialog box with an ID, IDD_SETLOANDATA. There are three static fields and three entry fields, one set each for loan amount, interest rate, and period. The entry field IDs are respectively IDC_AMOUNT, IDC_RATE, and IDC_YEARS.

3. Rename the OK button to Set Data.

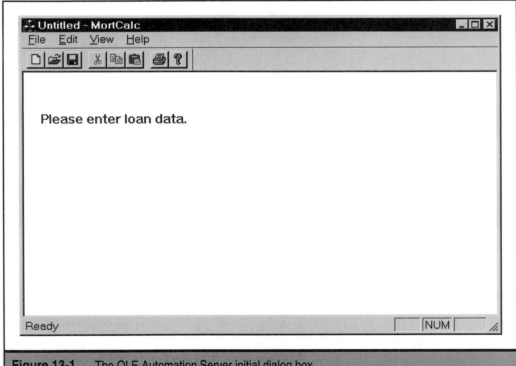

Figure 13-1.   The OLE Automation Server initial dialog box

Figure 13-2 shows this dialog box. Figure 13-3 shows the mortgage calculation results when a loan amount, rate, and period are entered.

4. Start the ClassWizard by double-clicking the dialog box while holding down the CTRL key.

5. Since a class does not exist yet, select Create A New Class in the Adding A Class dialog box. Click OK to get the New Class dialog box. The class name is specified as **CSetLoanDlg**, and the automation is left as none.

6. Click OK to return to the MFC ClassWizard dialog box. Three member variables are added in the Member Variables page. The details of each member variable are as follows: IDC_AMOUNT, m_amount, value, float; IDC_RATE, m_rate, value, float; and IDC_YEARS, m_years, value, int.

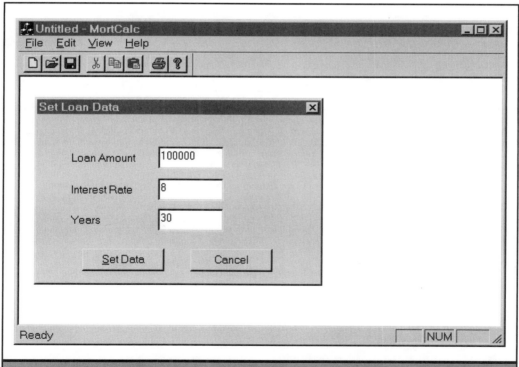

Figure 13-2.   The OLE Automation Server dialog box to set loan data

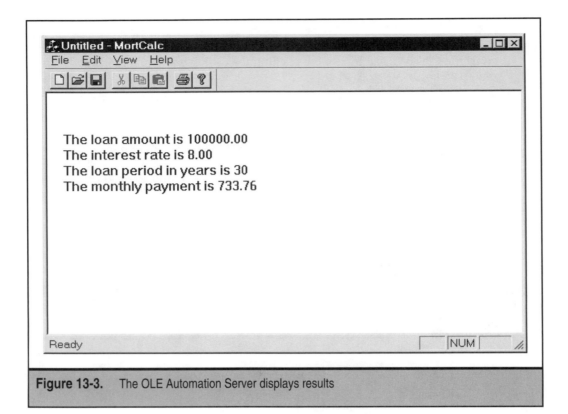

Figure 13-3. The OLE Automation Server displays results

7. Click OK to close the ClassWizard and generate the **CSetLoanDlg** class.

   Shown next are the header file and implementation file for the **CSetLoanDlg** class.

```
#if !defined(AFX_SETLOANDLG_H)
#define AFX_SETLOANDLG_H

#if _MSC_VER >= 1000
#pragma once
#endif // _MSC_VER >= 1000
// SetLoanDlg.h : header file

// CSetLoanDlg dialog

class CSetLoanDlg : public CDialog
{
```

```
// Construction
public:
    CSetLoanDlg(CWnd* pParent = NULL); // standard constructor

// Dialog Data
    //{{AFX_DATA(CSetLoanDlg)

    enum { IDD = IDD_SETLOANDATA };
    float       m_amount;
    float       m_rate;
    int         m_years;
    //}}AFX_DATA


// Overrides
    // ClassWizard generated virtual function overrides
    //{{AFX_VIRTUAL(CSetLoanDlg)
    protected:
    virtual void DoDataExchange(CDataExchange* pDX);
 //}}AFX_VIRTUAL

// Implementation
protected:

    // Generated message map functions
    //{{AFX_MSG(CSetLoanDlg)
    // NOTE: the ClassWizard will add member functions here
    //}}AFX_MSG
    DECLARE_MESSAGE_MAP()
};
//{{AFX_INSERT_LOCATION}}
#endif
```

The implementation file for the dialog class is shown next. Since the data is exchanged automatically by calling the **DoDataExchange** function, there is no custom code in this class.

```
// SetLoanDlg.cpp : implementation file

#include "stdafx.h"
#include "MortCalc.h"
#include "SetLoanDlg.h"

#ifdef _DEBUG
#define new DEBUG_NEW
```

```
#undef THIS_FILE
static char THIS_FILE[] = __FILE__;
#endif

// CSetLoanDlg dialog


CSetLoanDlg::CSetLoanDlg(CWnd* pParent /*=NULL*/)
    : CDialog(CSetLoanDlg::IDD, pParent)
{
    //{{AFX_DATA_INIT(CSetLoanDlg)
    m_amount = 0.0f;
    m_rate = 0.0f;

    m_years = 0;
    //}}AFX_DATA_INIT
}

void CSetLoanDlg::DoDataExchange(CDataExchange* pDX)
{
    CDialog::DoDataExchange(pDX);
    //{{AFX_DATA_MAP(CSetLoanDlg)
    DDX_Text(pDX, IDC_AMOUNT, m_amount);
    DDX_Text(pDX, IDC_RATE, m_rate);
    DDX_Text(pDX, IDC_YEARS, m_years);
    //}}AFX_DATA_MAP
}

BEGIN_MESSAGE_MAP(CSetLoanDlg, CDialog)
    //{{AFX_MSG_MAP(CSetLoanDlg)
    // NOTE: the ClassWizard will add message map macros here
    //}}AFX_MSG_MAP
END_MESSAGE_MAP()

// CSetLoanDlg message handlers
```

Next add the interface to invoke the previously discussed dialog box:

1. Add two menu items to the Edit menu: one to set the loan data through the dialog box and the other to calculate the monthly mortgage payment.

2. From ResourceView, select the Menu folder and open the IDR_ MAINFRAME menu.

3. Under the Edit menu, add two menu items with the following IDs and caption: IDM_SETLOAN/&Set Loan Data and IDM_PAYMENT/&Monthly Payment.

4. Bring up the ClassWizard and in the Message Maps tab select the **CMortCalcView** class.

5. For the IDM_SETLOAN object ID, double-click the **COMMAND** message and accept the default function name in the Add Member Function dialog box. Do the same for the IDM_PAYMENT object ID.

The next step is to add the OLE Automation feature for the application. To do this:

1. Select the Automation tab in the ClassWizard dialog box.

2. Select the **CMortCalcDoc** document class for the name, and click the Add Property button. This brings up the Add Property dialog box.

3. Select the **Get**/**Set** methods implementation.

4. For the loan amount property, give the external name as Principal, specify the type as float, and accept the default **Get** function name.

The loan information will be initialized by a single function, and hence there is no need for individual **Set** functions, which is why they are omitted. No parameters are needed for this function, so none is selected. Three more properties are added for interest rate (Rate/float/GetRate), period of loan (Period/long/GetPeriod), and monthly payment (Payment/float/GetPayment). This sample OLE Automation Server exposes two methods: one to reset the data and the other to set the loan data. They are added by clicking Add Methods and specifying details in the Add Method dialog box. The external and internal name for the first method is **Reset**, and its return type is void. It takes no parameters. The external and internal name for the second method is **SetLoanInfo**, and its return type is void. It takes three parameters whose name/type are Principal/float, Rate/float, and Period/long. Click OK in the ClassWizard, and the application is enabled to act as an OLE Automation Server. Of course, code has to be plugged into the respective empty member functions. The code is shown next.

The **CMortCalcDoc** class, which is the engine for this OLE Automation Server, is shown next. Shown first is the header file. Notice the highlighted code, which shows the member variables and member functions that were added and the OLE-related functions that were added by use of ClassWizard. Notice that there is no individual **Set** function, but instead one **SetLoanInfo** function that sets the loan information.

This sample can also be run as a stand-alone application. In order to be supported as such and perform the mortgage calculation, it needs some additional functions. These methods are **SetLoanData**, which sets the loan detail, **GetLoanData**, which retrieves the loan detail, and **Compute**, which calculates the monthly payment. These functions are manually added to the class. Notice that the **Compute** function is not an OLE Automation method, so the OLE Automation clients (which is discussed later in this chapter) cannot call the **Compute** method directly.

```
// MortCalcDoc.h : interface of the CMortCalcDoc class
//

#if !defined(AFX_MORTCALCDOC_H)
#define AFX_MORTCALCDOC_H

#if _MSC_VER >= 1000
#pragma once
#endif // _MSC_VER >= 1000


class CMortCalcDoc : public CDocument
{
protected: // create from serialization only
    CMortCalcDoc();
    DECLARE_DYNCREATE(CMortCalcDoc)

// Attributes
public:

// Operations
public:

    void    SetLoanData(float amount, float rate, int years);
    void    Compute();
    void    GetLoanData(float *P, float *R, int *Y, float *M);

// Overrides
    // ClassWizard generated virtual function overrides
    //{{AFX_VIRTUAL(CMortCalcDoc)
    public:
    virtual BOOL OnNewDocument();
    virtual void Serialize(CArchive& ar);
    //}}AFX_VIRTUAL

// Implementation
public:
    virtual ~CMortCalcDoc();
#ifdef _DEBUG
    virtual void AssertValid() const;
    virtual void Dump(CDumpContext& dc) const;
#endif
```

```
protected:
    float    flLoan;
    float    flRate;
    int      iNumofPayments;
    float    flMonthlyPayment;

// Generated message map functions
protected:
    DECLARE_MESSAGE_MAP()
    // Generated OLE dispatch map functions
    //{{AFX_DISPATCH(CMortCalcDoc)
    afx_msg float GetPrincipal();
    afx_msg float GetRate();
    afx_msg long GetPeriod();
    afx_msg float GetPayment();
    afx_msg void Reset();
    afx_msg void SetLoanInfo(float Principal,
                             float Rate, long Period);
    //}}AFX_DISPATCH
    DECLARE_DISPATCH_MAP()
    DECLARE_INTERFACE_MAP()
};



//{{AFX_INSERT_LOCATION}}

#endif
```

The implementation file is shown next. Looking at the MFC class hierarchy, you can see that the **CMortCalcDoc** class indirectly derives from **CCmdTarget**. To be exposed through Automation, the **CCmdTarget** derived class, **CMortCalcDoc** in this case, should call the **EnableAutomation** member function during construction of the class object, and it should also include a dispatch map. Since the Automation was exposed by use of AppWizard, the ClassWizard automatically adds the code. The class should also call **AfxOleLockApp** and **AfxOleUnlockApp** to increment and decrement the global count of active objects maintained by the framework. This prevents the user from closing the application while it still has active objects. If there are still active objects, the framework hides the application instead of completely shutting it down. Thus, during construction **AfxOleLockApp** is called, and during destruction **AfxOleUnlockApp** is called. The DISP_PROPERTY_EX macro defines the OLE Automation property by its external name, the accessing functions (in this sample the **Set** function is not supported), and the properties type. The DISP_FUNCTION macro defines the OLE Automation methods by its external name, member function name, return type, and parameters type (in this case, since there are multiple parameters, they are separated by spaces).

```
// MortCalcDoc.cpp:implementation of the CMortCalcDoc class
#include "stdafx.h"
#include "MortCalc.h"

#include "MortCalcDoc.h"

#ifdef _DEBUG
#define new DEBUG_NEW
#undef THIS_FILE
static char THIS_FILE[] = __FILE__;
#endif

// CMortCalcDoc

IMPLEMENT_DYNCREATE(CMortCalcDoc, CDocument)

BEGIN_MESSAGE_MAP(CMortCalcDoc, CDocument)
END_MESSAGE_MAP()

BEGIN_DISPATCH_MAP(CMortCalcDoc, CDocument)
    //{{AFX_DISPATCH_MAP(CMortCalcDoc)
    DISP_PROPERTY_EX(CMortCalcDoc, "Principal",
                    GetPrincipal, SetNotSupported, VT_R4)
    DISP_PROPERTY_EX(CMortCalcDoc, "Rate", GetRate,
                    SetNotSupported, VT_R4)
    DISP_PROPERTY_EX(CMortCalcDoc, "Period", GetPeriod,
                    SetNotSupported, VT_I4)
    DISP_PROPERTY_EX(CMortCalcDoc, "Payment", GetPayment,
                    SetNotSupported, VT_R4)
    DISP_FUNCTION(CMortCalcDoc, "Reset", Reset,
                 VT_EMPTY, VTS_NONE)
    DISP_FUNCTION(CMortCalcDoc, "SetLoanInfo", SetLoanInfo,
                 VT_EMPTY, VTS_R4 VTS_R4 VTS_I4)
    //}}AFX_DISPATCH_MAP
END_DISPATCH_MAP()
```

All OLE Automation Servers and ActiveX control servers require a unique class ID, which is defined here:

```
// Note: we add support for IID_IMortCalc to support
// typesafe binding from VBA.  This IID must match the GUID
// that is attached to the dispinterface in the .ODL file.

// {0109A0D5-1969-11D1-97B2-000000000000}
```

```
static const IID IID_IMortCalc =
{ 0x109a0d5, 0x1969, 0x11d1,
  { 0x97, 0xb2, 0x0, 0x0, 0x0, 0x0, 0x0, 0x0 } };

BEGIN_INTERFACE_MAP(CMortCalcDoc, CDocument)
    INTERFACE_PART(CMortCalcDoc, IID_IMortCalc, Dispatch)
END_INTERFACE_MAP()

// CMortCalcDoc construction/destruction

CMortCalcDoc::CMortCalcDoc()
{
    // TODO: add one-time construction code here

    EnableAutomation();
    AfxOleLockApp();


    flLoan = 0.0;
    flRate = 0.0;
    iNumofPayments = 0;
    flMonthlyPayment = 0.0;
}

CMortCalcDoc::~CMortCalcDoc()
{
    AfxOleUnlockApp();
}

BOOL CMortCalcDoc::OnNewDocument()
{
    if (!CDocument::OnNewDocument())
        return FALSE;

    // TODO: add reinitialization code here
    // (SDI documents will reuse this document)

    return TRUE;
}

// CMortCalcDoc serialization
void CMortCalcDoc::Serialize(CArchive& ar)
{
    if (ar.IsStoring())
```

```
    {
        // TODO: add storing code here
    }
    else
    {
        // TODO: add loading code here
    }
}


// CMortCalcDoc diagnostics
#ifdef _DEBUG
void CMortCalcDoc::AssertValid() const
{
    CDocument::AssertValid();
}

void CMortCalcDoc::Dump(CDumpContext& dc) const
{
    CDocument::Dump(dc);
}
#endif //_DEBUG
```

The next three functions are member functions of the **CMortCalcDoc** class. They set the loan data (notice that the year is converted to months, assuming monthly payment), compute the monthly payment, and return the loan data, including monthly payment. Please note that the include file *math.h,* which declares *pow* functions, is added in **StdAfx.h** and is not shown here.

```
// CMortCalcDoc commands
void CMortCalcDoc::SetLoanData(float amount,
                              float rate, int years)
{
    flLoan = amount;
    flRate = rate;
    iNumofPayments = years*12;
}


void CMortCalcDoc::Compute()
{

// P = principal, I = interest rate, L = years.
// J = I/(12*100)
// N = L*12 - number payments
// Monthly payment = P * (J/(1-(1+J)** -N))
```

```
        double J = flRate/(1200.0);


        double OnePlusJPowerMinusN = pow ((double)(1.0 + J),
                                    (double)-iNumofPayments);
        flMonthlyPayment = flLoan *
                           (float)(J/(1.0-OnePlusJPowerMinusN));
}

void CMortCalcDoc::GetLoanData(float *P, float *R,
                               int *Y, float *M)
{
    *P = flLoan;
    *R = flRate;
    *Y = iNumofPayments/12;
    *M = flMonthlyPayment;
}
```

The next six functions implement the OLE Automation properties and methods exposed by this MortCalc application. Since a method to compute the monthly payment is not exposed, the **SetLoanInfo** method during its processing sets the loan data and calls the **Compute** function.

```
float CMortCalcDoc::GetPrincipal()
{
    // TODO: Add your property handler here
    return flLoan;
}

float CMortCalcDoc::GetRate()
{
    // TODO: Add your property handler here
    return flRate;
}

long CMortCalcDoc::GetPeriod()
{
    // TODO: Add your property handler here
    return iNumofPayments/12;
}

float CMortCalcDoc::GetPayment()
{
    // TODO: Add your property handler here
```

```
        return flMonthlyPayment;
}

void CMortCalcDoc::Reset()
{
    // TODO: Add your dispatch handler code here
    flLoan = 0.0;
    flRate = 0.0;
    iNumofPayments = 0;
    flMonthlyPayment = 0.0;
}

void CMortCalcDoc::SetLoanInfo(float Principal,
                               float Rate, long Period)
{
    // TODO: Add your dispatch handler code here
    flLoan = Principal;
    flRate = Rate;
    iNumofPayments = Period*12;
    Compute();
}
```

As mentioned earlier, this OLE Automation Server application can also be a stand-alone application. The code in the **CMortCalcView** class provides an interface to the user to enter loan data, calculate the monthly payment, and display the results on the screen. The header file is shown, followed by the implementation file. The relevant code appears in bold.

```
// MortCalcView.h : interface of the CMortCalcView class

#if !defined(AFX_MORTCALCVIEW_H)
#define AFX_MORTCALCVIEW_H

#if _MSC_VER >= 1000
#pragma once
#endif // _MSC_VER >= 1000

class CMortCalcView : public CView
{
protected: // create from serialization only
    CMortCalcView();
    DECLARE_DYNCREATE(CMortCalcView)
// Attributes
public:
```

```
        CMortCalcDoc* GetDocument();
// Operations
public:
// Overrides
        // ClassWizard generated virtual function overrides
        //{{AFX_VIRTUAL(CMortCalcView)
        public:
        virtual void OnDraw(CDC* pDC);   // overridden to draw this view
        virtual BOOL PreCreateWindow(CREATESTRUCT& cs);
        protected:
        virtual BOOL OnPreparePrinting(CPrintInfo* pInfo);
        virtual void OnBeginPrinting(CDC* pDC, CPrintInfo* pInfo);
        virtual void OnEndPrinting(CDC* pDC, CPrintInfo* pInfo);
        //}}AFX_VIRTUAL

// Implementation
public:
        virtual ~CMortCalcView();
#ifdef _DEBUG
        virtual void AssertValid() const;
        virtual void Dump(CDumpContext& dc) const;
#endif

protected:

// Generated message map functions
protected:
        //{{AFX_MSG(CMortCalcView)
        afx_msg void OnPayment();
        afx_msg void OnSetloan();
        //}}AFX_MSG
        DECLARE_MESSAGE_MAP()
};

#ifndef _DEBUG  // debug version in MortCalcView.cpp
inline CMortCalcDoc* CMortCalcView::GetDocument()
   { return (CMortCalcDoc*)m_pDocument; }
#endif
//{{AFX_INSERT_LOCATION}}
#endif


// MortCalcView.cpp : implementation of the CMortCalcView class
//
```

```
#include "stdafx.h"
#include "MortCalc.h"

#include "MortCalcDoc.h"
#include "MortCalcView.h"


#include "SetLoanDlg.h"

#ifdef _DEBUG
#define new DEBUG_NEW
#undef THIS_FILE
static char THIS_FILE[] = __FILE__;
#endif

// CMortCalcView

IMPLEMENT_DYNCREATE(CMortCalcView, CView)

BEGIN_MESSAGE_MAP(CMortCalcView, CView)
    //{{AFX_MSG_MAP(CMortCalcView)
    ON_COMMAND(IDM_PAYMENT, OnPayment)
    ON_COMMAND(IDM_SETLOAN, OnSetloan)
    //}}AFX_MSG_MAP
    // Standard printing commands
    ON_COMMANDID_FILE_PRINT,CView::OnFilePrint)
    ON_COMMANDID_FILE_PRINT_DIRECT,CView::OnFilePrint)
    ON_COMMANDID_FILE_PRINT_PREVIEW,CView::OnFilePrintPreview)
END_MESSAGE_MAP()

// CMortCalcView construction/destruction

CMortCalcView::CMortCalcView()
{
    // TODO: add construction code here
}


CMortCalcView::~CMortCalcView()
{
}


BOOL CMortCalcView::PreCreateWindow(CREATESTRUCT& cs)
{
  // TODO: Modify the Window class or styles here by modifying
```

```
      //  the CREATESTRUCT cs
        return CView::PreCreateWindow(cs);
}

// CMortCalcView drawing

void CMortCalcView::OnDraw(CDC* pDC)
{
    CMortCalcDoc* pDoc = GetDocument();
    ASSERT_VALID(pDoc);

    // TODO: add draw code for native data here
    float P, R, M;
    int Y;
    char    szBuffer[256];
    pDoc->GetLoanData(&P, &R, &Y, &M);
    if (M == 0.0)
    {
        strcpy (szBuffer, "Please enter loan data.");
        pDC->TextOut(20, 50, szBuffer);
    }
    else
    {
        sprintf (szBuffer, "The loan amount is %.2f", P);
        pDC->TextOut(20, 50, szBuffer);
        sprintf (szBuffer, "The interest rate is %.2f", R);
        pDC->TextOut(20, 70, szBuffer);
        sprintf (szBuffer, "The loan period in years is %d",
                 Y);
        pDC->TextOut(20, 90, szBuffer);
        sprintf (szBuffer, "The monthly payment is %.2f", M);
        pDC->TextOut(20, 110, szBuffer);
    }
}


// CMortCalcView printing

BOOL CMortCalcView::OnPreparePrinting(CPrintInfo* pInfo)
{
    // default preparation
    return DoPreparePrinting(pInfo);
}

void CMortCalcView::OnBeginPrinting
```

```
                              (CDC* /*pDC*/, CPrintInfo* /*pInfo*/)
{
    // TODO: add extra initialization before printing
}

void CMortCalcView::OnEndPrinting
                      (CDC* /*pDC*/, CPrintInfo* /*pInfo*/)
{
    // TODO: add cleanup after printing
}

// CMortCalcView diagnostics

#ifdef _DEBUG
void CMortCalcView::AssertValid() const
{
    CView::AssertValid();
}

void CMortCalcView::Dump(CDumpContext& dc) const
{
    CView::Dump(dc);
}

CMortCalcDoc* CMortCalcView::GetDocument()
{
  ASSERT(m_pDocument->IsKindOf(RUNTIME_CLASS(CMortCalcDoc)));
  return (CMortCalcDoc*)m_pDocument;
}
#endif //_DEBUG

// CMortCalcView message handlers
void CMortCalcView::OnPayment()
{
    // TODO: Add your command handler code here
    CMortCalcDoc     *pDoc = GetDocument();
    ASSERT_VALID(pDoc);
    pDoc->Compute();
    Invalidate();
}

void CMortCalcView::OnSetloan()
{
    // TODO: Add your command handler code here
```

```
    CSetLoanDlg dbSetLoanDlg;

    if (dbSetLoanDlg.DoModal() == IDOK)
    {
        CMortCalcDoc      *pDoc = GetDocument();
        ASSERT_VALID(pDoc);


        pDoc->SetLoanData(dbSetLoanDlg.m_amount,
                          dbSetLoanDlg.m_rate,
                          dbSetLoanDlg.m_years);
    }
}
```

The main application class, **CMortCalcApp**, is shown next. The code related to the About dialog box is omitted. This code is automatically generated by the AppWizard, and it is worth looking at the OLE-related code.

```
// MortCalc.h : main header file for the MORTCALC application
//

#if !defined(AFX_MORTCALC_H)
#define AFX_MORTCALC_H

#if _MSC_VER >= 1000
#pragma once
#endif // _MSC_VER >= 1000

#ifndef __AFXWIN_H__
  #error include 'stdafx.h' before including this file for PCH
#endif

#include "resource.h"
// CMortCalcApp:
// See MortCalc.cpp for the implementation of this class

class CMortCalcApp : public CWinApp
{
public:
    CMortCalcApp();

// Overrides
    // ClassWizard generated virtual function overrides
    //{{AFX_VIRTUAL(CMortCalcApp)
```

```
    public:
    virtual BOOL InitInstance();
    //}}AFX_VIRTUAL

// Implementation
    COleTemplateServer m_server;
        // Server object for document creation
    //{{AFX_MSG(CMortCalcApp)
    afx_msg void OnAppAbout();
    DECLARE_MESSAGE_MAP()
};
#endif


// MortCalc.cpp

#include "stdafx.h"
#include "MortCalc.h"

#include "MainFrm.h"
#include "MortCalcDoc.h"
#include "MortCalcView.h"

#ifdef _DEBUG
#define new DEBUG_NEW
#undef THIS_FILE
static char THIS_FILE[] = __FILE__;
#endif

// CMortCalcApp

BEGIN_MESSAGE_MAP(CMortCalcApp, CWinApp)
    //{{AFX_MSG_MAP(CMortCalcApp)
    ON_COMMAND(ID_APP_ABOUT, OnAppAbout)
    // Standard file based document commands
    ON_COMMAND(ID_FILE_NEW, CWinApp::OnFileNew)
    ON_COMMAND(ID_FILE_OPEN, CWinApp::OnFileOpen)
    // Standard print setup command
    ON_COMMAND(ID_FILE_PRINT_SETUP, CWinApp::OnFilePrintSetup)
END_MESSAGE_MAP()

// CMortCalcApp construction
CMortCalcApp::CMortCalcApp()
{
    // TODO: add construction code here
```

```
    // Place all significant initialization in InitInstance
}

// The one and only CMortCalcApp object

CMortCalcApp theApp;

// {0109A0D3-1969-11D1-97B2-000000000000}
static const CLSID clsid =
{ 0x109a0d3, 0x1969, 0x11d1,
  { 0x97, 0xb2, 0x0, 0x0, 0x0, 0x0, 0x0, 0x0 } };
```

During initialization of the application, OLE DLLs are initialized by calling the **AfxOleInit** function. The call to **ConnectTemplate** registers this application's class ID in the Registry. The class ID shown earlier that is generated by the AppWizard is random and is statistically guaranteed to be unique. A regeneration of this application will produce a different class ID altogether.

```
// CMortCalcApp initialization
BOOL CMortCalcApp::InitInstance()
{
    // Initialize OLE libraries
    if (!AfxOleInit())
    {
        AfxMessageBox(IDP_OLE_INIT_FAILED);
        return FALSE;
    }

#ifdef _AFXDLL
    Enable3dControls();
#else
    Enable3dControlsStatic();
#endif

    // Change the registry key under which our settings
    // are stored. You should modify this string to be
    // something appropriate such as the name of your
    // company or organization.
    SetRegistryKey(_T("Local AppWizard-Generated Applications"));
    LoadStdProfileSettings();

    // Register the application's document templates.
    // Document templates serve as the connection
    // between documents, frame windows and views.
```

```
CSingleDocTemplate* pDocTemplate;
pDocTemplate = new CSingleDocTemplate(
    IDR_MAINFRAME,
    RUNTIME_CLASS(CMortCalcDoc),
    RUNTIME_CLASS(CMainFrame),
    RUNTIME_CLASS(CMortCalcView));
AddDocTemplate(pDocTemplate);

// Connect the COleTemplateServer to the document template.
//  The COleTemplateServer creates new documents on behalf
//  of requesting OLE containers by using information
//  specified in the document template.
m_server.ConnectTemplate(clsid, pDocTemplate, TRUE);
// Note: SDI applications register server objects
// only if /Embedding or /Automation is present
// on the command line.

// Parse command line for standard shell commands,
// DDE, file open
CCommandLineInfo cmdInfo;
ParseCommandLine(cmdInfo);

// Check to see if launched as OLE server
if (cmdInfo.m_bRunEmbedded || cmdInfo.m_bRunAutomated)
{
    // Register all OLE server (factories) as running.
    // This enables the OLE libraries to create objects
    // from other applications.
    COleTemplateServer::RegisterAll();

    // Application was run with /Embedding
    // or /Automation.  Don't show the
    //  main window in this case.
    return TRUE;
}

// When a server application is launched stand-alone,
// it is a good idea to update the system registry
// in case it has been damaged.
m_server.UpdateRegistry(OAT_DISPATCH_OBJECT);
COleObjectFactory::UpdateRegistryAll();

// Dispatch commands specified on the command line
```

```
    if (!ProcessShellCommand(cmdInfo))
        return FALSE;

    // The one and only window has been initialized,
    // so show and update it.
    m_pMainWnd->ShowWindow(SW_SHOW);
    m_pMainWnd->UpdateWindow();

    return TRUE;
}
```

After building this OLE server application, you need to register it with Windows. AppWizard creates a Registry text file that can be imported into the Registry. To import the Registry file, start Regedit and select Import Registry File from the File menu. In the file selection dialog box, navigate through the directory structure and select the *MortCalc.reg* file. Regedit imports the Registry file and displays an informational message. For convenience, the executable is also copied to a directory that is in the PATH statement.

OLE AUTOMATION CLIENTS

Next let's look at OLE Automation clients, which include the functionality provided by OLE Automation Servers. One OLE Automation client can include the functionality provided by many OLE Automation Servers as part of the same application.

There are two types of OLE Automation clients:

▼ Clients that obtain information about the methods and properties of the server at run time using the **IDispatch** interface.

▲ Clients that include information about the methods and properties of the server at compile time and use the **COleDispatchDriver** class and the ClassWizard. You can specify the type-library file describing the properties and functions of the server application's object. ClassWizard reads this file and creates the **COleDispatchDriver**-derived class, with member functions that your application can call to access the server application's objects.

PROGRAMMING EXAMPLE FOR AN OLE AUTOMATION CLIENT

The next sample discussed here is an Automation client application that drives the *MORTCALC* sample application developed earlier. When run, it displays a dialog box with entry fields to enter the loan details, such as the loan amount, interest rate, and period of loan, as shown in Figure 13-4.

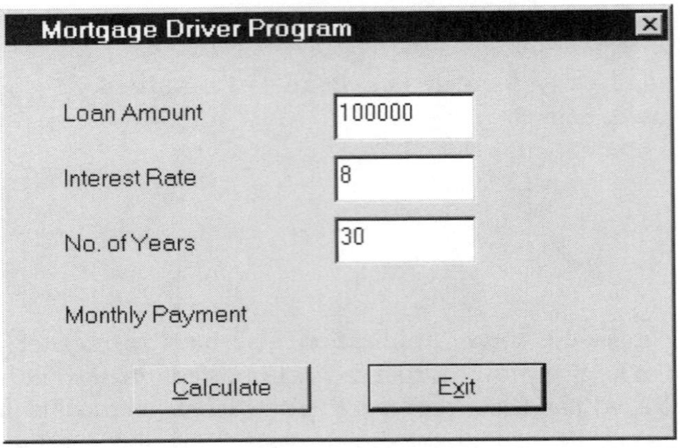

Figure 13-4. The OLE Automation client initial dialog box

When the Calculate button in the dialog box is clicked, it invokes the Automation Server method, which calculates the monthly payments. The application then retrieves the monthly payment property and displays the dialog box shown in Figure 13-5.

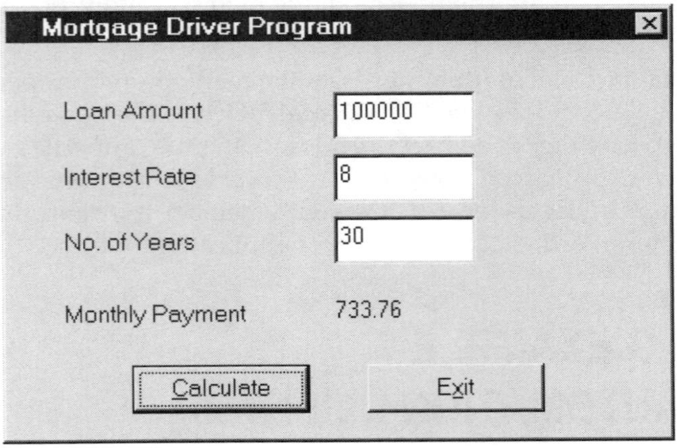

Figure 13-5. The OLE Automation client displays results

This dialog-based application is created by use of the AppWizard, and you are invited to follow along the steps to create the application:

1. Create a new MFC AppWizard (exe) project with the project name MortDriv.

2. In the MFC AppWizard—Step 1 dialog box, set the application type to Dialog Based Application Type.

3. In MFC AppWizard—Step 2—leave the ActiveX Controls check box unchecked and specify Mortgage Driver Program as the program heading.

4. Leave the rest of the information at default values and click Finish. Click OK in the New Project Information dialog box.

This creates all the necessary files for this project.

1. At this point an empty main dialog, IDD_MORTDRIV_DIALOG, should already be up. If not, create the dialog box by selecting the ResourceView tab in the Workspace window, opening the Dialog folder, and double-clicking IDD_MORTDRIV_DIALOG.

2. This brings up the dialog editor. Create three sets of static text and entry fields—one each for Loan Amount, Interest Rate, and No. of Years. The entry field IDs are respectively IDC_PRINCIPAL, IDC_RATE, and IDC_PERIOD.

3. After the monthly mortgage payment is calculated, the result is shown as static text in the dialog box. To realize this action, create two more static fields, one for prompt text (Monthly Payment) and the other for actual monthly payment. Specify the ID for the static text that displays actual monthly payment as IDC_PAYMENT. Specify a control ID, since this static text needs to be altered every time the monthly payment is calculated.

4. Change the property of the OK button by setting the text to Calculate and the ID to IDC_CALCULATE.

The Automation server MortCalc is accessed by the client through a proxy class that encapsulates the server. The ClassWizard provides an easy means for generating this proxy class from the Automation Server application's type library. To generate the proxy class:

1. Bring up the ClassWizard and click Add Class.

2. From the pull-down menu, select the From A Type Library option.

3. The Import From Type Library dialog box is displayed. Select the Automation Server type library by navigating through the directory structure and selecting the *MortCalc.tlb* file.

4. In the Confirm Classes dialog box, change the class name from **IMortCalc** to **CMortCalc** just to match the rest of the class names. Accept the rest of the module names as suggested by the panel.

5. Select OK to generate the proxy class. An object of this proxy class is added as a protected member variable of the application dialog class, as will be seen later.

6. Complete the rest of the client application functionality by adding member variables for each of the modifiable fields in the dialog box, namely, IDC_PRINCIPAL, IDC_RATE, IDC_PERIOD, and IDC_PAYMENT. The member variable name, category, and variable type for these are respectively m_principal/value/float, m_rate/value/float, m_period/value/int, and m_payment/value/CString.

7. In the Message Maps tab, the processing of the **BN_CLICKED** message for the IDC_CALCULATE button is set to the function **OnCalculate**. OLE needs to be initialized when the dialog is created. To make this happen, select the **CMortDrivDlg** object ID and double-click on the WM_CREATE message to add the **OnCreate** function.

8. Select OK in the ClassWizard dialog box to create the boilerplate code for the dialog box.

The dialog class header file and the implementation file are shown next. This is a standard dialog class. The noticeable difference is the addition of a **CMortCalc** object, **m_mortcalc**. **CMortCalc**, it may be recalled, is the wrapper class for the Automation Server. An object of the Automation Server wrapper class, **m_mortcalc** is added as a protected member variable. The methods and properties of the Automation Server are accessed by use of this Automation Server object.

```
// MortDrivDlg.h : header file
//
#if !defined(AFX_MORTDRIVDLG_H)
#define AFX_MORTDRIVDLG_H

#if _MSC_VER >= 1000
#pragma once
#endif // _MSC_VER >= 1000

// CMortDrivDlg dialog
class CMortDrivDlg : public CDialog
{
// Construction
public:
    CMortDrivDlg(CWnd* pParent = NULL);

// Dialog Data
    //{{AFX_DATA(CMortDrivDlg)
    enum { IDD = IDD_MORTDRIV_DIALOG };
    CString     m_payment;
```

```
    int         m_period;
    float       m_principal;
    float       m_rate;
    //}}AFX_DATA

    // ClassWizard generated virtual function overrides
    //{{AFX_VIRTUAL(CMortDrivDlg)
    protected:
    virtual void DoDataExchange(CDataExchange* pDX);
    //}}AFX_VIRTUAL

// Implementation
protected:
    HICON m_hIcon;
    CMortCalc    m_mortcalc;

    // Generated message map functions
    //{{AFX_MSG(CMortDrivDlg)
    virtual BOOL OnInitDialog();
    afx_msg void OnSysCommand(UINT nID, LPARAM lParam);
    afx_msg void OnPaint();
    afx_msg HCURSOR OnQueryDragIcon();
    afx_msg void OnCalculate();
    afx_msg int OnCreate(LPCREATESTRUCT lpCreateStruct);
    //}}AFX_MSG
    DECLARE_MESSAGE_MAP()
};
#endif
```

The implementation file is shown next. The code relating to the About dialog box processing is not shown. In the **OnCreate** function, the **IDispatch** object is created by calling the **CreateDispatch** member function. This creates the **IDispatch** object and attaches it to the **COleDispatchDriver** object. A pointer to the programmatic identifier to the Automation object, **MortCalc.Document** in this case, is passed. The only other function of interest is the button command processing for the Calculate button.

```
// MortDrivDlg.cpp : implementation file
//

#include "stdafx.h"
#include "MortDriv.h"

#include "MortCalc.h"
#include "MortDrivDlg.h"
```

```
#ifdef _DEBUG
#define new DEBUG_NEW
#undef THIS_FILE
static char THIS_FILE[] = __FILE__;
#endif

// CMortDrivDlg dialog

CMortDrivDlg::CMortDrivDlg(CWnd* pParent /*=NULL*/)
    : CDialog(CMortDrivDlg::IDD, pParent)
{
    //{{AFX_DATA_INIT(CMortDrivDlg)
    m_payment = _T("");
    m_period = 0;
    m_principal = 0.0f;
    m_rate = 0.0f;
    //}}AFX_DATA_INIT
    m_hIcon = AfxGetApp()->LoadIcon(IDR_MAINFRAME);
}

void CMortDrivDlg::DoDataExchange(CDataExchange* pDX)
{
    CDialog::DoDataExchange(pDX);
    //{{AFX_DATA_MAP(CMortDrivDlg)
    DDX_Text(pDX, IDC_PAYMENT, m_payment);
    DDX_Text(pDX, IDC_PERIOD, m_period);
    DDX_Text(pDX, IDC_PRINCIPAL, m_principal);
    DDX_Text(pDX, IDC_RATE, m_rate);
    //}}AFX_DATA_MAP
}

BEGIN_MESSAGE_MAP(CMortDrivDlg, CDialog)
    //{{AFX_MSG_MAP(CMortDrivDlg)
    ON_WM_SYSCOMMAND()
    ON_WM_PAINT()
    ON_WM_QUERYDRAGICON()
    ON_BN_CLICKED(IDC_CALCULATE, OnCalculate)
    ON_WM_CREATE()
    //}}AFX_MSG_MAP
END_MESSAGE_MAP()

// CMortDrivDlg message handlers

int CMortDrivDlg::OnCreate(LPCREATESTRUCT lpCreateStruct)
{
```

```
      if (CDialog::OnCreate(lpCreateStruct) == -1)
          return -1;
      // TODO: Add your specialized creation code here
      if (!m_mortcalc.CreateDispatch(_T("MortCalc.Document")))

      {
          AfxMessageBox("MortCalc Missing");
          return -1;
      }
      return 0;
}


BOOL CMortDrivDlg::OnInitDialog()
{
      CDialog::OnInitDialog();

      // Add "About..." menu item to system menu.

      // IDM_ABOUTBOX must be in the system command range.
      ASSERT((IDM_ABOUTBOX & 0xFFF0) == IDM_ABOUTBOX);
      ASSERT(IDM_ABOUTBOX < 0xF000);

      CMenu* pSysMenu = GetSystemMenu(FALSE);
      if (pSysMenu != NULL)
      {
          CString strAboutMenu;
          strAboutMenu.LoadString(IDS_ABOUTBOX);
          if (!strAboutMenu.IsEmpty())
          {
              pSysMenu->AppendMenu(MF_SEPARATOR);
              pSysMenu->AppendMenu(MF_STRING,
                                        IDM_ABOUTBOX,
                                        strAboutMenu);
          }
      }

      // Set the icon for this dialog.
      // The framework does this automatically
      //  when the application's main window is not a dialog
      SetIcon(m_hIcon, TRUE);            // Set big icon
      SetIcon(m_hIcon, FALSE);           // Set small icon

      // TODO: Add extra initialization here
      return TRUE;
}
```

```
void CMortDrivDlg::OnSysCommand(UINT nID, LPARAM lParam)
{
    if ((nID & 0xFFF0) == IDM_ABOUTBOX)
    {
        CAboutDlg dlgAbout;
        dlgAbout.DoModal();
    }

    else
    {
        CDialog::OnSysCommand(nID, lParam);
    }
}


void CMortDrivDlg::OnPaint()
{
    if (IsIconic())
    {
        CPaintDC dc(this); // device context for painting

        SendMessage(WM_ICONERASEBKGND,
                    (WPARAM) dc.GetSafeHdc(), 0);

        // Center icon in client rectangle
        int cxIcon = GetSystemMetrics(SM_CXICON);
        int cyIcon = GetSystemMetrics(SM_CYICON);
        CRect rect;
        GetClientRect(&rect);
        int x = (rect.Width() - cxIcon + 1) / 2;
        int y = (rect.Height() - cyIcon + 1) / 2;

        // Draw the icon
        dc.DrawIcon(x, y, m_hIcon);
    }
    else
    {
        CDialog::OnPaint();
    }
}

// The system calls this to obtain the cursor to
// display while the user drags
// the minimized window.
HCURSOR CMortDrivDlg::OnQueryDragIcon()
{
```

```
        return (HCURSOR) m_hIcon;
}
```

When the Calculate button is clicked, the data from the dialog box is updated and the **SetLoanInfo** method of the Automation Server is called to set the loan data. This will not only set the loan information but also compute the monthly payment. The Payment property is queried and displayed in the dialog box.

```
void CMortDrivDlg::OnCalculate()
{
    float    flPayment;
    char     szPayment[32];

    UpdateData(TRUE);

    m_mortcalc.SetLoanInfo(m_principal, m_rate, m_period);
    flPayment = m_mortcalc.GetPayment();
    sprintf(szPayment, "%.2f", flPayment);
    m_payment = szPayment;
    UpdateData (FALSE);
}
```

This part of the process is not shown here, but the OLE-related DLLs are initialized during the **InitInstance** processing of the application in *Mortdriv.cpp*.

Shown next is the ClassWizard-generated proxy class for the Automation Server:

```
// Machine generated IDispatch wrapper class(es)
// created with ClassWizard
// CMortCalc wrapper class

class CMortCalc : public COleDispatchDriver
{
public:
    CMortCalc() {}
    CMortCalc(LPDISPATCH pDispatch) :
        COleDispatchDriver(pDispatch) {}
    CMortCalc(const CMortCalc& dispatchSrc) :
        COleDispatchDriver(dispatchSrc) {}

// Attributes
public:
    float GetPrincipal();
    void SetPrincipal(float);
    float GetRate();
    void SetRate(float);
    long GetPeriod();
    void SetPeriod(long);
```

```
        float GetPayment();
        void SetPayment(float);

// Operations
public:
        void Reset();
        void SetLoanInfo(float Principal,float Rate,long Period);
};
```

The ClassWizard-generated implementation module follows:

```
// Machine generated IDispatch wrapper class(es)
// created with ClassWizard

#include "stdafx.h"
#include "mortcalc.h"

#ifdef _DEBUG
#define new DEBUG_NEW
#undef THIS_FILE
static char THIS_FILE[] = __FILE__;
#endif

// CMortCalc properties

float CMortCalc::GetPrincipal()
{
    float result;
    GetProperty(0x1, VT_R4, (void*)&result);
    return result;
}

void CMortCalc::SetPrincipal(float propVal)
{
    SetProperty(0x1, VT_R4, propVal);
}

float CMortCalc::GetRate()
{
    float result;
    GetProperty(0x2, VT_R4, (void*)&result);
    return result;
}

void CMortCalc::SetRate(float propVal)
```

```
{
    SetProperty(0x2, VT_R4, propVal);
}

long CMortCalc::GetPeriod()
{
    long result;
    GetProperty(0x3, VT_I4, (void*)&result);
    return result;
}

void CMortCalc::SetPeriod(long propVal)
{
    SetProperty(0x3, VT_I4, propVal);
}

float CMortCalc::GetPayment()
{
    float result;
    GetProperty(0x4, VT_R4, (void*)&result);
    return result;
}

void CMortCalc::SetPayment(float propVal)
{
    SetProperty(0x4, VT_R4, propVal);
}

// CMortCalc operations

void CMortCalc::Reset()
{
    InvokeHelper(0x5, DISPATCH_METHOD, VT_EMPTY, NULL, NULL);
}

void CMortCalc::SetLoanInfo(float Principal,
                           float Rate,
                           long Period)
{
    static BYTE parms[] =
        VTS_R4 VTS_R4 VTS_I4;
    InvokeHelper(0x6, DISPATCH_METHOD, VT_EMPTY, NULL, parms,
        Principal, Rate, Period);
}
```

OLE DRAG-AND-DROP

The concept of drag-and-drop is not unique to OLE. You can drag and drop a file in Windows Explorer if you want to copy a file, for example. OLE drag-and-drop is a more generalized drag-and-drop. Unlike in the Explorer, which deals primarily with files in its drag-and-drop operations, OLE drag-and-drop, like a Clipboard, can handle a wide variety of data, and the user interface mechanism is a lot simpler compared with the keystroke/mouse clicks required to copy data using the Clipboard.

By use of OLE drag-and-drop, data transfer can be from one location to another within the same document, or between different documents, or even between different applications. The source and the target for the drag-and-drop must be open and must be at least partially visible on the screen.

Function/Methods	Description
RegisterDragDrop	This registers the specified window as a potential target of an OLE drag-and-drop operation. This function calls the IUnknown::AddRef method.
RevokeDragDrop	This revokes the registration of the specified application window. This function calls the IUnknown::Release method.
DoDragDrop	This invokes different methods in IDropSource and IDropTarget interfaces and carries out a drag-and-drop operation.
IDropTarget::DragEnter	The DoDragDrop function calls this method to determine the effect of a drop the first time the user drags the mouse into the registered window of a drop target. To implement this method, you must determine whether the target can use the data in the source data object by checking the format and medium specified by the data object, the input value of pdwEffect, and the state of the modifier keys.
IDropTarget::DragOver	The DoDragDrop function calls this method each time the user moves the mouse across a given target window. You must provide features similar to those in IDropTarget::DragEnter.
IUnknown::AddRef	This increments the reference count for the calling interface on an object and is called for every new copy of a pointer to an interface on a given object.
IUnknown::Release	This decrements the reference count for the calling interface on an object. The memory allocated to the object is freed if the reference count for the object falls to zero.

Table 13-1. Functions and Methods Used in OLE Drag-and-Drop

A number of functions and methods are available for you to program the OLE drag-and-drop capability, and these are summarized in Table 13-1.

The source of drag-and-drop may be non-OLE applications. You can get source data from applications that do not support compound documents (or customize standard OLE drag-and-drop behavior) by creating a **COleDataSource** object and calling the **DoDragDrop** function from this object when the user starts a drag-and-drop operation. Similarly, the target for drag-and-drop could be non-OLE applications as well as OLE applications. You enable drop support in your OLE (or non-OLE) application by adding a member variable of type **COleDropTarget** (or a class derived from it) to each view in the application that you want to be a drop target and calling the new member variable's **Register** member function from the view class's function that handles the **WM_CREATE** message. You may override functions such as **OnDragEnter**, **OnDragLeave**, and so on. The programming details for implementing drag-and-drop mentioned earlier apply to both container and server applications. In most cases, OLE takes care of deleting the data involved in the drag-and-drop operation after that operation is complete.

PROGRAMMING EXAMPLE FOR OLE DRAG-AND-DROP

The next sample shows how to implement a simple drag-and-drop by providing OLE's **IDropTarget** interface. It is a dialog-based application that has two buttons and a status window. The dialog box is shown in Figure 13-6.

One of the buttons allows the user to enable the application for drag-and-drop, and the other button exits the application. When the application is enabled for drag-and-drop, the status window displays the status of drag-and-drop activities. When text is dropped, it

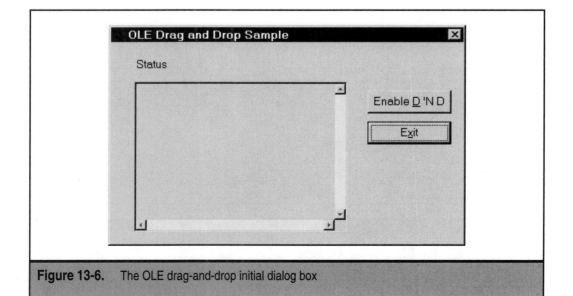

Figure 13-6.   The OLE drag-and-drop initial dialog box

displays the dropped text. To run the application, start it and click the Enable D'ND button to enable the application for drag-and-drop. The dialog box in Figure 13-7 appears.

Using the WordPad application, mark some text and then drag and drop it on this application. Notice the status window, which shows the drag-and-drop activities; when the text is dropped, it is displayed in the status window. Figure 13-8 shows the status when you attempt an invalid drag-and-drop operation, while Figure 13-9 shows the status for a valid drag-and-drop operation. The text in the WordPad application that is the source of the drag-and-drop is shown in Figure 13-10.

Two sets of code are shown here. One is the code related to the dialog box, which for the most part is very typical; the second is the implementation of the **IDropTarget** interface. The application dialog box–related code is shown next, starting with the header file and followed by the implementation code. The code of interest is highlighted. The About dialog box processing is not shown, for brevity.

A means to display text in the status window is provided by public method **SetStatus**. Since the implementation of **IDropTarget** displays the activities of drag-and-drop and there will be many calls to **DragOver**, the status window will be cluttered with **DragOver** activity information. To prevent this, only the first **DragOver** activity is displayed. To achieve this, a flag is maintained as a member variable, and the member functions are provided to set and query the status of the flag. Since the application allows the user to enable and disable drag-and-drop, a pointer to the **IDropTarget** object is maintained where the

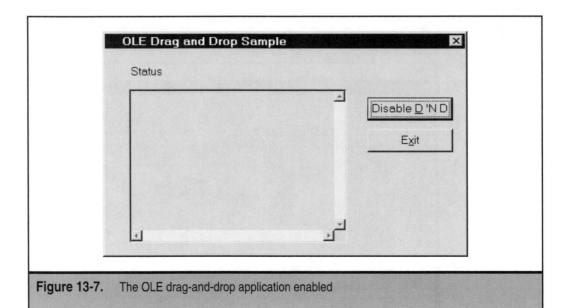

Figure 13-7. The OLE drag-and-drop application enabled

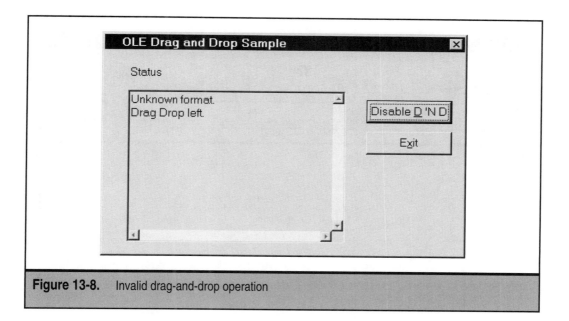

Figure 13-8. Invalid drag-and-drop operation

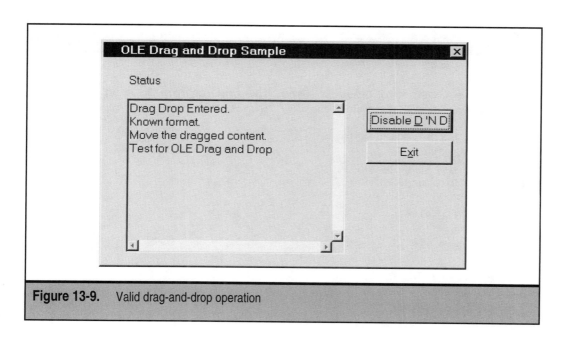

Figure 13-9. Valid drag-and-drop operation

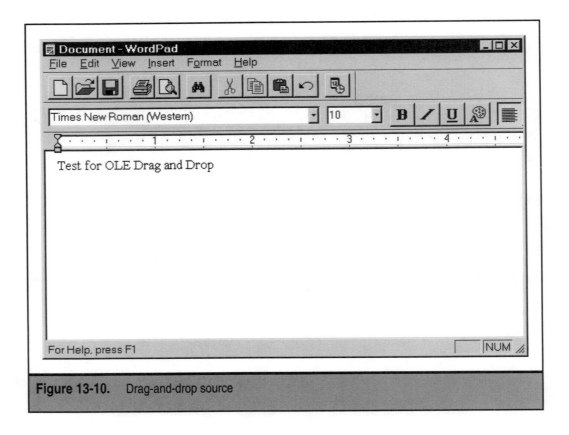

Figure 13-10. Drag-and-drop source

pointer to the constructed object is saved. The **OnDragDrop** function handles the drag-and-drop button in the dialog box.

```
// DragDropDlg.h : header file
//
#if !defined(AFX_DRAGDROPDLG_H)
#define AFX_DRAGDROPDLG_H

#if _MSC_VER >= 1000
#pragma once
#endif // _MSC_VER >= 1000

// CDragDropDlg dialog

class CDragDropTarget;
class CDragDropDlg : public CDialog
```

```
{
// Construction
public:
    CDragDropDlg(CWnd* pParent = NULL);
    void SetStatus(char *);
    void SetMoveFlag(BOOL);
    BOOL GetMoveFlag();

// Dialog Data
    //{{AFX_DATA(CDragDropDlg)
    enum { IDD = IDD_DRAGDROP_DIALOG };
    CEdit    m_status;
    //}}AFX_DATA

    // ClassWizard generated virtual function overrides
    //{{AFX_VIRTUAL(CDragDropDlg)
    protected:
    virtual void DoDataExchange(CDataExchange* pDX);
    //}}AFX_VIRTUAL

// Implementation
protected:
    HICON    m_hIcon;
    BOOL     fDragDropEnabled;
    BOOL     fMoveMsgDisplayed;
    CDragDropTarget *pCDDTarget;

    // Generated message map functions
    //{{AFX_MSG(CDragDropDlg)
    virtual BOOL OnInitDialog();
    afx_msg void OnSysCommand(UINT nID, LPARAM lParam);
    afx_msg void OnPaint();
    afx_msg HCURSOR OnQueryDragIcon();
    afx_msg void OnDragdrop();
    //}}AFX_MSG
    DECLARE_MESSAGE_MAP()
};
#endif
```

Shown next is the implementation file for the **CDragDropDlg** class. The About dialog box processing is not shown. The code of interest is highlighted:

```
// DragDropDlg.cpp : implementation file
//
```

```
#include "stdafx.h"
#include "DragDrop.h"
#include "DragDropDlg.h"
#include "DragDropTarget.h"

#ifdef _DEBUG
#define new DEBUG_NEW
#undef THIS_FILE
static char THIS_FILE[] = __FILE__;
#endif

// CDragDropDlg dialog

CDragDropDlg::CDragDropDlg(CWnd* pParent /*=NULL*/)
    : CDialog(CDragDropDlg::IDD, pParent)
{
    //{{AFX_DATA_INIT(CDragDropDlg)
    //}}AFX_DATA_INIT
    m_hIcon = AfxGetApp()->LoadIcon(IDR_MAINFRAME);

    fDragDropEnabled = FALSE;
}

void CDragDropDlg::DoDataExchange(CDataExchange* pDX)
{
    CDialog::DoDataExchange(pDX);
    //{{AFX_DATA_MAP(CDragDropDlg)
    DDX_Control(pDX, IDC_STATUS, m_status);
    //}}AFX_DATA_MAP
}

BEGIN_MESSAGE_MAP(CDragDropDlg, CDialog)
    //{{AFX_MSG_MAP(CDragDropDlg)
    ON_WM_SYSCOMMAND()
    ON_WM_PAINT()
    ON_WM_QUERYDRAGICON()
    ON_BN_CLICKED(IDC_DRAGDROP, OnDragdrop)
    //}}AFX_MSG_MAP
END_MESSAGE_MAP()

// CDragDropDlg message handlers

BOOL CDragDropDlg::OnInitDialog()
{
```

```
        CDialog::OnInitDialog();

        // Add "About..." menu item to system menu.
        // IDM_ABOUTBOX must be in the system command range.
        ASSERT((IDM_ABOUTBOX & 0xFFF0) == IDM_ABOUTBOX);
        ASSERT(IDM_ABOUTBOX < 0xF000);

        CMenu* pSysMenu = GetSystemMenu(FALSE);
        if (pSysMenu != NULL)
        {
            CString strAboutMenu;
            strAboutMenu.LoadString(IDS_ABOUTBOX);
            if (!strAboutMenu.IsEmpty())
            {
                pSysMenu->AppendMenu(MF_SEPARATOR);
                pSysMenu->AppendMenu(MF_STRING,
                                     IDM_ABOUTBOX,
                                     strAboutMenu);
            }
        }

        // Set the icon for this dialog.
        // The framework does this automatically
        //  when the application's main window is not a dialog
        SetIcon(m_hIcon, TRUE);            // Set big icon
        SetIcon(m_hIcon, FALSE);           // Set small icon

        // TODO: Add extra initialization here

        return TRUE;
}

void CDragDropDlg::OnSysCommand(UINT nID, LPARAM lParam)
{
        if ((nID & 0xFFF0) == IDM_ABOUTBOX)
        {
            CAboutDlg dlgAbout;
            dlgAbout.DoModal();
        }
        else
        {
            CDialog::OnSysCommand(nID, lParam);
        }
}
```

```
void CDragDropDlg::OnPaint()
{
    if (IsIconic())
    {
        CPaintDC dc(this); // device context for painting

        SendMessage(WM_ICONERASEBKGND,
                    (WPARAM)dc.GetSafeHdc(),0);

        // Center icon in client rectangle
        int cxIcon = GetSystemMetrics(SM_CXICON);
        int cyIcon = GetSystemMetrics(SM_CYICON);
        CRect rect;
        GetClientRect(&rect);
        int x = (rect.Width() - cxIcon + 1) / 2;
        int y = (rect.Height() - cyIcon + 1) / 2;

        // Draw the icon
        dc.DrawIcon(x, y, m_hIcon);
    }
    else
    {
        CDialog::OnPaint();
    }
}

// The system calls this to obtain the cursor
// to display while the user drags
//  the minimized window.
HCURSOR CDragDropDlg::OnQueryDragIcon()
{
    return (HCURSOR) m_hIcon;
}
```

To enable the application for OLE's drag-and-drop, an object derived from **IDropTarget** should be created and given to the operating system. After the object is created, the reference count is incremented and the **CoLockObjectExternal** is called to lock the object and to make sure that it stays in memory. Notice that this call must be made in the process in which the object actually resides. After locking the object in memory, the application informs the operating system that the specified window (in this case the dialog window) can be the target of an OLE drag-and-drop operation. This is done by calling the **RegisterDragDrop** function and giving the window handle of the window that can be the target for the drag-and-drop operation and the pointer to the **IDropTarget** object. This registration must be done whenever any window in the application is available as a drop target. However, this application has only one window, and it does not have to bother about it. To stop the window from being a target of an OLE drag-and-drop, the **RevokeDragDrop** function is called and given the handle of the window handle that should not be the target. This is followed by unlocking the lock placed on the **IDropTarget** object by calling **CoLockObjectExternal** and then **Release**. You will see later that the **Release** function actually discards the object when it's no longer referenced. The code here toggles the action of the button and changes the name of the button to show what action will be performed when it is clicked:

```
void CDragDropDlg::OnDragdrop()
{
    CButton *pButton;

    pButton = (CButton *)GetDlgItem(IDC_DRAGDROP);

    // TODO: Add your control notification handler code here
    if (fDragDropEnabled)
    {
        // Disable drag drop
        RevokeDragDrop(m_hWnd);
        CoLockObjectExternal(pCDDTarget, FALSE, TRUE);
        pCDDTarget->Release();

        fDragDropEnabled = FALSE;
        pButton->SetWindowText("Enable &D 'N D");

    }
    else
    {
        // Enable Drag drop
        pCDDTarget = new CDragDropTarget(this);
        pCDDTarget->AddRef();
        CoLockObjectExternal(pCDDTarget, TRUE, FALSE);
        RegisterDragDrop(m_hWnd, pCDDTarget);


        fDragDropEnabled = TRUE;
        pButton->SetWindowText("Disable &D 'N D");
    }
}
```

The next three member functions are helper functions that display text in the status window and provide the status of the state flag indicating whether the first **DragOver** message has been displayed in the status window.

```
void CDragDropDlg::SetStatus(char *pszStatus)
{
    m_status.SetSel(-1,0);
    m_status.ReplaceSel(pszStatus);
}

BOOL CDragDropDlg::GetMoveFlag()
{
    return(fMoveMsgDisplayed);
}

void CDragDropDlg::SetMoveFlag(BOOL f)
{
    fMoveMsgDisplayed = f;
}
```

Shown next is the implementation of the **Drop** target class that supports the OLE's
IDropTarget interface. When implemented in C++, this **Drop** target class is derived from
IDropTarget class, and all the virtual methods of **IDropTarget** class are implemented. To
display status in the status area, a pointer to the dialog class is provided when the class is
constructed. A member variable for keeping track of the reference count is maintained.
Note that this class must also implement the **IUnknown** interfaces:

```
#if !defined(CDRAGDROPTARGET_H)
#define CDRAGDROPTARGET_H

class CDragDropDlg;
class CDragDropTarget : public IDropTarget
{
protected:
    ULONG     m_ReferenceCount;
    BOOL      fKnownFormat;
    CDragDropDlg     *pDDDlg;

public:
    CDragDropTarget(CDragDropDlg *);
    ~CDragDropTarget();

    // IUnknown interface members

    STDMETHODIMP_(ULONG) AddRef();
    STDMETHODIMP_(ULONG) Release();
    STDMETHODIMP QueryInterface(REFIID , LPVOID* );
```

```
    // IDropTarget interface members

    STDMETHODIMP DragEnter(IDataObject *, DWORD,
                        POINTL, DWORD *);
    STDMETHODIMP DragOver(DWORD, POINTL, DWORD *);
    STDMETHODIMP DragLeave();
    STDMETHODIMP Drop(IDataObject *, DWORD,
                    POINTL, DWORD *);

};
#endif
```

The implementation of the **Drop** target class derived from **IDropTarget** is shown next. Notice the inclusion of *Oleidl.h*, which has the definitions needed. All COM interfaces are derived from the **IUnknown** interface. So is this class, which implements the methods of the **IUnknown** interface, which are **AddRef**, **QueryInterface**, and **Release**.

```
#include "stdafx.h"
#include <oleidl.h>
#include "DragDrop.h"
#include "DragDropDlg.h"
#include "DragDropTarget.h"

CDragDropTarget::CDragDropTarget(CDragDropDlg *pDlg)
{
  pDDDlg = pDlg;
  fKnownFormat = FALSE;
  m_ReferenceCount = 0;
}


CDragDropTarget::~CDragDropTarget()
{
}
```

AddRef increments the object's reference count by 1 when an interface or another application binds itself to the object. This reference count is maintained in the protected member variable, **m_ReferenceCount**.

```
STDMETHODIMP_(ULONG) CDragDropTarget::AddRef()
{
    m_ReferenceCount += 1;
    return (m_ReferenceCount);
}
```

QueryInterface queries the object about the features it supports by requesting pointers to a specific interface. Thus, if the ID of the requested interface is either **IUnknown** or **IDropTarget**, a pointer to this object is returned.

```
STDMETHODIMP CDragDropTarget::QueryInterface(
    REFIID iid, LPVOID* ppvObj)
{
    if (IsEqualIID(iid, IID_IUnknown) ||
        IsEqualIID(iid, IID_IDropTarget))
    {
        *ppvObj = this;
        AddRef();
        return S_OK;
    }

    return E_NOINTERFACE;
}
```

Release decrements the object's reference count by 1, and when there are no more references to the object, it is deleted.

```
STDMETHODIMP_(ULONG) CDragDropTarget::Release()
{
    m_ReferenceCount -= 1;
    if (m_ReferenceCount < 1)
    {
        delete this;
        return 0;
    }
    return m_ReferenceCount;
}
```

When the user drags the mouse the first time into the window that is registered for a drop target, the system calls **DragEnter**. The system provides a pointer to the source data object, the keyboard modifier, the pointer location, and a pointer to the effect of the drag-drop operation. In response, the application must check whether it can use the data provided by checking the format and media of the data object and the state of the modifier keys, and it must update the value of the effect pointed to by *pdwEffect*. If the application cannot handle the data, it updates the effect to DROPEFFECT_NONE. If it can handle the data, the effect is set to other DROPEFFECT values. The system in turn calls the drop source to show the visual feedback by displaying the appropriate pointer. In this sample, it checks whether the format is text:

```
STDMETHODIMP CDragDropTarget::DragEnter(
                              IDataObject *pDataObject,
                              DWORD grfKeyState,
                              POINTL pt,
                              DWORD *pdwEffect)
{
    FORMATETC    format;

    pDDDlg->SetMoveFlag(FALSE);

    format.cfFormat = CF_TEXT ;
    format.ptd = NULL ;
    format.dwAspect = DVASPECT_CONTENT ;
    format.lindex = -1 ;
    format.tymed = TYMED_HGLOBAL ;

    if (pDataObject->QueryGetData (&format) == S_OK)
    {
        fKnownFormat = TRUE;
        pDDDlg->SetStatus("Drag Drop Entered.\r\n");
        pDDDlg->SetStatus("Known format.\r\n");
            DragOver(grfKeyState, pt, pdwEffect) ;
    }
    else
    {
        *pdwEffect = DROPEFFECT_NONE ;
    }
    return S_OK ;
}
```

When the user moves the mouse across the target window, the system calls the **DragOver** method. The processing of this method is generally similar to that of **DragEnter**. Note that the system calls this function frequently, and it should be optimized. In this sample, the status window is updated only once, and for all future calls it is not updated:

```
STDMETHODIMP CDragDropTarget::DragOver(DWORD grfKeyState,
                                       POINTL pt,
                                       DWORD *pdwEffect)
{
    char    *pszStatus;
    if (!fKnownFormat)
```

```
    {
        *pdwEffect = DROPEFFECT_NONE;
        pszStatus = "Unknown format.\r\n";
    }
    else if ((grfKeyState & MK_CONTROL) &&
             (grfKeyState & MK_SHIFT))
    {
        *pdwEffect = DROPEFFECT_LINK;
        pszStatus = "Link the dragged content.\r\n";
    }
    else if (grfKeyState & MK_CONTROL)
    {
        *pdwEffect = DROPEFFECT_COPY;
        pszStatus = "Copy the dragged content.\r\n";
    }
    else
    {
        *pdwEffect = DROPEFFECT_MOVE;
        pszStatus = "Move the dragged content.\r\n";
    }

    if (!pDDDlg->GetMoveFlag())
    {
        pDDDlg->SetStatus(pszStatus);
        pDDDlg->SetMoveFlag(TRUE);
    }
    return S_OK;
}
```

DragLeave is called by the system when the user moves the mouse out of the target window that is enabled for the drop target, or if the user cancels the current drag-and-drop operation. In response to this, the application may remove any visual feedback that it provides to the user or release any reference to the data transfer object. In this sample, it displays information in the status window and resets some state flags:

```
STDMETHODIMP CDragDropTarget::DragLeave()
{
    fKnownFormat = FALSE;
    pDDDlg->SetStatus("Drag Drop left.\r\n");
    pDDDlg->SetMoveFlag(FALSE);
    return S_OK;
}
```

The **Drop** function is called by the system when the user completes the drag-and-drop operation. In turn the target application should incorporate the data in accordance with the modifier keys such as CTRL and SHIFT. In this sample, the data is obtained by calling the **GetData** method of the data object and providing the format and a storage medium structure. The data is pointed to by a global memory handle whose actual pointer is requested by locking the handle. The data is displayed in the status window, and the storage medium is freed by calling **ReleaseStgMedium**. Apart from this, the effect is updated, in this case by calling **DragOver**, such that the source application can do any necessary cleanup. Any visual effect that the target application provided should also be removed, and any reference to the data object is released. This application does not provide any visual feedback.

```
STDMETHODIMP CDragDropTarget::Drop(IDataObject *pDataObject,
                                   DWORD grfKeyState,
                                   POINTL pt,
                                   DWORD *pdwEffect)
{
    STGMEDIUM    Stg;
    FORMATETC    format;
    char         *pDDData;

    format.cfFormat = CF_TEXT ;
    format.ptd = NULL ;
    format.dwAspect = DVASPECT_CONTENT ;
    format.lindex = -1 ;
    format.tymed = TYMED_HGLOBAL ;

    pDataObject->GetData(&format, &Stg);
    pDDData = (char *)GlobalLock(Stg.hGlobal);

    pDDDlg->SetStatus(pDDData);
    pDDDlg->SetStatus("\r\n");

    ReleaseStgMedium(&Stg);
    DragOver(grfKeyState, pt, pdwEffect) ;
    return S_OK;
}
```

CONCLUSION

In this chapter, we looked at OLE Automation Servers and at an OLE Automation Server programming example. In the example, we also discussed how to make an OLE

Automation Server a stand-alone application. Next we looked at OLE Automation clients and an OLE Automation client programming example. This client example accessed the OLE Automation Server mentioned earlier. Finally, we took a closer look at a significant OLE user interface enhancement—OLE drag-and-drop—including a programming example that illustrated OLE drag-and-drop.

Chapter 14 covers another very important Windows 2000 programming topic—ActiveX.

CHAPTER 14

Using ActiveX

A ctiveX is one of the hot programming technologies of Windows 2000. With the increased use of the Web and intranets for business programming, you are likely to use ActiveX controls and containers because ActiveX controls enable you to include dynamic content. For instance, you might create an onscreen stock ticker where the stock prices are changing dynamically; this is only one example of the potential of ActiveX controls.

We covered ActiveX briefly in Chapter 12 and noted that ActiveX controls are an outgrowth of what used to be OLE custom controls. We will build upon ActiveX controls including properties, methods, and events in this chapter. We will look at a programming example where we create an ActiveX control. We will also examine containers and a container programming example. Since an ActiveX control you develop may access local resources, such as the file system on the local computer to which it has been downloaded, you have to take extra precautions to ensure that the control does not cause any damage. You should also know whether ActiveX controls you download to your computer are safe to use. There are ways, such as signing and marking ActiveX controls, that help improve the security aspects of using ActiveX controls. We will look at signing and marking ActiveX controls and at a related programming example.

ACTIVEX CONTROL AND CONTAINER COMMUNICATION

An ActiveX control inherits all the features of an MFC window object as it is derived from the base class, **COleControl**. This means that besides features such as firing events, the ActiveX control also inherits advanced features such as in-place activation, automation, and windowless controls.

The ActiveX control communicates with the container by firing *events*. The container operates an ActiveX control using the control's *properties* and *methods*. We looked at properties, methods, and events briefly in Chapter 12. Let's look at these in more detail here.

ActiveX Control Properties, Methods, and Events

Events are notifications from the control to the container of significant happenings in the control. Events can have associated parameters that provide additional data to the container. Some common events are mouse clicks on the control or the entry of keyboard data. There are two types of events—stock events and custom events. *Stock* events, such as single and double mouse clicks, are those for which there is built-in support in **COleControl**. *Custom* events are events, such as the receipt of a specific window message, for which there is no built-in support in **COleControl**, and for which you have to provide your own implementation. Your control class must map each event of the control to a member function that is called when the event occurs. Custom events can have the same name as stock events so long as you don't try to use both implementations in the same control. While containers normally are programmed to respond to events, keep in mind that the container can choose not to act on the events.

Properties are control attributes, such as the appearance of the control, that can be modified by a container or by a user of the control. Properties are similar to C++ class member variables and are data members of the ActiveX control. There are two types of properties—stock properties and custom properties. *Stock* properties, such as a control's caption, are those for which there is built-in support in **COleControl**. *Custom* properties are properties such as the appearance and state of a control, for which there is no built-in support in **COleControl**, and for which you have to provide your own implementation. Properties can have associated parameters to provide additional data. You can override the built-in notification functions of most stock properties. There are four ways of implementing custom properties, each with its own dispatch map macro (see the dispatch map later in this section), as shown in Table 14-1.

Sometimes it is useful to be able to set a property to be read-only or write-only. If you are creating a new control, you can designate the ActiveX control to be read-only or write-only using the ClassWizard, which inserts the function **SetNotSupported** or **GetNotSupported** in the dispatch map. If you want to change an existing property to be

Custom Property Implementation	Description	Dispatch Map Macro
Member variable implementation	The property's state is represented as a variable in the control class. No notification is made when the property value changes. This implementation creates the least amount of support code.	DISP_PROPERTY
Member variable with notification implementation	This implementation adds a notification function to the member variable implementation, which automatically is called when the property value changes.	DISP_PROPERTY_NOTIFY
Get/Set methods implementation	This implementation uses a Get member function that is called when the control user retrieves the current property value and uses a Set member function when the control user wants to change the property value. You can use the Get/Set member functions to validate a user's input or to dynamically derive a property value. You can also use the Get/Set member functions to implement a read-only or write-only property.	DISP_PROPERTY_EX
Parameterized implementation	This implementation lets you use a single property in your control to represent a homogenous set of property values (also called a property array).	DISP_PROPERTY_PARAM

Table 14-1.   Custom Property Implementation

read-only or write-only unconditionally, you can manually edit the dispatch map and remove the existing **Set/Get** functions. If you want to change an existing property to be read-only or write-only based on your application logic, then provide your implementation for the **Get/Set** functions and call **SetNotSupported** or **GetNotSupported** where appropriate. You can indicate that an error occurred in a method using the **ThrowError** member function of **COleControl**.

Sometimes you may want to ensure that your ActiveX control fits seamlessly within its container by matching the container's characteristics: fonts, background color, and so on. You can be notified and take action when the container's ambient property changes by overriding the **OnAmbientPropertyChanged** function, and you can get information about the container's ambient properties using the **GetAmbientProperty** function of **COleControl**.

The properties of an ActiveX control can be viewed and changed through a control properties dialog box. The properties dialog box can be displayed either by invoking the control's properties verb or by the container. It is possible to have a control with more than one property page, and you can add property pages to an existing control. You can allow the user to change the font of any text that may be present in your control by changing the font property. You can let the user choose from stock fonts, or you can include custom fonts.

Just as properties are similar to C++ class member variables, methods are similar to C++ class member functions and provide interfaces that are exposed to the container (and other applications). As with events and properties, there are two types of methods—stock methods and custom methods. *Stock* methods are those for which there is built-in support in **COleControl** (for example the **Refresh** method). *Custom* methods are methods for which there is no built-in support in **COleControl** and for which you have to provide your own implementation. You can indicate that an error occurred in a method by using the **ThrowError** member function of **COleControl**.

Properties and methods are exposed by use of a *dispatch map*. A dispatch map is a set of macros that expands into the declarations and calls needed to expose methods and properties. The dispatch map designates the internal and external names of object functions and properties, as well as the data types of the function arguments and properties. A dispatch map is analogous to a message map that maps functions to Windows message IDs, except that a dispatch map maps virtual member functions.

CREATING AN ACTIVEX CONTROL

Your ActiveX control must satisfy some basic requirements. It must

▼ Be a COM object

■ Export the **DLLRegisterServer** function

■ Export the **DLLUnRegisterServer** function

▲ Implement the **IUnknown** interface

You can create ActiveX controls using the Visual C++ ControlWizard. You can also create ActiveX controls using the ActiveX Template Library (ATL). The examples in this chapter will use the MFC method. The steps involved in creating an ActiveX control are summarized here:

1. Use the Visual C++ ControlWizard to create an ActiveX control shell.
2. Add stock and custom properties using ClassWizard.
3. Add stock and custom methods using ClassWizard.
4. Add stock and custom events using ClassWizard.
5. Create property pages.
6. Associate controls and the property pages using ClassWizard.
7. Add application-specific code where appropriate.
8. Compile and build the ActiveX control.
9. Register the ActiveX control.
10. Test your ActiveX control. You can use the Test container Microsoft provides. If you are using the ActiveX control with a Web page, you have to make up an object tag and specify the complete filename of your control in the *CODEBASE* parameter.

The following example expands on each of the preceding steps.

PROGRAMMING EXAMPLE TO ILLUSTRATE CREATING AN ACTIVEX CONTROL

In the next sample, an ActiveX control is created that maintains a list of addresses. The control has two property pages—one page containing custom properties such as Name, Address, and Remark—and the other page containing stock properties, foreground color, and background color. The control will have four methods: to add an address to the list, to view an address, to reset the address list, and to get the count of the number of addresses in the list. The control will also fire three events, one for each of the field changes.

One of the ways to create an ActiveX control is to use the Visual C++ ControlWizard. When you use the ControlWizard, it will create the shell required for the ActiveX control. This sample uses the ControlWizard to create all the necessary files in the project as follows:

1. Create a new project by clicking the New menu item in the File menu.
2. In the Projects tab, select MFC ActiveX ControlWizard and give the project name and location.
3. Use **Rec_ax** as the sample project name.

4. Click OK to bring up the MFC ActiveX ControlWizard—Step 1 of 2 dialog box. Information that appears as default is used here.

5. Click Next> to bring up the Step 2 of 2 dialog box.

6. The class and filename automatically generated by the ControlWizard can be changed. To change them, click the Edit Names... button and change the names of the Control's and Property Page's class name, header file, type name, implementation file, and type ID by replacing "Rec_ax" or "Recax" with "Records."

7. Complete the steps by clicking Finish.

8. Click OK in the New Project Information dialog box to create all the necessary files for the project.

You can now compile this project and build an ActiveX control, which, of course, does not yet have any functionality. The next step is to add functionality.

To add properties:

1. Select ClassWizard... from the View menu. This brings up the MFC ClassWizard dialog box.

2. On the Automation tab, select the **CRecordsCtrl** class name if it is not already selected.

3. Click the Add Property... button to bring up the Add Property dialog box. The control needs three custom properties: **Name**, **Address**, and **Remarks**. These properties are added one at a time as follows.

4. Enter **Name** in the External name field and select **CString** as the type.

5. The generated Variable name and Notification function are accepted and implemented as member variables when you select the Member Variable radio button.

6. Click OK to create this property.

7. Repeat steps 4–6 for the other two custom properties, Address and Remarks.

8. Add two more stock properties, the foreground and background color properties. In the Add Property dialog box, select these stock properties, ForeColor and BackColor, from the predefined list of the External names. Notice that the Stock radio button is automatically selected in the Implementation group box. Click OK to add this property.

The next step is to add methods. The methods added are **View**, **Add**, **Reset**, and **GetCount**. All methods except **GetCount** have a return type of **void**, and **GetCount** returns a **short**. To add a method:

1. Click Add Method....This brings up the Add Method dialog box.

2. Enter the name of the method in the External name box.

3. Accept the automatically generated Internal Name.

4. Select the return type and click OK.

Next the events are added. Three custom events are added to signal the change in the three properties. To add the events:

1. Click the ActiveX Events tab and then press the Add Event... button. This brings up the Add Event dialog box.

2. Specify the external name in the External name field and click OK. Enter the three external names **NameChanged**, **AddressChanged**, and **RemarksChanged**. Accept the automatically generated Internal name in all the three cases.

3. Close the MFC ClassWizard page by clicking the OK button and saving the changes.

Next the property page dialog box is created as follows:

1. Select the ResourceView in the Workspace, expand the Rec_ax resources folder, and then expand the Dialog folder.

2. Double-click IDD_PROPPAGE_REC_AX to bring up the default dialog box.

3. Delete the default static control and create three sets of controls—one each for **Name**, **Address**, **Remarks**—by adding static text and an entry field for each set.

4. Each set has a static control and an edit box control. The edit box control IDs are specified as **IDC_NAME**, **IDC_ADDR**, and **IDC_REM**. Note that the size of the property page should be limited to either 250 × 62 dialog units or 250 × 110 dialog units. The stock and color property pages are 250 × 62 dialog units, and the stock font property page is 250 × 110 dialog units.

Now that the property page has been created, these controls are tied to the properties, thereby enabling them to display and modify the properties. To do this:

1. Invoke the ClassWizard for this dialog and select the **CRecordsPropPage** class if it is not already selected.

2. Click the Member Variables tab. The list of Control IDs earlier defined in the property page dialog box appears.

3. For each control ID, add a variable by clicking Add Variable.... The member variable names for the Name control, Address control, and Remarks control are, respectively, **m_Name**, **m_Addr**, and **m_Rem**. Select the Value category and select the variable type of Cstring for all three controls.

4. Save the operations by clicking OK and closing the MFC ClassWizard dialog box.

We just discussed generating the ActiveX control code by use of ControlWizard. Shown next is the code that is generated and the code added to the ActiveX control files. Code that has been added or modified is shown in boldface. Shown first is the entry module for the ActiveX control. The class that is derived from **COleControlModule** is the main entry point to the control. The AppWizard by default overrides the **InitInstance** and **ExitInstance** member functions in this class, where the ActiveX control-related initialization and termination can be done.

This application does not perform any special initialization or termination. Before an ActiveX control can be used, it should be registered, with the control-related information placed in the Registry. The ActiveX control created using the ControlWizard automatically generates the code to register and unregister the control. These register and unregister entry points are exported (look in the module definition file), and applications that load these controls call these entry points to register or unregister. If the control is built by use of Visual C++, it automatically calls this function and registers the control. You can also manually register a control using the *Regsvr32.exe* program and passing the complete path and filename of the control. Alternatively, you can write a separate setup program. The setup program could load the control DLL (using **LoadLibrary**) and call the **DllRegisterServer** function. If you install and register an ActiveX control, you should also register *Olepro32.dll* (unless *Olepro32.dll* is already installed). In addition, if your control uses stock property pages, you should register *Mfcx0.dll* as well.

```
#if !defined(AFX_REC_AX_H)
#define AFX_REC_AX_H

#if _MSC_VER > 1000
#pragma once
#endif // _MSC_VER > 1000

// rec_ax.h : main header file for REC_AX.DLL

#if !defined( __AFXCTL_H__ )
    #error include 'afxctl.h' before including this file
#endif
#include "resource.h"       // main symbols

/////////////////////////////////////////////////////
// CRec_axApp : See rec_ax.cpp for implementation.

class CRec_axApp : public COleControlModule
{
public:
    BOOL InitInstance();
    int ExitInstance();
};
```

```
extern const GUID CDECL _tlid;
extern const WORD _wVerMajor;
extern const WORD _wVerMinor;

//{{AFX_INSERT_LOCATION}}

#endif

// rec_ax.cpp : Implementation of CRec_axApp and DLL registration.

#include "stdafx.h"
#include "rec_ax.h"

#ifdef _DEBUG
#define new DEBUG_NEW
#undef THIS_FILE
static char THIS_FILE[] = __FILE__;
#endif


CRec_axApp NEAR theApp;

const GUID CDECL BASED_CODE _tlid =
    { 0xe150326c, 0xebda, 0x11d0,
      { 0xa9, 0xee, 0x9, 0x92, 0, 0x54, 0, 0x30 } };
const WORD _wVerMajor = 1;
const WORD _wVerMinor = 0;

/////////////////////////////////////////////////
// CRec_axApp::InitInstance - DLL initialization
BOOL CRec_axApp::InitInstance()
{
    BOOL bInit = COleControlModule::InitInstance();
    if (bInit)
    {

        // TODO: Add your own module initialization code here.
    }
    return bInit;
}

/////////////////////////////////////////////////
// CRec_axApp::ExitInstance - DLL termination
int CRec_axApp::ExitInstance()
```

```
{
    // TODO: Add your own module termination code here.
    return COleControlModule::ExitInstance();
}


/////////////////////////////////////////////////
// DllRegisterServer - Adds entries to the system registry
STDAPI DllRegisterServer(void)
{
    AFX_MANAGE_STATE(_afxModuleAddrThis);

    if (!AfxOleRegisterTypeLib(AfxGetInstanceHandle(), _tlid))
        return ResultFromScode(SELFREG_E_TYPELIB);

    if (!COleObjectFactoryEx::UpdateRegistryAll(TRUE))
        return ResultFromScode(SELFREG_E_CLASS);

    return NOERROR;
}


/////////////////////////////////////////////////
// DllUnregisterServer - Removes entries from the system registry
STDAPI DllUnregisterServer(void)
{
    AFX_MANAGE_STATE(_afxModuleAddrThis);

    if (!AfxOleUnregisterTypeLib(_tlid, _wVerMajor, _wVerMinor))
        return ResultFromScode(SELFREG_E_TYPELIB);

    if (!COleObjectFactoryEx::UpdateRegistryAll(FALSE))
        return ResultFromScode(SELFREG_E_CLASS);

    return NOERROR;
}
```

Shown next is the ActiveX control class derived from **COleControl**. This has both the automatically generated code and the code that was added later:

```
// RecordsCtl.cpp : Implementation of the CRecordsCtrl ActiveX
// Control class.

#include "stdafx.h"
```

```
#include "rec_ax.h"
#include "RecordsCtl.h"
#include "RecordsPpg.h"

#ifdef _DEBUG
#define new DEBUG_NEW
#undef THIS_FILE
static char THIS_FILE[] = __FILE__;
#endif

IMPLEMENT_DYNCREATE(CRecordsCtrl, COleControl)
```

The type of custom property that has been implemented here is the member variable with notification. The ClassWizard creates the necessary code in the dispatch map. The notification code is automatically called by the framework when the property value is changed. Each custom property that is added to the control has an entry in the dispatch map. The ClassWizard also adds these notification functions as member functions inside the class, as can be seen in the code that follows.

Also added in the dispatch map are the four methods that were added through the ClassWizard: **View**, **Reset**, **Add**, and **GetCount**. The two stock properties that were added are also included here. The ClassWizard also adds the stub code for the methods.

```
/////////////////////////////////////////////////
// Message map

BEGIN_MESSAGE_MAP(CRecordsCtrl, COleControl)
    //{{AFX_MSG_MAP(CRecordsCtrl)
```

If the control needs to perform any initialization, it can be done during the creation of the control. To do this, the **ON_WM_CREATE** message is processed. It can be added either through ClassWizard or by adding the code that follows:

```
    ON_WM_CREATE()    //}}AFX_MSG_MAP
    ON_OLEVERB(AFX_IDS_VERB_PROPERTIES, OnProperties)
END_MESSAGE_MAP()


/////////////////////////////////////////////////
// Dispatch map

BEGIN_DISPATCH_MAP(CRecordsCtrl, COleControl)
    //{{AFX_DISPATCH_MAP(CRecordsCtrl)
    DISP_PROPERTY_NOTIFY(CRecordsCtrl, "Name", m_name,
                         OnNameChanged, VT_BSTR)
```

```
DISP_PROPERTY_NOTIFY(CRecordsCtrl, "Address",
                     m_address, OnAddressChanged,
                     VT_BSTR)
DISP_PROPERTY_NOTIFY(CRecordsCtrl, "Remarks",
                     m_remarks, OnRemarksChanged,
                     VT_BSTR)
```

The **VT_EMPTY** in the dispatch match here indicates that the function does not return anything. The **View** function created by following the preceding steps does not accept any parameters. However, the **View** function has been modified to accept a *short* to tell the function which element needs to be viewed. Hence the last parameter, which indicates what the input parameter for the function is, has been changed from **VTS_NONE** to **VTS_I2**. Thus the new declaration of the **View** function indicates that it takes a short as input and returns nothing.

```
DISP_FUNCTION(CRecordsCtrl, "View", View, VT_EMPTY, VTS_I2)
DISP_FUNCTION(CRecordsCtrl, "Reset", Reset, VT_EMPTY,
              VTS_NONE)
DISP_FUNCTION(CRecordsCtrl, "Add", Add, VT_EMPTY, VTS_NONE)
DISP_FUNCTION(CRecordsCtrl, "GetCount", GetCount, VT_I2,
              VTS_NONE)
DISP_STOCKPROP_BACKCOLOR()
DISP_STOCKPROP_FORECOLOR()
//}}AFX_DISPATCH_MAP
DISP_FUNCTION_ID(CRecordsCtrl, "AboutBox", DISPID_ABOUTBOX,
                 AboutBox, VT_EMPTY, VTS_NONE)
END_DISPATCH_MAP()
```

Seen next is the declaration of event maps. Recall that as the application was created, three custom events were created. Unlike the stock events, custom events should be handled by the control and are not automatically fired by the **COleControl** class. The event map entries for the custom events are represented by the EVENT_CUSTOM macro. When an event is created by use of the ClassWizard, it creates all the stub code necessary. Additional code should be written by the control developer to fire the event. The event map indicates to the user of this ActiveX control that this control is capable of firing these events. The events are fired by the function specified as the second parameter in the EVENT_CUSTOM macro.

```
///////////////////////////////////////////////
// Event map

BEGIN_EVENT_MAP(CRecordsCtrl, COleControl)
    //{{AFX_EVENT_MAP(CRecordsCtrl)
```

When the name, address, or remarks are changed, an event is fired. The default behavior of these functions does not take any parameter. This has been changed here to take a string, which will either be the new name, the new address, or the new remark. Since the signature of the firing functions changed, the event map is modified from **VTS_NONE** to **VTS_BSTR** to indicate that they take a string.

```
EVENT_CUSTOM("NameChanged", FireNameChanged, VTS_BSTR)
EVENT_CUSTOM("AddressChanged", FireAddressChanged, VTS_BSTR)
EVENT_CUSTOM("RemarksChanged", FireRemarksChanged, VTS_BSTR)
//}}AFX_EVENT_MAP
END_EVENT_MAP()
```

The next section declares the property pages for the control. This control has one custom property page and has a second stock property page. The entry for the custom property page has been added by the ClassWizard. The second is a stock property page provided by MFC. Of the three stock property pages available (**CLSID_CColorPropPage**, **CLSID_CFontPropPage**, and **CLSID_CPicturePropPage**), the color property page is used here. Notice that as the generated comment reminds us, the count should be increased every time a property page is added.

The ClassWizard creates a default property page ID table having one entry. This sample would like to take advantage of the stock color property that MFC supports. To do this, the proper page count is increased from 1 to 2 and the entry for the stock color property is added as follows:

```
/////////////////////////////////////////////////
// Property pages

// TODO: Add more property pages as needed.
//   Remember to increase the count!
BEGIN_PROPPAGEIDS(CRecordsCtrl, 2)
    PROPPAGEID(CRecordsPropPage::guid)


    PROPPAGEID(CLSID_CColorPropPage)
END_PROPPAGEIDS(CRecordsCtrl)
```

The next macro implements the control's class factory and the **GetClassID** function. This is followed by the IMPLEMENT_OLETYPELIB macro, which implements the **GetTypeLib** member function.

```
/////////////////////////////////////////////////
// Initialize class factory and guid
IMPLEMENT_OLECREATE_EX(CRecordsCtrl, "RECAX.RecordsCtrl.1",
    0xe150326f, 0xebda, 0x11d0, 0xa9, 0xee, 0x9, 0x92, 0,
```

```
    0x54, 0, 0x30)

//////////////////////////////////////////////
// Type library ID and version
IMPLEMENT_OLETYPELIB(CRecordsCtrl, _tlid, _wVerMajor, _wVerMinor)

//////////////////////////////////////////////
// Interface IDs

const IID BASED_CODE IID_DRecords =
        { 0xe150326d, 0xebda, 0x11d0, { 0xa9, 0xee, 0x9, 0x92,
          0, 0x54, 0, 0x30 } };
const IID BASED_CODE IID_DRecordsEvents =
        { 0xe150326e, 0xebda, 0x11d0, { 0xa9, 0xee, 0x9, 0x92,
          0, 0x54, 0, 0x30 } };

//////////////////////////////////////////////
// Control type information

static const DWORD BASED_CODE _dwRecordsOleMisc =
    OLEMISC_ACTIVATEWHENVISIBLE |
    OLEMISC_SETCLIENTSITEFIRST |
    OLEMISC_INSIDEOUT |
    OLEMISC_CANTLINKINSIDE |
    OLEMISC_RECOMPOSEONRESIZE;

IMPLEMENT_OLECTLTYPE(CRecordsCtrl, IDS_RECORDS, _dwRecordsOleMisc)


//////////////////////////////////////////////
// CRecordsCtrl::CRecordsCtrlFactory::UpdateRegistry -
// Adds or removes system registry entries for CRecordsCtrl

BOOL CRecordsCtrl::CRecordsCtrlFactory::UpdateRegistry(BOOL bRegister)
{
    // TODO: Verify that your control follows apartment-model
    // threading rules.
    // Refer to MFC TechNote 64 for more information.
    // If your control does not conform to the apartment-model
    // rules, then you must modify the code below, changing the
    // 6th parameter from afxRegApartmentThreading to 0

    if (bRegister)
        return AfxOleRegisterControlClass(
```

```
                AfxGetInstanceHandle(),
                m_clsid,
                m_lpszProgID,
                IDS_RECORDS,
                IDB_RECORDS,
                afxRegApartmentThreading,
                _dwRecordsOleMisc,
                _tlid,
                _wVerMajor,
                _wVerMinor);
        else
            return AfxOleUnregisterClass(m_clsid, m_lpszProgID);

}


/////////////////////////////////////////////////
// CRecordsCtrl::CRecordsCtrl - Constructor

CRecordsCtrl::CRecordsCtrl()
{
    InitializeIIDs(&IID_DRecords, &IID_DRecordsEvents);

    // TODO: Initialize your control's instance data here.
}



/////////////////////////////////////////////////
// CRecordsCtrl::~CRecordsCtrl - Destructor

CRecordsCtrl::~CRecordsCtrl()
{
    // TODO: Clean up your control's instance data here.
}
```

The **OnDraw** member function stub is replaced with the control-specific drawing functions. Here it basically sets the background and foreground colors and displays the number of records in the address book:

```
/////////////////////////////////////////////////
// CRecordsCtrl::OnDraw - Drawing function

void CRecordsCtrl::OnDraw(
            CDC* pdc, const CRect& rcBounds, const CRect& rcInvalid)
{
```

```
    // TODO: Replace the following code with your own drawing code.
    OLE_COLOR oleclr = GetBackColor();
    COLORREF clr = TranslateColor( oleclr );
    CBrush brush( clr );
    pdc->FillRect(rcBounds, &brush);
    oleclr = GetForeColor();
    clr = TranslateColor( oleclr );
    pdc->SetBkMode( TRANSPARENT );
    pdc->SetTextColor( clr );
    CRect rect = rcBounds;
    char buf[81];
    sprintf( buf, "Total Records: %d", GetCount() );
    pdc->DrawText( buf, -1, rect,
            DT_LEFT | DT_WORDBREAK );
}
```

A control may wish to initialize the property when the control is loaded, or it may wish to save a persistent value of the property when it is stored. This can be handled in the **DoPropExchange** member function. This member function is called when the control is loaded and when the control is stored. Since in this example the control does not care for any persistent data or in other words, does not stream the data, nothing is done. If the control needs to initialize or store the property, the **PX_** functions can be used.

```
/////////////////////////////////////////////////
// CRecordsCtrl::DoPropExchange - Persistence support

void CRecordsCtrl::DoPropExchange(CPropExchange* pPX)
{
    ExchangeVersion(pPX, MAKELONG(_wVerMinor, _wVerMajor));
    COleControl::DoPropExchange(pPX);

// TODO: Call PX_ functions for each persistent custom property.

}



/////////////////////////////////////////////////
// CRecordsCtrl::OnResetState - Reset control to default state

void CRecordsCtrl::OnResetState()
{
    // Resets defaults found in DoPropExchange
    COleControl::OnResetState();
```

```
    // TODO: Reset any other control state here.
    Reset();
}


/////////////////////////////////////////////////////
// CRecordsCtrl::AboutBox - Display an "About" box to the user

void CRecordsCtrl::AboutBox()
{
    CDialog dlgAbout(IDD_ABOUTBOX_RECORDS);
    dlgAbout.DoModal();
}
```

The preceding member function handles the AboutBox by displaying the About dialog box. The rest of the code deals with the properties change notification and the four methods defined by the control. In the case of the three notification member functions, additional code is added to fire the respective events signaling the respective property changes. These firing functions, **FireNameChanged**, **FireAddressChanged**, and **FireRemarksChanged**, are defined inline in the control's header file.

```
/////////////////////////////////////////////////////
// CRecordsCtrl message handlers

void CRecordsCtrl::OnNameChanged()
{
    // TODO: Add notification handler code
    SetModifiedFlag();
    FireNameChanged( m_name );
}


void CRecordsCtrl::OnAddressChanged()
{
    // TODO: Add notification handler code
    SetModifiedFlag();
    FireAddressChanged( m_address );
}


void CRecordsCtrl::OnRemarksChanged()
{
    // TODO: Add notification handler code
    SetModifiedFlag();
    FireRemarksChanged( m_remarks );
}
```

The control maintains the address list in three **CStringArray** classes that are created as private member variables in the control's **CRecordsCtrl** class. As addresses are added, they are stored in these **CStringArrays**, and if needed, they are retrieved.

The next four member functions implement the methods of the control: **View**, **Reset**, **Add**, and **GetCount**. In the case of **View**, after preliminary checks, it retrieves the selected record from the string array that is maintained for the list of addresses. In the case of **Reset**, it empties the address list, and in the case of **Add**, it adds the current data from the properties to the address list. **GetCount** returns the number of addresses maintained by the address list.

```cpp
void CRecordsCtrl::View(short idx)
{
    // TODO: Add your dispatch handler code here
    ASSERT( m_AllNames.GetSize() == m_AllAddresses.GetSize() );
    ASSERT( m_AllNames.GetSize() == m_AllRemarks.GetSize() );
    int cnt = m_AllNames.GetSize();
    if ( idx<0 || idx>=cnt )
    {
        MessageBeep( MB_ICONHAND );
        return;
        }
    m_name = m_AllNames[idx];
    m_address = m_AllAddresses[idx];
    m_remarks = m_AllRemarks[idx];
}


void CRecordsCtrl::Reset()
{
    // TODO: Add your dispatch handler code here
    m_AllNames.RemoveAll();
    m_AllAddresses.RemoveAll();
    m_AllRemarks.RemoveAll();
    m_name.Empty();
    m_address.Empty();
    m_remarks.Empty();
    InvalidateControl( );
}


void CRecordsCtrl::Add()
{
    // TODO: Add your dispatch handler code here
    ASSERT( m_AllNames.GetSize() == m_AllAddresses.GetSize() );
    ASSERT( m_AllNames.GetSize() == m_AllRemarks.GetSize() );
    m_AllNames.Add( m_name );
```

```
    m_AllAddresses.Add( m_address );
    m_AllRemarks.Add( m_remarks );
    InvalidateControl( );
}


short CRecordsCtrl::GetCount()
{
    // TODO: Add your dispatch handler code here
    ASSERT( m_AllNames.GetSize() == m_AllAddresses.GetSize() );
    ASSERT( m_AllNames.GetSize() == m_AllRemarks.GetSize() );
    return (short)m_AllNames.GetSize();
}
```

Any initialization that needs to be done during the creation of the control can be done in the **OnCreate** function, which is called before the creation of the control. The sample does not perform any special initialization.

```
int CRecordsCtrl::OnCreate(LPCREATESTRUCT lpCreateStruct)
{
    if (COleControl::OnCreate(lpCreateStruct) == -1)
        return -1;

    // TODO: Add your specialized creation code here

    return 0;
}
```

Earlier, after the property page was created, the controls in the property page were tied to the properties. When this was done, the ClassWizard generated the ActiveX control's property page class, which is derived from **COlePropertyPage**. The ClassWizard adds code to initialize the member variables and to handle the exchange of data between the dialog controls, the member variables, and the properties.

```
// RecordsPpg.cpp : Implementation of the CRecordsPropPage
// property page class.

#include "stdafx.h"
#include "rec_ax.h"
#include "RecordsPpg.h"

#ifdef _DEBUG
#define new DEBUG_NEW
#undef THIS_FILE
```

```
static char THIS_FILE[] = __FILE__;
#endif

IMPLEMENT_DYNCREATE(CRecordsPropPage, COlePropertyPage)

/////////////////////////////////////////////////
// Message map
BEGIN_MESSAGE_MAP(CRecordsPropPage, COlePropertyPage)
    //{{AFX_MSG_MAP(CRecordsPropPage)
    //}}AFX_MSG_MAP
END_MESSAGE_MAP()

/////////////////////////////////////////////////
// Initialize class factory and guid

IMPLEMENT_OLECREATE_EX(CRecordsPropPage, "RECAX.RecordsPropPage.1",
    0xe1503270, 0xebda, 0x11d0, 0xa9, 0xee, 0x9, 0x92, 0,
    0x54, 0, 0x30)


/////////////////////////////////////////////////
// CRecordsPropPage::CRecordsPropPageFactory::UpdateRegistry -
// Adds or removes system registry entries for CRecordsPropPage

BOOL CRecordsPropPage::
    CRecordsPropPageFactory::UpdateRegistry(BOOL bRegister)
{
    if (bRegister)
        return AfxOleRegisterPropertyPageClass
                (AfxGetInstanceHandle(),
                 m_clsid, IDS_RECORDS_PPG);
    else
        return AfxOleUnregisterClass(m_clsid, NULL);
}


/////////////////////////////////////////////////
// CRecordsPropPage::CRecordsPropPage - Constructor

CRecordsPropPage::CRecordsPropPage() :
    COlePropertyPage(IDD, IDS_RECORDS_PPG_CAPTION)
{
    //{{AFX_DATA_INIT(CRecordsPropPage)
    m_Addr = _T("");
```

```
    m_Name = _T("");
    m_Rem = _T("");
    //}}AFX_DATA_INIT
}
```

In the preceding code, the member variables are initialized during the construction of the property page. The next member function handles the exchange of data between the control, the member variable, and the property. The **DDX_Text** macro is the same as has been discussed in earlier samples. It exchanges data between the controls on the property page dialog box and the member variables in the class. The **DDP_Text** macro exchanges data between the member variables and the specified properties.

```
//////////////////////////////////////////////////
// CRecordsPropPage::DoDataExchange
void CRecordsPropPage::DoDataExchange(CDataExchange* pDX)
{
    //{{AFX_DATA_MAP(CRecordsPropPage)
    DDP_Text(pDX, IDC_ADDR, m_Addr, _T("Address") );
    DDX_Text(pDX, IDC_ADDR, m_Addr);
    DDP_Text(pDX, IDC_NAME, m_Name, _T("Name") );
    DDX_Text(pDX, IDC_NAME, m_Name);
    DDP_Text(pDX, IDC_REM, m_Rem, _T("Remarks") );
    DDX_Text(pDX, IDC_REM, m_Rem);
    //}}AFX_DATA_MAP
    DDP_PostProcessing(pDX);
}


//////////////////////////////////////////////////
// CRecordsPropPage message handlers
```

If the dialog needs to do any further initialization when started, the **WM_INITDIALOG** message can be processed. A processing function can be added using the ClassWizard or by adding the code that follows:

```
BOOL CRecordsPropPage::OnInitDialog()
{
    COlePropertyPage::OnInitDialog();

    // TODO: Add extra initialization here

    return TRUE;
}
```

This code is built in Visual Studio. After a successful build, Visual Studio registers the ActiveX control. This control can now be used in any ActiveX container, as is discussed next.

CREATING AN ACTIVEX CONTROL CONTAINER

An ActiveX control is an in-process server that can be used in any OLE container and is typically represented as a child window. Of course, the full functionality of the ActiveX control is available only if the container has been designed to take advantage of the ActiveX control. You can build your own container. Keep in mind that Microsoft Access (starting with version 2.0) and Microsoft Visual Basic (starting with version 4.0) are some of the products that fully support ActiveX controls.

The sequence of events that occurs at the control and the container when a user action triggers a **WM_PAINT** message depends on whether the control is in an active or inactive state (see Chapter 12 for a discussion on active and inactive states of a control). For an *active* control, the control's base class handles **WM_PAINT** in its **OnPaint** function, which by default calls your control's **OnDraw** function. For an *inactive* control, which usually is marked by the absence of a visible window (and hence cannot process a paint message), the container calls your control's **OnDraw** function directly. You have to handle painting of the control in the **OnDraw** function, which receives the window rectangle corresponding to the control and a device context (DC). If the control is active, the DC is that of the control; if the control is inactive, the DC is that of the container. Keep in mind that, although normally the DC is that of a screen DC, the DC could correspond to a metafile DC for print and print preview operations.

You can create a container application using the MFC AppWizard, and the process of creating a container is basically the same as creating any other MFC-based application that we have been using throughout this book.

PROGRAMMING EXAMPLE TO ILLUSTRATE CREATING A CONTAINER APPLICATION

The next step after creating the ActiveX control is to see how the control can be inserted in a container. Here we'll create a container application that will use the ActiveX control created earlier. This application is basically an address list application with the core of the address list functionality done by the ActiveX control developed earlier. This application provides the front end for accepting the data, inserting it, viewing particular data, and resetting the address book. It uses the methods that were shown in the earlier ActiveX control sample to provide these functionalities. It does not provide any interface to the end user to change the foreground and background colors, but it changes them every time an address is added to the list.

Figures 14-1 through 14-5 show what you will see when you run the sample. Figure 14-1 shows the first dialog box. It shows that there are no records currently present.

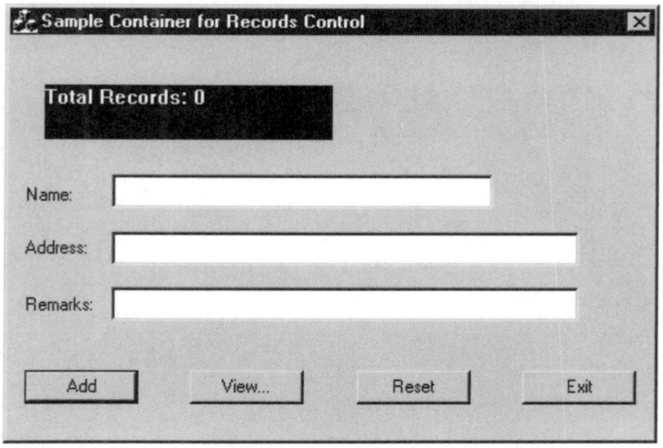

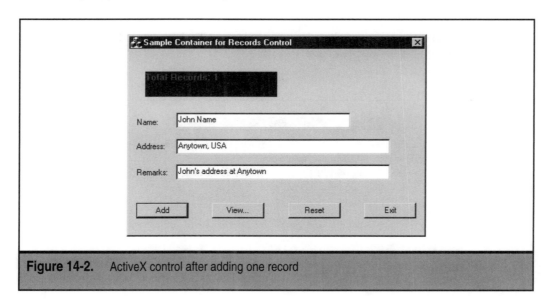

Figure 14-1.   Opening dialog of the ActiveX example

Figure 14-2 shows the dialog box after one record is added. Total Records now shows 1, and the background color has changed.

Figure 14-3 shows the dialog box after yet another record is added. Total Records now shows 2, and the background color has changed again.

Figure 14-4 shows the dialog box that appears when the View button is clicked. It provides an option to select a record by an index.

Figure 14-2.   ActiveX control after adding one record

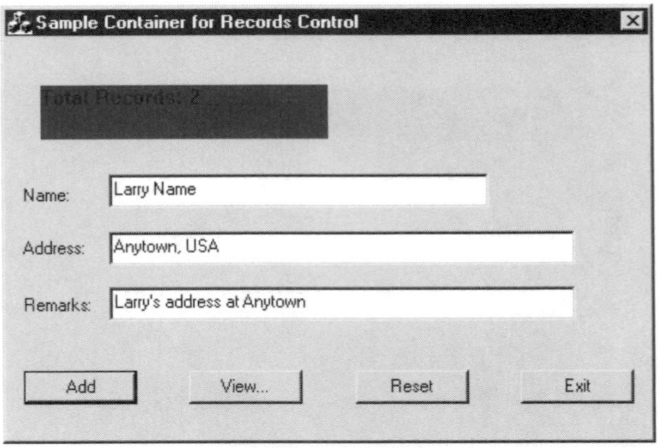

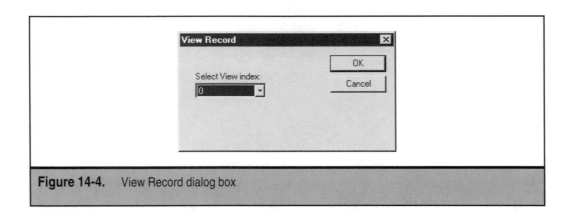

Figure 14-3. ActiveX control after adding second record

Figure 14-5 shows the effect of clicking Reset. All the records are deleted (reset), and Total Records now shows 0. Clicking View will now have no effect.

This application is created by use of the MFC AppWizard, and the steps are described here:

1. Create a new MFC AppWizard (EXE) project by specifying the project name (**Rec_cont**) and clicking OK.

2. In the MFC AppWizard-Step 1 dialog box, specify the type of the application to be a Dialog based Application.

Figure 14-4. View Record dialog box

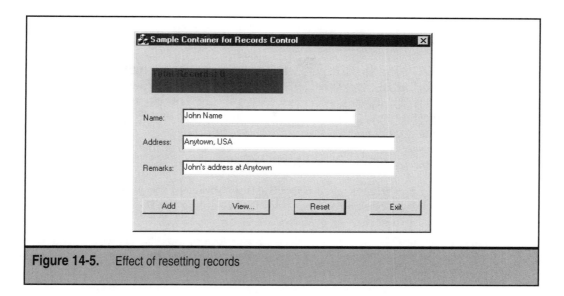

Figure 14-5.   Effect of resetting records

3. In the Step 2 dialog box, check the ActiveX Controls check box (by default it is checked) to indicate that this application will need additional support for ActiveX controls.

4. Accept the defaults for the rest of the steps and create the application framework by clicking Finish and then OK in the New Project Information dialog box. This will create the main application class, **CRec_contApp**, and a dialog class, **CRec_contDlg**.

The next step is to insert controls, including the ActiveX control, into the dialog box:

1. Select the ResourceView tab in the Workspace window.

2. Expanding the resource tree, double-click the IDD_REC_CONT_DIALOG dialog resource to open the dialog box.

3. Right-click the dialog box to select the Insert ActiveX Control… menu item. This will bring up the Insert ActiveX Control dialog box.

4. Select the Records Control ActiveX control and click OK. (Note if the ActiveX control developed earlier is not registered, then it will not appear in the list.) This will display the ActiveX control in the dialog box.

5. Insert three pairs of static and edit box controls, one each for Name, Address, and Remarks, in the dialog box. Also add four buttons: Add, View, Reset, and Exit.

When the container is operational, the user will be able to enter the name, address, and remark and click Add to add the information to the address list. When information is added, the ActiveX control displayed in the dialog box will increment to show the number of records in the address list. If users want to view a particular record, they can click the View button to bring up a (yet to be defined) dialog box that will prompt for the record number. When a record number is specified, the control will update this dialog box with data from that record number. The Reset button will empty the address list, and the Exit button will close the application.

Now that the dialog box is constructed, the ActiveX control that was created earlier needs to be imported. To import the ActiveX control, follow these steps:

1. Invoke the ClassWizard and import the type library of the ActiveX control created earlier by clicking Add Class... and selecting the From A Type Library... menu item.

2. This brings up the Import from Type Library dialog box. Navigating through the directory, select the *Rec_ax.tlb* type library file and click OK.

3. This brings up the Confirm Classes dialog box, which allows us to change the class name. Accept the default class names and close the dialog box by clicking OK. This generates the stub class or proxy class for the ActiveX control that is to be included in this container.

4. In the Member Variables page of the ClassWizard, select the ActiveX control ID to add a variable. MFC will prompt to insert a wrapper class into the project.

5. When you click OK, the Confirm Classes dialog box is displayed. The class name can be left alone to use the generated name, but this sample changes the class name to **CRecordControl**, changes the generated header file to *Recs.h*, and changes the implementation file to *Recs.cpp*.

6. Click OK to bring up the Add Member Variable dialog box. Name the member variable **m_RecCtrl** and click OK.

7. Add member variables for the Name, Address, and Remarks edit controls; for these select the Control category.

In the Message Maps tab of the ClassWizard dialog box, add member functions for the BN_CLICKED message of the Add, View, and Reset buttons. The ActiveX control that was inserted into this dialog box can generate three messages (that were exposed when the control was created in the previous example). These messages are also handled. To accomplish this, select the ActiveX control ID and double-click the individual messages. The ClassWizard brings up the Add Member Function panel with a suggested member function name for each message. Accept these suggested names.

The code related to this container application follows. Shown first is the main application class, **CRec_contApp**. There is nothing special in this code, and it is shown only for convenience. Notice the call to the **AfxEnableControlContainer** function in the application's **InitInstance** member function. This enables support for ActiveX controls in the application.

```
// rec_cont.h : main header file for the REC_CONT application
//

#if !defined(AFX_REC_CONT_H)
#define AFX_REC_CONT_H

#if _MSC_VER > 1000
#pragma once
#endif // _MSC_VER > 1000

#ifndef __AFXWIN_H__
  #error include 'stdafx.h' before including this file for PCH
#endif

#include "resource.h"        // main symbols

/////////////////////////////////////////////////
// CRec_contApp:
// See rec_cont.cpp for the implementation of this class
//

class CRec_contApp : public CWinApp
{
public:
    CRec_contApp();

// Overrides
    // ClassWizard generated virtual function overrides
    //{{AFX_VIRTUAL(CRec_contApp)
    public:
    virtual BOOL InitInstance();
    //}}AFX_VIRTUAL

// Implementation

    //{{AFX_MSG(CRec_contApp)
    //}}AFX_MSG
    DECLARE_MESSAGE_MAP()
};


/////////////////////////////////////////////////

//{{AFX_INSERT_LOCATION}}

#endif

// rec_cont.cpp : Defines the class behaviors for the application.
//
```

```
#include "stdafx.h"
#include "rec_cont.h"
#include "rec_contDlg.h"

#ifdef _DEBUG
#define new DEBUG_NEW
#undef THIS_FILE
static char THIS_FILE[] = __FILE__;
#endif

/////////////////////////////////////////////////
// CRec_contApp

BEGIN_MESSAGE_MAP(CRec_contApp, CWinApp)
    //{{AFX_MSG_MAP(CRec_contApp)
    //}}AFX_MSG
    ON_COMMAND(ID_HELP, CWinApp::OnHelp)
END_MESSAGE_MAP()

/////////////////////////////////////////////////
// CRec_contApp construction

CRec_contApp::CRec_contApp()
{
    // TODO: add construction code here.
    // Place all significant initialization in InitInstance
}

/////////////////////////////////////////////////
// The one and only CRec_contApp object

CRec_contApp theApp;

/////////////////////////////////////////////////
// CRec_contApp initialization

BOOL CRec_contApp::InitInstance()
{
    AfxEnableControlContainer();


#ifdef _AFXDLL
    Enable3dControls();
#else
    Enable3dControlsStatic();
#endif

    CRec_contDlg dlg;
    m_pMainWnd = &dlg;
    int nResponse = dlg.DoModal();
    if (nResponse == IDOK)
    {
```

```
        // TODO: Place code here to handle when the dialog is
        //  dismissed with OK
    }
    else if (nResponse == IDCANCEL)
    {
        // TODO: Place code here to handle when the dialog is
        //  dismissed with Cancel
    }

// Since the dialog has been closed, return FALSE so that we exit the
//  application, rather than start the application's message pump.
    return FALSE;
}
```

Shown next is the code related to the main dialog box of the application. It contains both the code generated by the ClassWizard and the code added later to handle various user actions. The class header file is shown for completeness. Notice the inclusion of *Recs.h*, which has the wrapper class for the ActiveX control. The way MFC deals with the ActiveX control is to create an intermediate wrapper class; the interface to the ActiveX control is through this wrapper class. One added member function, **ChangeColor**, is used internally during the processing of other member functions.

```
// rec_contDlg.h : header file
//{{AFX_INCLUDES()
#include "recs.h"
//}}AFX_INCLUDES

#if !defined(AFX_REC_CONTDLG_H)
#define AFX_REC_CONTDLG_H

#if _MSC_VER > 1000
#pragma once
#endif // _MSC_VER > 1000

/////////////////////////////////////////////////////
// CRec_contDlg dialog
class CRec_contDlg : public CDialog
{
// Construction
public:
        CRec_contDlg(CWnd* pParent = NULL);
// Dialog Data
        //{{AFX_DATA(CRec_contDlg)
        enum { IDD = IDD_REC_CONT_DIALOG };
        CEdit        m_Remarks;
        CEdit        m_Name;
        CEdit        m_Address;
        CRecordsControl        m_RecCtrl;
        //}}AFX_DATA
```

```
        // ClassWizard generated virtual function overrides
        //{{AFX_VIRTUAL(CRec_contDlg)
        protected:
        virtual void DoDataExchange(CDataExchange* pDX);
        //}}AFX_VIRTUAL

    void ChangeColor();

// Implementation
protected:
        HICON m_hIcon;

        // Generated message map functions
        //{{AFX_MSG(CRec_contDlg)
        virtual BOOL OnInitDialog();
        afx_msg void OnSysCommand(UINT nID, LPARAM lParam);
        afx_msg void OnPaint();
        afx_msg HCURSOR OnQueryDragIcon();
        afx_msg void OnBtnadd();
        afx_msg void OnBtnreset();
        afx_msg void OnBtnview();
        afx_msg void OnNameChangedRecordsctrl1
                    (LPCTSTR NewName);
        afx_msg void OnAddressChangedRecordsctrl1
                    (LPCTSTR NewAddress);
        afx_msg void OnRemarksChangedRecordsctrl1
                    (LPCTSTR NewRemarks);
        DECLARE_EVENTSINK_MAP()
        //}}AFX_MSG
        DECLARE_MESSAGE_MAP()
};

//{{AFX_INSERT_LOCATION}}
#endif //
```

The implementation file follows.

```
// rec_contDlg.cpp : implementation file
//
#include "stdafx.h"
#include "rec_cont.h"
#include "rec_contDlg.h"
#include "viewdlg.h"

#ifdef _DEBUG
#define new DEBUG_NEW
#undef THIS_FILE
static char THIS_FILE[] = __FILE__;
#endif
```

```
//////////////////////////////////////////////////
// CAboutDlg dialog used for App About

class CAboutDlg : public CDialog
{
public:
        CAboutDlg();

// Dialog Data
        //{{AFX_DATA(CAboutDlg)
        enum { IDD = IDD_ABOUTBOX };
        //}}AFX_DATA

        // ClassWizard generated virtual function overrides
        //{{AFX_VIRTUAL(CAboutDlg)
        protected:
        virtual void DoDataExchange(CDataExchange* pDX);
        //}}AFX_VIRTUAL

// Implementation
protected:
        //{{AFX_MSG(CAboutDlg)
        //}}AFX_MSG
        DECLARE_MESSAGE_MAP()
};

CAboutDlg::CAboutDlg() : CDialog(CAboutDlg::IDD)
{
        //{{AFX_DATA_INIT(CAboutDlg)
        //}}AFX_DATA_INIT
}

void CAboutDlg::DoDataExchange(CDataExchange* pDX)
{
        CDialog::DoDataExchange(pDX);
        //{{AFX_DATA_MAP(CAboutDlg)
        //}}AFX_DATA_MAP
}

BEGIN_MESSAGE_MAP(CAboutDlg, CDialog)
        //{{AFX_MSG_MAP(CAboutDlg)
                // No message handlers
        //}}AFX_MSG_MAP
END_MESSAGE_MAP()

//////////////////////////////////////////////////
// CRec_contDlg dialog

CRec_contDlg::CRec_contDlg(CWnd* pParent /*=NULL*/)
```

```
                : CDialog(CRec_contDlg::IDD, pParent)
{
        //{{AFX_DATA_INIT(CRec_contDlg)
        //}}AFX_DATA_INIT

        m_hIcon = AfxGetApp()->LoadIcon(IDR_MAINFRAME);
}

void CRec_contDlg::DoDataExchange(CDataExchange* pDX)
{
        CDialog::DoDataExchange(pDX);
        //{{AFX_DATA_MAP(CRec_contDlg)
        DDX_Control(pDX, IDC_EDITREMARKS, m_Remarks);
        DDX_Control(pDX, IDC_EDITNAME, m_Name);
        DDX_Control(pDX, IDC_EDITADDRESS, m_Address);
        DDX_Control(pDX, IDC_RECORDSCTRL1, m_RecCtrl);
        //}}AFX_DATA_MAP
}

BEGIN_MESSAGE_MAP(CRec_contDlg, CDialog)
        //{{AFX_MSG_MAP(CRec_contDlg)
        ON_WM_SYSCOMMAND()
        ON_WM_PAINT()
        ON_WM_QUERYDRAGICON()
    ON_BN_CLICKED(IDC_BTNADD, OnBtnadd)
    ON_BN_CLICKED(IDC_BTNRESET, OnBtnreset)
    ON_BN_CLICKED(IDC_BTNVIEW, OnBtnview)
        //}}AFX_MSG_MAP
END_MESSAGE_MAP()

/////////////////////////////////////////////////
// CRec_contDlg message handlers

BOOL CRec_contDlg::OnInitDialog()
{
        CDialog::OnInitDialog();

        // Add "About..." menu item to system menu.

        // IDM_ABOUTBOX must be in the system command range.
        ASSERT((IDM_ABOUTBOX & 0xFFF0) == IDM_ABOUTBOX);
        ASSERT(IDM_ABOUTBOX < 0xF000);

        CMenu* pSysMenu = GetSystemMenu(FALSE);
        if (pSysMenu != NULL)
        {
                CString strAboutMenu;
                strAboutMenu.LoadString(IDS_ABOUTBOX);
                if (!strAboutMenu.IsEmpty())
                {
```

```
                        pSysMenu->AppendMenu(MF_SEPARATOR);
                        pSysMenu->AppendMenu(MF_STRING, IDM_ABOUTBOX,
                                  strAboutMenu);
             }
     }

     // Set the icon for this dialog.  The framework does this automatically
     //  when the application's main window is not a dialog
     SetIcon(m_hIcon, TRUE);
     SetIcon(m_hIcon, FALSE);

     // TODO: Add extra initialization here

     return TRUE;
}

void CRec_contDlg::OnSysCommand(UINT nID, LPARAM lParam)
{
     if ((nID & 0xFFF0) == IDM_ABOUTBOX)
     {
             CAboutDlg dlgAbout;
             dlgAbout.DoModal();
     }
     else
     {
         CDialog::OnSysCommand(nID, lParam);
     }
}


void CRec_contDlg::OnPaint()
{
    if (IsIconic())
    {
        CPaintDC dc(this); // device context for painting

        SendMessage(WM_ICONERASEBKGND, (WPARAM) dc.GetSafeHdc(), 0);

        // Center icon in client rectangle
        int cxIcon = GetSystemMetrics(SM_CXICON);
        int cyIcon = GetSystemMetrics(SM_CYICON);
        CRect rect;
        GetClientRect(&rect);
        int x = (rect.Width() - cxIcon + 1) / 2;
        int y = (rect.Height() - cyIcon + 1) / 2;

        // Draw the icon
        dc.DrawIcon(x, y, m_hIcon);
    }
```

```
    else
    {
        CDialog::OnPaint();
    }
}


// The system calls this to obtain the cursor to display while the
// user drags the minimized window.
HCURSOR CRec_contDlg::OnQueryDragIcon()
{
    return (HCURSOR) m_hIcon;
}
```

When the Add button is pressed, the message is processed by the **OnBtnadd** member function. During the processing, the name, the address, and the remark are picked up from the dialog box and are passed on to the ActiveX control through the **SetName**, **SetAddress**, and **SetRemarks** member functions of the ActiveX control's wrapper class, which was generated by MFC. This wrapper class, as you may recall, is defined in the *Recs.h* and *Recs.cpp* modules. These **Set** functions set the properties of the control. Earlier, when the ActiveX control was created, it was created such that every time one of these properties was set, an event was fired. The firing, you may recall, was directed to be handled by **On*ChangedRecordsctrl1** functions (where * is either **Name**, **Address**, or **Remarks**) when the message map for the ActiveX control (IDC_RECORDSCTRL1) was defined. Notice in the code that the **On*ChangedRecordsctrl1** functions call the **ChangeColor** member function, which changes the foreground and background stock properties of this ActiveX control. Thus, for every addition of the record, the color stock property is changed thrice, once each for the Name, the Address, and the Remarks. This is overkill for this application but shows the capability to handle the firing at the property level. With the change in the foreground and background colors, the ActiveX control will paint the text in two different colors.

```
void CRec_contDlg::OnBtnadd()
{
    // TODO: Add your control notification handler code here
    CString sName, sAddr, sRem;
    m_Name.GetWindowText(sName);
    m_Address.GetWindowText(sAddr);
    m_Remarks.GetWindowText(sRem);
    m_RecCtrl.SetName( sName );
    m_RecCtrl.SetAddress( sAddr );
    m_RecCtrl.SetRemarks( sRem );
    m_RecCtrl.Add();
}
```

Clicking the Reset button invokes the Reset method of the ActiveX control:

```
void CRec_contDlg::OnBtnreset()
{
    // TODO: Add your control notification handler code here
    m_RecCtrl.Reset();
}
```

When the user clicks the View button, the application should present the number of records available in the address list to the user in a combo box in a separate View dialog box. The user can then select the record number that the user wants to view. Upon return from the View dialog box, that record is presented to the user. This is handled by the **OnBtnview** member function.

The total number of records is queried by calling the **GetCount** method of the ActiveX control, and it is passed to the View dialog box. The user's selection is maintained in a member variable of the View class, which is used to get the data and display it in the dialog box.

```
void CRec_contDlg::OnBtnview()
{
    // TODO: Add your control notification handler code here
    int cnt = m_RecCtrl.GetCount();
    if ( cnt <= 0 )
        return;
    CViewDlg* pViewDlg = new CViewDlg( cnt-1, this );
    int nResponse = pViewDlg->DoModal();
    if (nResponse == IDOK)
    {
        m_RecCtrl.View( pViewDlg->m_ViewIdx );
        m_Name.SetWindowText(m_RecCtrl.GetName());
        m_Address.SetWindowText(m_RecCtrl.GetAddress());
        m_Remarks.SetWindowText(m_RecCtrl.GetRemarks());
    }
    delete pViewDlg;
}


BEGIN_EVENTSINK_MAP(CRec_contDlg, CDialog)
    //{{AFX_EVENTSINK_MAP(CRec_contDlg)
    ON_EVENT(CRec_contDlg, IDC_RECORDSCTRL1, 1 /* NameChanged */,
            OnNameChangedRecordsctrl1, VTS_BSTR)
    ON_EVENT(CRec_contDlg, IDC_RECORDSCTRL1, 2 /* AddressChanged */,
            OnAddressChangedRecordsctrl1, VTS_BSTR)
    ON_EVENT(CRec_contDlg, IDC_RECORDSCTRL1, 3 /* RemarksChanged */,
```

```
                        OnRemarksChangedRecordsctrl1, VTS_BSTR)
    //}}AFX_EVENTSINK_MAP
END_EVENTSINK_MAP()

void CRec_contDlg::OnNameChangedRecordsctrl1(LPCTSTR NewName)
{
    // TODO: Add your control notification handler code here
    ChangeColor();
}

void CRec_contDlg::OnAddressChangedRecordsctrl1(LPCTSTR NewAddress)
{
    // TODO: Add your control notification handler code here
    ChangeColor();
}

void CRec_contDlg::OnRemarksChangedRecordsctrl1(LPCTSTR NewRemarks)
{
    // TODO: Add your control notification handler code here
    ChangeColor();
}
void CRec_contDlg::ChangeColor()
{
    static char i=0;
    if ( i )
    {
       m_RecCtrl.SetBackColor( RGB(0,100,0) );
       m_RecCtrl.SetForeColor( RGB(100,0,0) );
       i=0;
    }
    else
    {
       m_RecCtrl.SetBackColor( RGB(0,0,80) );
       m_RecCtrl.SetForeColor( RGB(120,120,0) );
       i=1;

    }
}
```

The code for the View dialog box is shown here. The constructor takes the number of records in the address list. A member variable, **m_ViewIdx**, is used to keep track of the selection made by the user:

```
#if !defined(AFX_VIEWDLG_H)
#define AFX_VIEWDLG_H

#if _MSC_VER >= 1000
```

```
#pragma once
#endif // _MSC_VER >= 1000
// ViewDlg.h : header file
//


/////////////////////////////////////////////////
// CViewDlg dialog

class CViewDlg : public CDialog
{
// Construction
public:
    CViewDlg(int MaxViewIdx, CWnd* pParent = NULL);

// Dialog Data
    //{{AFX_DATA(CViewDlg)
    enum { IDD = IDD_VIEWDLG };
    int         m_ViewIdx;
    //}}AFX_DATA


// Overrides
    // ClassWizard generated virtual function overrides
    //{{AFX_VIRTUAL(CViewDlg)
    protected:
    virtual void DoDataExchange(CDataExchange* pDX);
    //}}AFX_VIRTUAL

// Implementation
protected:

    // Generated message map functions
    //{{AFX_MSG(CViewDlg)
    virtual void OnOK();
    virtual void OnCancel();
    virtual BOOL OnInitDialog();
    //}}AFX_MSG
    DECLARE_MESSAGE_MAP()

private:
   int m_MaxViewIdx;
};

//{{AFX_INSERT_LOCATION}}

#endif //
```

The implementation file is shown next. The integer passed in the constructor is used to initialize the combo box list during the dialog initialization, **OnInitDialog**. The selection in the combo box is handled through **DDX_CBIndex**, which transfers the index to the member variable **m_ViewIdx**. Since the index is also the record number in the address list, this works well for this application.

```cpp
// ViewDlg.cpp : implementation file
//

#include "stdafx.h"
#include "rec_cont.h"
#include "ViewDlg.h"

#ifdef _DEBUG
#define new DEBUG_NEW
#undef THIS_FILE
static char THIS_FILE[] = __FILE__;
#endif

/////////////////////////////////////////////////////
// CViewDlg dialog


CViewDlg::CViewDlg(int MaxViewIdx, CWnd* pParent /*=NULL*/)
    : CDialog(CViewDlg::IDD, pParent)
{
    //{{AFX_DATA_INIT(CViewDlg)
    m_ViewIdx = -1;
    //}}AFX_DATA_INIT
    ASSERT( MaxViewIdx >= 0 );
    m_MaxViewIdx = MaxViewIdx;
}


void CViewDlg::DoDataExchange(CDataExchange* pDX)
{
    CDialog::DoDataExchange(pDX);
    //{{AFX_DATA_MAP(CViewDlg)
    DDX_CBIndex(pDX, IDC_VIEWIDX, m_ViewIdx);
    //}}AFX_DATA_MAP
}
```

```
BEGIN_MESSAGE_MAP(CViewDlg, CDialog)
    //{{AFX_MSG_MAP(CViewDlg)
    //}}AFX_MSG_MAP
END_MESSAGE_MAP()

/////////////////////////////////////////////////
// CViewDlg message handlers

void CViewDlg::OnOK()
{
    // TODO: Add extra validation here

    CDialog::OnOK();
}

void CViewDlg::OnCancel()
{
    // TODO: Add extra cleanup here

    CDialog::OnCancel();
}

BOOL CViewDlg::OnInitDialog()
{
    CDialog::OnInitDialog();

    // TODO: Add extra initialization here
    CComboBox* pCBox = (CComboBox*)GetDlgItem( IDC_VIEWIDX );
    int i;
    char buf[10];
    for (i=0; i<=m_MaxViewIdx; i++)
    {
        sprintf( buf, "%d", i );
        pCBox->AddString( buf );
    }
    pCBox->SetCurSel(0);

     return TRUE; }
```

ACTIVEX CONTROL SECURITY

As mentioned at the beginning of this chapter, an ActiveX control you develop may access the local resources such as the file system on the local computer to which it is downloaded. Similarly, an ActiveX control you download to your computer may access your computer's resources. Thus, there is a potential for damage in both situations, and you have to take extra precautions to ensure that the control does not create any damage. One of the obvious possibilities is that a virus could be passed in an ActiveX control. As an author of an ActiveX control, you can *sign* a control, which lets the users of your control know that the control was signed by use of a certificate dialog box when the control is downloaded. You can also *mark* your control: You can mark your control as safe for initializing. You can also mark your control as safe for scripting. Signing and marking are independent steps. As a user downloads an ActiveX control, a certificate dialog box assures that the control has been signed. A marked control implies that the author deems it is safe for initializing and/or scripting. Let's first look at signing and marking from a developer's perspective. Then we will look at signing and marking from a user's perspective.

Signing an ActiveX Control

An ActiveX control can be signed either individually (by the developer) or by a company. In either case, a *certificate* is required. A certificate can be obtained from a certificate authority such as VeriSign (you can find more details at **http://digitalid.verisign.com/ codesign.htm**). VeriSign verifies data about the individual or corporation before issuing a certificate. Individuals are issued Class 2 certificates, and corporations are issued Class 3 certificates. A yearly fee is associated with the certificates.

Once a certificate is obtained, you can sign a control using the SIGNCODE program included with the ActiveX SDK. Note that you have to sign a control every time you modify the control. You do not have to sign a control if your company handles this.

Signing is thus a way for a control user to trace back to the individual or corporation that developed or is responsible for the control.

New in Internet Explorer 5.0

Internet Explorer 5.0 actually has four security levels: high, medium, medium-low, and low. Medium-low is the same as medium except for the absence of prompts. Another enhancement in IE 5.0 is that sites can be classified into four categories: Restricted, Trusted, Local intranet, and Internet. You can set the security levels differently for the different site categories.

Marking an ActiveX Control

As a developer, you mark a control to let a user of your control know that your control can be safely initialized and/or scripted. There is no way to specify that your control is safe for specific environments such as specific Web browsers. Once a control is marked safe, it is presumed safe in all environments in which the control could be used. This may require some extra testing and validation on your part before you can mark a control.

You can mark a control by adding entries to the Registry manually or by letting the control add the Registry entries when the control registers itself or by using the **IObjectSafety** OLE interface. For more details on how to mark a control using each of the preceding methods and for an overall description of signing and marking ActiveX controls, refer to an excellent article available from Microsoft at **http://www.microsoft.com/intdev/controls/signmark.htm**.

Using Signed and Marked ActiveX Controls

Now let's look at signing and marking from a user's perspective. We will take the example of an ActiveX control being downloaded using the Internet Explorer. Internet Explorer provides three security levels: high, medium, and none. High is the default. Table 14-2 summarizes the results when an ActiveX control with initialization and scripting is downloaded by Internet Explorer.

Internet Explorer Security Setting	Unsigned/ Unmarked	Signed, Not Marked	Signed and Marked
High	This downloads but does not display the control; it prevents the control from being used. This displays a dialog box asking the user to change security settings.	This downloads the control and displays a certificate. The control will run without initialization and without scripting.	This downloads the control and displays a certificate. The control will run with initialization and scripting.
Medium	This downloads and provides an option to the user to install the control.	This user is provided with separate options to accept the control without marking for initialization and scripting.	This control will run with initialization and scripting.
None	There is no warning dialog box. The control will run with initialization and scripting.		

Table 14-2.   ActiveX Controls and Internet Explorer

Now let's take a look at an ActiveX security programming example.

PROGRAMMING EXAMPLE TO ILLUSTRATE SIGNING AND MARKING ACTIVEX CONTROLS

The following code shows how to mark an ActiveX control. It takes the control developed earlier and adds code to mark the control during registration. The code that has been added to the control developed earlier is highlighted here. Part of the code that did not change is not shown here.

```cpp
// RecordsCtl.cpp : Implementation of the
// CRecordsCtrl ActiveX Control class.

#include "stdafx.h"
#include "rec_ax.h"
#include "RecordsCtl.h"
#include "RecordsPpg.h"

#ifdef _DEBUG
#define new DEBUG_NEW
#undef THIS_FILE
static char THIS_FILE[] = __FILE__;
#endif


IMPLEMENT_DYNCREATE(CRecordsCtrl, COleControl)


/////////////////////////////////////////////
// Message map

BEGIN_MESSAGE_MAP(CRecordsCtrl, COleControl)
    //{{AFX_MSG_MAP(CRecordsCtrl)
    ON_WM_CREATE()
    //}}AFX_MSG_MAP
    ON_OLEVERB(AFX_IDS_VERB_PROPERTIES, OnProperties)
END_MESSAGE_MAP()


/////////////////////////////////////////////
// Dispatch map
```

```
BEGIN_DISPATCH_MAP(CRecordsCtrl, COleControl)
    //{{AFX_DISPATCH_MAP(CRecordsCtrl)
    DISP_PROPERTY_NOTIFY(CRecordsCtrl, "Name", m_name,
                         OnNameChanged, VT_BSTR)
    DISP_PROPERTY_NOTIFY(CRecordsCtrl, "Address", m_address,
                         OnAddressChanged, VT_BSTR)
    DISP_PROPERTY_NOTIFY(CRecordsCtrl, "Remarks", m_remarks,
                         OnRemarksChanged, VT_BSTR)
    DISP_FUNCTION(CRecordsCtrl, "View", View, VT_EMPTY, VTS_I2)
    DISP_FUNCTION(CRecordsCtrl, "Reset", Reset, VT_EMPTY,
                 VTS_NONE)
    DISP_FUNCTION(CRecordsCtrl, "Add", Add, VT_EMPTY, VTS_NONE)
    DISP_FUNCTION(CRecordsCtrl, "GetCount", GetCount, VT_I2,
                 VTS_NONE)
    DISP_STOCKPROP_BACKCOLOR()
    DISP_STOCKPROP_FORECOLOR()
    //}}AFX_DISPATCH_MAP
    DISP_FUNCTION_ID(CRecordsCtrl, "AboutBox", DISPID_ABOUTBOX,
                    AboutBox, VT_EMPTY, VTS_NONE)
END_DISPATCH_MAP()


/////////////////////////////////////////////////
// Event map

BEGIN_EVENT_MAP(CRecordsCtrl, COleControl)
    //{{AFX_EVENT_MAP(CRecordsCtrl)
    EVENT_CUSTOM("NameChanged", FireNameChanged, VTS_BSTR)
    EVENT_CUSTOM("AddressChanged", FireAddressChanged, VTS_BSTR)
    EVENT_CUSTOM("RemarksChanged", FireRemarksChanged, VTS_BSTR)
    //}}AFX_EVENT_MAP
END_EVENT_MAP()


/////////////////////////////////////////////////
// Property pages

// TODO: Add more property pages as needed.
//   Remember to increase the count!
BEGIN_PROPPAGEIDS(CRecordsCtrl, 2)
    PROPPAGEID(CRecordsPropPage::guid)
    PROPPAGEID(CLSID_CColorPropPage)
END_PROPPAGEIDS(CRecordsCtrl)
```

```
/////////////////////////////////////////////////
// Initialize class factory and guid

IMPLEMENT_OLECREATE_EX(CRecordsCtrl, "RECAX.RecordsCtrl.1",
 0xe150326f, 0xebda,0x11d0,0xa9,0xee,0x9,0x92,0,0x54,0,0x30)
```

Marking the ActiveX control is essentially adding entries in the Registry. When the control is registered, the following three keys are added to the Registry. Adding these keys to the Registry would indicate that the control is marked and would suppress the security warnings that Microsoft Internet Explorer would otherwise prompt.

```
#define MARKINGKEY  \
"CLSID\\{E150326F-EBDA-11D0-A9EE-099200540030}\\Implemented Categories\\"
#define MARKSAFEINIT "{7DD95802-9882-11CF-9FA9-00AA006C42C4}"
#define MARKSAFESCRIPT "{7DD95801-9882-11CF-9FA9-00AA006C42C4}"
```

The CLSID of the ActiveX control may be obtained from the Registry using the OLE/COM viewer (*Oleview.exe*). As part of the marking, a new key called *Implemented Categories* is created under the ActiveX control's CLSID. Under Implemented Categories, two keys are created, one to mark the control as safe for data initialization, and the other to mark it as safe for scripting. These keys are defined in **MAKESAFEINIT** and **MAKESAFESCRIPT**, and they should be exactly as they appear.

```
// Type library ID and version

IMPLEMENT_OLETYPELIB(CRecordsCtrl, _tlid, _wVerMajor, _wVerMinor)

// Interface IDs
const IID BASED_CODE IID_DRecords =
        { 0xe150326d, 0xebda, 0x11d0, { 0xa9, 0xee,
          0x9, 0x92, 0, 0x54, 0, 0x30 } };
const IID BASED_CODE IID_DRecordsEvents =
        { 0xe150326e, 0xebda, 0x11d0, { 0xa9, 0xee,
          0x9, 0x92, 0, 0x54, 0, 0x30 } };

/////////////////////////////////////////////////
// Control type information

static const DWORD BASED_CODE _dwRecordsOleMisc =
    OLEMISC_ACTIVATEWHENVISIBLE |
    OLEMISC_SETCLIENTSITEFIRST |
    OLEMISC_INSIDEOUT |
    OLEMISC_CANTLINKINSIDE |
    OLEMISC_RECOMPOSEONRESIZE;
```

```
IMPLEMENT_OLECTLTYPE(CRecordsCtrl, IDS_RECORDS,
                     _dwRecordsOleMisc)


// CRecordsCtrl::CRecordsCtrlFactory::UpdateRegistry -
// Adds or removes system registry entries for CRecordsCtrl

BOOL CRecordsCtrl::CRecordsCtrlFactory::
                   UpdateRegistry(BOOL bRegister)
{
    if (bRegister)
    {
      BOOL brc =
          AfxOleRegisterControlClass(
            AfxGetInstanceHandle(),
              m_clsid,
              m_lpszProgID,
              IDS_RECORDS,
              IDB_RECORDS,
              afxRegApartmentThreading,
              _dwRecordsOleMisc,
              _tlid,
              _wVerMajor,
              _wVerMinor);

      // mark our ActiveX control as safe for MSIE
      /* Create or just open the key... */
      HKEY hRegistryKey;
      DWORD dwDisposition;
      CString sMarking = MARKINGKEY;
      sMarking += MARKSAFEINIT;
      long lRc = RegCreateKeyEx( HKEY_CLASSES_ROOT,
                            sMarking,
                            0L,
                            "",
                            REG_OPTION_NON_VOLATILE,
                            KEY_ALL_ACCESS,
                            NULL,
                            &hRegistryKey,
                            &dwDisposition  );
      if ( lRc != ERROR_SUCCESS )

      {
```

```
            AfxMessageBox( "Failed to register implemented categories"
                           " for safe initialization." );
    }
          else
       RegCloseKey( hRegistryKey );

    sMarking = MARKINGKEY;
    sMarking += MARKSAFESCRIPT;
    lRc = RegCreateKeyEx( HKEY_CLASSES_ROOT,
                          sMarking,
                          0L,
                          "",
                          REG_OPTION_NON_VOLATILE,
                          KEY_ALL_ACCESS,
                          NULL,
                          &hRegistryKey,
                          &dwDisposition  );
    if ( lRc != ERROR_SUCCESS )
    {
       AfxMessageBox( "Failed to register implemented categories"
                      " for safe scripting." );
    }
    else
       RegCloseKey( hRegistryKey );

    return brc;
  }
   else
       return AfxOleUnregisterClass(m_clsid, m_lpszProgID);
}
```

The rest of the code remains unchanged and is not shown.

ACTIVEX CONTROL TIPS

Keep the following tips in mind when you are designing and developing ActiveX controls:

▼ Keep the buttons and other control elements as small as possible. This helps in faster downloading when your controls are used in Web-based environments.

■ It is not always possible to restrict the ActiveX control to have just small control elements, and you will need to deal with BLOBs, such as bitmap images or AVI files. In such cases, structure the control and the container application so that the user does not have to wait for the complete downloading of images or video data, by incrementally retrieving the data and overlapping asynchronous data retrieval with user interaction. To download control properties asynchronously, you can click the Loads Properties Asynchronously button in the Advanced ActiveX Features dialog box of the ControlWizard.

■ For really large downloads, try to indicate the progress and expected completion time to the user.

■ Building and displaying a window is very time-consuming. Keep in mind that your ActiveX control does not need its own window. Your control can be set up for windowless activation. Your control can use the container's window services if appropriate.

■ Many times the control needs its own window. However, by default, the entire control area is painted. You can speed up repainting by repainting only what is required with the control's **OnDraw** function.

■ Quite often there is a requirement for the control to be drawn in both screen and metafile DCs. To facilitate the drawing in both DCs, make sure that you only use member functions supported in both DCs, and keep in mind that the coordinate system may not be using pixels.

■ You can make your ActiveX control user friendly by providing context-sensitive help for the control's property, event, and so on, by modifying the ODL file for the control.

▲ If your control is drawn exactly the same way when it is active or inactive, then you can eliminate the redrawing of the control at state transitions. This not only saves some processing and time, but it also avoids the flicker that accompanies redrawing the control. You can specify the Flicker-Free Activation option in the Advanced ActiveX features page of ControlWizard or specify it programmatically by setting the noFlickerActivate flag in the flags returned by **GetControlFlags**.

CONCLUSION

In this chapter, we built upon ActiveX controls, introduced in Chapter 12. We discussed ActiveX control properties, methods, and events. We looked at a programming example where we created an ActiveX control. We also examined containers and a container programming example. We looked at ways to improve the security aspects of using ActiveX controls, such as signing and marking ActiveX controls, and we discussed a related programming example.

In the next chapter, we will look at another common Windows 2000 communications mechanism: sockets.

CHAPTER 15

Windows Sockets

ontinuing our communications focus, let's look at one of the most important communications programming mechanisms Windows 2000 provides—Windows Sockets (WinSock).

In this chapter, we will look at Windows Sockets programming using the WinSock APIs. We will also look at MFC library support for Windows Sockets. Sockets programming sometimes involves communicating between computers with different architectures, which introduces some unique issues. We will cover these issues. We will also look at a sample socket program using WinSock APIs. The CD accompanying this book has two additional socket examples based on MFC.

SOCKET BASICS

A *socket* is a communications endpoint. Since the typical communication is between a client and a server, there are two endpoints, one at the client end and the other at the server end. Correspondingly, there are two sockets and the two sockets make up a connection for two-way transfer of data between the client and the server.

We looked at the OSI 7 layer communications model in Chapter 3, in particular Figure 3-1, which shows how the communications functions in Windows 2000 map to the OSI model. Note that WinSock fits in at the session level. As specified in the model, each layer is built on top of the functions provided in the layers below it. The WinSock layer, for example, uses the transport layer protocols such as Transmission Control Protocol (TCP), which in turn uses network layer protocols such as Internet Protocol (IP). For simplicity, the protocols are combined and we specify that WinSock uses TCP/IP, although this is not the only protocol supported by Windows Sockets. Windows Sockets provides a communications programming mechanism that you can use to develop applications that are independent of network specifics such as protocols. In fact, Windows Sockets also supports Novell's IPX/SPX, Compaq's (formerly Digital's) DECnet, and other protocols besides TCP/IP.

There are basically two types of sockets—a stream socket and a datagram socket. *Stream sockets* are used for the bidirectional transmission of a large stream of data. The data stream could be record streams or byte streams, depending on the protocol. Streams are normally used for transmitting and receiving data that is *unduplicated* (packets are sent and received only once) and *sequenced* (the order in which the data packets are sent is preserved). Stream sockets guarantee data delivery. *Datagram sockets* are used primarily for broadcast functions.

Your socket application will use a *port* to communicate with another socket application. Multiple communications functions may be carried on in different windows simultaneously. For example, the user may be performing FTP in one window while running your socket application or another communications program in another. A mechanism is necessary to ensure that data of your application is not mixed up with the data of the FTP application. The mechanism that ensures the separation is the port. Common communications functions such as FTP use a reserved port (reserved ports are listed in *Winsock2.h*). You can specify a port that is not a reserved port and is not being used, or you can let a port be assigned for you by passing zero as the port value.

Each socket also has a socket address, which typically is the IP address of the machine your application is running on (unless the machine your application is running on uses multiple network cards for connecting to different networks).

Each socket has a handle, and Windows defines a special data type—called SOCKET—for the handle. The SOCKET handle is conceptually the same as the HWND handle for a window. Each socket also operates in one of two modes—blocking mode or nonblocking mode. Blocking is discussed later, in the section "Blocking."

As with many other areas of Windows programming, you can program Windows Sockets using APIs or the MFC library. The APIs used for programming Windows Sockets functions are collectively called the WinSock APIs.

WINSOCK APIs

Windows 2000 actually provides 44 socket-related API functions, which can be grouped into four categories as follows:

- ▼ Database functions
- ■ Socket functions
- ■ Conversion functions
- ▲ Extension functions

The socket APIs are implemented as DLLs. *Winsock.dll* is the 16-bit version, and *Wsock32.dll* is the 32-bit version used by Windows Sockets version 1.1 applications. *WS2_32.dll* is used by Sockets version 2 applications. Let's look at socket functions in greater detail.

Socket Database Functions

The socket database functions provide the ability for your socket application to retrieve information about a computer that you want to communicate with, a protocol (such as TCP or UDP), or a service.

Socket database functions are part of the so-called "getXbyY" function family (except **GetHostName**). You get information about X (which could be a host, protocol, or service)

Note for UNIX Programmers

Many UNIX systems support sockets. Windows Sockets is based on Berkeley Software Distribution (BSD) sockets. If you have programmed using sockets in the UNIX environment, the concepts are pretty much the same for Windows Sockets. There are differences in the details, however. For example, in UNIX, socket descriptors are file descriptors, while Windows uses a special data type (SOCKETS). UNIX socket (and file) handles are nonnegative integers, while there is no such restriction in Windows.

by providing Y (which could be a name, address, port, and so on). Socket database functions are summarized in Table 15-1.

Socket Database Function	Description
gethostbyaddr	This gets information about a host computer using its IP address. This function successively checks the local computer, checks a HOSTS file, queries a DNS server, and tries NETBIOS name resolution to locate a host computer with the given address.
gethostbyname	This gets information about a host using its name. This function checks the local computer, checks a HOSTS file, queries a DNS server, and tries NETBIOS name resolution to locate a host computer with the given name.
gethostname	This gets the name of the local host computer.
getprotobyname	This gets information about a protocol using the name of the protocol.
getprotobynumber	This gets information about a protocol using the number or ID of the protocol.
getservbyname	This gets information about a service using the name of the service.
getservbyport	This gets information about a service using a port number.

Table 15-1. Socket Database Functions

Socket Conversion Functions

When you write socket applications that communicate across machines with different architectures or where the byte order of the data in the network is different from that of the host computer your application is running on, you need conversion routines to convert data from host byte order to network byte order and vice versa. You can write your own conversion routines, but it is easier to use the built-in conversion functions. See the section "Byte Ordering" later in this chapter for more details about byte-order differences and a list of conversion functions.

Socket Extensions

When Microsoft developed its Windows Sockets on the basis of BSD sockets, it added an important variation to handle asynchronous communication. Besides the GUI, one of the features that sets Windows apart from other operating systems is its message-driven architecture. Message handling is essentially asynchronous in nature. Your application, for example, has a message queue that gets messages posted asynchronously while some other part of your application is executing. Microsoft extended the asynchronous notion to sockets and defined a set of extension functions to sockets that provide asynchronous access to network events as well as provide overlapped I/O. These extension functions are summarized in Table 15-2.

TIP: Do not confuse WinSock APIs and WNet APIs. Although both APIs are for network-related functions, the WinSock family deals with socket connections, while the WNet family lets you programmatically list, connect, and disconnect network resources such as disks and printers.

Socket Extension Function	Description
WSAAccept	This is an extended version of the accept function.
WSAAsyncGetHostByAddr	This is an async version of GetHostByAddr. (Refer to the socket database functions for this and other "getXbyY" functions.)
WSAAsyncGetHostByName	This is an async version of GetHostByName.
WSAAsyncGetProtoByName	This is an async version of GetProtoByName.

Table 15-2. Socket Extension Functions

Socket Extension Function	Description
WSAAsyncGetProtoByNumber	This is an async version of GetProtoByNumber.
WSAAsyncGetServByName	This is an async version of GetServByName.
WSAAsyncGetServByPort	This is an async version of GetServByPort.
WSAAsyncSelect	This is an async version of the select function.
WSACancelAsyncRequest	This cancels an outstanding WSAAsyncGetXByY function call.
WSACleanup	This ends the use of underlying DLL (*WS2_32.dll*).
WSACloseEvent	This closes an event object's handle.
WSAConnect	This is an extended version of the connect function. It establishes an active connection for stream sockets and establishes a default destination address for datagram sockets.
WSACreateEvent	This creates an event object and gets its handle.
WSADuplicateSocket	This enables a socket to be shared between processes.
WSAEnumNetworkEvents	This discovers occurrences of network events for a socket since the previous invocation of WSAEnumNetworkEvents.
WSAEnumProtocols	This retrieves information about available protocols in the local computer.
WSAEventSelect	This associates network events with an event object. The event object is signaled when the network events occur.
WSAGetLastError	This gets the details of the error that occurred during the last socket operation. Do not use this function to check for an error on receipt of an asynchronous message (use the *lParam* field of the message instead).

Table 15-2.   Socket Extension Functions *(continued)*

Socket Extension Function	Description
WSAGetOverlappedResult	This gets the result of the last overlapped operation on the socket.
WSAGetQOSByName	This initializes quality of service (QOS) parameters based on a template.
WSAHtonl	This is an extended version of htonl; see Table 15-3 for a description of htonl.
WSAHtons	This is an extended version of htons; see Table 15-3 for a description of htons.
WSAIoctl	This is an extended version of ioctl capable of handling overlapped sockets.
WSAJoinLeaf	This joins a leaf node to a multipoint session.
WSANtohl	This is an extended version of ntohl; see Table 15-3 for a description of ntohl.
WSANtohs	This is an extended version of ntohs; see Table 15-3 for a description of ntohs.
WSARecv	This is an extended version of recv that allows multiple buffers for scatter/gather I/O, supports overlapped sockets, and provides the flags parameter for both input and output.
WSARecvFrom	This is an extended version of RecvFrom that allows multiple buffers for scatter/gather I/O, supports overlapped sockets, and provides the flags parameter for both input and output.
WSAResetEvent	This resets an event object to not signaled.
WSASend	This is an extended version of the send function that allows multiple buffers for scatter/gather I/O and supports overlapped sockets.
WSASendTo	This is an extended version of SendTo that allows multiple buffers for scatter/gather I/O and supports overlapped sockets.
WSASetEvent	This sets an event object to signaled.

Table 15-2.   Socket Extension Functions *(continued)*

Socket Extension Function	Description
WSASetLastError	This sets the error code. (The error code is returned by WSAGetLastError; see WSAGetLastError in this table.)
WSASocket	This is an extended version of the socket function. It supports overlapped sockets and allows the socket to create or join a socket group.
WSAStartup	This is the first sockets call your application issues to initialize the sockets DLL; you can specify the desired sockets version.
WSAWaitForMultipleEvents	This waits for multiple event objects to be signaled.
WSAAddressToString	This converts an address structure into a human-readable numeric string.
WSAEnumNameSpaceProviders	This retrieves the list of available Name Registration and Resolution service providers.
WSAGetServiceClassInfo	This retrieves all of the class-specific information pertaining to a service class.
WSAGetServiceClassNameBy ClassId	This returns the name of the service associated with the given type.
WSAInstallServiceClass	This creates a new service class type and stores its class-specific information.
WSALookupServiceBegin	This initiates a client query to retrieve name information as constrained by a WSAQUERYSET data structure.
WSALookupServiceEnd	This finishes a client query started by WSALookupServiceBegin and frees resources associated with the query.
WSALookupServiceNext	This retrieves the next unit of name information from a client query initiated by WSALookupServiceBegin.
WSARemoveServiceClass	This permanently removes a service class type.

Table 15-2. Socket Extension Functions *(continued)*

Socket Extension Function	Description
WSASetService	This registers or removes from the Registry a service instance within one or more name spaces.
WSAStringToAddress	This converts a human-readable numeric string to a socket address structure suitable for passing to Windows Sockets routines.

Table 15-2. Socket Extension Functions *(continued)*

COMMON SOCKET STRUCTURES

Common socket structures used by the WinSock functions mentioned earlier include **sockaddr_in, hostent, protoent,** and **servent**. The **sockaddr_in** and **hostent** structures are used in the programming example included later in this chapter. **sockaddr_in** is used for storing an IP port and address of a computer that is a socket endpoint. **sockaddr_in** is an Internet-specific format of the more general **sockaddr** structure. **hostent** is used for host information (including local host). **protoent** is used for protocol information. **servent** is used for service information. Let's look at each of these structures.

sockaddr_in

SOCKADDR_IN structure is used by Windows Sockets to specify a local or remote endpoint address to which to connect a socket.

```
struct sockaddr_in{short sin_family;
                    unsigned short sin_port;
                    struct in_addr sin_addr;
                    char sin_zero[8];
};
```

where

sin_family is the address family and must be AF_INET

sin_port is the IP port

sin_addr is the IP address, which is of type **in_addr** (**in_addr** structure is defined in *Winsock2.h*)

sin_zero is padding to match the size of this structure to **sockaddr**

hostent

This structure returns host-related data such as the host name (and any aliases) and a list of addresses of the host. Windows 2000 allocates this structure and returns a pointer to the structure on host-related calls such as **GetHostByAddr**. Since your application did not allocate the structure, do not free the structure or any of its components. One copy of this structure is allocated per thread, and the structure is reused by Windows Sockets API calls. For example, if you follow one **GetHostByAddr** call with another, the host information of the second call will overlay the first. So if you want to save any data, you should store elsewhere the information you need that is returned by the API call before you issue another call. The **hostent** structure is shown here:

```
struct hostent { char FAR * h_nam;
                 char FAR * FAR * h_aliases;
                 short h_addrtype;
                 short h_len;
                 char FAR * FAR * h_addrlst ;
};
```

where

> *h_nam* is the host name. The name that is returned depends on whether you use a name-resolution system such as DNS. If you use DNS, the name returned is the Fully Qualified Domain Name (FQDN). If you use a local *hosts* file, the name returned is the first entry after the IP address.
>
> *h_aliases* is an array of aliases
>
> *h_addrtype* is the type of returned address
>
> *h_len* is the address length in bytes
>
> *h_addrlst* is a list of addresses for the host in network byte order

protoent

This structure returns protocol data for protocols used with sockets such as TCP or UDP. The protocol data includes the protocol name, including aliases, and the protocol number (in host byte order). The use of this structure is very similar to that of **hostent**. Windows 2000 allocates **protoent** and returns a pointer to the structure on protocol-related calls such as **GetProtoByName**. Since your application did not allocate the structure, do not free the structure or any of its components. One copy of this structure is allocated per thread, and the structure is reused by Windows Sockets API calls. For example, if you follow one **GetProtoByName** call with another, the protocol information of the second call will overlay the first. To save any data, you should store elsewhere the information you

need that is returned by the API call before you issue another call. The **protoent** structure
is shown here:

```
struct protoent { char FAR * p_nam;
                  char FAR * FAR * p_aliases;
                  short p_protno;
};
```

where

> *p_nam* is the protocol name
>
> *p_aliases* is an array of aliases
>
> *p_protno* is the protocol number or ID (in host byte order)

servent

This structure returns service-related data such as the service name (and any aliases), a
port number for contacting the service, and the protocol that can be used with the service.

```
struct servent { char FAR * s_nam;
                 char FAR * FAR *  s_aliases;
                 short s_portno;
                 char FAR * s_protnam;
};
```

where

> *s_nam* is the service name
>
> *s_aliases* is an array of aliases
>
> *s_portno* is the port number (in network byte order) for contacting the service
>
> s_*protnam* is the protocol name to be used with the service

SOCKETS API PROGRAMMING

Having looked at available sockets API functions and the common data structures they
use, let's take a look at how we can actually program using sockets. Socket communication typically has three phases. In the first phase, you commonly perform setup functions,
such as creating and binding a socket and locating and establishing a socket connection
with a remote computer. In the second phase, you send and receive data. If you are writing a service-type socket application, you can create a socket and listen for incoming
socket connections from clients. If you have multiple clients trying to establish connec-

tions simultaneously, you can ask that the connection requests be backlogged. In the final phase, you perform cleanup functions, such as shutting down and closing the socket connection. Most of the APIs you would use for database socket functions are listed in Table 15-1. Table 15-2 lists the APIs for performing asynchronous communications using Windows socket extensions.

You can also perform a *broadcast* (also called a *multicast*) of a message to a list of IP addresses.

NEW IN WINDOWS 2000: Windows 2000 introduced enhancements related to Quality of Service (QOS) in Windows 2000. Please refer to the function **WSAGetQOSByName**, which is used to initialize a **QUALITYOFSERVICE** structure based on a named template, or to retrieve an enumeration of the available template names. Also refer to the **QUALITYOFSERVICE** structure for additional details.

SOCKETS PROGRAMMING USING MFCs

MFC socket objects encapsulate Windows Sockets object handles and provide classes to perform operations on the encapsulated handle. You can use the MFC library classes **CSocket** and **CAsyncSocket** for sockets programming. **CAsyncSocket** is derived from the **CObject** class, and **CSocket** is derived from **CAsyncSocket**. **CAsyncSocket** is a lower-level class compared with **CSocket**. With **CAsyncSocket** you have to take care of some low-level network functions such as blocking, byte order differences (see the "Byte Ordering" section), and so on. **CSocket** takes care of these functions for you. **CAsyncSocket** provides callbacks to notify you of network events. So if you want low-level control and efficiency, use **CAsyncSocket**. Otherwise, use the more general **CSocket**. **CSocket** handles the low-level details using a **CArchive** object (with an associated **CSocketFile** object. You generally attach the **CSocketFile** object to a **CArchive** object to simplify sending and receiving data using MFC serialization).

You can derive your own classes from these two classes and override the member functions they contain such as **OnConnect**, **OnSend**, **OnAccept**, and so on.

The following are the major steps for stream socket communications using **CAsyncSocket** or **CSocket**:

1. Call the object's constructor. You can use either the stack or the heap for the object.

2. Call the **create** member function to create the socket. (This step is not required if you are not creating a socket but are accepting a socket connection). The socket could be either a stream socket or a datagram socket (see the discussion on socket types in the "Socket Basics" section at the beginning of the chapter). You can also specify a port for the socket. You normally would specify a port

for server socket applications but accept the default for client socket applications.

3. Call the **connect** member function. (If you are writing a server socket application that will start and wait for clients to connect, then you would use the **listen** and **accept** member functions.)

4. Perform socket communications functions that are application dependent by use of member functions such as **send** and **receive**. You may also override notifications such as **OnSend**, and so on. If you are using **CSocket**, you will be using a **CArchive** object (with an associated **CSocketFile** object) for sending data and perhaps another **CArchive** for receiving data.

5. Destroy the socket object. If you used the heap in step 1, then you have to explicitly delete the object. If you used the stack in step 1, the destructor is called when the function goes out of scope. The destructor automatically calls the **close** member function.

ISSUES IN SOCKETS PROGRAMMING

There are special issues you may need to be aware of in sockets programming. Depending on the approach you take (MFC versus API, **CAsyncSocket** versus **CSocket**), some of the issues may be taken care of automatically. The issues in sockets programming include byte-order differences, blocking, and string conversion.

Byte Ordering

Bytes are stored (or ordered) within a word in two ways. You can have the *most* significant byte on the left end of a word (also called "big-endian"), or you can have the *least* significant byte on the left end of a word (also called "little-endian"). Computers using the Intel x86 architecture use the little-endian method, while computers using the Motorola architecture (Macs) and computers using the RISC architecture (many UNIX systems) use the big-endian method. The common byte order on TCP/IP networks is also big-endian (also called "network byte order"). When you are developing a sockets application, you may be communicating from a computer using one of the methods for byte ordering to another computer using the other method. If you use **CArchive** (by using a **CSocket**), the conversion is automatically done for you. If not, you have to do the conversion in your application. Windows 2000 provides conversion functions summarized in Table 15-3.

Sockets version 2 includes functions such as **WSAHtonl**, **WSAHtons**, which are WinSock extension functions that perform the conversion of byte orders.

Conversion Function	Description
htonl	Converts a 32-bit long number from host byte order to network byte order
htons	Converts a 16-bit short number from host byte order to network byte order
ntohl	Converts a 32-bit long number from network byte order to host byte order
ntohs	Converts a 16-bit short number from network byte order to host byte order

Table 15-3. Socket Conversion Functions

Blocking

As mentioned earlier, a socket can be in one of two modes—blocking mode or nonblocking mode. *Blocking mode* is synchronous. For example, if you call the **receive** function, your thread will not receive control until the receive is completed. If your socket is unable to receive data immediately, it waits (it is blocked) for the sending application to send the data if you use the blocking version of **CSocket** or **CAsyncSocket**. While most of the time the **receive** function should be able to receive the data, there is always the possibility that the receive may be significantly delayed if there are computer, network, or application problems. If you have users using your socket application, then you may not want them to wait on the blocked socket.

You can avoid users waiting on a blocked socket in one of two ways. First, you can use nonblocking versions of **CSocket** or **CAsyncSocket**. Alternatively, you can create a worker thread to handle socket communications including receive and send, and have the user interface thread interface with the user. The worker thread could be blocked, if necessary. For more details about user interface threads, worker threads, and multithreading, refer to Chapter 9.

String Conversion

Just as you could be performing socket communications between computers whose architectures could be using different byte ordering, you could also be communicating across computers using different character sets such as ANSI, MBCS, and UNICODE. (See Appendix A for more details about character sets.) If you use **CAsyncSocket**, you must perform the string conversions in your application. If you use **CSocket**, then the associated **CArchive** object handles string conversion using the **CString** class.

PROGRAMMING EXAMPLE USING SOCKETS

The *EchoCS* sample program shown next is a client/server program based on Windows Sockets. The client accepts a string from the user and sends that string to the server through a socket interface, and a thread listening at the echo port at the server sends back the same string to the client, which displays the string on the console. The sample is designed as a single executable that, based on the input parameters, behaves either as a server or a client. Starting the executable with the *–d* parameter will start the executable as a server, and starting it with the *–c* and *hostname* parameters (where *hostname* is the name of the host where the server is running) will start it as a client. Figures 15-1 through 15-5 show the startup and communication using sockets between the client and the server. The text typed in the client window is echoed at the server, and the same text is sent back to the client. Note that for this example, the client and the server were both the same machine. The server was started first with the command **echocs –d** at the command prompt. The client was started next with the command **echocs –c 127.0.0.1**. You can try this example on different machines by substituting the appropriate address for "127.0.0.1." Keep in mind though, that there may be problems in running this example if either the client or the server is behind a firewall that does not permit such functions. The complete project is available in the CD-ROM; notice the inclusion there of wsock32.lib for linking.

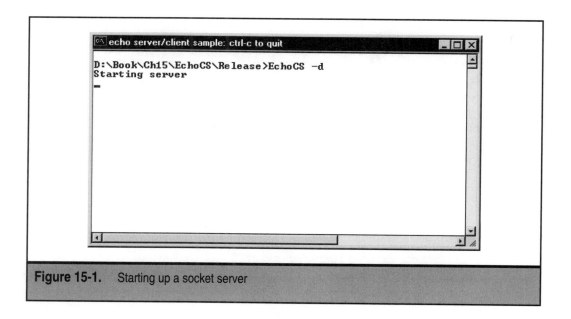

Figure 15-1.   Starting up a socket server

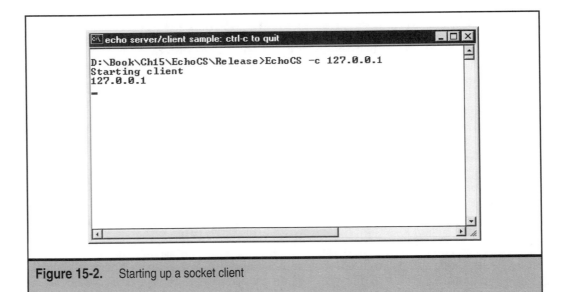

Figure 15-2. Starting up a socket client

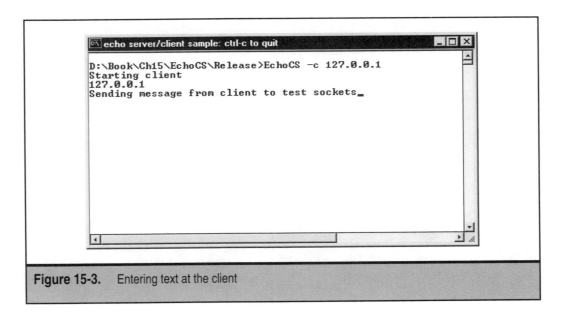

Figure 15-3. Entering text at the client

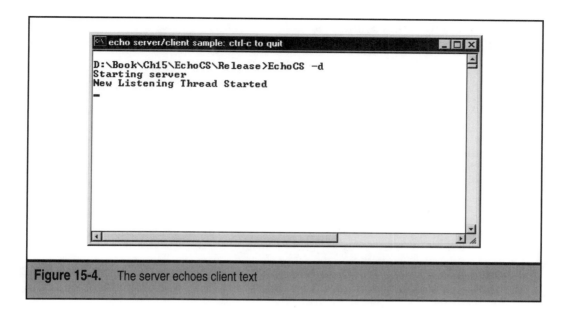

Figure 15-4. The server echoes client text

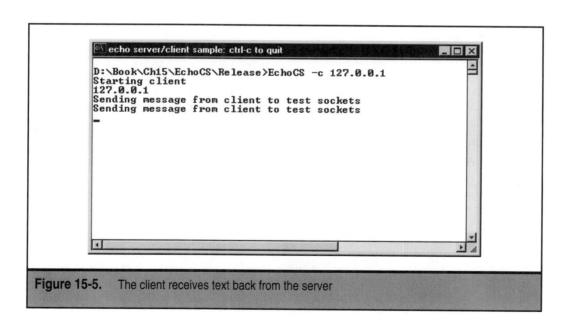

Figure 15-5. The client receives text back from the server

To use Windows Sockets, the *Winsock.h* header file is included. For simplicity the thread information and the socket handle are defined as global.

```c
#include <stdio.h>
#include <stdlib.h>
#include <windows.h>
#include <winsock.h>

// Function declarations
BOOL InitWinSock( char *szError );
int RunServer();
SOCKET StartServer( UINT nPort, char *szError );
BOOL WINAPI ClientThread( LPVOID lp );
int RunClient( char *szHost );
SOCKET ConnectToServer(char *name, UINT nPort, char *szError);
BOOL  SendToSocket(SOCKET hSocket, char *buf, int nSize, char *szError);
int ReadFromSocket(SOCKET hSocket, char *szBuffer, UINT nLength,
                    char *szError );
BOOL WINAPI ControlHandler(DWORD dwCtrlType);
void TerminateWinSock( SOCKET hSocket );

// thread structure
typedef struct
{
    SOCKET hSocket;
    BOOL bTerminate;
} ThreadStruct;

// global thread struct
ThreadStruct g_Info;
SOCKET g_hSocket = INVALID_SOCKET;       // global client/server socket
```

The main program checks the input parameters, initializes the sockets environment, and depending on the input parameter, is run either as a server or as a client. It also adds a console control handler to handle events generated by pressing CTRL-C or CTRL-BREAK, closing the console, logon, logoff, or shutdown. This is done to handle such events gracefully and close the application. When such an event occurs, the control of the program is transferred to the control handler function, which is **ControlHandler** in this sample.

```c
int main( int argc, char *argv[] )
{
    BOOL bServer = TRUE;
    char *szHost;
    char szError[1024];

    if( argc == 3 )
    {
        if( !strcmp( argv[1], "-c") )
```

```
        {
            bServer = FALSE;
            szHost = argv[2];
        }
    }
    else if ( argc > 3 )
    {
        // invalid args.
        puts("For server: \n\tusage: echocs [-d]\nFor client:\n\tusage:\
            echocs -c host\n");
        return 1;
    }

    if( !InitWinSock( szError ) )
    {
        puts(szError);
        return 1;
    }
    // set control event handler and console title
    SetConsoleCtrlHandler( ControlHandler, TRUE );
    SetConsoleTitle("echo server/client sample: ctrl-c to quit");

    if( bServer )
    {
        // server
        return RunServer();
    }
    else
    {
        // client
        return RunClient( szHost );
    }
    return 0; // never reached
}
```

The next function, **InitWinSock**, initializes the Windows Sockets environment by calling **WSAStartup**, which must be the first Windows Sockets function called by a WinSock application or DLL. This allows the application or DLL to specify the Windows Sockets version required and to retrieve the information for Windows Sockets as implemented in the current environment. This API checks the version requested by the application and returns "success" if the requested version is equal to or higher than the lowest version supported by the Windows Sockets implementation. It returns this version information in the **WSAData** structure passed in the API and expects the caller to look in the data and decide. This negotiation allows both the caller and the Windows Sockets DLL to support a range of Windows Sockets versions. In this sample, version 1.1 is requested. If the API returns "failure," the error is returned to the caller. It should be noted that the API returns the error code directly, and the standard mechanism of getting the error through

WSAGetLastError cannot be used, since the Windows Sockets DLL may not have established the client data area where the last error is stored.

```
/////////////////////////////////////////////////////////////////
// InitWinSock
//          starts up winsock.dll or wsock32.dll
BOOL InitWinSock( char *szError )
{

    WSADATA wsData;
    int iRC;

    // change 1,1 to 2,0 if using 2.0
    WORD wVersion = MAKEWORD(1,1);  // winsock version

    if( (iRC = WSAStartup(wVersion, &wsData)) !=   0 )
    {
        if( szError )
        {
            sprintf(szError,"WSAStartup failed: WSA ERROR: %d\r\n",
                    iRC);
        }
        return FALSE;
    }
    return TRUE;
}
```

The main program calls the **RunServer** function shown next if the application is started as a server. This function calls the **StartServer** function, which creates a listening socket on the specified port and returns the listening socket. The listening socket is created by use of the **socket** function call. The address family is specified as AF_INET, and a stream socket type is specified. This function call, which is bound to the specific transport service provider, allocates the socket descriptor and any related resources. The first available service provider that supports the requested combination of address family, socket type, and protocol is used. A socket of type SOCK_STREAM provides a full duplex connection and must be in a connected state before any data can be sent or received on it. A connection to another socket is created by use of the **connect** function call. After the connection, data can be transferred or received by use of **send** or **recv** function calls. After the socket is created, that socket is bound to associate a local address with the socket. When a socket is created by use of the **socket** function call, it exists in the address space without a name assigned to it. The **bind** function call establishes the local association of the socket by assigning a local name to an unnamed socket. The name is specified by use of the **SOCKADDR** structure. The **SOCKADDR** structure varies depending on the protocol selected. The **sockaddr_in** is used for TCP/IP. Note that except for the family field, all fields are expressed in network byte order. Helper functions **htonl** and **htons** are used to convert to network byte order. The **ZeroMemory** API is used to initialize the data structure.

After binding, the socket is placed in a listening state by use of the **listen** function call. This places the socket in a state where it is listening for incoming connections. To accept connections, the socket created earlier and a maximum backlog of incoming connections is given to the **listen** function call. If a connection request arrives and the queue is full, the client will receive an error. Though the backlog parameter is an *int,* the underlying service limits the backlog to a reasonable value. Even if the caller specifies an unreasonable value, it is replaced by the closest reasonable value.

The server then goes in a loop selecting the socket and accepting the connection. The **select** function call determines the status of the socket, waiting, if necessary, to perform synchronous I/O. The connection is accepted by use of the **accept** function call, and when the connection is accepted, a thread is started to handle the client connection. The **accept** function call extracts the first connection on the queue of pending connections on the given socket. It creates a new socket and returns the handle to the new socket. This newly created socket will handle the connection. The information about the socket is passed to the thread through the *thread* parameter.

```
/////////////////////////////////////////////////////
// RunServer
//          Server stuff
int RunServer()
{
    char szError[1024];

    puts("Starting server");
    g_hSocket = StartServer( 7, szError ); // echo port is 7
    struct sockaddr_in client;
    if( g_hSocket == INVALID_SOCKET )
    {
        puts(szError);
        return 1;
    }

    // loop forever
    // pressing ctrl+c will call the control handler, which will
    // terminate the process.
    while ( TRUE )
    {
        int nLength = sizeof(client);
        DWORD dwThreadId;
        g_Info.bTerminate = FALSE;

        fd_set fds;
        int nError;
        struct timeval timeout;

        timeout.tv_sec = 1;      //  1 second timeout
```

```
            timeout.tv_usec = 0;
            ////////////////////////////////////////////////////////////////
            // NOTE; we use select to avoid blocking on accept forever.
            //             It prevents Ctrl-C from calling the control handler.
            FD_ZERO(&fds);
            FD_SET( g_hSocket, &fds );
            nError = select( g_hSocket + 1, &fds, NULL, NULL, &timeout );

            if( nError == WSAEINTR )
                continue;  // interrupted: no harm done
            else if( nError < 0 )
            {
                // error:
                return 1;
            }

            if( FD_ISSET( g_hSocket, &fds ) )
            {
                // accept connection.
                if( (g_Info.hSocket = accept(g_hSocket,
                    (struct sockaddr *)&client,
                    &nLength)) < 0)
                {
                    puts("accept failed: exiting...");
                    return 1;
                }
                // start a thread to handle client connnection
                if (NULL == CreateThread( (LPSECURITY_ATTRIBUTES) NULL,
                                          0,
                                          (LPTHREAD_START_ROUTINE) ClientThread,
                                          (LPVOID)&g_Info,
                                          0,
                                          &dwThreadId ))
                {
                    puts("can't create thread");
                    TerminateWinSock( g_hSocket );
                    return 1;
                }
              // wait 1 second for thread to initialize
                Sleep(1000);
            }
        }
    return 0;
}
////////////////////////////////////////////////////////////////
// StartServer
//      creates a listening socket on the specified port.
//          returns the listening socket.
SOCKET StartServer( UINT nPort, char *szError )
```

```
{
    SOCKET hSocket;
    struct sockaddr_in server;
    if( (hSocket =  socket(AF_INET, SOCK_STREAM, 0)) < 0 )
    {
        sprintf(szError, "socket failed");
        return INVALID_SOCKET;
    }
    // fill in server structure
    ZeroMemory( (char *)&server, sizeof(server));
    server.sin_family = AF_INET;
    server.sin_addr.s_addr = htonl(INADDR_ANY);
    server.sin_port = htons(nPort);

    // bind address to socket
    if( bind( hSocket, (struct sockaddr *)&server, sizeof(server)) < 0 )
    {
        sprintf(szError, "bind failed");
        return INVALID_SOCKET;
    }

    if( listen(hSocket, 5) < 0 )
    {
        sprintf(szError, "listen failed");
        return INVALID_SOCKET;
    }
    return hSocket;
}
```

The thread function that handles the client connection is shown next. It basically does a select on the socket and then reads data from the socket by calling **ReadFromSocket**; if it reads data from the socket, it sends that data back to the client by calling **SendToSocket**. The socket is finally closed by use of the **closesocket** function call. This releases the socket descriptor such that further reference to this socket will fail.

```
////////////////////////////////////////////////////////////////////////////
// ClientThread
//          A thread function to handle each client connection.
//
BOOL WINAPI ClientThread( LPVOID lp )
{
    ThreadStruct* pInfo = (ThreadStruct *)lp;
    SOCKET hSocket = pInfo->hSocket;
    char szBuffer[1024];
    char szError[1024];
    fd_set fds;
    int nError, nLength;
    struct timeval timeout;
```

```
       timeout.tv_sec = 1;       //  1 second timeout
       timeout.tv_usec = 0;

       while( ! pInfo->bTerminate )
       {
           ZeroMemory( szBuffer, 1024 );
           ZeroMemory( szError, 1024 );
           FD_ZERO(&fds);
           FD_SET( hSocket, &fds );
           nError = select( hSocket + 1, &fds, NULL, NULL, &timeout );
           if( nError == WSAEINTR )
               continue;  // interrupt
           else if( nError < 0 )
           {
               break;
           }
       if( FD_ISSET( hSocket, &fds) )
           {
               // read from client
               if((nLength = ReadFromSocket(hSocket, szBuffer, 1024, szError))>0)
               {
                   // send whatever we just read: this is an echo server
                   if( !SendToSocket(hSocket, szBuffer, nLength, szError) )
                   {
                       puts(szError);
                       break;
                   }
               }
               else
               {
                   puts(szError);
                   break;
               }
           }
       }

       // close connection and exit
       closesocket(hSocket);
       return TRUE;
}
```

Up to now we have seen the operation of the server side of the sample. The **RunClient** function is called when the sample is executed as a client. This function sets up a connection to the server by calling the **ConnectToServer** function. In **ConnectToServer** the server name, which is actually an input to the sample program when it is started, is verified if it is in the numeric dot format. If not, the address of the host is queried by use of the **GetHostByName** function call. The **sockaddr_in** structure is initialized with the information of the server. A stream socket is created by use of the **socket** function call, and the connection is established with the server by use of the **connect** function call. This call will initiate an active connection to the server, since the type of the socket is stream socket. After the completion of this call, the socket is ready to send and receive data to the server. This socket handle is then used to send data to the server using **SendToSocket** and to read data from the server using **ReadFromSocket**. If data is received, it is displayed on the console, or else an error message is displayed. These functions are shown next.

```
// RunClient
int RunClient( char *szHost )
{
    char szError[1024];
    char szBuffer[1024];
    // client
    puts("Starting client");
    puts(szHost);

    // connect to server
    g_hSocket = ConnectToServer( szHost, 7, szError );

    if( g_hSocket == INVALID_SOCKET )
    {
        puts(szError);
        return 1;
    }
    // loop forever
    while( TRUE )
    {
        ZeroMemory( szBuffer, 1024 );
        ZeroMemory( szError, 1024 );
        gets(szBuffer);
        if( SendToSocket(g_hSocket, szBuffer, strlen(szBuffer), szError) )
        {
            if( ReadFromSocket(g_hSocket, szBuffer, 1024, szError ) < 0 )
            {
                puts(szError);
                return 1;
            }
            puts(szBuffer);
        }
    }
  return 0;
}
// ConnectToServer:
//     connects to a server on a specified port number
//     returns the connected socket
SOCKET ConnectToServer(char *name, UINT nPort, char *szError)
{
  SOCKET hSocket;
```

```
struct sockaddr_in server;
struct hostent far *hp;
if( !name || !*name )
      return INVALID_SOCKET;

if( isdigit(name[0]))
{
    ZeroMemory((char *) &server, sizeof(server));
    server.sin_family      = AF_INET;
    server.sin_addr.s_addr = inet_addr(name);
    server.sin_port    = htons(nPort);
}
else
{
  if ( (hp = (struct hostent far *) gethostbyname(name)) == NULL)
  {
      sprintf(szError,"Error: gethostbyname failed: %s.",name);
      return INVALID_SOCKET;
  }

  ZeroMemory((char *)&server, sizeof(server));
  CopyMemory((char *) &server.sin_addr,hp->h_addr,hp->h_length);
  server.sin_family = hp->h_addrtype;
  server.sin_port = htons(nPort);
}
/* create socket */
if( (hSocket = socket(AF_INET, SOCK_STREAM, 0)) < 1)
{
   sprintf(szError,"socket failed to create stream socket");
   return INVALID_SOCKET;
}

// connect to server.
if (connect(hSocket,(struct sockaddr *)&server, sizeof(server))< 0)
{
   sprintf(szError,"connect failed to connect to requested address.");
   return INVALID_SOCKET;
}
  return hSocket;
}
```

The next two functions send and receive data to and from the server. The **SendToSocket** function calls the **send** function to send data on a connected socket. If no error occurs, the **send** function returns the total number of bytes sent, which can be less than the number of bytes in the buffer. The **SendToSocket** function checks if all the bytes are sent and if needed, repeats the send after adjusting the buffer and buffer length. Though the **send** function may complete successfully, it does not mean that the data was successfully delivered.

Note that for message-oriented sockets, care must be taken not to exceed the maximum packet size of the underlying provider. This maximum size can be queried by use of the **GetSockOpt** function call.

```
// SendToSocket
//          sends a buffer (buf) of size nSize to the specified socket
//          returns TRUE or FALSE.
BOOL   SendToSocket(SOCKET hSocket, char *buf,
                    int nSize, char *szError)
{
  int    rv;
  /* write it all */
  while ((rv = send(hSocket, buf, nSize,0)) != nSize)
  {
     if (rv == -1)
     {
        sprintf(szError,"error sending to server. WSA ERROR: %d\r\n",
                WSAGetLastError());
        return FALSE;
     }

     if (rv == nSize)
        break;
     buf += rv;
     nSize -= rv;
  }
  return TRUE;
}
```

The **ReadFromSocket** function reads data from the socket by use of the **recv** function call. The **recv** function call receives data on a specified socket. The data is received in the given buffer, whose length is also specified. If the data or message available is larger than the buffer, then the behavior depends on the protocol. For reliable protocols, the buffer is filled with as much data as possible, and the **recv** function generates the **WSAEMSGSIZE** error. The data is retained until it is successfully read by calling the **recv** function with a large enough buffer. For unreliable protocols like UDP, the excess data is lost. The **recv** function call can be used to read data either on a connection-oriented socket or on a connectionless socket. If the socket is a connection-oriented socket, it must be connected before receiving data using the **recv** function. If the socket is a connectionless socket, the socket must be bound before receiving data using the **recv** function.

```
// ReadFromSocket
// Reads some bytes from the specified socket
// into szBuffer of size nLength.
//
int ReadFromSocket(SOCKET hSocket, char *szBuffer,
                   UINT nLength, char *szError )
```

```
{
    int rv = recv(hSocket, (LPSTR)szBuffer, nLength, 0);

    if( rv <= 0 )
        sprintf( szError, "recv failed");
    return rv;
}
```

The next function handles any control event generated by the user by pressing either CTRL-C or CTRL-BREAK, closing the console, logging off, or shutting down the system. Since a console control handler was set in the main program, the system will pass control to this function when a control event occurs. This function basically terminates the program gracefully by terminating the Windows Sockets and performing a cleanup function. The **TerminateWinSock** function cancels blocking calls by calling the **WSACancelBlockingCall** API. Note that this function has been removed from the Windows Sockets 2 specification. If the socket is active, it is closed and the use of Windows Sockets DLL is terminated by calling the **WSACleanup** API. The application must call **WSACleanup** to deregister itself from Windows Sockets and allow it to free any resources allocated on behalf of the application or DLL. When **WSACleanup** is called, any pending blocking or asynchronous calls issued by any thread in this process are canceled without posting any notification messages or signaling any event objects. Even if **CloseSocket** was not called, calling **WSACleanup** will reset and deallocate any open socket.

```
// ControlHandler
//      Control event handler: Ctrl-C, etc.
BOOL WINAPI ControlHandler(DWORD dwCtrlType)
{
  switch(dwCtrlType)
    {
    case CTRL_C_EVENT:              // Ctrl-C pressed
    case CTRL_BREAK_EVENT:          // ctrl+break pressed
    case CTRL_CLOSE_EVENT:          // window closing
    case CTRL_LOGOFF_EVENT:         // user logoff
    case CTRL_SHUTDOWN_EVENT:       // system shutdown
            TerminateWinSock( g_hSocket );  // unload winsock
        break;
    }
  return(TRUE);
}
```

```
/////////////////////////////////////////////////
// TerminateWinSock
// call this function with the current socket or INVALID_SOCKET
void TerminateWinSock( SOCKET hSocket )
{
    // cancel blocking calls, if any
    WSACancelBlockingCall();

    // close socket
    if( hSocket != INVALID_SOCKET )
        closesocket(hSocket);

    g_Info.bTerminate = TRUE;
    // allow threads to terminate, if any.
    Sleep(2000);
    Sleep(3000);

    // unload winsock
    WSACleanup();
}
```

CONCLUSION

In this chapter, we looked at Windows Sockets programming using the WinSock APIs. We also looked at MFC support for Windows Sockets. We covered unique issues related to sockets programming involving communicating between computers with different architectures. We also looked at a sample socket program using WinSock APIs. The CD accompanying this book has two additional socket examples based on MFC.

In the next chapter we will look at Internet-related programming using ISAPI.

CHAPTER 16

Internet Programming

ontinuing our communications focus, let's take a look at Internet-related programming and Windows 2000. With the advent of intranets and the continued popularity of Web browsers, more and more corporate applications are being developed for a Web-centric intranet environment. As a business programmer, you can expect to spend a lot of time developing intranet applications using the World Wide Web. There are two aspects of programming Web applications—the client side and the server side.

In this chapter, we will take a look at the programming aspects of both server and client Internet programming in the Windows 2000 environment. We will start with a brief review of Web and Internet Server API (ISAPI) basics, compare ISAPI and another method for Internet-related programming—Common Gateway Interface (CGI)—and look at the steps involved in developing the two types of ISAPI applications—filters and extensions. We will also discuss programming aspects at the client. In particular, we will look at the Windows Internet extensions and some examples of programming typical Internet functions such as FTP, Gopher, and HTTP.

WEB PROGRAMMING BASICS

There are two aspects of programming Web applications—the client side and the server side. The typical environments used for client-side programming include Java, ActiveX, VBScript, Win32 Internet Extensions (WinInet), and so on. Windows Internet extensions provide an alternative to programming using Windows Sockets (covered in Chapter 15) and TCP/IP. WinInet is covered in the section "Internet Client Programming" later in this chapter. ActiveX and programming examples using ActiveX are covered in Chapters 12 and 14. The typical environments for the server side include CGI, ISAPI, and so on. A simple interaction between a Web client and a Web server is shown in Figure 16-1.

The client could be a browser such as Netscape or Internet Explorer. It could also consist of stand-alone applications developed by use of languages such as Java/ActiveX, or it could include browsers with embedded Java applets/ActiveX controls. The client interacts with the user and sends a request to a Web/Internet server such as Microsoft's Internet Information Server (IIS) or the Peer Web Server. This server is an add-on function on top of the base operating system such as Windows 2000 server and runs as a Windows 2000 service. The client/server communications typically use the HTTP protocol. The Web server receives the client request and invokes an extension or filter function written by use of ISAPI. ISAPI extensions and filters are DLLs that are invoked just like any other DLLs. The extension uses MFC ODBC classes to access a database. (ODBC, which stands for Open Database Connectivity, is one of two common mechanisms for Windows applications to access databases, the other being Data Access Objects (DAO). ODBC is covered in detail in Chapter 20, and ADO is covered in Chapter 21.) The data from the database is passed from the database to the client through the ISAPI extension and the Web server. IIS supports ISAPI on Windows Server versions starting with Windows NT version 3.51. Peer Web Server supports ISAPI on Windows NT 2000 Professional and Windows 95. Most business Internet/intranet programming is likely to use IIS and Windows 2000 Server Editions.

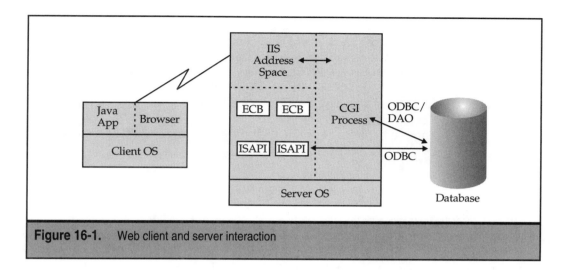

Figure 16-1.   Web client and server interaction

Other terms you should be familiar with in Windows 2000 Internet programming are *Active Server Pages (ASP), cookies,* and *CGI.*

ASP provides server-side scripting capabilities (in the same way as *VBScript* provides client-side scripting). ASPs typically are in-process servers. ASP is attracting a lot of attention, but as an advanced Windows 2000 programmer, you should still be familiar with the ISAPI.

Table 16-1 compares programming ISAPI versus ASP scripts/server-side COM components.

ISAPI	ASP Scripts/Server-Side COM Components
Highest possible performance.	Performance is normally less than can be obtained with ISAPI.
Provides low-level control by providing access to the full Win32 API functionality including multithreading.	Programming is typically at a higher level with some low-level details masked by abstraction. For example, session abstraction can be used here unlike ISAPI.
Development tends to take longer time, since most programming is performed at a low level with C/C++.	Development is relatively faster due to the use of higher-level scripts.

Table 16-1.   Comparing ISAPI and ASP Scripts/Server-Side COM Programming

Cookies are mechanisms for data exchange between an Internet server and client. Cookies are typically used to contain client state data, which is used by the server to return appropriate data consistent with the client's state.

CGI has been used in UNIX systems for a while. Although IIS supports CGI, it is for compatibility purposes only. If you are developing Web applications for the Windows environment, you are better off using ISAPI. See "ISAPI and CGI" for a comparison of ISAPI and CGI.

Now that we know where ISAPI fits in Web programming, let's take a closer look at ISAPI.

ISAPI BASICS

ISAPI is part of the Win32 API family. It allows you to develop two types of applications that work in conjunction with IIS to extend IIS functionality—*extensions* and *filters*. An ISAPI *extension* is typically used to return a programmatically built HTML page (dynamic content) in response to a client request. The HTML page could contain data from a database accessed from within the extension. An ISAPI *filter* can be used to intercept the two-way data flow between the client and the server, and to select or modify the data for purposes such as authentication, compression, encryption, and so on. ISAPI applications are developed as DLLs that are invoked at run time by an Internet/Web server to enhance the functionality of the Internet/Web server.

ISAPI AND CGI

CGI and ISAPI provide somewhat equivalent functions, and the fact that you use CGI or ISAPI at the server side is transparent to the client (as it should be). Although Windows 2000 supports CGI, it is for compatibility purposes only.

Table 16-2 shows the equivalence between CGI and ISAPI constructs.

Note for UNIX Programmers

Many UNIX systems support CGI. If you have CGI applications or if you want to develop Internet server-based applications that can execute across many Internet/Web servers, then CGI is more portable than ISAPI. If you are programming essentially for the Windows environment, ISAPI can provide some advantages over CGI, such as improved performance. Programming styles for CGI and ISAPI are very similar, and you can convert CGI to ISAPI (see Table 16-2).

CGI Application	ISAPI Application
Each CGI application/script runs as a separate process.	ISAPI extensions and filters are DLLs and are loaded within the process of the Internet/Web server.
Receive client data primarily through *stdin*.	Receive client data primarily through the *lpbData* member of ECB.
Access necessary variables such as userid using the *getenv* C run-time function.	Access necessary variables through ECB or calling *GetServerVariable*.
Send data to client by writing to *stdout*.	Send data to client using the *WriteClient* function.
Provide status information using *stdout*.	Provide status using *WriteClient* or *ServerSupportFunction*.
Client invocation reference for a CGI application is "http://.../cgi.exe?Param1+Param2."	Client invocation reference for an ISAPI application is "http://.../isapi.dll.exe?Param1+Param2."
The main entry point is *main*.	The main entry point is *HttpExtensionProc* or *HttpFilterProc*.

Table 16-2. Comparing CGI and ISAPI

TIP: While loading the ISAPI applications in the server process space improves performance, it also opens the possibility that the code you write in the DLL can cause problems such as memory/resource leaks, which could affect the server. Since the server may be up for an extended time, these problems could have cumulative effects. You should pay extra attention when developing ISAPI applications to avoid such problems.

Next, let's take a look at developing ISAPI applications.

DEVELOPING USING ISAPI

You would typically use Visual C++ and MFC to develop ISAPI extensions and filters. A simple way to develop an ISAPI extension or filter is to use the ISAPI Extension Wizard, which, like the application and class wizards, generates code that you can build on. The code generated by the ISAPI Extension Wizard is MFC compatible.

ISAPI Application Data Structures

To better understand the execution flow in an ISAPI application, we need to understand the data structures used in ISAPI applications. The primary data structure used in ISAPI is the **EXTENSION_CONTROL_BLOCK**.

The **EXTENSION_CONTROL_BLOCK** structure contains data members as well as function pointers as shown here:

```
typedef struct _EXTENSION_CONTROL_BLOCK {

    DWORD      cbSize;                            //IN
    DWORD      dwVersion;                         //IN
    HCONN      ConnID;                            //IN
    DWORD      dwHttpStatusCode;                  //OUT
    CHAR       lpszLogData[HSE_LOG_BUFFER_LEN];   //OUT
    LPSTR      lpszMethod;                        //IN
    LPSTR      lpszQueryString;                   //IN
    LPSTR      lpszPathInfo;                      //IN
    LPSTR      lpszPathTranslated;                //IN
    DWORD      cbTotalBytes;                      //IN
    DWORD      cbAvailable;                       //IN
    LPBYTE     lpbData;                           //IN
    LPSTR      lpszContentType;                   //IN

    BOOL ( WINAPI * GetServerVariable )
        ( HCONN    hConn,
         LPSTR    lpszVariableName,
         LPVOID   lpvBuffer,
         LPDWORD  lpdwSize );

    BOOL ( WINAPI * WriteClient )
        ( HCONN    ConnID,
         LPVOID   Buffer,
         LPDWORD  lpdwBytes,
         DWORD    dwReserved );

    BOOL ( WINAPI * ReadClient )
        ( HCONN    ConnID,
         LPVOID   lpvBuffer,
         LPDWORD  lpdwSize );

    BOOL ( WINAPI * ServerSupportFunction )
        ( HCONN    hConn,
         DWORD    dwHSERRequest,
         LPVOID   lpvBuffer,
```

```
        LPDWORD    lpdwSize,
        LPDWORD    lpdwDataType );

} EXTENSION_CONTROL_BLOCK, *LPEXTENSION_CONTROL_BLOCK;
```

where

cbSize contains the size of the ECB structure.

dwVersion contains the version information (the HIWORD contains the major version number and the LOWORD contains the minor version number).

ConnID contains a unique number assigned to identify each connection by the HTTP server. You normally do not need to modify the *cbSize, dwVersion,* and *ConnID* fields.

dwHttpStatusCode contains the current transaction status when the request is complete. The value contained can be one of HTTP_STATUS_BAD_REQUEST, HTTP_STATUS_ AUTH_REQUIRED, HTTP_STATUS_FORBIDDEN, HTTP_STATUS_NOT_FOUND, HTTP_STATUS_SERVER_ERROR, or HTTP_STATUS_NOT_IMPLEMENTED.

lpszLogData contains log information of the current transaction in a buffer of size HSE_LOG_BUFFER_LEN. This log information will be entered in the HTTP server log.

lpszMethod is the method with which the request was made. This is equivalent to the CGI variable **REQUEST_METHOD**.

lpszQueryString contains the query information.
lpszPathInfo contains client-provided path information.
lpszPathTranslated contains the translated path.

cbTotalBytes contains the total number of bytes to be received from the client. If the data to be received from the client is four gigabytes or more, use CHttpServerContext:: ReadClient repeatedly until all the data from the client is read.

cbAvailable contains the available number of bytes. If *cbTotalBytes* is the same as *cbAvailable,* the buffer point to variable *lpbData* contains all the data sent by the client. Otherwise, use CHttpServerContext::ReadClient repeatedly until all the data from the client is read.

lpbData points to a buffer of size *cbAvailable* containing the data sent by the client.
lpszContentType contains the content type of the client data.

The functions in the ECB are summarized in Table 16-3.

Your ISAPI application may also need environment data such as the user ID and the password of the current client request. Such data is available through server variables. For example, the user ID is available in **REMOTE_USER**, and the password is available in **HTTP_AUTHORIZATION** (in UUEncoded format). Windows 2000 basic authentication should be on for this data to be available.

ECB	Description
GetServerVariable	Copies connection or server information
WriteClient	Sends information to the client
ReadClient	Reads information from the client
ServerSupportFunction	Provides server-specific and general-purpose functions

Table 16-3.   ECB Functions and Descriptions

Developing ISAPI Extensions

When you use the extension wizard, the skeleton extension it creates includes an APP variable to initialize MFC and an extension variable to initialize the ISAPI extension. You can build on the skeleton and add code to its three main important function entry points shown here:

1. **GetExtensionVersion**
2. **HttpExtensionProc**
3. **TerminateExtension**

The first two are mandatory, and the third is optional.

GetExtensionVersion identifies the name and version of the extension. This function is the first one called (and is called only once) when the ISAPI extension is loaded. You would typically initialize variables with this function. You can also use the version information to ensure that a compatible version of the extension is loaded. **GetExtensionVersion** returns TRUE upon successful function execution and FALSE otherwise. Setting FALSE will cause the extension DLL not to be loaded.

HttpExtensionProc is used to process client requests and is called once for each client request. **HttpExtensionProc** uses callback functions to read client data. **HttpExtensionProc** uses the **EXTENSION_CONTROL_BLOCK** structure (this structure was described earlier under "ISAPI Application Data Structures").

TerminateExtension is used to perform cleanup activities. This function is the last one called (and is called only once) when the ISAPI extension is unloaded. One of the most common cleanup activities is to free memory and other resources. Using a flag passed to the function, you can decide if the extension must be unloaded or whether the unloading can be deferred. The flag HSE_TERM_ADVISORY_UNLOAD provides an option for the extension to decide if it should be unloaded immediately. The extension returns TRUE to accept immediate unloading and FALSE to prevent immediate unloading. Deferred unloading may be useful if the extension wants to keep open connections it made (which are costly to break and reestablish), such as a database connection. The flag

HSE_TERM_MUST_UNLOAD doesn't provide an option and indicates that the extension will be immediately unloaded.

Developing ISAPI Filters

Developing ISAPI filters is very similar to developing ISAPI extensions. The two main functions of an ISAPI filter are **GetFilterVersion** and **HttpFilterProc**, which perform similar functions as **GetExtensionVersion** and **HttpExtensionProc** for ISAPI extensions. You can load ISAPI filters automatically when W3 service (W3SVC) starts by adding the full path name where the filter DLL resides to the Registry key:

```
HKEY_LOCAL_MACHINES\System\CurrentControlSet\Services\W3SVC\Parameters\Filter DLLs
```

If you want to use multiple filters, separate the path names by a comma. When the Internet/Web server starts up, it loads all the listed DLLs and calls **GetFilterVersion** for each filter DLL. The events for which the DLLs should be notified and the priority order of invoking the filter DLLs (when multiple filters are to be invoked for the same event) are established at this time.

When an event occurs, the server invokes **HttpFilterProc** for each filter registered for the event. The filter then performs the appropriate function (encryption, event logging, authentication, and so on).

Filter Enhancements Introduced in IIS 4.0

If you are programming for IIS 4.0 or later, note that the filter information is loaded from the Metabase (a new storage location introduced in IIS 4.0), rather than the Registry. The filter information in the Registry should be in the Metabase. Filters can also be applied either globally or to a particular Web site. A new entry point function, **TerminateFilter**, has been introduced. IIS 4.0 also introduced new filter notifications, new server variables, new ServerSupportFunction commands, and new members in the **HTTP_FILTER_LOG** structure. For more details, refer to the latest Microsoft Developer Network information for IIS and ISAPI.

NEW IN WINDOWS 2000:   Windows 2000 includes Web services functionality in IIS 5.0 as well as services that were available in IIS 4.0 as an option such as certificate server and index server. Windows 2000 also includes ADO 2.1. One of the performance improvement features in IIS 5.0 is Site Socket Pooling, which permits sites bound to different IP addresses—but sharing the same port number—to share the same set of sockets. By contrast, in IIS 4.0, each Web site was bound to a different IP address, which meant that each site had its own socket. Since sockets can use significant amounts of nonpaged memory, this binding mechanism placed a limit on the number of sites that can be connected.

TIP: Even though Site Socket Spooling is the default behavior for IIS 5.0, the default can be changed for critical sites that require a dedicated socket by setting DisableSocketPooling to TRUE. You can make this change at the site level, so that other sites can continue to take advantage of the new socket pooling feature.

Cookie Programming with ISAPI

Cookies are sent as part of the HTTP header. They are not normally persistent across browser sessions. However, the server can override this default behavior by specifying an expiration attribute that causes the browser to store the cookie across browser sessions until expiration. While the primary purpose of using cookies is to pass client-state data, concerns have been expressed about cookies because the data transfer happens transparently to the user and cookies could be potentially used to pass non–state-related client data. These concerns have led some browser makers to enable the user to disable cookie support. When you are programming with cookies, you need to account for the possibility that the client may not respond as anticipated. Cookies are typically transmitted in the clear (without encryption) between the client and the server, and are also not protected when stored at the client. You have to take this into account when you decide the type of data you want to pass using cookies and avoid passing sensitive information.

You can send and retrieve cookies in your ISAPI extension or filter DLL. The HTTP header cookie information is added (to be sent to the client) in an ISAPI application by use of the **AddResponseHeaders** member function (in the **HTTP_FILTER_CONTEXT** structure passed to the ISAPI application) or as an additional header in the call to **ServerSupportFunction**. A cookie sent by the client is retrieved by use of the **GetHeader** member function (in the **HTTP_FILTER_PREPROC_HEADERS** structure) or by use of the **GetServerVariable** member function (in the **HTTP_FILTER_CONTEXT** and **EXTENSION_CONTROL_BLOCK** structures).

ISAPI and Database Programming

As mentioned earlier, your ISAPI applications must be thread safe. Hence, if you need to perform database access from your ISAPI application, you can use ODBC, but not DAO. MFC DAO classes and the DAO SDK aren't thread safe. Alternatively, you can use the Internet Database Connector feature of the IIS or write a CGI application.

ISAPI and COM Programming

IIS maintains a pool of I/O threads. The threads from this pool are used to call an ISAPI's callback functions. However, IIS allocates threads from the pool in no particular sequence with respect to your particular application. Thus, it is possible that the thread that calls your initialization code in **DllMain** or **GetExtensionVersion** may not be the same thread that calls **HttpExtensionProc**. In addition, it is also likely that different threads will call **HttpExtensionProc** from one request to another.

This fact imposes some conditions as well as determines some design options on how you program your application. Since COM initialization affects the thread in which it is called, you should never initialize COM within **CoInitialize** or **CoInitializeEx** unless you will be uninitializing it before your callback function returns. You have three design options to use COM from ISAPI:

1. You can do all of the initialization and uninitialization from within **HttpExtensionProc** for each request.

2. You can avoid initializing COM. This will allow your ISAPI filter or extension to run in a multithreaded apartment because IIS initializes one of its threads at start time.

3. You can create your own pool of threads and initialize them when the ISAPI extension is loaded.

Option 3 is preferable to option 1 because option 1 forces initialization on each request (and leaves your code vulnerable to other ISAPI extensions that may have initialized COM on the IIS thread).

Additional ISAPI-Related Considerations

Since IIS runs as a service and ISAPI applications are DLLs, debugging your ISAPI application development becomes somewhat of a challenge. Some major challenges are the absence of a desktop (since the DLL is part of a service) and the fact that the DLL executes in the local system context. There are some tips you can use in developing and debugging your ISAPI applications. The following is an abbreviated summary of some points in Microsoft Knowledge Base article Q152054. Refer to the article for more details:

▼ If you are developing ISAPI extensions, you are likely to make changes and create new versions of your extension code. The default behavior of IIS is to cache ISAPI extensions (to improve performance), which means you have to bring down IIS and bring it back up again to test your extension changes. A better solution is to force IIS to disable caching extensions. You can do this by setting the Registry key

```
HKEY_LOCAL_MACHINE\System\CurrentControlSet\Services\
                W3SVC\Parameters\CacheExtensions
```

to zero. Remember to set it to 1 (enable caching) after development is done, as the overhead of loading and unloading extensions is significant. If you are debugging an ISAPI filter, you must stop the IIS service using the administration tool, overlay the old version of your filter with the new version, and restart the service.

■ Output debugging text using the **OutputDebugString** function, and view debug strings using the utility DBMON included with the Win32 SDK.

■ Log error messages or trace execution flow using the Windows 2000 event log or your own log file. If you use your own log file and Win32 file functions, you have to ensure that for important messages, you can also use the message box. However, as mentioned earlier, there is no default desktop. To cause the message box to appear in the logged-in user's desktop, you need to specify MB_SERVICE_NOTIFICATION | MB_TOPMOST (refer to the Win32 SDK's online help for message boxes).

▲ You can also debug by running IIS as a console application (rather than a service) and use the Visual C++ debugger.

If there are current applications written as OLE servers, the ActiveX SDK includes a sample application called OLE2ISAPI, which uses ISAPI to communicate with the Web server and behaves like an OLE client to the OLE server application.

Another server programming technique that you should be aware of is *Server Side Includes (SSI)*. SSI is a set of HTML extensions that are in the form of directives to the Internet/Web server. An example of an SSI directive is *#include,* which lets one HTML file reference another HTML file. When the client requests an HTML file that references another HTML file, the Internet/Web server retrieves the original file and the reference. Although there are other directives, IIS 2.0 supports only the #include directive.

Before we look at Internet client-side programming, you should be aware of another server programming technique—Active Server Pages (ASP). ASP makes it possible to combine ActiveX scripts and ActiveX components to create dynamic content. ASP files, which have the *.asp* extension, consist of HTML tags, Script commands, and text. These files can be referenced as URLs from a browser. ASP scripting is handled by the Internet/Web server, and an expanded HTML page is then sent to the client. Active Server pages can be used as components of an Advanced Data Connector application.

INTERNET CLIENT PROGRAMMING

There are several ways to program clients that use the Internet. If the primary end-user application is a browser, you can write add-on functions, such as Java applets or ActiveX controls, to work in conjunction with the browser. With more operating systems providing native Java support, you can write stand-alone programs using Java. You can also use Windows Sockets and TCP/IP. (Windows Sockets is covered in Chapter 15.) For programmers who want to perform simple Internet functions such as FTP, HTTP, and Gopher without knowing Sockets and TCP/IP, Microsoft also provides Windows Internet (WinInet) extensions. WinInet lets the programmer access Internet resources just as he or she accesses local resources such as hard drives. Some of the functions you can perform with WinInet include these:

▼ Upload or download files using FTP

■ Download HTML pages using HTTP

▲ Use Gopher to access Internet resources

Programming examples to perform each of the preceding functions are included in the "Internet Programming Examples" section that follows. The client programming is the same whether there is an external network connection between client and server (Internet) or whether the connection is through an internal network (intranet).

MFC WinInet Classes

You can write a WinInet client application by calling the Win32 functions directly or by using the MFC WinInet classes. MFC provides WinInet classes that encapsulate the underlying Win32 functions. WinInet support is included with Windows CE starting with version 2.12. Note that WinInet functions are not officially supported by Microsoft when run from any service including IIS. However, workarounds exist. For additional information, refer to the Microsoft Knowledge Base article ID: Q238425. There are also global "**Afx**" functions that are useful in Internet client programming. These classes/ functions are summarized in Table 16-4.

WinInet Class/ Global Function	Description
CInternetSession	This creates and initializes one or more simultaneous Internet sessions. This class can also be used to interface with a proxy server.
CInternetConnection	This manages an Internet server connection. This class is the base class for CFtpConnection, CHttpConnection, and CGopherConnection. You need a CInternetSession object and a CInternetConnection object to communicate with an Internet server.
CFtpConnection	This manages your application's FTP connection to an Internet server. This class lets your application access directories and files on the Internet server. A CFtpConnection object is created when you invoke CInternetSession::GetFtpConnection.
CHttpConnection	This manages your application's HTTP connection to an Internet server. This class lets your application communicate with the Internet server using the HTTP protocol and perform functions such as downloading HTML pages. A CHttpConnection object is created when you invoke CInternetSession::GetHttpConnection.

Table 16-4.   WinInet Classes and Global Functions

Winlnet Class/ Global Function	Description
CGopherConnection	This manages your application's connection to a Gopher Internet server for Gopher functions. A CGopherConnection object is created when you invoke CInternetSession::GetGopherConnection.
CInternetFile	This provides a base class for the CHttpFile and CGopherFile file classes. This class (and the derived classes) provides access to remote files. A CInternetFile object is created when you invoke CGopherConnection::OpenFile or CHttpConnection::OpenRequest or CFtpConnection::OpenFile.
CHttpFile	This lets your application access and read files residing on an HTTP server.
CGopherFile	This lets your application access and read files residing on a Gopher server.
CFileFind	CFileFind is the base class for two other MFC classes designed to search particular server types—CGopherFileFind and CFtpFileFind (see the next entry).
CFtpFileFind	This is used in FTP server file searches. This class includes member functions to begin a search, locate files, and return the URLs/descriptive information about files.
CGopherFileFind	This is used in Gopher server file searches. This class includes member functions to begin a search, locate files, and return the URLs/ descriptive information about files.
CGopherLocator	This gets a Gopher locator from a Gopher server, which is then used by CGopherFileFind. A Gopher locator contains attributes determining file/server types. You must get a Gopher server's locator before you can retrieve information from the Gopher server.

Table 16-4. Winlnet Classes and Global Functions *(continued)*

WinInet Class/ Global Function	Description
CInternetException	This object is used when you encounter an exception condition on an Internet operation. The CInternetException class includes a public data member that contains the exception's error code and another public data member that contains the context identifier of the Internet application associated with the exception.
AfxParseURL	This parses a URL string and returns the type of service and its components. The function returns a nonzero return code upon successful parsing and zero otherwise.
AfxGetInternetHandleType	This determines the type of an Internet handle, such as INTERNET_HANDLE_TYPE_INTERNET or INTERNET_HANDLE_TYPE_FTP_FIND. The complete list of types is defined in *Wininet.h*.
AfxThrowInternet Exception	This throws an Internet exception and specifies the context and the error associated with the exception.

Table 16-4. WinInet Classes and Global Functions *(continued)*

In case you are wondering, there is no file find function for HTTP servers as there are for FTP and Gopher, because HTTP does not support direct file access and search.

TIP: **CInternetSession::OpenURL()** will fail if you use a URL that specifies a filename that contains spaces. This is because the specifications for a URL designate certain unsafe characters (including space) that must be escaped when they are present in a URL. To get around this problem, do not convert unsafe characters to their escape sequences when using the file protocol. To see sample code that shows how to handle this problem and for more information, refer to Microsoft Knowledge Base article: Q172551.

Adding Security with WinInet

The ability to add security is of paramount importance for business applications using the Internet. You can also add security to your Internet clients using Secure HTTP as part of your WinInet application. Security in the current WinInet environment is provided by

Schannel.dll, which uses the SSL/PCT authentication protocol. With Windows NT 2000, you can choose Kerberos security as well. Using WinInet provides an easier way to implement security than using the Security Support Provider Interface (SSPI) directly (WinInet invokes SSPI under the covers). You add security by calling the **InternetConnect** API with the INTERNET_FLAG_SECURE flag turned on. Some versions of Windows NT and the Internet Information Server version 1.0 imposed a restriction of 32K data size when communicating using the Secure Sockets Layer, which caused a problem with large HTML pages. If you encounter this problem, make sure you apply the appropriate service pack.

Internet Programming Examples

For those who always wanted to write an Internet client application but were afraid to learn sockets programming, MFC includes the Win32 Internet Extensions (WinInet) for creating FTP, HTTP, and other Internet client applications. WinInet classes encapsulate FTP, HTTP, and Gopher protocols, and provide a simple set of member functions that can be used to write powerful client applications to download files over the Internet. These applications can use the Win32 functions directly, or use the MFC WinInet classes.

FTP Sample

The sample program shown next is a very simple application that retrieves a file from an FTP site using the File Transfer Protocol. The size of the program shows the simplicity of using the WinInet classes. When the sample is run, the FTP site and the file to be downloaded are given as parameters. The program FTPs to that site as an anonymous user and downloads that file. The program can be easily upgraded to log on with a given user ID and password.

After checking for the parameters, the program first creates and initializes an Internet session by creating a **CInternetSession** object. The session identifies itself as *FtpSample* to the server. Among other things that can be specified while creating an Internet session are a context identifier for the operation, the access type required, the name of a preferred proxy, a list of server addresses that may be bypassed when using proxy access cache, and asynchronous options. These options are defaulted here. Next the application connects to the FTP server by calling the **GetFtpConnection** member function and specifying the FTP server address. This establishes an FTP connection and returns a pointer to a **CFtpConnection** object. When you're establishing a connection to an FTP server, a logon user name and password can be specified by passing these parameters to **GetFtpConnection**. This function only establishes an FTP connection and does not perform any operation on the server. By default it uses "anonymous" as the user name and the user's e-mail name as the password. If this method fails, it throws an exception of object type **CInternetException**. The filename that needs to be retrieved from the FTP site is parsed and is passed to the **GetFile** member function of the **CFtpConnection**. This member function gets the file from the FTP server and stores it on the local machine. The default transfer type is binary. If the transfer mode is specified to be ASCII (FILE_TRANSFER_TYPE_ASCII), the translation of the file data also converts the control and formatting characters to Windows equivalents. The default context identifier can be overridden. Make sure that this sample is run outside of a firewall, because it does not handle firewalls. A sample parameter could be *ftp.microsoft.com dirmap.txt,* which downloads the directory map of Microsoft's FTP site.

```cpp
#include <afxinet.h>
#include <iostream.h>
#include <string.h>

int main(int argc, char **argv)
{
    CFtpConnection *pftpCon = NULL;
    if (argc!=3)
    {
        cerr << "usage: ftpsample <ftp server> <remote file directory path>" << endl;
        exit(0);
    }
    CInternetSession session("FtpSample");
    try
    {

    pftpCon = session.GetFtpConnection(
                argv[1] // ftp server
                );

        char * pszLocalFile=strrchr(argv[2],'/');
        if (pszLocalFile==0)
        {
            pszLocalFile=argv[2];
        }
        else
        {
            pszLocalFile=pszLocalFile+1;
        }
        cout << "downloading "
            << argv[2]
            << " from  site(" << argv[1] << ")"
            << endl;

        BOOL bRetVal=pftpCon->GetFile(
            argv[2], // remote file path
            pszLocalFile // local file
            );
        if (bRetVal)
        {
            cout << "downloaded!" << endl;
        }
        else
        {
            cout << "download failed!!" << endl;
        }
```

```
        }
        catch (CInternetException *pEX)
        {
            cout << "Error : " << pEX->m_dwError
                << " Refer WININET.H" << endl;
        }
        if (pftpCon)
        {
            delete pftpCon;
        }
        session.Close();
        return(0);
}
```

After the file is downloaded, the FTP connection is deleted, and the Internet session is closed by calling the **Close** member function. The **CFtpConnection** class has other useful member functions such as **SetCurrentDirectory**, **GetCurrentDirectory**, **RemoveDirectory**, and **CreateDirectory**, which help to navigate through the directories at the FTP site and to manage directories. Files can also be placed at an FTP site by use of the **PutFile** member function.

There is another class that might be of interest when you're dealing with FTP. This is the **CFtpFileFind** class, which helps in Internet file searches at the FTP site, using its member functions **FileFind**, **FindNextFile**, and **GetFileURL**. This class derives from **CFileFind**.

HTTP Sample

The next sample is similar to the previous one, except that it retrieves a file using HTTP rather than FTP. This sample takes a URL and retrieves the top page from the HTTP server. It then prints the top page on the console. The output can be redirected to a file, and it can be viewed by use of a Web browser. The program can be modified to retrieve a specific page. The code is shown next.

The code first checks for the parameters and initializes an Internet session by creating a **CInternetSession** object. The session identifies itself as HTTPSample to the HTTP server. As mentioned earlier, a context identifier for the operation, the access type required, the name of a preferred proxy, a list of server addresses that may be bypassed when using proxy access, and cache and asynchronous options can be specified during the creation of the Internet session. This sample accepts the default options and then establishes an HTTP connection by calling the **GetHttpConnection** member function and passing in the HTTP server name. This returns a pointer to a **CHttpConnection** object. Optionally, a user name and password can be specified while connecting to the HTTP server. If a port number is not specified, the **CHttpConnection** class uses the protocol-specific port, port 80 in the case of HTTP. This function only establishes a connection and does not perform any operation on the server. An HTTP connection is then opened by calling the **OpenRequest** member function, which returns a pointer to a **CHttpFile** object. The request type is set to the "GET" verb, and the top page is requested. The rest of the parameters are defaulted. A set of flags can also be specified to force a download on the requested object instead of getting it from a local cache (INTERNET_FLAG_RELOAD), not to cache the object (INTERNET_FLAG_DONT_CACHE), to add the object to the persistent cache (INTERNET_FLAG_MAKE_PERSISTENT), to use secure transaction semantics (INTERNET_FLAG_SECURE), and not to handle redirections automatically (INTERNET_FLAG_NO_AUTO_REDIRECT). The context identifier can also be overridden to identify this operation to the **OnStatusCallback** member function. The request is then sent to the HTTP server by calling the **SendRequest** member function, and the status of the request is queried by calling the **QueryInfoStatusCode** member function. If there are no errors, the file is read by calling the **ReadString** member function of the **CInternetFile** class from which **CHttpFile** is derived. The information is then displayed on the console. After the object is downloaded from the HTTP server, the file object is closed by calling **Close( )**, and the Internet session is also closed.

```
#include <afxinet.h>
#include <iostream.h>
#include <string.h>

int main(int argc, char **argv)
{
    if (argc!=2)
    {
        cerr << "usage: httpsample <web server>" << endl;
        cerr<<"(example) httpsample www.microsoft.com"<<endl;
        exit(0);
    }
    CInternetSession session("HTTPSample");
    try
    {
        CHttpConnection *phttpCon=session.GetHttpConnection(argv[1]);

        CHttpFile *pFile=phttpCon->OpenRequest(
                        CHttpConnection::HTTP_VERB_GET,
                        "/", NULL, 1,
                         NULL, NULL,
                        INTERNET_FLAG_RELOAD);
        pFile->SendRequest();
        DWORD statusCode;
        if (pFile->QueryInfoStatusCode(statusCode)==0)
        {
            DWORD dRC=GetLastError();
            cout << "Error retrieving status."
                << "Error: " << dRC << endl;
        }
```

```
        else
        {
            if (statusCode==HTTP_STATUS_OK)
            {
                CString aLine;
                while (pFile->ReadString(aLine))
                {
                    cout << aLine << endl;
                }
            }
            else
            {
                cout << "Error occurred in the HTTP request."
                    << "Error number : "

                    << statusCode << endl
                    << "Program Terminating"
                    << endl;
                char szError[512];
                while (pFile->ReadString(szError, 511))
                {
                    cout << szError;
                }

            }

            pFile->Close();
            delete pFile;
            delete phttpCon;
        }
    }
    catch (CInternetException *pEX)
    {
        switch(pEX->m_dwError)
        {
            case ERROR_INTERNET_NAME_NOT_RESOLVED:
            {
                cout << "Server name could not be resolved."
                    << endl;
                break;
            }
            case ERROR_INTERNET_TIMEOUT:
            {
                cout << "Connection timed out." << endl;
```

```
                break;
            }
        default:
            {
                cout << "Win Inet Error: " << pEX->m_dwError
                    << "Look in WININET.H" << endl;
            }
        }
    }
    }
    session.Close();
    return(0);
}
```

Gopher Sample

The next sample deals with the Gopher protocol. To run the sample program, just start the program and provide two parameters on the command line: the Gopher site and the file to display. The program connects to the Gopher site, dumps all the screen names available, and then displays the requested file on the console. For example, to display what is available at the Voice of America Gopher site, you can type **gopherapp gopher.voa.gov /README-VOA.** This would display the screen names available at that Gopher site and then open the README-VOA file and display it. With the popularity of the World Wide Web sites, the importance of the Gopher sites has diminished.

The code for the preceding sample is shown next. As in other applications, an Internet session is first established, and a Gopher connection is created by calling the **GetGopherConnection** member function. A pointer to the Gopher server name is passed. A user name, password, and port number can also be optionally passed to the **GetGopherConnection** member function. This member function creates a Gopher connection and returns a pointer to that connection. A Gopher locator object is created by calling the **CreateLocator** member function of the **CGopherConnection** object. This gets a Gopher locator from the Gopher server, determines the locator's type, and makes the locator available to the **CGopherFileFind** class. A Gopher server's locator must be gotten before the application can retrieve information from the server. To get the screen names, a **CGopherFileFind** object is created by passing in the Gopher connection object to the **CGopherFileFind** constructor. The **FileFind** member function is used to find the first file. The **GetScreenName** member function gets the name of the Gopher screen that is printed until all of them are displayed. To retrieve a file, the Gopher locator created earlier with the filename is used to open the file using the **OpenFile** member function of the Gopher connector. This returns a pointer to a **CGopherFile** object, which is used to read the file and display it on the console.

```
#include <afxinet.h>
#include <iostream.h>
#include <string.h>
```

```
int main(int argc, char **argv)
{
    if (argc < 3)
    {
        cerr << "Usage: gopherapp <gopher server> "
             << "<full file to display>"
             << endl
             << "Ex: gopherapp wiretap.spies.com 0/About_Gopher"
             << endl;
        exit(0);
    }
    CInternetSession session("GopherSample");
    CGopherConnection *pgopherCon =
        session.GetGopherConnection(argv[1]);

    CGopherLocator CGLocator = pgopherCon->CreateLocator(NULL,
                               argv[2], GOPHER_TYPE_TEXT_FILE);

    CGopherFileFind *pFile=new CGopherFileFind(pgopherCon);

    BOOL bRetVal=pFile->FindFile(argv[1]);

    while (bRetVal)
    {
        cout << pFile->GetScreenName() << endl;
        bRetVal=pFile->FindNextFile();
    }

    try
    {
        CGopherFile *pCGFile = pgopherCon->OpenFile(CGLocator);
        CString aLine;
        while(pCGFile->ReadString(aLine))
        {
            cout << aLine << endl;
        }

    }
    catch(CInternetException *pEX)
    {
        cout << "Error Win32 " << pEX->m_dwError << endl;
    }
    delete pFile;
    delete pgopherCon;
```

```
    session.Close();
    return(0);
}
```

Notice the *Afxinet.h* file that has been included in all the applications. This header file has all the relevant information about the WinInet classes.

In general when an application performs a time-consuming task, it is good to show the progress to the user. This is particularly true in the case of Internet applications, where the tasks are relatively much slower than other applications. The MFC library classes that we used in the samples shown earlier provide a means to display status to the user. The next sample takes the HTTP sample program that was discussed earlier and extends it to show the progress as the activities of the program proceed. The changes made are highlighted.

An application can establish a callback function that the Internet session can call to notify the status. The **CInternetSession** class provides a member function, **EnableStatusCallback**, which can be used to establish a status callback routine. Once enabled for status callback, the Internet session calls the **OnStatusCallback** member function to indicate the status of the operation. To handle this, the **OnStatusCallback** member function should be overridden by deriving a class from the **CInternetSession**. In the sample that follows, the application's own **CMyHttpSession** class is derived from **CInternetSession**, and the **OnStatusCallback** member function is overridden. Whenever the **OnStatusCallback** member function is called, the Internet session passes the context for which this callback was called, the status, and some additional information related to the status. The context can be thought of as a token or identification of the operation. This context identifier is provided by the application when certain operations are performed. For example, a context can be passed when calling the **GetFile** member function of the **CFtpConnection** class, when calling the **OpenRequest** member function of the **CHttpConnection** class, or when calling the **OpenFile** member function of the **CGopherConnection** class. By default all these contexts are set to 1, and that default is used by this application. If the application performs multiple requests at the same time— for example, opening two requests on an HTTP connection—then each can have a different context identifying itself. When the **OnStatusCallback** function is called, the respective context identifies the respective operation. This is particularly useful in asynchronous operations.

This application displays the status information on the console as it arrives.

```
#include <afxinet.h>
#include <iostream.h>
#include <string.h>

// Create our own class derived from CInternetSession
// to handle OnStatusCallback.
class CMyHttpSession : public CInternetSession
{
 public:
  CMyHttpSession(LPCTSTR pszAppName);
  virtual void OnStatusCallback(DWORD dwContext, DWORD dwInternetStatus,
  LPVOID lpvStatusInfomration,
```

```
   DWORD dwStatusInformationLen);
};

CMyHttpSession::CMyHttpSession(LPCTSTR pszAppName)
  : CInternetSession(pszAppName,1,INTERNET_OPEN_TYPE_PRECONFIG)
{
}

void CMyHttpSession::OnStatusCallback(DWORD dwContext, DWORD dwInternetStatus,
  LPVOID lpvStatusInformation, DWORD dwStatusInformationLen )
  {
  if ((dwInternetStatus == INTERNET_STATUS_RESOLVING_NAME))
  {
  cerr << "Resolving server name." << endl;
  }
  else if ((dwInternetStatus == INTERNET_STATUS_NAME_RESOLVED))
  {
  cerr << "Server name resolved." << endl;
  }
  else if ((dwInternetStatus == INTERNET_STATUS_CONNECTING_TO_SERVER))
  {
  cerr << "Connecting to server." << endl;
  }
  else if ((dwInternetStatus == INTERNET_STATUS_CONNECTED_TO_SERVER))
  {
  cerr << "Connected to server." << endl;
  }
  else if ((dwInternetStatus == INTERNET_STATUS_SENDING_REQUEST))
  {
  cerr << "Sending request." << endl;
  }
  else if ((dwInternetStatus == INTERNET_STATUS_REQUEST_SENT))
  {
  cerr << "Request sent." << endl;
  }
  else if ((dwInternetStatus == INTERNET_STATUS_RECEIVING_RESPONSE))
  {
  cerr << "Response receiving." << endl;
  }
  else if ((dwInternetStatus == INTERNET_STATUS_RESPONSE_RECEIVED))
  {
  cerr << "Response received." << endl;
  }
  else if ((dwInternetStatus == INTERNET_STATUS_CLOSING_CONNECTION))
  {
  cerr << "Closing connection." << endl;
  }

  else if ((dwInternetStatus == INTERNET_STATUS_CONNECTION_CLOSED))
```

```
 {
 cerr << "Connection closed." << endl;
 }
 }

int main(int argc, char **argv)
{
 if (argc!=2)
 {
 cerr << "usage: httpsample <web server>" << endl;
 cerr << "(example) httpsample www.microsoft.com" << endl;
 exit(0);
 }
 CMyHttpSession session("HTTPSample");
 try
 {
 session.EnableStatusCallback(TRUE);
 CHttpConnection *phttpCon=session.GetHttpConnection(argv[1]);

 CHttpFile *pFile=phttpCon->OpenRequest(
 CHttpConnection::HTTP_VERB_GET,
 "/"
 );
 pFile->SendRequest();
 DWORD statusCode;
 if (pFile->QueryInfoStatusCode(statusCode)==0)
 {
 DWORD dRC=GetLastError();
 cout << "Error retrieving status."
 << "Error: " << dRC << endl;
 }
 else
 {
 if (statusCode==HTTP_STATUS_OK)
 {
 CString aLine;
 while (pFile->ReadString(aLine))
 {
 cout << aLine << endl;
 }


 else
 {
 cout << "Error occurred in the HTTP request. "
 << "Error number : "
 << statusCode << endl;
 << "Program Terminating"
 << endl;
```

```
char szError[512];
while (pFile->ReadString(szError, 511))
{
cout << szError;
}
}
pFile->Close();
delete pFile;
delete phttpCon;
}
}
catch (CInternetException *pEX)
{
switch(pEX->m_dwError)
{
case ERROR_INTERNET_NAME_NOT_RESOLVED:
{
cout << "Server name could not be resolved." << endl;
break;
}
case ERROR_INTERNET_TIMEOUT:
{
cout << "Connection timed out." << endl;
break;
}
default:
{
cout << "Win Inet Error: " << pEX->m_dwError
<< "Look in WININET.H" << endl;
}
}
}
session.Close();
return(0);
}
```

CONCLUSION

In this chapter, we looked at the programming aspects of both server and client Internet programming in the Windows 2000 environment. We started with a brief review of Web and ISAPI basics, compared ISAPI and CGI, and looked at the steps involved in developing the two types of ISAPI applications—filters and extensions. We also discussed programming aspects at the client. In particular, we looked at the Windows Internet extensions and some examples of programming typical Internet functions such as FTP, Gopher, and HTTP.

PART IV

Windows 2000 Multimedia and Database Programming

CHAPTER 17

Multimedia Programming

Now we'll cover some really exciting and useful topics. We will start with the exciting part, multimedia programming, where we will look at the different ways you can program audio and video. We will look at examples where you write your own audio CD player and video players. We will also look at using OpenGL for sophisticated 3-D graphics programming. Then we will look at useful topics that you are most likely to use as a business programmer—accessing databases using Open Database Connectivity (ODBC) and ActiveX Data Objects (ADO).

We will look at multimedia programming in this chapter. The term "multimedia" is a generic term, and as the name implies, it deals with different media types. The two major categories of multimedia are audio and video. Windows 2000 provides a number of ways to incorporate audio and video support in your application.

We will start with a brief review of multimedia basics, including time formats. Then we will look at some audio programming methods—using the media control interface and MCIWnd. Next we will examine an audio programming example, a CD player. Then we will discuss video programming methods and look at a video programming example that plays AVI video clips.

There are numerous audio and video multimedia devices with varying functions and features. Windows 2000 attempts both to provide a common programming interface and to enable you to take advantage of device-specific functions by substituting default data structures with custom data structures. Your application can then use the additional fields in the structures to provide increased functionality.

MULTIMEDIA PROGRAMMING BASICS

Before we look at multimedia programming aspects, let's briefly review the formats used to represent audio and video. We'll also look at the time formats used for multimedia programming.

You can program your application to play audio content of different devices. Some devices use audio content that is already stored in files such as waveform files (with the *.wav* extension). A device such as a CD-ROM player uses audio content stored on the CD. Video content is available in different formats such as AVI, MPEG, and so on. Still images and graphics are not covered here. Graphics using GDI programming are covered in Chapter 5, and sophisticated graphics using OpenGL are covered in Chapter 19. We will also not cover animation in this chapter. Animation using advanced controls is covered in Chapter 7.

Time Formats

Whenever we play audio or video, we need some method of specifying the play duration and to identify significant positions within the audio or video content (which tend to be large compared with other forms of computer content). Popular time formats used are *milliseconds, tracks* (commonly used with audio), and *frames* (commonly used with video). There are also other time formats such as SMPTE (Society of Motion Picture and Television Engineers) 24. Windows 2000 provides several macros to set and retrieve time formats. The macros are summarized in Table 17-1. Note that MCI stands for *Multimedia Control Interface,* which is an interface that Windows 2000 provides for audio-related programming. MCI is covered in detail later in this chapter in the section "Media Control Interface."

The macros and messages mentioned in Table 17-1 are specific to setting or changing time formats of MCI devices. You can also set the time format using the more general **MCI_SET** command, which sets device information, including time formats. You can set the **dwTimeFormat** member of the **MCI_SET_PARMS** structure to an appropriate constant. The valid values for the **dwTimeFormat** depend on the device type. Some common device types, the device constants defined for the device types in *Mmsystem.h,* and the time formats that can be used with them are shown in Table 17-2. Note that SMPTE has come up with a number of time formats based on number of frames, such as SMPTE 24 (which has 24 frames), SMPTE 25 (which has 25 frames), and so on.

Time Macro	Purpose
MCIWndSetTimeFormat	This sets the time format of an MCI device to a format supported by the device. Alternatively, you can explicitly send the MCIWNDM_SETTIMEFORMAT message or use one of the MCIWndUseTime/MCIWndUseFrames macros if appropriate.
MCIWndUseTime	This sets the time format of an MCI device to milliseconds. Alternatively, you can explicitly send the MCIWNDM_SETTIMEFORMAT message or use the MCIWndSetTimeFormat macro.
MCIWndUseFrames	This sets the time format of an MCI device to frames. Alternatively, you can explicitly send the MCIWNDM_SETTIMEFORMAT message or use the MCIWndSetTimeFormat macro.
MCIWndGetTimeFormat	This retrieves the current time format for a file or an MCI device in string and numeric forms. Alternatively, you can explicitly send the MCIWNDM_GETTIMEFORMAT message.

Table 17-1.   Time Macros and Their Purposes

Device Type	Device Constant	Applicable Time Formats
digitalvideo	MCI_DEVTYPE_DIGITAL_VIDEO	MCI_FORMAT_FRAMES (frames) MCI_FORMAT_MILLISECONDS (milliseconds)
vcr	MCI_DEVTYPE_VCR	MCI_FORMAT_FRAMES (frames) MCI_FORMAT_MILLISECONDS (milliseconds) MCI_FORMAT_HMS (hours/minutes/seconds) MCI_FORMAT_MSF (minutes/seconds/frames) MCI_FORMAT_SMPTE_24 (SMPTE 24 frame) MCI_FORMAT_SMPTE_25 (SMPTE 25 frame) MCI_FORMAT_SMPTE_30 (SMPTE 30 frame) MCI_FORMAT_SMPTE_30DROP (SMPTE 30 drop-frame) MCI_FORMAT_TMSF (tracks/minutes/seconds/frames)
videodisc	MCI_DEVTYPE_VIDEODISC	MCI_FORMAT_FRAMES (frames) MCI_FORMAT_MILLISECONDS (milliseconds) MCI_FORMAT_HMS (hours/minutes/seconds)
waveaudio	MCI_DEVTYPE_WAVEFORM_AUDIO	MCI_FORMAT_BYTES (bytes specific to a pulse code modulation data format) MCI_FORMAT_SAMPLES (samples) MCI_FORMAT_MILLISECONDS (milliseconds)
cdaudio	MCI_DEVTYPE_CD_AUDIO	MCI_FORMAT_MILLISECONDS (milliseconds) MCI_FORMAT_MSF (minutes/seconds/frames) MCI_FORMAT_TMSF (tracks/minutes/seconds/frames)
sequencer (MIDI sequencer)	MCI_DEVTYPE_SEQUENCER	MCI_FORMAT_MILLISECONDS (milliseconds) MCI_FORMAT_SMPTE_24 (SMPTE 24 frame) MCI_FORMAT_SMPTE_25 (SMPTE 25 frame) MCI_FORMAT_SMPTE_30 (SMPTE 30 frame) MCI_FORMAT_SMPTE_30DROP (SMPTE 30 drop-frame)

Table 17-2. Common Device Types, Associated Device Constants, and Applicable Time Formats

AUDIO PROGRAMMING

Windows 2000 provides different ways of audio-related programming in your applications. You can use some high-level functions, such as **MCIWnd**, **MessageBeep**, **PlaySound**, and **sndPlaySound** (**sndPlaySound** offers a subset of the functionality of the **PlaySound** function and is being maintained for backward compatibility). The amount of code you need to add is reduced, but you also lose some control when you use the high-level functions. These functions are appropriate when you do not need the low-level control and the functions are adequate for your requirements.

Windows 2000 also provides the Multimedia Control Interface (MCI), an interface that includes a set of functions and commands that can be used to control audio (and other multimedia) devices. While using MCI may make your program code bigger than when you use high-level audio functions, the extra control you get can let you perform functions that may not be possible with high-level functions. For example, you cannot play large waveform files that do not fit completely in memory using the high-level functions, whereas you can use the media control interface to play such files.

Media Control Interface

While the capabilities of multimedia devices vary, MCI attempts to provide a standard generic interface to all multimedia devices. MCI provides two ways to communicate with a multimedia device (also called an *MCI device*). The two ways are command messages and command strings. The command message interface uses message-passing and is meant to be used by applications requiring a C-language interface. The command message interface uses the **mciSendCommand** function. Alternatively you can send string commands, parameters for the string commands, and a buffer for any returned information. The command string interface uses the **mciSendString** function. Use of the two functions is not mutually exclusive. You can use both in your application. The command string format is easier to use, while the command message format generally offers better performance. The commands you can send to the multimedia device include *play* and *close.*

The MCI functions and their descriptions are summarized in Table 17-3.

MCI Function	Description
MciGetCreatorTask	Retrieves a handle to the creator task responsible for opening the specified device
MciGetDeviceID	Retrieves the device identifier assigned to a device when the device was opened
MciGetErrorString	Retrieves the string that contains descriptive text information about specific MCI error code
MciGetYieldProc	Retrieves the address of the current yield callback function associated with the MCI_WAIT flag
MciSendCommand	Sends a command message to an MCI device
MciSendString	Sends a command string to an MCI device
MciSetYieldProc	Sets the address of a callback function to be called periodically when an MCI device is waiting for a command to finish

Table 17-3. MCI Functions and Associated Descriptions

Of these, **mciSendCommand** and **mciSendString** are by far the most commonly used. Let's take a closer look at these two functions. The prototype for the **mciSendCommand** function is shown here:

```
MCIERROR mciSendCommand( MCIDEVICEID DevID,
                         UINT uMsg,
                         DWORD fdwCmd,
                         DWORD dwParm

);
```

where

DevID is the device identifier to which the command message is sent.

uMsg is the specific command message.

fdwCmd specifies the flags for the command message.

dwParm points to the address of a structure that contains message command parameters.

The **mciSendCommand** function returns zero if successful and an error otherwise. The low-order word of the returned doubleword value contains the error return value. You can use the **mciGetErrorString** function to retrieve the string that contains descriptive text from the error value returned. If the error is device specific, the high-order word of the return value is the driver identifier; it is zero otherwise.

The prototype for the **mciSendString** function is shown here:

```
MCIERROR mciSendString( LPCTSTR lpszCmd,
                        LPTSTR lpszRtnString,
                        UINT cchRtn,
                        HANDLE hwndCallback
    );
```

where

lpszCmd is the MCI command string address.

lpszRtnString is the address of the buffer that will receive return information. You can set lpszRtnString to NULL, if you have no return information.

cchRtn is the return buffer size (in characters).

hwndCallback contains the handle of a callback window.

The **mciSendString** function returns zero if successful and an error otherwise. The low-order word of the returned doubleword value contains the error return value. You can use the **mciGetErrorString** function to retrieve the string that contains descriptive text from the error value returned. If the error is device specific, the high-order word of the return value is the driver identifier; it is zero otherwise. The simple programming sequence for both the **mciSendString** and the **mciSendCommand** functions is to use the *open, play,* and *close* commands in that order. If at any point you get an error, then call **mciGetErrorString** to get descriptive text that can be displayed to the user by use of a function such as **MessageBox**.

The **mciSendString** function is easier to program than the **mciSendCommand** function, but it is also somewhat less efficient (as the strings specified in **mciSendString** have to be parsed and interpreted, unlike the **mciSendCommand** function). The programming examples later in the chapter use both the **mciSendString** and the **mciSendCommand** functions.

Programming Using MCIWnd

You can use the functions, messages, and macros associated with the **MCIWnd** window class to perform audio and video playback and to record in your applications. The functions used with an **MCIWnd** class include the following:

MCIWnd-Related Function	Description
GetOpenFileNamePreview	This lets a user select files and preview some files, such as an AVI file.
GetSaveFileNamePreview	This is the same as GetOpenFileNamePreview, except that the dialog box displayed is the Save As dialog box, instead of the File Open dialog box.
MCIWndCreate	This registers the MCIWnd window class (you don't need a separate call to MCIWndRegisterClass) and creates an MCIWnd window. MCIWndCreate also opens an MCI device or file. This returns a window handle that you should use in MCIWnd macros.
MCIWndRegisterClass	This registers the MCI window class. If you use this function, use the CreateWindow or CreateWindowEx function to create an MCIWnd window (instead of using MCIWndCreate).

The most important of the **MCIWnd** functions is the **MCIWndCreate** function, whose prototype is shown here:

```
HWND MCIWndCreate( HWND hwndParnt,
                   HINSTANCE hInst,
                   DWORD dwStyle,
                   LPSTR szFl
);
```

where

hwndParnt is the parent window's handle (when this value is not NULL, **MCIWndCreate** automatically creates a child window).

hInst is the instance handle associated with the new MCIWnd window.

dwStyle specifies one or more flags that define the window style. You can use the window styles you specify for the window-create function commonly used, **CreateWindowEx**. **MCIWndCreate** also provides some additional flags that are unique to **MCIWndCreate**. **MCIWndCreate** is used in the programming example covered later in the chapter.

szFl is the name of the MCI device or data file to be opened.

MCIWndCreate returns the handle to the MCI window that is created if successful and zero otherwise.

Other Audio Programming Methods

You can also use the **MessageBeep** function for audio programming. You can specify the type of sound you want with **MessageBeep** (such as *SystemAsterisk*, *SystemExclamation*, and so on) by including the value in the *uType* parameter, as shown in the **MessageBeep** prototype here:

```
BOOL MessageBeep( UINT uType
);
```

Most of the choices in the Sounds icon in the Control Panel can be used with **MessageBeep**, including a simple beep. **MessageBeep** plays the waveform file identified in the Registry for the type of sound selected asynchronously. If **MessageBeep** is unable to play the selected waveform file, it attempts to play the system default sound. **MessageBeep** is commonly used along with the **MessageBox** function to play a sound when a message box is displayed. **MessageBeep** returns a nonzero value when successful and zero otherwise.

While **MessageBeep** gives you the ability to play a set of predefined sounds, sometimes you may want to play the sound from other sources, such as a waveform file, that have not been predefined. You can use the **PlaySound** function to play sounds specified by a file, resource, or system event. The prototype for it is shown here:

```
BOOL PlaySound( LPCSTR pszSound,
                HMODULE hmod,
                DWORD fdwSound
);
```

where

pszSound specifies the name of the sound file or system event alias or resource identifier.

hmod contains the handle of the executable file that contains the resource to be loaded (used only if the sound source is a resource).

fdwSound specifies one or more flags. The flags are used to indicate whether the sound source is a waveform file (SND_FILENAME), a system event (SND_ALIAS), or resource (SND_RESOURCE), and whether any currently playing sound should be interrupted (SND_NOSTOP), and so on.

PlaySound returns TRUE, if successful, and FALSE otherwise. If you specify a file-name for the sound, **PlaySound** searches for the file in a specific order (the current directory, the Windows directory, the Windows system directory, directories listed in the PATH environment variable, and so on), which is the same as that used by the **OpenFile** function. If **PlaySound** cannot find the sound you specified, it will attempt to play the default system event sound.

So far, we have been looking at representation of sound in the waveform format. Sound is also represented using the Musical Instrument Digital Interface (MIDI) protocol format. The primary difference between the two forms of representation is that waveforms record and reproduce sounds as is (without conversion to a notational format), which takes up a lot of space. MIDI, on the other hand, is actually a notational representation (much like a music sheet). A device capable of understanding the MIDI instructions (a MIDI synthesizer) can reproduce the sound from MIDI instructions. MCI includes a MIDI sequencer that can play (but not record) MIDI. Windows 2000 includes low-level functions such as **midiOutOpen** and **midiOutClose**, but these are not addressed in this book.

In addition to the methods mentioned earlier, Windows 2000 also provides some other low-level functions such as **waveOutOpen, waveOutWrite**, and **waveOutClose**. You normally should be able to address your audio programming needs using high-level functions and MCI. These low-level functions are not covered in this book.

Audio Programming Example

The *CDPlayer* sample application controls and plays a CD audio device. When the sample application is started, it opens the CD player, checks the CD, and displays the track and length information in a status window. It has buttons on the dialog box that can be used to control the CD player. Figures 17-1 through 17-3 show the dialog box when you run the *CDPlayer* sample. Figure 17-1 shows the dialog box when the *CDPlayer* program is started. The status window includes information obtained by querying the CD, such as the number of tracks present and the total time it would take to play the CD. Figure 17-2 shows the effect of clicking the Eject button. This ejects the CD and changes the button label to "Retract." Clicking the Retract button retracts the CD (if the CD-ROM drive supports it) and changes the button label to "Eject." Figure 17-3 shows the effect of pressing Pause. Pressing Pause changes the Pause label to "Resume" and pauses the playing of the CD.

MCI supports command strings and command messages to control a media device. Both commands can be used in an application. To illustrate both sets of media control interface APIs available in Windows 2000, this application uses both the command message format and command string format of the API. Though the command string format is easier to use, the command message format generally offers better performance.

The application is created by use of the AppWizard, and it is a dialog-based AppWizard executable. Since there is nothing significant in the main application class, the code for the main application is not shown here. The application dialog box class has all the functionality and is shown here. Shown first is the header file.

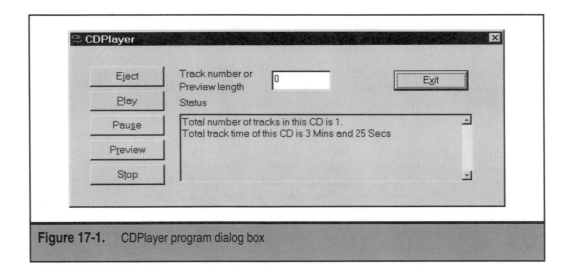

Figure 17-1. CDPlayer program dialog box

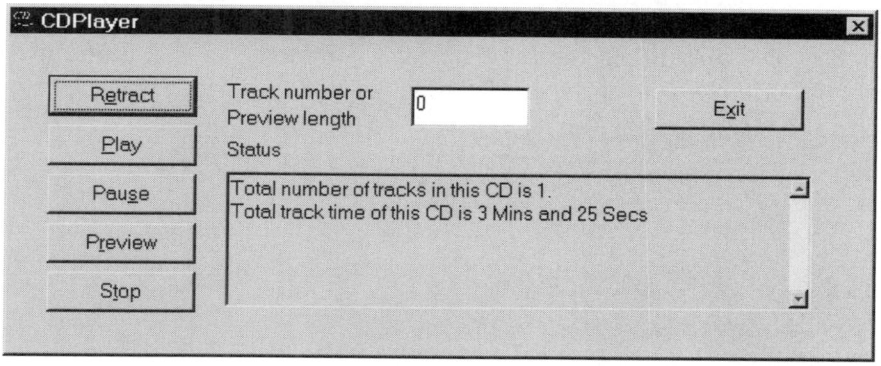

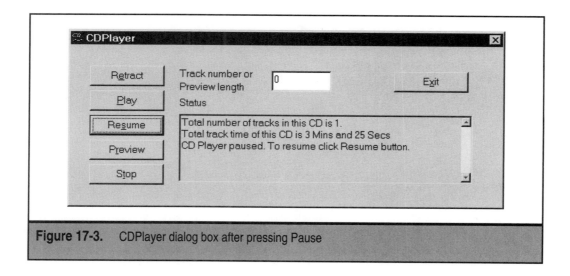

Figure 17-2. CDPlayer dialog box after pressing Eject

This is a standard class definition file created by the ClassWizard. Member variables to retain the total tracks, device ID, whether the CD player door is open, whether the CD player is in a paused state, and a character buffer for holding the status information are declared here. Notice the member functions added by the ClassWizard that are invoked when the buttons are clicked on the dialog box. When the dialog box is initialized, the CD

Figure 17-3. CDPlayer dialog box after pressing Pause

player device is opened, and the device ID is queried and stored in the member variable. This device ID is then used throughout the operation of the CD player. The number of tracks in the CD is also queried and initialized. A common character buffer to hold the status of the CD player is used.

```
// CDPlayerDlg.h : header file

#if !defined(AFX_CDPLAYERDLG_H)
#define AFX_CDPLAYERDLG_H

#if _MSC_VER >= 1000
#pragma once
#endif // _MSC_VER >= 1000

/////////////////////////////////////////////////////////////////////////////
// CCDPlayerDlg dialog

class CCDPlayerDlg : public CDialog
{
// Construction
public:
    CCDPlayerDlg(CWnd* pParent = NULL);    // standard constructor

// Dialog Data
    //{{AFX_DATA(CCDPlayerDlg)
    enum { IDD = IDD_CDPLAYER_DIALOG };
    CEdit    m_status;
    short    m_track;
    //}}AFX_DATA

    // ClassWizard generated virtual function overrides
    //{{AFX_VIRTUAL(CCDPlayerDlg)
    protected:
    virtual void DoDataExchange(CDataExchange* pDX);    // DDX/DDV support
    //}}AFX_VIRTUAL

// Implementation
protected:
    HICON m_hIcon;

    MCIDEVICEID    uDevID;
    short    sTotalTracks;
    BOOL     fDoorOpen;
    BOOL     fPaused;
    char     szStatus[256];
    // Generated message map functions
    //{{AFX_MSG(CCDPlayerDlg)
    virtual BOOL OnInitDialog();
    afx_msg void OnSysCommand(UINT nID, LPARAM lParam);
```

```
        afx_msg void OnPaint();
        afx_msg HCURSOR OnQueryDragIcon();
        afx_msg void OnPlay();
        afx_msg void OnPreview();
        afx_msg void OnDoor();
        afx_msg void OnPause();
        afx_msg void OnExit();
        afx_msg void OnStop();
        //}}AFX_MSG
        DECLARE_MESSAGE_MAP()
};
//{{AFX_INSERT_LOCATION}}
#endif //
```

The *CDPlayer* dialog box code is shown next. The framework code is generated by the ClassWizard. This generated code performs standard functions like handling the paint message, handling the About panel, and so on. First the code for the About dialog box is shown. This code is generated by ClassWizard, and no change has been made.

```cpp
// CDPlayerDlg.cpp : implementation file
//

#include "stdafx.h"
#include "CDPlayer.h"
#include "CDPlayerDlg.h"

#ifdef _DEBUG
#define new DEBUG_NEW
#undef THIS_FILE
static char THIS_FILE[] = __FILE__;
#endif

/////////////////////////////////////////////////////////////////////////////
// CAboutDlg dialog used for App About

class CAboutDlg : public CDialog
{
public:
    CAboutDlg();

// Dialog Data
    //{{AFX_DATA(CAboutDlg)
    enum { IDD = IDD_ABOUTBOX };
    //}}AFX_DATA

    // ClassWizard generated virtual function overrides
    //{{AFX_VIRTUAL(CAboutDlg)
    protected:
    virtual void DoDataExchange(CDataExchange* pDX);
```

```
    //}}AFX_VIRTUAL

// Implementation
protected:
    //{{AFX_MSG(CAboutDlg)
    //}}AFX_MSG
    DECLARE_MESSAGE_MAP()
};

CAboutDlg::CAboutDlg() : CDialog(CAboutDlg::IDD)
{
    //{{AFX_DATA_INIT(CAboutDlg)
    //}}AFX_DATA_INIT
}

void CAboutDlg::DoDataExchange(CDataExchange* pDX)
{
    CDialog::DoDataExchange(pDX);
    //{{AFX_DATA_MAP(CAboutDlg)
    //}}AFX_DATA_MAP
}

BEGIN_MESSAGE_MAP(CAboutDlg, CDialog)
    //{{AFX_MSG_MAP(CAboutDlg)
    // No message handlers
    //}}AFX_MSG_MAP
END_MESSAGE_MAP()
```

The *CDPlayer* dialog box code follows:

```
////////////////////////////////////////////////////////////////////////
// CCDPlayerDlg dialog

CCDPlayerDlg::CCDPlayerDlg(CWnd* pParent /*=NULL*/)
    : CDialog(CCDPlayerDlg::IDD, pParent)
{
    //{{AFX_DATA_INIT(CCDPlayerDlg)
    m_track = 0;
    //}}AFX_DATA_INIT
    m_hIcon = AfxGetApp()->LoadIcon(IDR_MAINFRAME);
}

void CCDPlayerDlg::DoDataExchange(CDataExchange* pDX)
{
    CDialog::DoDataExchange(pDX);
    //{{AFX_DATA_MAP(CCDPlayerDlg)
    DDX_Control(pDX, IDC_STATUS, m_status);
    DDX_Text(pDX, IDC_TRACK, m_track);
    //}}AFX_DATA_MAP
}
```

```
BEGIN_MESSAGE_MAP(CCDPlayerDlg, CDialog)
    //{{AFX_MSG_MAP(CCDPlayerDlg)
    ON_WM_SYSCOMMAND()
    ON_WM_PAINT()
    ON_WM_QUERYDRAGICON()
    ON_BN_CLICKED(IDC_PLAY, OnPlay)
    ON_BN_CLICKED(IDC_PREVIEW, OnPreview)
    ON_BN_CLICKED(IDC_DOOR, OnDoor)
    ON_BN_CLICKED(IDC_PAUSE, OnPause)
    ON_BN_CLICKED(IDOK, OnExit)
    ON_BN_CLICKED(IDC_STOP, OnStop)
    //}}AFX_MSG_MAP
END_MESSAGE_MAP()

////////////////////////////////////////////////////////////////////////
// CCDPlayerDlg message handlers

BOOL CCDPlayerDlg::OnInitDialog()
{
    CDialog::OnInitDialog();

    // Add "About..." menu item to system menu.
    // IDM_ABOUTBOX must be in the system command range.
    ASSERT((IDM_ABOUTBOX & 0xFFF0) == IDM_ABOUTBOX);
    ASSERT(IDM_ABOUTBOX < 0xF000);

    CMenu* pSysMenu = GetSystemMenu(FALSE);
    if (pSysMenu != NULL)
    {
        CString strAboutMenu;
        strAboutMenu.LoadString(IDS_ABOUTBOX);
        if (!strAboutMenu.IsEmpty())
        {
            pSysMenu->AppendMenu(MF_SEPARATOR);
            pSysMenu->AppendMenu(MF_STRING, IDM_ABOUTBOX, strAboutMenu);
        }
    }

    // Set the icon for this dialog.  The framework does this automatically
    //  when the application's main window is not a dialog
    SetIcon(m_hIcon, TRUE);             // Set big icon
    SetIcon(m_hIcon, FALSE);            // Set small icon
```

The following additional steps are done during initialization: First the CD audio device is opened by sending the **MCI_OPEN** command message. The multimedia device *cdaudio*, which represents the CD player device, is passed in the **MCI_OPEN_PARMS** structure. The command message to open the multimedia device is **MCI_OPEN**. When this command message is sent, the device is opened and the device ID is returned in the *wDeviceID* field of the **MCI_OPEN_PARMS** structure. The device name can be specified in either case, but there cannot be any leading or trailing spaces. The MCI_OPEN_TYPE flag must be specified whenever a device is specified in the **mciSendCommand** function. The multimedia device can also be opened by specifying the device-type constants. For the CD player the device-type constant is MCI_DEVTYPE_CD_AUDIO.

Next the time format for the CD player is set to TMSF (track/minute/second/frame). For CD audio-type devices the preferred positioning is relative to tracks. That is, users want to play by tracks and not by minutes or frames. To specify a position relative to a track, the time format should be set to TMSF. As an exercise other time formats can be tried and results checked. The time format is set by sending the **MCI_SET** command message and MCI_SET_TIME_FORMAT flag.

This *CDPlayer* application enables the user to open the CD audio device by clicking on a button on the dialog box. For the application to open the CD audio device through software, the CD audio device should support this feature. To find out if the CD audio device supports this, the **MCI_GETDEVCAPS** command message is sent with the MCI_GETDEVCAPS_CAN_EJECT flag. Based on the result, the Eject button is grayed out on the dialog box if necessary. Though it serves no useful purpose here, the code also queries if the device can play. The **mciSendCommand** API returns zero if successful or a nonzero value if it failed. The error string can easily be obtained by calling the **mciGetErrorString** API and passing in the error code, the buffer for the error string, and the buffer size. This makes it convenient to handle errors and display them. Though it is wise to check for errors after each command, this application assumes successful completion at some places for simplicity.

One of the most useful command messages is the **MCI_STATUS**. This command message can be sent to find the status of the CD audio device—such as the track length, current mode (play, pause, open, and so on), readiness, whether there is a CD present, and so forth. This application gets the total number of tracks in the CD and the total track length. This information is displayed in the dialog box. Notice the limitation of this application that it expects a CD to be present in the CD audio device when this application is started. However, this can be easily changed by checking whether the CD is present and then proceeding according to the result.

```
// TODO: Add extra initialization here

    DWORD dwRC;
    MCI_OPEN_PARMS OpenParms;
    MCI_SET_PARMS SetParms;

    fDoorOpen = FALSE;
    fPaused = FALSE;

    OpenParms.lpstrDeviceType = "cdaudio";
    if (dwRC = mciSendCommand(NULL, MCI_OPEN | MCI_WAIT,
        MCI_OPEN_TYPE, (DWORD) &OpenParms))
    {
        return (FALSE);
```

```
    }
    uDevID = OpenParms.wDeviceID;
    SetParms.dwTimeFormat = MCI_FORMAT_TMSF;
    if (dwRC = mciSendCommand(uDevID, MCI_SET,
        MCI_SET_TIME_FORMAT, (DWORD) &SetParms))
    {
        mciSendCommand(uDevID, MCI_CLOSE, 0, NULL);
        return (FALSE);
    }
    MCI_GETDEVCAPS_PARMS CapsParms;
    CapsParms.dwCallback = 0;
    CapsParms.dwItem = MCI_GETDEVCAPS_CAN_PLAY;
    if (dwRC = mciSendCommand(uDevID, MCI_GETDEVCAPS,
                MCI_GETDEVCAPS_CAN_PLAY | MCI_GETDEVCAPS_ITEM,
                (DWORD)&CapsParms))
    {
        CHAR szError[128+1];
        mciGetErrorString(dwRC, szError, sizeof(szError));
        AfxMessageBox(szError);
    }

    CapsParms.dwItem = MCI_GETDEVCAPS_CAN_EJECT;
    if (dwRC = mciSendCommand(uDevID, MCI_GETDEVCAPS,
                MCI_GETDEVCAPS_CAN_EJECT | MCI_GETDEVCAPS_ITEM,
                (DWORD)&CapsParms))
    {
        CHAR szError[256];
        mciGetErrorString(dwRC, szError, sizeof(szError));
        AfxMessageBox(szError);
    }

    // If the drive cannot eject the CD, gray the Eject button.
    if (!CapsParms.dwReturn)
    {
        GetDlgItem(IDC_DOOR)->EnableWindow(FALSE);
    }

    MCI_STATUS_PARMS StatusParms;
    StatusParms.dwItem = MCI_STATUS_NUMBER_OF_TRACKS;
    if (dwRC = mciSendCommand(uDevID, MCI_STATUS,
                MCI_STATUS_ITEM, (DWORD)&StatusParms))
    {// May be no disk in the CD drive.
        sTotalTracks = 0;
    }
    else
    {
        sTotalTracks = (short)StatusParms.dwReturn;
    }
```

```
        StatusParms.dwItem = MCI_STATUS_LENGTH;
        if (dwRC = mciSendCommand(uDevID, MCI_STATUS,
                   MCI_STATUS_ITEM, (DWORD)&StatusParms))
        {// May be no disk in the CD drive
            StatusParms.dwReturn = 0;
        }
        wsprintf (szStatus,
                   "Total number of tracks in this CD is %d.\r\n\
                    Total track time of this CD is %d Mins and %d Secs\r\n",
                   sTotalTracks,
                   MCI_MSF_MINUTE(StatusParms.dwReturn),
                   MCI_MSF_SECOND(StatusParms.dwReturn));
        m_status.SetSel(-1,0);
        m_status.ReplaceSel(szStatus);

        return TRUE;  // return TRUE unless you set the focus to a control
}

void CCDPlayerDlg::OnSysCommand(UINT nID, LPARAM lParam)
{
    if ((nID & 0xFFF0) == IDM_ABOUTBOX)
    {
        CAboutDlg dlgAbout;
        dlgAbout.DoModal();
    }
    else
    {
        CDialog::OnSysCommand(nID, lParam);
    }
}

// If you add a minimize button to your dialog, you will need the code below
//  to draw the icon.  For MFC applications using the document/view model,
//  this is automatically done for you by the framework.

void CCDPlayerDlg::OnPaint()
{
    if (IsIconic())
    {
        CPaintDC dc(this); // device context for painting

        SendMessage(WM_ICONERASEBKGND, (WPARAM) dc.GetSafeHdc(), 0);

        // Center icon in client rectangle
        int cxIcon = GetSystemMetrics(SM_CXICON);
        int cyIcon = GetSystemMetrics(SM_CYICON);
        CRect rect;
        GetClientRect(&rect);
        int x = (rect.Width()—cxIcon + 1) / 2;
        int y = (rect.Height()—cyIcon + 1) / 2;
```

```
        // Draw the icon
        dc.DrawIcon(x, y, m_hIcon);
    }
    else
    {
        CDialog::OnPaint();
    }
}


// The system calls this to obtain the cursor to display while the user drags
// the minimized window.
HCURSOR CCDPlayerDlg::OnQueryDragIcon()
{
    return (HCURSOR) m_hIcon;
}
```

When the user clicks on the Play button, the selected track's length is queried and the status message is displayed. If the user selects a track number greater than the total number of tracks, the entire CD is played. To play a track, the **MCI_PLAY** command message is sent. Depending on the track, additional flags, such as MCI_FROM and MCI_TO, are specified. If both these flags are specified, then the CD audio device will play starting from the From track specified in the **MCI_PLAY_PARMS** until the To track. If the To track is not specified, it will play until the end of the CD. If the MCI_FROM flag is not specified, it will start playing from the current track. After issuing the **MCI_PLAY** command message, the function returns immediately without waiting for the track to be completed. This should be the preferred way in order to yield to the Windows message loop.

If the track specified is less than or equal to zero, a waveform sound is played. The sound depends on the Registry entry for the MB_ICONHAND sound type.

```
void CCDPlayerDlg::OnPlay()
{
    // TODO: Add your control notification handler code here
    DWORD dwRC;
    MCI_PLAY_PARMS PlayParms;
    MCI_STATUS_PARMS StatusParms;

    UpdateData(TRUE);
    if (m_track <= 0)
    {
        MessageBeep(MB_ICONHAND);
        MessageBox("Track number should be greater than 0",
                   "Error", MB_ICONHAND);
        return;
    }
    if (m_track <= sTotalTracks)
    {
        StatusParms.dwItem = MCI_STATUS_LENGTH;
        StatusParms.dwTrack = m_track;
```

```
    if (dwRC = mciSendCommand(uDevID, MCI_STATUS,
            MCI_STATUS_ITEM | MCI_TRACK,
            (DWORD)&StatusParms))
    {
        CHAR szError[128+1];
        mciGetErrorString(dwRC, szError, sizeof(szError));
        AfxMessageBox(szError);
    }
    wsprintf (szStatus,
            "Length of track %d is %d Mins and %d Secs\r\n",
        m_track,
        MCI_MSF_MINUTE(StatusParms.dwReturn),
        MCI_MSF_SECOND(StatusParms.dwReturn));
}
else
{
    strcpy (szStatus, "Playing all tracks.\r\n");
}
m_status.SetSel(-1,0);
m_status.ReplaceSel(szStatus);

dwRC = 0;
PlayParms.dwFrom = 0L;
PlayParms.dwTo = 0L;
if (m_track < sTotalTracks)
{
    PlayParms.dwFrom = MCI_MAKE_TMSF(m_track, 0, 0, 0);
    PlayParms.dwTo = MCI_MAKE_TMSF(m_track + 1, 0, 0, 0);
    PlayParms.dwCallback = (DWORD) NULL;
    dwRC = mciSendCommand(uDevID, MCI_PLAY,
        MCI_FROM | MCI_TO , (DWORD)(LPVOID) &PlayParms);
}
else if (m_track == sTotalTracks)
{
    PlayParms.dwFrom = MCI_MAKE_TMSF(m_track, 0, 0, 0);
    PlayParms.dwCallback = (DWORD) NULL;
    dwRC = mciSendCommand(uDevID, MCI_PLAY,
        MCI_FROM, (DWORD)(LPVOID) &PlayParms);
}
else
{   // Play all tracks
    PlayParms.dwFrom = MCI_MAKE_TMSF(1, 0, 0, 0);
    PlayParms.dwCallback = (DWORD) NULL;
    dwRC = mciSendCommand(uDevID, MCI_PLAY,
        MCI_FROM, (DWORD)(LPVOID) &PlayParms);
}
if (dwRC)
    {
        CHAR szError[128+1];
```

```
            mciGetErrorString(dwRC, szError, sizeof(szError));
            AfxMessageBox(szError);
            mciSendCommand(uDevID, MCI_CLOSE, 0, NULL);
    }
}
```

When the Preview button is selected, the CD audio device plays each track for a specified number of seconds. This is done by seeking each track, playing it for the specified amount of time, and then seeking the next track. The **MCI_SEEK** command message is used to jump to the track specified in the **MCI_SEEK_PARM** structures. This application takes a simple method of sleeping for a given number of milliseconds, thereby not yielding to the message loop. A better method would be to use the notification method by specifying the MCI_NOTIFY flag and giving a callback window handle in the **MCI_PLAY_PARMS** structure. MCI commands usually return immediately, even if the command could take several minutes to complete the action, as in the case of playing a track. If needed, the program can wait until the command is completed by specifying the MCI_WAIT flag. This will cause the device to wait until the command action is completed.

```
void CCDPlayerDlg::OnPreview()
{
    // TODO: Add your control notification handler code here
    DWORD dwRC;
    UpdateData(TRUE); // Get the preview time.
    for (int i = 1; i <= sTotalTracks; i++)
    {
        MCI_PLAY_PARMS PlayParms;
        MCI_SEEK_PARMS SeekParms;

        SeekParms.dwTo = i;
        dwRC = mciSendCommand(uDevID, MCI_SEEK,
            MCI_TO, (DWORD)(LPVOID) &SeekParms);

        if (i < sTotalTracks)
        {
            PlayParms.dwFrom = MCI_MAKE_TMSF(i, 0, 0, 0);
            PlayParms.dwTo = MCI_MAKE_TMSF(i + 1, 0, 0, 0);
            PlayParms.dwCallback = (DWORD) NULL;
            dwRC = mciSendCommand(uDevID, MCI_PLAY,
                MCI_FROM | MCI_TO , (DWORD)(LPVOID) &PlayParms);
        }
        else
        {
            PlayParms.dwFrom = MCI_MAKE_TMSF(i, 0, 0, 0);
            PlayParms.dwCallback = (DWORD) NULL;
            dwRC = mciSendCommand(uDevID, MCI_PLAY,
                    MCI_FROM, (DWORD)(LPVOID) &PlayParms);
        }
```

```
        Sleep(m_track*1000); // Data in track is the preview seconds.
    }
    dwRC = mciSendCommand(uDevID, MCI_STOP, 0, NULL);
    wsprintf (szStatus,
              "%d seconds preview of CD Player ended.\r\n",
               m_track);
    m_status.SetSel(-1,0);
    m_status.ReplaceSel(szStatus);


}
```

When the Eject button is pressed, the CD is ejected from the CD audio device and the button is renamed "Retract." When the Retract button is pressed, it retracts the CD audio device door. Unlike earlier commands that were used, the application uses the command string format API, **mciSendString**. Using **mciSendString** is much easier, since the string form of the command is directly sent to the device. When the CD is ejected, the track information is reset; when the CD is loaded, information related to the track is reread and displayed on the status area.

```
void CCDPlayerDlg::OnDoor()
{
    // TODO: Add your control notification handler code here
    CButton *pDoorButton;
    MCI_STATUS_PARMS StatusParms;
    DWORD dwRC;

    // Assume that the CD is in the drive and the door is closed
    // to start with.

    if (fDoorOpen)
    {
        mciSendString( "set cdaudio door closed wait",
                       NULL, 0, NULL );
        pDoorButton = (CButton *)GetDlgItem(IDC_DOOR);
        pDoorButton->SetWindowText("&Eject");
        fDoorOpen = FALSE;

        while (1)
        {   // Loop till device is ready
            memset (&StatusParms, ''\0'', sizeof(StatusParms));
            StatusParms.dwItem = MCI_STATUS_MODE;
            if (dwRC = mciSendCommand(uDevID, MCI_STATUS,
                    MCI_STATUS_ITEM | MCI_WAIT,
                    (DWORD)&StatusParms))
            {
                break; // error assume no media!
            }
            else
            {
```

```
                if (StatusParms.dwReturn == MCI_MODE_NOT_READY ||
                    StatusParms.dwReturn == MCI_MODE_OPEN)
                {
                    continue; // Still not ready continue.
                }
                else
                {
                    break;        // Ready to query.
                }
            }
        }
        memset (&StatusParms, ''\0'', sizeof(StatusParms));
        StatusParms.dwItem = MCI_STATUS_NUMBER_OF_TRACKS;
        if (mciSendCommand(uDevID, MCI_STATUS, MCI_STATUS_ITEM |
                        MCI_WAIT, (DWORD)&StatusParms))
        {// May be no disk in the CD drive.
            sTotalTracks = 0;
        }
        else
        {
            sTotalTracks = (short)StatusParms.dwReturn;
        }


        StatusParms.dwItem = MCI_STATUS_LENGTH;
        if (mciSendCommand(uDevID, MCI_STATUS, MCI_STATUS_ITEM,
                        (DWORD)&StatusParms))
        {// May be no disk in the CD drive
            StatusParms.dwReturn = 0;
        }
        wsprintf (szStatus,
                "Total number of tracks in this CD is %d.\r\n\
Total track time of this CD is %d Mins and %d Secs\r\n",
                sTotalTracks,
                MCI_MSF_MINUTE(StatusParms.dwReturn),
                MCI_MSF_SECOND(StatusParms.dwReturn));
        m_status.SetSel(-1,0);
        m_status.ReplaceSel(szStatus);

    }
    else
    {
        mciSendString( "set cdaudio door open", NULL, 0, NULL );
        pDoorButton = (CButton *)GetDlgItem(IDC_DOOR);
        pDoorButton->SetWindowText("R&etract");
        fDoorOpen = TRUE;
        sTotalTracks = 0;   // The CD is taken out. Reset total tracks.
    }
}
```

When the Pause button is pressed, it pauses the currently playing CD and changes the button text to "Resume." When the Resume button is pressed, the currently selected track continues to play. Here again the string format of the API is used.

```
void CCDPlayerDlg::OnPause()
{
    // TODO: Add your control notification handler code here
    CButton *pPauseButton;
    DWORD dwRC;
    char    szCmdBuffer[32];

    // Assume that the CD is in the drive and the door is closed
    // to start with.

    if (fPaused)
    {
        if (m_track < sTotalTracks)
        {
            wsprintf (szCmdBuffer,
                        "play cdaudio to %d",
                        m_track+1);
        }
        else
        {
            strcpy (szCmdBuffer, "play");
        }

        if (dwRC = mciSendString( szCmdBuffer, NULL, 0, NULL ))
        {
            CHAR szError[128+1];
            mciGetErrorString(dwRC, szError, sizeof(szError));
            AfxMessageBox(szError);
        }
        else
        {
            pPauseButton = (CButton *)GetDlgItem(IDC_PAUSE);
            pPauseButton->SetWindowText("Pau&se");
            fPaused = FALSE;
            strcpy (szStatus, "CD Player resumed.\r\n");
            m_status.SetSel(-1,0);
            m_status.ReplaceSel(szStatus);
        }
```

```
    }
    else
    {
        if(dwRC = mciSendString( "pause cdaudio", NULL, 0, NULL ))
        {
            CHAR szError[128+1];
            mciGetErrorString(dwRC, szError, sizeof(szError));
            AfxMessageBox(szError);
        }
        else
        {
            pPauseButton = (CButton *)GetDlgItem(IDC_PAUSE);
            pPauseButton->SetWindowText("Re&sume");
            fPaused = TRUE;
            strcpy (szStatus, "CD Player paused. To resume click Resume \
button.\r\n");
            m_status.SetSel(-1,0);
            m_status.ReplaceSel(szStatus);
        }
    }
}


void CCDPlayerDlg::OnStop()
{
    // TODO: Add your control notification handler code here
    mciSendCommand(uDevID, MCI_STOP, 0, NULL);

}
```

The **MCI_STOP** command message stops playing the CD. The difference between **MCI_PAUSE** and **MCI_STOP** is that **MCI_STOP** resets the current track position to zero, whereas **MCI_PAUSE** remembers the current track position and can resume at that point.

```
void CCDPlayerDlg::OnExit()
{
    // TODO: Add your control notification handler code here

    mciSendCommand(uDevID, MCI_CLOSE, 0, NULL);

    CDialog::OnOK();

}
```

When exiting the application, the CD audio device is closed by sending the **MCI_CLOSE** command message, which relinquishes the device. The device should be closed when exiting the application. Not doing so can leave the device inaccessible.

Though the sample application deals with the CD audio device, the MCI commands (both the message form and the string form) can be used to control any supported multimedia device including waveform audio devices, MIDI sequencers, digital video devices, and CD audio devices.

The libraries related to multimedia are *Vfw32.lib* and *Winmm.lib,* which are included as input to the project while building. Also not shown here is the inclusion of the *Vfw.h* header file, which is included in the *Stdafx.h* header file. This header file has all the definitions needed for multimedia.

VIDEO PROGRAMMING EXAMPLE

The next sample is an application that loads, plays, and controls an AVI file. When the application is started, a dialog box is displayed with buttons to open, play, pause, stop, step forward, step reverse, and change the speed of an AVI file. It also allows input of the From and To location of the AVI segment to be played and provides a status area. Figure 17-4 shows the dialog box.

The application creates an *MCIWnd* window and uses it to play the AVI file. Like the CDPlayer sample application, this is also a dialog-based application whose framework is created by use of the AppWizard and ClassWizard. Since all the functionality that this application tries to show is in the *AVIPlayerDlg* dialog box, code related to this dialog box class is shown next. Shown is the class definition file for the **AVIPlayerDlg** class. The class maintains the information about the AVI window, its status, and the file information in member variables. Information conveyed by the user or to the user through the

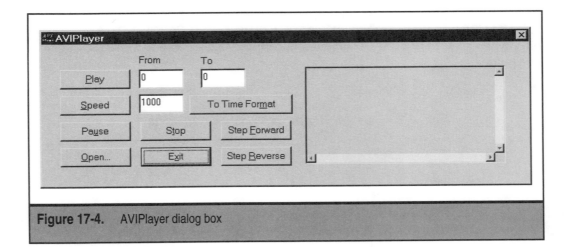

Figure 17-4. AVIPlayer dialog box

user interface, such as the frame numbers, speed, and status, is also maintained in member variables.

```cpp
// AVIPlayerDlg.h : header file
#if !defined(AFX_AVIPLAYERDLG_H)
#define AFX_AVIPLAYERDLG_H
#if _MSC_VER >= 1000
#pragma once
#endif // _MSC_VER >= 1000


/////////////////////////////////////////////////////////////////////////////
// CAVIPlayerDlg dialog

class CAVIPlayerDlg : public CDialog
{
// Construction
public:
    CAVIPlayerDlg(CWnd* pParent = NULL);    // standard constructor

// Dialog Data
    //{{AFX_DATA(CAVIPlayerDlg)
    enum { IDD = IDD_AVIPLAYER_DIALOG };
    CEdit    m_status;
    long     m_from;
    short    m_speed;
    long     m_to;
    //}}AFX_DATA


    // ClassWizard generated virtual function overrides
    //{{AFX_VIRTUAL(CAVIPlayerDlg)
    protected:
    virtual void DoDataExchange(CDataExchange* pDX);
    //}}AFX_VIRTUAL

// Implementation
protected:
    HICON m_hIcon;
    BOOL     fPaused;
    BOOL     fTimeFormat;
    char     szStatus[256];
    char     szAVIFile[MAX_PATH];
    HWND     m_hwndAVIWindow;

    // Generated message map functions
    //{{AFX_MSG(CAVIPlayerDlg)
    virtual BOOL OnInitDialog();
    afx_msg void OnSysCommand(UINT nID, LPARAM lParam);
    afx_msg void OnPaint();
    afx_msg HCURSOR OnQueryDragIcon();
```

```
        afx_msg void OnOpen();
        afx_msg void OnPause();
        afx_msg void OnPlay();
        afx_msg void OnSpeed();
        afx_msg void OnStepf();
        afx_msg void OnStepr();
        afx_msg void OnStop();
        afx_msg void OnTimeformat();
        virtual void OnOK();
        //}}AFX_MSG
        DECLARE_MESSAGE_MAP()
};


//{{AFX_INSERT_LOCATION}}

#endif // !defined(AFX_AVIPLAYERDLG_H)
```

The implementation file for the **AVIPlayerDlg** class is shown next. Apart from the code for the application dialog box, it also has code to deal with the About panel. During **OnInitDialog** processing, the member variables are initialized and displayed in the dialog box by calling **UpdateData**. **OnSystemCommand**, **OnPaint**, and **OnQueryDragIcon** are handled by the code generated by the ClassWizard and are unchanged, since no additional processing is required in this application.

```
// AVIPlayerDlg.cpp : implementation file
//

#include "stdafx.h"
#include "AVIPlayer.h"
#include "AVIPlayerDlg.h"

#ifdef _DEBUG
#define new DEBUG_NEW
#undef THIS_FILE
static char THIS_FILE[] = __FILE__;
#endif

/////////////////////////////////////////////////////////////////////////////
// CAboutDlg dialog used for App About

class CAboutDlg : public CDialog
{
public:
    CAboutDlg();

// Dialog Data
    //{{AFX_DATA(CAboutDlg)
    enum { IDD = IDD_ABOUTBOX };
    //}}AFX_DATA
```

```
    // ClassWizard generated virtual function overrides
    //{{AFX_VIRTUAL(CAboutDlg)
    protected:
    virtual void DoDataExchange(CDataExchange* pDX);
    //}}AFX_VIRTUAL

// Implementation
protected:
    //{{AFX_MSG(CAboutDlg)
    //}}AFX_MSG
    DECLARE_MESSAGE_MAP()
};

CAboutDlg::CAboutDlg() : CDialog(CAboutDlg::IDD)
{
    //{{AFX_DATA_INIT(CAboutDlg)
    //}}AFX_DATA_INIT
}

void CAboutDlg::DoDataExchange(CDataExchange* pDX)
{
    CDialog::DoDataExchange(pDX);
    //{{AFX_DATA_MAP(CAboutDlg)
    //}}AFX_DATA_MAP
}

BEGIN_MESSAGE_MAP(CAboutDlg, CDialog)
    //{{AFX_MSG_MAP(CAboutDlg)
        // No message handlers
    //}}AFX_MSG_MAP
END_MESSAGE_MAP()

/////////////////////////////////////////////////////////////////////////
// CAVIPlayerDlg dialog


CAVIPlayerDlg::CAVIPlayerDlg(CWnd* pParent /*=NULL*/)
    : CDialog(CAVIPlayerDlg::IDD, pParent)
{
    //{{AFX_DATA_INIT(CAVIPlayerDlg)
    m_from = 0;
    m_speed = 0;
    m_to = 0;
    //}}AFX_DATA_INIT
    // Note that LoadIcon does not require a subsequent DestroyIcon in Win32
    m_hIcon = AfxGetApp()->LoadIcon(IDR_MAINFRAME);
}
```

```
void CAVIPlayerDlg::DoDataExchange(CDataExchange* pDX)
{
    CDialog::DoDataExchange(pDX);
    //{{AFX_DATA_MAP(CAVIPlayerDlg)
    DDX_Control(pDX, IDC_MLE_STATUS, m_status);
    DDX_Text(pDX, IDC_EDIT_FROM, m_from);
    DDX_Text(pDX, IDC_EDIT_SPEED, m_speed);
    DDX_Text(pDX, IDC_EDIT_TO, m_to);
    //}}AFX_DATA_MAP
}

BEGIN_MESSAGE_MAP(CAVIPlayerDlg, CDialog)
    //{{AFX_MSG_MAP(CAVIPlayerDlg)
    ON_WM_SYSCOMMAND()
    ON_WM_PAINT()
    ON_WM_QUERYDRAGICON()
    ON_BN_CLICKED(IDC_OPEN, OnOpen)
    ON_BN_CLICKED(IDC_PAUSE, OnPause)
    ON_BN_CLICKED(IDC_PLAY, OnPlay)
    ON_BN_CLICKED(IDC_SPEED, OnSpeed)
    ON_BN_CLICKED(IDC_STEPF, OnStepf)
    ON_BN_CLICKED(IDC_STEPR, OnStepr)
    ON_BN_CLICKED(IDC_STOP, OnStop)
    ON_BN_CLICKED(IDC_TIMEFORMAT, OnTimeformat)
    //}}AFX_MSG_MAP
END_MESSAGE_MAP()

///////////////////////////////////////////////////////////////////////////
// CAVIPlayerDlg message handlers

BOOL CAVIPlayerDlg::OnInitDialog()
{
    CDialog::OnInitDialog();

    // Add "About..." menu item to system menu.

    // IDM_ABOUTBOX must be in the system command range.
    ASSERT((IDM_ABOUTBOX & 0xFFF0) == IDM_ABOUTBOX);
    ASSERT(IDM_ABOUTBOX < 0xF000);

    CMenu* pSysMenu = GetSystemMenu(FALSE);
    if (pSysMenu != NULL)
    {
        CString strAboutMenu;
        strAboutMenu.LoadString(IDS_ABOUTBOX);
        if (!strAboutMenu.IsEmpty())
        {
            pSysMenu->AppendMenu(MF_SEPARATOR);
            pSysMenu->AppendMenu(MF_STRING, IDM_ABOUTBOX, strAboutMenu);
```

```
        }
    }

    // Set the icon for this dialog.  The framework does this automatically
    //  when the application's main window is not a dialog
    SetIcon(m_hIcon, TRUE);            // Set big icon
    SetIcon(m_hIcon, FALSE);           // Set small icon

    // TODO: Add extra initialization here

    fPaused = FALSE;
    fTimeFormat = FALSE;
    m_to = 0;
    m_from = 0;
    m_speed = 1000;

    UpdateData(FALSE);

    return TRUE;
}

void CAVIPlayerDlg::OnSysCommand(UINT nID, LPARAM lParam)
{
    if ((nID & 0xFFF0) == IDM_ABOUTBOX)
    {
        CAboutDlg dlgAbout;
        dlgAbout.DoModal();
    }
    else
    {
        CDialog::OnSysCommand(nID, lParam);
    }
}


void CAVIPlayerDlg::OnPaint()
{
    if (IsIconic())
    {
        CPaintDC dc(this); // device context for painting

        SendMessage(WM_ICONERASEBKGND, (WPARAM) dc.GetSafeHdc(), 0);

        // Center icon in client rectangle
        int cxIcon = GetSystemMetrics(SM_CXICON);
        int cyIcon = GetSystemMetrics(SM_CYICON);
        CRect rect;
        GetClientRect(&rect);
        int x = (rect.Width()—cxIcon + 1) / 2;
```

```
        int y = (rect.Height()—cyIcon + 1) / 2;

        // Draw the icon
        dc.DrawIcon(x, y, m_hIcon);
    }
    else
    {
        CDialog::OnPaint();
    }
}


// The system calls this to obtain the cursor to
// display while the user drags
// the minimized window.
HCURSOR CAVIPlayerDlg::OnQueryDragIcon()
{
    return (HCURSOR) m_hIcon;
}
```

When the Open button is pressed, a file dialog box is displayed by calling the
DoModal member function of the **CFileDialog** class. The class is initialized to display all
the files with the *.avi* extension and to pad *.avi* as the extension if the user does not provide
one. When the user selects an AVI file, an **MCIWnd** window is created and the selected
file is passed to it by calling the **MCIWndCreate** function. This function registers the
MCIWnd window class and creates an **MCIWnd** window to which various MCI
command messages can be sent. The window is created without any menus
(MCIWNDF_NOMENU), is created without the play bar that allows you to control
the play (MCIWNDF_NOPLAYBAR), and is requested to show the mode on the title bar
MCIWNDF_SHOWMODE). The menu and play bar are not shown, since this application
controls the entire functionality of the AVI file. As an exercise, the style can be modified
and the effect can be observed. The AVI file is also passed to the function, and when the
MCIWnd window is created, the AVI file is loaded.

```
void CAVIPlayerDlg::OnOpen()
{
    // TODO: Add your control notification handler code here
    CFileDialog    Filedlg (TRUE, "avi", "*.avi", OFN_HIDEREADONLY,
                "Video files (*.AVI)", this);
    if (IDOK == Filedlg.DoModal())
    {
        strcpy (szAVIFile, Filedlg.GetPathName());
        m_hwndAVIWindow = MCIWndCreate(NULL,
                            AfxGetInstanceHandle(),
                            MCIWNDF_NOMENU |
                            MCIWNDF_SHOWMODE |
                            MCIWNDF_NOPLAYBAR,
                            szAVIFile);
        long lAVILength = MCIWndGetLength(m_hwndAVIWindow);
```

```
        wsprintf (szStatus, "Window opened with %s.\r\n The file has
          %ld frames.\r\n", szAVIFile, lAVILength);
        m_status.SetSel(-1,0);
        m_status.ReplaceSel(szStatus);
    }
    else
    {
        return;
    }
}
```

When the Play button is pressed, the segment information (either frames or time) is retrieved and the segment is played by calling the **MCIWndPlay**, **MCIWndPlayTo**, **MCIWndPlayFrom**, or **MCIWndPlayFromTo** macro. Depending on the segment information, one of these macros is used. These macros in turn send a **MCI_PLAY**, **MCIWNDM_PLAYFROM**, or **MCIWNDM_PLAYTO** message to the **MCIWnd** window. In the case of **MCIWndPlayFromTo** the system first seeks to the starting segment by sending a **MCI_SEEK** message and then sending a **MCI_PLAYTO** message. The **MCI_PLAY** message plays from the current location till the end of the content, **MCIWNDM_PLAYTO** plays from the current location till the specified location, and **MCIWNDM_PLAYFROM** plays from the specified location till the end of the content. Note that if the From location is after the To location, the content is played in the reverse direction. After sending the message, the status edit control is updated with the status information.

```
void CAVIPlayerDlg::OnPlay()
{
    // TODO: Add your control notification handler code here
    UpdateData(TRUE);

    if (m_from == 0 && m_to == 0)
    {   // Play the entire segment
        MCIWndPlay(m_hwndAVIWindow);
        strcpy (szStatus, "Playing the AVI file\r\n");
    }
    else if (m_from == 0 && m_to != 0)
    {   // Play up to m_to segment
        MCIWndPlayTo(m_hwndAVIWindow, m_to);
        wsprintf (szStatus, "Playing up to %d\r\n", m_to);
    }
    else if (m_from !=0 && m_to == 0)
    {   // Play from m_from segment
        MCIWndPlayFrom(m_hwndAVIWindow, m_from);
        wsprintf (szStatus, "Playing from %d\r\n", m_from);
    }
    else
    {   // Play the selected segment
        MCIWndPlayFromTo(m_hwndAVIWindow, m_from, m_to);
        wsprintf (szStatus, "Playing from %d to %d\r\n",
```

```
                            m_from, m_to);
    }
    m_status.SetSel(-1,0);
    m_status.ReplaceSel(szStatus);
}
```

When the Pause button is pressed, the application sends an **MCI_PAUSE** or **MCI_RESUME** message to the **MCIWnd** window by calling the **MCIWndPause** or **MCIWndResume** macro. It also changes the button text from "Pause" to "Resume" or the other way around, depending on the current state. Information as to whether the player is paused is maintained in a member variable. To stop the player, the **MCI_STOP** message is sent to the **MCIWnd** window by use of the **MCIWndStop** macro.

```
void CAVIPlayerDlg::OnPause()
{
    // TODO: Add your control notification handler code here
    CButton *pPauseButton;

    if (fPaused)
    {
        MCIWndResume(m_hwndAVIWindow);
        pPauseButton = (CButton *)GetDlgItem(IDC_PAUSE);
        pPauseButton->SetWindowText("Pau&se");
        fPaused = FALSE;
        strcpy (szStatus, "Play resumed.\r\n");
    }
    else
    {
        MCIWndPause(m_hwndAVIWindow);
        pPauseButton = (CButton *)GetDlgItem(IDC_PAUSE);
        pPauseButton->SetWindowText("Re&sume");
        fPaused = TRUE;
        strcpy (szStatus,
                "Play paused.\r\nTo resume click Resume button.\r\n");
    }

    m_status.SetSel(-1,0);
    m_status.ReplaceSel(szStatus);
}

void CAVIPlayerDlg::OnStop()
{
    // TODO: Add your control notification handler code here
    MCIWndStop(m_hwndAVIWindow);
    strcpy(szStatus, "Play stopped\r\n");
    m_status.SetSel(-1,0);
    m_status.ReplaceSel(szStatus);

}
```

The speed of the player can be controlled by sending the **MCIWNDM_SETSPEED** message. This *AVIPlayer* application provides a way to change the speed at which the player plays back the AVI file. The speed can be provided by the application through the Speed edit control in the dialog box and by setting the speed by clicking on the Speed button. A value of 1000 indicates a normal speed, any value above 1000 can be specified for more speed, and any value lower than 1000 but greater than 0 can be specified for less speed.

```
void CAVIPlayerDlg::OnSpeed()
{
    // TODO: Add your control notification handler code here
    UpdateData(TRUE);

    if( MCIWndSetSpeed (m_hwndAVIWindow, m_speed))
    {
        strcpy (szStatus, "Speed setting command failed\r\n");
    }
    else
    {
        wsprintf (szStatus, "Player speed set to %d\r\n", m_speed);
    }
    m_status.SetSel(-1,0);
    m_status.ReplaceSel(szStatus);

}


void CAVIPlayerDlg::OnStepf()
{
    // TODO: Add your control notification handler code here
    MCIWndStep(m_hwndAVIWindow, 1);
    strcpy(szStatus, "Step forward\r\n");
    m_status.SetSel(-1,0);
    m_status.ReplaceSel(szStatus);

}
```

Two buttons to step through the AVI player are provided. The Step Forward button steps one frame forward, and Step Reverse steps one frame backward. The step can be modified to other values. For example, a step value of 5 will step forward five frames, and −5 will step five frames backward.

```
void CAVIPlayerDlg::OnStepr()
{
    // TODO: Add your control notification handler code here
```

```
    MCIWndStep(m_hwndAVIWindow, -1);
    strcpy(szStatus, "Step backward\r\n");
    m_status.SetSel(-1,0);
    m_status.ReplaceSel(szStatus);


}


void CAVIPlayerDlg::OnTimeformat()
{
    // TODO: Add your control notification handler code here
    CButton *pTimeFormatButton;

    if (fTimeFormat)
    {   // Currently in Time Format
        MCIWndUseFrames(m_hwndAVIWindow);
        pTimeFormatButton = (CButton *)GetDlgItem(IDC_TIMEFORMAT);
        pTimeFormatButton->SetWindowText("To Ti&me Format");
        fTimeFormat = FALSE;
        strcpy (szStatus, "Changed to Frame Format\r\n");
    }
    else
    {   // Currently in Frame Format
        MCIWndUseTime(m_hwndAVIWindow);
        pTimeFormatButton = (CButton *)GetDlgItem(IDC_TIMEFORMAT);
        pTimeFormatButton->SetWindowText("To Fra&me Format");
        fTimeFormat = TRUE;
        strcpy (szStatus, "Changed to Time Format.\r\n");
    }

    m_status.SetSel(-1,0);
    m_status.ReplaceSel(szStatus);


}
```

This application allows the user to change the time format for the player. By default the time format is set to *frames*. But the time format can also be set to *ms* or milliseconds. Messages like **MCIWND_PLAYTO** and **MCIWND_PLAYFROM** are affected by the time format setting. Thus, if the time format is set to frames and "10" and "100," respectively, appear in the From and To entry fields, all frames from 10 until 100 are played. On the other hand, if the time format is set to *ms*, then the player will play 90ms of the segment beginning at 10ms from the start. Formats other than *frames* and *ms* can be set provided the MCI device supports them. To set the time format to *frames*, the **MCIWndUseFrames** macro is used; to set to *ms*, **MCIWndUseTime** is used.

Finally, when the user chooses the Exit button, the **MCIWnd** window is closed by sending an **MCI_CLOSE** message by use of the **MCIWndClose** macro. This closes the file associated with the **MCIWnd** window, but still keeps the window open and can be associated with a different file. Since this application processes the Exit button to exit, it also destroys the **MCIWnd** window by sending the **WM_CLOSE** message using the **MCIWndDestroy** macro. This macro destroys the **MCIWnd** window. (It also closes the MCI file associated with the window, and hence the **MCIWndClose** macro is irrelevant here.)

```
void CAVIPlayerDlg::OnOK()
{
    // TODO: Add extra validation here
    MCIWndClose(m_hwndAVIWindow);
    CDialog::OnOK();
}
```

If you do not have an AVI file to load, look at some of the television networks' Web sites, such as **www.abcnews.com**. They typically have AVI files for their news coverage.

The libraries related to multimedia are *Vfw32.lib* and *Winmm.lib,* which are included as input to the project while building. Also not shown here is the inclusion of the *Vfw.h* header file, which is included in the *Stdafx.h* header file. This header file has all the definitions needed for multimedia.

Video Capture

Although video capture started with Video for Windows (VfW) back with Windows 3.1, enormous strides have been made since then. To overcome the limitations of VfW, Microsoft introduced a new driver model called the Windows Driver Model (WDM). This model supports enhanced video capture features including very fast data transfer rates and support for multiple streams. WDM works in conjunction with DirectShow (formerly called ActiveMovie). WDM also supports minidrivers. Minidrivers provide device-specific functions for video components such as television tuners, video decoders, and video encoders and are typically developed by the hardware manufacturers and work in conjunction with streaming class drivers provided by Microsoft.

WINDOWS 2000 SUPPORT FOR DVD

DVD, which is expanded as both Digital Video Disc and Digital Versatile Disc, is more than another storage medium. It also encompasses associated technologies that makes it useful for storing audio and video entertainment content as well as storing large quantities (up to 17GB) of data on a single DVD disc. The associated technologies include compression technologies such as MPEG-2 for video and AC-3 for audio, Universal Disc Format (UDF, a new method to format DVD discs), and a new streaming class device driver that conforms to the new Windows Driver Model (WDM) defined by Microsoft. These DVD-specific technologies are integrated with Microsoft's "Direct" family including technologies such as DirectDraw, DirectSound, and DirectShow. The integration of these technologies and the different Windows 2000 components that provide complete DVD support is shown in Figure 17-5.

CONCLUSION

We started with a brief review of multimedia basics, including time formats. Then we looked at some audio programming methods such as using the media control interface and **MCIWnd**. We looked at a CD player programming example. Then we looked at video programming methods and looked at a video programming example that plays AVI video clips.

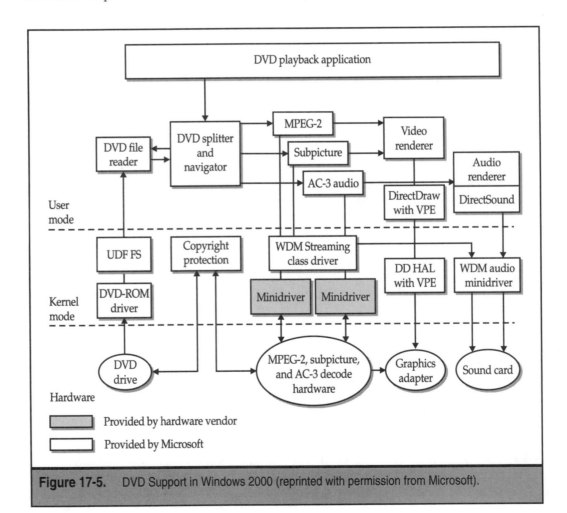

Figure 17-5. DVD Support in Windows 2000 (reprinted with permission from Microsoft).

CHAPTER 18

OpenGL Programming

We looked at graphics programming using GDI in Chapter 6. While GDI can help you with some graphics, its capabilities are somewhat limited. If you want to program sophisticated three-dimensional graphics and want to include special effects such as shading, lighting, texture mapping, and so on, you need OpenGL.

OpenGL is an offshoot of IRIS GL graphics workstations developed by Silicon Graphics. It is now a standard supported across many computer systems, including many UNIX systems and Windows 2000. The OpenGL language standard, including language features and conformance testing, is controlled by the OpenGL Architecture Review Board (OpenGL ARB), an industry consortium whose members include Silicon Graphics, Microsoft, IBM, Intel, and DEC. The OpenGL language itself is independent of hardware and underlying software, such as operating systems and windowing systems. You can port OpenGL applications written for one environment to another (see the section "Porting OpenGL Applications" later in this chapter). OpenGL is heavily used where three-dimensional object visualization and sophisticated graphics are required, such as in CAD/CAM applications.

We will start with a brief review of OpenGL basics and then look at OpenGL data structures, OpenGL functions, and programming examples to draw and transform two-dimensional and three-dimensional objects. We will conclude the chapter with a look at porting OpenGL across environments.

OPENGL BASICS

OpenGL can handle geometric objects, images, and text. In OpenGL, the geometric objects are defined as sequences of vertices across different planes. The images are a collection of pixels. OpenGL support for text includes different fonts.

OpenGL handles geometric objects (which are made up of vertices) by *rasterizing* (the process of converting vector graphics to images consisting of pixels) and storing the pixels in a frame buffer. A *vertex* is a point, such as the endpoint of a line or a corner in a polygon. Besides the coordinates of the vertex, OpenGL also lets you associate other attributes, such as color and texture, with each vertex. OpenGL processes *primitives*, which are functions, to connect vertices and form geometric objects such as lines, poly-

Note for UNIX Programmers

As mentioned earlier, OpenGL is standards based, and there are UNIX systems that support OpenGL. If you have used OpenGL in UNIX systems or developed IRIS GL applications, then the language part of your OpenGL application in Windows 2000 is pretty much the same. However, the windowing subsystems are different—X Window in UNIX and the Windows subsystem in Windows 2000. The operating system calls in your OpenGL application will also be different.

gons, and so on. Primitive processing includes evaluation, transforming vertices, lighting, and clipping to a viewport. Processed primitives are rasterized, resulting in a series of frame buffer addresses and associated points. The rasterized output is stored as pixels in the frame buffer after some final processing, such as blending incoming pixel colors with existing colors. The OpenGL primitives execute in the order you specify them to complete the drawing of the geometric object. You can further control the final output using *modes* (see modes in the "OpenGL Programming Concepts" section).

OpenGL can handle image pixels directly (instead of using vertices). OpenGL provides pixel update functions to handle images. The pixels are either used in the rasterization stage or stored directly in frame buffers. You can use the standard GDI text functions to draw text if you are working with a single-buffered OpenGL window. If you are using a double-buffered window (see "Double Buffering" in the section "OpenGL Programming Concepts"), you can draw text by creating display lists for characters in a font and executing the appropriate display list when the characters (of the text you want to display) are drawn.

These functions are just the beginning. OpenGL also provides transformation matrices, lighting equation coefficients, antialiasing methods, and so on, to significantly enhance the graphics effects in the final output.

OpenGL, like other Windows 2000 functions, is implemented in a client/server fashion. Your application runs at the client and invokes the OpenGL APIs. The OpenGL client module communicates with an OpenGL server module and passes your application's OpenGL commands. The OpenGL server module invokes the Win32 Device Driver Interface (DDI) to drive the display driver. The OpenGL server may be on the same machine as the client, or it may be separated by a network. An OpenGL server typically maintains several OpenGL contexts. A *context* is an encapsulated OpenGL state that an OpenGL client connects to.

Graphics are typically resource intensive, and hardware accelerators are available to improve specific graphics functions. Windows 2000 provides a mechanism for you to take advantage of such devices where available. However, Microsoft did not want its OpenGL implementation tied to specific hardware. So Windows 2000 OpenGL includes a *generic* implementation that is software based. You can take advantage of special hardware and device drivers by setting and using flags in appropriate data structures. The client module invokes hardware-specific device drivers at the client level. At the server level, hardware-specific device drivers (instead of the Win32 DDI) are used by the server module to drive the display driver. Unlike in most other programming areas in Windows 2000, you should check on the availability of add-ons before developing your OpenGL applications and take advantage of them where appropriate. While the add-ons may enhance your application's performance and other capabilities, keep in mind that the add-ons also make it more difficult to port your OpenGL application to another OpenGL environment where the add-on is not available or is not supported. Also note that resource-intensive OpenGL applications (including some OpenGL screen-savers) executed on a client machine only affect other applications at the client, whereas the same applications executed at the server may affect a number of users.

Windows 2000 implementation of OpenGL supports color processing in one of two ways—RGBA mode and color-index mode. Unlike GDI, where most applications use color indexing and logical palettes, OpenGL applications usually work better in the RGBA mode. RGBA tends to perform better than color indexing, particularly for shading, lighting, texture mapping, and so on. RGBA works better for OpenGL applications for both true-color devices and palette-based devices. Situations in which you may want to use color-index mode in your application include porting an existing application that uses color-index mode or using color-map animation (which is not possible on true-color devices).

OpenGL does not handle end-user input (which your application can do by use of the GUI mechanisms discussed in Part II). In addition, OpenGL does not configure frame buffers (frame buffers are configured by the windowing subsystem) or initialize itself (initialization of OpenGL occurs when the windowing subsystem allocates a window for OpenGL).

OpenGL applications can print a rendered scene in one of two ways. The more difficult method (and the only method available prior to Windows NT 4.0) is to render the scene into a DIB section and then print the DIB section. Starting with Windows NT 4.0, OpenGL applications can print directly to a printer device context if a metafile spooler is used (by using a metafile device context when creating a rendering context). Keep in mind, though, that most OpenGL output requires more memory than is typically found in most printers. As such, OpenGL prints graphics in bands, which causes OpenGL printing to take more time than other output.

OPENGL PROGRAMMING CONCEPTS

You should be familiar with many concepts that are almost unique to OpenGL to be able to write OpenGL programs. The concepts include rendering contexts; modes; double buffering; and OpenGL internal matrices such as projection, model view, and texture. These concepts are briefly addressed here.

Rendering Contexts

Rendering contexts are the link between OpenGL and the Windows 2000 windowing system. All your application's OpenGL calls pass through an OpenGL rendering context.

An application specifies a Windows 2000 device context when it creates a rendering context. You can create a rendering context after you set the pixel format (see **PIXELFORMATDESCRIPTOR** in the "OpenGL Data Structures" section) for the device context (and the rendering context has the same pixel format as the device context). This rendering context is now ready for drawing on the device referenced by the specified device context. Keep in mind, however, that this does not mean that the rendering context must use the device context created with it. It can use another device context as long as that device context references the same device and has the same pixel format.

Also, the preceding discussion does not mean that a rendering context is basically the same as a device context. A *device* context contains information related to GDI, while a *rendering* context contains information related to OpenGL. In addition, a device context is specified explicitly in a GDI call, while a rendering context is implicit in an OpenGL call.

A thread that makes OpenGL calls must have one (and only one) current rendering context. A rendering context can be current to only one thread. However, a window to which OpenGL outputs are being sent can have multiple rendering contexts drawing to it at one time. An application's OpenGL calls without a current rendering context have no effect. The typical sequence involving rendering contexts is as follows:

1. A rendering context is created.
2. The rendering context created is set as a thread's current rendering context.
3. The thread then performs initialization related to OpenGL.
4. The thread calls OpenGL rendering functions.
5. When OpenGL processing is complete, the rendering context is made not current (the rendering context is detached).
6. The rendering context is destroyed (when not needed).

Now let's look at the multithreading implications of OpenGL applications.

Multithreading OpenGL Applications

You can use multiple threads in your OpenGL application. If your application has multiple threads, then each thread that makes OpenGL calls must have its own (and only one) current rendering context. With multithreaded applications, you should take steps to ensure that one thread does not affect the output of another thread. For example, one thread may clear the window prior to displaying its OpenGL image, and this may inadvertently clear an image of another thread. Another example would be that if you were to call **SwapBuffers** in one thread application, it could overwrite another thread's output. A common way to handle multithreaded OpenGL applications is to designate one thread for clearing and swapping the window, and to let other threads communicate with the designated thread. Multithreading and thread communication and synchronization are covered in detail in Chapter 9.

Now let's look at another OpenGL programming concept—modes.

Modes

Modes are OpenGL capabilities that can be used to enhance the final output. Modes are enabled by the **glEnable** function and disabled by the **glDisable** function. Modes are specified as parameters to these functions. A number of modes are possible; the following table lists only a small, selected subset of the modes.

Mode Parameter	Description
GL_BLEND	Blends the source RGBA color values with the RGBA values in the destination buffer using **glBlendFunc**
GL_TEXTURE_2D	Performs two-dimensional texturing using **glTexImage2D**
GL_SCISSOR_TEST	Performs drawing functions only within the rectangle specified by the **glScissor** function
GL_POLYGON_ SMOOTH	Applies filtering specified by **glPolygonMode**

Double Buffering

Microsoft implementation of OpenGL supports double buffering. There are two buffers—an onscreen buffer and an offscreen buffer. By default, all your OpenGL drawing commands draw to the offscreen buffer. When the drawing is complete, the contents of the offscreen buffer are copied to the onscreen buffer (by use of the **SwapBuffers** function). Double buffering smoothes image transitions.

OPENGL DATA STRUCTURES

A pixel format specifies properties of an OpenGL drawing surface, such as whether the pixel buffer is single or double buffered, whether the pixel data is in RGBA or color-index form, and so on.

The **PIXELFORMATDESCRIPTOR** structure describes the pixel format of a drawing surface. It is probably the most important data structure related to OpenGL in Windows 2000. The **PIXELFORMATDESCRIPTOR** structure is shown here:

```
typedef struct tagPIXELFORMATDESCRIPTOR { // pfd
    WORD  nSize;
    WORD  nVersion;
    DWORD dwFlags;
    BYTE  iPixelType;
    BYTE  cColorBits;
    BYTE  cRedBits;
    BYTE  cRedShift;
    BYTE  cGreenBits;
    BYTE  cGreenShift;
    BYTE  cBlueBits;
    BYTE  cBlueShift;
    BYTE  cAlphaBits;
    BYTE  cAlphaShift;
```

```
    BYTE   cAccumBits;
    BYTE   cAccumRedBits;
    BYTE   cAccumGreenBits;
    BYTE   cAccumBlueBits;
    BYTE   cAccumAlphaBits;
    BYTE   cDepthBits;
    BYTE   cStencilBits;
    BYTE   cAuxBuffers;
    BYTE   iLayerType;
    BYTE   bReserved;
    DWORD  dwLayerMask;
    DWORD  dwVisibleMask;
    DWORD  dwDamageMask;
} PIXELFORMATDESCRIPTOR;
```

where

nSize is the size of the **PIXELFORMATDESCRIPTOR** structure and is set by use of **sizeof(PIXELFORMATDESCRIPTOR)**.

nVersion is the version of the **PIXELFORMATDESCRIPTOR** structure and is set to 1.

dwFlags is a set of bit flags that specify pixel buffer properties, such as whether the buffer supports GDI or OpenGL, whether the pixel format is supported by GDI or a device/driver or hardware, and so on. Most of the flags are not mutually exclusive (exceptions are noted in the description), and you can set a combination of bit flags to suit your application. The flag values and associated description are listed in Table 18-1.

Flag Value	Description
PFD_DRAW_TO_WINDOW	The buffer can draw to a window/device surface.
PFD_DRAW_TO_BITMAP	The buffer can draw to a memory bitmap.
PFD_SUPPORT_GDI	The buffer supports GDI. This flag is mutually exclusive with PFD_DOUBLEBUFFER in the current generic implementation.
PFD_SUPPORT_OPENGL	The buffer supports OpenGL.
PFD_GENERIC_ACCELERATED	The pixel format is supported by a device driver that provides acceleration in the generic implementation.

Table 18-1.   Pixel Buffer Property Flags and Descriptions

Flag Value	Description
PFD_GENERIC_FORMAT	The pixel format is supported by the generic implementation (implementation by GDI without hardware acceleration).
PFD_NEED_PALETTE	The buffer uses RGBA pixels on a palette-managed device. You need a logical palette for this pixel type. Colors in the palette should be specified according to the values of cRedBits, cRedShift, and so on (see cRedBits, cRedShift, and so on, later in this section).
PFD_NEED_SYSTEM_PALETTE	This flag is used with hardware palettes. Some restrictions include support for one hardware palette in 256-color mode only, and that the hardware palette must be in a fixed order (for example, 3-3-2) in RGBA mode or must match the logical palette in color-index mode. To use hardware palettes, call SetSystemPaletteUse in your program to force a one-to-one mapping of the logical palette and the system palette. You can clear this flag if your OpenGL hardware supports multiple hardware palettes and the device driver can assign spare hardware palettes for OpenGL.
PFD_DOUBLEBUFFER	The buffering uses double buffers (mutually exclusive with PFD_SUPPORT_GDI). See PFD_SUPPORT_GDI earlier in this table.
PFD_STEREO	The buffering is stereoscopic (there are separate left and right buffers). This flag is not supported in the current generic implementation.
PFD_SWAP_LAYER_BUFFERS	This specifies whether a device can swap individual layer planes with pixel formats. The layer planes could include double-buffered overlay or underlay planes. When this flag is not set, all layer planes are swapped together as a group. This flag must be set for the wglSwapLayerBuffers function to be supported.

Table 18-1 .   Pixel Buffer Property Flags and Descriptions *(continued)*

Flag Value	Description
PFD_DEPTH_DONTCARE	Selected pixel format can either have or not have a depth buffer
PFD_DOUBLEBUFFER_DONTCARE	Selected pixel format can be either single or double buffered
PFD_STEREO_DONTCARE	Selected pixel format can be either monoscopic or stereoscopic

Table 18-2. ChoosePixelFormat Function Flags

You can specify the bit flags listed in Table 18-2 when calling **ChoosePixelFormat** (which attempts to find the closest pixel format supported by a device context to that specified in your application).

With the **glAddSwapHintRectWIN** extension function, the two flags in Table 18-3 are included for the **PIXELFORMATDESCRIPTOR** pixel format structure.

Flag Value	Description
PFD_SWAP_COPY	This flag causes the content of the back buffer to be copied to the front buffer in the double-buffered main color plane without affecting the contents of the back buffer. PFD_SWAP_COPY is a hint to the device driver, which may opt not to support the function.
PFD_SWAP_EXCHANGE	This flag causes the exchange of the back buffer's content with the front buffer's content in the double-buffered main color plane. PFD_SWAP_COPY is a one-way copy from the back buffer to the front buffer, while PFD_SWAP_EXCHANGE is a two-way copy between the front and back buffers. PFD_SWAP_EXCHANGE is a hint to the device driver, which may opt not to support the function.

Table 18-3. Flags Enabled by glAddSwapHintRectWIN Function

iPixelType specifies the type of pixel data. The types are defined in Table 18-4.

cColorBits is the number of color bitplanes in each color buffer. For RGBA pixel types, it is the size of the color buffer, excluding the alpha bitplanes. For color-index pixels, it is the size of the color-index buffer.

cRedBits is the number of red bitplanes in each RGBA color buffer.

cRedShift is the shift count for red bitplanes in each RGBA color buffer.

cGreenBits is the number of green bitplanes in each RGBA color buffer.

cGreenShift is the shift count for green bitplanes in each RGBA color buffer.

cBlueBits is the number of blue bitplanes in each RGBA color buffer.

cBlueShift is the shift count for blue bitplanes in each RGBA color buffer.

cAlphaBits is the number of alpha bitplanes in each RGBA color buffer (alpha bitplanes are not supported).

cAlphaShift is the shift count for alpha bitplanes in each RGBA color buffer (alpha bitplanes are not supported).

cAccumBits is the total number of bitplanes in the accumulation buffer.

cAccumRedBits is the number of red bitplanes in the accumulation buffer.

cAccumGreenBits is the number of green bitplanes in the accumulation buffer.

cAccumBlueBits is the number of blue bitplanes in the accumulation buffer.

cAccumAlphaBits is the number of alpha bitplanes in the accumulation buffer.

cDepthBits is the depth of the Z-axis (depth) buffer.

cStencilBits is the depth of the stencil buffer.

cAuxBuffers is the number of auxiliary buffers (auxiliary buffers are not supported in Release 1.0 of the generic implementation).

iLayerType is ignored. This parameter is included for compatibility.

Flag Value	Description
PFD_TYPE_RGBA	These are RGBA pixels. Each pixel has four components (in red, green, blue, and alpha order).
PFD_TYPE_ COLORINDEX	These are color-index pixels. Each pixel uses a color-index value.

Table 18-4. Pixel Types

bReserved is the number of overlay and underlay planes. Bits 0 through 3 specify up to 15 overlay planes, and bits 4 through 7 specify up to 15 underlay planes.

dwLayerMask is ignored. This parameter is included for compatibility.

dwVisibleMask is the transparent color value of the index of an underlay plane. When the pixel type is RGBA, *dwVisibleMask* is a transparent RGB color value. When the pixel type is a color index, it is a transparent index value.

dwDamageMask is ignored. This parameter is included for compatibility.

OPENGL FUNCTIONS

OpenGL implementation is in the form of a library of functions. Although there are a lot of OpenGL functions, many functions are variations of each other with different data types for arguments. For example, there are two variations to the scaling function—**glScaled**, which uses double-precision arguments, and **glScalef**, which uses floating-point arguments. Keep in mind, however, that extensions supported in one rendering context are not necessarily supported in a different rendering context. The OpenGL functions can be classified as follows:

▼ *Core* OpenGL functions are for basic functions such as object shape description, matrix transformation, and so on. These core functions are prefixed by "gl" (such as **glDrawBuffer**).

■ *Utility* OpenGL functions provide functions including texture support, rendering cylinders and other geometric objects, and so on. Utility functions are prefixed by "glu" (such as **gluPerspective**).

■ *Auxiliary* OpenGL functions are for simple window management and are prefixed by "aux" (such as **auxSphere**).

■ *WGL* functions connect OpenGL to a windowing subsystem and are prefixed by "wgl" (such as **wglGetCurrentDC**).

▲ *Win32* functions are related to OpenGL.

There are more than 300 core OpenGL functions (counting variations of functions) besides a lot of utility and auxiliary functions. Refer to MSDN and other OpenGL documentation such as the *OpenGL Reference Manual* and *OpenGL Programming Guide* (these are the official books on OpenGL published by the OpenGL ARB) for more details about these functions. Table 18-5 summarizes the Win32 functions related to OpenGL and their descriptions.

ENABLING MFC APPLICATIONS TO USE OPENGL

Before we look at programming examples, let's briefly review the steps involved for an MFC application to use OpenGL. These steps are a brief extract from the *MFCOGL.EXE* sample that is included on MSDN. This sample program is also available by anonymous FTP from **ftp.microsoft.com** in the SOFTLIB/MSLFILES directory.

OpenGL Function	Description
ChoosePixel Format	This chooses a pixel format supported by a device context that is closest to a given pixel format specification. Although the closest format is chosen, the choice may not be acceptable, and you have to ensure that the selection is valid. For example, the closest format to a 24-bit RGB color format supported by the device context may be an 8-bit color format, but this may not be acceptable to your application.
DescribePixel Format	This loads the pixel format data of the specified pixel format and device in a PIXELFORMATDESCRIPTOR structure.
GetEnhMetaFile PixelFormat	This retrieves enhanced metafile pixel format data. You have to ensure that the buffer used to store the pixel format data is large enough.
GetPixelFormat	This obtains the index of the currently selected pixel format of the specified device context.
SetPixelFormat	This sets the pixel format of the specified device context to the specified format.
SwapBuffers	This exchanges contents of front (onscreen) and back (offscreen) buffers.

Table 18-5.   OpenGL Win32 Functions

1. Include required headers (such as *Gl.h*, *Glu.h*, and *Glaux.h*) and add required libraries (such as *Opengl32.lib*, *Glu32.lib*, and *Glaux.lib*) to the link project settings.
2. If your application uses palettes, add your implementations for the **OnPaletteChanged** and **OnQueryNewPalette** functions in the **CMainFrame** class.
3. Derive classes from **Cwnd**, including view classes.
4. Include implementations for initialization, window sizing (if necessary), and so on.
5. Include implementation for OpenGL rendering code.
6. Include implementation for cleanup.

Let's now take a look at some programming examples using OpenGL.

OPENGL PROGRAMMING EXAMPLES

Three sample programs related to OpenGL will be discussed here. The first sample program displays three 2-D objects—a triangle, a rectangle, and a pentagon—using OpenGL.

In the second sample program a graphic object is transformed, and in the third sample, 3-D objects are drawn and transformed. The samples are AppWizard-generated SDI applications. There is no dependency of MFC when using OpenGL, and OpenGL can be used directly using the normal Windows SDK. For ease of programming the examples, however, use MFC.

Programming Example to Display 2-D Objects

The code for the first sample program is shown next. Figure 18-1 shows the 2-D objects displayed by this programming example.

It is basically an SDI application framework created by use of AppWizard. The only relevant changes that are made are in the view module that is shown.

There are a few standard steps that must be taken in an OpenGL application. They will be discussed as the sample application is discussed. The header file for the view class is shown next. A set of member variables, some relevant to OpenGL and others not, are added. Additional message handlers for **WM_CREATE**, **WM_DESTROY**, **WM_SIZE**, and **WM_MOUSEMOVE** are added, the use of which will become clear later.

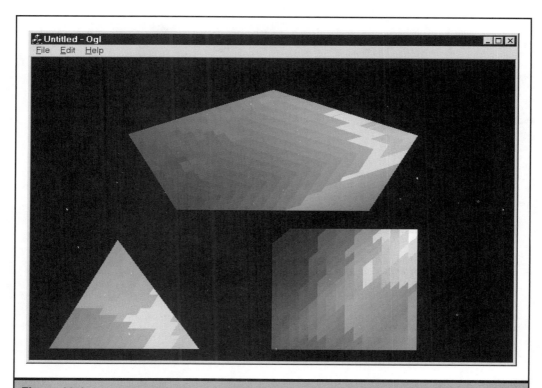

Figure 18-1.   Display of 2-D OpenGL objects

```
// OglView.h : interface of the COglView class
//
#if !defined(AFX_OGLVIEW_H)
#define AFX_OGLVIEW_H

#if _MSC_VER >= 1000
#pragma once
#endif // _MSC_VER >= 1000

class COglView : public CView
{
protected: // create from serialization only
    COglView();
    DECLARE_DYNCREATE(COglView)

// Attributes
public:
    COglDoc* GetDocument();
// Operations
public:
// Overrides
    // ClassWizard generated virtual function overrides
    //{{AFX_VIRTUAL(COglView)
    public:
    virtual BOOL PreCreateWindow(CREATESTRUCT& cs);
    protected:
    virtual void OnDraw(CDC* pDC);
    //}}AFX_VIRTUAL
// Implementation
public:
    virtual ~COglView();
#ifdef _DEBUG
    virtual void AssertValid() const;
    virtual void Dump(CDumpContext& dc) const;
#endif
protected:
    int m_pixelformat;
    HGLRC m_hglRendContext;

    GLfloat vdColor1[3];
    GLfloat vdColor2[3];
    GLfloat vdColor3[3];
    GLfloat vdColor4[3];
    GLfloat vdColor5[3];
    GLfloat vdColor6[3];
    GLfloat vdColor7[3];
    GLfloat vdColor8[3];

    GLfloat *clrArray[8];
```

```
        BOOL InitPixelFormat(HDC hDC);
        void InitPFDStruc(PIXELFORMATDESCRIPTOR *ppfd);

// Generated message map functions
protected:
    //{{AFX_MSG(COglView)
    afx_msg int OnCreate(LPCREATESTRUCT lpCreateStruct);
    afx_msg void OnDestroy();
    afx_msg void OnPaint();
    afx_msg void OnSize(UINT nType, int cx, int cy);
    afx_msg void OnMouseMove(UINT nFlags, CPoint point);
    //}}AFX_MSG
    DECLARE_MESSAGE_MAP()
};

#ifndef _DEBUG  // debug version in OglView.cpp
inline COglDoc* COglView::GetDocument()
   { return (COglDoc*)m_pDocument; }
#endif

/////////////////////////////////////////////////////////////////////////////

//{{AFX_INSERT_LOCATION}}

#endif //
```

The implementation code for the view is shown next. When the view is created, the member variables are initialized. The member variable **m_pixelformat** maintains the chosen pixel format index. The member variable **m_hglRendContext** maintains the OpenGL rendering context. An array of colors is also maintained, which is used to add some interesting effects to the graphic objects that are drawn.

```
// OglView.cpp : implementation of the COglView class
//
#include "stdafx.h"
#include "Ogl.h"

#include "OglDoc.h"
#include "OglView.h"

#ifdef _DEBUG
#define new DEBUG_NEW
#undef THIS_FILE
static char THIS_FILE[] = __FILE__;
#endif

/////////////////////////////////////////////////////////////////////////////
// COglView
```

```
IMPLEMENT_DYNCREATE(COglView, CView)

BEGIN_MESSAGE_MAP(COglView, CView)
    //{{AFX_MSG_MAP(COglView)
    ON_WM_CREATE()
    ON_WM_DESTROY()
    ON_WM_PAINT()
    ON_WM_SIZE()
    ON_WM_MOUSEMOVE()
    //}}AFX_MSG_MAP
END_MESSAGE_MAP()

/////////////////////////////////////////////////////////////////////////
// COglView construction/destruction

COglView::COglView()
{
    // TODO: add construction code here
    m_pixelformat = 0;
m_hglRendContext = NULL;

    vdColor1[0] = 1.0;
    vdColor1[1] = 0.0;
    vdColor1[2] = 0.0;
    vdColor2[0] = 0.0;
    vdColor2[1] = 1.0;
    vdColor2[2] = 0.0;
    vdColor3[0] = 1.0;
    vdColor3[1] = 1.0;
    vdColor3[2] = 0.0;
    vdColor4[0] = 0.0;
    vdColor4[1] = 1.0;
    vdColor4[2] = 1.0;
    vdColor5[0] = 1.0;
    vdColor5[1] = 0.0;
    vdColor5[2] = 1.0;
    vdColor6[0] = 0.0;
    vdColor6[1] = 1.0;
    vdColor6[2] = 1.0;
    vdColor7[0] = 1.0;
    vdColor7[1] = 1.0;
    vdColor7[2] = 1.0;
    vdColor8[0] = 0.0;
    vdColor8[1] = 0.0;
    vdColor8[2] = 0.0;

    clrArray[0] = vdColor1;
    clrArray[1] = vdColor2;
    clrArray[2] = vdColor3;
```

```
        clrArray[3] = vdColor4;
        clrArray[4] = vdColor5;
        clrArray[5] = vdColor6;
        clrArray[6] = vdColor7;
        clrArray[7] = vdColor8;
}

COglView::~COglView()
{
}
```

An OpenGL window has its own pixel format; thus, to draw into the window, the device contexts retrieved for the client area of an OpenGL window should be used. Therefore an OpenGL window should be created with the WS_CLIPCHILDREN and WS_CLIPSIBLINGS styles. Furthermore, the window class attribute should not include the CS_PARENTDC style. This is the first standard step and is performed by the **PreCreateWindow** member function.

```
    BOOL COglView::PreCreateWindow(CREATESTRUCT& cs)
{
    // TODO: Modify the Window class or styles here by modifying
    //   the CREATESTRUCT cs

    cs.style |= (WS_CLIPCHILDREN | WS_CLIPSIBLINGS);
    return CView::PreCreateWindow(cs);
}

/////////////////////////////////////////////////////////////////////////////
// COglView drawing

void COglView::OnDraw(CDC* pDC)
{
    COglDoc* pDoc = GetDocument();
    ASSERT_VALID(pDoc);

    // TODO: add draw code for native data here
}

/////////////////////////////////////////////////////////////////////////////
// COglView diagnostics

#ifdef _DEBUG
void COglView::AssertValid() const
{
    CView::AssertValid();
}

void COglView::Dump(CDumpContext& dc) const
{
```

```
    CView::Dump(dc);
}

COglDoc* COglView::GetDocument() // non-debug version is inline
{
    ASSERT(m_pDocument->IsKindOf(RUNTIME_CLASS(COglDoc)));
    return (COglDoc*)m_pDocument;
}
#endif //_DEBUG
```

The next step is to create a rendering context and make it current. But before a rendering context is created, the window's pixel format should be set. This is handled by the **OnCreate** member function. The actual setting of the pixel format is done in the **InitPixelFormat** member function. To set a pixel format, a **PIXELFORMATDESCRIPTOR** data structure is initialized with the requirements for this application, and a close match is requested from the system by calling the **ChoosePixelFormat** function. This function attempts to match an appropriate pixel format supported by a device context to the given pixel format and returns a pixel format index. The application may check to see if the returned pixel format matches the application's requirement. The **DescribePixelFormat** function can be used to get information about the pixel format given the pixel format index. This application overlooks this and assumes that it gets the correct or closest matching pixel format. **SetPixelFormat** is then used to set the pixel format for the device context. If the application does not get a pixel format, it tries to use the first pixel format but checks that it is valid before using it by calling **DescribePixelFormat**.

After the pixel format is set, a rendering context is created by calling the **wglCreateContext** function. This creates a new rendering context that is made the current rendering context by calling the **wglMakeCurrent** function. Note that a rendering context is not the same as a device context. Typically a rendering context is created once and is used throughout the application. It is finally freed at the end. On the other hand, a device context is created when needed and freed immediately after that. This is to improve performance, since creation of a rendering context is quite expensive. When the application no longer needs the rendering context, it should be deleted by calling the **wglDeleteContext** function. This is done when the window is destroyed in the **OnDestroy** handler.

```
////////////////////////////////////////////////////////////////////////
// COglView message handlers

int COglView::OnCreate(LPCREATESTRUCT lpCreateStruct)
{
    if (CView::OnCreate(lpCreateStruct) == -1)
        return -1;

    // TODO: Add your specialized creation code here
    HDC hDC = ::GetDC(GetSafeHwnd());
```

```
        if (InitPixelFormat(hDC) == FALSE)
            return 0;
    m_hglRendContext = wglCreateContext(hDC);
    wglMakeCurrent(hDC, m_hglRendContext);
    return 0;
}


 BOOL COglView::InitPixelFormat(HDC hDC)
{
    PIXELFORMATDESCRIPTOR   PixForDesc;

    InitPFDStruc(&PixForDesc);
    m_pixelformat = ChoosePixelFormat( hDC, &PixForDesc);
    if (m_pixelformat == 0)
    {
        m_pixelformat = 1;
        if (DescribePixelFormat(hDC,  m_pixelformat,
            sizeof(PIXELFORMATDESCRIPTOR), &PixForDesc) == 0)
        {
            return FALSE;
        }
    }

    if (SetPixelFormat(hDC, m_pixelformat, &PixForDesc) == FALSE)
    {
        return FALSE;
    }

    return TRUE;

}
```

Only those fields that are supported are filled in the **PIXELFORMATDESCRIPTOR** structure. The two variations of *dwFlags* that are seen in the code are discussed at the end.

```
void COglView::InitPFDStruc(PIXELFORMATDESCRIPTOR *ppfd)
{
    memset(ppfd, 0, sizeof(PIXELFORMATDESCRIPTOR));
    ppfd->nSize = sizeof(PIXELFORMATDESCRIPTOR);
    ppfd->nVersion = 1;
#if 1
    ppfd->dwFlags = PFD_DRAW_TO_WINDOW |
                    PFD_SUPPORT_OPENGL |
                    PFD_DOUBLEBUFFER;
#else
    ppfd->dwFlags = PFD_DRAW_TO_WINDOW |
                    PFD_SUPPORT_OPENGL |
                    PFD_DRAW_TO_BITMAP ;
#endif
```

```
    ppfd->iPixelType = PFD_TYPE_RGBA;
    ppfd->cColorBits = 24;
    ppfd->cDepthBits = 16;
    ppfd->iLayerType = PFD_MAIN_PLANE;
}
```

The objects are painted in the **OnPaint** handler member function shown next. First the buffers that are currently enabled for color are cleared by calling the **glClear** function. Then three polygons—a triangle, a rectangle, and a pentagon—are drawn by use of the **glVertex2f** function. For each vertex, the color is specified by calling the **glColor3fv** function. The **glBegin** and **glEnd** functions delimit the vertices of a primitive-like point, line, and so on. The **glVertex** function commands should only be used within the **glBegin**/**glEnd** pair. Note that the application just sets the color of the vertex. OpenGL will automatically interpolate the color between the vertices. Finally the **glFlush** function is called to force execution of the previous graphic functions, which in this case are graphic primitives. Note that depending on the OpenGL implementation, the buffering of commands can be in a network buffer, graphic accelerator card, and so on. This application uses double buffering, and the call to **SwapBuffers** exchanges the front and the back buffers displaying the graphic objects.

```
void COglView::OnPaint()
{
    CPaintDC dc(this); // device context for painting
    // TODO: Add your message handler code here
    glClear(GL_COLOR_BUFFER_BIT);
    glBegin(GL_POLYGON);
        glColor3fv(clrArray[0]);
        glVertex2f(20.0f, 20.0f);
        glColor3fv(clrArray[1]);
        glVertex2f(175.0f, 20.0f);
        glColor3fv(clrArray[2]);
        glVertex2f(90.0f, 200.0f);
    glEnd();
    glBegin(GL_POLYGON);
        glColor3fv(clrArray[3]);
        glVertex2f(250.0f, 20.0f);
        glColor3fv(clrArray[4]);
        glVertex2f(400.0f, 20.0f);
        glColor3fv(clrArray[5]);
        glVertex2f(400.0f, 220.0f);
        glColor3fv(clrArray[6]);
        glVertex2f(250.0f, 220.0f);
    glEnd();
    glBegin(GL_POLYGON);
        glColor3fv(clrArray[7]);
        glVertex2f(150.0f, 250.0f);
```

```
        glColor3fv(clrArray[0]);
        glVertex2f(350.0f, 250.0f);
        glColor3fv(clrArray[1]);
        glVertex2f(400.0f, 375.0f);
        glColor3fv(clrArray[2]);
        glVertex2f(250.0f, 450.0f);
        glColor3fv(clrArray[3]);
        glVertex2f(100.0f, 375.0f);
    glEnd();
    glFlush();
#if 1
    SwapBuffers (wglGetCurrentDC());
#endif
    // Do not call CView::OnPaint() for painting messages
}
```

A *viewport* is the area in the window within which the OpenGL can draw. In this application whenever the window is resized, the entire client area of the window is set to be the viewport. The **gluOrtho2D** function defines the 2-D orthographic matrix. The aspect ratio passed to this function draws the graphic objects relative to the screen, so when the viewport becomes larger, the graphic objects appear larger, too.

```
void COglView::OnSize(UINT nType, int cx, int cy)
{
    CView::OnSize(nType, cx, cy);

    // TODO: Add your message handler code here
      glViewport(0, 0, cx, cy);
    if (cy == 0)
    {
        cy = 1;
    }
    glMatrixMode(GL_PROJECTION);
    glLoadIdentity();
    gluOrtho2D(0.0, (GLdouble)500.0*(cx/cy), 0.0, 500.0);
    glMatrixMode(GL_MODELVIEW);
    glLoadIdentity();
    glDrawBuffer(GL_BACK);
}
```

Just to add some dynamic features to the graphic objects that are drawn, the mouse movement is tracked and the events are handled by the next function. Earlier in the application, the code sets the color of the vertices, and OpenGL interpolates the color between the vertices. The vertex color is taken from a color array. This color array is manipulated in this function so that every time the mouse is moved, the color of the graphic objects drawn changes. This function can be commented out, and the difference can be seen.

```
void COglView::OnMouseMove(UINT nFlags, CPoint point)
{
    // TODO: Add your message handler code here and/or call default
    GLfloat *glfTemp;
    glfTemp = clrArray[0];
    for(int j=0; j<7; j++)
    {
        clrArray[j] = clrArray[j+1];
    }
    clrArray[7] = glfTemp;
    Invalidate(FALSE);
    CView::OnMouseMove(nFlags, point);
}

void COglView::OnDestroy()
{
    CView::OnDestroy();

    // TODO: Add your message handler code here
    HGLRC hRC;

    hRC = ::wglGetCurrentContext();
    ::wglMakeCurrent(NULL, NULL);
    if (hRC)
    {
        ::wglDeleteContext(hRC);
    }
}
```

This application used double buffering, which prevents the flicker every time the graphic objects are drawn. The difference between double buffering and drawing directly to the bitmap can be seen by changing the #if preprocessor directives and building the application not to use double buffering.

Programming Example to Transform 2-D Objects

The next sample extends the previous sample to illustrate pushing and popping the matrices, which are useful when you are transforming certain graphic objects while leaving the others in place. When the application is run and the mouse is moved over the application windows, the triangle object rotates about the lower-left corner of the screen, while the other two objects just change color. Part of the code that has changed is shown next. Figure 18-2 shows the transformation of 2-D objects of this programming example.

To keep track of angle of rotation, a protected member variable **theta** is added in the view class. This is initialized to 0.0 degrees in the view constructor and is incremented by

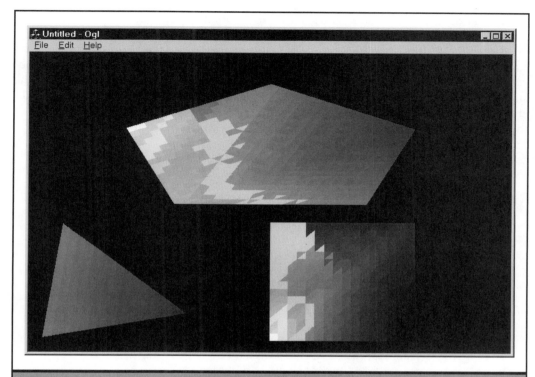

Figure 18-2. Transforming an OpenGL 2-D object

5 degrees every time the application gets a mouse move message. The function that draws the graphic objects is shown next.

The idea of the application is to transform just the triangle. The transformation functions **glRotated** and **glTranslated** can be used to achieve these desired effects. The **glRotated** function computes a matrix that performs a counterclockwise rotation of the object by a given degree about the axis between the origin and the given vector. The **glTranslated** function moves the coordinate system origin to the point specified by the new coordinates. In both cases the current matrix is multiplied by the transformation matrix, and the resulting matrix replaces the current matrix. Thus, if the current matrix is not saved, then the result of one graphic object's translation will also be reflected in all other future graphic objects that are drawn. To overcome this situation, OpenGL maintains a stack of matrices. (The stack depth is 32 for the GL_MODELVIEW mode and 2 for the GL_PROJECTION and GL_TEXTURE modes.) It also provides two functions, **glPushMatrix** and **glPopMatrix**, that save and restore the current matrix. The **glPushMatrix** function pushes the current matrix in the stack, makes a copy of it, and leaves it at the top of the stack. The **glPopMatrix** function pops the top matrix from the stack, thereby making the next matrix current.

Before the triangle is transformed, the current matrix is saved by pushing it in the stack. The transformation is applied and the triangle is drawn. Before the next graphic object is drawn, the transformed matrix is replaced with the old matrix that was saved in the stack. Thus, the transformation only applies to the triangle graphic object and not the others. To gain more understanding, it would be worth trying out the application without the **glPushMatrix**/**glPopMatrix** functions. Then it would transform all three objects.

```
void COglView::OnPaint()
{
    CPaintDC dc(this); // device context for painting
    // TODO: Add your message handler code here

    glLoadIdentity();
    glClear(GL_COLOR_BUFFER_BIT);

    glPushMatrix();
        glRotated(theta, 0.0, 0.0, 1.0);
//      glTranslated(100.0, 100.0, 0);

        glBegin(GL_POLYGON);
                    glColor3fv(clrArray[0]);
                    glVertex2f(20.0f, 20.0f);
                    glColor3fv(clrArray[1]);
                    glVertex2f(175.0f, 20.0f);
                    glColor3fv(clrArray[2]);
                    glVertex2f(90.0f, 200.0f);
        glEnd();
    glPopMatrix();

    glBegin(GL_POLYGON);
        glColor3fv(clrArray[3]);
        glVertex2f(250.0f, 20.0f);
        glColor3fv(clrArray[4]);
        glVertex2f(400.0f, 20.0f);
        glColor3fv(clrArray[5]);
        glVertex2f(400.0f, 220.0f);
        glColor3fv(clrArray[6]);
        glVertex2f(250.0f, 220.0f);
    glEnd();

    glBegin(GL_POLYGON);
        glColor3fv(clrArray[7]);
```

```
        glVertex2f(150.0f, 250.0f);
        glColor3fv(clrArray[0]);
        glVertex2f(350.0f, 250.0f);
        glColor3fv(clrArray[1]);
        glVertex2f(400.0f, 375.0f);
        glColor3fv(clrArray[2]);
        glVertex2f(250.0f, 450.0f);
        glColor3fv(clrArray[3]);
        glVertex2f(100.0f, 375.0f);
    glEnd();
    glFlush();

    SwapBuffers (wglGetCurrentDC());

    // Do not call CView::OnPaint() for painting messages
}
```

When the mouse is moved, the angle of rotation is incremented by 5.0 degrees.

```
void COglView::OnMouseMove(UINT nFlags, CPoint point)
{
    // TODO: Add your message handler code here and/or call default

    GLfloat *glfTemp;
    glfTemp = clrArray[0];

    for(int j=0; j<7; j++)
    {
        clrArray[j] = clrArray[j+1];
    }
    clrArray[7] = glfTemp;
    theta += 5.0;
    Invalidate(FALSE);
    CView::OnMouseMove(nFlags, point);
}
```

Programming Example to Draw and Transform 3-D Objects

The next sample draws two 3-D graphic objects and transforms them. Figures 18-3 and 18-4 show the 3-D objects of this programming example.

Most of the code follows a pattern similar to that seen earlier. The changes related to the 3-D object are highlighted here. Notice that in the **OnPaint** function the Z buffer is enabled by calling the **glEnable** function. Since we are enabling the Z buffer, it is cleared before drawing by calling **glClear** and adding GL_DEPTH_BUFFER_BIT to the parameter. The rest of the logic of pushing and popping the matrix is similar to the earlier example.

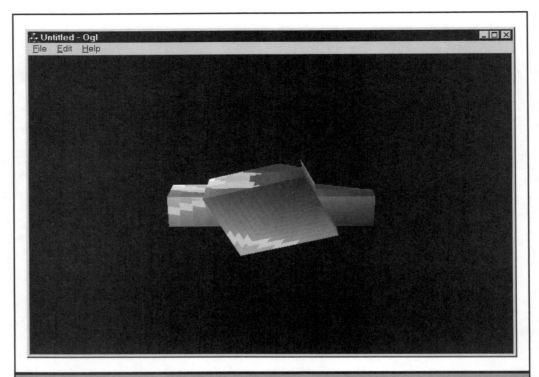

Figure 18-3.   Display of a 3-D OpenGL object

The coordinates of the two boxes are calculated with respect to the origin being at the center of the 3-D box. You can modify and experiment with the sample by changing the axis of rotation of the 3-D boxes. Check the commented-out lines in the **OnPaint( )** function in the following example.

```cpp
// OglView.cpp : implementation of the COglView class
//

#include "stdafx.h"
#include "Ogl.h"

#include "OglDoc.h"
#include "OglView.h"

#ifdef _DEBUG
#define new DEBUG_NEW
#undef THIS_FILE
```

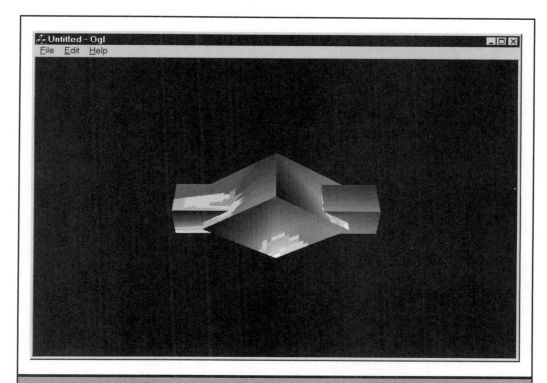

Figure 18-4. Transforming a 3-D OpenGL object

```
static char THIS_FILE[] = __FILE__;
#endif

/////////////////////////////////////////////////////////////////////////
// COglView

IMPLEMENT_DYNCREATE(COglView, CView)

BEGIN_MESSAGE_MAP(COglView, CView)
        //{{AFX_MSG_MAP(COglView)
        ON_WM_CREATE()
        ON_WM_DESTROY()
        ON_WM_PAINT()
        ON_WM_SIZE()
        ON_WM_MOUSEMOVE()
        //}}AFX_MSG_MAP
END_MESSAGE_MAP()
```

```
/////////////////////////////////////////////////////////////////////////
// COglView construction/destruction

COglView::COglView()
{
        // TODO: add construction code here
    theta = 5.0;
    m_pixelformat = 0;
    m_hglRendContext = NULL;

    vdColor1[0] = 1.0;
    vdColor1[1] = 0.0;
    vdColor1[2] = 0.0;
    vdColor2[0] = 0.0;
    vdColor2[1] = 1.0;
    vdColor2[2] = 0.0;
    vdColor3[0] = 1.0;
    vdColor3[1] = 1.0;
    vdColor3[2] = 0.0;
    vdColor4[0] = 0.0;
    vdColor4[1] = 1.0;
    vdColor4[2] = 1.0;
    vdColor5[0] = 1.0;
    vdColor5[1] = 0.0;
    vdColor5[2] = 1.0;
    vdColor6[0] = 0.0;
    vdColor6[1] = 1.0;
    vdColor6[2] = 1.0;
    vdColor7[0] = 1.0;
    vdColor7[1] = 1.0;
    vdColor7[2] = 1.0;
    vdColor8[0] = 0.0;
    vdColor8[1] = 0.0;
    vdColor8[2] = 0.0;

    clrArray[0] = vdColor1;
    clrArray[1] = vdColor2;
    clrArray[2] = vdColor3;
    clrArray[3] = vdColor4;
    clrArray[4] = vdColor5;
    clrArray[5] = vdColor6;
    clrArray[6] = vdColor7;
    clrArray[7] = vdColor8;

}

COglView::~COglView()
{
}
```

```
BOOL COglView::PreCreateWindow(CREATESTRUCT& cs)
{
    // TODO: Modify the Window class or styles here by modifying
    //  the CREATESTRUCT cs

    cs.style |= (WS_CLIPCHILDREN | WS_CLIPSIBLINGS);
        return CView::PreCreateWindow(cs);
}

/////////////////////////////////////////////////////////////////////////
// COglView drawing

void COglView::OnDraw(CDC* pDC)
{
        COglDoc* pDoc = GetDocument();
        ASSERT_VALID(pDoc);

        // TODO: add draw code for native data here
}

/////////////////////////////////////////////////////////////////////////
// COglView diagnostics

#ifdef _DEBUG
void COglView::AssertValid() const
{
        CView::AssertValid();
}

void COglView::Dump(CDumpContext& dc) const
{
        CView::Dump(dc);
}

COglDoc* COglView::GetDocument() // non-debug version is inline
{
        ASSERT(m_pDocument->IsKindOf(RUNTIME_CLASS(COglDoc)));
        return (COglDoc*)m_pDocument;
}
#endif //_DEBUG

/////////////////////////////////////////////////////////////////////////
// COglView message handlers

int COglView::OnCreate(LPCREATESTRUCT lpCreateStruct)
{
    if (CView::OnCreate(lpCreateStruct) == -1)
        return -1;
```

```
    // TODO: Add your specialized creation code here
    HDC hDC = ::GetDC(GetSafeHwnd());
    if (InitPixelFormat(hDC) == FALSE)
        return 0;
    m_hglRendContext = wglCreateContext(hDC);
    wglMakeCurrent(hDC, m_hglRendContext);
    return 0;
}

void COglView::OnDestroy()
{
        CView::OnDestroy();
        // TODO: Add your message handler code here
    HGLRC hRC;

    hRC = ::wglGetCurrentContext();
    ::wglMakeCurrent(NULL, NULL);
    if (hRC)
    {
        ::wglDeleteContext(hRC);
    }
}

BOOL COglView::InitPixelFormat(HDC hDC)
{
    PIXELFORMATDESCRIPTOR    PixForDesc;

    InitPFDStruc(&PixForDesc);
    m_pixelformat = ChoosePixelFormat( hDC, &PixForDesc);
    if (m_pixelformat == 0)
    {
        m_pixelformat = 1;
        if (DescribePixelFormat(hDC,  m_pixelformat,
            sizeof(PIXELFORMATDESCRIPTOR), &PixForDesc) == 0)
        {
            return FALSE;
        }
    }
    if (SetPixelFormat(hDC, m_pixelformat, &PixForDesc) == FALSE)
    {
        return FALSE;
    }
    return TRUE;
}

void COglView::InitPFDStruc(PIXELFORMATDESCRIPTOR *ppfd)
{
    memset(ppfd, 0, sizeof(PIXELFORMATDESCRIPTOR));

    ppfd->nSize = sizeof(PIXELFORMATDESCRIPTOR);
```

```
        ppfd->nVersion = 1;
        ppfd->dwFlags = PFD_DRAW_TO_WINDOW |
                        PFD_SUPPORT_OPENGL |
                        PFD_DOUBLEBUFFER;

        ppfd->iPixelType = PFD_TYPE_RGBA;
        ppfd->cColorBits = 24;
        ppfd->cDepthBits = 16;
        ppfd->iLayerType = PFD_MAIN_PLANE;

}

void COglView::OnPaint()
{
    CPaintDC dc(this); // device context for painting

    // TODO: Add your message handler code here
    glEnable( GL_DEPTH_TEST );
    glClear( GL_COLOR_BUFFER_BIT | GL_DEPTH_BUFFER_BIT);
    glMatrixMode( GL_MODELVIEW );
    glLoadIdentity();

    glTranslated( 0.0, 0.0, -9.0 );
    glRotated( theta, 1.0, 0.0, 0.0 ); // Spin along the X axis
// The next two lines can be uncommented to see rotation along Y and Z axis
//  glRotated( theta, 0.0, 1.0, 0.0 ); // Spin along the Y axis
//  glRotated( theta, 0.0, 0.0, 1.0 ); // Spin along the Z axis


    glPushMatrix();
// Commented-out lines can be uncommented to see rotation along X and Z axis
//      glRotated( theta, 1.0, 0.0, 0.0); // Spin along the X axis
        glRotated( theta, 0.0, 1.0, 0.0); // Spin along the Y axis
//      glRotated( theta, 0.0, 0.0, 1.0); // Spin along the Z axis

        glTranslated( 0.0, 0.05, 0.0 ); // Translate only along the Y axis
        DrawBox(0.5f, 0.5f, 0.5f);
    glPopMatrix();

    DrawBox(1.0f, 0.30f, 0.25f);
    glFlush();
    SwapBuffers( wglGetCurrentDC() );
        // Do not call CView::OnPaint() for painting messages
}

void COglView::OnSize(UINT nType, int cx, int cy)
{
    CView::OnSize(nType, cx, cy);

    // TODO: Add your message handler code here
```

```
        glViewport(0, 0, cx, cy);
        if (cy == 0)
        {
            cy = 1;
        }
        glMatrixMode(GL_PROJECTION);
        glLoadIdentity();
        gluPerspective(30.0f, cx/cy, 1.0, 20.0);
        glMatrixMode(GL_MODELVIEW);
        glLoadIdentity();
        glDrawBuffer(GL_BACK);
}


void COglView::OnMouseMove(UINT nFlags, CPoint point)
{
        // TODO: Add your message handler code here and/or call default

#if 0
    GLfloat *glfTemp;

    glfTemp = clrArray[0];
    for(int j=0; j<7; j++)
    {
        clrArray[j] = clrArray[j+1];
    }
    clrArray[7] = glfTemp;
#endif
    theta += 5.0;
    Invalidate(FALSE);
    CView::OnMouseMove(nFlags, point);
}

void COglView::DrawBox(GLfloat x, GLfloat y, GLfloat z)
{
    glBegin(GL_POLYGON);
        glColor3fv(clrArray[0]);
        glVertex3f(x,y,z);
        glColor3fv(clrArray[1]);
        glVertex3f(-x,y,z);
        glColor3fv(clrArray[2]);
        glVertex3f(-x,-y,z);
        glColor3fv(clrArray[3]);
        glVertex3f(x,-y,z);
    glEnd();
    glBegin(GL_POLYGON);
        glColor3fv(clrArray[4]);
        glVertex3f(x,y,-z);
```

```
        glColor3fv(clrArray[5]);
        glVertex3f(-x,y,-z);
        glColor3fv(clrArray[6]);
        glVertex3f(-x,-y,-z);
        glColor3fv(clrArray[7]);
        glVertex3f(x,-y,-z);
    glEnd();
    glBegin(GL_POLYGON);
        glColor3fv(clrArray[0]);
        glVertex3f(-x,y,z);
        glColor3fv(clrArray[1]);
        glVertex3f(-x,y,-z);
        glColor3fv(clrArray[2]);
        glVertex3f(-x,-y,-z);
        glColor3fv(clrArray[3]);
        glVertex3f(-x,-y,z);
    glEnd();
    glBegin(GL_POLYGON);
        glColor3fv(clrArray[4]);
        glVertex3f(x,y,z);
        glColor3fv(clrArray[5]);
        glVertex3f(x,y,-z);
        glColor3fv(clrArray[6]);
        glVertex3f(x,-y,-z);
        glColor3fv(clrArray[7]);
        glVertex3f(x,-y,z);
    glEnd();
    glBegin(GL_POLYGON);
        glColor3fv(clrArray[0]);
        glVertex3f(x,y,z);
        glColor3fv(clrArray[1]);
        glVertex3f(x,y,-z);
        glColor3fv(clrArray[2]);
        glVertex3f(-x,y,-z);
        glColor3fv(clrArray[3]);
        glVertex3f(-x,y,z);
    glEnd();
    glBegin(GL_POLYGON);
        glColor3fv(clrArray[4]);
        glVertex3f(x,-y,z);
        glColor3fv(clrArray[5]);
        glVertex3f(x,-y,-z);
        glColor3fv(clrArray[6]);
        glVertex3f(-x,-y,-z);
        glColor3fv(clrArray[7]);
        glVertex3f(-x,-y,z);
    glEnd();
}
```

Now that you have seen how to develop OpenGL applications, let's conclude this chapter with how to port an OpenGL application from one environment to another.

PORTING OPENGL APPLICATIONS

As mentioned earlier, the OpenGL standard helps in porting OpenGL applications from one environment to another. If you are porting OpenGL within Windows 2000 environments, you should be able to make your application work by recompiling your OpenGL application source in the new environment (due to implementation differences, your application binaries are not normally portable).

If you are porting from a UNIX (or other) OpenGL environment to Windows 2000 or vice versa, then you have a lot more work to do. A typical OpenGL application will include OpenGL statements, calls to the operating system, calls to the windowing system, and potentially some calls for accessing databases. The OpenGL calls, for the most part, are standard. However, you may have to replace calls to the X Window subsystem in UNIX with equivalent calls to the Windows subsystem (for example, the **glXgetConfig** GLX X Window function may need to be replaced by the equivalent **Describe PixelFormat** function). While most GLX/Xlib functions have an equivalent Windows function, some GLX/Xlib functions are not applicable in a Windows environment (such as **glXlsDirect**) or have no equivalent Windows function (such as **glxWaitGl**). You may need to delete or rewrite functions that have no direct equivalents. You may need similar replacements for the operating system and database access calls.

CONCLUSION

We started with a brief review of OpenGL basics. We then looked at OpenGL data structures, OpenGL functions, and programming examples to draw and transform two-dimensional and three-dimensional objects. We concluded the chapter with a look at porting OpenGL across environments.

In the next chapter we will switch from multimedia to databases and take a look at database access by use of ODBC.

CHAPTER 19

Database Programming Using ODBC

et's look now at another important programming aspect of Windows 2000 that you are likely to use a lot in business programming—accessing databases. Almost all business applications store and retrieve data from databases. Windows 2000 provides two primary ways to access databases—ActiveX Data Objects (ADO) and Open Database Connectivity (ODBC). In this chapter, we will discuss ODBC. (We will look at ADO in Chapter 20.)

We will examine the need for ODBC, review ODBC basics, look at MFC library support for ODBC, review the steps involved in executing an ODBC API application, and see programming examples illustrating ODBC.

WHY ODBC?

Database applications belong to one of three categories: interactive, embedded, and module. *Interactive* database applications are typically ready-made database front-ends that include a GUI and that access a database in response to user queries. A *module* is a stand-alone usage. The most common form for database application development purposes is the *embedded* application, where an application program is developed with programming language statements interspersed with embedded database access statements. The most common language used for embedding is the Structured Query Language (SQL). SQL is a widely accepted standard followed by almost all relational database product vendors. A recent enhancement to the standard addresses the *call level interface (CLI)*. ODBC (also referred to as ODBC/SQL-3 CLI) provides database transparency to your application. As shown in Figure 19-1, your application interfaces with the ODBC driver manager using the same ODBC APIs or ODBC MFC library classes, regardless of which database it is accessing. This architecture permits easy access to heterogeneous databases as long as there is an ODBC driver for them. The databases need not be local to the machine your application is executing on, as indicated by the network connections between the drivers and the databases in Figure 19-1. When the database is on a network, a network library such as NetLib or SQLNet, in addition to the ODBC drivers, is also required to access the data.

Note for UNIX Programmers

You can port Windows applications written to the Win32 API to run on UNIX using porting tools. If you are porting ODBC applications, you have to make sure that you are using the appropriate version of the ODBC driver for the UNIX system you are porting to.

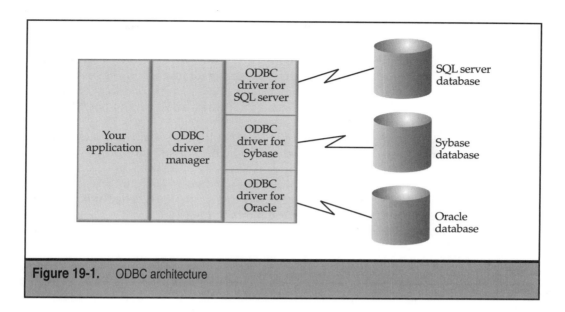

Figure 19-1.   ODBC architecture

ODBC BASICS

An ODBC *data source* is a set of data together with the location of the data, information to access the data, and any intervening network connection. Your ODBC application can access multiple data sources at the same time. Examples of ODBC data sources could be a SQL server on the network or a local access database. Data sources must be registered and configured before they can be accessed by ODBC applications, and this function is typically performed by the ODBC administrator. See the programming example later in this chapter for more details about the ODBC administrator.

Your application must first establish a *connection* with the data source, and all communication with the data source is through that connection. You terminate the connection after you have finished accessing the data source. Besides being able to access multiple data sources at the same time, you can also have multiple connections at any given time to one data source.

Visual C++ includes ODBC drivers for a number of Microsoft databases, including SQL Server, Access, and FoxPro. Visual C++ also includes ODBC drivers for Microsoft's other products, such as Excel, and non-Microsoft databases, such as dBASE and Paradox. ODBC drivers are available from other vendors, too. When you connect to an ODBC data source using an ODBC driver, your application connects to the driver, which in turn connects to the ODBC data source. Typically the ODBC driver performs a translation from the format in which it receives the application's request to the format suitable for the target database. However, ODBC level 2 supports a *pass-through* function whereby the application request is sent to the target database without format translation.

ODBC data sources can be updated in *transaction* mode. In this mode, a series of updates to the ODBC data source can be bunched together so that either they are all performed *(commit transactions),* or none of the updates is performed *(rollback transactions).* This feature is useful to synchronize data across data sources. Many, but not all, ODBC data sources support transaction mode processing.

When you are updating data in a data source that could be accessed by multiple users, you may want to ensure that the integrity of the data in the data source is preserved by using *locking,* which prevents simultaneous update access by more than one user.

You can either access records from a data source a record at a time or access multiple records with one call. Accessing multiple records with a single call is called *bulk row fetching* (see the "Bulk Row Fetching" section later in this chapter).

Now that we have a basic understanding of what ODBC is, let's look at some advantages and disadvantages of using ODBC compared with direct SQL access, which are summarized in Table 19-1.

TIP: Both 16- and 32-bit ODBC drivers are available. Make sure that you use the 32-bit version when you are developing 32-bit applications for Windows 2000.

ODBC Advantages	ODBC Disadvantages
Transparent access to a variety of databases.	Small degradation in performance compared with invoking SQL directly, due to translation by the ODBC drivers.
No precompilation step required (unlike embedded SQL).	Vendor SQL extensions not supported at ODBC level 1. Some extensions may be accessed in ODBC level 2 using pass-through.
Besides SQL statements, your application can also initiate the execution of other database functions, such as stored procedures.	Absence of precompilation makes it difficult to detect or enforce coding standards.

Table 19-1. Advantages and Disadvantages of ODBC

MFC AND ODBC

MFC database classes let your application access data from any ODBC source database for which an ODBC driver is available. MFC provides the following classes for developing ODBC applications:

▼ CDatabase

■ CRecordset

■ CFieldExchange

■ CRecordView

■ CLongBinary

▲ CDBException

Let's look at these classes in detail.

CDatabase

A **CDatabase** class is derived from **CObject** and is used to construct a **CDatabase** object. The **CDatabase** object represents the connection between your application and the ODBC data source through which all interactions occur. The **CDatabase** class provides member functions to open and close the ODBC data source as well as to perform transactions. The important member functions of **CDatabase** are summarized in Table 19-2.

CRecordset

You typically derive an application-specific recordset class from the **CRecordset** class to create a **CRecordset** object, which is a set of records selected from an ODBC data source. There are two types of recordsets: *dynasets* and *snapshots*. A dynaset is a recordset where the data reflects updates made to the record by your application or other applications. For example, when you scroll to a record in a dynaset, it reflects changes made to the record after the recordset was created. A snapshot is a static view of the data as of the time the recordset was created and is not updated. You can specify the type of recordset you want in the **Open** member function.

With either type of recordset, you can perform functions such as scrolling, filtering, and sorting of the records in the recordset. The important member functions of **CRecordset** are summarized in Table 19-3.

Recordset Locking

To ensure that updates to the ODBC data source are coordinated between multiple users of the data source, you can use *locking*. The typical update sequence is to use the **Edit** member function of **CRecordset** to get the data, update the desired fields, and use the **Update** member function to update the data. You can choose between two types of locking—*optimistic*

CDatabase Member Function	Description
Open	This opens a database connection after a database object is constructed and before recordsets are constructed.
OpenEx	This is a more general version of Open supporting more options.
Close	This closes a connection. Close does not destroy the CDatabase object, which can be reused for another connection to the same or even a different ODBC data source. You have to close associated recordsets before closing the connection.
BeginTrans	This starts a new transaction. The data source must support transaction processing. You can check if your driver supports transactions for a given database using the CanTransact member function. BeginTrans may lock data records in the data source. A transaction consists of one or more calls to the AddNew, Edit, Delete, and Update member functions of a CRecordset object (see the "CRecordset" section).
CommitTrans	This commits updates of the current transaction.
Rollback	This cancels updates of the current transaction.
ExecuteSQL	This executes a SQL statement. You normally would retrieve and update data in the data source using recordset objects. However, there may be a need to execute some SQL statements directly. You use ExecuteSQL for such purposes. ExecuteSQL does not return any data.

Table 19-2. CDatabase Member Functions

and *pessimistic*. In optimistic locking mode, the lock is placed only for the **Update** call. In pessimistic locking mode, the lock is placed when the **Edit** member function is called, and the lock remains in place (affecting other potential users) until the **Update** member function is called. While the lock duration in optimistic mode is much shorter than in pessimistic mode, your application has to account for the possibility that some other application may apply a lock between the time your application called the **Edit** member function and called the **Update** member function. You can choose between the two locking modes using the **SetLockingMode** member function.

CRecordset Member Function	Description
AddNew	This prepares a new record using the recordset's field data members. The record's fields are initially set to NULL. After assigning values, call the Update member function (see Update member function in this table). You cannot use this member function in bulk row fetching.
Edit	This edits field data member values for existing records.
Update	This commits new records after AddNew or existing records after Edit.
Delete	This deletes a record.

Table 19-3. CRecordset Member Functions

Consistent with the MFC design, the MFC library doesn't support all the functionality of the native APIs. You can call ODBC and ADO APIs directly from your MFC applications for functionality not supported by the MFC library (just as you can directly call any Win32 APIs). One such example would be the ODBC catalog functions, such as **::SQLTables**.

Bulk Row Fetching

Bulk row fetching lets multiple records be retrieved during a single fetch. You have to derive a class from the **CRecordset** class to implement bulk row fetching. The number of records you want to retrieve with a single fetch is specified as a parameter of the **SetRowsetSize** member function. You must also set the **CRecordset::useMultiRowFetch** option in the *dwOptions* parameter of the **Open** member function. Bulk row fetching uses *bulk record field exchange* to transfer data between the data source and the recordset. Bulk record field exchange uses arrays to store the multiple rows of data. You can assign the memory buffers to hold the multiple data rows, or the buffers can be allocated automatically. You assign the buffers by specifying the **CRecordset::user AllocMultiRowBuffers** option. **CRecordset** does not include a member function for bulk row data updates. If you want to update bulk row data, you have to use ODBC APIs directly. In addition, ClassWizard does not support bulk record field exchange. This implies that you must declare field data members and override **DoBulkFieldExchange**. Repositioning within records retrieved using bulk row fetching is by rowset.

CFieldExchange

The **CFieldExchange** class supports the record field exchange (RFX) and bulk record field exchange (bulk RFX) routines. You will not normally use this class unless you are implementing bulk row fetching or writing custom RFX routines. The member functions provided by **CFieldExchange** are **IsFieldType**, which helps determine whether the current operation can be performed on a particular field or parameter, and **SetFieldType**, which specifies the type of access for a parameter or column as input, output, and so on.

CRecordView

A **CRecordView** object enables the records from an ODBC data source to be displayed in controls of a dialog box. **CRecordView** uses dialog data exchange (DDX) and record field exchange (RFX) to automate the movement of data between the controls and the fields of the recordset. The **CRecordView** class is commonly created with the AppWizard, which also creates an associated **CRecordset** class. You can also create the **CRecordView** class using ClassWizard.

CLongBinary

The **CLongBinary** class is used in constructing a **CLongBinary** object. A **CLongBinary** object can be used if you are working with *binary large objects (BLOBs)*. A common example of a BLOB is a bitmap. If you want to store a BLOB as a field in a table row, declare a field data member of type **CLongBinary** in your recordset class. Once the **CLongBinary** object is constructed and ready to use, RFX queries the data source for the size of the binary large object, allocates storage, and stores an HGLOBAL handle to the data in the **m_hData** data member of the **CLongBinary** object. RFX also stores the actual size of the data object in the **m_dwDataLength** data member of the **CLongBinary** object.

CDBException

The **CDBException** class includes the **m_nRetCode** data member that contains an ODBC return code in case of an exception. The data member **m_strError** contains an alphanumeric string that has the error description. You can also throw **CDBException** objects from your code with the **AfxThrowDBException** global function.

ODBC Application Using ODBC APIs

The sequence of steps followed by an ODBC application using ODBC APIs are summarized here:

1. Allocate the environment, connection, and statement handles using **SQLAllocHandle**. Allocating the environment handle initializes the ODBC call-level interface, and this function must be called before any other ODBC call is made. Allocating the connection handle causes memory to be allocated

for the connection. Allocating a statement handle provides access to statement information, such as the cursor name, error messages, and SQL status information. The ODBC driver is then loaded and connected to the ODBC data source. You can access multiple ODBC data sources in your application, and you can create multiple connections to the same data source as long as the ODBC driver supports these functions. Also, if the driver is thread safe (that is, if the driver is capable of being invoked by multiple simultaneous threads), you can pass the environment, connection, and statement handles across different threads in your application.

2. Perform application processing such as requesting recordsets, managing transactions, or submitting SQL statements.

3. Receive results of requests from the ODBC data source such as recordsets and responses to SQL queries.

4. Process the received results. This may result in requesting additional recordsets or submitting additional SQL statements.

5. When you are done processing, free the environment, connection, and statement handles using **SQLFreeHandle**.

ODBC PROGRAMMING EXAMPLE

The *MyPhone* sample shown here provides a graphical interface for a Microsoft Access database that contains a list of names, phone numbers, and comments. This sample uses the document/view architecture and is created by use of the AppWizard. It also uses the MFC library database classes based on ODBC, which significantly reduces the complexity of the application. In later samples, this application will be extended to give the ability to add and delete the records in the database. The example shows the records from the database accessed and displayed on a dialog box. You can navigate through the records in the database using the Next Record, Previous Record, First Record, and Last Record menu selections or icons. Figure 19-2 shows the first record in the database when the example program starts execution.

Note that the First Record and Previous Record icons are grayed out, indicating that the record shown is the first record. You can also add and delete records to the database using the Add and Delete options in the Record pull-down menu. When you select Add, the example program clears all the entry fields in the dialog box, as shown in Figure 19-3.

The MFC library database classes are based on ODBC, and thus they provide access to any database so long as an ODBC driver is available for that database. The application based on ODBC can access data from many different data formats and different local and remote configurations, thereby elevating the application above the details of the database.

The database for this sample application consists of four columns: first and last names, phone number, and a comment. The first step is to register the database that will be used, with an ODBC data source name. This data source name will be referred to by

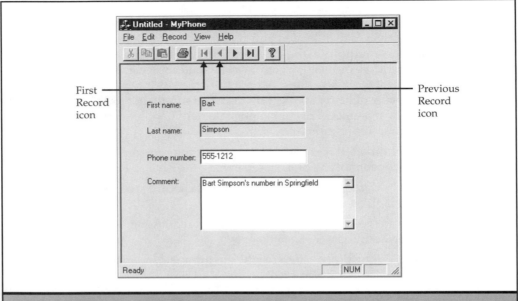

Figure 19-2. Displaying records from the database

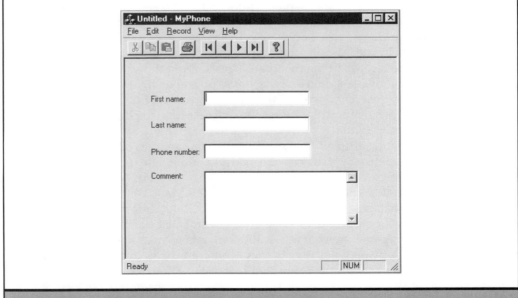

Figure 19-3. Adding a record clears the dialog box fields

the sample application. This registration is done by use of the ODBC Data Source Administrator tool . This tool is available by selecting Control Panel | Administrative Tools | Data Sources(ODBC) from the Start menu. Alternatively, the database can also be registered by a custom-written application. To register the data source using ODBC:

1. Select Start | Settings | Control Panel | Administrative Tools | Data Sources(ODBC). This will bring up the ODBC Data Source Administrator window.

2. Go to the User DSN page, and click the Add button to add the new data source. The database that will be added is a Microsoft Access database.

3. Select Microsoft Access Driver and click Finish in the Create New Data Source dialog box. This will bring up the ODBC Microsoft Access Setup window.

4. Type in **Phone Directory** as the data source name, and add descriptive text for the data source name.

5. In the Database group box, click Select and provide the database name, which is **PhoneList.mdb**. (Make sure the fully qualified filename is provided. It may make it easier to navigate through the directories and locate the database file.)

6. Click OK on all the dialog boxes to exit the ODBC Data Source Administrator.

Figure 19-4 shows the ODBC Data Source Administrator menu after registration is complete and the Phone Directory has been added.

The procedure to create this application through the AppWizard is as follows:

1. Start the Microsoft Visual C++ and select New from the File menu to create a new project.

2. Click the Projects tab, and select MFC AppWizard (exe) as the project type.

3. Type in the project name as **MyPhone** and click OK. The AppWizard creates the project directory, and the MFC AppWizard—Step 1 dialog box appears.

4. Make this application a single document application by clicking the Single Document radio button, and then click Next to go to the Step 2 Of 6 dialog box.

5. Click Database View Without File Support, and then click the Data Source... button.

6. In the Database Options dialog box, click the ODBC radio button and select the Phone Directory. Registering the database in the earlier step resulted in the availability of the data source. Clicking OK will bring up the Select Database Tables dialog box.

7. Select the *PhoneBook* table and click OK. This will bring you back to the Step 2 Of 6 dialog box.

8. On the rest of the pages select Next to accept the defaults. (In the last page, the filenames can be changed if needed. To illustrate this, the **CMyPhoneView**

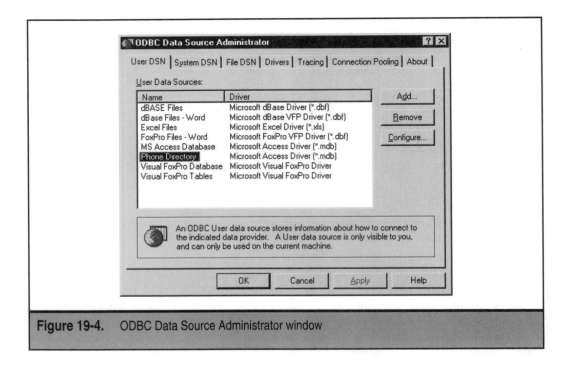

Figure 19-4. ODBC Data Source Administrator window

class name is changed to **CMyPhoneForm**, and the files, both header and implementation, are renamed from the default *MyPhoneView* to *MyPhoneForm*.) When the Finish button is clicked, the AppWizard will create the files related to the project.

Shown next is the standard application class derived from the **CWinApp** class. The only significant code to notice here is the registration of the application's document template with the framework. This document template serves as the connection between document, frame window, and view. This module also has the code to process the About dialog box.

```
// MyPhone.h : main header file for the MYPHONE application
//
#if !defined(AFX_MYPHONE_H)
#define AFX_MYPHONE_H

#if _MSC_VER >= 1000
#pragma once
#endif // _MSC_VER >= 1000

#ifndef __AFXWIN_H__
    #error include 'stdafx.h' before including this file for PCH
#endif
```

```
#include "resource.h"          // main symbols

/////////////////////////////////////////////
// CMyPhoneApp:
// See MyPhone.cpp for the implementation of this class
//

class CMyPhoneApp : public CWinApp
{
public:
    CMyPhoneApp();

// Overrides
    // ClassWizard generated virtual function overrides
    //{{AFX_VIRTUAL(CMyPhoneApp)
    public:
    virtual BOOL InitInstance();
    //}}AFX_VIRTUAL

// Implementation

    //{{AFX_MSG(CMyPhoneApp)
    afx_msg void OnAppAbout();
        // NOTE - the ClassWizard will add and remove member functions here.
        //    DO NOT EDIT what you see in these blocks of generated code!
    //}}AFX_MSG
    DECLARE_MESSAGE_MAP()
};

//{{AFX_INSERT_LOCATION}}
#endif

// MyPhone.cpp : Defines the class behaviors for the application.
//

#include "stdafx.h"
#include "MyPhone.h"

#include "MainFrm.h"
#include "MyPhoneSet.h"
#include "MyPhoneDoc.h"
#include "MyPhoneForm.h"

#ifdef _DEBUG
#define new DEBUG_NEW
#undef THIS_FILE
static char THIS_FILE[] = __FILE__;

#endif
```

```
//////////////////////////////////////////////
// CMyPhoneApp

BEGIN_MESSAGE_MAP(CMyPhoneApp, CWinApp)
    //{{AFX_MSG_MAP(CMyPhoneApp)
    ON_COMMAND(ID_APP_ABOUT, OnAppAbout)
        // NOTE - the ClassWizard will add and remove mapping macros here.
        //    DO NOT EDIT what you see in these blocks of generated code!
    //}}AFX_MSG_MAP
    // Standard print setup command
    ON_COMMAND(ID_FILE_PRINT_SETUP, CWinApp::OnFilePrintSetup)
END_MESSAGE_MAP()

//////////////////////////////////////////////
// CMyPhoneApp construction

CMyPhoneApp::CMyPhoneApp()
{
    // TODO: add construction code here,
    // Place all significant initialization in InitInstance
}

//////////////////////////////////////////////
// The one and only CMyPhoneApp object

CMyPhoneApp theApp;

//////////////////////////////////////////////
// CMyPhoneApp initialization

BOOL CMyPhoneApp::InitInstance()
{
    AfxEnableControlContainer();

#ifdef _AFXDLL
    Enable3dControls();
#else
    Enable3dControlsStatic();
#endif

// Change the registry key under which our settings are stored.
// You should modify this string to be something appropriate
// such as the name of your company or organization.
    SetRegistryKey(_T("Local AppWizard-Generated Applications"));
    LoadStdProfileSettings();

    CSingleDocTemplate* pDocTemplate;
    pDocTemplate = new CSingleDocTemplate(
        IDR_MAINFRAME,
        RUNTIME_CLASS(CMyPhoneDoc),
```

```
        RUNTIME_CLASS(CMainFrame),          // main SDI frame window
        RUNTIME_CLASS(CMyPhoneForm));
    AddDocTemplate(pDocTemplate);

    CCommandLineInfo cmdInfo;
    ParseCommandLine(cmdInfo);

    // Dispatch commands specified on the command line
    if (!ProcessShellCommand(cmdInfo))
        return FALSE;

    // The one and only window has been initialized,
    // so show and update it.
    m_pMainWnd->ShowWindow(SW_SHOW);
    m_pMainWnd->UpdateWindow();

    return TRUE;
}

/////////////////////////////////////////////////
// CAboutDlg dialog used for App About

class CAboutDlg : public CDialog
{
public:
    CAboutDlg();

// Dialog Data
    //{{AFX_DATA(CAboutDlg)
    enum { IDD = IDD_ABOUTBOX };
    //}}AFX_DATA

    // ClassWizard generated virtual function overrides
    //{{AFX_VIRTUAL(CAboutDlg)
    protected:
    virtual void DoDataExchange(CDataExchange* pDX);    // DDX/DDV support
    //}}AFX_VIRTUAL

// Implementation
protected:
    //{{AFX_MSG(CAboutDlg)
        // No message handlers
    //}}AFX_MSG
    DECLARE_MESSAGE_MAP()
};

CAboutDlg::CAboutDlg() : CDialog(CAboutDlg::IDD)
{
    //{{AFX_DATA_INIT(CAboutDlg)
    //}}AFX_DATA_INIT
```

```
}

void CAboutDlg::DoDataExchange(CDataExchange* pDX)
{
    CDialog::DoDataExchange(pDX);
    //{{AFX_DATA_MAP(CAboutDlg)
    //}}AFX_DATA_MAP
}

BEGIN_MESSAGE_MAP(CAboutDlg, CDialog)
    //{{AFX_MSG_MAP(CAboutDlg)
        // No message handlers
    //}}AFX_MSG_MAP
END_MESSAGE_MAP()

// App command to run the dialog
void CMyPhoneApp::OnAppAbout()
{
    CAboutDlg aboutDlg;
    aboutDlg.DoModal();
}
```

Shown next is the code for the **CMyPhoneDoc** class, which is derived from the **CDocument** class of the framework. This is pretty much boilerplate code. Just notice the member data **m_myPhoneSet**. In a typical application the document stores the data and serializes it to a file, reading all the data into memory once and writing it back to disk. But in the database application the data is stored in the database and is commonly viewed one record at a time. So instead of serializing the data, the document encapsulates the recordset object. The recordset object **m_myPhoneSet** is encapsulated in the document and is automatically constructed when the document object is constructed, and deleted when the document object is deleted. This sample has only one recordset related to the phone list, so we have only one recordset object. The document can encapsulate more than one recordset object if the application has more than one recordset. Thus, the document acts as a proxy or front-end for the database.

```
// MyPhoneDoc.h : interface of the CMyPhoneDoc class
//
#if !defined(AFX_MYPHONEDOC_H)
#define AFX_MYPHONEDOC_H

#if _MSC_VER >= 1000
#prama once
#endif // _MSC_VER >= 1000
#include "MyPhoneSet.h"


class CMyPhoneDoc : public CDocument
{
protected: // create from serialization only
```

```
        CMyPhoneDoc();
        DECLARE_DYNCREATE(CMyPhoneDoc)

// Attributes
public:
        CMyPhoneSet m_myPhoneSet;

// Operations
public:

// Overrides
        // ClassWizard generated virtual function overrides
        //{{AFX_VIRTUAL(CMyPhoneDoc)
        public:
        virtual BOOL OnNewDocument();
        //}}AFX_VIRTUAL

// Implementation
public:
        virtual ~CMyPhoneDoc();
#ifdef _DEBUG
        virtual void AssertValid() const;
        virtual void Dump(CDumpContext& dc) const;
#endif

protected:

// Generated message map functions
protected:
        //{{AFX_MSG(CMyPhoneDoc)
                // NOTE - the ClassWizard will add and remove member functions here.
                //      DO NOT EDIT what you see in these blocks of generated code!
        //}}AFX_MSG
        DECLARE_MESSAGE_MAP()
};


#endif

// MyPhoneDoc.cpp : implementation of the CMyPhoneDoc class
//
#include "stdafx.h"
#include "MyPhone.h"
#include "MyPhoneSet.h"
#include "MyPhoneDoc.h"

#ifdef _DEBUG
#define new DEBUG_NEW
#undef THIS_FILE
static char THIS_FILE[] = __FILE__;
```

```
#endif

/////////////////////////////////////////////
// CMyPhoneDoc

IMPLEMENT_DYNCREATE(CMyPhoneDoc, CDocument)

BEGIN_MESSAGE_MAP(CMyPhoneDoc, CDocument)
    //{{AFX_MSG_MAP(CMyPhoneDoc)
        // NOTE - the ClassWizard will add and remove mapping macros here.
        //    DO NOT EDIT what you see in these blocks of generated code!
    //}}AFX_MSG_MAP
END_MESSAGE_MAP()

/////////////////////////////////////////////
// CMyPhoneDoc construction/destruction

CMyPhoneDoc::CMyPhoneDoc()
{
    // TODO: add one-time construction code here
}

CMyPhoneDoc::~CMyPhoneDoc()
{
}

BOOL CMyPhoneDoc::OnNewDocument()
{
    if (!CDocument::OnNewDocument())
        return FALSE;
    // TODO: add reinitialization code here
    // (SDI documents will reuse this document)

    return TRUE;
}
/////////////////////////////////////////////
// CMyPhoneDoc diagnostics
#ifdef _DEBUG
void CMyPhoneDoc::AssertValid() const
{
    CDocument::AssertValid();
}

void CMyPhoneDoc::Dump(CDumpContext& dc) const
{
    CDocument::Dump(dc);
}
#endif //_DEBUG
```

Shown next are the **CMyPhoneSet** class-related modules. This class deals with the set of records selected from the database known as recordsets. Notice that the application-specific recordset, **CMyPhoneSet** class, is derived from **CRecordset**, which is typical. Recordsets select records from a data source, and these records can be scrolled through and updated if needed. A filter can also be specified to selectively retrieve the records from the data source. The records in the recordset can be sorted, and the recordset can be parameterized to customize its selection with information not known until run time.

In the **CMyPhoneSet** class, notice that the columns of the phone book table appear as member variables. The AppWizard has bound all of the columns in the table to member variables in this class. These member variables are called *field data members*. The names for these member variables, as you can see, are automatically assigned by AppWizard. It also assigns the correct C++ or class library data type to them according to the column type. As expected, they are mapped to the **CString** type. Though AppWizard creates these automatically, not all columns need to be exposed to the user. Fields that need not be exposed can be removed from this list. This customization can be done through the ClassWizard.

To use a recordset, the ClassWizard constructs a recordset object and calls the **Open** member function to run the recordset's query and select the records. When this process is completed, the recordset is closed and the object is destroyed. In the following example these processes are triggered by the framework. The **GetDefaultConnect** member function, which is overridden here automatically by the ClassWizard, is called by the framework to get the default connect string for the data source on which the recordset is based. The ClassWizard implements this function by identifying the same data source that was identified to the ClassWizard to get information about tables and columns. The other member function that is overridden here is **GetDefaultSQL**, which is also called by the framework to get the default SQL statement on which the recordset is based. The default SQL statement was indirectly defined by the ClassWizard when the recordset class was declared with it. The data exchange between the recordset and the data source is achieved by the **DoFieldExchange** member function. The framework calls this member function to automatically exchange data between the field data members of the recordset object and the corresponding columns of the current record on the data source.

```
// MyPhoneSet.h : interface of the CMyPhoneSet class
//
#if !defined(AFX_MYPHONESET_H)
#define AFX_MYPHONESET_H

#if _MSC_VER >= 1000
#pragma once
#endif // _MSC_VER >= 1000

class CMyPhoneSet : public CRecordset
{
public:
    CMyPhoneSet(CDatabase* pDatabase = NULL);
```

```
        DECLARE_DYNAMIC(CMyPhoneSet)

// Field/Param Data
    //{{AFX_FIELD(CMyPhoneSet, CRecordset)
    CString     m_FirstName;
    CString     m_LastName;
    CString     m_Phone;
    CString     m_Notes;
    //}}AFX_FIELD

// Overrides
    // ClassWizard generated virtual function overrides
    //{{AFX_VIRTUAL(CMyPhoneSet)
    public:
    virtual CString GetDefaultConnect();    // Default connection string
    virtual CString GetDefaultSQL();      // default SQL for Recordset
    virtual void DoFieldExchange(CFieldExchange* pFX);    // RFX support
    //}}AFX_VIRTUAL

// Implementation
#ifdef _DEBUG
    virtual void AssertValid() const;
    virtual void Dump(CDumpContext& dc) const;
#endif

};

#endif

// MyPhoneSet.cpp : implementation of the CMyPhoneSet class
//

#include "stdafx.h"
#include "MyPhone.h"
#include "MyPhoneSet.h"

#ifdef _DEBUG
#define new DEBUG_NEW
#undef THIS_FILE
static char THIS_FILE[] = __FILE__;
#endif

/////////////////////////////////////////////////
// CMyPhoneSet implementation

IMPLEMENT_DYNAMIC(CMyPhoneSet, CRecordset)

CMyPhoneSet::CMyPhoneSet(CDatabase* pdb)
```

```
        : CRecordset(pdb)
{
    //{{AFX_FIELD_INIT(CMyPhoneSet)
    m_FirstName = _T("");
    m_LastName = _T("");
    m_Phone = _T("");
    m_Notes = _T("");
    m_nFields = 4;
    //}}AFX_FIELD_INIT
    m_nDefaultType = snapshot;
}

CString CMyPhoneSet::GetDefaultConnect()
{
    return _T("ODBC;DSN=Phone Directory");
}

CString CMyPhoneSet::GetDefaultSQL()
{
    return _T("[PhoneBook]");
}

void CMyPhoneSet::DoFieldExchange(CFieldExchange* pFX)
{
    //{{AFX_FIELD_MAP(CMyPhoneSet)
    pFX->SetFieldType(CFieldExchange::outputColumn);
    RFX_Text(pFX, _T("[FirstName]"), m_FirstName);
    RFX_Text(pFX, _T("[LastName]"), m_LastName);
    RFX_Text(pFX, _T("[Phone]"), m_Phone);
    RFX_Text(pFX, _T("[Notes]"), m_Notes);
    //}}AFX_FIELD_MAP
}

/////////////////////////////////////////////////
// CMyPhoneSet diagnostics

#ifdef _DEBUG
void CMyPhoneSet::AssertValid() const
{
    CRecordset::AssertValid();
}

void CMyPhoneSet::Dump(CDumpContext& dc) const
{
    CRecordset::Dump(dc);
}
#endif //_DEBUG
```

Discussed next are the procedures to create the form that displays the phone numbers and how to bind the controls on the dialog box to the recordset fields. In ResourceView, the MyPhone folder is expanded and then the Dialog folder is expanded. IDD_MYPHONE_ FORM is opened by double-clicking it. The default static control that says "TODO: Place form controls on this dialog" is selected and deleted. Four pairs of static controls and edit controls are created, one each for First name, Last name, Phone number, and Comment. They are named IDC_FIRSTNAME, IDC_LASTNAME, IDC_PHONENUMBER, and IDC_ NOTES. The style for the First name and Last name edit controls is set to read-only. The resource file is saved. The next step is to bind the controls to the recordset fields to indicate which control maps to which column in the table. This is done by use of the ClassWizard's "foreign object" mechanism. Typically ClassWizard binds controls in a dialog box or form to member variables of the class derived from **CDialog** or **CFormView**. In the case of **CRecordView**, the controls are bound to data members of the recordset class associated with the record view. In this case the class derived from **CRecordView**, **CMyPhoneForm**, has a data member for **CMyPhoneSet**. The control bindings go through **m_pSet** to the corresponding field data members of **CMyPhoneSet**.

To bind a control in the dialog box to a recordset data member, the CTRL key is held down and the left mouse button (in right-handed button configuration) is double-clicked on the control in the dialog box. The ClassWizard's Add Member Variable dialog box appears with a proposed field name selected. This proposed name is accepted. All the controls in the dialog box are bound and the work is saved.

The **CMyPhoneForm** class-related code is shown next:

```
// MyPhoneForm.h : interface of the CMyPhoneForm class
//

#if !defined(AFX_MYPHONEFORM_H)
#define AFX_MYPHONEFORM_H

#if _MSC_VER >= 1000
#pragma once
#endif // _MSC_VER >= 1000

class CMyPhoneSet;

class CMyPhoneForm : public CRecordView
{
protected: // create from serialization only


    CMyPhoneForm();
    DECLARE_DYNCREATE(CMyPhoneForm)

public:
    //{{AFX_DATA(CMyPhoneForm)
    enum { IDD = IDD_MYPHONE_FORM };
    CEdit    m_ctlLastName;
```

```cpp
    CEdit     m_ctlFirstName;
    CMyPhoneSet* m_pSet;
    //}}AFX_DATA

// Attributes
public:
    CMyPhoneDoc* GetDocument();

// Operations
public:

// Overrides
    // ClassWizard generated virtual function overrides
    //{{AFX_VIRTUAL(CMyPhoneForm)
    public:
    virtual CRecordset* OnGetRecordset();
    virtual BOOL PreCreateWindow(CREATESTRUCT& cs);
    virtual BOOL OnMove(UINT nIDMoveCommand);
    protected:
    virtual void DoDataExchange(CDataExchange* pDX);    // DDX/DDV support
    virtual void OnInitialUpdate(); // called first time after construct
    virtual BOOL OnPreparePrinting(CPrintInfo* pInfo);
    virtual void OnBeginPrinting(CDC* pDC, CPrintInfo* pInfo);
    virtual void OnEndPrinting(CDC* pDC, CPrintInfo* pInfo);
    //}}AFX_VIRTUAL

// Implementation
public:


    virtual ~CMyPhoneForm();
#ifdef _DEBUG
    virtual void AssertValid() const;
    virtual void Dump(CDumpContext& dc) const;
#endif

protected:

// Generated message map functions
protected:


  //{{AFX_MSG(CMyPhoneForm)
  //}}AFX_MSG
    DECLARE_MESSAGE_MAP()
};

#ifndef _DEBUG  // debug version in MyPhoneForm.cpp
```

```
inline CMyPhoneDoc* CMyPhoneForm::GetDocument()
   { return (CMyPhoneDoc*)m_pDocument; }
#endif


/////////////////////////////////////////////

#endif //

// MyPhoneForm.cpp : implementation of the CMyPhoneForm class
//

#include "stdafx.h"
#include "MyPhone.h"

#include "MyPhoneSet.h"
#include "MyPhoneDoc.h"
#include "MyPhoneForm.h"

#ifdef _DEBUG
#define new DEBUG_NEW
#undef THIS_FILE
static char THIS_FILE[] = __FILE__;
#endif


/////////////////////////////////////////////


// CMyPhoneForm



IMPLEMENT_DYNCREATE(CMyPhoneForm, CRecordView)


BEGIN_MESSAGE_MAP(CMyPhoneForm, CRecordView)
    //{{AFX_MSG_MAP(CMyPhoneForm)
    //}}AFX_MSG_MAP
    // Standard printing commands
    ON_COMMAND(ID_FILE_PRINT, CRecordView::OnFilePrint)
    ON_COMMAND(ID_FILE_PRINT_DIRECT, CRecordView::OnFilePrint)
    ON_COMMAND(ID_FILE_PRINT_PREVIEW, CRecordView::OnFilePrintPreview)
END_MESSAGE_MAP()

/////////////////////////////////////////////
// CMyPhoneForm construction/destruction
```

```
CMyPhoneForm::CMyPhoneForm()
     : CRecordView(CMyPhoneForm::IDD)
{
    //{{AFX_DATA_INIT(CMyPhoneForm)
    m_pSet = NULL;
    //}}AFX_DATA_INIT
    // TODO: add construction code here
}


CMyPhoneForm::~CMyPhoneForm()


{
}

void CMyPhoneForm::DoDataExchange(CDataExchange* pDX)
{
    CRecordView::DoDataExchange(pDX);
    //{{AFX_DATA_MAP(CMyPhoneForm)
    DDX_Control(pDX, IDC_LASTNAME, m_ctlLastName);
    DDX_Control(pDX, IDC_FIRSTNAME, m_ctlFirstName);
    DDX_FieldText(pDX, IDC_FIRSTNAME, m_pSet->m_FirstName, m_pSet);
    DDX_FieldText(pDX, IDC_LASTNAME, m_pSet->m_LastName, m_pSet);
    DDX_FieldText(pDX, IDC_PHONENUMBER, m_pSet->m_Phone, m_pSet);
    DDX_FieldText(pDX, IDC_NOTES, m_pSet->m_Notes, m_pSet);
    //}}AFX_DATA_MAP
}


BOOL CMyPhoneForm::PreCreateWindow(CREATESTRUCT& cs)
{
    // TODO: Modify the Window class or styles here by modifying
    //   the CREATESTRUCT cs
    return CRecordView::PreCreateWindow(cs);
}


void CMyPhoneForm::OnInitialUpdate()
{
    m_pSet = &GetDocument()->m_myPhoneSet;
    m_pSet->m_strSort="FirstName"; // sort by first name
    CRecordView::OnInitialUpdate();
}


/////////////////////////////////////////////////////
// CMyPhoneForm printing

BOOL CMyPhoneForm::OnPreparePrinting(CPrintInfo* pInfo)
{
    // default preparation
    return DoPreparePrinting(pInfo);
}
```

```
void CMyPhoneForm::OnBeginPrinting(CDC* /*pDC*/, CPrintInfo* /*pInfo*/)
{
    // TODO: add extra initialization before printing
}

void CMyPhoneForm::OnEndPrinting(CDC* /*pDC*/, CPrintInfo* /*pInfo*/)
{
    // TODO: add cleanup after printing
}

/////////////////////////////////////////////////
// CMyPhoneForm diagnostics

#ifdef _DEBUG
void CMyPhoneForm::AssertValid() const
{
    CRecordView::AssertValid();
}

void CMyPhoneForm::Dump(CDumpContext& dc) const
{
    CRecordView::Dump(dc);
}

CMyPhoneDoc* CMyPhoneForm::GetDocument() // non-debug version is inline
{
    ASSERT(m_pDocument->IsKindOf(RUNTIME_CLASS(CMyPhoneDoc)));
    return (CMyPhoneDoc*)m_pDocument;
}
#endif //_DEBUG

/////////////////////////////////////////////////
// CMyPhoneForm database support
CRecordset* CMyPhoneForm::OnGetRecordset()
{
    return m_pSet;
}


/////////////////////////////////////////////////
// CMyPhoneForm message handlers

BOOL CMyPhoneForm::OnMove(UINT nIDMoveCommand)
{
    // TODO: Add your specialized code here and/or call the base class
    return CRecordView::OnMove(nIDMoveCommand);
}
```

The **OnInitialUpdate** member function that is overridden here is called by the framework after the view is attached to the document but before the view is initially displayed. When this is called, the sort order for the recordset is set by setting the **m_strSort** data member of the recordset. The string that appears in the SQL **ORDER BY** clause is set here. In this sample the records are sorted by the **FirstName** column. Later, when the **Open** member function of the recordset class is called, the records are retrieved and sorted by this column. Also notice that the **OnGetRecordset** member function is overridden here. This function should be overridden, and a recordset object or a pointer to a recordset object should be returned. Since this sample uses the ClassWizard, **OnGetRecordSet** is automatically overridden and the pointer to the recordset is returned.

At this stage, take a look at the **CRecordView** class implementation file, *Dbview.cpp*, that is shipped with Visual C++. When the user navigates through the records, the framework calls the **OnMove** member function, whose default implementation is shown in the *Dbview.cpp* file. If anything special needs to be done in response to scrolling of the record, it can be done here in the **OnMove** overridden function. This sample does not do any special processing but simply uses the default processing. The **OnMove** member function first gets the recordset from the application and checks if the record needs to be updated. If so, it collects the data from the dialog box and then updates the data to the database by calling the **Update** member function of the **CRecordset** class. Before a record is updated, the **Edit** member function of the **CRecordset** class should be called to allow changes to the current record. If a new record is added, then the **AddNew** member function of **CRecordset** should be called before calling the **Update** member function. The **Update** member function updates the record. Only those fields that are changed are updated. The record is then moved after proper boundary checking. The move can be done forward, backward, to the first record, to the last record, and to the *n*th record relative to the current one by calling a variety of move-related member functions in the **CRecordset** class like **MoveNext**, **MovePrev**, **MoveFirst**, **MoveLast**, and **Move**. Helper functions like **IsEOF** and **IsBOF** help in determining the boundaries. Based on the original design, SQL provided only forward scrolling, but ODBC extends scrolling capabilities. However, the available level of scrolling support depends on the ODBC driver that is used by the application.

Earlier you saw how to implement sorting of the record by setting the **m_strSort** member data in the **CRecordset** class. A similar feature is also available to filter the records so that only a certain set of records is selected according to the filter. This is achieved by setting the **m_strFilter** member data in the **CRecordset** class. This is set to the contents of the SQL **WHERE** clause. For example, to locate the phone numbers of all the Johns, the filter can be set to

```
m_pSet->m_strFilter = "Firstname = 'John'";
```

This filter is also useful for joining tables, in which case the filter would be set as follows, where Table1 and Table2 are two tables and Column1 and Column2 are columns in Table1 and Table2 that are to be joined:

```
m_pSet->m_strFilter = "Table1.Column1=Table2.Column2";
```

Most of the functions that are needed for this simple sample program are done by default by the framework, and this sample does not need to bother about doing them. If an application is written without using AppWizard, then it should perform all these steps. By now you can see the advantages of using the AppWizard and ClassWizard for simple applications.

The preceding sample lets the user view the database and update an existing phone number or notes. The next example extends this sample to add a new record to the database. Since there is no change in the database schema, the changes to be made are very simple and are limited to the **CMyPhoneForm** class. The changes to the **CMyPhoneForm** class in *Myphoneform.h* and *MYphoneform.cpp* are highlighted in the following code:

```cpp
// MyPhoneForm.h : interface of the CMyPhoneForm class
//

#if !defined(AFX_MYPHONEFORM_H)
#define AFX_MYPHONEFORM_H

#if _MSC_VER >= 1000
#pragma once
#endif // _MSC_VER >= 1000

class CMyPhoneSet;


class CMyPhoneForm : public CRecordView
{
protected: // create from serialization only
    CMyPhoneForm();
    DECLARE_DYNCREATE(CMyPhoneForm)

public:
    //{{AFX_DATA(CMyPhoneForm)
    enum { IDD = IDD_MYPHONE_FORM };
    CEdit       m_ctlLastName;
    CEdit       m_ctlFirstName;
    CMyPhoneSet* m_pSet;
    //}}AFX_DATA

// Attributes
public:
    CMyPhoneDoc* GetDocument();

// Operations
public:

// Overrides
    // ClassWizard generated virtual function overrides
    //{{AFX_VIRTUAL(CMyPhoneForm)
```

```
    public:
    virtual CRecordset* OnGetRecordset();
    virtual BOOL PreCreateWindow(CREATESTRUCT& cs);
    virtual BOOL OnMove(UINT nIDMoveCommand);
    protected:
    virtual void DoDataExchange(CDataExchange* pDX);    // DDX/DDV support
    virtual void OnInitialUpdate(); // called first time after construct
    virtual BOOL OnPreparePrinting(CPrintInfo* pInfo);
    virtual void OnBeginPrinting(CDC* pDC, CPrintInfo* pInfo);
    virtual void OnEndPrinting(CDC* pDC, CPrintInfo* pInfo);
    //}}AFX_VIRTUAL

// Implementation
public:
    virtual ~CMyPhoneForm();
#ifdef _DEBUG
    virtual void AssertValid() const;
    virtual void Dump(CDumpContext& dc) const;
#endif

protected:
    BOOL m_bAddMode;

// Generated message map functions
protected:

    //{{AFX_MSG(CMyPhoneForm)
    afx_msg void OnRecordAdd();
    //}}AFX_MSG
    DECLARE_MESSAGE_MAP()
};

#ifndef _DEBUG  // debug version in MyPhoneForm.cpp
inline CMyPhoneDoc* CMyPhoneForm::GetDocument()
    { return (CMyPhoneDoc*)m_pDocument; }
#endif

#endif

// MyPhoneForm.cpp : implementation of the CMyPhoneForm class
//

#include "stdafx.h"
#include "MyPhone.h"

#include "MyPhoneSet.h"
#include "MyPhoneDoc.h"
#include "MyPhoneForm.h"
```

```
#ifdef _DEBUG
#define new DEBUG_NEW
#undef THIS_FILE
static char THIS_FILE[] = __FILE__;
#endif

/////////////////////////////////////////////////

// CMyPhoneForm

IMPLEMENT_DYNCREATE(CMyPhoneForm, CRecordView)

BEGIN_MESSAGE_MAP(CMyPhoneForm, CRecordView)
    //{{AFX_MSG_MAP(CMyPhoneForm)
    ON_COMMAND(ID_RECORD_ADD, OnRecordAdd)
    //}}AFX_MSG_MAP
    // Standard printing commands
    ON_COMMAND(ID_FILE_PRINT, CRecordView::OnFilePrint)
    ON_COMMAND(ID_FILE_PRINT_DIRECT, CRecordView::OnFilePrint)
    ON_COMMAND(ID_FILE_PRINT_PREVIEW, CRecordView::OnFilePrintPreview)
END_MESSAGE_MAP()

/////////////////////////////////////////////////
// CMyPhoneForm construction/destruction


CMyPhoneForm::CMyPhoneForm()
    : CRecordView(CMyPhoneForm::IDD)
{
    //{{AFX_DATA_INIT(CMyPhoneForm)
    m_pSet = NULL;
    //}}AFX_DATA_INIT
    // TODO: add construction code here
    m_bAddMode=FALSE;
}


CMyPhoneForm::~CMyPhoneForm()
{
}

void CMyPhoneForm::DoDataExchange(CDataExchange* pDX)
{
    CRecordView::DoDataExchange(pDX);
    //{{AFX_DATA_MAP(CMyPhoneForm)
    DDX_Control(pDX, IDC_LASTNAME, m_ctlLastName);
    DDX_Control(pDX, IDC_FIRSTNAME, m_ctlFirstName);
    DDX_FieldText(pDX, IDC_FIRSTNAME, m_pSet->m_FirstName, m_pSet);
    DDX_FieldText(pDX, IDC_LASTNAME, m_pSet->m_LastName, m_pSet);
```

```
        DDX_FieldText(pDX, IDC_PHONENUMBER, m_pSet->m_Phone, m_pSet);
        DDX_FieldText(pDX, IDC_NOTES, m_pSet->m_Notes, m_pSet);
        //}}AFX_DATA_MAP
}

BOOL CMyPhoneForm::PreCreateWindow(CREATESTRUCT& cs)
{
        // TODO: Modify the Window class or styles here by modifying
        //  the CREATESTRUCT cs

        return CRecordView::PreCreateWindow(cs);
}

void CMyPhoneForm::OnInitialUpdate()
{
        m_pSet = &GetDocument()->m_myPhoneSet;
        m_pSet->m_strSort="FirstName"; // sort by first name
        CRecordView::OnInitialUpdate();
}

/////////////////////////////////////////////////
// CMyPhoneForm printing

BOOL CMyPhoneForm::OnPreparePrinting(CPrintInfo* pInfo)
{
        // default preparation
        return DoPreparePrinting(pInfo);
}

void CMyPhoneForm::OnBeginPrinting(CDC* /*pDC*/, CPrintInfo* /*pInfo*/)
{
        // TODO: add extra initialization before printing
}

void CMyPhoneForm::OnEndPrinting(CDC* /*pDC*/, CPrintInfo* /*pInfo*/)
{
        // TODO: add cleanup after printing
}

/////////////////////////////////////////////////
// CMyPhoneForm diagnostics

#ifdef _DEBUG
void CMyPhoneForm::AssertValid() const
{
        CRecordView::AssertValid();
}

void CMyPhoneForm::Dump(CDumpContext& dc) const
```

```
{
    CRecordView::Dump(dc);
}

CMyPhoneDoc* CMyPhoneForm::GetDocument() // non-debug version is inline
{
    ASSERT(m_pDocument->IsKindOf(RUNTIME_CLASS(CMyPhoneDoc)));
    return (CMyPhoneDoc*)m_pDocument;
}
#endif //_DEBUG

/////////////////////////////////////////////////
// CMyPhoneForm database support
CRecordset* CMyPhoneForm::OnGetRecordset()
{
    return m_pSet;
}


/////////////////////////////////////////////////
// CMyPhoneForm message handlers

    void CMyPhoneForm::OnRecordAdd()
    {
    // TODO: Add your command handler code here
    if (m_bAddMode) {
    OnMove(ID_RECORD_FIRST);
    }
    m_pSet->AddNew();
    m_pSet->SetFieldNull(NULL, FALSE);
    m_pSet->SetFieldNull(NULL, FALSE);
    m_bAddMode=TRUE;
    m_ctlFirstName.SetReadOnly(FALSE);
    m_ctlLastName.SetReadOnly(FALSE);
    UpdateData(FALSE);
}

BOOL CMyPhoneForm::OnMove(UINT nIDMoveCommand)
{
    // TODO: Add your specialized code here and/or call the base class
    if (m_bAddMode) {
        if (!UpdateData()) {
            return FALSE;
        }
        try {
            m_pSet->Update();
        } catch (CDBException e) {
            AfxMessageBox(e.m_strError);
            return FALSE;
```

```
        }
        m_pSet->Requery();
        UpdateData(FALSE);
        m_ctlFirstName.SetReadOnly(TRUE);
        m_ctlLastName.SetReadOnly(TRUE);
        m_bAddMode=FALSE;
        return TRUE;
    } else {
        return CRecordView::OnMove(nIDMoveCommand);
    }
}
```

To add a new phone number, select Add from the Record pull-down menu. This transforms the application to add mode. In add mode, all fields including the first name and last name can be entered, unlike in view mode, where only the phone number and the notes can be updated. A state flag, **m_bAddMode**, maintains the current mode of the application. The Add menu command is handled by the **OnRecordAdd** member function. To add a new record, the **AddNew** member function is first called. This does the preparation work for adding a new record to the table. The fields in the record are initially set to NULL fields. This should be followed by a call to the **Update** member function to save the record to the data source. This call is done in the **OnMove** member function, which is called when the user navigates to a different record. When **OnMove** is called, it calls **UpdateData** to set the values of the new record's field data members. The **Update** member function is later called to save the record. Note that only after calling the **Update** member function is the data stored. If **Update** is not called, the new record will be lost. The **Requery** member function is called to refresh the recordset. Optionally the **AddNew** call can be placed within a transaction if the database supports transactions.

The next example takes the preceding sample and extends the functionality to provide the Delete and Refresh capabilities. Here again the changes are made only to the **CMyPhoneForm** class. Shown next is the additional code to implement the **OnRecordDelete** and **OnRecordRefresh** member functions. Since the header file is very similar to the earlier header file except for the addition of two new member functions, it is not shown.

```
BEGIN_MESSAGE_MAP(CMyPhoneForm, CRecordView)
    //{{AFX_MSG_MAP(CMyPhoneForm)
    ON_COMMAND(ID_RECORD_ADD, OnRecordAdd)
    ON_COMMAND(ID_RECORD_DELETE, OnRecordDelete)
    ON_COMMAND(ID_RECORD_REFRESH, OnRecordRefresh)
    //}}AFX_MSG_MAP
    // Standard printing commands
    ON_COMMAND(ID_FILE_PRINT, CRecordView::OnFilePrint)
    ON_COMMAND(ID_FILE_PRINT_DIRECT, CRecordView::OnFilePrint)
    ON_COMMAND(ID_FILE_PRINT_PREVIEW, CRecordView::OnFilePrintPreview)
END_MESSAGE_MAP()
```

```
void CMyPhoneForm::OnRecordDelete()
{
    // TODO: Add your command handler code here
    try {
        m_pSet->Delete();
    } catch (CDBException e) {
        AfxMessageBox(e.m_strError);
        return;
    }

    m_pSet->MoveNext();

    if (m_pSet->IsEOF()) {
        m_pSet->MoveLast();
    }
    if (m_pSet->IsBOF()) {
        m_pSet->SetFieldNull(NULL);
    }
    UpdateData(FALSE);
}



void CMyPhoneForm::OnRecordRefresh()
{
    // TODO: Add your command handler code here
    m_pSet->Requery();
    m_ctlFirstName.SetReadOnly(TRUE);
    m_ctlLastName.SetReadOnly(TRUE);
    m_bAddMode=FALSE;
    UpdateData(FALSE);
}
```

The **OnRecordDelete** member function is called when the Delete menu item is selected. This function deletes the current record displayed on the screen by calling the **Delete** member function. The **Delete** member function deletes the current record from the open recordset object. After successful deletion, the field data members are set to a NULL value, and an explicit call to one of the recordset navigation member functions must be made. Here the code calls the **MoveNext** member function and checks the boundary to adjust for the current record appropriately. Unlike **AddNew**, **Delete** has no corresponding **Update** call, since it immediately marks the record as deleted both in the recordset and on the data source. In the sample, notice that if the record that was deleted is scrolled back, the fields are shown as <Deleted>. Looking at the *Dbview.cpp* module, which is shipped with Visual C++, would make this immediately clear. If the record is deleted, the code in *Dbview.cpp* displays the string "<Deleted>". Another way to handle this is to check if the record is deleted by calling the **IsDeleted** member function while scrolling through the records and to jump over the deleted records. The recordset can also be refreshed by calling the **Requery** member function. To refresh the records, this sample provides another menu item called Refresh.

The **OnRecordRefresh** member function is called when the Refresh menu item is selected. This function refreshes the recordset, which moves the current record to the beginning of the recordset. The refresh is done by calling the **Requery** member function. **Requery** rebuilds the recordset, and if records are returned, the first record is made the current record. If the data source can be accessed by multiple users, then the recordset should be refreshed by calling **Requery** to reflect the change to the data source.

This sample can easily be extended to search for a specific record. For example, if it needs to search for the phone number given the first name, then a filter can be added before getting the recordset. The filter can be set as discussed previously in the **m_strFilter** member data.

CONCLUSION

Quite often the ODBC application that you develop needs to be distributed and run in a number of environments. When you are distributing your ODBC applications, you have to ensure that the environment that will run your application uses the same ODBC driver, ODBC administrator functions, and so on that you have used for your application to work successfully in the other environment.

We looked at the need for ODBC, reviewed ODBC basics, looked at MFC library support for ODBC, reviewed the steps involved in executing an ODBC API application, and looked at a programming example illustrating ODBC.

Chapter 20 looks at how you can use a similar mechanism—ADO—and compares ODBC and ADO.

CHAPTER 20

Database Programming Using ADO

A ctiveX Data Objects (ADO) is part of the Microsoft's Universal Data Access strategy as well as part of Microsoft Data Access Components (MDAC). ADO simplifies data access programming by exposing data from an underlying OLE DB provider. The most commonly used OLE DB provider is the OLE DB Provider for ODBC Drivers, which exposes ODBC Data sources to ADO. ADO is a language-neutral object model, which means it can be used with a number of different programming mechanisms, including Visual Basic, Visual C++, and others.

Note that the earlier edition of this book covered DAO. Since that time, DAO has been deemphasized by Microsoft as a data access mechanism, and hence DAO has been dropped and has been replaced by ADO.

ADO OBJECTS

ADO is made up of seven objects (Connection, Command, Recordset, Parameters, Properties, Fields, and Errors as shown in Figure 20-1.

The top-level objects (Connection, Command, and Recordset) are objects that you can create and destroy independent of other objects. The lower-level objects (Field, Error, and Property) exist only within the context of their parent objects. That is, you cannot independently create these objects. As far the Parameter object, you can create the Parameter object independent of its parent, the Command object. However, it must be associated with a command object before you can use it.

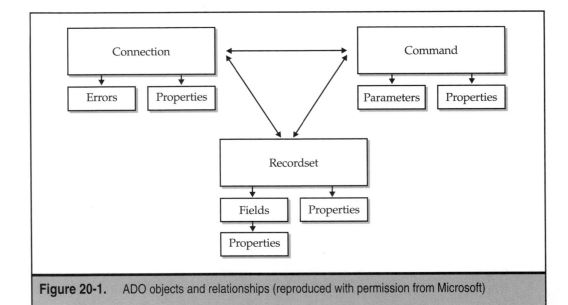

Figure 20-1.   ADO objects and relationships (reproduced with permission from Microsoft)

An ADO application uses the Connection object to establish connections with a database, the Command object to issue commands such as queries and updates to the database, and the Recordset object to view and manipulate the data returned from the database. Let us look at each of the objects.

Recordset Objects

Recordset objects are used to hold the results of executing commands such as retrieving data from a data source. Executing queries on a data source can result in one of the following:

▼   Generation of a Recordset object. For example, executing a single SELECT statement may generate a Recordset object.

■   Generation of multiple Recordset objects. For example, executing a batch of SELECT statements or a stored procedure may generate more than one Recordset object.

▲   No Recordset objects are generated. For example, executing data definition language queries will not generate Recordset objects.

If a command, such as SELECT, generates rows, a default Recordset object will be generated and returned. This may be sufficient for some purposes. However, sometimes you may want to create a new Recordset object if you want a more complex Recordset object. If you create your own Recordset object, you must bind it to the Connection, and then open the cursor and retrieve data.

Cursors

When you retrieve and update data, you do so through a relative position in the data source called the *cursor*. ADO defines four cursor types, as shown in Table 20-1.

Cursor Type	Description
Dynamic cursor	Allows you to view additions, changes, and deletions by other users.
Keyset cursor	Similar to a dynamic cursor, except that only data changes by other users are visible. You cannot view records that other users add or access records that other users delete.

Table 20-1.   Cursor Types and Descriptions

Cursor Type	Description
Static cursor	Additions, changes, or deletions by other users are not visible. Provides a static copy of a set of records that you can use to find data or generate reports. This is the only type of cursor allowed when you open a client-side Recordset object.
Forward-only cursor	Additions, changes, or deletions by other users are not visible. Allows only scrolling forward through the Recordset. This improves performance in situations where you need to make only a single forward pass through a Recordset.

Table 20-2.   Cursor Types and Descriptions *(continued)*

You can set the Cursor type prior to opening the Recordset. Alternatively, you can pass a **CursorType** argument with the **Open** method. Support for cursor types depends on the data source providers. If you do not specify a cursor type, the default cursor that ADO uses is the forward-only cursor.

Connection Objects

You gain access from your application to a data source through a *connection*. Connection objects are used to establish connection sessions with data sources. Connection objects provide a mechanism for initializing and establishing the connection, executing queries and transactions. The **Open** method is used to establish a connection. The State property is used to determine the current state of the connection.

Command Objects

A command is issued across an established connection to retrieve, add, delete, or update data in a data source. The command language used with the Command object is dependent on the underlying provider for the data source. For relational databases, the command language is generally SQL. If the data source is not a relational database, SQL statements may not be supported by the data source. For this reason, the command object is optional.

The Command object opens a new connection or reuses an existing connection depending on what you specify in the ActiveConnection property. If you set the ActiveConnection property and point to a Connection object, the Command object uses the existing connection from the Connection object. If you specify the ActiveConnection property with a connection string, a new connection is established for the Command object. The same Connection object can be used by more than one Command object.

You use the CommandText property to specify the query string. A query string can be a standard SQL statement, such as SELECT, INSERT, DELETE, or UPDATE, or a DDL statement, such as CREATE or DROP. A query string can also be the name of a stored procedure or table.

Command Parameters

Parameter objects represent parameters associated with commands or the input/output arguments and the return values of stored procedures. Parameters are used to alter some behavior of the command by changing some aspects of the working of the command.

Error Objects

Operation involving ADO objects can generate one or more errors. Note that error objects are typically created as a result of errors detected by providers such as database providers. ADO, itself, may detect other errors, which may be detected at run time and communicated to your application using regular run-time exception handling mechanisms.

ADOR and ADODB Objects

The ADOR library is a lightweight client that allows the manipulation of an existing recordset on the client. It does not include the server-side objects such as Connection, Command, Error, or Parameters. The ADOR functionality is distributed with the ADO client components.

The ADODB library contains server-side objects such as Connection, Command, Error, and Parameters. These objects are typically used within server-side components to communicate with the database.

Remote Data Service (RDS) for ADO

RDS for ADO is used to transport ActiveX Data Object recordsets from a server to a client computer. Once transported, the resulting recordset can be cached on the client computer and the client can be disconnected from the server. Caching recordsets cuts down the traffic between the client and the server. RDS uses a subset of the ADO Object model, the ADOR.Recordset, to provide a low-overhead, high-performance way to marshal recordset data over a network or the Web.

ADO, RDO, AND DAO

As mentioned earlier, Microsoft's preferred data access method is ADO, which supercedes DAO and RDO. It is for this reason that the chapter on DAO in the previous edition of this book has been replaced with a chapter on ADO. What if you have developed applications using DAO or RDO? Microsoft provides a 200-page migration guide to migrate DAO applications to ADO. This guide, titled "Migrating from DAO to ADO: Using ADO with the Microsoft Jet Provider," is available on MSDN. MSDN also includes documentation to help with migration from RDO to ADO.

ADO PROGRAMMING CONSIDERATIONS

ADO objects, such as the Recordset object, return data as VARIANT data type. When you use ADO with C++, you have to convert these Variant types returned by the methods to C++ native types. This conversion, besides involving additional coding details, may degrade performance as well. To facilitate this conversion, ADO 2.0 exposes an interface called **IADORecordBinding** that lets you bind a specific field of a Recordset object to a C++ data type. The **BindToRecordset** method of the **IADORecordBinding** interface binds fields to C/C++ variables. The **AddNew** method adds a new row to the bound Recordset object. The **Update** method populates fields in new rows of the Recordset object, or updates fields in existing rows, with the value of the C/C++ variables. The **IADORecordBinding** interface is implemented by the Recordset object.

As mentioned earlier, the Visual C++ Extensions for ADO map fields of a Recordset object to C/C++ variables. A mapping between a field and a variable is called a *binding entry*. Macros provide binding entries for numeric, fixed-length, and variable-length data. These macros are called *binding entry macros*. The binding entries and C/C++ variables are declared in a class derived from the Visual C++ Extensions class, **CADORecordBinding**. The **CADORecordBinding** class is defined internally by the binding entry macros.

You can use ADO functionality with different languages such as Visual Basic, Visual C++, and Visual J++. Keeping in mind that ADO documentation such as the ADO API Reference describes the functionality of the ADO application programming interface (API) using a syntax similar to Microsoft Visual Basic, you should use the ADO for Visual C++ Syntax Indexes, which provide Visual C++ language-specific syntax.

ADO PROGRAMMING EXAMPLE

ADO can be used to manipulate the database in several ways. Of all the methods, **#import** is the most powerful. The next few programming samples show how to use ADO to view, add, update, and delete data in databases. Emphasis is given to manipulating ADO through **#import**. Most of these examples use the Phone Directory access database that was used in Chapter 19. If the Phone Directory data source is not registered, please refer to the ODBC chapter on how to register it.

Microsoft ships a few Office 2000 Developer controls that make the viewing of the database tables very, very easy. The first sample shows how to use two of the Office 2000 Developer controls, Microsoft ADO Data Control, version 6.0 (OLE DB) and Microsoft DataGrid Control, version 6.0 (OLE DB). Using this control, it is really simple to view the contents of a database table. The steps that follow show how to go about creating the project. These steps assume that a data source Phone Directory is already registered.

Using Visual C++ version 6.0, create a dialog-based project. When the AppWizard completes creating the project, it will bring up the dialog box editor and a simple dialog box. Then follow these steps:

1. Go to the Project menu and select the Add To Project menu item. Then select the Components and Controls… submenu item. This will bring up the Components and Controls Gallery dialog box.

2. Double-click Registered ActiveX Controls. This will show all the registered ActiveX controls.

3. Select the Microsoft ADO Data Control, version 6.0 (OLE DB) component and click Insert to insert the control in the project. This will bring up a prompt dialog. Select OK on the prompt dialog.

4. This will bring up the Confirm Classes dialog box. Click OK to accept the default data and to generate all the classes from the ActiveX control.

5. If you now have the dialog box editor controls open, you can see another icon being added to the controls.

6. Repeat the process to add the Microsoft DataGrid Control, version 6.0 (OLE DB). After you add the second control, the Components and Controls Gallery is closed.

7. Back in the dialog box editor, delete the default static text and rearrange the default OK and Cancel buttons to the bottom of the dialog.

8. From the Controls tool box, select the Microsoft DataGrid Control and place it in the dialog box. Place the Microsoft ADO Data Control beneath that.

9. Now that you have the dialog box ready, you next need to set the properties of these controls. To set the property of the ADO Data Control, select it and select the Properties menu item from the View menu (or by using the ALT-ENTER accelerator).

10. This brings up the Properties dialog box for the Microsoft DataGrid control. Go to the Control tab and specify the source for the connection. Select Use ODBC Data Source Name and select the Phone Directory data source. This is the access data source that was earlier registered in the ODBC chapter. Since this data source does not have any authentication, the authentication is skipped. However, if you are selecting some other data source that needs authentication, you can specify it in the Authentication tab.

11. Go to the RecordSource tab and specify the SQL command that this control needs to perform. This sample needs to display all the records from the table. So enter **select * from PhoneBook** in the Command Text (SQL) edit box. The All tab can be used to verify/modify the properties of the control.

12. The next step is to connect this ADO Data control to the DataGrid control. To do this, click the DataGrid control and bring up the Properties panel. Select the Control tab and specify "Phone Directory" as the caption. Select the All tab and click the DataSource property. Select IDC_ADODC1, which is the control ID of the ADO Data control. This indicates that the data source for this DataGrid control is to be derived from the ADO Data control specified by the ID that was selected.

The project can now be saved and built. When the sample is run, it queries the Phone Directory data source and displays all the records from that data source. Notice that during the whole process, we did not add any code to do this. But when you look at the directory, you can tell that a whole lot of code has been generated for you. You can take a look at the code on the accompanying CD-ROM. Figure 20-2 shows the listing of all the records from the Phone Directory data source when the program is run. Figure 20-3 shows the records scrolled using the Microsoft ADO Data Control.

With little additional code, the sample created here can be extended to do a search of a given record. To do this, bring up the resource editor and add sets of static fields and entry fields for first name and last name. Add appropriate member variables for these fields through the ClassWizard to collect the first and last name information. Also add member variables for the ADO Data control and the DataGrid control. Rename the OK button to Search. The sample will bring up all the records from the data source and display in the DataGrid control. The user can specify the first and/or last name; when the Search button is clicked, the DataGrid control will be updated with the records satisfying the search condition. For simplicity the conditions are *and*ed for the search. Figure 20-4 shows how to specify search data, and Figure 20-5 shows the results of the search.

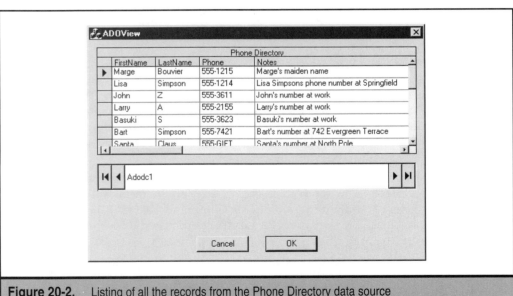

Figure 20-2. Listing of all the records from the Phone Directory data source

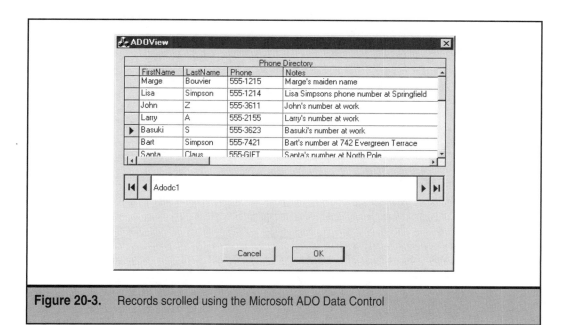

Figure 20-3. Records scrolled using the Microsoft ADO Data Control

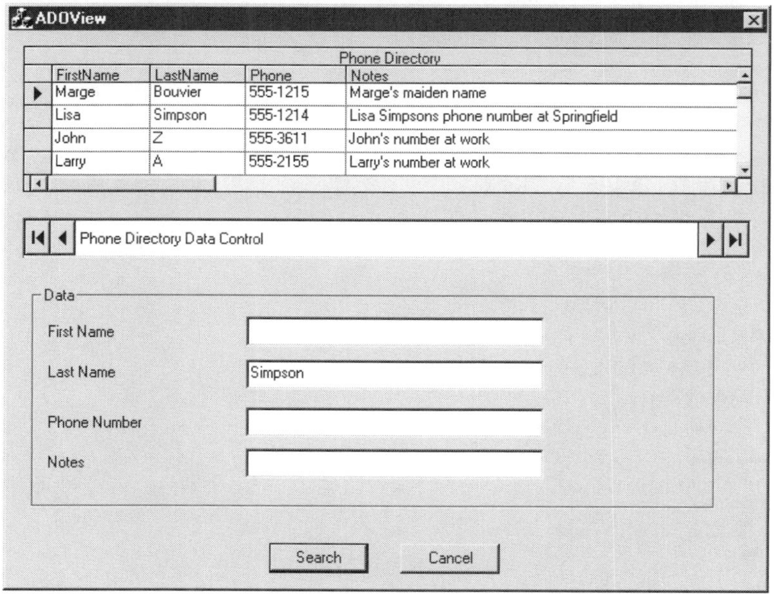

Figure 20-4. Specifying search data

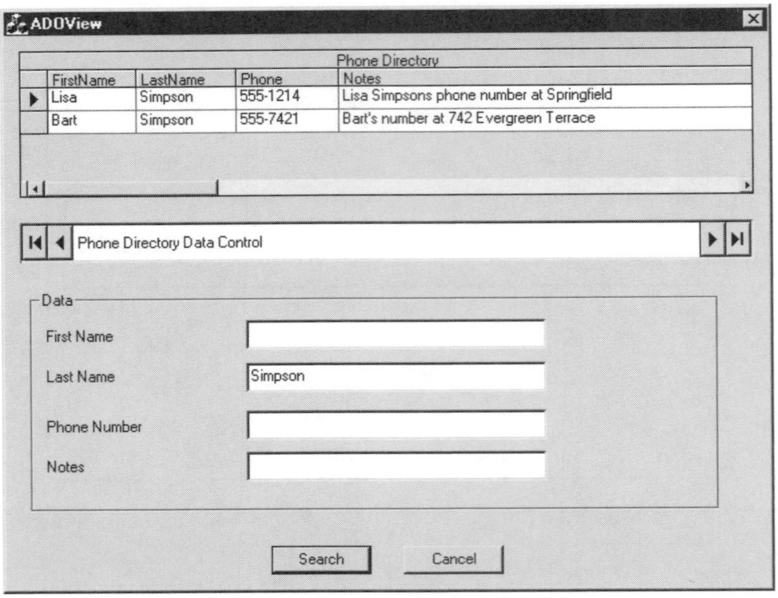

Figure 20-5. Results of the search

The code related to the dialog class, which is the only code that has been modified, is shown next. For the rest of the modules, please look on the CD-ROM in the subdirectory *ADOView2* for this chapter. The *adodc.h* header file contains the ADO Data Control class, and the *datagrid.h* contains the DataGrid Control class.

```
// ADOViewDlg.h : header file
//{{AFX_INCLUDES()
#include "adodc.h"
#include "datagrid.h"
//}}AFX_INCLUDES

#if !defined(AFX_ADOVIEWDLG_H)
#define AFX_ADOVIEWDLG_H

#if _MSC_VER > 1000
#pragma once
#endif // _MSC_VER > 1000

// CADOViewDlg dialog
class CADOViewDlg : public CDialog
```

```
{
// Construction
public:
    CADOViewDlg(CWnd* pParent = NULL);

// Dialog Data
    //{{AFX_DATA(CADOViewDlg)
    enum { IDD = IDD_ADOVIEW_DIALOG };
    CAdodc      m_pddatactrl;
    CDataGrid   m_pdDataGrid;
    CString     m_firstname;
    CString     m_lastname;
    //}}AFX_DATA

    // ClassWizard generated virtual function overrides
    //{{AFX_VIRTUAL(CADOViewDlg)
    protected:
    virtual void DoDataExchange(CDataExchange* pDX);    // DDX/DDV support
    //}}AFX_VIRTUAL

// Implementation
protected:
    HICON m_hIcon;

    // Generated message map functions
    //{{AFX_MSG(CADOViewDlg)
    virtual BOOL OnInitDialog();
    afx_msg void OnPaint();
    afx_msg HCURSOR OnQueryDragIcon();
    afx_msg void OnSearch();
    //}}AFX_MSG
    DECLARE_MESSAGE_MAP()
};

//{{AFX_INSERT_LOCATION}}
#endif // !defined(AFX_ADOVIEWDLG_H)
```

The dialog box class is shown next, with the relevant code shown in boldface:

```
// ADOViewDlg.cpp : implementation file
#include "stdafx.h"
#include "ADOView.h"
#include "ADOViewDlg.h"

#ifdef _DEBUG
#define new DEBUG_NEW
```

```
#undef THIS_FILE
static char THIS_FILE[] = __FILE__;
#endif

// CADOViewDlg dialog

CADOViewDlg::CADOViewDlg(CWnd* pParent /*=NULL*/)
    : CDialog(CADOViewDlg::IDD, pParent)
{
    //{{AFX_DATA_INIT(CADOViewDlg)
    m_firstname = _T("");
    m_lastname = _T("");
    //}}AFX_DATA_INIT
    // Note that LoadIcon does not require a subsequent DestroyIcon in Win32
    m_hIcon = AfxGetApp()->LoadIcon(IDR_MAINFRAME);
}
void CADOViewDlg::DoDataExchange(CDataExchange* pDX)
{
    CDialog::DoDataExchange(pDX);
    //{{AFX_DATA_MAP(CADOViewDlg)
    DDX_Control(pDX, IDC_ADODC1, m_pddatactrl);
    DDX_Control(pDX, IDC_DATAGRID1, m_pdDataGrid);
    DDX_Text(pDX, IDC_FIRSTNAME, m_firstname);
    DDX_Text(pDX, IDC_LASTNAME, m_lastname);
    //}}AFX_DATA_MAP
}

BEGIN_MESSAGE_MAP(CADOViewDlg, CDialog)
    //{{AFX_MSG_MAP(CADOViewDlg)
    ON_WM_PAINT()
    ON_WM_QUERYDRAGICON()
    ON_BN_CLICKED(ID_SEARCH, OnSearch)
    //}}AFX_MSG_MAP
END_MESSAGE_MAP()

// CADOViewDlg message handlers

BOOL CADOViewDlg::OnInitDialog()
{
    CDialog::OnInitDialog();
    SetIcon(m_hIcon, TRUE);
    SetIcon(m_hIcon, FALSE);
    return TRUE;
}
```

```
// If you add a minimize button to your dialog, you will need the code below
//   to draw the icon.  For MFC applications using the document/view model,
//   this is automatically done for you by the framework.

void CADOViewDlg::OnPaint()
{
    if (IsIconic())
    {
        CPaintDC dc(this); // device context for painting

        SendMessage(WM_ICONERASEBKGND, (WPARAM) dc.GetSafeHdc(), 0);

        // Center icon in client rectangle
        int cxIcon = GetSystemMetrics(SM_CXICON);
        int cyIcon = GetSystemMetrics(SM_CYICON);
        CRect rect;
        GetClientRect(&rect);
        int x = (rect.Width() - cxIcon + 1) / 2;
        int y = (rect.Height() - cyIcon + 1) / 2;

        // Draw the icon
        dc.DrawIcon(x, y, m_hIcon);
    }
    else
    {
        CDialog::OnPaint();
    }
}

// The system calls this to obtain the cursor to display while the user drags
//   the minimized window.
HCURSOR CADOViewDlg::OnQueryDragIcon()
{
    return (HCURSOR) m_hIcon;
}
```

When the user clicks the Search button, the data from the dialog box is picked up by calling the **UpdateDate()** method and a SQL statement is created to satisfy the user's query. This new SQL statement is set as the source of the records by calling the **SetRecordSource** method. This sets up the filter for the records, and only those that satisfy the query are available in the adodc control after the **Refresh** method. To have all the records selected, you can leave both the name fields blank.

```
void CADOViewDlg::OnSearch()
{
    UpdateData();
```

```
CString sql("select * from PhoneBook");
if ((m_firstname.GetLength() != 0) && (m_lastname.GetLength() != 0))
{
    sql = sql + " where FirstName=\'" + m_firstname + "'" "and LastName=\'" +
        m_lastname + "'";
}
else if(m_firstname.GetLength() != 0)
{
    sql = sql + " where FirstName=\'" + m_firstname + "'";
}
else if(m_lastname.GetLength() != 0)
{
    sql = sql + " where LastName=\'" + m_lastname + "'";
}
m_pddatactrl.SetRecordSource(sql);
m_pddatactrl.Refresh();
}
```

This same sample can be extended to add, update, and delete records. A peek at the *adodc.h* file will show the method that returns the C_Recordset object, which we can use to manipulate the data in the data source. However, instead of using ADO through these controls, we would next see how to go about programming ADO using the **#import** method, which provides a lot more flexibility.

The next three samples use the same data source but have different interfaces than the one that was discussed earlier. The subdirectory *ADOAdd* contains the sample that allows the user to add a new record to the database. This sample is later extended to update a record and delete a record. These extended samples are available in the subdirectories *ADOUpdate* and *ADODelete* respectively. As we discuss these samples, only the code that is relevant to the discussion is shown. The complete project is available on the CD-ROM. Figure 20-6 shows the screen before adding a new record. Figure 20-7 shows the screen after adding the record. Figure 20-8 shows the screen after refresh with records sorted by last name.

The sample uses the **#import** method of manipulating the ADO using Visual C++. The information from the Microsoft ADO type library is incorporated by using the **#import** directive. This directive would convert the contents of the type library to usable C++ classes, which can be used in the code to manipulate the database. Based on the information in the type library, the directive also generates the definitions for the GUIDs and the enumerated types. It creates a header file and an implementation file that is compiled along with the rest of the user-developed code. In the sample that follows, we import *msado15.dll*; it generates two files, *msado.tlh*, which is the header file, and *msado.thi*, which is the implementation file.

Shown next is the main application class. The only significant code to notice here involves the initialization and termination of OLE. Before manipulating the ADO objects, the code must initialize OLE; it must later uninitialize it during termination. In a dialog-based application like this one, the **InitInstance** method is a convenient place to do

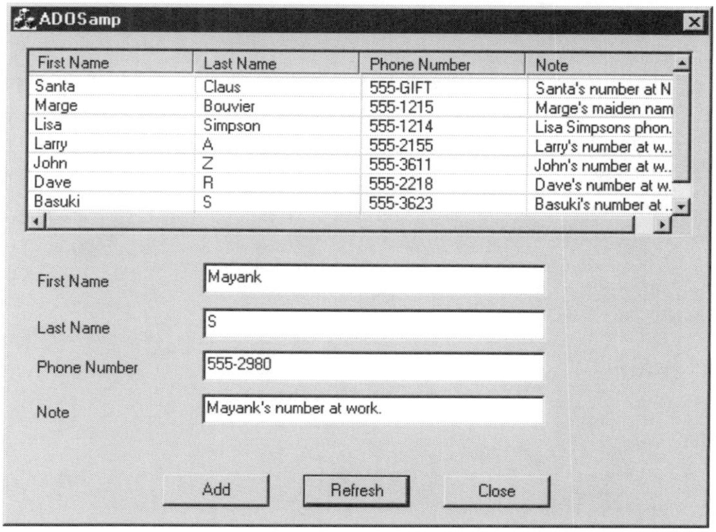

Figure 20-6. Adding a new record

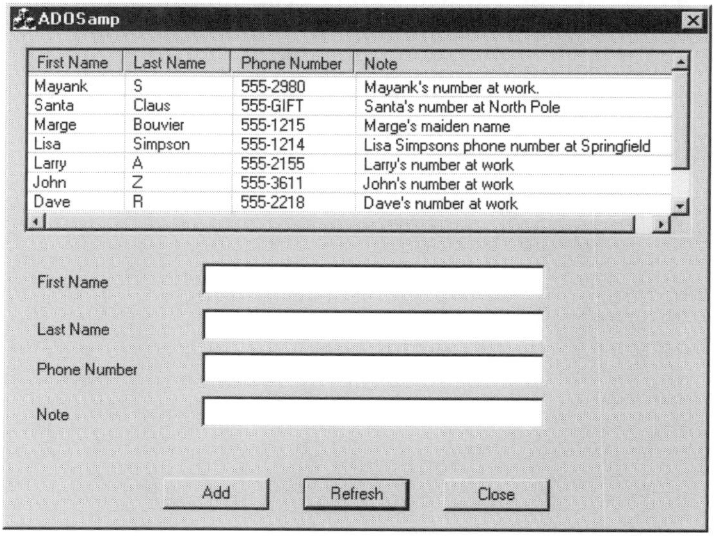

Figure 20-7. Results of adding the record

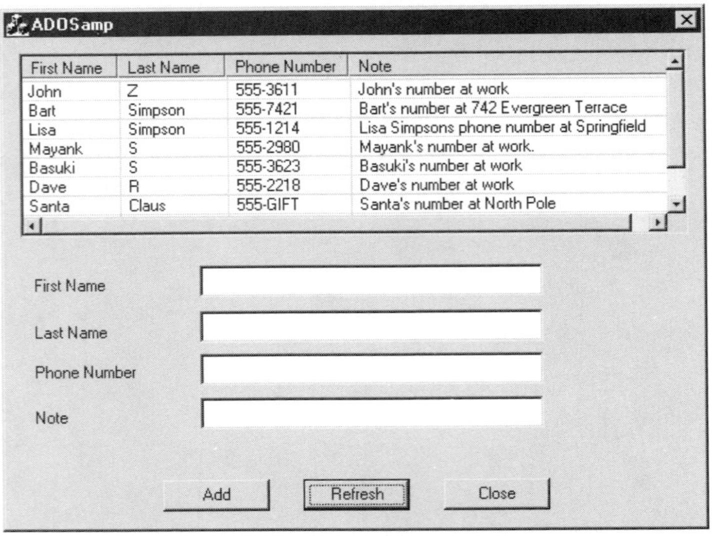
ADOSamp
First Name
Last Name
Phone Number
Note
John
Z
555-3611
John's number at work
Bart
Simpson
555-7421
Bart's number at 742 Evergreen Terrace
Lisa
Simpson
555-1214
Lisa Simpsons phone number at Springfield
Mayank
S
555-2980
Mayank's number at work.
Basuki
S
555-3623
Basuki's number at work
Dave
R
555-2218
Dave's number at work
Santa
Claus
555-GIFT
Santa's number at North Pole
First Name
Last Name
Phone Number
Note
Add
Refresh
Close

Figure 20-8. Refreshed list of records sorted by last name

this. A popular method for initializing and uninitializing OLE involves defining a struct with in-line code to initialize. When the object is destructed during termination, the uninitialize call is automatically made. In a non-dialog-based application or a C-based application, the initialization and termination can be done at other convenient locations. The only thing to remember is to initialize OLE before manipulating the ADO object and to terminate it when it is no longer needed.

```
// ADOSamp.cpp : Defines the class behaviors for the application.

#include "stdafx.h"
#include "ADOSamp.h"
#include "ADOSampDlg.h"

#ifdef _DEBUG
#define new DEBUG_NEW
#undef THIS_FILE
static char THIS_FILE[] = __FILE__;
#endif

/////////////////////////////////////////////////////////////////////////////
// CADOSampApp

BEGIN_MESSAGE_MAP(CADOSampApp, CWinApp)
```

```
    //{{AFX_MSG_MAP(CADOSampApp)
        // NOTE - the ClassWizard will add and remove mapping macros here.
        //    DO NOT EDIT what you see in these blocks of generated code!
    //}}AFX_MSG
    ON_COMMAND(ID_HELP, CWinApp::OnHelp)
END_MESSAGE_MAP()
// CADOSampApp construction
CADOSampApp::CADOSampApp()
{
    // TODO: add construction code here,
    // Place all significant initialization in InitInstance
}

// The one and only CADOSampApp object

CADOSampApp theApp;

// CADOSampApp initialization

BOOL CADOSampApp::InitInstance()
{
    AfxEnableControlContainer();

    // Standard initialization
    // If you are not using these features and wish to reduce the size
    //  of your final executable, you should remove from the following
    //  the specific initialization routines you do not need.

#ifdef _AFXDLL
    Enable3dControls();
#else
    Enable3dControlsStatic();
#endif

    // Initialize and unInitialize OLE
    struct InitOle
    {
        InitOle()
        {
            ::CoInitialize(NULL);
        }
        ~InitOle ()
        {
            ::CoUninitialize();
        }
    } _init_InitOle_;

    CADOSampDlg dlg;
    m_pMainWnd = &dlg;
```

```
    int nResponse = dlg.DoModal();
    if (nResponse == IDOK)
    {
        // TODO: Place code here to handle when the dialog is
        //  dismissed with OK
    }
    else if (nResponse == IDCANCEL)
    {
        // TODO: Place code here to handle when the dialog is
        //  dismissed with Cancel
    }
    return FALSE;
}
```

Shown next is the dialog class, with relevant code in boldface. The application contains a list control where the data retrieved from the database is displayed. It also has four entry fields where the user can enter data for a new record. Member variables for these are defined in the class. The variables related to the ADO objects, the connection to the data store, a pointer to a recordset, and a pointer to a command pointer are also maintained. Instances of these objects are created during the initialization of the dialog box and maintained for use later during various stages of processing.

```
// ADOSampDlg.h : header file

#if !defined(AFX_ADOSAMPDLG_H)
#define AFX_ADOSAMPDLG_H

#if _MSC_VER > 1000
#pragma once
#endif // _MSC_VER > 1000

/////////////////////////////////////////////////////////////////////////
// CADOSampDlg dialog

class CADOSampDlg : public CDialog
{
// Construction
public:
    CADOSampDlg(CWnd* pParent = NULL);

// Dialog Data
    //{{AFX_DATA(CADOSampDlg)
    enum { IDD = IDD_ADOSAMP_DIALOG };
    CListCtrl    m_rslistctrl;
    CString      m_fn;
    CString      m_ln;
    CString      m_note;
    CString      m_pn;
    //}}AFX_DATA
```

```
    // ClassWizard generated virtual function overrides
    //{{AFX_VIRTUAL(CADOSampDlg)
    protected:
    virtual void DoDataExchange(CDataExchange* pDX);    // DDX/DDV support
    //}}AFX_VIRTUAL

// Implementation
protected:
    HICON m_hIcon;

    // Generated message map functions
    //{{AFX_MSG(CADOSampDlg)
    virtual BOOL OnInitDialog();
    afx_msg void OnPaint();
    afx_msg HCURSOR OnQueryDragIcon();
    afx_msg void OnAdd();
    afx_msg void OnRefresh();
    afx_msg void OnClose();
    //}}AFX_MSG
    DECLARE_MESSAGE_MAP()

private:
    void InsertOneItem(LPTSTR szFirstName, LPTSTR szLastName, LPTSTR
szPhoneNumber, LPTSTR szNote);
    _ConnectionPtr pConn;
    _RecordsetPtr pRecordSet;
    _CommandPtr pCmd;
    CPBRecordSet rs;
};
#endif
```

In the preceding class, notice the **CPBRecordSet** variable. This class is defined in *ADOSamp.h* header file, and just that class definition is shown here. ADO objects return the data as VARIANT data types. To deal with these data types in C++, they need to be converted to C++ data types. As you can see, additional code is needed to convert the data from VARIANT to C++ native types. Luckily, the Visual C++ Extensions for ADO provide interfaces for retrieving data into native C/C++ data types without going through a VARIANT data type. They also provide preprocessor macros that simplify using these interfaces.

To bind the fields in a recordset to a C/C++ variable, a class, which is derived from **CADORecordBinding**, is created. Two macros, **BEGIN_ADO_BINDING** and **END_ADO_BINDING** are used to contain the mapping of the VARIANT type to the C/C++ native type. For each field that needs to be mapped, an appropriate binding macro is used. Since we have variable-length data, the **ADO_VARIABLE_LENGTHENTRY2** macro is used. The first parameter is a one-based index of the field in the recordset that is being mapped. Next comes an enumerated data type that corresponds to the OLE DB type. The value of the field in the recordset will be converted to this OLE DB type if necessary.

This is followed with a name of the C/C++ variable, which in our sample is a character array, and its size.

A flag follows that holds the status to indicate the validity of the contents of the buffer. During data conversion, for example retrieving a record, the program should check this status variable before processing the data provided in the buffer. Conversely, when adding/updating a record, the program should set the validity of the field to enable ADO to process the data in the buffer. Last, a Boolean flag indicates whether the ADO should update the field or not. If this flag is set to **true**, the ADO updates the corresponding field in the recordset with the value contained in the buffer. Since this application expects all fields to be updated, it sets that flag to true. The *icrsint.h* header file needs to be included to use the Visual C++ Extensions for ADO.

```
// ADOSamp.h : main header file for the ADOSAMP application
#include <icrsint.h>
    :
    :
    :
class CPBRecordSet : public CADORecordBinding
{
BEGIN_ADO_BINDING(CPBRecordSet)
    ADO_VARIABLE_LENGTH_ENTRY2(1, adVarChar, m_firstname, sizeof(m_firstname),
lfnStatus, true)
    ADO_VARIABLE_LENGTH_ENTRY2(2, adVarChar, m_lastname, sizeof(m_lastname),
llnStatus, true)
    ADO_VARIABLE_LENGTH_ENTRY2(3, adVarChar, m_phonenumber, sizeof(m_phonenumber),
lphoneStatus, true)
    ADO_VARIABLE_LENGTH_ENTRY2(4, adVarChar, m_note, sizeof(m_note), lnoteStatus,
true)
END_ADO_BINDING()

public:
    CHAR    m_firstname[64];
    ULONG   lfnStatus;
    CHAR    m_lastname[64];
    ULONG   llnStatus;
    CHAR    m_phonenumber[14];
    ULONG   lphoneStatus;
    CHAR    m_note[128];
    ULONG   lnoteStatus;
};
    :
    :
    :
```

Shown next is the implementation of the application. Notice the **#import** directive at the top of the module. This directive will generate the necessary class wrappers for the ADO object by creating two modules: a header file with a *.tlh* extension and an implementation file with a *.thi* extension. The contents of the type library are all defined under a name space. This name space is specified by the type library developer and can be part of the type library. If the code imports from just one type library, then there is no name clash, and we can ignore the name space, as is done in this sample. However, if the code imports more than one type library, it cannot guarantee that the names of the objects in the type libraries will not clash. In such cases, it is wise to use the name space for the objects.

The import directive also redefines EOF. Visual C++ has already defined EOF as a constant using **#define**. EOF is also defined within ADO as a property of type Variant_Bool. To avoid the name collision, the rename attribute is used to rename EOF to adoEOF. This (or some other method, such as using #undef EOF to undefine the EOF definition before importing the DLL) is required to avoid compile errors. This sample assumes that the type library is available in a specific directory. You can also let the compiler hunt for the type library in a variety of directories by not specifying a path. In that case, the path information should be added to the PATH, INCLUDE, or LIB environment variable.

```cpp
// ADOSampDlg.cpp : implementation file
//
#import "c:\Program Files\Common Files\System\ADO\msado15.dll" \
    no_namespace rename("EOF", "EndOfFile")
#include <stdio.h>
#include <icrsint.h>

#include "stdafx.h"
#include "ADOSamp.h"
#include "ADOSampDlg.h"

#ifdef _DEBUG
#define new DEBUG_NEW
#undef THIS_FILE
static char THIS_FILE[] = __FILE__;
#endif

// CADOSampDlg dialog

CADOSampDlg::CADOSampDlg(CWnd* pParent /*=NULL*/)
    : CDialog(CADOSampDlg::IDD, pParent)
{
    //{{AFX_DATA_INIT(CADOSampDlg)
    m_fn = _T("");
    m_ln = _T("");
    m_note = _T("");
    m_pn = _T("");
    //}}AFX_DATA_INIT
    m_hIcon = AfxGetApp()->LoadIcon(IDR_MAINFRAME);
}

void CADOSampDlg::DoDataExchange(CDataExchange* pDX)
{
    CDialog::DoDataExchange(pDX);
    //{{AFX_DATA_MAP(CADOSampDlg)
```

```
    DDX_Control(pDX, IDC_RECORDSET, m_rslistctrl);
    DDX_Text(pDX, IDC_FN, m_fn);
    DDX_Text(pDX, IDC_LN, m_ln);
    DDX_Text(pDX, IDC_NOTE, m_note);
    DDX_Text(pDX, IDC_PN, m_pn);
    //}}AFX_DATA_MAP
}

BEGIN_MESSAGE_MAP(CADOSampDlg, CDialog)
    //{{AFX_MSG_MAP(CADOSampDlg)
    ON_WM_PAINT()
    ON_WM_QUERYDRAGICON()
    ON_BN_CLICKED(IDC_ADD, OnAdd)
    ON_BN_CLICKED(IDC_REFRESH, OnRefresh)
    ON_BN_CLICKED(IDC_CLOSE, OnClose)
    //}}AFX_MSG_MAP
END_MESSAGE_MAP()

void static DisplayError(_com_error &e)
    {
        char    szError[512];
        sprintf(szError, "Error:\nCode = %08lx\nCode meaning = %s\nSource =
%s\nDescription = %s\n", e.Error(),e.ErrorMessage(),(LPCSTR) e.Source(), (LPCSTR)
e.Description());
        MessageBox(NULL,(LPCTSTR)szError, "Error", MB_OK);
    }

// CADOSampDlg message handlers

BOOL CADOSampDlg::OnInitDialog()
{
    HRESULT hResult;
    CDialog::OnInitDialog();

    // Set the icon for this dialog.  The framework does this automatically
    //  when the application's main window is not a dialog
    SetIcon(m_hIcon, TRUE);            // Set big icon
    SetIcon(m_hIcon, FALSE);           // Set small icon
```

The next few lines initialize the list control where the retrieved data is shown. The records have four columns; these columns are created and the headings are set here. These lines also set the extended style of the list control to assume a look like that of spreadsheet cells.

```
// Set up the List Ctrl
    CRect rect;
    LVCOLUMN lvcolumn;
    m_rslistctrl.GetWindowRect(&rect);
    lvcolumn.mask = LVCF_FMT | LVCF_SUBITEM | LVCF_TEXT | LVCF_WIDTH;
    lvcolumn.fmt = LVCFMT_LEFT;
```

```
        lvcolumn.cx = rect.Width()/4; lvcolumn.pszText = "First Name";
        lvcolumn.iSubItem = 1;
        m_rslistctrl.InsertColumn(1, &lvcolumn);

        lvcolumn.pszText = "Last Name";
        lvcolumn.iSubItem = 2;
        m_rslistctrl.InsertColumn(2, &lvcolumn);

        lvcolumn.pszText = "Phone Number";
        lvcolumn.iSubItem = 3;
        m_rslistctrl.InsertColumn(3, &lvcolumn);

        lvcolumn.pszText = "Note";
        lvcolumn.iSubItem = 4;
        m_rslistctrl.InsertColumn(4, &lvcolumn);

        DWORD dwStyle = m_rslistctrl.SendMessage (LVM_GETEXTENDEDLISTVIEWSTYLE,0,0);
        dwStyle |= LVS_EX_FULLROWSELECT | LVS_EX_GRIDLINES;
        m_rslistctrl.SendMessage(LVM_SETEXTENDEDLISTVIEWSTYLE, 0, dwStyle);
// End - Setup the List Ctrl
```

Next we define and instantiate the ADO objects. These objects, once instantiated, can be used to manipulate the ADO. Notice that we have defined these variables in the **ADOSampDlg** class as member variables. Here an actual instance is created by calling the **CreateInstance** method. The GUID of the object is retrieved by calling the extension function **__uuidof**, and this GUID is passed to **CreateInstance**. If a name space is in effect, then the object should be qualified with the name space, which in the Connection object would have been ADODB::Connection. One of the services that the Visual C++ Extensions for ADO provide is to bind or associate fields in the Recordset object to a class. Once this is done, every time the current row changes in the Recordset, all the fields that are bound will also be copied to the necessary variable in the class. If there is a need, the bind process will also convert the data types appropriately. The **BindToRecordset** method is used to bind the fields to the **CPBRecordSet** class. Various methods such as **AddNew, Update** in the **IADORecordBinding** help to manipulate the data in the Recordset.

```
        IADORecordBinding    *picRs = NULL;
        try
        {
            hResult = pConn.CreateInstance( __uuidof(Connection ));
            hResult = pRecordSet.CreateInstance( __uuidof(Recordset));
            hResult = pCmd.CreateInstance(__uuidof(Command));
```

After actual instance of the Connection object is instantiated, a connection is opened by calling the **Open** method. The Open object takes a connection string where the information about data source is specified. Other parameters passed to the Open object are the userid, password, and connection options. The data source opened here does not require any authentication, and no userid or password are provided. There are two options available for how to open the connection. The connection can be opened asynchronously, by

adAsyncConnect, in which case the call returns right away before a connection is established, or synchronously, by **adConnectUnspecified**, in which case the call returns after establishing the connection. The asynchronous connection will be useful when the application needs to initialize many things, in which case you can start the connection and proceed to initialize other things in your application. If an asynchronous connection is used, the application can use the **ConnectComplete** event to determine if the connection is established.

To define a command to be executed against the data source, a **Command** object is used. The Command object has a **CommandText** property where the command to be executed can be set. In this sample, the command is to select all the records from the PhoneBook data source. Using the **ActiveConnection** property, the data source connection is set to the connection opened earlier.

At this stage, we are all set to open the Recordset object. The **Open** method is called to open the records from the data store. The first parameter can be a Command object, a SQL statement, a table name, or a stored procedure call, for instance. Here the Command object is passed. The second parameter is an optional parameter; **vtMissing** can be used for any optional argument in the COM type library, and that is what is used here. Next is the cursor type that the ODBC provider should use when opening the Recordset. This particular sample is a stand-alone program and does not expect multiple users to access the database. Because it is so simple, a static cursor, **adOpenStatic** is used. With a static cursor, a *static* copy of the records that satisfy the query is retrieved, and hence additions, updates, and deletion made by other users will not be visible to this user. If there is such a need, a dynamic cursor should be used. For this sample, however, a static cursor should be good enough. Since the selection cursor affects the performance, the cursor should be chosen carefully.

The next parameter specifies the type of lock to be placed on the records during editing. The sample requests optimistic batch updates by specifying **adLockBatchOptimistic**. The last parameter tells how a first argument should be interpreted. The application wants to bind the Recordset fields to a class. So the IADORecordBinding object needs to be queried from the Recordset object. Once we have this IADORecordBinding object, the object rs of type **CPBRecordSet** class is bound by calling the **BindToRecordset** method. With this done, we can add a new record and update an existing record by calling the **AddNew** and **Update** methods. Before we call this method, the data in the **CPBRecordSet** class object should be set, particularly the status fields. The records in the Recordset can be sorted and filtered by setting the **Sort** and **Filter** properties respectively.

```
pConn->Open("dsn=Phone Directory;", "", "", adConnectUnspecified);
pCmd->CommandText = "select * from PhoneBook";
pCmd->ActiveConnection = pConn;
    pRecordSet->CursorLocation = adUseClient;
    pRecordSet->Open((IDispatch *) pCmd, vtMissing,
    adOpenStatic, adLockBatchOptimistic, adCmdUnspecified);
if (FAILED (hResult = pRecordSet->
            QueryInterface(__uuidof(IADORecordBinding),
                        (LPVOID*)&picRs)))
    {
```

```
                _com_issue_error(hResult);
        }
        if (FAILED (hResult = picRs->BindToRecordset(&rs)))
        {
            _com_issue_error(hResult);
        }
        pRecordSet->Sort = "FirstName";
//          pRecordSet->Filter = "phone LIKE '5*'";
```

With the records retrieved from the data source, the next few lines enumerate all the records starting from the first and insert them in the list control. When there are no longer any records available, the EOF property is set to TRUE.

```
        pRecordSet->MoveFirst();
        while (VARIANT_FALSE == pRecordSet->EndOfFile)
        {
            InsertOneItem(rs.m_firstname, rs.m_lastname, rs.m_phonenumber, rs.m_note);
            pRecordSet->MoveNext();
        }
//          pRecordSet->Filter = (long) adFilterNone;
        picRs->Release();
    }
    catch (_com_error &e)
    {
        DisplayError(e);
    }


return TRUE;  // return TRUE  unless you set the focus to a control
}


// If you add a minimize button to your dialog, you will need the code below
//  to draw the icon.  For MFC applications using the document/view model,
//  this is automatically done for you by the framework.

void CADOSampDlg::OnPaint()
{
    if (IsIconic())
    {
        CPaintDC dc(this); // device context for painting

        SendMessage(WM_ICONERASEBKGND, (WPARAM) dc.GetSafeHdc(), 0);

        // Center icon in client rectangle
        int cxIcon = GetSystemMetrics(SM_CXICON);
        int cyIcon = GetSystemMetrics(SM_CYICON);
        CRect rect;
        GetClientRect(&rect);
        int x = (rect.Width() - cxIcon + 1) / 2;
        int y = (rect.Height() - cyIcon + 1) / 2;
        // Draw the icon
```

```
        dc.DrawIcon(x, y, m_hIcon);
    }
    else
    {
        CDialog::OnPaint();
    }
}
HCURSOR CADOSampDlg::OnQueryDragIcon()
{
    return (HCURSOR) m_hIcon;
}
```

The method is called when the user clicks the Add button on the dialog box. The code makes sure that the data is provided to create a new record. If there is valid data, it updates the data in the rs object, which is derived from **CADORecordsetBinding**. Notice that it sets the status flags to **adFldOK** to indicate that the field is OK. If the status flag is not set to OK, the field will not be updated in the Recordset. Since the addition operation needs the IADORecordBinding object, it is queried and the operations are carried over with that object. To add a new record, the **AddNew** method is called. Later, by calling the **Update** method, the newly added record is saved in the Recordset. If the Recordset supports this, multiple changes can be made before updating all the changes in the batch. To update all the changes, the **UpdateBatch** method is called. In this simple application, the batch update is made after every addition of new records. When updating the batch, we can specify which records are affected by the update operation. The sample uses overkill by indicating that all the records are affected, though the current record would be sufficient. The code then adds the new record to the list control and resets the fields in the panel.

```
void CADOSampDlg::OnAdd()
{
    UpdateData();
    if(strcmp(m_fn, "") &&
        strcmp (m_ln, "") &&
        strcmp (m_pn, "") &&
        strcmp (m_note, ""))
    {
        HRESULT hResult;
        IADORecordBinding    *picRs = NULL;

        try
        {
            if (FAILED (hResult = pRecordSet->
                            QueryInterface(__uuidof(IADORecordBinding),
                                           (LPVOID*)&picRs)))
            {
                _com_issue_error(hResult);
            }

            strcpy (rs.m_firstname, m_fn);
```

```
                rs.lfnStatus = adFldOK;
                strcpy (rs.m_lastname, m_ln);
                rs.llnStatus = adFldOK;
                strcpy (rs.m_phonenumber, m_pn);
                rs.lphoneStatus = adFldOK;
                strcpy (rs.m_note, m_note);
                rs.lnoteStatus = adFldOK;
                if (FAILED(hResult = picRs->AddNew(&rs)))
                {
                    _com_issue_error(hResult);
                }
                picRs->Update(&rs);
                pRecordSet->UpdateBatch(adAffectAll);
                InsertOneItem(rs.m_firstname, rs.m_lastname,
                              rs.m_phonenumber, rs.m_note);
                m_fn = "";
                m_ln = "";
                m_pn = "";
                m_note = "";
                UpdateData(false);
                picRs->Release();
            }
            catch (_com_error &e)
            {
                DisplayError(e);
            }
        }
        else
        {
            MessageBox("Enter First Name, Last Name, Phone Number and Note");
        }
    }
```

When the user clicks the Refresh button, the next method is called. The idea is to requery the data from the data source, change the sort order, and update the list control. When you click the Refresh button, you can see the entries being resorted by last name.

```
void CADOSampDlg::OnRefresh()
{
    HRESULT hResult;
    IADORecordBinding    *picRs = NULL;

    m_rslistctrl.DeleteAllItems();
    try
    {
        pCmd->CommandText = "select * from PhoneBook";
        pCmd->ActiveConnection = pConn;
        if (FAILED (hResult = pRecordSet->
                        QueryInterface(__uuidof(IADORecordBinding),
                                        (LPVOID*)&picRs)))
```

```
        {
            _com_issue_error(hResult);
        }
        pRecordSet->Sort = "LastName";
        pRecordSet->MoveFirst();
        while (VARIANT_FALSE == pRecordSet->EndOfFile)
        {
            InsertOneItem(rs.m_firstname, rs.m_lastname,
                          rs.m_phonenumber, rs.m_note);
            pRecordSet->MoveNext();
        }
        pRecordSet->Filter = (long) adFilterNone;
        picRs->Release();
    }
    catch (_com_error &e)
    {
        DisplayError(e);
    }

}
```

When the application is closed, the Recordset and the connection to the data source
are closed. When a Recordset is closed, it relinquishes any exclusive access it might have
had to any data through this object. Actually closing a Connection object by calling the
Close method will also close the active Recordset object associated with this connection.
Thus the **Close** on the Recordset is more for good programming practice. When the program terminates, the OLE uninitialize is automatically called because of the way it was
initialized earlier.

```
void CADOSampDlg::OnClose()
{
    pRecordSet->Close();
    pConn->Close();
    EndDialog(1);
}
void CADOSampDlg::InsertOneItem(LPTSTR szFirstName, LPTSTR szLastName, LPTSTR
szPhoneNumber, LPTSTR szNote)
{
        int inewitem;
        LVITEM lvitem;

        lvitem.mask = LVIF_TEXT;
        lvitem.iItem =  0;
        lvitem.iSubItem = 0;
        lvitem.pszText = szFirstName;
        inewitem = m_rslistctrl.InsertItem(&lvitem);

        lvitem.mask = LVIF_TEXT;
        lvitem.iItem =  0;
        lvitem.iSubItem = 1;
        lvitem.pszText = szLastName;
```

```
        m_rslistctrl.SetItem(&lvitem);

        lvitem.mask = LVIF_TEXT;
        lvitem.iItem =   0;
        lvitem.iSubItem = 2;
        lvitem.pszText = szPhoneNumber;
        m_rslistctrl.SetItem(&lvitem);

        lvitem.mask = LVIF_TEXT;
        lvitem.iItem =   0;
        lvitem.iSubItem = 3;
        lvitem.pszText = szNote;
        m_rslistctrl.SetItem(&lvitem);
}
```

The method shown here is just a utility method to add a record in the list control.

The sample just discussed adds a record to the data source. The next sample extends the previous sample to update an existing record (see Figures 20-9 and 20-10).

The phone number is used as an index and assumed to be unmodifiable. The sample is available in the *ADOUpdate* subdirectory. Most of the code that has not changed is not shown, and the code of interest is shown in boldface.

```
// ADOSampDlg.cpp : implementation file
//
#import "c:\Program Files\Common Files\System\ADO\msado15.dll" \
   no_namespace rename("EOF", "EndOfFile")
#include <stdio.h>
#include <icrsint.h>

#include "stdafx.h"
#include "ADOSamp.h"
#include "ADOSampDlg.h"

#ifdef _DEBUG
#define new DEBUG_NEW
#undef THIS_FILE
static char THIS_FILE[] = __FILE__;
#endif

/////////////////////////////////////////////////////////////////////////////
// CADOSampDlg dialog

CADOSampDlg::CADOSampDlg(CWnd* pParent /*=NULL*/)
    : CDialog(CADOSampDlg::IDD, pParent)
{
    //{{AFX_DATA_INIT(CADOSampDlg)
    m_fn = _T("");
    m_ln = _T("");
    m_note = _T("");
    m_pn = _T("");
```

```
    //}}AFX_DATA_INIT
    // Note that LoadIcon does not require a subsequent DestroyIcon in Win32
    m_hIcon = AfxGetApp()->LoadIcon(IDR_MAINFRAME);
}

void CADOSampDlg::DoDataExchange(CDataExchange* pDX)
{
    CDialog::DoDataExchange(pDX);
    //{{AFX_DATA_MAP(CADOSampDlg)
    DDX_Control(pDX, IDC_RECORDSET, m_rslistctrl);
    DDX_Text(pDX, IDC_FN, m_fn);
    DDX_Text(pDX, IDC_LN, m_ln);
    DDX_Text(pDX, IDC_NOTE, m_note);
    DDX_Text(pDX, IDC_PN, m_pn);
    //}}AFX_DATA_MAP
}
```

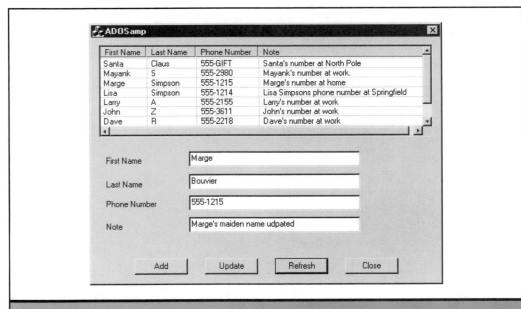

Figure 20-9. Updating a record

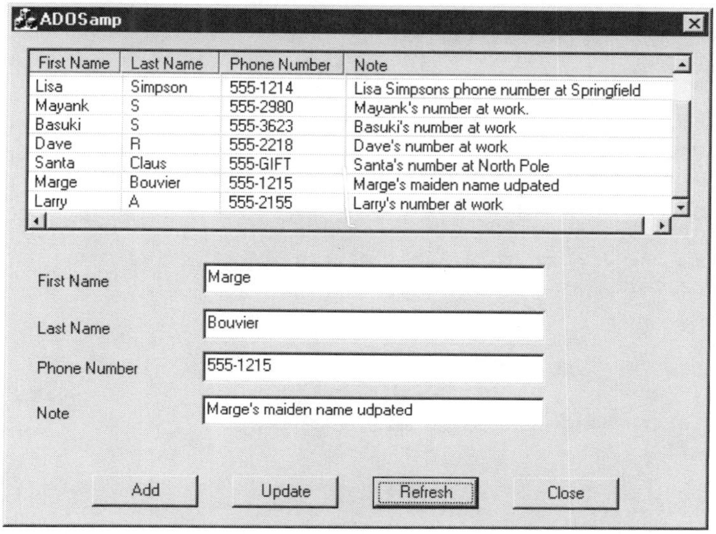

Figure 20-10.   Results of update

The message map requests notification when the user clicks the list control that displays the records from the data store. It also requests notification when the user clicks the Update button.

```
BEGIN_MESSAGE_MAP(CADOSampDlg, CDialog)
    //{{AFX_MSG_MAP(CADOSampDlg)
    ON_WM_PAINT()
    ON_WM_QUERYDRAGICON()
    ON_BN_CLICKED(IDC_ADD, OnAdd)
    ON_BN_CLICKED(IDC_REFRESH, OnRefresh)
    ON_BN_CLICKED(IDC_CLOSE, OnClose)
        ON_NOTIFY(NM_CLICK, IDC_RECORDSET, OnClickRecordset)
        ON_BN_CLICKED(IDC_UPDATE, OnUpdate)
    //}}AFX_MSG_MAP
END_MESSAGE_MAP()
```

```
void static DisplayError(_com_error &e)
{
// No change in the dialog initialization code.
// See code earlier
}


// CADOSampDlg message handlers

BOOL CADOSampDlg::OnInitDialog()
{
// No change in the dialog initialization code.
// See code earlier
}


void CADOSampDlg::OnPaint()
{
// No change in the dialog initialization code.
// See code earlier
}


HCURSOR CADOSampDlg::OnQueryDragIcon()
{
// No change in the dialog initialization code.
// See code earlier
}


void CADOSampDlg::OnAdd()
{
// No change in the dialog initialization code.
// See code earlier
}
```

None of the methods have any change in the code. To change a record, the user will select the record from the list control. This triggers a call to the **OnClickRecordset** method, which retrieves the records and updates the fields in the dialog box. The user can then make changes to the name and note fields and update the record.

```
void CADOSampDlg::OnClickRecordset(NMHDR* pNMHDR, LRESULT* pResult)
{
    LPNMITEMACTIVATE pSelectedItem;

    pSelectedItem = (LPNMITEMACTIVATE)pNMHDR;
    if (pSelectedItem->iItem >= 0) // If we have an item selected.
    {
        m_fn = m_rslistctrl.GetItemText(pSelectedItem->iItem,
                                        0);
        m_ln = m_rslistctrl.GetItemText(pSelectedItem->iItem,
                                        1);
        m_pn = m_rslistctrl.GetItemText(pSelectedItem->iItem,
                                        2);
```

```
            m_note = m_rslistctrl.GetItemText(pSelectedItem->iItem,
                                               3);
        }
        UpdateData(false);
        *pResult = 0;
    }
```

When a record is requested to be updated, the **OnUpdate** method is called. This method retrieves the data from the dialog box by calling the **UpdateData** method. With this data, it searches for the record in the record set. In order to make this program work in many environments, the code does a very basic search by means of setting the filter for the Recordset. A more elegant method is to seek for the record, but this requires support for indexing and seeking from the underlying service provider. Not all providers provide these facilities. So before performing the operation, the code checks if the Recordset supports the *index* and *seek* properties by calling the **Supports** method. The index property tells which column is currently the index in the Recordset object. Before a column can be used as an index, it should have been declared on the base table that the Recordset object represents. For the **Seek** method to work, the Recordset should support the index property. If the underlying provider does not support the Index property, then the **Seek** method is not available. The code to **Seek** if indexing is supported is shown here, though it is not compiled. The **Seek** method is called by providing a key value, which is the phone number in this case, and a seek option. It later checks if the seek ran to the end of the available records, and if so it displays a message. Of course the code here is **#if 0** and hence not compiled. It is offered only to show another possible option. The next section of the code shows the search being done sequentially. This is definitely not a suggested option but is shown to illustrate the record navigation using the **MoveNext** method.

```
void CADOSampDlg::OnUpdate()
{
    if (m_rslistctrl.GetSelectedCount() > 0)
    {
        // A record is selected
        HRESULT hResult;
        IADORecordBinding   *picRs = NULL;
        UpdateData();
        try
        {
            if (FAILED (hResult = pRecordSet->
                    QueryInterface(__uuidof(IADORecordBinding),
                                    (LPVOID*)&picRs)))
            {
                _com_issue_error(hResult);
            }

            if (pRecordSet->Supports(adIndex) &&
                pRecordSet->Supports(adSeek) )
            {
#if 0
```

```
                            strcpy (rs.m_firstname, m_fn);
                            rs.lfnStatus = adFldOK;
                            strcpy (rs.m_lastname, m_ln);
                            rs.llnStatus = adFldOK;
                            strcpy (rs.m_phonenumber, m_pn);
                            rs.lphoneStatus = adFldOK;
                            strcpy (rs.m_note, m_note);
                            rs.lnoteStatus = adFldOK;
                            pRecordSet->Index = "phone";
                            pRecordSet->MoveFirst();
                            _variant_t phonenumber((LPCTSTR)m_pn);
                            pRecordSet->Seek(phonenumber, adSeekAfterEQ);
                            if (pRecordSet->EndOfFile)
                            {
                                MessageBox("Record not found");
                            }
#endif
                    }
                    else
                    {
#if 0
                        pRecordSet->MoveFirst();
                        while (pRecordSet->EndOfFile == VARIANT_FALSE)
                        {
                            if (!strcmp(rs.m_phonenumber, m_pn))
                            {
                                break;
                            }
                            pRecordSet->MoveNext();
                        }
                        if (pRecordSet->EndOfFile != VARIANT_TRUE)
                        {
                            // We did not go past all the records.
                            strcpy (rs.m_firstname, m_fn);
                            rs.lfnStatus = adFldOK;
                            strcpy (rs.m_lastname, m_ln);
                            rs.llnStatus = adFldOK;
                            strcpy (rs.m_note, m_note);
                            rs.lnoteStatus = adFldOK;
                            picRs->Update(&rs);
                            pRecordSet->UpdateBatch(adAffectAll);
                        }
                        else
                        {
                            MessageBox("Record not found");
                        }
#else
```

The next section of the code locates the record that needs to be updated and updates it. It sets the filter of the Recordset and checks if there are any records available in the Recordset. If so, it moves to the first record in case there are multiple records satisfying the filter. It updates the data by setting the appropriate variable in the binding class and sets the status flag to indicate that the records need to be picked for update. It then calls the **Update** method to update the record in the Recordset and calls the **UpdateBatch** method to update the batch to the data store. The filter is reset such that the filter set earlier will not affect any future cursoring in the Recordset.

```
            char szFilter[512];
            sprintf(szFilter, "Phone = '%s'", m_pn);
            pRecordSet->Filter = szFilter;

            if (pRecordSet->RecordCount > 0)
            {
                // We did not go past all the records.
                pRecordSet->MoveFirst();
                strcpy (rs.m_firstname, m_fn);
                rs.lfnStatus = adFldOK;
                strcpy (rs.m_lastname, m_ln);
                rs.llnStatus = adFldOK;
                strcpy (rs.m_note, m_note);
                rs.lnoteStatus = adFldOK;
                picRs->Update(&rs);
                pRecordSet->UpdateBatch(adAffectAll);
                pRecordSet->Filter = (long) adFilterNone;
            }
            else
            {
                MessageBox("Record not found");
            }
#endif
            }
            picRs->Release();
        }
        catch (_com_error &e)
        {
            DisplayError(e);
        }
    }
    else
    {
        // No records selected.
        MessageBox("Please select a record to update.");
    }
}


void CADOSampDlg::OnRefresh()
{
// No change in the dialog initialization code.
// See code earlier
}
```

```
void CADOSampDlg::OnClose()
{
    pRecordSet->Close();
    pConn->Close();
    EndDialog(1);
}
```

```
void CADOSampDlg::InsertOneItem(LPTSTR szFirstName, LPTSTR szLastName, LPTSTR
szPhoneNumber, LPTSTR szNote)
{
// No change in the dialog initialization code.
// See code earlier
}
```

The next sample, available in the *ADODelete* subdirectory, extends the previous ADOUpdate sample with an additional button to delete a selected record. To delete a record, the record is selected from the list control (see Figure 20-11) and the Delete button is clicked. When the Delete button is clicked, the selected record is deleted and the user is prompted whether the transaction should be committed (see Figure 20-12). The user can choose not to commit the transaction, in which case the transaction is rolled back; otherwise,

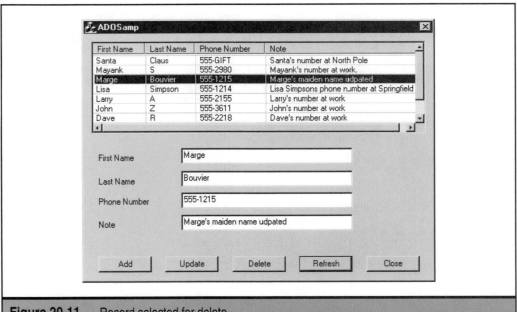

Figure 20-11. Record selected for delete

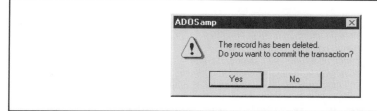

Figure 20-12. Warning message before committing the delete

the transaction is committed (see Figure 20-13). The records can be refreshed, or the sample can be restarted to check if the record was deleted. Only the relevant code is shown; and lines that have not changed from earlier samples are not shown.

```
// ADOSampDlg.cpp :  implementation file
//
#import "c:\Program Files\Common Files\System\ADO\msado15.dll" \
   no_namespace rename("EOF", "EndOfFile")
#include <stdio.h>
#include <icrsint.h>

#include "stdafx.h"
#include "ADOSamp.h"
#include "ADOSampDlg.h"

#ifdef _DEBUG
#define new DEBUG_NEW
#undef THIS_FILE
static char THIS_FILE[] = __FILE__;
#endif

// CADOSampDlg dialog

CADOSampDlg::CADOSampDlg(CWnd* pParent /*=NULL*/)
    : CDialog(CADOSampDlg::IDD, pParent)
{
    //{{AFX_DATA_INIT(CADOSampDlg)
    m_fn = _T("");
    m_ln = _T("");
    m_note = _T("");
    m_pn = _T("");
    //}}AFX_DATA_INIT
    // Note that LoadIcon does not require a subsequent DestroyIcon in Win32
    m_hIcon = AfxGetApp()->LoadIcon(IDR_MAINFRAME);
}
```

```
void CADOSampDlg::DoDataExchange(CDataExchange* pDX)
{
    CDialog::DoDataExchange(pDX);
    //{{AFX_DATA_MAP(CADOSampDlg)
    DDX_Control(pDX, IDC_RECORDSET, m_rslistctrl);
    DDX_Text(pDX, IDC_FN, m_fn);
    DDX_Text(pDX, IDC_LN, m_ln);
    DDX_Text(pDX, IDC_NOTE, m_note);
    DDX_Text(pDX, IDC_PN, m_pn);
    //}}AFX_DATA_MAP
}
```

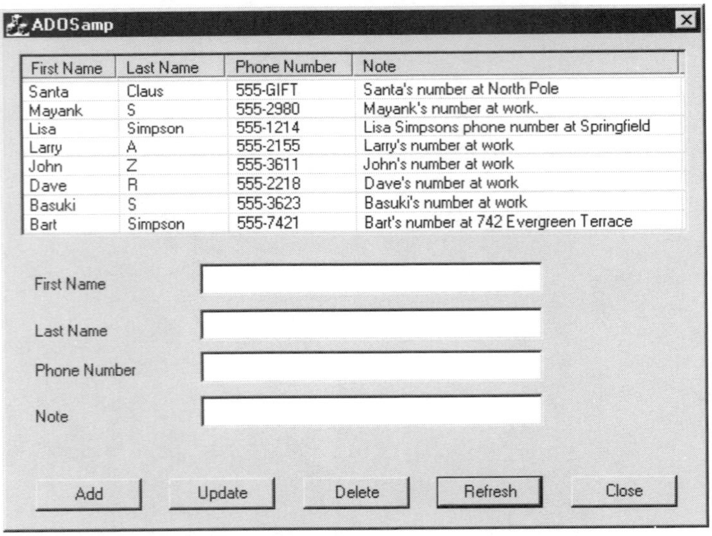

Figure 20-13. Screen after the delete

The message map requests the **OnDelete** method to be called when the Delete button is clicked.

```
BEGIN_MESSAGE_MAP(CADOSampDlg, CDialog)
    //{{AFX_MSG_MAP(CADOSampDlg)
    ON_WM_PAINT()
    ON_WM_QUERYDRAGICON()
    ON_BN_CLICKED(IDC_ADD, OnAdd)
    ON_BN_CLICKED(IDC_REFRESH, OnRefresh)
    ON_BN_CLICKED(IDC_CLOSE, OnClose)
    ON_NOTIFY(NM_CLICK, IDC_RECORDSET, OnClickRecordset)
    ON_BN_CLICKED(IDC_UPDATE, OnUpdate)
        ON_BN_CLICKED(IDC_DELETE, OnDelete)
    //}}AFX_MSG_MAP
END_MESSAGE_MAP()


void static DisplayError(_com_error &e)
{
// No change in the dialog initialization code.
// See code earlier
}


// CADOSampDlg message handlers

BOOL CADOSampDlg::OnInitDialog()
{
// No change in the dialog initialization code.
// See code earlier
}
void CADOSampDlg::OnPaint()
{
// No change in the dialog initialization code.
// See code earlier
}
HCURSOR CADOSampDlg::OnQueryDragIcon()
{
    return (HCURSOR) m_hIcon;
}
```

```
void CADOSampDlg::OnAdd()
{
// No change in the dialog initialization code.
// See code earlier
}
void CADOSampDlg::OnUpdate()
{
// No change in the dialog initialization code.
// See code earlier
}
```

When the Delete button is clicked, the data from the selected record is picked up and the cursor is moved to that record by setting the filter of the Recordset appropriately. The record is then deleted by calling the **Delete** method and indicating which record the operation applied to. In this case, the code indicates that the operation affects only the current record by specifying **adAffectCurrent** as the parameter. The Delete method marks the record for deletion from the cache, and when the **UpdateBatch** method is called, the actual deletion occurs. Notice that the whole operation is enveloped in a transaction by the **BeginTrans**, **CommitTrans**, and **RollbackTrans** methods. With these methods, the changes in a connection object can be saved or cancelled. Most database applications need to access and update records in multiple tables over many lines of code. In such scenarios, it is critical to complete the whole operation as a single unit of work. Partial updates to certain tables may leave the database in an inconsistent state, which may not be what the application expects. This point is extremely important in a client/server or multitiered application, since there is a real possibility of communication failing between operations. Customers will really be upset if in a financial transaction such as cash withdrawal from an ATM machine, the account is debited without dispensing the cash! To solve these problems, ADO provides a mechanism whereby multiple database operations can form units of work and the complete unit of work can be done as a single database operation. This is achieved by calling the **BeginTrans** method of the Connection object. **BeginTrans** starts a new transaction. The ADO operations done after **BeginTrans** are considered a single unit of work. When the changes are to be saved to the data source, the **CommitTrans** method is called, and if the changes are to be cancelled, **RollbackTrans** is called. You can notice that after deleting the record from the Recordset, the code prompts the user whether the user wants to commit the changes. If the user wishes to cancel the deletion, then **RollbackTrans** is called to roll back the changes.

Support of transactions for data sources depends on the providers. Some providers do not support transactions, although all industrial-strength providers do so. Some providers also support nested transactions, such that calling the **BeginTrans** method with a transaction starts a new nested transaction. A call to **CommitTrans** or **RollbackTrans** in a nested transaction applies to the innermost level of the nested transaction.

```
void CADOSampDlg::OnDelete()
{
    if (m_rslistctrl.GetSelectedCount() > 0)
    {
        // A record is selected
```

```
        HRESULT hResult;
        IADORecordBinding    *picRs = NULL;
        UpdateData();
        pConn->BeginTrans();
        try
        {
            if (FAILED (hResult = pRecordSet->
                        QueryInterface(__uuidof(IADORecordBinding),
                                        (LPVOID*)&picRs)))
            {
                _com_issue_error(hResult);
            }
            char szFilter[512];
            sprintf(szFilter, "FirstName='%s' AND LastName='%s' AND Phone = \
                        '%s'",m_fn, m_ln, m_pn);
            pRecordSet->Filter = szFilter;
            if (pRecordSet->RecordCount > 0)
            {
                pRecordSet->Delete(adAffectCurrent);
                pRecordSet->UpdateBatch(adAffectCurrent);
                if ((AfxMessageBox("The record has been deleted.\nDo you want\
                                    to commit the transaction?", MB_YESNO) ==
                    IDNO))
                {
                    pConn->RollbackTrans();
                }
                else
                {
                    pConn->CommitTrans();
                }
            }
            else
            {
                MessageBox("Record not found");
            }
            pRecordSet->Filter = (long) adFilterNone;
            picRs->Release();
        }
        catch (_com_error &e)
        {
            DisplayError(e);
            pConn->RollbackTrans();
        }
    }
    else
    {
        // No records selected.
        MessageBox("Please select a record to delete.");
    }
```

```
}

void CADOSampDlg::OnRefresh()
{// No change in the dialog initialization code.
// See code earlier
}

void CADOSampDlg::OnClose()
{
    pRecordSet->Close();
    pConn->Close();
    EndDialog(1);
}
void CADOSampDlg::OnClickRecordset(NMHDR* pNMHDR, LRESULT* pResult)
{
// No change in the dialog initialization code.
// See code earlier
}
void CADOSampDlg::InsertOneItem(LPTSTR szFirstName, LPTSTR szLastName,
                                LPTSTR szPhoneNumber, LPTSTR szNote)
{
// No change in the dialog initialization code.
// See code earlier
}
```

CONCLUSION

In this chapter, we looked at another method to access databases from your application in addition to ODBC, which we looked at in Chapter 19. As mentioned earlier, ADO is the preferred method recommended by Microsoft, and you should consider using it if you are thinking of using DAO or RDO.

In the next chapter we will look at a major enhancement in Windows 2000 compared to Windows NT—Security.

CHAPTER 21

Windows 2000 Security Features

With the growing use of the Web for developing applications that let a company's customers and partners transact electronically with the company, security has become a key factor. Besides traditional authentication, used to identify users and allow them access, Web-based e-commerce applications require other functions such as digital signing, nonrepudiation, capability to foil attempts to capture data while in transit, and capability to reject illegal users attempting to masquerade as legal users. Windows 2000 makes it possible for these security functions to be provided using a comprehensive security architecture that is integrated with other Windows 2000 components such as Active Directory. This security architecture supports a number of key security technologies such as Public Key Cryptography.

WINDOWS 2000 SECURITY ARCHITECTURE

Microsoft Windows 2000 security architecture, which is an enhancement to Windows NT security architecture, has been designed to enable end users and independent software vendors develop end-to-end security solutions in open distributed environments. End-to-end security is achieved using the industry standard set of security services: authentication, access control, confidentiality, integrity, and non-repudiation. The core components of Windows 2000 security architecture are secure operating system services, distributed system security services, and security management services.

Secure operating systems implement the trusted computing base for the end system, which enforces the required security policy for its trusted subjects and trusted objects. Windows NT has been rated at C2 level of assurance by the US national security administration.

Windows 2000 has implemented the distributed system security services based on the following:

▼ Microsoft Cryptographic Application Programming Interface (CAPI) framework providing a set of security APIs to enable application developers implement new security applications, and a set of security SPIs to enable system vendors implement specialized Cryptographic Security Provider (CSP) plug-ins.

Examples of CSPs are: Smart Card CSPs implementing Digital Signature services with protected private keys, hardware cryptographic accelerators for bulk data encryption and decryption services, and CSPs for the recently proposed new FIP Standard Advanced Encryption System (AES) cryptographic algorithm.

Secure applications use the CAPI APIs to obtain confidentiality, integrity, and digital signature services. CAPI APIs are covered in detail later in this chapter.

■ Secure Messaging interface for providing support for industry standard secure communication protocols, such as IPSec, SSL, TLS, and S/MIME. These secure communication protocols have been implemented using the CAPI APIs.

- Secure Authentication protocol services based on support for secret key based Kerberos and public key based X509.3 protocols. The objective of Windows NT/2000 security architecture is to support Mobile Users with Single Logon to the entire security domain. Windows NT/2000 supports multiple authentication mechanisms, ranging from passwords sufficiently secure for use inside a physically protected LAN environment to X509.3 certificates on smart cards providing strong authentication for mobile users in open Internet environments.

▲ Secure Directory services, based on Windows 2000 Active Directory, to store the security attributes of all the trusted subjects and trusted objects of each security domain.

Windows 2000 Security Management tools enables configuration and enforcement of the security policy for all the trusted subjects and trusted objects of each security domain. These security management tools are part of the Windows NT/2000 Zero Administration system facilitating ease-of-use to the security administrators.

It is outside the scope of this chapter to discuss these core security architectural features in depth. These topics have been covered extensively at Microsoft Web sites devoted to Windows 2000 security topics. Our main objective in this chapter is to explain how all the security architectural features work together to enforce end-to-end security for a user's typical business transaction in open, distributed environments and to illustrate the same through programming examples.

Now let's look at technologies supported by the Windows 2000 security architecture such as public key cryptography.

PUBLIC KEY CRYPTOGRAPHY

Cryptography is the science of mathematically combining plain text and an encryption key to generate encrypted data. The encrypted data is also called *cipher text*. The power of cryptography stems from the fact that it is computationally impossible to reverse the encryption process and derive the plain text data from cipher text in finite time. While some older cryptographic algorithms have been cracked using powerful computers, more complex cryptographic algorithms that use longer key lengths have been developed. Traditional or *symmetric* cryptography uses the same key for encryption and decryption. By contrast, in *asymmetric* or *public key* cryptography, two different keys are used. One key is used for encryption, and a different matching key is used for decryption. The encryption key is also called the *public key*, and the decryption key is also called the *private key*. The encryption key is made available publicly to anyone who wishes to send encrypted text or messages to the person possessing the matching decryption or private key. Typically, as the name suggests, the private key is held privately and is not divulged to others, though some organizations may have some policies to keep another copy of the private key apart from the user.

Windows 2000 introduces a comprehensive public key infrastructure (PKI) to the Windows platform. This PKI utilizes the existing Windows-based public key cryptographic services and provides an integrated set of services and administrative tools for creating, deploying, and managing the PK-based applications. As an applications developer, you can take advantage of Windows 2000 security mechanisms starting with shared secrets all the way to PK-based security mechanisms as appropriate. The different components that make up Windows 2000 PKI support include the CryptoAPI, Active Directory, and Microsoft Certificate Server. We will cover Windows 2000 security topics including CryptoAPI and Certificate Server in this chapter. Active Directory is covered in Chapter 10.

USES OF PUBLIC KEY CRYPTOGRAPHY

Public key cryptography is used to satisfy a number of requirements brought about by the increased use of the Internet, such as confidentiality, authentication, nonrepudiation, and data integrity. These can be achieved by encryption and digital signatures. We will briefly cover these topics here.

Let's take a simple example, where you would like to authorize your bank to pay some amount to a third party and furthermore you want all these transactions to take place over the Internet. The following points need to be addressed:

▼ **Confidentiality**   You may not want others know to whom you are paying, as this information could be sensitive.

■ **Authentication**   The bank needs to authenticate that the person accessing your account and instructing it to pay from your account is indeed you.

■ **Integrity**   The data received by the bank must indeed be the data sent by you. You do not want an instruction to send $200 to become an instruction to send $450!

▲ **Nonrepudiation**   The bank wants to make sure that you do not deny that you wrote this electronic check.

By a combination of both digital signatures and encryption, these concerns can be addressed.

Digital Signatures

To understand digital signatures, let us start with *message digests*, also called *hash values*. A hash value is a small amount of binary data, normally 160 bits long. It is generated using a hashing algorithm, as shown in Figure 21-1.

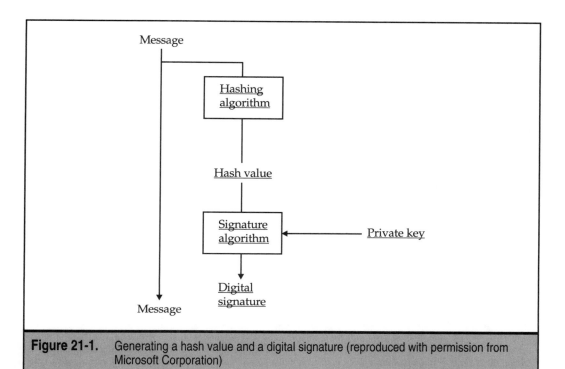

Figure 21-1. Generating a hash value and a digital signature (reproduced with permission from Microsoft Corporation)

Hash values have these characteristics (regardless of the algorithm used):

▼ A hash value has a fixed length, independent of the size of the message from which the hash value was derived.

■ No two different messages will generate the same hash value. This is true even if the two messages differ only by one bit. While theoretically it is possible that two messages could generate the same hash value, the probability of this occurring with the consequential impact is so low that we will discount this possibility.

■ All hashing algorithms are fully deterministic, which means that the same hash value is generated every time a specific message is hashed using the same algorithm.

▲ All hashing algorithms are one-way generators, which means that it is not practically feasible to recover the original message given its hash value.

Now that we have covered hash values, observe that digital signatures are created using the signer's private key to sign the hash value, as shown in Figure 21-1.

Once a message and a digital signature have been created as in Figure 21-1, both the message and the signature are sent to a recipient. The recipient can verify the digital signature, as shown in Figure 21-2.

The ability to verify the message using a public key ensures that only someone who has the private key could have signed the message. If the signed data is changed either during transmission or intentionally by someone other than the private key holder, the verification fails.

This functionality is useful whenever there is a requirement to ensure that the document is from a known individual and that the document has not been tampered with. One such example is secure e-mail.

Authentication

Authentication is the process by which we can verify that the user accessing your application online is in fact the person who he or she claims to be. The most common authentication mechanism used today is a shared secret mechanism such as a userid, password combination. However, as public key cryptography becomes more common, better authentication mechanisms based on public key cryptography will become available.

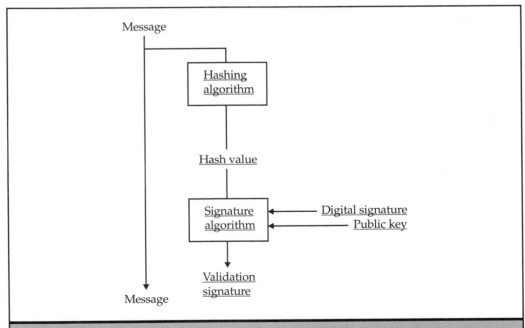

Figure 21-2.   Verifying a digital signature (reproduced with permission from Microsoft Corporation)

Authentication using public key cryptography can be accomplished in a number of ways. Let's say that party A wants to ensure that the other communicating party, B, is in fact B. The different ways to authenticate B are:

▼ A can send simple text to B. B uses its private key to encrypt the text and send it back to A. A can use B's public key to decrypt the information returned by B. If the decrypted text matches the text that A sent, then B is authenticated, since only B has access to B's private key.

■ Alternatively, A can send B text encrypted with B's public key. B decrypts using B's private key and sends it back to A. If the messages sent and received match, B is authenticated, since only B could have decrypted the message using its private key. Attempts to capture the communications between A and B for purposes of replay attacks can be frustrated by varying the text sent for authentication.

▲ Public keys can also be combined with shared secrets for authentication. A can generate a random number and send it to B encrypted using B's public key. B decrypts the message and extracts A's random number. B can do likewise and send A another random number. The two random numbers can be combined to form a shared secret known only to A and B. Since A and B used their private keys to decrypt, both A and B are authenticated.

Encryption

While encrypting and decrypting authentication messages using public key cryptography or asymmetric algorithms is fine, using the same mechanisms to encrypt and decrypt regular data exchanges may not be advisable, particularly when large amounts of data need to exchanged. This is because encryption and decryption using public and private keys are computationally intensive and this introduces a significant overhead in large data exchanges.

One way around this fact is to use a separate, more efficient symmetric encryption algorithm to encrypt data and then use the asymmetric algorithm to encrypt the key that encrypted the data. The key that is used to encrypt the data is called the *session key*. This session key can be created once for each communication session and can be exchanged between the communicating entities. The initial exchange between the communicating entities exchanges the session encryption key, and this initial exchange itself is encrypted and decrypted using public and private keys.

Integrity

Integrity ensures that the message was not tampered with in any way en route from the sender to the receiver. Public key cryptography mechanisms ensure that such tampering (even if it is just one bit) can be detected. When the message or text is sent, the message can be signed by the sender using the sender's private key, which can be verified.

Thus in public key cryptography, the public key is used to encrypt and verify the signature, while a private key is used to decrypt and sign.

PUBLIC KEY CRYPTOGRAPHY AND DIGITAL CERTIFICATES

So far, we have assumed that the sender and the receiver have public and private keys, but we did not worry about how the keys were issued to the communicating entities and who issues them. Keys are commonly distributed using digital certificates, and the management and distribution of digital certificates is handled by *certificate authorities (CAs)*.

A CA verifies the identities of the entities to whom it issues digital certificates and acts as the guarantor of the binding between a public key and the entity owning the corresponding private key. Thus when you verify the signature of a message using someone's public key, all you really know is that the message was signed using that person's private key. You trust the CA and accept the CA's word that the specific public key belongs to a specific entity mentioned in the digital certificate. The ITU-T X.509 standard is the most common standard governing digital certificates.

Windows 2000 uses a hierarchical CA model. In this model, the CA at the top of a hierarchy is generally referred to as a root CA. This does not mean that there will be only one root CA. There could be multiple disjoint hierarchies, each with its own root. It is also possible to merge two disjoint hierarchies by issuing a certificate from one of the root CAs certifying the other root CA to be an intermediate CA. Below the root level are subordinate CAs, of which there could be multiple levels. The CAs at the bottom-most level are typically called *issuing CAs,* while the other subordinate CAs are called *intermediate CAs.* The trust flows down, whereby each child is certified by its parent.

WINDOWS 2000 PKI SUPPORT

Windows 2000 provides extensive support for public key cryptography. An overview of the PKI components in Windows 2000 is shown in Figure 21-3.

A brief description of the components shown in Figure 21-3 follows. Microsoft Certificate services permit the deployment of one or more CAs. The CAs can either be an enterprise CA or an external CA. CAs, which support certificate management functions such as enrollment and revocation, are integrated with the Active Directory, which provides CA policy and location information. Active Directories also allow certificate and revocation information to be published. The Domain controller (DC) and Kerberos Key Distribution Center (KDC) handle normal domain trust and authorization functions such as client logons. Microsoft Certificate Services is included with Windows 2000 server editions. The components shown in Figure 21-1 can be distributed across one or more physical server machines as appropriate.

An overview of public key application services is shown in Figure 21-4.

Figure 21-4 shows the details of Certificate Management Services interface with other devices and services. For a developer of Windows 2000 applications, the most interesting

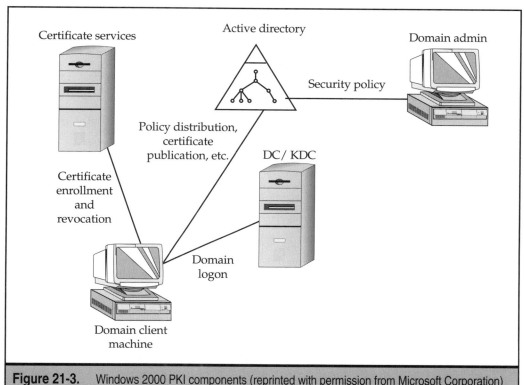

Figure 21-3.   Windows 2000 PKI components (reprinted with permission from Microsoft Corporation)

aspect of Figure 21-4 is the key role played by the CryptoAPI. Just as the hardware ab-straction layer shields the specifics of the underlying hardware from the rest of the Win-dows 2000 Executive, CryptoAPIs provide a standard interface to cryptographic functionality while shielding the specifics of Cryptographic Service Providers (CSPs), which provide installable cryptographic functionality. Such functionality can be pro-vided either by software or by specialized hardware devices. Figure 21-4 shows a hard-ware CSP supporting a smart card reader. This smart card support is the basis for Windows 2000 smart card logon support. For more information about smart card support by Microsoft products, see **www.microsoft.com/smartcard** and **www.smartcardsys.com**.

The certificate management services mentioned earlier are built on top of crypto-ser-vices. The installation of certificate services steps the administrator through the process of setting up the CA hierarchy. The CA setup process involves setting up a domain fol-lowed by setting up one or more root CAs and finally all the intermediate and issuing CAs.

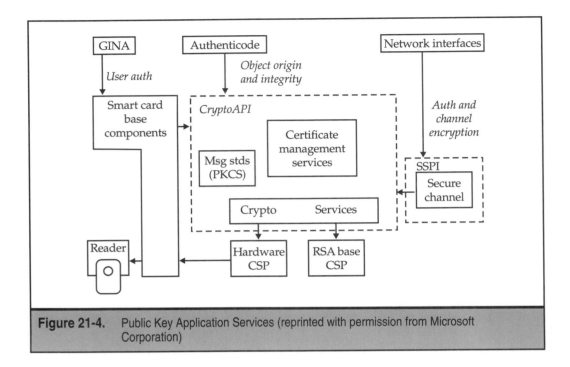

Figure 21-4. Public Key Application Services (reprinted with permission from Microsoft Corporation)

Figure 21-4 also shows how other services take advantage of the CryptoAPI to provide additional functionality. Secure Channel (Schannel) provides network authentication and encryption using TLS and SSL protocols. Authenticode, which supports object signing and verification, is primarily used to determine the origin and integrity of components downloaded from the Internet.

APPLICATION SERVICES PROVIDED BY WINDOWS 2000 PKI

Windows 2000 PKI support provides you a number of services to help you build PKI applications for Windows 2000. These services include key pair generation, key recovery, certificate enrollment, and more.

Key Generation

The CryptoAPI defines standard interfaces for generating and managing keys. These interfaces are supported by the CSPs. Using installable CSPs, the CryptoAPI supports key generation and management for a variety of cryptographic algorithms. Mechanisms for storing key material vary by CSP. The Microsoft-provided software CSPs, also called *base* CSPs, store key material in an encrypted form on a per-user or per-computer basis. Smart card CSPs store the public-key pair in the smart card tamper-resistant hardware and provide access by requiring entry of a PIN code.

The key storage and protection mechanisms are transparent to your application. You reference all key pairs through a key-set name that is unique in the context of a CSP. You also use flags provided as part of the CryptoAPI interface. For example, you use the CRYPT_EXPORTABLE flag for private-key export from the CSP and the CRYPT_ USER_PROTECT flag for determining user-notification behavior when using the private key.

Key Recovery

Key recovery, as the name implies, involves recovering persistent keys that are lost or that need to be recovered without the knowledge or consent of the owning entity. The former happens when an employee loses a key and needs to be able to read archived data such as e-mail encrypted using the key. The latter situation typically happens in law-enforcement situations.

Note that same key recovery procedure could potentially be used for recovering data exchange keys used to encrypt data as well as keys used for identification or digital signature. A word of caution is appropriate for the latter, since it is possible to use a recovered identification key for impersonation purposes. Microsoft Exchange currently provides support for recovery of key-exchange keys only. However, third-party CSPs are available that provide general support for key recovery.

Certificate Enrollment

Windows 2000 PKI support for certificate enrollment is standards based. Windows 2000 PKI supports the industry-standard PKCS-10 certificate request messages and PKCS-7 responses containing the resulting certificate or certificate chain. At this time, certificates that support RSA keys and signatures, Digital Signature Algorithm (DSA) keys and signatures, and Diffie-Hellman keys are supported. Microsoft has indicated that the certificate enrollment process will evolve in a manner consistent with the Certificate Request Syntax (CRS) draft current in the IETF PKIX working group.

Windows 2000 PKI supports Microsoft enterprise CA or third-party CAs. Enrollment support is implemented in a transport-independent manner. Underlying transport mechanisms could include RPC, DCOM, and e-mail. The PKI supports multiple enrollment methods, including Web-based enrollment, an enrollment wizard, and policy-driven autoenrollment, which occurs as part of a user's logon processing.

As part of its PKI support, Windows 2000 includes an enrollment control *(Xenroll.dll).* This DLL provides support for PKCS-10 and PKCS-7 messages. This control allows the calling application to specify the attributes included in the PKCS-10 message and allows use of an existing key pair or generation of a new key pair. You can access the DLL in scripts for Web-based enrollment. You can also call the DLL programmatically to support the different transport mechanisms mentioned earlier. The enrollment process is assumed to be asynchronous, and the enrollment control provides state management to match issued certificates against pending requests. This provides a means of creating an internal binding between the certificate, the CSP that generated the key pair, and the key pair container name.

Certificate Renewal

As in the case of enrollment, Microsoft has indicated its intent that its certificate renewal functions will be standards based. Industry-standard message protocols are included in the IETF PKIX CRS draft but have not yet become a standard. Renewal is currently supported in the Windows 2000 PKI for automatically enrolled certificates. For other mechanisms, a renewal is treated as a new enrollment request.

Certificate renewal is very similar to enrollment in that renewal assumes that the requesting entity wants a new certificate with the same attributes as an existing, valid certificate, but with extended validity dates. A renewal may use the existing public key or a new public key. A renewal request can be processed more efficiently, since it can take advantage of existing trust relationships inherent in an existing certificate without having to reverify the existing certificate attributes.

Key Backup and Restore

Recognizing that key pairs and certificates are mission-critical data, Windows 2000 PKI supports the ability to back up and restore both certificates and associated key pairs through the certificate-management administrative tools. Using the certificate manager for exporting a certificate, a user can opt to export the associated key pair. If this option is selected, the information is exported as an encrypted (based on a user-supplied password) PKCS-12 message. This may later be imported to the system, or another system, to restore the certificate and, if selected, key pairs.

Support for key pair export is implemented by the CSP. Microsoft's base CSPs support key pair export but also make it user controlled through an exportable flag, which is set at key generation. Third-party CSPs may or may not support private key export. For example, smart card CSPs do not generally support this operation. For software CSPs with nonexportable keys, the alternative is to maintain a complete system-image backup, including all Registry information.

Certificate Revocation

Certificates may need to be revoked for a variety of reasons such as fraud, compromise of a private key, or change of status since certificate issuance. Windows 2000 PKI support for certificate revocation is also standards based and incorporates support for industry-standard Certificate Revocation Lists (CRLs). Since verification in a PK environment is distributed, revocation information must also be distributed. Windows 2000 uses the Active Directory for this distribution. Enterprise CAs support certificate revocation and CRL publication to the Active Directory. Domain clients can obtain this information and cache it locally to use when verifying certificates; thus distribution of verification is extended to the client level. This implies that published CRLs must be accessible to clients over the network. This same distribution and verification mechanism also supports CRLs published by commercial CAs or third-party certificate server products.

Roaming Support

Roaming is the ability of a user to use the same PK-based applications on different computers within the enterprise Windows environment. This ability can be made possible if the user's cryptographic keys and certificates are available wherever he or she logs on. Windows 2000 PKI supports roaming in two ways. First, if the Microsoft base CSPs are used, roaming of keys and certificates is supported by using roaming profiles. This is transparent to the user once roaming profiles are enabled. This method will not work in instances where the key data is preserved on hardware devices and not available as software. In such cases, hardware token devices, such as smart cards, support roaming, provided that they incorporate a physical certificate store. The smart card CSPs that ship with the Windows 2000 platform support this functionality. The user carries the hardware token to the new location.

PK SECURITY POLICY IN WINDOWS 2000

Security policies are policies that can be applied to sites, domains, etc., and affect the associated security groups of users and computers. It is important to note that PK security policy is only one aspect of an overall Windows security policy and is integrated into this structure. PK security policy provides a mechanism to centrally define and manage policy and enforce it globally. For example, trust in root CAs may be set by policy to establish trust relationships used by domain clients in verifying PK certificates. As another example, the administrator can set usage properties associated with the CA. If specified, these restrict the purposes for which the CA-issued certificates are valid. Restrictions are specified according to object identifiers (OIDs), as defined for ExtendedKeyUsage extensions in the IETF PKIX Part 1 draft. As another example, Windows 2000 policy mechanisms have been defined to support an automated certificate enrollment process. An organization should be familiar with and tailor these PK policies as part of establishing a Windows 2000–based PK environment.

PK-BASED APPLICATIONS

PK-based functionality has been incorporated in a number of application areas. A number of Microsoft products also support the protocols and standards needed to implement a PK-based infrastructure.

Internet Security

Security is a key consideration in Web-based applications given the distributed anonymous environment provided by the Internet where an organization can exercise little direct control over users. PK-based applications have been developed for authenticating clients and servers, and protecting the confidentiality of the data as it travels around the public Internet. Windows 2000 supports the Secure Sockets Layer (SSL) and the emerging

IETF standard Transport Layer Security (TLS) protocols. SSL and TLS are flexible security protocols that can be layered on top of other transport protocols. They rely on PK-based authentication technology and use PK-based key negotiation to generate a unique encryption key for each client/server session.

SSL and TLS are supported on the Windows platform by the secure channel (Schannel) SSPI provider (see earlier Figure 21-4). Microsoft Internet Explorer and Internet Information Services both use Schannel for this functionality. Because Schannel is integrated with Microsoft's SSPI architecture, it is available for use with multiple protocols to support authenticated and/or encrypted communications.

Using SSL and TLS protocols, it is possible for both clients and servers to have identification certificates issued by mutually trusted CAs. In this scenario, certificates can be exchanged along with data that proves possession of the corresponding private key. Each side can then validate the certificate and verify possession of the private key, as mentioned earlier (using the public key of the certificate holder). The advantage of this method is that the identifying information included in the certificate can then be used to make supplemental access-control decisions. For example, the server can decide what data the client can access. Windows 2000 PKI integrates support for these types of server functions as a standard feature of Windows 2000 Server. User certificates can be mapped on a one-to-one or many-to-one basis against security principals (User objects) in the Active Directory.

Secure E-Mail

PK-based secure e-mail products have been available for a while and are being adopted by more and more users. Among the products that support secure e-mail are Microsoft Exchange and Microsoft Outlook. The most common uses of PK technology by secure e-mail vendors are for digital signatures and large data encryption (these topics are covered earlier in the chapter). The problem of interoperability between certificates issued by different vendors is being tackled by the latest S/MIME standard (S/MIME version 3). The current status is that SSL/TLS and S/MIME are relatively mature and fairly widely adopted and work well across multiple vendor products. However, newer applications such as code signing and digitally signed forms have not yet reached the same level of maturity and interoperability.

Microsoft recommends that companies interested in PK technology start with S/MIME-based secure e-mail using Microsoft Exchange Server. Exchange Server 5.5 (SP1) together with Outlook 98 offers an S/MIME-based e-mail solution. This solution provides secure e-mail, along with key recovery features and the ability to have multiple Key Management servers and a certificate trust hierarchy.

CRYPTOAPI ARCHITECTURE

The CryptoAPI interface is the primary interface available for you to develop applications that use the security functions in Windows 2000. Figure 21-5 shows the CryptoAPI architecture.

As shown in Figure 21-5, five major functional areas make up the architecture of the CryptoAPI. A summary of these five areas along with their descriptions is shown in Table 21-1.

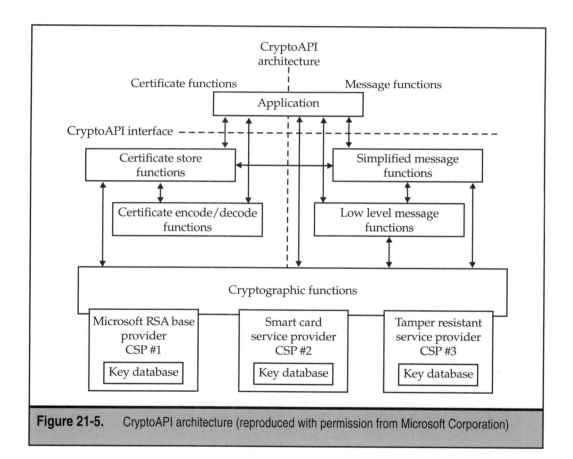

Figure 21-5.   CryptoAPI architecture (reproduced with permission from Microsoft Corporation)

CryptoAPI Architecture Functional Area	Description
Base cryptographic functions	There are three subfunctions in this functional area. These are: *Context functions* Context functions are used to connect to a CSP. Using these functions, you can choose a specific CSP by name or find a specific CSP that can provide a needed class of functionality. *Key generation functions* Key generation functions are used to generate and store cryptographic keys. These functions include full support for changing chaining modes, initialization vectors, and other encryption features. *Key exchange functions* Key exchange functions are used to exchange or transmit keys.
Simplified message functions	Simplified message functions wrap low-level CryptoAPI functions into a single function to accomplish a specified task. Simplified message functions are used to: Encrypt and decrypt messages and data. Sign messages and data. Verify the authenticity of signatures on received messages and related data. An example of a simplified message function is **CryptDecodeMessage**, which decodes a cryptographic message.
Certificate store functions	Certificate store functions provide the capability to store, retrieve, enumerate, verify, and use the information stored in the certificates.
Certificate encode/decode functions	Certificate encode/decode functions, as the name implies, support encryption, decryption, and hashing operations. An example of a certificate encode/decode function is **CryptDecrypt**, which decrypts a section of ciphertext by using the specified encryption key.
Low-level message functions	Low-level message functions are used to perform essentially the same tasks as those performed by the simplified message functions; they offer greater flexibility at the cost of invoking more function calls. Unless you have a specific reason, the use of these low-level message functions is not recommended in most applications.

Table 21-1.   CryptoAPI Functions and Descriptions

CryptoAPI Usage Guidelines

The entire collection of all the functions, taken together, composes the CryptoAPI. CryptoAPI functions are exposed by the operating system's *Advapi32.dll* and *Crypt32.dll* files. You can invoke any of the functions, regardless of the functional area to which it belongs, directly. The only restriction, as shown in previous Figure 21-3, is that you cannot directly invoke a CSP.

Access to CSP functionality is through base cryptographic functions. When you invoke the base cryptographic functions, a parameter is available for you to specify the CSP you want to use. For example, the *HCRYPTPROV* parameter of the **CryptDeriveKey** function lets you specify the handle of the CSP you want to access. This parameter is not mandatory. You can set this parameter to NULL to select a default CSP. You get the CSP handle by calling **CryptAcquireContext** and specifying a provider type and, optionally, a provider name.

While accessing CSP functions, you may want to take care not to tie your applications to specific details of the CSP implementation such as memory required or specifics about data types and sizes. This is because the CSP may provide an improved version in the future, and your application may cease to work. Alternatively, you may want your application to work with more than one CSP and let the user choose CSPs. Tying your application to the details of a specific CSP may prevent your application from working with multiple CSPs.

Cryptographic Service Providers

As mentioned earlier, the actual cryptography-related implementation of standards and algorithms is provided by Cryptographic Service Providers (CSPs). A CSP has both a name and a type. A name has to be unique, although there is likely to be more than one CSP for the same type. Microsoft ships software-based CSPs along with Windows 2000. The simplest of these CSPs is named Base Cryptographic Provider and has the type PROV_RSA_FULL. Besides the Base Cryptographic provider, Microsoft also provides the following other CSPs:

▼ Microsoft Strong Cryptographic Provider

■ Microsoft Enhanced Cryptographic Provider

■ Microsoft DSS Cryptographic Provider

■ Microsoft Base DSS and Diffie-Hellman Cryptographic Provider

■ Microsoft DSS and Diffie-Hellman/Schannel Cryptographic Provider

▲ Microsoft RSA/Schannel Cryptographic Provider

The Windows 2000 Microsoft CSPs have received the Federal Information Processing Standard (FIPS) 140-1 Level 1 certification by the National Institute of Standards and Technology (NIST). The primary differences between the base CSP and enhanced CSPs are that the enhanced versions support longer key lengths and support all variations of the Data Encryption Standard (DES), including DES and Triple DES (2 and 3 keys). Additional details about the CSPs are available on MSDN.

It is important to note that CSPs can implement their functions in a number of different ways, although their implementation is transparent to your application. Some CSPs may supply a DLL and a signature file. The signature file ensures that the CryptoAPI recognizes the CSP, and the CryptoAPI periodically validates the signature file to ensure that it has not been tampered with. Other CSPs may be implemented as a Win32 service that can be called through a local RPC. Yet other CSPs may implement some of their functions using hardware such as smart cards or coprocessors accessed through device drivers. For example, Windows 2000 includes smart card CSPs from Gemplus SCA and Schlumberger Limited.

PROGRAMMING EXAMPLES

The next sample is a dialog-based application that initializes the user's cryptographic environment and allows the user to encrypt, decrypt, sign, or verify a file. The sample requests the names of the input file and the output file to operate on. For encryption, a key is generated and is encrypted with the user's public key. The encrypted key is placed at the beginning of the output file and is followed with the encrypted contents of the input file. For decryption, the encrypted key is read and imported into the key container and is used to decrypt the rest of the data. As the data is decrypted, it is written to the output file. For signing, the data from the input file is read and a hash value is generated. The hash value is encrypted, that is, it is signed with the user's private key. The signed hash is placed at the beginning of the output file and is followed with the original data. To verify a signed file, the input file is opened and the signature is read. The file content following the signature is hashed, and the signature is verified.

```
// CryptoDlg.h

#if !defined(AFX_CRYPTODLG_H)
#define AFX_CRYPTODLG_H

#if _MSC_VER > 1000
#pragma once
#endif // _MSC_VER > 1000
#include <stdio.h>
#include <wincrypt.h>

// CCryptoDlg dialog

class CCryptoDlg : public CDialog
{
// Construction
public:
    CCryptoDlg(CWnd* pParent = NULL);
```

```
// Dialog Data
    //{{AFX_DATA(CCryptoDlg)
    enum { IDD = IDD_CRYPTO_DIALOG };
    CEdit     m_status;
    CEdit     m_fileout;
    CEdit     m_filein;
    CString   m_password;
    //}}AFX_DATA

    // ClassWizard generated virtual function overrides
    //{{AFX_VIRTUAL(CCryptoDlg)
    protected:
    virtual void DoDataExchange(CDataExchange* pDX);
    //}}AFX_VIRTUAL

// Implementation
protected:
    HICON m_hIcon;

    // Generated message map functions
    //{{AFX_MSG(CCryptoDlg)
    virtual BOOL OnInitDialog();
    afx_msg void OnPaint();
    afx_msg HCURSOR OnQueryDragIcon();
    afx_msg void OnBrowsein();
    afx_msg void OnBrowseout();
    afx_msg void OnDecrypt();
    afx_msg void OnEncrypt();
    afx_msg void OnSign();
    afx_msg void OnVerify();
    afx_msg void AppendMsg(LPCTSTR);
    virtual void OnCancel();
    //}}AFX_MSG
    DECLARE_MESSAGE_MAP()

private:
    HCRYPTPROV    hProvider;
    HCRYPTKEY     hExchangeKey;
    HCRYPTKEY     hSigningKey;
    BYTE          szContainerName[128];
    DWORD         dwLen;

    void CloseFileHandles (FILE *f1, FILE *f2);
};

#endif // !defined(AFX_CRYPTODLG_H)
```

The dialog class implementation is shown next. Notice the inclusion of *wincrypt.h*. This header file has all the declarations needed for cryptographic functions of this sample. Application modules using the CAPI features of Windows 2000 should use this include file.

```cpp
// CryptoDlg.cpp

#include "stdafx.h"
#include "wincrypt.h"
#include "Crypto.h"
#include "CryptoDlg.h"

#ifdef _DEBUG
#define new DEBUG_NEW
#undef THIS_FILE
static char THIS_FILE[] = __FILE__;
#endif

// CCryptoDlg dialog

CCryptoDlg::CCryptoDlg(CWnd* pParent /*=NULL*/)
    : CDialog(CCryptoDlg::IDD, pParent)
{
    //{{AFX_DATA_INIT(CCryptoDlg)
    m_password = _T("");
    //}}AFX_DATA_INIT
    // Note that LoadIcon does not require a subsequent DestroyIcon in Win32
    m_hIcon = AfxGetApp()->LoadIcon(IDR_MAINFRAME);
}

void CCryptoDlg::DoDataExchange(CDataExchange* pDX)
{
    CDialog::DoDataExchange(pDX);
    //{{AFX_DATA_MAP(CCryptoDlg)
    DDX_Control(pDX, IDC_STATUS, m_status);
    DDX_Control(pDX, IDC_OUTFILE, m_fileout);
    DDX_Control(pDX, IDC_INFILE, m_filein);
    DDX_Text(pDX, IDC_PASSWORD, m_password);
    //}}AFX_DATA_MAP
}
```

```
BEGIN_MESSAGE_MAP(CCryptoDlg, CDialog)
    //{{AFX_MSG_MAP(CCryptoDlg)
    ON_WM_PAINT()
    ON_WM_QUERYDRAGICON()
    ON_BN_CLICKED(IDC_BROWSEIN, OnBrowsein)
    ON_BN_CLICKED(IDC_BROWSEOUT, OnBrowseout)
    ON_BN_CLICKED(IDC_DECRYPT, OnDecrypt)
    ON_BN_CLICKED(IDC_ENCRYPT, OnEncrypt)
    ON_BN_CLICKED(IDC_SIGN, OnSign)
    ON_BN_CLICKED(IDC_VERIFY, OnVerify)
    //}}AFX_MSG_MAP
END_MESSAGE_MAP()

// CCryptoDlg message handlers

BOOL CCryptoDlg::OnInitDialog()
{
    CDialog::OnInitDialog();
    CHAR    szMessage[256];
    DWORD   dwRC;

    // Set the icon for this dialog.  The framework does this automatically
    //  when the application's main window is not a dialog
    SetIcon(m_hIcon, TRUE);            // Set big icon
    SetIcon(m_hIcon, FALSE);           // Set small icon
```

To perform cryptographic operations such as encrypt, decrypt, sign, or verify, a user should have a key container with proper key pairs. The **CryptAcquireContext** API gets a handle to a particular key container within a specific Cryptographic Service Provider. This API returns a handle that is used in CryptoAPIs to identify the CSP. Since this handle is required to use the crypto functions, the first call any crypto application would make will be to the **CryptAcquireContext** API. When requesting a handle, the application specifies the name of the CSP and the provider type. A CSP has a unique name, but the provider type may not be unique. If the application does not specify a CSP, the API will try to load the default named provider from a list of named providers associated with the logged-on user; in the event that one is not available, it will try to load from the list associated with the computer. Windows 2000 comes with a CSP by the name "Microsoft Base Cryptographic Provider v1.0," which is used here. A number of predefined provider types are also available; one such predefined provider type, PROV_RSA_FULL, is used in this sample. This provider type supports both encryption and signing. The RSA algorithm is used for public key operations by this provider. The last parameter in this API is generally set to zero, but it may also be a set of predefined flags with special meaning to a particular CSP.

If the key container is available, then this API returns a handle. However, if the specified key container is not available, then the API returns an error. This API actually returns a range of errors, but for simplicity, this sample ignores very generic errors such as invalid parameters, not enough memory, and other obvious errors. If a key container is not available, it returns the error NTE_BAD_KEYSET. The **CryptAcquireContext** API can also be used to create a new key container by specifying the CRYPT_NEWKEYSET flag. The Cryptographic Service Providers store all keys in a key container and are persisted on some storage medium such a hard disk or smart card. If a name for the key container is not specified, the user's logon name is used for the key container name. It may be useful for applications to create their own key containers and key pairs.

```
if (!(CryptAcquireContext(&hProvider, NULL,
                          MS_DEF_PROV,
                          PROV_RSA_FULL, 0)))
{
    AppendMsg("Container does not exist.  Creating a new \
            container.\r\n");
    if (!(CryptAcquireContext(&hProvider, NULL,
                              MS_DEF_PROV, PROV_RSA_FULL,
                              CRYPT_NEWKEYSET)))
    {
        sprintf(szMessage, "Error creating new container. RC = %X\r\n",
            GetLastError());
        AppendMsg(szMessage);
        return FALSE;
    }
```

In order to retrieve various attributes of the CSP, the **CryptGetProvParam** API can be used. This API can be called with a flag to indicate the attribute of interest, and that attribute value will be returned. To illustrate the use of this API, the container name of the newly created container is queried and displayed here. This API is not thread-safe and should be used with care in a multithreaded application.

```
    if (!(CryptGetProvParam(hProvider, PP_CONTAINER, szContainerName,
                            &dwLen, 0)))
    {
        AppendMsg("Error getting the container name");
    }
    else
    {
        sprintf(szMessage, "The name of the new container is %s.\r\n",
            szContainerName);
        AppendMsg(szMessage);
    }
}
```

For any asymmetric key cryptographic operation, a public/private key pair is required. The key pairs have two components; one is the private key, which is not divulged to any one, and the other is the public key, which is made public. The private key is used for decrypting and signing, while the public key is used for encrypting and verifying. The key pair owner, whether an application or a user, generally distributes the public key such that other applications or users can send messages or data encrypted using this public key. These messages can only be decrypted by the private key, which is kept safe by the application or user. The private key can also be used by the owner to sign messages or data that can be verified by anyone using the signer's public key.

Though the same key pair can be used for both decryption and signing, it is very useful to keep two key pairs, one for decryption and the other for the signature. Situations could arise in which the key owner could be required by law to divulge the private key to decrypt encrypted information meant for that key owner. However, if the user has the same key pair for both signing and decryption, then when the user divulges the private key, the receiver of the private key can impersonate the owner by signing messages and data. Another reason for having two key pairs is that some CSPs use one algorithm for key exchange and a different algorithm for signing. When data is signed and encrypted with the same key pair, it becomes more vulnerable than data that is signed and encrypted with two different keys. Data is typically signed and encrypted during an encrypted and signed message exchange in which the data is encrypted and the session key is placed along with the signature. Hence it is very wise to keep two key pairs, one meant for decrypting messages, and one meant for signing messages.

Of the two general ways of encrypting contents, using symmetric algorithms and using asymmetric algorithms, the symmetric algorithms are substantially faster. However, they are relatively weak when compared to asymmetric algorithms. A compromise that is generally used in a cryptographic data exchange is to encrypt the message using a symmetric key and a symmetric algorithm and then to encrypt that symmetric key using the public key and asymmetric algorithm. This sample program uses this way of encrypting data. In order to encrypt the symmetric key that was used for encrypting data, an asymmetric key is required. This key pair is called a *key exchange* key pair and is identified by a flag, **AT_KEYEXCHANGE**.

Having initialized the CSP, the sample gets the handle to the key exchange key pair by calling the **CryptGetUserKey** API. If the key pair is not available, a new key pair for key exchange is created by calling the **CryptGenKey** API.

```
    // Check if key pairs exist and if not create them.
if (!(CryptGetUserKey(hProvider, AT_KEYEXCHANGE, &hExchangeKey)))
{
    if (dwRC = GetLastError())
    {
        if (dwRC == NTE_NO_KEY)
        {
            if (!(CryptGenKey(hProvider, AT_KEYEXCHANGE, 0,
                        &hExchangeKey)))
```

```
            {
                sprintf(szMessage,
                        "Error generating exchange key. RC = %X\r\n",
                        GetLastError());
                AppendMsg(szMessage);
                return TRUE;
            }
          }
        }
      }
```

The sample repeats for a signing key pair. It checks if a signing key pair is available and if not, it creates a signing key pair.

```
    if (!(CryptGetUserKey(hProvider, AT_SIGNATURE, &hSigningKey)))
    {
        if (dwRC = GetLastError())
        {
            if (dwRC == NTE_NO_KEY)
            {
                if (!CryptGenKey(hProvider, AT_SIGNATURE, 0,
                                &hSigningKey))
                {
                    sprintf(szMessage,
                            "Error generating signing key. RC = %X\r\n",
                            GetLastError());
                    AppendMsg(szMessage);
                    return TRUE;
                }
            }
        }
    }
    return TRUE;
}
```

Thus during initialization all the data required for the rest of the program are initialized and, if not available, created and maintained as class member variables for ready access later.

```
void CCryptoDlg::OnPaint()
{
    if (IsIconic())
    {
        CPaintDC dc(this); // device context for painting
```

```
        SendMessage(WM_ICONERASEBKGND, (WPARAM) dc.GetSafeHdc(), 0);

        // Center icon in client rectangle
        int cxIcon = GetSystemMetrics(SM_CXICON);
        int cyIcon = GetSystemMetrics(SM_CYICON);
        CRect rect;
        GetClientRect(&rect);
        int x = (rect.Width() - cxIcon + 1) / 2;
        int y = (rect.Height() - cyIcon + 1) / 2;

        // Draw the icon
        dc.DrawIcon(x, y, m_hIcon);
    }
    else
    {
        CDialog::OnPaint();
    }
}


HCURSOR CCryptoDlg::OnQueryDragIcon()
{
    return (HCURSOR) m_hIcon;
}
```

The next two methods aid in navigating through the file system using the file dialog and retrieving the file for operation.

```
void CCryptoDlg::OnBrowsein()
{
    CString strPath("");
    CFileDialog m_File(TRUE, NULL, NULL, OFN_FILEMUSTEXIST);

    if (m_File.DoModal() == IDOK)
    {
        strPath = m_File.GetPathName();
    }

    m_filein.SetWindowText((LPCTSTR)strPath);
}


void CCryptoDlg::OnBrowseout()
```

```
{
    CString strPath("");
    CFileDialog m_File(FALSE, NULL, NULL,
                       OFN_OVERWRITEPROMPT |
                       OFN_PATHMUSTEXIST);

    if (m_File.DoModal() == IDOK)
    {
        strPath = m_File.GetPathName();
    }

    m_fileout.SetWindowText((LPCTSTR)strPath);
}
```

When the user clicks Encrypt in the dialog box, the **OnEncrypt** function is called, which encrypts the specified file and writes it to the output file. The common way of encrypting a file is using a symmetric algorithm. The symmetric key that is used for encryption is also called the *session key*. The layout of the encrypted file is as follows: If a session key is generated, then the encrypted session key is included in the file. In that case, the first four bytes hold the length of the encrypted session key. The encrypted session key itself follows this. The encrypted data is then placed in the file. If a session key is derived using a password string, then the encrypted session key is not placed in the file but can be derived from the same password later for decryption.

The first thing that needs to be done before encrypting is to get a session key. A session key can be either generated by calling the **CryptGenKey** API or derived using a password string and using the **CryptDeriveKey** API. A session key is generally considered transient; unlike the key exchange key or signing key, it is not persisted in the key container. If some data that is encrypted with a session key needs to be decrypted, then the session key should be exported and persisted. When session keys are exported, they are exported in a secure manner by encrypting them with the user's public key, and hence to regain the session key, the user should have the private key that corresponds to the public key that encrypted the session key. Given that there are two methods of creating a session key, which one to use depends on what is appropriate to the application. The advantage of the session key generated by calling the **CryptGenKey** API is that it uses a random key that is less predictable. However, the disadvantage is that when this key is exported and reimported, it can only be imported by the user who exported it. The reason is that when the session key is exported, it is encrypted using the user's public key. Another user who does not posses this user's private key cannot import this session key. The consequence is that the encrypted file can be decrypted only by the user who encrypted that file. If for some reason the user who encrypted the file loses the key exchange key pair, either because of hardware failure or by deleting the key container, then the original file is not recoverable from the encrypted file. On the other hand, if the session key is generated by a password using the **CryptDeriveKey** API, users other than the one who encrypted the file can decrypt it.

867

```
void CCryptoDlg::OnEncrypt()
{
    CHAR      szMessage[256];
    BYTE *    pKeyBlob = NULL;
    DWORD     dwKeyBlobLen;
    HCRYPTKEY    hSessionKey = NULL;
    HCRYPTHASH  hHash = NULL;
    BYTE     *pEncryptBuffer = NULL;
    FILE *hSource      = NULL;
    FILE *hDestination = NULL;
    CString filein;
    CString fileout;
```

The application checks to see if a password has been provided for encryption. If a password is not provided, the code calls the **CrypGenKey** API to generate a random session key. This is the same API that was used earlier for generating the user's key pairs but with different parameters. This sample uses block encryption where a block of data is sent for encryption each time. The algorithm that it uses for encryption is the RC2 block cipher, and this algorithm is passed in as a parameter for generating the key.

```
UpdateData();
do {
    if (m_password.IsEmpty())
    {
        if (!CryptGenKey (hProvider, CALG_RC2, CRYPT_EXPORTABLE,
                          &hSessionKey))
        {
            sprintf(szMessage,
                    "Error generating session key. RC = %X\r\n",
                    GetLastError());
            AppendMsg(szMessage);
            break;
        }
```

If a session key is generated, then the session key is exported so that it can be written to the output file. Although this discussion makes many references to the keys, what actually happens is that keys are used only through their handles. The raw key itself, the bits of data, is not handled by the application. Generally keys are stored in the key containers and are referenced only by their handles. However, transient keys such as the session key are not persisted in the key container. Since a symmetric algorithm is used for encryption, the key that is used for encryption should be remembered in order to decrypt the data later. As the session key generated here is random, it needs to be exported and persisted. To export the key, the **CryptExportKey** API is used. This API exports the requested key to a key blob.

Key blobs (binary large objects) are secure means of exporting a key and exchanging it with other applications. A blob consists of a header information and the key itself. Since the key is encrypted, it is safe to exchange the key using the key blob. There are five types of key blobs to which the keys can be exported. The SIMPLEBLOB that is used here is used to export the session key. When the key is exported, the session key is encrypted with the user's public key.

The **CryptExportKey** API is used to export the session key. Since we may not know the size of the buffer that is needed for the key blob, a NULL parameter can be passed. When the API sees a NULL parameter for the buffer, it returns the buffer size required to fulfill the request. A buffer of appropriate size is allocated, and the API is called again. Many of the CAPIs use this technique to first query the size of the buffer needed, next allocate a buffer of the required size, and then reissue the call. This must be done to accommodate different CSPs as well as the different algorithms.

```
CryptExportKey (hSessionKey, hExchangeKey,
                SIMPLEBLOB, 0,  NULL, &dwKeyBlobLen);
if ((pKeyBlob = (BYTE *) malloc (dwKeyBlobLen)) == NULL)
{
    AppendMsg("Error allocating memory");
    break;
}
if (!CryptExportKey (hSessionKey, hExchangeKey,
                SIMPLEBLOB, 0,  pKeyBlob, &dwKeyBlobLen))
{
    sprintf(szMessage,
            "Error exporting session key. RC = %X\r\n",
             GetLastError());
    AppendMsg(szMessage);
    break;
}
}
```

As discussed earlier, if the data should be decrypted by a different user than the one who encrypted it, a password can be used to encrypt the data, as in this sample. The code shown next details how the password is used to encrypt the data. Essentially, the session key is derived from the password instead of being random. In order to derive a session key, the password or any pass phrase string is first hashed. In order to do this, a hash object is first created by calling the **CryptCreateHash** API. This returns a hash object similar to objects used in other hash-related APIs. This API is discussed in more detail later in the description of this sample where I discuss signing. The hash of the given password string is calculated by calling the **CryptHashData** API.

```
    else
    {
        if (!CryptCreateHash(hProvider, CALG_MD5, 0, 0, &hHash))
        {
            sprintf(szMessage,
                    "Error creating a hash object. RC = %X\r\n",
                    GetLastError());
            AppendMsg(szMessage);
            break;
        }
        if (!CryptHashData(hHash, (BYTE *)((LPCTSTR)m_password),
                           m_password.GetLength(), 0))
        {
            sprintf(szMessage,
                    "Error hashing the data. RC = %X\r\n",
                    GetLastError());
            AppendMsg(szMessage);
            break;
        }
```

Once the data is hashed, the session key can be derived from the hash object by calling the **CryptDeriveKey** API. This API generates a session key and guarantees that the same session key will be generated for a given CSP, algorithm, and set of hash data. As before, the algorithm requested is the RC2 block cipher algorithm.

```
        if (!(CryptDeriveKey(hProvider, CALG_RC2, hHash,
                             0, &hSessionKey)))
        {
            sprintf(szMessage,
                    "Error generating session key. RC = %X\r\n",
                    GetLastError());
            AppendMsg(szMessage);
            break;
        }
        CryptDestroyHash(hHash);
    }
    // Allocate the a buffer to read data into and encrypt
    // The size of each block of data is 1024 bytes
    pEncryptBuffer = (BYTE *) malloc (1024 + 8);

    // Open the input and output files
    m_filein.GetWindowText(filein);
    m_fileout.GetWindowText(fileout);
```

```
if ((hSource = fopen ((LPCTSTR)filein, "rb")) == NULL)
{
    // Error opening the input file
    AppendMsg ("Cannot open the source file.\r\n");
    break;
}
if ((hDestination = fopen ((LPCTSTR)fileout, "wb")) == NULL)
{
    // Error opening the output file
    AppendMsg ("Cannot open the output file.\r\n");
    break;
}
```

The input and output files are opened, and if a session key was generated, then the session key blob length and the session key blob are written to the output file. This is followed with blocks of encrypted data. To encrypt the data, a block of 1,024 bytes is read and passed on to the **CryptEncrypt** API. The handle to the session key is passed as the first parameter. The second parameter is the handle to a hash object.

In certain cases, the application would like to encrypt the data as well as sign it when completed. In such a situation, the application can provide a hash object and the **CryptEncrypt** API would compute the hash of the data as it encrypts them. At the end of the encryption cycle, the application can call the **CryptGetHashParam** API and sign the hash using the **CryptSignHash** API. In this sample, however, the encrypted file is not signed and hence a zero is passed in. The logic of this sample reads a block of data from the input file and encrypts that block. This is done repeatedly until the end of the file is reached. The encryption engine needs to know when the last block of data is being encrypted, since it does additional work for the last block. The next parameter is reserved for future use. The buffer to be encrypted is passed in, and the API sends back the encrypted data in the same buffer, which is written back to the output file. The next parameter is a pointer to a DWORD, which on input indicates the number of bytes to be encrypted and on return from the API indicates the length in bytes of the encrypted data. If the buffer is smaller than what is needed, then the application can allocate a buffer of the size indicated by this parameter. The last parameter is the size of the input buffer.

```
if (m_password.IsEmpty())
{
    fwrite(&dwKeyBlobLen, sizeof(DWORD), 1, hDestination);
    fwrite(pKeyBlob, 1, dwKeyBlobLen, hDestination);
}
// Now read blocks of data from the file and encrypt each block.

do
{
    DWORD dwBytesRead = 0;
    if (dwBytesRead = fread (pEncryptBuffer, 1, 1024, hSource))
```

```
        {
            // if data is read
            if (!(CryptEncrypt(hSessionKey, 0, feof(hSource), 0,
                               pEncryptBuffer, &dwBytesRead, 1024+8)))
            {
                sprintf(szMessage,
                        "Error encrypting data. RC = %X\r\n",
                        GetLastError());
                AppendMsg(szMessage);
                break;
            }
            // Write the encrypted data to the file
            fwrite (pEncryptBuffer, 1,  dwBytesRead, hDestination);
        }
    } while (!feof(hSource));
    AppendMsg ("File encrypted succesfully.\r\n");
} while (0);
if (pKeyBlob)
    free (pKeyBlob);
if (pEncryptBuffer)
    free (pEncryptBuffer);
CloseFileHandles(hSource, hDestination);
if (hSessionKey)
    CryptDestroyKey(hSessionKey);
}
```

After writing the encrypted data, the sample cleans up the resources allocated. The **CryptDestroyKey** API should be called to release the handle reference to the session key. The handle in this sample refers to a session key, and in this case the CSP destroys the key and typically cleans up the memory and frees it. This is also true for public keys that might have been imported into the key container. The handle to these keys is freed, although the public/private key pairs are really not destroyed. While this may not seem to involve a lot of resources, some of the CSPs are implemented in hardware, where the available resources are really limited.

When the user clicks Decrypt in the dialog box, the **OnDecrypt** function is called, which decrypts the specified file and writes the decrypted file to the output file. The flow of this function is very similar to that of the **OnEncrypt** function.

```
void CCryptoDlg::OnDecrypt()
{
    CHAR     szMessage[256];
    BYTE *   pKeyBlob = NULL;
    DWORD    dwKeyBlobLen;
    HCRYPTKEY    hSessionKey = NULL;
    HCRYPTHASH   hHash = NULL;
```

```
FILE *hSource      = NULL;
FILE *hDestination = NULL;
CString filein;
CString fileout;
BYTE    *pDecryptBuffer = NULL;


UpdateData ();

// Open the input and output files
do {

    m_filein.GetWindowText (filein);
    m_fileout.GetWindowText (fileout);

    if ((hSource = fopen ((LPCTSTR)filein, "rb")) == NULL)
    {
        // Error opening the input file
        AppendMsg ("Cannot open the source file.\r\n");
        break;
    }
    if ((hDestination = fopen ((LPCTSTR)fileout, "wb")) == NULL)
    {
        // Error opening the output file
        AppendMsg ("Cannot open the output file.\r\n");
        break;
    }
```

If a password is not provided, it is assumed that the original file was encrypted with a session key, which in turn is encrypted and placed at the beginning of the file. It may be recalled that the first DWORD at the beginning of the file gives the size of the key blob that encrypted the file. The key blob length is read, and a buffer to hold the key blob is allocated. The code marginally protects itself by making sure that the number of bytes indicated at the top of the file is not greater than the file size itself. While this is not a foolproof method, it marginally protects the user.

```
if (m_password.IsEmpty())
{
    // Read the session key
    LONG fileLen = 0;
    fseek(hSource, 0, SEEK_END);
    fileLen = ftell(hSource);
    fseek(hSource, 0, SEEK_SET);
    fread (&dwKeyBlobLen, sizeof(DWORD), 1, hSource);
```

```
if (dwKeyBlobLen >= (DWORD)fileLen)
{
    AppendMsg("Invalid source file.\r\n");
    break;
}
if ((pKeyBlob = (BYTE *)malloc (dwKeyBlobLen)) == NULL)
{
    sprintf(szMessage,
            "Error allocating %ld bytes of memory\r\n",
            dwKeyBlobLen);
    AppendMsg(szMessage);
    break;
}
fread (pKeyBlob, 1, dwKeyBlobLen, hSource);
if (ferror(hSource))
{
    AppendMsg("Error reading the encrypted session key.\r\n");
    break;
}
```

Once the key blob is read, it needs to be imported. Remember that this key blob is a secure container for the session key, which is encrypted with the user's public key. The **CryptImportKey** API is used to import the session key from the key blob into the CSP.

```
// Import the encrypted key
if (!(CryptImportKey(hProvider, pKeyBlob,
                     dwKeyBlobLen, 0, 0, &hSessionKey)))
{
    sprintf(szMessage,
            "Error importing the key. RC = %X\r\n",
            GetLastError());
    AppendMsg(szMessage);
    break;
}
}
```

If a password was used to derive the session key during encryption, the same password is used again to derive the session key.

```
else
{
    // We have a password.  Use it to derive the session key
    if (!(CryptCreateHash(hProvider, CALG_MD5, 0, 0, &hHash)))
```

```
    {
        sprintf(szMessage,
                "Error creating a hash object. RC = %X\r\n",
                GetLastError());
        AppendMsg(szMessage);
        break;
    }
    if (!(CryptHashData(hHash, (BYTE *)((LPCTSTR)m_password),
                        m_password.GetLength(), 0)))
    {
        sprintf(szMessage,
                "Error hashing the data. RC = %X\r\n",
                GetLastError());
        AppendMsg(szMessage);
        break;
    }
    if (!(CryptDeriveKey(hProvider, CALG_RC2, hHash, 0,
                         &hSessionKey)))
    {
        sprintf(szMessage,
                "Error generating session key. RC = %X\r\n",
                GetLastError());
        AppendMsg(szMessage);
        break;
    }
    CryptDestroyHash(hHash);
    hHash = NULL;
}
```

Once the handle to the session key is retrieved, a buffer to read and decrypt the data is allocated and the contents of the file are read and decrypted repeatedly until all data in the file is decrypted. The **CryptDecrypt** API is used for decryption; the parameters used for this API are similar to those used for **CryptEncrypt**. As in the case of the encrypt function, an optional handle to a hash object can be sent to the **CryptDecrypt** API, in which case the signature can be verified after the decryption is completed by calling the **CryptVerifySignature** API.

```
pDecryptBuffer = (BYTE *) malloc (1024 + 8);
do
{
    DWORD dwBytesRead = 0;
    if (dwBytesRead = fread (pDecryptBuffer, 1, 1024, hSource))
    {
        // if data is read
```

```
            if (!(CryptDecrypt(hSessionKey, 0, feof(hSource), 0,
                            pDecryptBuffer, &dwBytesRead)))
            {
                sprintf(szMessage,
                        "Error decrypting data. RC = %X\r\n",
                        GetLastError());
                AppendMsg(szMessage);
                break;
            }
            // Write the encrypted data to the file
            fwrite (pDecryptBuffer, 1,  dwBytesRead, hDestination);
        }
    } while (!feof(hSource));
    AppendMsg ("File decrypted succesfully.\r\n");
}while (0);
if (pKeyBlob)
    free (pKeyBlob);
if (pDecryptBuffer)
    free (pDecryptBuffer);
if (hHash)
    CryptDestroyHash(hHash);
CloseFileHandles(hSource, hDestination);
if (hSessionKey)
    CryptDestroyKey(hSessionKey);
}
```

After completion of the decryption, all the resources are freed. Shown next is the code that gets executed when the Sign button is clicked in the dialog box. This function reads the input file, signs it, and produces an output file with the signature attached at the beginning of the file.

Signing data becomes necessary if an application wants to detect tampering with the data or establish the authenticity of the data. Since signing of the data is done with a private key, and given that the private key is not divulged, one can rely on the authenticity and integrity of signed data. Signing data consists of two steps: first the data is hashed and then the resulting hash value is encrypted with the private key of the private/public key pair. Since the corresponding public key is publicly available, anyone can verify the signature.

```
void CCryptoDlg::OnSign()
{
    CHAR      szMessage[256];
    INT       iBytesRead;
    DWORD     dwSignatureBufLen;
    HCRYPTHASH  hHash = NULL;
```

```
BYTE     *pSignatureBuffer = NULL;
FILE *hSource      = NULL;
FILE *hDestination = NULL;
CString filein;
CString fileout;

UpdateData();
do {
    // Open the input and output files
    m_filein.GetWindowText(filein);
    m_fileout.GetWindowText(fileout);
    if ((hSource = fopen ((LPCTSTR)filein, "rb")) == NULL)
    {
        // Error opening the input file
        AppendMsg ("Cannot open the source file.\r\n");
        break;
    }
    if ((hDestination = fopen ((LPCTSTR)fileout, "wb")) == NULL)
    {
        // Error opening the output file
        AppendMsg ("Cannot open the output file.\r\n");
        break;
    }
```

As mentioned earlier, signing data first requires us to hash the data. The CAPI framework provides a hash object that can be created by calling **CryptCreateHash**. A hash object acts like a container to which the data to be hashed can be sequentially sent by calling the **CryptHashData** API. As data flows into the container, it is continuously digested to create a hash value.

Hash values, which are also referred to as message digests, have some interesting properties. Hash values are small fixed-length binary strings. Depending on the algorithm that is chosen for hashing, the length of the resulting hash is either 128 bits for the MD2, MD4, or MD5 algorithm or 160 bits for SHA. Thus no matter what the length of the source data, the hash is always of fixed length. These algorithms are currently proved to produce distinct hash value for any two strings of data that differ, even by a bit. On the other hand, for a given algorithm, given data will always produce the same hash value. It is also impossible to reverse-engineer the data from the hash value.

To create a hash object, the handle to the CSP provider is passed along with the preferred algorithm. A variety of algorithms are supported by the Microsoft base CSP. This sample uses the MD5 algorithm. Since MD5 is a nonkeyed algorithm for which no key is involved, the next parameter is set to zero. The parameter after that is for future use, and the last parameter is the address to which the handle to the hash object is copied.

```
if (!CryptCreateHash(hProvider, CALG_MD5, 0, 0, &hHash))
{
    sprintf(szMessage,
            "Error creating a hash object. RC = %X\r\n",
            GetLastError());
    AppendMsg(szMessage);
    break;
}
DWORD dwRC = ERROR_SUCCESS;
```

Once the hash object is created, the hash is computed by repeatedly adding data to the hash object by calling the **CryptHashData** API. This file is read and the data is added to the hash object to compute the hash. Each time the data is added to the hash object, the data buffer along with the length of the data is sent to the API. The Microsoft base CSP ignores the last parameter, which is therefore set to zero.

```
do
{
    iBytesRead = fread (szMessage, 1, 256, hSource);
    if (!CryptHashData(hHash, (BYTE *)szMessage, iBytesRead, 0))
    {
        dwRC = GetLastError();
        sprintf(szMessage,
                "Error hashing the data. RC = %X\r\n", dwRC);
        AppendMsg(szMessage);
        break;
    }
} while (!feof(hSource));
if (dwRC != ERROR_SUCCESS)
    break;
```

Once the hash value is computed, it can be signed by calling the **CryptSignHash** API. Signing is done by the private key. Typically a user would use two sets of key pairs, one for signing, created by sending the **AT_SIGNATURE** flag, and the other for key exchange, created by sending **AT_ KEYEXCHANGE**. Both the key pairs contain a private key, and hence both can be used for signing. Typically if the user owns the data to be signed, then the signing key pair is used for signing. If the user does not own the data, as in the case of a session key that was generated, the key exchange key pair is used. In this sample, the signing key pair is used, since the user owns the data the source file contains. The **CryptSignHash** API is called twice in tandem, first to get the size of signature buffer to be allocated and again to get the signature.

```
        if (!(CryptSignHash(hHash, AT_SIGNATURE, NULL, 0, NULL,
                        &dwSignatureBufLen)))
        {
            sprintf(szMessage,
                    "Error hashing the data. RC = %X\r\n",
                    GetLastError());
            AppendMsg(szMessage);
            break;
        }
        pSignatureBuffer = (BYTE *) malloc (dwSignatureBufLen);
        if (!(CryptSignHash(hHash, AT_SIGNATURE, NULL, 0, pSignatureBuffer,
                        &dwSignatureBufLen)))
        {
            sprintf(szMessage,
                    "Error hashing the data. RC = %X\r\n",
                    GetLastError());
            AppendMsg(szMessage);
            break;
        }
        CryptDestroyHash(hHash);
        hHash = NULL;
```

After signing, the signature data is retrieved and written to the top of the file with the size of the signature first. The file pointer is then reset, and the rest of the file is copied. The expectation is that the verification function would read the size of the signature, retrieve the signature, and verify the data. When the program is done using the hash object, it is destroyed by calling the **CryptDestroyHash** API. For security reasons, the hash should be destroyed. The underlying CSP typically cleans the memory and frees it.

```
        // Write the signature length and the signature.
        fwrite(&dwSignatureBufLen, sizeof(DWORD), 1, hDestination);
        fwrite(pSignatureBuffer, 1, dwSignatureBufLen, hDestination);
        // Copy the rest of the source file next.
        fseek (hSource, 0, SEEK_SET);    // go to the beginning of the file.
        int ch;
        while ((ch = fgetc(hSource)) != EOF)
            fputc(ch, hDestination);
        AppendMsg("File signed successfully.\r\n");
    } while(0);
    if (hHash)
        CryptDestroyHash(hHash);
    CloseFileHandles(hSource, hDestination);
    if (pSignatureBuffer)
        free (pSignatureBuffer);
}
```

The next function shown, **OnVerify**, is executed when the user selects the Verify button on the dialog box. The flow of this function is very similar to that of the **OnSign** function discussed earlier. The signature is first read from the top of the file and verified against the data in the file. Signature verification allows the application to detect tampering of the data as well as establish the authenticity of the data. In its simplest form, verifying a signature consists of two steps. First the data whose signature is to be verified is hashed and the hash value is compared to the value derived by decrypting the signature using the signer's public key. If the values match, then the verification is considered successful.

```
void CCryptoDlg::OnVerify()
{
    CHAR      szMessage[256];
    INT       iBytesRead;
    DWORD     dwSignatureLen;
    BYTE      *pSignatureBuffer = NULL;
    HCRYPTHASH  hHash = NULL;
    HCRYPTKEY   hPublicKey = NULL;
    FILE *hSource      = NULL;
    FILE *hDestination = NULL;
    CString filein;
    CString fileout;

    UpdateData();
    do {
        // Open the input and output files
        m_filein.GetWindowText(filein);
        m_fileout.GetWindowText(fileout);
        if ((hSource = fopen ((LPCTSTR)filein, "rb")) == NULL)
        {
            // Error opening the input file
            AppendMsg ("Cannot open the source file.\r\n");
            break;
        }
        if ((hDestination = fopen ((LPCTSTR)fileout, "wb")) == NULL)
        {
            // Error opening the output file
            AppendMsg ("Cannot open the output file.\r\n");
            break;
        }
        if (!CryptCreateHash(hProvider, CALG_MD5, 0, 0, &hHash))
        {
            sprintf(szMessage,
                    "Error creating a hash object. RC = %X\r\n",
                    GetLastError());
```

```
        AppendMsg(szMessage);
        break;
    }
    if (!(CryptGetUserKey(hProvider, AT_SIGNATURE, &hPublicKey)))
    {
        sprintf(szMessage,
                "Error getting the sign verification key. RC = %X\r\n",
                GetLastError());
        AppendMsg(szMessage);
        break;
    }
```

The process of verification requires a hash object as well as the signer's public key. The code shown here creates the hash object and retrieves the handle to the public key of the signing key. Note that the **AT_SIGNATURE** key was used to sign the data earlier. An attempt is made to make sure that the signature is within the file limits, and if not an error is displayed.

```
        LONG fileLen = 0;
        fseek(hSource, 0, SEEK_END);
        fileLen = ftell(hSource);
        fseek(hSource, 0, SEEK_SET);
        fread(&dwSignatureLen, sizeof(DWORD), 1, hSource);
        if (dwSignatureLen >= (DWORD)fileLen)
        {
            AppendMsg("Invalid source file.\r\n");
            break;
        }
        if ((pSignatureBuffer = (BYTE *)malloc(dwSignatureLen)) == NULL)
        {
            sprintf(szMessage,
                    "Error allocating %ld bytes of memory\r\n",
                    dwSignatureLen);
            AppendMsg(szMessage);
            break;
        }
        fread(pSignatureBuffer, 1, dwSignatureLen, hSource);
        if (ferror(hSource))
        {
            AppendMsg("Error reading the signature.\r\n");
            break;
        }
        DWORD dwRC = ERROR_SUCCESS;
        do
        {
```

```
    iBytesRead = fread (szMessage, 1, 256, hSource);
    if (!CryptHashData(hHash, (BYTE *)szMessage, iBytesRead, 0))
    {
        dwRC = GetLastError();
        sprintf(szMessage,
                "Error hashing the data. RC = %X\r\n", dwRC);
        AppendMsg(szMessage);
        break;
    }
} while (!feof(hSource));
```

After extraction of the signature, the rest of the file is hashed by sending the data to the **CryptHashData** API. After adding the last block of data to the hash object, the code verifies the signature by calling the **CryptVerifySignature** API. The handle to the hash object along with the signature data, its length, and a handle to the public key whose matching private key signed the original data is sent to the API.

```
if (dwRC != ERROR_SUCCESS)
    break;
if (!(CryptVerifySignature(hHash, pSignatureBuffer,
                           dwSignatureLen, hPublicKey, NULL, 0)))
{
    dwRC = GetLastError();
    if (dwRC == NTE_BAD_SIGNATURE)
        AppendMsg ("Signature verification failed.\r\n");
    else
    {
        sprintf(szMessage,
                "Signature verification failed. RC = %X\r\n",
                dwRC);
        AppendMsg(szMessage);
    }
    break;
}
AppendMsg ("Signature verification was successful.\r\n");
int ch;
```

Once the signature is successfully validated, the rest of the file is extracted and written to the user-specified output file.

```
fseek(hSource, sizeof(DWORD)+dwSignatureLen, SEEK_SET);
while ((ch = fgetc(hSource)) != EOF)
    fputc(ch, hDestination);
AppendMsg ("Output file created without signature.\r\n");
```

```
    } while (0);
    if (hHash)
        CryptDestroyHash(hHash);
    if (hPublicKey)
        CryptDestroyKey(hPublicKey);
    CloseFileHandles(hSource, hDestination);
    if (pSignatureBuffer)
        free (pSignatureBuffer);
}
```

When the user cancels the dialog panels, all the resources associated with the CSP, such as the handle to the key exchange key pair, the handle to the signing key pair and the handle to the CSP, are freed. The **CryptDestroyKey** API is used to free the keys, and the **CryptReleaseContext** API is used to release the handle to the provider. Once the handle is released, it can no longer be used.

```
void CCryptoDlg::OnCancel()
{
    if (hExchangeKey)
        CryptDestroyKey(hExchangeKey);
    if (hSigningKey)
        CryptDestroyKey(hSigningKey);
    if (hProvider)
        CryptReleaseContext(hProvider, 0);
    CDialog::OnCancel();
}


void CCryptoDlg::AppendMsg(LPCTSTR msg)
{
    m_status.SetSel(-1, 0);
    m_status.ReplaceSel(msg);
    return;
}
```

AppendMsg and **CloseFileHandles** are utility functions that append a message to the status field in the dialog box and close any file handles that remain open.

```
void CCryptoDlg::CloseFileHandles(FILE *hFile1, FILE *hFile2)
{
    if (hFile1)
        fclose (hFile1);
    if (hFile2)
        fclose (hFile2);
}
```

To try out the failure situations for this sample, you can create two user IDs on the Windows 2000 system. Log onto Windows 2000 and encrypt or sign a file. Now take the output file, which is either encrypted or signed, to be used with another user ID. Log off and log back again as a different user and try to decrypt or verify the files that were earlier encrypted or signed. These operations should fail, since the key exchange key pair and the signing key pair are different for the new user. However, if the file were encrypted using a password, the second user would still be able to decrypt, since the session key is derived from the password.

The key container for a user or application can be deleted by calling the **CryptAcquireContext** API and passing in **CRYPT_DELETEKEYSET** as the last parameter. The code snippet shown next would delete the key container with the default name for the Microsoft Base CSP. Great care should be taken before deleting the key pairs. Once the key pairs are deleted, there is no way to recover any encrypted file that used the corresponding public key.

```
CryptAcquireContext(&hProv, NULL, MS_DEF_PROV,
                 PROV_RSA_FULL,
                 CRYPT_DELETEKEYSET);
```

The preceding sample is a very generic sample that illlustrates how some basic cryptographic functions work. In this sample, functions such as signing and verifying do not work across two users or applications. Neither do they accommodate file encryption/decryption across two users or applications. For two users to exchange an encrypted file, the file should be encrypted with a password. It cannot be encrypted with a random key. The reason for this is that the random session key used during encryption as well as the verification code uses the current user's public key. However, it is not difficult to extend the application to use the recipient's public key. The only issue here is to import the recipient's public key into the CSP before performing the operations. Though the public keys are treated as key blobs in this sample, practical applications deal with digital certificates to access another person's public key. A simple definition of a digital certificate is that it associates a public key with an entity that possesses the corresponding private key, and that it is signed by a certificate authority.

While some applications might want to perform cryptographic functions on static files, these cryptographic functions are more useful in communications programs where the data or messages are encrypted and signed when flowing between two processes. A good extension to the named pipe sample that was discussed in Chapter 9 is to add security to the data flow between the server and the client. During initialization, both the client and the server can initialize their cryptographic environment and exchange each other's public keys. Or they can export each other's public key blobs and, when the server and client start, import each other's public keys. With this done, any message that is to be sent between server and client can be encrypted and signed before sending. The other end verifies and decrypts the message before displaying it to the user.

CONCLUSION

In this chapter, we looked at different security features in Windows 2000, many of which are new in Windows 2000, not present in Windows NT. While we covered different components of security such as smart cards, PK cryptography, digital certificates, certificate authorities, CryptoAPIs, and security applications, it is important to keep in mind that a complete security solution involves all components working together. It is also important to keep in mind that there is normally a trade-off between enhanced security and user convenience.

This concludes all the chapters of this text. So far we have presumed implicitly that all the applications being developed were for the English language market using the English language version of Windows 2000. An appendix follows that discusses the different aspects of developing applications for the international market using Windows 2000.

There is more to Windows 2000 than meets the eye. As you get to use Windows 2000 more, you will soon appreciate all the functions and features it supports. As someone said, "Software, like wine, gets better with age." We have been through many operating systems, starting with IBM's MVS, VM, and so on, through the many UNIX variants, DOS, Windows, and Windows 2000. Windows 2000 has picked up some of the best elements of operating systems. Programming using Windows 2000 is bound to be a rewarding experience from a programming-pleasure as well as a financial viewpoint.

PART V

Appendixes

APPENDIX A

Internationalization

One of the buzzwords of the '90s is "globalization." You undoubtedly have heard about a global economy, shrinking borders, the Internet bringing people together, and so on. All point to the fact that communication, distribution, and many other business functions now span the world. Consider two examples. Talking about shrinking borders, today you can buy a stock from the Tokyo stock exchange, turn around and sell it on the London stock exchange (and hopefully make a profit), and have the money taken from and deposited to your account in the United States—all through phone call(s) in a matter of minutes while you are vacationing on your boat in the Bahamas.

Let's take a simpler example. Books like this will be sold as is in some countries and after translation in other countries. What does this globalization mean to you as a programmer? You may have faced this question already. Even if you haven't, the chances are increasing that the program you write will execute in more than one country. If you are a product developer, then it would make good business sense to sell the product you have already developed (and spent development dollars on) in other markets. Even if you are not a product developer, if you work for a multinational organization, then the application you develop may need to run outside the United States. More and more international programmers routinely participate in programming newsgroups, and the road shows and conferences that software companies conduct to promote their products now include many international stops as well. I hope I have given you enough incentive to look at the topic of programming for the world in this chapter.

You may ask, "How come I have successfully developed programs all these years without worrying about all this international programming stuff?"

If you are like many programmers, you probably developed your application just fine without worrying about international programming, because Windows 2000 lets you develop applications at least three ways (using the default code page, multibyte characters, and Unicode), and you have been using one of the three.

THE PROBLEM

Chances are, the programs you are developing every day will not work in Germany, Japan, or China. To understand why, let's start with the ANSI character set. In ANSI, each character is represented by 8 bits. With 8 bits, the maximum number of different characters you can represent is 2^8, which is 256 characters. Even if you count A through Z, a through z, the numbers 0–9, and special characters such as $, *, and so on, the total number is well within 256. Thus, the ANSI character set is large enough to handle the English language and other languages using the same character set. But what if the language needs more than 256 characters? There are a lot of languages based on other character sets such as Cyrillic and Kanji. You cannot represent ANSI and Cyrillic characters in the same set with just 8 bits. The problem gets worse when you consider some eastern languages whose alphabets are actually pictorial symbols—and there are thousands of these symbols.

Now that you know what the problem is, let's look at some solutions that will let you develop programs that will not only work in the United States, but also will require little or no effort to make them work elsewhere. We will look at four solutions and their programming aspects:

▼ Using code pages

■ Using multibyte character sets (MBCS)

■ Using Unicode

▲ Of course, you can create a portable source and use a switch to generate applications for different environments

CODE PAGES

The first solution, which still permits use of only one byte per character, is the computer version of divide and conquer—using *code pages*. Each single-byte code page could still represent only 256 characters, but different code pages are used to support different character sets. Thus, there are a number of ANSI and OEM character sets, and corresponding code pages. Different versions of the same product are created, each one using a different code page. For example, the U.S. version of the Windows 95 operating system uses a code page that is different from the code page that can represent Cyrillic characters. Windows 2000 is available in several international versions, including Chinese, French, German, Japanese, and so on. The most common code page used in the United States is OEM code page 437. The code page for Japanese is 932. As a programmer, you do not have to do any special programming involving code pages, unlike MBCS and Unicode (discussed later in the chapter). You can tell the current code page by use of the C run-time function **_getmbcp**.

This solution works fine as long as you have applications that need to work with only one code page at a time. If within your application you want to support more than one code page at the same time, then you have problems. Consider, for example, a server in one of the European countries serving clients that run with different code pages within the same or different countries (a common situation). With the increased use of the Internet and intranets, more and more applications need to be able to handle this type of situation.

MULTIBYTE CHARACTER SETS (MBCS)

By default you program using a character set where a single byte is a single character—a *single-byte character set (SBCS)*. A logical solution is to have more than one byte represent the characters in the character set, if all the characters cannot be represented by one byte. Two bytes are used in *double-byte character sets (DBCS)*—keep in mind that two bytes are only for *some* characters, not all. Of course, you are not restricted to two bytes. You can have multibyte character sets too, but DBCS is by far the most common. In fact, Visual C++ only supports up to two bytes per character (DBCS). If you want to develop a new application for the international market, you are better off using Unicode. But if you already have an application that you want to quickly enable for markets that will be satisfied with MBCS support, you may want to look at MBCS-enabling your application.

Programming Aspects of DBCS

Visual C++ and MFC support DBCS. You have to watch out for data type differences (in particular, character strings) and run-time function differences. Character strings are a problem in DBCS. This is because each character in the string could be either a complete character or a partial character. How can you tell? By looking at each byte. If the byte has a value in a reserved range and is the first of two bytes that make up the character (the first byte is also called the *lead byte*), then the character uses two bytes. The reserved range is dependent on the code page (for example, 0×81 through 0×9F for the code page 932). Although you can check for the lead byte yourself (find out the code page and use a table that specifies the appropriate range), it is a lot easier for you to use the function **IsDBCSLeadByteEx** to check if a byte is a lead byte. You can use the Input Method Editor to create double-byte characters (as well as single-byte characters). You use _MBCS in your build to specify that you are building an MBCS-enabled application. Some of the things you need to watch out for in DBCS programming are as follows:

▼ Operations such as inserting, deleting, and counting characters are normally synonymous with byte operations. In DBCS, you have to ensure that you deal with characters, not bytes.

■ In instances where you used **str** functions (such as **strlen** to get the number of characters in a string), you need to use **_mbs** functions (**strlen** will not return the right result on a string with both one-byte and two-byte characters).

■ Develop your application on an MBCS-enabled version of Windows 2000 to ensure that Visual C++ will accept DBCS characters.

■ Ensure that the application uses the right code page. You can change the default code page using the resource compiler's /c option.

▲ Ensure that you have the right target locale (country and language). You can use the pragma setlocale to change the default as required.

UNICODE

Developed by the Unicode Consortium, a nonprofit consortium sponsored by a number of computer companies, *Unicode* is a fixed-width encoding scheme where each character is represented by 16 bits. The number of characters that can be represented by Unicode is thus 2^{16} or 65,536.

Using Unicode, we can represent all the characters from character sets like ANSI, characters from the Cyrillic character set, special-purpose characters such as publishing characters, and mathematical symbols—in short, everything we want to represent (as of now). For a complete description of the Unicode standard, the characters represented, and so on, refer to *The Unicode Standard, Version 3.0 by* The Unicode Consortium (New York, Addison-Wesley, 2000).

The Win32 API and Windows 2000 support Unicode. Windows 2000 uses Unicode extensively in its internal operations. For example, all text strings in GDI are in Unicode, and NTFS uses Unicode for file, path, and directory names; object names; and all system information files.

The subsystems take care of many of the conversions. For instance, the Win32 subsystem converts American Standard Code for Information Interchange (ASCII) characters it receives into Unicode strings and converts them back to ASCII, if necessary, for output.

Note for UNIX Programmers

Unicode is supported on many UNIX systems such as Digital UNIX. If you have done Unicode programming before in UNIX, then it is essentially the same in Windows 2000.

The differences between SBCS, MBCS, and Unicode are summarized in Table A-1.

Programming Using Unicode

Unicode programming is not a whole new way of programming. Using it is not as difficult as learning a new programming language. You just have to be aware of the differences in data types, function types, string handling, and so on between using Unicode and not using Unicode.

To represent character constants, you normally would use **char**, which would take up one byte. In Unicode you use **wchar_t**, and the same character constant would take up two bytes (the Unicode character set is also called the *wide character set,* and the prefix "W" is used in functions and data types to indicate that the function or data type is Unicode related). A string such as "example string" becomes a Unicode string by prefixing it with "L"; that is, the Unicode string is "Lexample string." You can include Unicode fonts in your program by using UNICODE_CHARSET for **lfCharSet** in your **LOGFONT** structure.

SBCS	MBCS	Unicode
All characters use one byte.	Not all characters use two bytes.	All characters use two bytes.
Use str functions.	Use _mbs functions.	Use _wcs functions.
Don't include _MBCS or _UNICODE.	Include _MBCS for build.	Include _UNICODE for build.

Table A-1.   SBCS, MBCS, and Unicode Programming Differences

If you used the **CString** class to handle strings, you can continue to use **CString**, because **CString** is Unicode enabled.

To specify that your application uses Unicode, you use the #define _Unicode.

TIP: The libraries for the MFC library's Unicode support are copied only by selecting Custom Installation.

Win32 APIs and Unicode

Win32 APIs that use characters are actually implemented three ways:

▼ The most common, the ANSI version, is implemented with the suffix "A."

■ The Unicode version is implemented with the suffix "W."

▲ A portable version that can be compiled for either Unicode or ANSI is implemented without a suffix.

For example, if you specifically want the ANSI version of **SetWindowLong**, you call **SetWindowLongA**. When you specifically want the Unicode version, you call **SetWindowLongW**.

At times, you may need to translate strings from one form to another. Win32 includes functions that let you perform these translations, as summarized in Table A-2.

NEW IN WINDOWS 2000:   In the **MultiByteToWideChar** and **WideCharToMultiByte** functions, Windows 2000 supports the CP_SYMBOL value for the CodePage parameter that denotes Symbol code page (42). In the **WideCharToMultiByte** function, Windows 2000 supports the value WC_NO_BEST_FIT_CHARS for the dwFlags parameter, which causes Unicode characters that do not translate directly to multibyte equivalents to be translated to the default characters.

Function	Purpose
MultiByteToWideChar	Translates MBCS strings to Unicode strings
WideCharToMultiByte	Translates Unicode strings to MBCS strings
CharToOem or CharToOemBuff	Translates an ANSI or Unicode string to OEM characters
OemToChar or OemToCharBuff	Translates OEM characters to an ANSI or Unicode string

Table A-2.   Win32 String Translation Functions

WRITING PORTABLE APPLICATIONS

You don't have to choose between SBCS, MBCS, and Unicode. You can write portable applications and build your application in different ways—SBCS, MBCS, or Unicode—without changing your program source. The Microsoft run-time library provides mappings for many data types, routines that you can use to write generic code that can be compiled for single byte, multibyte, or Unicode. You make the selection between single byte, multibyte, or Unicode using a #define statement. You would also include the header file *Tchar.h*. As mentioned before, an ANSI character is **char**, while a Unicode character is **wchar_t**. You can use a generic character type **TCHAR**, and *Tchar.h* takes care of portability by switching the typedef as shown next:

```
#ifdef UNICODE
        typedef wchar_t TCHAR;
#else
        typedef unsigned char TCHAR;
#endif
```

Similar portability mappings occur for other data types besides the simple character type, as shown in Table A-3.

Similarly, *Tchar.h* maps generic macros prefixed with _tcs to str (SBCS), _mbs (DBCS), or wcs (Unicode) functions as appropriate. Thus, what may appear in an SBCS program as

```
char * strcat(char *, const char *);
```

would appear in a Unicode program as

```
wchar_t * wcscat(wchar_t *, const wchar_t *);
```

For a complete list of the mappings, refer to the *Microsoft Visual C++: Run-Time Library Reference* (Microsoft Press, 1997).

Data Type	SBCS	MBCS	Unicode
_TINT	int	int	wint_t
_TSCHAR	Signed char	Signed char	wchar_t
_TUCHAR	Unsigned char	Unsigned char	wchar_t
_TXCHAR	Signed char	Unsigned char	wchar_t
_T or _TEXT	Not required	Not required	Prefixed by "L"

Table A-3. Data Types Portability Mapping

AN INTERNATIONALIZATION TECHNIQUE

When your program can be used internationally, you have to ensure that the end-user interface is usable in the countries you expect your program to run. A German user must see all end-user interface text, such as dialog titles, static controls, text in other controls, messages, and so on in German. A French user would like to see all the user interface text in French.

One way of doing this would be to develop your program as you normally would, send all the relevant source to the countries you want your program to run in, and get some programmer there to change all the user interface text and rebuild the application. The advantage of this approach is that your program development is not slowed by the development and testing related to international requirements. But there are also problems with this approach. First, you may not be able to find the skills you need in all the countries—and even if you do, the countries may not have all the latest versions necessary to be able to develop the application. Second, you have multiple versions of your sources, and replicating future changes across different sources in different countries is a major problem.

The typical compromise is to ship the international versions a little bit after the U.S. version. Instead of shipping the complete source overseas, you just get the text of the various user interface elements translated here or abroad, and structure your application so that it can be quickly built by use of the translated user interface elements. The following program shows how to separate user interface text from your main executable so that changes to the user interface can be handled without changing or rebuilding your program. There are two ways you can get the program to pick up different user interface elements. You can swap text files and rebuild the *Intl* DLL, or you can copy the already generated DLLs to *Intl* DLL and rerun your application.

The Intl example is a simple example that displays an application window with a title. The menu has two choices: one brings up a dialog panel, and the other exits the program. The dialog panel gets an input from the user and displays that in a message box. The output of the program using the English version of the user interface elements is shown in Figures A-1 and A-2.

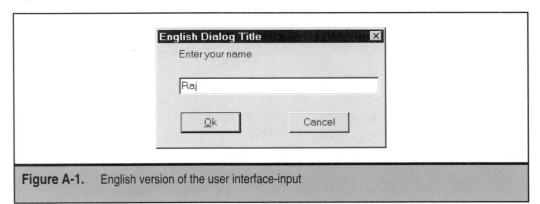

Figure A-1. English version of the user interface-input

Figure A-2.   English version of the user interface-output

The French version was then substituted by copying *French.dll* to *Intl.dll*. When the program is run, the French version of the user interface is shown. (For simplicity, the letter "F" prefixes all user interface elements, but in the real world you would insert the translated text into the *French.txt* file.) The output using the French version is shown in Figures A-3 and A-4.

Finally, the German version is used, and that output is shown in Figures A-5 and A-6.

Now let's take a detailed look at the program to see how this is done.

The program's header files *Menus.h* and *Dialogs.h* are shown next:

```
// menus.h
// Constants for menu commands

#define IDM_NAME        1001
#define IDM_EXIT        1002

#define IDS_PROG_TITLE    2001
#define IDS_NAME_PROMPT 2002
#define IDS_MESSAGE_1    2003

// dialogs.h
#define IDC_NAME          101
#define IDC_LABEL         104
```

Figure A-3.   French version of the user interface-input

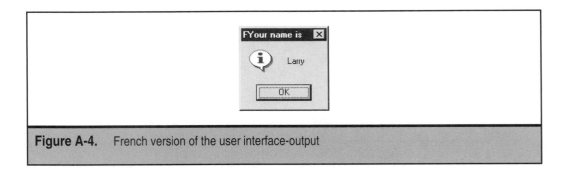

Figure A-4.   French version of the user interface-output

When developing software for international use, it is crucial to isolate all the language-dependent entities like prompt text, messages, icons, and so on, so that you do not end up creating one executable for each language. Obviously, having one executable for each language would be a maintenance nightmare, particularly when your program works in many other languages.

The Intl example shows one of the programming techniques that can be used to isolate all the strings and create a *resource DLL*. This resource DLL can then be loaded from the executable and used. When the time comes to translate the program to another language, the translators, who are typically translators and not programmers, can just translate the text files. These text files are included in the resource files, which can be compiled into a resource DLL. The program can then load the resource DLL and use it.

The idea behind the program is to show how the textual strings can be isolated to a resource file. The program is made up of one executable and one DLL. The executable is made of just the *Intl.cpp* module and the related header files *Dialog.h* and *Menus.h*. It does not include the resource file in the build process. That is part of the resource DLL, which will be discussed later.

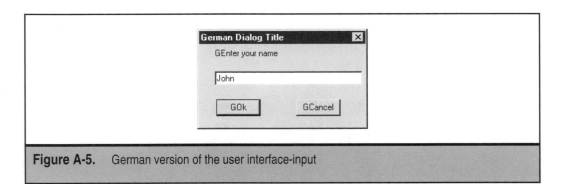

Figure A-5.   German version of the user interface-input

Figure A-6.   German version of the user interface-output

The *Intl.cpp* module essentially has two classes. The **CWindow** class is the application's main class, and **CNameDialog** is the dialog panel class. The other class is the application class **CApp**.

```
// INTL.CPP

#include <afxwin.h>
#include <afxdlgs.h>
#include "dialogs.h"
#include "menus.h"


// Define the application object class
class CApp : public CWinApp
{
public:
    virtual BOOL InitInstance ();
};

// Define the window class
class CWindow : public CFrameWnd
{
public:
    CWindow();
    afx_msg void OnName();
    afx_msg void OnExit();
    DECLARE_MESSAGE_MAP()
};
```

What has been done here is the standard definition of our application class and the frame window class. The member function **OnName( )** will display a dialog panel, and **OnExit( )** will exit the application.

```cpp
// Define the Name Dialog Class
class CNameDialog: public CDialog
{
private:
    CString m_nameString;
public:
    CNameDialog( CString defaultString = NULL,
        CWnd* pParentWnd = NULL )
        : CDialog( "NameDlg", pParentWnd )
        { m_nameString = defaultString; }

    virtual void OnOK();
    virtual BOOL OnInitDialog();
    CString& GetInputString()
        { return m_nameString; }
};


// OnInitDialog is called just before the dialog
// appears on the screen.

BOOL CNameDialog::OnInitDialog()
{
    SetDlgItemText( IDC_NAME, m_nameString );
    return TRUE;
}


void CNameDialog::OnOK()
{
    GetDlgItemText( IDC_NAME,
        m_nameString.GetBuffer(128), 128 );
    m_nameString.ReleaseBuffer();
    EndDialog( IDOK );
}
```

Next the dialog class **CNameDialog** is defined. Note that the string "NameDlg" is really immaterial for translation, and it could have been a dialog identification number instead. The **CNameDialog** constructor initializes the prompt string that would appear in the edit field of the dialog panel. The member function **GetInputString( )** returns the stored string inline. The **OnInitDialog( )** member function basically initializes the edit field in the dialog panel. The **OnOK( )** member function picks up the string and stores it in the member variable **m_nameString**.

Next the **CWindow** constructor is defined:

```
// CWindow constructor
CWindow::CWindow()
{
            CString title;
            title.LoadString(IDS_PROG_TITLE);
            Create( NULL, "",
            WS_OVERLAPPEDWINDOW,
            rectDefault, NULL, "MainMenu" );
            SetWindowText(title);
}
```

The interesting piece of code starts here. Typically, when the frame window is created, the window title is explicitly given as a parameter to the **Create( )**. In the code here, a **CString** title is defined, and the title string is loaded from the resource file. This dynamically loaded string is used as the title. In the example here, the frame is created without any title text, and it is set later with **SetWindowText( )**. This is done assuming that some dynamic change to the loaded text will be made. If there is nothing to be made, the title can be directly passed in the **Create( )** member function.

```
void CWindow::OnName()
{
            CString namePrompt;
            CString messageText;
            namePrompt.LoadString(IDS_NAME_PROMPT);
            CNameDialog nameDialog( namePrompt, this );

            if( nameDialog.DoModal() == IDOK )
            {
              messageText.LoadString(IDS_MESSAGE_1);
              MessageBox( nameDialog.GetInputString(),messageText,
                  MB_ICONINFORMATION );
            }
}
```

The **OnName( )** member function processes the menu selection "Name Dialog." It loads the prompt text from the resource file and uses it to create the dialog panel. When the user is done with the dialog panel, the program retrieves the data entered in the edit field and displays the entered data in a message box. Note that the title for the message box is also loaded from the resource file.

The item to look at next is the **InitInstance** method of the main application class **CApp**:

```
// Initialize the CApp m_pMainWnd data member
BOOL CApp::InitInstance()
{
```

```
        HINSTANCE          ResourceHandle;

        ResourceHandle = AfxLoadLibrary ("Intl.DLL");
        AfxSetResourceHandle (ResourceHandle);

        m_pMainWnd = new CWindow();
        m_pMainWnd -> ShowWindow( m_nCmdShow );
        m_pMainWnd -> UpdateWindow();
        return( TRUE );
}
```

Here a resource instance handle, **ResourceHandle**, is defined, and the resource DLL *Intl.dll* is loaded using **AfxLoadLibrary**. **AfxSetResourceHandle** takes this handle and sets it as the application's resource handle. All resources that are needed by the application will use this resource handle. The rest of the code is the standard code.

As was seen earlier, the *Intl.exe* did not contain any resource files associated with the executable. The resources are separated and a resource DLL is created as discussed next. The files that create the resource DLL *Intl.dll* are *Resource.c, Intl.rc, Dialogs.dlg, Dialogs.h, Menus.h,* and *Intl.txt.*

```
// This is a dummy file used for creating the Resource DLL
void dialogs ()
{
}
```

The preceding is the *Resource.c* file. This is just a dummy file to create a DLL. It contains no code and the only reason for its existence is to create a DLL.

```
// Intl.rc
// The resource file for INTL.CPP sample

#include <windows.h>
#include <afxres.h>

#include "dialogs.h"
#include "dialogs.dlg"
#include "menus.h"
#include "intl.txt"


MainMenu MENU
BEGIN
    POPUP TXT_M_FILE
    BEGIN
      MENUITEM TXT_MI_NAME, IDM_NAME
      MENUITEM TXT_MI_EXIT, IDM_EXIT
```

```
        END
END
STRINGTABLE
BEGIN
    IDS_PROG_TITLE,        TXT_STR_PROG_TITLE
    IDS_NAME_PROMPT,       TXT_STR_NAME_PROMPT
    IDS_MESSAGE_1,         TXT_STR_MESSAGE_1
END
```

Just shown is the *Intl.rc* module. Apart from including the standard header files related to the resource ID, notice that it also includes a text file, *Intl.txt*. At places where text is to appear in the resource, it is substituted with a macro. So instead of specifying the MainMenu as

```
MainMenu MENU
BEGIN
    POPUP "&File"
    BEGIN
      MENUITEM "&Name dialog", IDM_NAME
      MENUITEM "&Exit", IDM_EXIT
    END
END
```

it specifies it as

```
MainMenu MENU
BEGIN
    POPUP TXT_M_FILE
    BEGIN
      MENUITEM TXT_MI_NAME, IDM_NAME
      MENUITEM TXT_MI_EXIT, IDM_EXIT
    END
END
```

where TXT_M_FILE, TXT_MI_NAME, and TXT_MI_EXIT are defined in the *Intl.txt* file, as shown next:

```
// This file contains the English text related to
// the International program.

// Main Window related text
#define TXT_M_FILE          "&File"
#define TXT_MI_NAME         "&Name dialog"
#define TXT_MI_EXIT         "&Exit"
```

```
// Name dialog related text
#define TXT_DIALOG_TITLE      "English Dialog Title"
#define TXT_OK                "&Ok"
#define TXT_CANCEL            "Cancel"
#define TXT_PROMPT1_STRING    "Enter your name"


// String Table text

#define TXT_STR_PROG_TITLE    "Sample for Internationalization"
#define TXT_STR_NAME_PROMPT   "Type your name here"
#define TXT_STR_MESSAGE_1     "Your name is"
```

With this structure, just the text file—*Intl.txt*—which contains minimal programming details, can be given to the translators for translation.

When this program is compiled and run, the characters appear in English text. Also found in the project are two more text files, *German.txt* and *French.txt*. These files are similar to *Intl.txt*, but the texts are German and French texts, respectively. The same English texts as found in *Intl.txt* are just prefixed with "G" in *German.txt* and "F" in *French.txt*. To create the German version of the resource file, just copy *German.txt* to *Intl.txt*, and rebuild the resource *DLL Intl.dll*. Now without making any change or rebuild of the executable, a German version of the program is created. While the sizes of the program and resource shown here are small and trivial, in a real project this would substantially increase the maintainability of the project.

There are some drawbacks in this approach to keep in mind. When translated, some strings, such as titles, may become too long and may not fit in the available space. You may also have a problem with the text direction (right to left versus left to right, as well as horizontal versus vertical). In such cases, you can create individual dialogs as needed.

GUIDELINES FOR INTERNATIONAL PROGRAMMING

If you use the technique illustrated by this program, here are a few guidelines that you will find useful:

▼ The way numbers, dates, time, and currency are represented is different in different countries. You should account for this by using locale information and preferences. There are Win32 functions, such as **GetProfileInt**, **GetSystemDefaultSystemLCID**, and **GetLocaleInfoW**, to retrieve locale and preference information. There are also Win32 functions, such as **GetDateFormatW**, to convert dates to local formats.

■ Even though dialogs may have the same string repeated, use different string IDs for multiple occurrences of one string with the same name. This is because a given string may have a different meaning when translated, and the different instances where the string is used in dialogs may not always translate to the same target string.

- To find out whether your application is running on an MBCS-enabled operating system, set a flag at program startup, and do not issue repeated API calls.

- A translated string (particularly in German) may be longer than the source string. To ensure that the translated string will fit, allow approximately 30 percent extra space at the end of static text controls.

- Keep the fonts available in your target systems in mind, as not all fonts will be available (by default). Try to use a least common subset.

- Do not mix localized strings with those that are not localized. Assume that the string is localized if you are not sure.

- Use *stringtable* resources to specify strings. Include strings in your application's RC file. This will avoid source code changes that will be required as a result of string changes due to translation.

- ▲ Keep in mind that even if you have taken care of all the programming issues, you may have difficulty testing. The real test is when a program meant for another market runs using the keyboard, the display, the code page, the international user, and so on. In many instances, you will not be able to test your application without the right equipment. In such cases, make sure to allocate some extra time to get your software to the other market and tested under the right conditions.

CONCLUSION

As mentioned at the start of the chapter, advanced programmers are most likely to be required to write programs that will work internationally. There are some other cultural aspects that influence your application, but for which no general-purpose solution exists. The basic units of measurement for height, weight, distances, calendars, and so on vary among countries. Some basic assumptions that are true in the United States may not be true elsewhere (for example, identifying a person by use of a social security number). The algorithms and keys you may have used in your application in the United States will not work properly elsewhere. You can try to modularize your code as was shown in the example to minimize country-specific changes.

APPENDIX B

Preparing for 64-bit Windows

A s the demand and race for more powerful computers grows constantly, hardware manufacturers have responded with solutions. The most familiar one is probably the ever-increasing clock speed, which currently exceeds 1.2GHz. Equally important, but growing on a slower scale, is word length. Intel's first set of computers started with 8 bits. Over the years it has expanded to 16 and then 32 bits. While 32 bits is now the most common, 64-bit designs are available. One of these is the Alpha chip from Compaq (formerly DEC). Intel is working on a 64-bit version called IA-64 (formerly code-named "Merced") and has demonstrated some early designs. Besides the hardware itself, support is required in the operating systems.

Besides new capabilities and features, Windows 2000 also includes preparatory steps in anticipation of 64-bit Windows. As an example, for Windows 2000, the definitions of the Win32 API elements have been updated with new Win64-compatible types. One of the major problems that Microsoft will face in going to the 64-bit environment is compatibility of existing applications; to minimize this problem, Microsoft is providing details of data types that will be used in the 64-bit environment to help facilitate development of applications that will be easy to migrate to 64-bit Windows. It is not necessary, and in fact very expensive, to make all data types 64 bits. That would be a waste of memory, and almost all applications do not need it at this time. The most important data type that will benefit from the expansion to 64 bits is the pointer. This provides the mechanism to support addresses beyond the 4GB limit imposed by 32-bit Windows. All pointers are 64 bits on a 64-bit platform. While it is certain that Microsoft will move to 64-bit programming, please keep in mind that the specifics discussed in this appendix may change when they are actually introduced.

Note For UNIX Programmers

Some versions of UNIX already have 64-bit support. If you have been through a 32-bit-to-64-bit migration on UNIX, the technical details will be very similar.

GETTING READY FOR 64-BIT WINDOWS

There are a number of programming aspects relating to getting ready for 64-bit Windows. These include using new data types, the 64-bit programming environment, the tools, Win32 API changes, etc. Microsoft provides updated information in MSDN with each new update relating to 64-bit Windows. Let's look at these in some detail.

Data Types

You should be aware of these types and use them to the extent possible, as it is likely that the applications you develop will still be running when the 64-bit environment is introduced. Since these new types are derived from the basic C-language integer and long types, you can use these data types in your current Win32-based application. When 64-bit Windows is available, you can recompile your current Win32 application as a Win64 application.

These data types are broadly classified as follows:

▼ Fixed-precision data types

■ Pointer-precision types

▲ Specific-precision pointers

These types were added to **Basetsd.h**. Figure B-1 summarizes the new data types.

Programming Environment

Microsoft is striving to keep the 64-bit programming environment—including the APIs, Dev. Studio, C++ language support, etc.—as close as possible to the 32-bit environment to minimize the learning curve required. The Platform SDK, starting with Windows 2000 beta 2, has added support for these new data types. These new data types allow pointers and pointer-associated variables to reflect the precision of the platform. The migration path that Microsoft envisions is the three-step process, shown here:

1. Start including the new data types when you are developing new Win32 applications or updating old ones.

2. Compile your application with the 64-bit compiler and test it in preparation for migrating to the real 64-bit environment.

3. When you are ready for the actual 64-bit environment, build all your applications for the 64-bit environment and migrate to that environment.

Tools to Prepare for 64-bit Windows

As mentioned earlier, with each new update of MSDN, you can expect more and more tools to help you prepare for 64-bit Windows. The Platform SDK includes a 64-bit toolkit that ships with the a 64-bit MIDL compiler, Midl.exe, for generating native 64-bit stubs (as well as 32-bit stubs). To generate 64-bit stubs, use the /env win64 switch. The default will generate dual stubs that run on both platforms.

The Windows header files have been modified so that you can use them for both Win32 and Win64 code. The Win64-specific types and macros are defined in a new header file, *Basetsd.h*. This file is in the set of header files included by Windows.h. Basetsd.h includes the new data-type definitions you can use to make your application word-size independent.

The 64-bit compiler introduces a new macro, _WIN64, for a 64-bit platform. The current _WIN32 and _WIN16 are also supported for compatibility. However, you have to

Fixed Precision	
{PRIVATE} **Type**	**Definition**
DWORD32	32-bit unsigned integer
DWORD64	64-bit unsigned integer
INT32	32-bit signed integer
INT64	64-bit signed integer
LONG32	32-bit signed integer
LONG64	64-bit signed integer
UINT32	Unsigned **INT32**
UINT64	Unsigned **INT64**
ULONG32	Unsigned **LONG32**
ULONG64	Unsigned **LONG64**
Pointer Precision	
DWORD_PTR	Unsigned long type for pointer precision.
HALF_PTR	Half the size of a pointer. Use within a structure that contains a pointer and two small fields.
INT_PTR	Signed integral type for pointer precision.
LONG_PTR	Signed long type for pointer precision.
SIZE_T	The maximum number of bytes to which a pointer can refer. Use for a count that must span the full range of a pointer.
SSIZE_T	Signed **SIZE_T**.
UHALF_PTR	Unsigned **HALF_PTR**.
UINT_PTR	Unsigned **INT_PTR**.
ULONG_PTR	Unsigned **LONG_PTR**.
Specific Pointer-Precision Types	
POINTER_32	A 32-bit pointer. On a 32-bit system, this is a native pointer. On a 64-bit system, this is a truncated 64-bit pointer.
POINTER_64	A 64-bit pointer. On a 64-bit system, this is a native pointer. On a 32-bit system, this is a sign-extended 32-bit pointer. Note that it is not safe to assume the state of the high pointer bit.

Figure B-1. New data types and descriptions (reproduced with permission from Microsoft)

watch out for code that may be presuming that there are only two environments—the 16 and 32 bits. For example:

```
#ifdef _WIN32 // Win32 code

...

#else        // Win16 code

...

#endif
```

will not work right, and this is not something that will be caught automatically.

Platform SDK also includes a 64-bit compiler that you can use to identify pointer truncation, improper type casts, and other problems that you will encounter that are related to 64 bits. The most common warning you will get when you use the 64-bit compiler is:

```
warning C4311: 'type cast' : pointer truncation from 'unsigned char *'
to 'unsigned long '
```

The compiler includes a warning option to assist porting to LLP64 data model (data model used for 64-bit applications, which is a different model used with 32-bit applications). The -Wp64 -W3 switch enables warnings such as the 4311 previously mentioned.

Other vendors besides Microsoft are also getting ready for the 64-bit environment. CodeWarrior for MIPS 2, by Metroworks Inc., is hosted on Windows 95 and Windows NT. CodeWarrior for MIPS 2 supports both C and C++ languages. It has an integrated development environment that includes an editor, project manager, class browser, and 32-bit and 64-bit compilers.

Programming Considerations

The Win32 and Win64 API elements are virtually identical. So for the most part your job is to identify the specific differences and watch out for some rules in preparing for the 64-bit environment. Microsoft includes the following rules in MSDN:

▼ If you're developing a device driver and your device supports more than 4GB, you can use the Mm64BitPhysicalAddresses value to determine if 64-bit addressing is needed.

■ If you have window or class private data that contains pointers, use the new functions listed in the following table:

New Windows Function	Description
GetClassLongPtr	This function supersedes the GetClassLong function. It is used to retrieve a pointer or a handle.

New Windows Function	Description
GetWindowLongPtr	This function supersedes the GetWindowLong function and retrieves information about the specified window.
SetClassLongPtr	This function supersedes the SetClassLong function and replaces the specified value at the specified offset in the extra class memory or the WNDCLASSEX structure for the class to which the specified window belongs.
SetWindowLongPtr	This function supersedes the SetWindowLong function and changes an attribute of the specified window. The function also sets a value at the specified offset in the extra window memory.

■ If you cast a pointer to test some bits, set or clear bits, use the UINT_PTR or INT_PTR type instead of casting pointers to INT, LONG, ULONG, or DWORD.

■ Remember that LPARAM, WPARAM, and LRESULT types change size with the platform and will be 64 bits long in the new environment (as these typically hold pointers). Mixing these types with DWORD, ULONG, UINT, INT, etc., may lead to inadvertent truncation.

■ If you want to truncate a pointer to a 32-bit value, use the PtrToLong or PtrToUlong functions. These functions are defined in **Basetsd.h** and they disable the pointer truncation warning for the duration of the call.

■ Do not create functions that accept DWORD parameters for polymorphic data. If the data can be a pointer or an integral value, use the UINT_PTR or PVOID type instead.

▲ Access all window and class data using the FIELD_OFFSET macro instead of using hard-coded offsets.

CONCLUSION

Although Windows is somewhat late to 64 bits, the direction is clear and Microsoft is taking the steps to 64-bit–enable Windows as quickly as possible. As a developer you should have enough lead time to hone your skills to the new 64-bit environment.

INDEX

DestroyMenu, 40
Developer Studio. *see* Microsoft
  Developer Studio
development environment, 17–18
device context (DC)
    ActiveX controls and, 606
    compared with rendering
      contexts, 733
    GDIs and, 134–135
Device Driver Interface (DDI), 731
device driver kits (DDKs), 13
device drivers, architecture of,
  12–13
device space, 157
DFS (distributed file system), 465
DHCP. *see* Dynamic Host
  Configuration Protocol (DHCP)
dial-up networking, 74–75
dialog boxes
    characteristics of, 40–41
    programming, 41–43
dialog data exchange (DDX), 770
dialog functions, 42
dialog procedures, 42
DialogBox API, 41–42
Diffie-Hellman algorithm, 851
digital certificates, 848
Digital Signature Algorithm
  (DSA), 851
digital signatures
    creating, 846
    hash values and, 844–845
    verifying, 846
Digital Video Disc (DVD), 727–728
directory functions, programming,
  83–84
directory services. *see also* Active
  Directory (AD)
    Active Directory, 26
    defined, 448
    Novell Directory Services, 448
directory system agent (DSA), 449
DirectShow, 727
DisconnectNamedPipe, 429, 441
discretionary access-control list
  (DACL), 451
disk mirroring, fault tolerance
  and, 27
DisplayUserInfo, 475
distinguished names (DN)
    defined, 448
    finding objects with, 450
Distributed COM (DCOM), 23–24
distributed computing, 73–74

Distributed Computing
  Environment (DCE), 73
distributed file system (DFS), 465
DLL redirection, 122
dllexport/dllimport, 313–314
DLLs. *see* dynamic link libraries
  (DLLs)
DN. *see* distinguished names (DN)
DNS (Domain Naming Service), 71
document types, in Registry, 482
DoDataExchange, 539
DoDragDrop, 569
DoFieldExchange, 781
Domain Naming Service (DNS), 71
DoModal, 106, 722
double buffering, OpenGL, 731, 734
drag-and-drop functionality, OLE,
  521–522, 568–569
DSA (Digital Signature
  Algorithm), 851
DSA (directory system agent), 449
duplexing, 27
DuplicateHandle, 413
DVD (Digital Video Disc), 727–728
dynamic cursor, 801
Dynamic Domain Name Service
  (DDNS), 27
Dynamic Host Configuration
  Protocol (DHCP)
    programming, 71
    TCP/IP configuration, 70
    Windows 2000 networking, 27
dynamic link libraries (DLLs),
  304–324
    comparing with application
      development, 306–307
    DCOM and, 24
    entry/exit functions, 312–313
    exporting/importing
      functions, 313–316
    freeing, 309
    invoking, 308–309, 311
    ISAPI and, 664
    KnownDLLS, 310–311
    loading, 316–319
    overview of, 304
    pro/cons, 304–306
    search order for, 310
    version control, 319–323
    Win16 DLLs vs. Win32
      DLLs, 307
    Windows 2000 DLLs and
      functions, 305
dynamic local storage, 347

dynamic object interfaces, ADSI,
  460–462
dynasets, ODBC recordsets, 767

▼ E

EAP (Extensible Authentication
  Protocol), 125–126
early binding, 522
EBCDIC (Extended Binary Coded
  Decimal Interchange Code), 61
Edit box, 192
EFS (Encrypted File System), 100.
  see also encryption
embedded database
  applications, 764
EnableAutomation, 543
EnableWindow, 37
Encrypted File System (EFS), 100.
  see also encryption
encryption
    APIs for, 102
    cleaning up after, 871–872
    decrypting, 874–875
    example of, 101–103
    items that cannot be encrypted,
      100–101
    overview of, 847
    signing data and, 870
    using symmetric algorithms
      for, 866
    Visual C++ Wizard and,
      104–114
EndPaint, 166
enhancements. *see* programming
  enhancements
EnterCriticalSection, 354
EnumElements, 518
EnumFontFamiliesEx, 144,
  148–150, 152
EnumFontFamiliesProc, 144
EnumFontsProcInsert-
  FontName, 150
EnumOneLevel, 502
error objects, ADO, 803
events
    APIs for, 363
    thread objects, 363–373
Executive OS code, 9–15
    Input/Output (I/O) Manager
      and, 12–13
    local procedure calls and, 15
    memory manager and, 10–12

multimedia programming
audio programming, 694–716
Media Control Interface
(MCI), 695–697
MIDI format, 699
overview of, 694–695
sample program (CDPlayer)
for, 700–716
using MCIWnd, 697–698
using MessageBeep, 698–699
using PlaySound, 699
basics of, 692–694
DVD support, 727–728
time formats for, 692–694
device types, 694
time macros and
functions, 693
video programming example
(AVIPlayer), 716–727
multiprocessing
I/O problems and, 95
support for, 8
symmetric and asymmetric, 327
multitasking, 326
multithreading
defined, 326
OpenGL, 733
mutexes
APIs for, 363
thread objects and, 363

 N

name mangling, 306
named pipes
communications function of, 65
comparing with mailslots, 67
programming, 65–66
sample program for, 420–444
naming contexts, 448
NBNS (NetBIOS Name Servers), 72
NDIS (Network Device Interface
Specification), 58
NDS (Novell Directory Services), 448
NetBEUI. see NetBIOS Extended
User Interface (NetBEUI)
NetBIOS. see Network Basic Input
Output System (NetBIOS)
NetBIOS Extended User Interface
(NetBEUI), 58, 69, 70
NetBIOS Name Servers (NBNS), 72
NetGroup, 451
Netscape, 664
NetServer, 451
NetShare, 451

network adapter cards, 56. see also
network interface card (NIC)
Network Basic Input Output
System (NetBIOS)
communications
enhancements and, 124
session layer and, 60
Network Device Interface
Specification (NDIS), 58
network interface card (NIC), 58.
see also network adapter cards
network layer, ISO model, 58–59
network programming, 22–23
network redirector. see Remote
Access Server (RAS)
New Technology File System
(NTFS), 79–80
comparing with FAT, 80
data access and, 25
overview of, 79
NIC (network interface card), 58.
see also network adapter cards
NMCUSTOMDRAW, 277
non-automation interfaces,
ADSI, 463
notification functions, 92–95
notification messages, 37
Novell Directory Services
(NDS), 448
NTFS. see New Technology File
System (NTFS)
NWLink, transport layer and, 58

O

Object Identifier (OID), 450
object linking and embedding
(OLE), 532–584. see also ActiveX
controls
binding supported by, 522–523
comparing OLE 1.0 with OLE
2.0, 515, 519
drag-and-drop functionality of,
521–522, 568–569
drag-and-drop program,
569–583
in-place activation or visual
editing with, 515
MFC library and, 524
OLE Automation
Client program, 557–567
client/server
communication, 534
definition of, 24
GUIDs, 534

overview of, 523–524, 533
Server program, 535–557
overview of, 24, 514
programming aspects of, 524
structured storage, 515–519
using a moniker for broken
links, 519–521
Windows 2000 COM
enhancements, 532–533
Object Manager, 13–14
ODBC. see Open Database
Connectivity (ODBC)
OID (Object Identifier), 450
OLE. see object linking and
embedding (OLE)
OLEDB
ADOs and, 800
writing ADSI client
applications with, 464–465
OnBtnadd, 618
OnBtnview, 619
OnCancelBeep, 406
On*ChangedRecordsctrl1, 618
OnChangeEdit, 204, 206
OnClearSendData, 430
OnClose, 204
OnCreate, 561, 746
OnDecrypt, 871
OnDelete, 837
OnDragDrop, 572
OnDragEnter, 569
OnDragLeave, 569
OnDraw, 606, 631
OnEncrypt, 866, 871
OnExit, 419
OnGetRecordset, 789
OnInitDialog, 181, 204, 217, 622, 718
OnInitialUpdate, 789
OnMove, 789, 795
OnNewThread, 395
OnPaint, 166, 606, 718, 748,
753–754
OnQueryDragIcon, 718
OnRecordAdd, 795
OnRecordDelete, 795–796
OnRecordRefresh, 795, 797
OnSend, 429, 439
OnSet, 217
OnSetTimer, 405
OnSign, 879
OnSize, 226
OnSysCommand, 216
OnSystemCommand, 718
OnToolBarToolTip, 230
OnUpdate, 831

X

ABOUT THE CD

The CD-ROM that accompanies this book contains all of the source code and executable files from this book. These code examples and executables are in the *Book Samples* subdirectory, with one directory for each applicable chapter. For your convenience, they are ready for use, rather than being compressed. They also come with complete project files.